PEARSON ALWAYS LEARNING

Microeconomics for Economics 251

Third Custom Edition
with contributions from Kelly Blanchard, Ph.D.
at Purdue University, West Lafayette, IN

Taken from:
Microeconomics, Tenth Edition
by Michael Parkin

D1500465

Cover Art: Courtesy of Photodisc, DigitalVision/Getty Images

Taken from:

Microeconomics, Tenth Edition
by Michael Parkin
Copyright © 2012, 2010, 2008, 2005, 2003 by Pearson Education, Inc.
Published by Addison-Wesley
Boston, Massachusetts 02116

Copyright © 2011 by Pearson Learning Solutions
All rights reserved.

Pearson Learning Solutions, 501 Boylston Street, Suite 900, Boston, MA 02116
A Pearson Education Company
www.pearsoned.com

Printed in the United States of America

3 4 5 6 7 8 9 10   V092 16 15 14 13 12

000200010270728684

CY

ISBN 10: 1-256-31838-8
ISBN 13: 978-1-256-31838-5

*Summary (Key Points and Key Terms), Study Plan
Problems and Applications, and Additional Problems
and Applications appear at the end of each chapter.*

After studying this chapter,
you will be able to:

◆ Define economics and distinguish between microeconomics and macroeconomics

◆ Explain the two big questions of economics

◆ Explain the key ideas that define the economic way of thinking

◆ Explain how economists go about their work as social scientists and policy advisers

1

WHAT IS ECONOMICS?

You are studying economics at a time of extraordinary challenge and change. The United States, Europe, and Japan, the world's richest nations, are still not fully recovered from a deep recession in which incomes shrank and millions of jobs were lost. Brazil, China, India, and Russia, poorer nations with a combined population that dwarfs our own, are growing rapidly and playing ever-greater roles in an expanding global economy.

The economic events of the past few years stand as a stark reminder that we live in a changing and sometimes turbulent world. New businesses are born and old ones die. New jobs are created and old ones disappear. Nations, businesses, and individuals must find ways of coping with economic change.

Your life will be shaped by the challenges that *you* face and the opportunities that *you* create. But to face those challenges and seize the opportunities they present, you must understand the powerful forces at play. The economics that you're about to learn will become your most reliable guide. This chapter gets you started. It describes the questions that economists try to answer and the ways in which they think as they search for the answers.

◆ Definition of Economics

A fundamental fact dominates our lives: We want more than we can get. Our inability to get everything we want is called **scarcity**. Scarcity is universal. It confronts all living things. Even parrots face scarcity!

Not only do I want a cracker—we all want a cracker!

© The New Yorker Collection 1985
Frank Modell from cartoonbank.com. All Rights Reserved.

Think about the things that *you* want and the scarcity that *you* face. You want to live a long and healthy life. You want to go to a good school, college, or university. You want to live in a well-equipped, spacious, and comfortable home. You want the latest smart phone and a faster Internet connection for your laptop or iPad. You want some sports and recreational gear—perhaps some new running shoes, or a new bike. And you want more time, much more than is available, to go to class, do your homework, play sports and games, read novels, go to the movies, listen to music, travel, and hang out with your friends.

What you can afford to buy is limited by your income and by the prices you must pay. And your time is limited by the fact that your day has 24 hours.

You want some other things that only governments provide. You want to live in a peaceful and secure world and safe neighborhood and enjoy the benefits of clean air, lakes, and rivers.

What governments can afford is limited by the taxes they collect. Taxes lower people's incomes and compete with the other things they want to buy.

What everyone can get—what *society* can get—is limited by the productive resources available. These resources are the gifts of nature, human labor and ingenuity, and all the previously produced tools and equipment.

Because we can't get everything we want, we must make *choices*. You can't afford *both* a laptop *and* an iPhone, so you must *choose* which one to buy. You can't spend tonight *both* studying for your next test *and* going to the movies, so again, you must *choose* which one to do. Governments can't spend a tax dollar on *both* national defense *and* environmental protection, so they must *choose* how to spend that dollar.

Your choices must somehow be made consistent with the choices of others. If you choose to buy a laptop, someone else must choose to sell it. Incentives reconcile choices. An **incentive** is a reward that encourages an action or a penalty that discourages one. Prices act as incentives. If the price of a laptop is too high, more will be offered for sale than people want to buy. And if the price is too low, fewer will be offered for sale than people want to buy. But there is a price at which choices to buy and sell are consistent.

Economics is the social science that studies the *choices* that individuals, businesses, governments, and entire societies make as they cope with *scarcity* and the *incentives* that influence and reconcile those choices.

*[handwritten: * make consistent. * cause to coexist in harmony.]*

The subject has two parts:

- Microeconomics
- Macroeconomics

Microeconomics is the study of the choices that individuals and businesses make, the way these choices interact in markets, and the influence of governments. Some examples of microeconomic questions are: Why are people downloading more movies? How would a tax on e-commerce affect eBay?

Macroeconomics is the study of the performance of the national economy and the global economy. Some examples of macroeconomic questions are: Why is the U.S. unemployment rate so high? Can the Federal Reserve make our economy expand by cutting interest rates?

◆ REVIEW QUIZ

1 List some examples of the scarcity that you face.
2 Find examples of scarcity in today's headlines.
3 Find an illustration of the distinction between microeconomics and macroeconomics in today's headlines.

You can work these questions in Study Plan 1.1 and get instant feedback.

◆ Two Big Economic Questions

Two big questions summarize the scope of economics:

- How do choices end up determining *what*, *how*, and *for whom* goods and services are produced?
- Can the choices that people make in the pursuit of their own *self-interest* also promote the broader *social interest*?

What, How, and For Whom?

Goods and services are the objects that people value and produce to satisfy human wants. *Goods* are physical objects such as cell phones and automobiles. *Services* are tasks performed for people such as cell-phone service and auto-repair service.

What? What we produce varies across countries and changes over time. In the United States today, agriculture accounts for 1 percent of total production, manufactured goods for 22 percent, and services (retail and wholesale trade, health care, and education are the biggest ones) for 77 percent. In contrast, in China today, agriculture accounts for 11 percent of total production, manufactured goods for 49 percent, and services for 40 percent. Figure 1.1 shows these numbers and also the percentages for Brazil, which fall between those for the United States and China. What determines these patterns of production? How do choices end up determining the quantities of cell phones, automobiles, cell-phone service, auto-repair service, and the millions of other items that are produced in the United States and around the world?

How? Goods and services are produced by using productive resources that economists call **factors of production**. Factors of production are grouped into four categories:

- Land
- Labor
- Capital
- Entrepreneurship

Land The "gifts of nature" that we use to produce goods and services are called **land**. In economics, land is what in everyday language we call *natural resources*. It includes land in the everyday sense

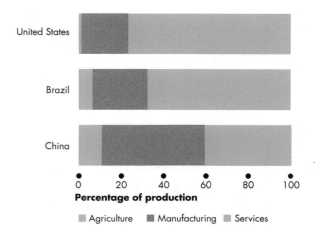

FIGURE 1.1   What Three Countries Produce

United States

Brazil

China

0   20   40   60   80   100
Percentage of production

■ Agriculture   ■ Manufacturing   ■ Services

Agriculture and manufacturing is a small percentage of production in rich countries such as the United States and a large percentage of production in poorer countries such as China. Most of what is produced in the United States is services.

Source of data: CIA Factbook 2010, Central Intelligence Agency.

[myeconlab animation]

together with minerals, oil, gas, coal, water, air, forests, and fish.

Our land surface and water resources are renewable and some of our mineral resources can be recycled. But the resources that we use to create energy are nonrenewable—they can be used only once.

Labor The work time and work effort that people devote to producing goods and services is called **labor**. Labor includes the physical and mental efforts of all the people who work on farms and construction sites and in factories, shops, and offices.

The *quality* of labor depends on **human capital**, which is the knowledge and skill that people obtain from education, on-the-job training, and work experience. You are building your own human capital right now as you work on your economics course, and your human capital will continue to grow as you gain work experience.

Human capital expands over time. Today, 87 percent of the adult population of the United States have completed high school and 29 percent have a college or university degree. Figure 1.2 shows these measures of the growth of human capital in the United States over the past century.

[handwritten note: measure of economic value of an employee's skill set.]

FIGURE 1.2   A Measure of Human Capital

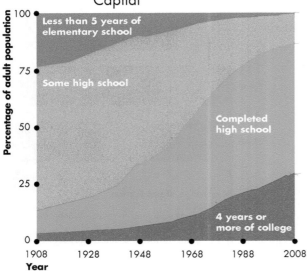

In 2008 (the most recent data), 29 percent of the population had 4 years or more of college, up from 2 percent in 1908. A further 58 percent had completed high school, up from 10 percent in 1908.

Source of data: U.S. Census Bureau, *Statistical Abstract of the United States*, 2010.

myeconlab animation

mom made resources.

Capital The tools, instruments, machines, buildings, and other constructions that businesses use to produce goods and services are called **capital**.

In everyday language, we talk about money, stocks, and bonds as being "capital." These items are *financial* capital. Financial capital plays an important role in enabling businesses to borrow the funds that they use to buy physical capital. But because financial capital is not used to produce goods and services, it is not a productive resource.

Entrepreneurship The human resource that organizes labor, land, and capital is called **entrepreneurship**. Entrepreneurs come up with new ideas about what and how to produce, make business decisions, and bear the risks that arise from these decisions.

What determines the quantities of factors of production that are used to produce goods and services?

For Whom? Who consumes the goods and services that are produced depends on the incomes that people earn. People with large incomes can buy a wide range of goods and services. People with small incomes have fewer options and can afford a smaller range of goods and services.

People earn their incomes by selling the services of the factors of production they own:

- Land earns **rent**.
- Labor earns **wages**.
- Capital earns **interest**.
- Entrepreneurship earns **profit**.

Which factor of production earns the most income? The answer is labor. Wages and fringe benefits are around 70 percent of total income. Land, capital, and entrepreneurship share the rest. These percentages have been remarkably constant over time.

Knowing how income is shared among the factors of production doesn't tell us how it is shared among individuals. And the distribution of income among individuals is extremely unequal. You know of some people who earn very large incomes: Angelina Jolie earns $10 million per movie; and the New York Yankees pays Alex Rodriguez $27.5 million a year.

You know of even more people who earn very small incomes. Servers at McDonald's average around $7.25 an hour; checkout clerks, cleaners, and textile and leather workers all earn less than $10 an hour.

You probably know about other persistent differences in incomes. Men, on average, earn more than women; whites earn more than minorities; college graduates earn more than high-school graduates.

We can get a good sense of who consumes the goods and services produced by looking at the percentages of total income earned by different groups of people. The 20 percent of people with the lowest incomes earn about 5 percent of total income, while the richest 20 percent earn close to 50 percent of total income. So on average, people in the richest 20 percent earn more than 10 times the incomes of those in the poorest 20 percent.

Why is the distribution of income so unequal? Why do women and minorities earn less than white males?

Economic Instability The years between 1993 and 2007 were a period of remarkable economic stability, so much so that they've been called the *Great Moderation*. During those years, the U.S. and global economies were on a roll. Incomes in the United States increased by 30 percent and incomes in China tripled. Even the economic shockwaves of 9/11

Economics in Action
A Credit Crunch

Flush with funds and offering record low interest rates, banks went on a lending spree to home buyers. Rapidly rising home prices made home owners feel well off and they were happy to borrow and spend. Home loans were bundled into securities that were sold and resold to banks around the world.

In 2006, as interest rates began to rise and the rate of rise in home prices slowed, borrowers defaulted on their loans. What started as a trickle became a flood. As more people defaulted, banks took losses that totaled billions of dollars by mid-2007.

Global credit markets stopped working, and people began to fear a prolonged slowdown in economic activity. Some even feared the return of the economic trauma of the *Great Depression* of the 1930s when more than 20 percent of the U.S. labor force was unemployed. The Federal Reserve, determined to avoid a catastrophe, started lending on a very large scale to the troubled banks.

brought only a small dip in the strong pace of U.S. and global economic growth.

But in August 2007, a period of financial stress began. A bank in France was the first to feel the pain that soon would grip the entire global financial system.

Banks take in people's deposits and get more funds by borrowing from each other and from other firms. Banks use these funds to make loans. All the banks' choices to borrow and lend and the choices of people and businesses to lend to and borrow from banks are made in self-interest. But does this lending and borrowing serve the social interest? Is there too much borrowing and lending that needs to be <u>reined</u> in, or is there too little and a need to stimulate more? → keep under control restrain

When the banks got into trouble, the Federal Reserve (the Fed) bailed them out with big loans backed by taxpayer dollars. Did the Fed's bailout of troubled banks serve the social interest? Or might the Fed's rescue action encourage banks to repeat their dangerous lending in the future?

Banks weren't the only recipients of public funds. General Motors was saved by a government bailout. GM makes its decisions in its self-interest. The government bailout of GM also served the firm's self-interest. Did the bailout also serve the social interest?

 REVIEW QUIZ

1 Describe the broad facts about *what*, *how*, and *for whom* goods and services are produced.
2 Use headlines from the recent news to illustrate the potential for conflict between self-interest and the social interest.

You can work these questions in Study Plan 1.2 and get instant feedback.

We've looked at four topics and asked many questions that illustrate the big question: Can choices made in the pursuit of self-interest also promote the social interest? We've asked questions but not answered them because we've not yet explained the economic principles needed to do so.

By working through this book, you will discover the economic principles that help economists figure out when the social interest is being served, when it is not, and what might be done when it is not being served. We will return to each of the unanswered questions in future chapters.

◆ The Economic Way of Thinking

The questions that economics tries to answer tell us about the *scope of economics*, but they don't tell us how economists *think* and go about seeking answers to these questions. You're now going to see how economists go about their work.

We're going to look at six key ideas that define the *economic way of thinking*. These ideas are

- A choice is a *tradeoff*.
- People make *rational choices* by comparing *benefits* and *costs*.
- *Benefit* is what you gain from something.
- *Cost* is what you *must give up* to get something.
- Most choices are "*how-much*" choices made at the *margin*.
- Choices respond to *incentives*.

A Choice Is a Tradeoff

Because we face scarcity, we must make choices. And when we make a choice, we select from the available alternatives. For example, you can spend Saturday night studying for your next economics test or having fun with your friends, but you can't do both of these activities at the same time. You must choose how much time to devote to each. Whatever choice you make, you could have chosen something else.

You can think about your choices as tradeoffs. A **tradeoff** is an exchange—giving up one thing to get something else. When you choose how to spend your Saturday night, you face a tradeoff between studying and hanging out with your friends.

Making a Rational Choice

Economists view the choices that people make as rational. A **rational choice** is one that compares costs and benefits and achieves the greatest benefit over cost for the person making the choice.

Only the wants of the person making a choice are relevant to determine its rationality. For example, you might like your coffee black and strong but your friend prefers his milky and sweet. So it is rational for you to choose espresso and for your friend to choose cappuccino.

The idea of rational choice provides an answer to the first question: *What* goods and services will be produced and in what quantities? The answer is those that people rationally choose to buy!

But how do people choose rationally? Why do more people choose an iPod rather than a Zune? Why has the U.S. government chosen to build an interstate highway system and not an interstate high-speed railroad system? The answers turn on comparing benefits and costs.

Benefit: What You Gain

The **benefit** of something is the gain or pleasure that it brings and is determined by **preferences**—by what a person likes and dislikes and the intensity of those feelings. If you get a huge kick out of "Guitar Hero," that video game brings you a large benefit. And if you have little interest in listening to Yo Yo Ma playing a Vivaldi cello concerto, that activity brings you a small benefit.

Some benefits are large and easy to identify, such as the benefit that you get from being in school. A big piece of that benefit is the goods and services that you will be able to enjoy with the boost to your earning power when you graduate. Some benefits are small, such as the benefit you get from a slice of pizza.

Economists measure benefit as the most that a person is *willing to give up* to get something. You are willing to give up a lot to be in school. But you would give up only an iTunes download for a slice of pizza.

Cost: What You *Must Give Up*   *best alternative*

The **opportunity cost** of something is the highest-valued alternative that must be given up to get it.

To make the idea of opportunity cost concrete, think about *your* opportunity cost of being in school. It has two components: the things you can't afford to buy and the things you can't do with your time.

Start with the things you can't afford to buy. You've spent all your income on tuition, residence fees, books, and a laptop. If you weren't in school, you would have spent this money on tickets to ball games and movies and all the other things that you enjoy. But that's only the start of your opportunity cost. You've also given up the opportunity to get a job. Suppose that the best job you could get if you weren't in school is working at Citibank as a teller earning $25,000 a year. Another part of your opportunity cost of being in school is all the things that you could buy with the extra $25,000 you would have.

A person has a comparative advantage in an activity if that person can perform the activity at a lower opportunity cost than anyone else.

The Economic Way of Thinking   7

As you well know, being a student eats up many hours in class time, doing homework assignments, preparing for tests, and so on. To do all these school activities, you must give up many hours of what would otherwise be leisure time spent with your friends.

So the opportunity cost of being in school is all the good things that you can't afford and don't have the spare time to enjoy. You might want to put a dollar value on that cost or you might just list all the items that make up the opportunity cost.

The examples of opportunity cost that we've just considered are all-or-nothing costs—you're either in school or not in school. Most situations are not like this one. They involve choosing *how much* of an activity to do.

How Much? Choosing at the Margin

You can allocate the next hour between studying and instant messaging your friends, but the choice is not all or nothing. You must decide how many minutes to allocate to each activity. To make this decision, you compare the benefit of a little bit more study time with its cost—you make your choice at the **margin**.

The benefit that arises from an increase in an activity is called **marginal benefit**. For example, your marginal benefit from one more night of study before a test is the boost it gives to your grade. Your marginal benefit doesn't include the grade you're already achieving without that extra night of work.

The *opportunity cost* of an *increase* in an activity is called **marginal cost**. For you, the marginal cost of studying one more night is the cost of not spending that night on your favorite leisure activity.

To make your decisions, you compare marginal benefit and marginal cost. If the marginal benefit from an extra night of study exceeds its marginal cost, you study the extra night. If the marginal cost exceeds the marginal benefit, you don't study the extra night.

Choices Respond to Incentives

Economists take human nature as given and view people as acting in their self-interest. All people— you, other consumers, producers, politicians, and public servants—pursue their self-interest.

Self-interested actions are not necessarily *selfish* actions. You might decide to use your resources in ways that bring pleasure to others as well as to yourself. But a self-interested act gets the most benefit for *you* based on *your* view about benefit.

The central idea of economics is that we can predict the self-interested choices that people make by looking at the *incentives* they face. People undertake those activities for which marginal benefit exceeds marginal cost; and they reject options for which marginal cost exceeds marginal benefit.

For example, your economics instructor gives you a problem set and tells you these problems will be on the next test. Your marginal benefit from working these problems is large, so you diligently work them. In contrast, your math instructor gives you a problem set on a topic that she says will never be on a test. You get little marginal benefit from working these problems, so you decide to skip most of them.

Economists see incentives as the key to reconciling self-interest and social interest. When our choices are *not* in the social interest, it is because of the incentives we face. One of the challenges for economists is to figure out the incentives that result in self-interested choices being in the social interest.

Economists emphasize the crucial role that institutions play in influencing the incentives that people face as they pursue their self-interest. Laws that protect private property and markets that enable voluntary exchange are the fundamental institutions. You will learn as you progress with your study of economics that where these institutions exist, self-interest can indeed promote the social interest.

economic cost = opportunity cost

REVIEW QUIZ

1 Explain the idea of a tradeoff and think of three tradeoffs that you have made today.

2 Explain what economists mean by rational choice and think of three choices that you've made today that are rational.

3 Explain why opportunity cost is the best forgone alternative and provide examples of some opportunity costs that you have faced today.

4 Explain what it means to choose at the margin and illustrate with three choices at the margin that you have made today.

5 Explain why choices respond to incentives and think of three incentives to which you have responded today.

You can work these questions in Study Plan 1.3 and get instant feedback.

Social interest and self interest can come into conflict.

◆ Economics as Social Science and Policy Tool

Economics is both a social science and a toolkit for advising on policy decisions.

Economist as Social Scientist

As social scientists, economists seek to discover how the economic world works. In pursuit of this goal, like all scientists, economists distinguish between positive and normative statements.

Positive Statements A *positive* statement is about what *is*. It says what is currently believed about the way the world operates. A positive statement might be right or wrong, but we can test it by checking it against the facts. "Our planet is warming because of the amount of coal that we're burning" is a positive statement. We can test whether it is right or wrong.

A central task of economists is to test positive statements about how the economic world works and to weed out those that are wrong. Economics first got off the ground in the late 1700s, so it is a young science compared with, for example, physics, and much remains to be discovered. *fact based*

Normative Statements A *normative* statement is about what *ought to be*. It depends on values and cannot be tested. Policy goals are normative statements. For example, "We ought to cut our use of coal by 50 percent" is a normative policy statement. You may agree or disagree with it, but you can't test it. It doesn't assert a fact that can be checked. *Judgment based*

Unscrambling Cause and Effect Economists are particularly interested in positive statements about cause and effect. Are computers getting cheaper because people are buying them in greater quantities? Or are people buying computers in greater quantities because they are getting cheaper? Or is some third factor causing both the price of a computer to fall and the quantity of computers bought to increase?

To answer such questions, economists create and test economic models. An **economic model** is a description of some aspect of the economic world that includes only those features that are needed for the purpose at hand. For example, an economic model of a cell-phone network might include features such as the prices of calls, the number of cell-

phone users, and the volume of calls. But the model would ignore cell-phone colors and ringtones.

A model is tested by comparing its predictions with the facts. But testing an economic model is difficult because we observe the outcomes of the simultaneous change of many factors. To cope with this problem, economists look for natural experiments (situations in the ordinary course of economic life in which the one factor of interest is different and other things are equal or similar); conduct statistical investigations to find correlations; and perform economic experiments by putting people in decision-making situations and varying the influence of one factor at a time to discover how they respond.

Economist as Policy Adviser

Economics is useful. It is a toolkit for advising governments and businesses and for making personal decisions. Some of the most famous economists work partly as policy advisers.

For example, Jagdish Bhagwati of Columbia University has advised governments and international organizations on trade and economic development issues.

Christina Romer of the University of California, Berkeley, is on leave and serving as the chief economic adviser to President Barack Obama and head of the President's Council of Economic Advisers.

All the policy questions on which economists provide advice involve a blend of the positive and the normative. Economics can't help with the normative part—the policy goal. But for a given goal, economics provides a method of evaluating alternative solutions—comparing marginal benefits and marginal costs and finding the solution that makes the best use of the available resources.

◼ REVIEW QUIZ

1 Distinguish between a positive statement and a normative statement and provide examples.
2 What is a model? Can you think of a model that you might use in your everyday life?
3 How do economists try to disentangle cause and effect?
4 How is economics used as a policy tool?

You can work these questions in Study Plan 1.4 and get instant feedback.

→ Ought to
Used to say what is the right thing to do.
Used to say what you expect or would like to happen.

SUMMARY

Key Points

Definition of Economics (p. 2)

- All economic questions arise from scarcity—from the fact that wants exceed the resources available to satisfy them.
- Economics is the social science that studies the choices that people make as they cope with scarcity.
- The subject divides into microeconomics and macroeconomics.

Working Problem 1 will give you a better understanding of the definition of economics.

Two Big Economic Questions (pp. 3–5)

- Two big questions summarize the scope of economics:

  1. How do choices end up determining *what*, *how*, and *for whom* goods and services are produced?

  2. When do choices made in the pursuit of *self-interest* also promote the *social interest*?

Working Problems 2 and 3 will give you a better understanding of the two big questions of economics.

The Economic Way of Thinking (pp. 6–7)

- Every choice is a tradeoff—exchanging more of something for less of something else.
- People make rational choices by comparing benefit and cost.
- Cost—*opportunity cost*—is what you must give up to get something.
- Most choices are "how much" choices made at the *margin* by comparing marginal benefit and marginal cost.
- Choices respond to incentives.

Working Problems 4 and 5 will give you a better understanding of the economic way of thinking.

Economics as Social Science and Policy Tool (p. 8)

- Economists distinguish between positive statements—what is—and normative statements—what ought to be.
- To explain the economic world, economists create and test economic models.
- Economics is a toolkit used to provide advice on government, business, and personal economic decisions.

Working Problem 6 will give you a better understanding of economics as social science and policy tool.

Key Terms

Benefit, 6	Interest, 4	Preferences, 6
Capital, 4	Labor, 3	Profit, 4
Economic model, 8	Land, 3	Rational choice, 6
Economics, 2	Macroeconomics, 2	Rent, 4
Entrepreneurship, 4	Margin, 7	Scarcity, 2
Factors of production, 3	Marginal benefit, 7	Tradeoff, 6
Goods and services, 3	Marginal cost, 7	Wages, 4
Human capital, 3	Microeconomics, 2	
Incentive, 2	Opportunity cost, 6	

STUDY PLAN PROBLEMS AND APPLICATIONS

myeconlab You can work Problems 1 to 6 in MyEconLab Chapter 1 Study Plan and get instant feedback.

Definition of Economics (Study Plan1.1)

1. Apple Inc. decides to make iTunes freely available in unlimited quantities.
   a. Does Apple's decision change the incentives that people face?
   b. Is Apple's decision an example of a microeconomic or a macroeconomic issue?

Two Big Economic Questions (Study Plan1.2)

2. Which of the following pairs does not match?
   a. Labor and wages
   b. Land and rent
   c. Entrepreneurship and profit
   d. Capital and profit

3. Explain how the following news headlines concern self-interest and the social interest.
   a. Starbucks Expands in China
   b. McDonald's Moves into Salads
   c. Food Must Be Labeled with Nutrition Data

The Economic Way of Thinking (Study Plan1.3)

4. The night before an economics test, you decide to go to the movies instead of staying home and working your MyEconLab Study Plan. You get 50 percent on your test compared with the 70 percent that you normally score.
   a. Did you face a tradeoff?
   b. What was the opportunity cost of your evening at the movies?

5. **Costs Soar for London Olympics**
   The regeneration of East London, the site of the 2012 Olympic Games, is set to add extra £1.5 billion to taxpayers' bill.
   Source: *The Times*, London, July 6, 2006
   Is the cost of regenerating East London an opportunity cost of hosting the 2012 Olympic Games? Explain why or why not.

Economics as Social Science and Policy Tool

(Study Plan1.4)

6. Which of the following statements is positive, which is normative, and which can be tested?
   a. The United States should cut its imports.
   b. China is the largest trading partner of the United States.
   c. If the price of antiretroviral drugs increases, HIV/AIDS sufferers will decrease their consumption of the drugs.

ADDITIONAL PROBLEMS AND APPLICATIONS

myeconlab You can work these problems in MyEconLab if assigned by your instructor.

Definition of Economics

7. **Hundreds Line up for 5 p.m. Ticket Giveaway**
   By noon, hundreds of Eminem fans had lined up for a chance to score free tickets to the concert.
   Source: *Detroit Free Press*, May 18, 2009
   When Eminem gave away tickets, what was free and what was scarce? Explain your answer.

Two Big Economic Questions

8. How does the creation of a successful movie influence *what, how*, and *for whom* goods and services are produced?

9. How does a successful movie illustrate self-interested choices that are also in the social interest?

The Economic Way of Thinking

10. Before starring in *Iron Man*, Robert Downey Jr. had appeared in 45 movies that grossed an average of $5 million on the opening weekend. In contrast, *Iron Man* grossed $102 million.
    a. How do you expect the success of *Iron Man* to influence the opportunity cost of hiring Robert Downey Jr.?
    b. How have the incentives for a movie producer to hire Robert Downey Jr. changed?

11. What might be an incentive for you to take a class in summer school? List some of the benefits and costs involved in your decision. Would your choice be rational?

Economics as Social Science and Policy Tool

12. Look at today's *Wall Street Journal*. What is the leading economic news story? With which of the big economic questions does it deal and what tradeoffs does it discuss or imply?

13. Provide two microeconomic statements and two macroeconomic statements. Classify your statements as positive or normative. Explain why.

APPENDIX

Graphs in Economics

After studying this appendix,
you will be able to:

◆ Make and interpret a scatter diagram

◆ Identify linear and nonlinear relationships and
relationships that have a maximum and a
minimum

◆ Define and calculate the slope of a line

◆ Graph relationships among more than two
variables

◆ Graphing Data

A graph represents a quantity as a distance on a line.
In Fig. A1.1, a distance on the horizontal line represents temperature, measured in degrees Fahrenheit. A
movement from left to right shows an increase in
temperature. The point 0 represents zero degrees
Fahrenheit. To the right of 0, the temperature is positive. To the left of 0 the temperature is negative (as
indicated by the minus sign). A distance on the vertical line represents height, measured in thousands of
feet. The point 0 represents sea level. Points above 0
represent feet above sea level. Points below 0 represent feet below sea level (indicated by a minus sign).

In Fig. A1.1, the two scale lines are perpendicular
to each other and are called *axes*. The vertical line is
the *y*-axis, and the horizontal line is the *x*-axis. Each
axis has a zero point, which is shared by the two axes
and called the *origin*.

To make a two-variable graph, we need two pieces
of information: the value of the variable *x* and the
value of the variable *y*. For example, off the coast of
Alaska, the temperature is 32 degrees—the value of *x*.
A fishing boat is located at 0 feet above sea level—the
value of *y*. These two bits of information appear as
point *A* in Fig. A1.1. A climber at the top of Mount
McKinley on a cold day is 20,320 feet above sea level
in a zero-degree gale. These two pieces of information
appear as point *B*. On a warmer day, a climber might
be at the peak of Mt. McKinley when the temperature
is 32 degrees, at point *C*.

We can draw two lines, called *coordinates*, from
point *C*. One, called the *x*-coordinate, runs from *C* to
the vertical axis. This line is called "the *x*-coordinate"

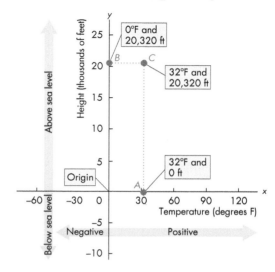

Graphs have axes that measure quantities as distances.
Here, the horizontal axis (*x*-axis) measures temperature, and
the vertical axis (*y*-axis) measures height. Point *A* represents
a fishing boat at sea level (0 on the *y*-axis) on a day when
the temperature is 32°F. Point *B* represents a climber at the
top of Mt. McKinley, 20,320 feet above sea level at a
temperature of 0°F. Point *C* represents a climber at the top
of Mt. McKinley, 20,320 feet above sea level at a temperature of 32°F.

 myeconlab   animation

because its length is the same as the value marked off
on the *x*-axis. The other, called the *y*-coordinate, runs
from *C* to the horizontal axis. This line is called "the
y-coordinate" because its length is the same as the
value marked off on the *y*-axis.

We describe a point on a graph by the values of
its *x*-coordinate and its *y*-coordinate. For example, at
point *C*, *x* is 32 degrees and *y* is 20,320 feet.

A graph like that in Fig. A1.1 can be made using
any quantitative data on two variables. The graph can
show just a few points, like Fig. A1.1, or many
points. Before we look at graphs with many points,
let's reinforce what you've just learned by looking at
two graphs made with economic data.

Economists measure variables that describe *what*,
how, and *for whom* goods and services are produced.
These variables are quantities produced and prices.
Figure A1.2 shows two examples of economic graphs.

FIGURE A1.2   Two Graphs of Economic Data

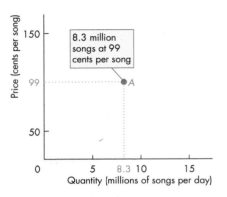

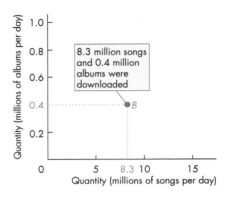

The graph in part (a) tells us that in January 2010, 8.3 million songs per day were downloaded from the iTunes store at a price of 99 cents a song.

The graph in part (b) tells us that in January 2010, 8.3 million songs per day and 0.4 million albums per day were downloaded from the iTunes store.

(a) iTunes downloads: quantity and price   **(b) iTunes downloads: songs and albums**

 animation

Figure A1.2(a) is a graph about iTunes song downloads in January 2010. The *x*-axis measures the quantity of songs downloaded per day and the *y*-axis measures the price of a song. Point *A* tells us what the quantity and price were. You can "read" this graph as telling you that in January 2010, 8.3 million songs a day were downloaded at a price of 99¢ per song.

Figure A1.2(b) is a graph about iTunes song and album downloads in January 2010. The *x*-axis measures the quantity of songs downloaded per day and the *y*-axis measures the quantity of albums downloaded per day. Point *B* tells us what these quantities were. You can "read" this graph as telling you that in January 2010, 8.3 million songs a day and 0.4 million albums were downloaded.

The three graphs that you've just seen tell you how to make a graph and how to read a data point on a graph, but they don't improve on the raw data. Graphs become interesting and revealing when they contain a number of data points because then you can visualize the data.

Economists create graphs based on the principles in Figs. A1.1 and A1.2 to reveal, describe, and visualize the relationships among variables. We're now going to look at some examples. These graphs are called scatter diagrams.

Scatter Diagrams

A **scatter diagram** is a graph that plots the value of one variable against the value of another variable for a number of different values of each variable. Such a graph reveals whether a relationship exists between

two variables and describes their relationship.

The table in Fig. A1.3 shows some data on two variables: the number of tickets sold at the box office and the number of DVDs sold for eight of the most popular movies in 2009.

What is the relationship between these two variables? Does a big box office success generate a large volume of DVD sales? Or does a box office success mean that fewer DVDs are sold?

We can answer these questions by making a scatter diagram. We do so by graphing the data in the table. In the graph in Fig. A1.3, each point shows the number of box office tickets sold (the *x* variable) and the number of DVDs sold (the *y* variable) of one of the movies. There are eight movies, so there are eight points "scattered" within the graph.

The point labeled *A* tells us that Star Trek sold 34 million tickets at the box office and 6 million DVDs. The points in the graph form a pattern, which reveals that larger box office sales are associated with larger DVD sales. But the points also tell us that this association is weak. You can't predict DVD sales with any confidence by knowing only the number of tickets sold at the box office.

Figure A1.4 shows two scatter diagrams of economic variables. Part (a) shows the relationship between income and expenditure, on average, during a ten-year period. Each point represents income and *act of spending* expenditure in a given year. For example, point *A* shows that in 2006, income was $31 thousand and expenditure was $30 thousand. This graph shows that as income increases, so does expenditure, and the relationship is a close one.

FIGURE A1.3   A Scatter Diagram

Movie	Tickets	DVDs
	(millions)	
Twilight	38	10
Transformers: Revenge of the Fallen	54	9
Up	39	8
Harry Potter and the Half-Blood Prince	40	7
Star Trek	34	6
The Hangover	37	6
Ice Age: Dawn of the Dinosaurs	26	5
The Proposal	22	5

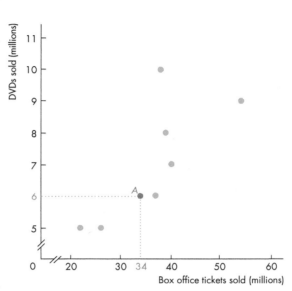

The table lists the number of tickets sold at the box office and the number of DVDs sold for eight popular movies. The scatter diagram reveals the relationship between these two variables. Each point shows the values of the two variables for a specific movie. For example, point A shows the point for *Star Trek*, which sold 34 million tickets at the box office and 6 million DVDs. The pattern formed by the points shows that there is a tendency for large box office sales to bring greater DVD sales. But you couldn't predict how many DVDs a movie would sell just by knowing its box office sales.

 animation

Figure A1.4(b) shows a scatter diagram of U.S. inflation and unemployment during the 2000s. Here, the points for 2000 to 2008 show no relationship between the two variables, but the high unemployment rate of 2009 brought a low inflation rate that year.

You can see that a scatter diagram conveys a wealth of information, and it does so in much less space than we have used to describe only some of its features. But you do have to "read" the graph to obtain all this information.

FIGURE A1.4   Two Economic Scatter Diagrams

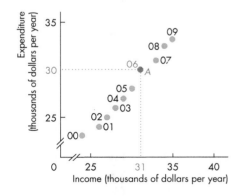

(a) Income and expenditure

(b) Unemployment and inflation

The scatter diagram in part (a) shows the relationship between income and expenditure from 2000 to 2009. Point A shows that in 2006, income was $31 (thousand) on the x-axis and expenditure was $30 (thousand) on the y-axis. This graph shows that as income rises, so does expenditure and the relationship is a close one.

The scatter diagram in part (b) shows a weak relationship between unemployment and inflation in the United States during most of the 2000s.

econlab animation

Breaks in the Axes The graph in Fig. A1.4(a) has breaks in its axes, as shown by the small gaps. The breaks indicate that there are jumps from the origin, 0, to the first values recorded.

The breaks are used because the lowest values of income and expenditure exceed $20,000. If we made this graph with no breaks in its axes, there would be a lot of empty space, all the points would be crowded into the top right corner, and it would be difficult to see whether a relationship exists between these two variables. By breaking the axes, we are able to bring the relationship into view.

Putting a break in one or both axes is like using a zoom lens to bring the relationship into the center of the graph and magnify it so that the relationship fills the graph.

Misleading Graphs Breaks can be used to highlight a relationship, but they can also be used to mislead—to make a graph that lies. The most common way of making a graph lie is to put a break in the axis and either to stretch or compress the scale. For example, suppose that in Fig. A1.4(a), the *y*-axis that measures expenditure ran from zero to $35,000 while the *x*-axis was the same as the one shown. The graph would now create the impression that despite a huge increase in income, expenditure had barely changed.

To avoid being misled, it is a good idea to get into the habit of always looking closely at the values and the labels on the axes of a graph before you start to interpret it.

Correlation and Causation A scatter diagram that shows a clear relationship between two variables, such as Fig. A1.4(a), tells us that the two variables have a high correlation. When a high correlation is present, we can predict the value of one variable from the value of the other variable. But correlation does not imply causation.

Sometimes a high correlation is a coincidence, but sometimes it does arise from a causal relationship. It is likely, for example, that rising income causes rising expenditure (Fig. A1.4a) and that high unemployment makes for a slack economy in which prices don't rise quickly, so the inflation rate is low (Fig. A1.4b).

You've now seen how we can use graphs in economics to show economic data and to reveal relationships. Next, we'll learn how economists use graphs to construct and display economic models.

◆ Graphs Used in Economic Models

The graphs used in economics are not always designed to show real-world data. Often they are used to show general relationships among the variables in an economic model.

An *economic model* is a stripped-down, simplified description of an economy or of a component of an economy such as a business or a household. It consists of statements about economic behavior that can be expressed as equations or as curves in a graph. Economists use models to explore the effects of different policies or other influences on the economy in ways that are similar to the use of model airplanes in wind tunnels and models of the climate.

You will encounter many different kinds of graphs in economic models, but there are some repeating patterns. Once you've learned to recognize these patterns, you will instantly understand the meaning of a graph. Here, we'll look at the different types of curves that are used in economic models, and we'll see some everyday examples of each type of curve. The patterns to look for in graphs are the four cases in which

- Variables move in the same direction.
- Variables move in opposite directions.
- Variables have a maximum or a minimum.
- Variables are unrelated.

Let's look at these four cases.

Variables That Move in the Same Direction

Figure A1.5 shows graphs of the relationships between two variables that move up and down together. A relationship between two variables that move in the same direction is called a **positive relationship** or a **direct relationship**. A line that slopes upward shows such a relationship.

Figure A1.5 shows three types of relationships: one that has a straight line and two that have curved lines. All the lines in these three graphs are called curves. Any line on a graph—no matter whether it is straight or curved—is called a *curve*.

A relationship shown by a straight line is called a **linear relationship**. Figure A1.5(a) shows a linear relationship between the number of miles traveled in

FIGURE A1.5   Positive (Direct) Relationships

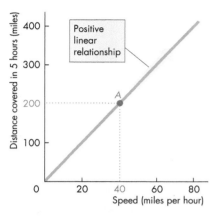

(a) Positive linear relationship

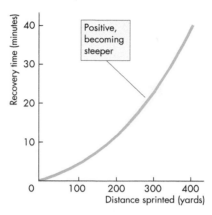

(b) Positive, becoming steeper

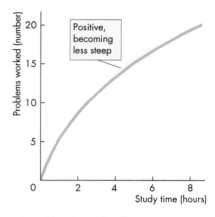

(c) Positive, becoming less steep

Each part shows a positive (direct) relationship between two variables. That is, as the value of the variable measured on the x-axis increases, so does the value of the variable measured on the y-axis. Part (a) shows a linear positive relationship—as the two variables increase together, we move along a straight line.

Part (b) shows a positive relationship such that as the two variables increase together, we move along a curve that becomes steeper.

Part (c) shows a positive relationship such that as the two variables increase together, we move along a curve that becomes flatter.

🅧 myeconlab animation

5 hours and speed. For example, point *A* shows that we will travel 200 miles in 5 hours if our speed is 40 miles an hour. If we double our speed to 80 miles an hour, we will travel 400 miles in 5 hours.

Figure A1.5(b) shows the relationship between distance sprinted and recovery time (the time it takes the heart rate to return to its normal resting rate). This relationship is an upward-sloping one that starts out quite flat but then becomes steeper as we move along the curve away from the origin. The reason this curve becomes steeper is that the additional recovery time needed from sprinting an additional 100 yards increases. It takes less than 5 minutes to recover from sprinting 100 yards but more than 10 minutes to recover from 200 yards.

Figure A1.5(c) shows the relationship between the number of problems worked by a student and the amount of study time. This relationship is an upward-sloping one that starts out quite steep and becomes flatter as we move along the curve away from the origin. Study time becomes less productive as the student spends more hours studying and becomes more tired.

Variables That Move in Opposite Directions

Figure A1.6 shows relationships between things that move in opposite directions. A relationship between variables that move in opposite directions is called a **negative relationship** or an **inverse relationship.**

Figure A1.6(a) shows the relationship between the hours spent playing squash and the hours spent playing tennis when the total time available is 5 hours. One extra hour spent playing tennis means one hour less spent playing squash and vice versa. This relationship is negative and linear.

Figure A1.6(b) shows the relationship between the cost per mile traveled and the length of a journey. The longer the journey, the lower is the cost per mile. But as the journey length increases, even though the cost per mile decreases, the fall in the cost is smaller the longer the journey. This feature of the relationship is shown by the fact that the curve slopes downward, starting out steep at a short journey length and then becoming flatter as the journey length increases. This relationship arises because some of the costs are fixed, such as auto insurance, and the fixed costs are spread over a longer journey.

FIGURE A1.6   Negative (Inverse) Relationships

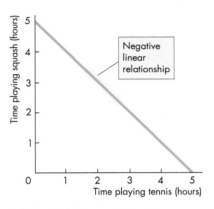
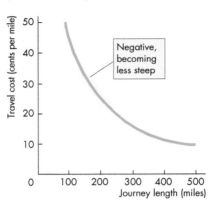
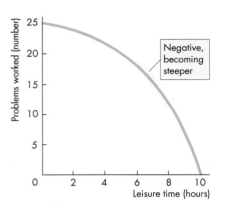

(a) Negative linear relationship   (b) Negative, becoming less steep   (c) Negative, becoming steeper

Each part shows a negative (inverse) relationship between two variables. Part (a) shows a linear negative relationship. The total time spent playing tennis and squash is 5 hours. As the time spent playing tennis increases, the time spent playing squash decreases, and we move along a straight line.

Part (b) shows a negative relationship such that as the journey length increases, the travel cost decreases as we move along a curve that becomes less steep.

Part (c) shows a negative relationship such that as leisure time increases, the number of problems worked decreases as we move along a curve that becomes steeper.

 animation

Figure A1.6(c) shows the relationship between the amount of leisure time and the number of problems worked by a student. Increasing leisure time produces an increasingly large reduction in the number of problems worked. This relationship is a negative one that starts out with a gentle slope at a small number of leisure hours and becomes steeper as the number of leisure hours increases. This relationship is a different view of the idea shown in Fig. A1.5(c).

Variables That Have a Maximum or a Minimum

Many relationships in economic models have a maximum or a minimum. For example, firms try to make the maximum possible profit and to produce at the lowest possible cost. Figure A1.7 shows relationships that have a maximum or a minimum.

Figure A1.7(a) shows the relationship between rainfall and wheat yield. When there is no rainfall, wheat will not grow, so the yield is zero. As the rainfall increases up to 10 days a month, the wheat yield

increases. With 10 rainy days each month, the wheat yield reaches its maximum at 40 bushels an acre (point *A*). Rain in excess of 10 days a month starts to lower the yield of wheat. If every day is rainy, the wheat suffers from a lack of sunshine and the yield decreases to zero. This relationship is one that starts out sloping upward, reaches a maximum, and then slopes downward.

Figure A1.7(b) shows the reverse case—a relationship that begins sloping downward, falls to a minimum, and then slopes upward. Most economic costs are like this relationship. An example is the relationship between the cost per mile and speed for a car trip. At low speeds, the car is creeping in a traffic snarl-up. The number of miles per gallon is low, so the cost per mile is high. At high speeds, the car is traveling faster than its efficient speed, using a large quantity of gasoline, and again the number of miles per gallon is low and the cost per mile is high. At a speed of 55 miles an hour, the cost per mile is at its minimum (point *B*). This relationship is one that starts out sloping downward, reaches a minimum, and then slopes upward.

FIGURE A1.7   Maximum and Minimum Points

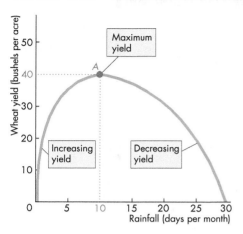

(a) Relationship with a maximum

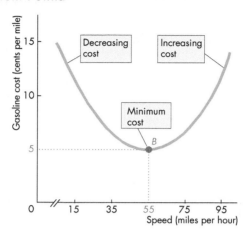

(b) Relationship with a minimum

Part (a) shows a relationship that has a maximum point, *A*. The curve slopes upward as it rises to its maximum point, is flat at its maximum, and then slopes downward.

Part (b) shows a relationship with a minimum point, *B*. The curve slopes downward as it falls to its minimum, is flat at its minimum, and then slopes upward.

myeconlab   animation

Variables That Are Unrelated

There are many situations in which no matter what happens to the value of one variable, the other variable remains constant. Sometimes we want to show the independence between two variables in a graph, and Fig. A1.8 shows two ways of achieving this.

In describing the graphs in Fig. A1.5 through Fig. A1.7, we have talked about curves that slope upward or slope downward, and curves that become less steep or steeper. Let's spend a little time discussing exactly what we mean by *slope* and how we measure the slope of a curve.

FIGURE A1.8   Variables That Are Unrelated

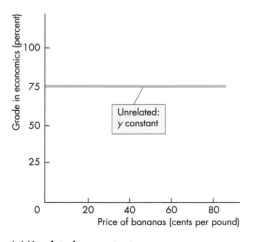

(a) Unrelated: *y* constant

(b) Unrelated: *x* constant

This figure shows how we can graph two variables that are unrelated. In part (a), a student's grade in economics is plotted at 75 percent on the *y*-axis regardless of the price of bananas on the *x*-axis. The curve is horizontal.

In part (b), the output of the vineyards of France on the *x*-axis does not vary with the rainfall in California on the *y*-axis. The curve is vertical.

myeconlab   animation

◆ The Slope of a Relationship

We can measure the influence of one variable on another by the slope of the relationship. The **slope** of a relationship is the change in the value of the variable measured on the y-axis divided by the change in the value of the variable measured on the x-axis. We use the Greek letter Δ (*delta*) to represent "change in." Thus Δy means the change in the value of the variable measured on the y-axis, and Δx means the change in the value of the variable measured on the x-axis. Therefore the slope of the relationship is

$$\text{Slope} = \frac{\Delta y}{\Delta x}.$$

If a large change in the variable measured on the y-axis (Δy) is associated with a small change in the variable measured on the x-axis (Δx), the slope is large and the curve is steep. If a small change in the variable measured on the y-axis (Δy) is associated with a large change in the variable measured on the x-axis (Δx), the slope is small and the curve is flat.

We can make the idea of slope clearer by doing some calculations.

The Slope of a Straight Line

The slope of a straight line is the same regardless of where on the line you calculate it. The slope of a straight line is constant. Let's calculate the slope of the positive relationship in Fig. A1.9. In part (a),

---

FIGURE A1.9   The Slope of a Straight Line

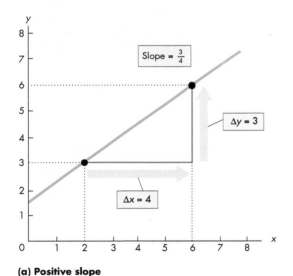

(a) Positive slope

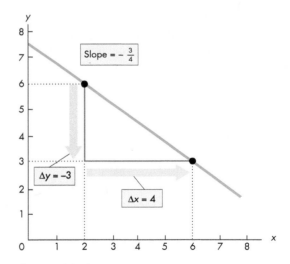

(b) Negative slope

To calculate the slope of a straight line, we divide the change in the value of the variable measured on the y-axis (Δy) by the change in the value of the variable measured on the x-axis (Δx) as we move along the line.

Part (a) shows the calculation of a positive slope. When x increases from 2 to 6, Δx equals 4. That change in x

brings about an increase in y from 3 to 6, so Δy equals 3. The slope ($\Delta y/\Delta x$) equals 3/4.

Part (b) shows the calculation of a negative slope. When x increases from 2 to 6, Δx equals 4. That increase in x brings about a decrease in y from 6 to 3, so Δy equals –3. The slope ($\Delta y/\Delta x$) equals –3/4.

when x increases from 2 to 6, y increases from 3 to 6. The change in x is +4—that is, Δx is 4. The change in y is +3—that is, Δy is 3. The slope of that line is

$$\frac{\Delta y}{\Delta x} = \frac{3}{4}.$$

In part (b), when x increases from 2 to 6, y decreases from 6 to 3. The change in y is *minus* 3—that is, Δy is –3. The change in x is *plus* 4—that is, Δx is 4. The slope of the curve is

$$\frac{\Delta y}{\Delta x} = \frac{-3}{4}.$$

Notice that the two slopes have the same magnitude (3/4), but the slope of the line in part (a) is positive (+3/+4 = 3/4) while that in part (b) is negative (–3/+4 = –3/4). The slope of a positive relationship is positive; the slope of a negative relationship is negative.

The Slope of a Curved Line

The slope of a curved line is trickier. The slope of a curved line is not constant, so the slope depends on where on the curved line we calculate it. There are two ways to calculate the slope of a curved line: You can calculate the slope at a point, or you can calculate the slope across an arc of the curve. Let's look at the two alternatives.

Slope at a Point To calculate the slope at a point on a curve, you need to construct a straight line that has the same slope as the curve at the point in question. Figure A1.10 shows how this is done. Suppose you want to calculate the slope of the curve at point A. Place a ruler on the graph so that the ruler touches point A and no other point on the curve, then draw a straight line along the edge of the ruler. The straight red line is this line, and it is the tangent to the curve at point A. If the ruler touches the curve only at point A, then the slope of the curve at point A must be the same as the slope of the edge of the ruler. If the curve and the ruler do not have the same slope, the line along the edge of the ruler will cut the curve instead of just touching it.

Now that you have found a straight line with the same slope as the curve at point A, you can calculate the slope of the curve at point A by calculating the slope of the straight line. Along the straight line, as x

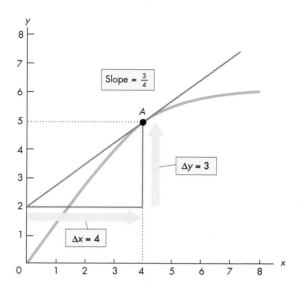

FIGURE A1.10   Slope at a Point

To calculate the slope of the curve at point A, draw the red line that just touches the curve at A—the tangent. The slope of this straight line is calculated by dividing the change in y by the change in x along the red line. When x increases from 0 to 4, Δx equals 4. That change in x is associated with an increase in y from 2 to 5, so Δy equals 3. The slope of the red line is 3/4, so the slope of the curve at point A is 3/4.

myeconlab   animation

increases from 0 to 4 (Δx is 4) y increases from 2 to 5 (Δy is 3). Therefore the slope of the straight line is

$$\frac{\Delta y}{\Delta x} = \frac{3}{4}.$$

So the slope of the curve at point A is 3/4.

Slope Across an Arc An arc of a curve is a piece of a curve. Fig. A1.11 shows the same curve as in Fig. A1.10, but instead of calculating the slope at point A, we are now going to calculate the slope across the arc from point B to point C. You can see that the slope of the curve at point B is greater than at point C. When we calculate the slope across an arc, we are calculating the average slope between two points. As we move along the arc from B to C, x increases from 3 to 5 and y increases from 4.0 to 5.5. The change in x is 2 (Δx is 2), and the change in y is 1.5 (Δy is 1.5).

FIGURE A1.11   Slope Across an Arc

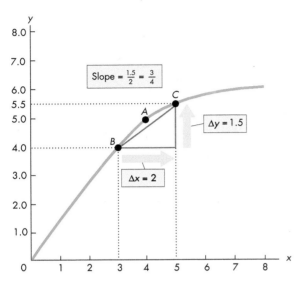

To calculate the average slope of the curve along the arc BC, draw a straight line from point B to point C. The slope of the line BC is calculated by dividing the change in y by the change in x. In moving from B to C, the increase in x is 2 (Δx equals 2) and the change in y is 1.5 (Δy equals 1.5). The slope of the line BC is 1.5 divided by 2, or 3/4. So the slope of the curve across the arc BC is 3/4.

myeconlab animation

Therefore the slope is

$$\frac{\Delta y}{\Delta x} = \frac{1.5}{2} = \frac{3}{4}.$$

So the slope of the curve across the arc BC is 3/4.

This calculation gives us the slope of the curve between points B and C. The actual slope calculated is the slope of the straight line from B to C. This slope approximates the average slope of the curve along the arc BC. In this particular example, the slope across the arc BC is identical to the slope of the curve at point A, but the calculation of the slope of a curve does not always work out so neatly. You might have fun constructing some more examples and a few counter examples.

You now know how to make and interpret a graph. So far, we've limited our attention to graphs of two variables. We're now going to learn how to graph more than two variables.

Graphing Relationships Among More Than Two Variables

We have seen that we can graph the relationship between two variables as a point formed by the *x*- and *y*-coordinates in a two-dimensional graph. You might be thinking that although a two-dimensional graph is informative, most of the things in which you are likely to be interested involve relationships among many variables, not just two. For example, the amount of ice cream consumed depends on the price of ice cream and the temperature. If ice cream is expensive and the temperature is low, people eat much less ice cream than when ice cream is inexpensive and the temperature is high. For any given price of ice cream, the quantity consumed varies with the temperature; and for any given temperature, the quantity of ice cream consumed varies with its price.

Figure A1.12 shows a relationship among three variables. The table shows the number of gallons of ice cream consumed each day at two different temperatures and at a number of different prices of ice cream. How can we graph these numbers?

To graph a relationship that involves more than two variables, we use the *ceteris paribus* assumption.

Ceteris Paribus

Ceteris paribus (often shortened to *cet par*) means "if all other relevant things remain the same." To isolate the relationship of interest in a laboratory experiment, a scientist holds everything constant except for the variable whose effect is being studied. Economists use the same method to graph a relationship that has more than two variables.

Figure A1.12 shows an example. There, you can see what happens to the quantity of ice cream consumed when the price of ice cream varies but the temperature is held constant.

The curve labeled 70°F shows the relationship between ice cream consumption and the price of ice cream if the temperature remains at 70°F. The numbers used to plot that curve are those in the first two columns of the table. For example, if the temperature is 70°F, 10 gallons are consumed when the price is $2.75 a scoop and 18 gallons are consumed when the price is $2.25 a scoop.

The curve labeled 90°F shows the relationship between ice cream consumption and the price of ice cream if the temperature remains at 90°F. The

all else equal

FIGURE A1.12   Graphing a Relationship Among Three Variables

Price (dollars per scoop)	Ice cream consumption (gallons per day)	
	70°F	90°F
2.00	25	50
2.25	18	36
2.50	13	26
2.75	**10**	**20**
3.00	7	14
3.25	5	10
3.50	3	6

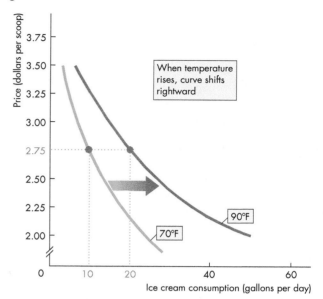

Ice cream consumption depends on its price and the temperature. The table tells us how many gallons of ice cream are consumed each day at different prices and two different temperatures. For example, if the price is $2.75 a scoop and the temperature is 70°F, 10 gallons of ice cream are consumed.

To graph a relationship among three variables, the value of one variable is held constant. The graph shows the relationship between price and consumption when temperature is held constant. One curve holds temperature at 70°F and the other holds it at 90°F.

A change in the price of ice cream brings a movement along one of the curves—along the blue curve at 70°F and along the red curve at 90°F.

When the temperature *rises* from 70°F to 90°F, the curve that shows the relationship between consumption and price *shifts* rightward from the blue curve to the red curve.

numbers used to plot that curve are those in the first and third columns of the table. For example, if the temperature is 90°F, 20 gallons are consumed when the price is $2.75 a scoop and 36 gallons are consumed when the price is $2.25 a scoop.

When the price of ice cream changes but the temperature is constant, you can think of what happens in the graph as a movement along one of the curves. At 70°F there is a movement along the blue curve and at 90°F there is a movement along the red curve.

When Other Things Change

The temperature is held constant along each of the curves in Fig. A1.12, but in reality the temperature

changes. When that event occurs, you can think of what happens in the graph as a shift of the curve. When the temperature rises from 70°F to 90°F, the curve that shows the relationship between ice cream consumption and the price of ice cream shifts rightward from the blue curve to the red curve.

You will encounter these ideas of movements along and shifts of curves at many points in your study of economics. Think carefully about what you've just learned and make up some examples (with assumed numbers) about other relationships.

With what you have learned about graphs, you can move forward with your study of economics. There are no graphs in this book that are more complicated than those that have been explained in this appendix.

MATHEMATICAL NOTE
Equations of Straight Lines

If a straight line in a graph describes the relationship between two variables, we call it a linear relationship. Figure 1 shows the *linear relationship* between a person's expenditure and income. This person spends $100 a week (by borrowing or spending previous savings) when income is zero. Out of each dollar earned, this person spends 50 cents (and saves 50 cents).

All linear relationships are described by the same general equation. We call the quantity that is measured on the horizontal axis (or x-axis) x, and we call the quantity that is measured on the vertical axis (or y-axis) y. In the case of Fig. 1, x is income and y is expenditure.

A Linear Equation

The equation that describes a straight-line relationship between x and y is

$$y = a + bx.$$

In this equation, a and b are fixed numbers and they are called *constants*. The values of x and y vary, so these numbers are called *variables*. Because the equation describes a straight line, the equation is called a *linear equation.*

The equation tells us that when the value of x is zero, the value of y is a. We call the constant a the y-axis intercept. The reason is that on the graph the straight line hits the y-axis at a value equal to a. Figure 1 illustrates the y-axis intercept.

For positive values of x, the value of y exceeds *a*. The constant b tells us by how much y increases above a as x increases. The constant b is the slope of the line.

Slope of Line

As we explain in the chapter, the *slope* of a relationship is the change in the value of y divided by the change in the value of x. We use the Greek letter Δ (delta) to represent "change in." So Δy means the change in the value of the variable measured on the y-axis, and Δx means the change in the value of the variable measured on the x-axis. Therefore the slope of the relationship is

$$\text{Slope} = \frac{\Delta y}{\Delta x}$$

To see why the slope is b, suppose that initially the value of x is x_1, or $200 in Fig. 2. The corresponding value of y is y_1, also $200 in Fig. 2. The equation of the line tells us that

$$y_1 = a + bx_1. \tag{1}$$

Now the value of x increases by Δx to $x_1 + \Delta x$ (or $400 in Fig. 2). And the value of y increases by Δy to $y_1 + \Delta y$ (or $300 in Fig. 2).

The equation of the line now tells us that

$$y_1 + \Delta y = a + b(x_1 + \Delta x). \tag{2}$$

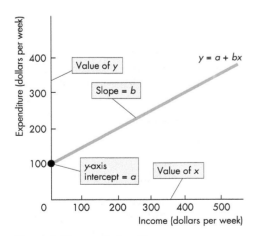

Figure 1 Linear relationship

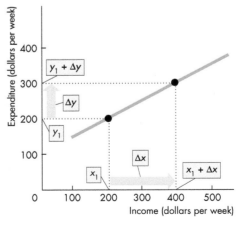

Figure 2 Calculating slope

To calculate the slope of the line, subtract equation (1) from equation (2) to obtain

$$\Delta y = b\Delta x \qquad (3)$$

and now divide equation (3) by Δx to obtain

$$\Delta y/\Delta x = b.$$

So the slope of the line is b.

Position of Line

The y-axis intercept determines the position of the line on the graph. Figure 3 illustrates the relationship between the y-axis intercept and the position of the line. In this graph, the y-axis measures saving and the x-axis measures income.

When the y-axis intercept, a, is positive, the line hits the y-axis at a positive value of y—as the blue line does. Its y-axis intercept is 100. When the y-axis intercept, a, is zero, the line hits the y-axis at the origin—as the purple line does. Its y-axis intercept is 0. When the y-axis intercept, a, is negative, the line hits the y-axis at a negative value of y—as the red line does. Its y-axis intercept is –100.

As the equations of the three lines show, the value of the y-axis intercept does not influence the slope of the line. All three lines have a slope equal to 0.5.

Positive Relationships

Figure 1 shows a positive relationship—the two variables x and y move in the same direction. All positive relationships have a slope that is positive. In the equation of the line, the constant b is positive. In this example, the y-axis intercept, a, is 100. The slope b equals $\Delta y/\Delta x$, which in Fig. 2 is 100/200 or 0.5. The equation of the line is

$$y = 100 + 0.5x.$$

Negative Relationships

Figure 4 shows a negative relationship—the two variables x and y move in the opposite direction. All negative relationships have a slope that is negative. In the equation of the line, the constant b is negative. In the example in Fig. 4, the y-axis intercept, a, is 30. The slope, b, equals $\Delta y/\Delta x$, which is –20/2 or –10. The equation of the line is

$$y = 30 + (-10)x$$

or

$$y = 30 - 10x.$$

Example

A straight line has a y-axis intercept of 50 and a slope of 2. What is the equation of this line?
The equation of a straight line is

$$y = a + bx$$

where a is the y-axis intercept and b is the slope. So the equation is

$$y = 50 + 2x.$$

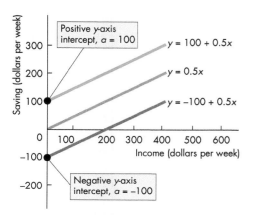

Figure 3 The y-axis intercept

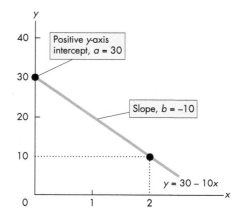

Figure 4 Negative relationship

REVIEW QUIZ

1 Explain how we "read" the three graphs in Figs A1.1 and A1.2.
2 Explain what scatter diagrams show and why we use them.
3 Explain how we "read" the three scatter diagrams in Figs A1.3 and A1.4.
4 Draw a graph to show the relationship between two variables that move in the same direction.
5 Draw a graph to show the relationship between two variables that move in opposite directions.
6 Draw a graph to show the relationship between two variables that have a maximum and a minimum.

7 Which of the relationships in Questions 4 and 5 is a positive relationship and which is a negative relationship?
8 What are the two ways of calculating the slope of a curved line?
9 How do we graph a relationship among more than two variables?
10 Explain what change will bring a *movement along* a curve.
11 Explain what change will bring a *shift* of a curve.

You can work these questions in Study Plan 1.A and get instant feedback.

SUMMARY

Key Points

Graphing Data (pp. 11–14)

- A graph is made by plotting the values of two variables x and y at a point that corresponds to their values measured along the x-axis and the y-axis.
- A scatter diagram is a graph that plots the values of two variables for a number of different values of each.
- A scatter diagram shows the relationship between the two variables. It shows whether they are positively related, negatively related, or unrelated.

Graphs Used in Economic Models (pp. 14–17)

- Graphs are used to show relationships among variables in economic models.
- Relationships can be positive (an upward-sloping curve), negative (a downward-sloping curve), positive and then negative (have a maximum point), negative and then positive (have a minimum point), or unrelated (a horizontal or vertical curve).

The Slope of a Relationship (pp. 18–20)

- The slope of a relationship is calculated as the change in the value of the variable measured on the y-axis divided by the change in the value of the variable measured on the x-axis—that is, $\Delta y/\Delta x$.
- A straight line has a constant slope.
- A curved line has a varying slope. To calculate the slope of a curved line, we calculate the slope at a point or across an arc.

Graphing Relationships Among More Than Two Variables (pp. 20–21)

- To graph a relationship among more than two variables, we hold constant the values of all the variables except two.
- We then plot the value of one of the variables against the value of another.
- A *cet par* change in the value of a variable on an axis of a graph brings a movement along the curve.
- A change in the value of a variable held constant along the curve brings a shift of the curve.

Key Terms

Ceteris paribus, 20
Direct relationship, 14
Inverse relationship, 15
Linear relationship, 14
Negative relationship, 15
Positive relationship, 14
Scatter diagram, 12
Slope, 18

STUDY PLAN PROBLEMS AND APPLICATIONS

myeconlab You can work Problems 1 to 11 in MyEconLab Chapter 1A Study Plan and get instant feedback.

Use the following spreadsheet to work Problems 1 to 3. The spreadsheet provides data on the U.S. economy: Column A is the year, column B is the inflation rate, column C is the interest rate, column D is the growth rate, and column E is the unemployment rate.

	A	B	C	D	E
1	1999	2.2	4.6	4.8	4.2
2	2000	3.4	5.8	4.1	4.0
3	2001	2.8	3.4	1.1	4.7
4	2002	1.6	1.6	1.8	5.8
5	2003	2.3	1.0	2.5	6.0
6	2004	2.7	1.4	3.6	5.5
7	2005	3.4	3.2	3.1	5.1
8	2006	3.2	4.7	2.7	4.6
9	2007	2.8	4.4	2.1	4.6
10	2008	3.8	1.4	0.4	5.8
11	2009	−0.4	0.2	−2.4	9.3

1. Draw a scatter diagram of the inflation rate and the interest rate. Describe the relationship.
2. Draw a scatter diagram of the growth rate and the unemployment rate. Describe the relationship.
3. Draw a scatter diagram of the interest rate and the unemployment rate. Describe the relationship.

Use the following news clip to work Problems 4 to 6.

Clash of the Titans **Tops Box Office With Sales of $61.2 Million:**

Movie	Theaters (number)	Revenue (dollars per theater)
Clash of the Titans	3,777	16,213
Tyler Perry's Why Did I Get Married	2,155	13,591
How To Train Your Dragon	4,060	7,145
The Last Song	2,673	5,989

Source: Bloomberg.com, April 5, 2010

4. Draw a graph of the relationship between the revenue per theater on the y-axis and the number of theaters on the x-axis. Describe the relationship.
5. Calculate the slope of the relationship between 4,060 and 2,673 theaters.
6. Calculate the slope of the relationship between 2,155 and 4,060 theaters.

7. Calculate the slope of the following relationship.

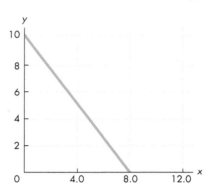

Use the following relationship to work Problems 8 and 9.

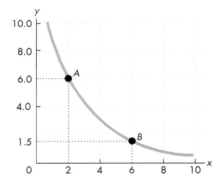

8. Calculate the slope of the relationship at point A and at point B.
9. Calculate the slope across the arc AB.

Use the following table to work Problems 10 and 11. The table gives the price of a balloon ride, the temperature, and the number of rides a day.

Price (dollars per ride)	Balloon rides (number per day)		
	50°F	**70°F**	**90°F**
5	32	40	50
10	27	32	40
15	18	27	32

10. Draw a graph to show the relationship between the price and the number of rides, when the temperature is 70°F. Describe this relationship.
11. What happens in the graph in Problem 10 if the temperature rises to 90°F?

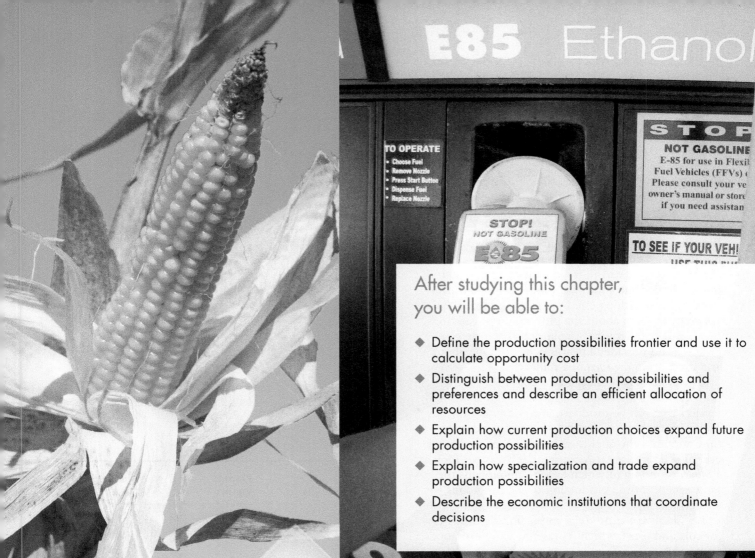

2

THE ECONOMIC PROBLEM

 (duplicate reference removed)

After studying this chapter,
you will be able to:

◆ Define the production possibilities frontier and use it to calculate opportunity cost

◆ Distinguish between production possibilities and preferences and describe an efficient allocation of resources

◆ Explain how current production choices expand future production possibilities

◆ Explain how specialization and trade expand production possibilities

◆ Describe the economic institutions that coordinate decisions

Why does food cost much more today than it did a few years ago? One reason is that we now use part of our corn crop to produce ethanol, a clean biofuel substitute for gasoline. Another reason is that drought in some parts of the world has decreased global grain production. In this chapter, you will study an economic model—the production possibilities frontier—and you will learn why ethanol production and drought have increased the cost of producing food. You will also learn how to assess whether it is a good idea to increase corn production to produce fuel; how we can expand our production possibilities; and how we gain by trading with others.

Production Possibilities and Opportunity Cost

Every working day, in mines, factories, shops, and offices and on farms and construction sites across the United States, 138 million people produce a vast variety of goods and services valued at $50 billion. But the quantities of goods and services that we can produce are limited both by our available resources and by technology. And if we want to increase our production of one good, we must decrease our production of something else—we face a tradeoff. You are going to learn about the production possibilities frontier, which describes the limit to what we can produce and provides a neat way of thinking about and illustrating the idea of a tradeoff.

The **production possibilities frontier** (*PPF*) is the boundary between those combinations of goods and services that can be produced and those that cannot. To illustrate the *PPF*, we focus on two goods at a time and hold the quantities produced of all the other goods and services constant. That is, we look at a *model* economy in which everything remains the same except for the production of the two goods we are considering.

Let's look at the production possibilities frontier for cola and pizza, which represent *any* pair of goods or services.

Production Possibilities Frontier

The *production possibilities frontier* for cola and pizza shows the limits to the production of these two goods, given the total resources and technology available to produce them. Figure 2.1 shows this production possibilities frontier. The table lists some combinations of the quantities of pizza and cola that can be produced in a month given the resources available. The figure graphs these combinations. The *x*-axis shows the quantity of pizzas produced, and the *y*-axis shows the quantity of cola produced.

The *PPF* illustrates *scarcity* because we cannot attain the points outside the frontier. These points describe wants that can't be satisfied. We can produce at any point *inside* the *PPF* or *on* the *PPF*. These points are attainable. Suppose that in a typical month, we produce 4 million pizzas and 5 million cans of cola. Figure 2.1 shows this combination as point *E* and as possibility *E* in the table. The figure

FIGURE 2.1   Production Possibilities Frontier

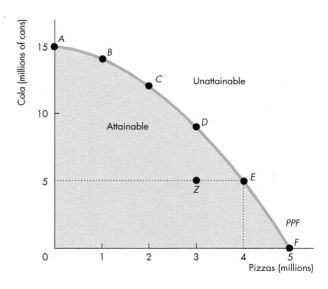

Possibility	Pizzas (millions)		Cola (millions of cans)
A	0	and	15
B	1	and	14
C	2	and	12
D	3	and	9
E	4	and	5
F	5	and	0

The table lists six production possibilities for cola and pizzas. Row *A* tells us that if we produce no pizzas, the maximum quantity of cola we can produce is 15 million cans. Points *A*, *B*, *C*, *D*, *E*, and *F* in the figure represent the rows of the table. The curve passing through these points is the production possibilities frontier (*PPF*).

The *PPF* separates the attainable from the unattainable. Production is possible at any point *inside* the orange area or *on* the frontier. Points outside the frontier are unattainable. Points inside the frontier, such as point *Z*, are inefficient because resources are wasted or misallocated. At such points, it is possible to use the available resources to produce more of either or both goods.

myeconlab   animation

*[handwritten top-left margin: Sunk cost. *it is money spend regardless of your choices → irreversible cost. It is a cost that has already been incurred and cannot be recovered]*

[handwritten top-right: Sunk cost concept → lecture 3 CH 1]

also shows other production possibilities. For example, we might stop producing pizza and move all the people who produce it into producing cola. Point *A* in the figure and possibility *A* in the table show this case. The quantity of cola produced increases to 15 million cans, and pizza production dries up. Alternatively, we might close the cola factories and switch all the resources into producing pizza. In this situation, we produce 5 million pizzas. Point *F* in the figure and possibility *F* in the table show this case.

Production Efficiency

We achieve **production efficiency** if we produce goods and services at the lowest possible cost. This outcome occurs at all the points *on the PPF*. At points *inside* the *PPF*, production is inefficient because we are giving up more than necessary of one good to produce a given quantity of the other good.

For example, at point *Z* in Fig. 2.1, we produce 3 million pizzas and 5 million cans of cola. But we have enough resources to produce 3 million pizzas and 9 million cans of cola. Our pizzas cost more cola than necessary. We can get them for a lower cost. Only when we produce *on the PPF* do we incur the lowest possible cost of production.

Production is *inefficient* inside the *PPF* because resources are either *unused* or *misallocated* or both.

Resources are *unused* when they are idle but could be working. For example, we might leave some of the factories idle or some workers unemployed.

[handwritten margin: not active ← must. without purpose]

Resources are *misallocated* when they are assigned to tasks for which they are not the best match. For example, we might assign skilled pizza chefs to work in a cola factory and skilled cola producers to work in a pizza shop. We could get more pizzas *and* more cola from these same workers if we reassigned them to the tasks that more closely match their skills.

Tradeoff Along the *PPF*

Every choice *along* the *PPF* involves a *tradeoff*. On the *PPF* in Fig. 2.1, we trade off cola for pizzas.

Tradeoffs arise in every imaginable real-world situation in which a choice must be made. At any given point in time, we have a fixed amount of labor, land, capital, and entrepreneurship. By using our available technologies, we can employ these resources to produce goods and services, but we are limited in what we can produce. This limit defines a boundary

between what we can attain and what we cannot attain. This boundary is the real-world's production possibilities frontier, and it defines the tradeoffs that we must make. On our real-world *PPF*, we can produce more of any one good or service only if we produce less of some other goods or services.

When doctors want to spend more on AIDS and cancer research, they face a tradeoff: more medical research for less of some other things. When Congress wants to spend more on education and health care, it faces a tradeoff: more education and health care for less national defense or less homeland security. When an environmental group argues for less logging, it is suggesting a tradeoff: greater conservation of endangered wildlife for less paper. When you want to study more, you face a tradeoff: more study time for less leisure or sleep.

All tradeoffs involve a cost—an opportunity cost.

Opportunity Cost   *[handwritten: = lost / Produced]*

The **opportunity cost** of an action is the highest-valued alternative forgone. The *PPF* makes this idea precise and enables us to calculate opportunity cost. Along the *PPF*, there are only two goods, so there is only one alternative forgone: some quantity of the other good. Given our current resources and technology, we can produce more pizzas only if we produce less cola. The opportunity cost of producing an additional pizza is the cola we *must* forgo. Similarly, the opportunity cost of producing an additional can of cola is the quantity of pizza we must forgo.

In Fig. 2.1, if we move from point *C* to point *D*, we get 1 million more pizzas but 3 million fewer cans of cola. The additional 1 million pizzas *cost* 3 million cans of cola. One pizza costs 3 cans of cola.

We can also work out the opportunity cost of moving in the opposite direction. In Fig. 2.1, if we move from point *D* to point *C*, the quantity of cola produced increases by 3 million cans and the quantity of pizzas produced decreases by 1 million. So if we choose point *C* over point *D*, the additional 3 million cans of cola *cost* 1 million pizzas. One can of cola costs 1/3 of a pizza.

Opportunity Cost Is a Ratio Opportunity cost is a ratio. It is the decrease in the quantity produced of one good divided by the increase in the quantity produced of another good as we move along the production possibilities frontier.

[handwritten bottom-center:
Jobs   70   80   90
Benefits   90 ≤ 90   80 = 80
best alternative, cost   80 = 80   90 = 90
*   10   -10]*

[handwritten bottom-right:
Explicit costs = monetary expenses.
Implicit costs = value of forgone alternative.]

Because opportunity cost is a ratio, the opportunity cost of producing an additional can of cola is equal to the *inverse* of the opportunity cost of producing an additional pizza. Check this proposition by returning to the calculations we've just worked through. When we move along the *PPF* from *C* to *D*, the opportunity cost of a pizza is 3 cans of cola. The inverse of 3 is 1/3. If we decrease the production of pizza and increase the production of cola by moving from *D* to *C*, the opportunity cost of a can of cola must be 1/3 of a pizza. That is exactly the number that we calculated for the move from *D* to *C*.

Increasing Opportunity Cost The opportunity cost of a pizza increases as the quantity of pizzas produced increases. The outward-bowed shape of the *PPF* reflects increasing opportunity cost. When we produce a large quantity of cola and a small quantity of pizza—between points *A* and *B* in Fig. 2.1—the frontier has a gentle slope. An increase in the quantity of pizzas costs a small decrease in the quantity of cola—the opportunity cost of a pizza is a small quantity of cola.

When we produce a large quantity of pizzas and a small quantity of cola—between points *E* and *F* in Fig. 2.1—the frontier is steep. A given increase in the quantity of pizzas *costs* a large decrease in the quantity of cola, so the opportunity cost of a pizza is a large quantity of cola.

The *PPF* is bowed outward because resources are not all equally productive in all activities. People with many years of experience working for PepsiCo are good at producing cola but not very good at making pizzas. So if we move some of these people from PepsiCo to Domino's, we get a small increase in the quantity of pizzas but a large decrease in the quantity of cola.

Similarly, people who have spent years working at Domino's are good at producing pizzas, but they have no idea how to produce cola. So if we move some of these people from Domino's to PepsiCo, we get a small increase in the quantity of cola but a large decrease in the quantity of pizzas. The more of either good we try to produce, the less productive are the additional resources we use to produce that good and the larger is the opportunity cost of a unit of that good.

Economics in Action
Increasing Opportunity Cost on the Farm

Sanders Wright, a homesick Mississippi native, is growing cotton in Iowa. The growing season is short, so his commercial success is unlikely. Cotton does not grow well in Iowa, but corn does. A farm with irrigation can produce 300 bushels of corn per acre—twice the U.S. average.

Ronnie Gerik, a Texas cotton farmer, has started to grow corn. Ronnie doesn't have irrigation and instead relies on rainfall. That's not a problem for cotton, which just needs a few soakings a season. But it's a big problem for corn, which needs an inch of water a week. Also, corn can't take the heat like cotton, and if the temperature rises too much, Ronnie will be lucky to get 100 bushels an acre.

An Iowa corn farmer gives up almost no cotton to produce his 300 bushels of corn per acre—corn has a low opportunity cost. But Ronnie Gerick gives up a huge amount of cotton to produce his 100 bushels of corn per acre. By switching some land from cotton to corn, Ronnie has increased the production of corn, but the additional corn has a high opportunity cost.

"Deere worker makes 'cotton pickin' miracle happen," WCFCourier.com; and "Farmers stampede to corn," USA Today.

REVIEW QUIZ

1 How does the production possibilities frontier illustrate scarcity?
2 How does the production possibilities frontier illustrate production efficiency?
3 How does the production possibilities frontier show that every choice involves a tradeoff?
4 How does the production possibilities frontier illustrate opportunity cost?
5 Why is opportunity cost a ratio?
6 Why does the *PPF* bow outward and what does that imply about the relationship between opportunity cost and the quantity produced?

You can work these questions in Study Plan 2.1 and get instant feedback.

We've seen that what we can produce is limited by the production possibilities frontier. We've also seen that production on the *PPF* is efficient. But we can produce many different quantities on the *PPF*. How do we choose among them? How do we know which point on the *PPF* is the best one?

Using Resources Efficiently

We achieve *production efficiency* at every point on the *PPF*, but which point is best? The answer is the point on the *PPF* at which goods and services are produced in the quantities that provide the greatest possible benefit. When goods and services are produced at the lowest possible cost and in the quantities that provide the greatest possible benefit, we have achieved **allocative efficiency.**

The questions that we raised when we reviewed the four big issues in Chapter 1 are questions about allocative efficiency. To answer such questions, we must measure and compare costs and benefits.

The *PPF* and Marginal Cost

The **marginal cost** of a good is the opportunity cost of producing one more unit of it. We calculate marginal cost from the slope of the *PPF*. As the quantity of pizzas produced increases, the *PPF* gets steeper and the marginal cost of a pizza increases. Figure 2.2 illustrates the calculation of the marginal cost of a pizza.

Begin by finding the opportunity cost of pizza in blocks of 1 million pizzas. The cost of the first million pizzas is 1 million cans of cola; the cost of the second million pizzas is 2 million cans of cola; the cost of the third million pizzas is 3 million cans of cola, and so on. The bars in part (a) illustrate these calculations.

The bars in part (b) show the cost of an average pizza in each of the 1 million pizza blocks. Focus on the third million pizzas—the move from *C* to *D* in part (a). Over this range, because 1 million pizzas cost 3 million cans of cola, one of these pizzas, on average, costs 3 cans of cola—the height of the bar in part (b).

Next, find the opportunity cost of each additional pizza—the marginal cost of a pizza. The marginal cost of a pizza increases as the quantity of pizzas produced increases. The marginal cost at point *C* is less than it is at point *D*. On average over the range from *C* to *D*, the marginal cost of a pizza is 3 cans of cola. But it exactly equals 3 cans of cola only in the middle of the range between *C* and *D*.

The red dot in part (b) indicates that the marginal cost of a pizza is 3 cans of cola when 2.5 million pizzas are produced. Each black dot in part (b) is interpreted in the same way. The red curve that passes through these dots, labeled *MC*, is the marginal cost curve. It shows the marginal cost of a pizza at each quantity of pizzas as we move along the *PPF*.

FIGURE 2.2   The *PPF* and Marginal Cost

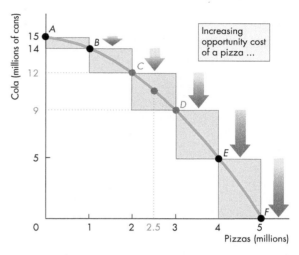

(a) PPF and opportunity cost

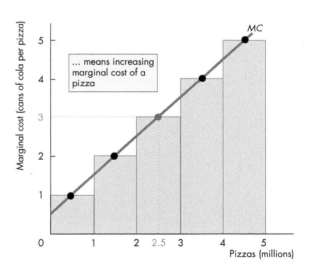

(b) Marginal cost

Marginal cost is calculated from the slope of the *PPF*. As the quantity of pizzas produced increases, the *PPF* gets steeper and the marginal cost of a pizza increases. The bars in part (a) show the opportunity cost of pizza in blocks of 1 million pizzas. The bars in part (b) show the cost of an average pizza in each of these 1 million blocks. The red curve, *MC*, shows the marginal cost of a pizza at each point along the *PPF*. This curve passes through the center of each of the bars in part (b).

Preferences and Marginal Benefit

The **marginal benefit** from a good or service is the benefit received from consuming one more unit of it. This benefit is subjective. It depends on people's **preferences**—people's likes and dislikes and the intensity of those feelings.

Marginal benefit and *preferences* stand in sharp contrast to *marginal cost* and *production possibilities.* Preferences describe what people like and want and the production possibilities describe the limits or constraints on what is feasible.

We need a concrete way of illustrating preferences that parallels the way we illustrate the limits to production using the *PPF.*

The device that we use to illustrate preferences is the **marginal benefit curve,** which is a curve that shows the relationship between the marginal benefit from a good and the quantity consumed of that good. Note that the *marginal benefit curve is unrelated* to the *PPF* and cannot be derived from it.

We measure the marginal benefit from a good or service by the most that people are *willing to pay* for an additional unit of it. The idea is that you are willing to pay less for a good than it is worth to you but you are not willing to pay more: The most you are willing to pay for something is its marginal benefit.

It is a general principle that the more we have of any good or service, the smaller is its marginal benefit and the less we are willing to pay for an additional unit of it. This tendency is so widespread and strong that we call it a principle—the *principle of decreasing marginal benefit.*

The basic reason why marginal benefit decreases is that we like variety. The more we consume of any one good or service, the more we tire of it and would prefer to switch to something else.

Think about your willingness to pay for a pizza. If pizza is hard to come by and you can buy only a few slices a year, you might be willing to pay a high price to get an additional slice. But if pizza is all you've eaten for the past few days, you are willing to pay almost nothing for another slice.

You've learned to think about cost as opportunity cost, not as a dollar cost. You can think about marginal benefit and willingness to pay in the same way. The marginal benefit, measured by what you are willing to pay for something, is the quantity of other goods and services that you are willing to forgo. Let's continue with the example of cola and pizza and illustrate preferences this way.

FIGURE 2.3   Preferences and the Marginal Benefit Curve

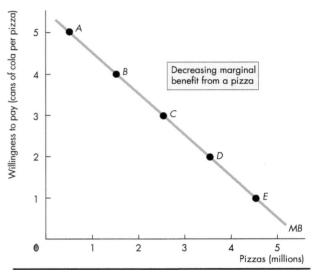

Possibility	Pizzas (millions)	Willingness to pay (cans of cola per pizza)
A	0.5	5
B	1.5	4
C	2.5	3
D	3.5	2
E	4.5	1

The smaller the quantity of pizzas available, the more cola people are willing to give up for an additional pizza. With 0.5 million pizzas available, people are willing to pay 5 cans of cola per pizza. But with 4.5 million pizzas, people are willing to pay only 1 can of cola per pizza. Willingness to pay measures marginal benefit. A universal feature of people's preferences is that marginal benefit decreases.

Ⓧ myeconlab   animation

Figure 2.3 illustrates preferences as the willingness to pay for pizza in terms of cola. In row *A*, with 0.5 million pizzas available, people are willing to pay 5 cans of cola per pizza. As the quantity of pizzas increases, the amount that people are willing to pay for a pizza falls. With 4.5 million pizzas available, people are willing to pay only 1 can of cola per pizza.

Let's now use the concepts of marginal cost and marginal benefit to describe allocative efficiency.

FIGURE 2.4   Efficient Use of Resources

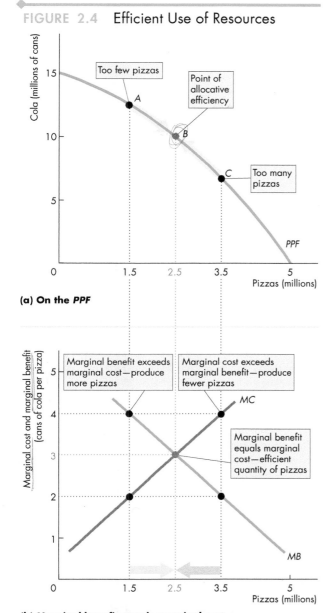

(a) On the PPF

(b) Marginal benefit equals marginal cost

review The greater the quantity of pizzas produced, the smaller is the marginal benefit (MB) from pizza—the less cola people are willing to give up to get an additional pizza. But the greater the quantity of pizzas produced, the greater is the marginal cost (MC) of a pizza—the more cola people must give up to get an additional pizza. When marginal benefit equals marginal cost, resources are being used efficiently.

 animation

Allocative Efficiency

At *any* point on the *PPF*, we cannot produce more of one good without giving up some other good. At the *best* point on the *PPF*, we cannot produce more of one good without giving up some other good that provides greater benefit. We are producing at the point of allocative efficiency—the point on the *PPF* that we prefer above all other points.

Suppose in Fig. 2.4, we produce 1.5 million pizzas. The marginal cost of a pizza is 2 cans of cola, and the marginal benefit from a pizza is 4 cans of cola. Because someone values an additional pizza more highly than it costs to produce, we can get more value from our resources by moving some of them out of producing cola and into producing pizza.

Now suppose we produce 3.5 million pizzas. The marginal cost of a pizza is now 4 cans of cola, but the marginal benefit from a pizza is only 2 cans of cola. Because the additional pizza costs more to produce than anyone thinks it is worth, we can get more value from our resources by moving some of them away from producing pizza and into producing cola.

Suppose we produce 2.5 million pizzas. Marginal cost and marginal benefit are now equal at 3 cans of cola. This allocation of resources between pizzas and cola is efficient. If more pizzas are produced, the forgone cola is worth more than the additional pizzas. If fewer pizzas are produced, the forgone pizzas are worth more than the additional cola.

REVIEW QUIZ

1   What is marginal cost? How is it measured?
2   What is marginal benefit? How is it measured?
3   How does the marginal benefit from a good change as the quantity produced of that good increases?
4   What is allocative efficiency and how does it relate to the production possibilities frontier?
5   What conditions must be satisfied if resources are used efficiently?

You can work these questions in Study Plan 2.2 and get instant feedback.   myeconlab

You now understand the limits to production and the conditions under which resources are used efficiently. Your next task is to study the expansion of production possibilities.

◆ Economic Growth

During the past 30 years, production per person in the United States has doubled. The expansion of production possibilities is called **economic growth**. Economic growth increases our *standard of living,* but it doesn't overcome scarcity and avoid opportunity cost. To make our economy grow, we face a trade-off—the faster we make production grow, the greater is the opportunity cost of economic growth.

The Cost of Economic Growth

Economic growth comes from technological change and capital accumulation. **Technological change** is the development of new goods and of better ways of producing goods and services. **Capital accumulation** is the growth of capital resources, including *human capital.*

Technological change and capital accumulation have vastly expanded our production possibilities. We can produce automobiles that provide us with more transportation than was available when we had only horses and carriages. We can produce satellites that provide global communications on a much larger scale than that available with the earlier cable technology. But if we use our resources to develop new technologies and produce capital, we must decrease our production of consumption goods and services. New technologies and new capital have an opportunity cost. Let's look at this opportunity cost.

Instead of studying the *PPF* of pizzas and cola, we'll hold the quantity of cola produced constant and examine the *PPF* for pizzas and pizza ovens. Figure 2.5 shows this *PPF* as the blue curve PPF_0. If we devote no resources to producing pizza ovens, we produce at point *A*. If we produce 3 million pizzas, we can produce 6 pizza ovens at point *B*. If we produce no pizza, we can produce 10 ovens at point *C*.

The amount by which our production possibilities expand depends on the resources we devote to technological change and capital accumulation. If we devote no resources to this activity (point *A*), our *PPF* remains the blue curve PPF_0 in Fig. 2.5. If we cut the current pizza production and produce 6 ovens (point *B*), then in the future, we'll have more capital and our *PPF* will rotate outward to the position shown by the red curve PPF_1. The fewer resources we use for producing pizza and the more resources we use for producing ovens, the greater is the expansion of our future production possibilities.

FIGURE 2.5   Economic Growth

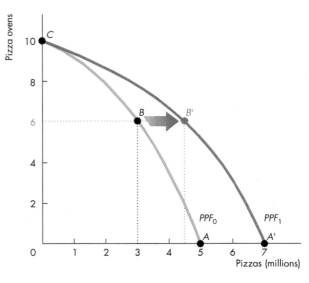

PPF_0 shows the limits to the production of pizzas and pizza ovens, with the production of all other goods and services remaining the same. If we devote no resources to producing pizza ovens and produce 5 million pizzas, our production possibilities will remain the same at PPF_0. But if we decrease pizza production to 3 million and produce 6 ovens, at point *B*, our production possibilities expand. After one period, the *PPF* rotates outward to PPF_1 and we can produce at point *B'*, a point outside the original PPF_0. We can rotate the *PPF* outward, but we cannot avoid opportunity cost. The opportunity cost of producing more pizzas in the future is fewer pizzas today.

⬦ myeconlab animation

Economic growth brings enormous benefits in the form of increased consumption in the future, but it is not free and it doesn't abolish scarcity.

In Fig. 2.5, to make economic growth happen we must use some resources to produce new ovens, which leaves fewer resources to produce pizzas. To move to *B'* in the future, we must move from *A* to *B* today. The opportunity cost of more pizzas in the future is fewer pizzas today. Also, on the new *PPF*, we still face a tradeoff and opportunity cost.

The ideas about economic growth that we have explored in the setting of the pizza industry also apply to nations. Hong Kong and the United States provide a striking case study.

Economics in Action

Hong Kong Catching Up to the United States

In 1969, the production possibilities per person in the United States were more than four times those in Hong Kong (see the figure). The United States devotes one fifth of its resources to accumulating capital and in 1969 was at point *A* on its *PPF*. Hong Kong devotes one third of its resources to accumulating capital and in 1969, Hong Kong was at point *A* on its *PPF*.

Since 1969, both countries have experienced economic growth, but because Hong Kong devotes a bigger fraction of its resources to accumulating capital, its production possibilities have expanded more quickly.

By 2009, production possibilities per person in Hong Kong had reached 94 percent of those in the United States. If Hong Kong continues to devote more resources to accumulating capital than we do (at point *B* on its 2009 *PPF*), it will continue to grow more rapidly. But if Hong Kong decreases capital accumulation (moving to point *D* on its 2009 *PPF*), then its rate of economic growth will slow.

Hong Kong is typical of the fast-growing Asian economies, which include Taiwan, Thailand, South Korea, China, and India. Production possibilities expand in these countries by between 5 and almost 10 percent a year.

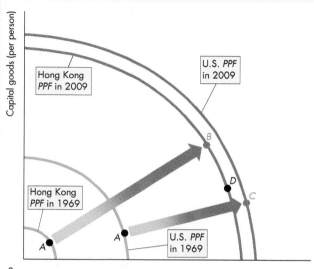

Economic Growth in the United States and Hong Kong

If such high economic growth rates are maintained, these other Asian countries will continue to close the gap between themselves and the United States, as Hong Kong is doing.

A Nation's Economic Growth

The experiences of the United States and Hong Kong make a striking example of the effects of our choices about consumption and capital goods on the rate of economic growth.

If a nation devotes all its factors of production to producing consumption goods and services and none to advancing technology and accumulating capital, its production possibilities in the future will be the same as they are today.

To expand production possibilities in the future, a nation must devote fewer resources to producing current consumption goods and services and some resources to accumulating capital and developing new technologies. As production possibilities expand, consumption in the future can increase. The decrease in today's consumption is the opportunity cost of tomorrow's increase in consumption.

REVIEW QUIZ

1 What generates economic growth?
2 How does economic growth influence the production possibilities frontier?
3 What is the opportunity cost of economic growth?
4 Why has Hong Kong experienced faster economic growth than the United States?
5 Does economic growth overcome scarcity?

You can work these questions in Study Plan 2.3 and get instant feedback.

Next, we're going to study another way in which we expand our production possibilities—the amazing fact that *both* buyers and sellers gain from specialization and trade.

◆ Gains from Trade

People can produce for themselves all the goods and services that they consume, or they can produce one good or a few goods and trade with others. Producing only one good or a few goods is called *specialization*. We are going to learn how people gain by specializing in the production of the good in which they have a *comparative advantage* and trading with others.

Comparative Advantage and Absolute Advantage

A person has a **comparative advantage** in an activity if that person can perform the activity at a lower opportunity cost than anyone else. Differences in opportunity costs arise from differences in individual abilities and from differences in the characteristics of other resources.

No one excels at everything. One person is an outstanding pitcher but a poor catcher; another person is a brilliant lawyer but a poor teacher. In almost all human endeavors, what one person does easily, someone else finds difficult. The same applies to land and capital. One plot of land is fertile but has no mineral deposits; another plot of land has outstanding views but is infertile. One machine has great precision but is difficult to operate; another is fast but often breaks down.

Although no one excels at everything, some people excel and can outperform others in a large number of activities—perhaps even in all activities. A person who is more productive than others has an **absolute advantage**.

Absolute advantage involves comparing productivities—production per hour—whereas comparative advantage involves comparing opportunity costs.

A person who has an absolute advantage does not have a *comparative* advantage in every activity. John Grisham is a better lawyer and a better author of fast-paced thrillers than most people. He has an absolute advantage in these two activities. But compared to others, he is a better writer than lawyer, so his *comparative* advantage is in writing.

Because ability and resources vary from one person to another, people have different opportunity costs of producing various goods. These differences in opportunity cost are the source of comparative advantage.

Let's explore the idea of comparative advantage by looking at two smoothie bars: one operated by Liz and the other operated by Joe.

Liz's Smoothie Bar Liz produces smoothies and salads. In Liz's high-tech bar, she can turn out either a smoothie or a salad every 2 minutes—see Table 2.1. If Liz spends all her time making smoothies, she can produce 30 an hour. And if she spends all her time making salads, she can also produce 30 an hour. If she splits her time equally between the two, she can produce 15 smoothies and 15 salads an hour. For each additional smoothie Liz produces, she must decrease her production of salads by one, and for each additional salad she produces, she must decrease her production of smoothies by one. So

> Liz's opportunity cost of producing 1 smoothie is 1 salad,

and

> Liz's opportunity cost of producing 1 salad is 1 smoothie.

Liz's customers buy smoothies and salads in equal quantities, so she splits her time equally between the two items and produces 15 smoothies and 15 salads an hour.

Joe's Smoothie Bar Joe also produces smoothies and salads, but his bar is smaller than Liz's. Also, Joe has only one blender, and it's a slow, old machine. Even if Joe uses all his resources to produce smoothies, he can produce only 6 an hour—see Table 2.2. But Joe is good at making salads. If he uses all his resources to make salads, he can produce 30 an hour.

Joe's ability to make smoothies and salads is the same regardless of how he splits an hour between the two tasks. He can make a salad in 2 minutes or a smoothie in 10 minutes. For each additional smoothie

TABLE 2.1   Liz's Production Possibilities

Item	Minutes to produce 1	Quantity per hour
Smoothies	2	30
Salads	2	30

TABLE 2.2   Joe's Production Possibilities

Item	Minutes to produce 1	Quantity per hour
Smoothies	10	6
Salads	2	30

Joe produces, he must decrease his production of salads by 5. And for each additional salad he produces, he must decrease his production of smoothies by 1/5 of a smoothie. So

> Joe's opportunity cost of producing 1 smoothie is 5 salads,

and

> Joe's opportunity cost of producing 1 salad is 1/5 of a smoothie.

Joe's customers, like Liz's, buy smoothies and salads in equal quantities. So Joe spends 50 minutes of each hour making smoothies and 10 minutes of each hour making salads. With this division of his time, Joe produces 5 smoothies and 5 salads an hour.

Liz's Comparative Advantage In which of the two activities does Liz have a comparative advantage? Recall that comparative advantage is a situation in which one person's opportunity cost of producing a good is lower than another person's opportunity cost of producing that same good. Liz has a comparative advantage in producing smoothies. Her opportunity cost of a smoothie is 1 salad, whereas Joe's opportunity cost of a smoothie is 5 salads.

Joe's Comparative Advantage If Liz has a comparative advantage in producing smoothies, Joe must have a comparative advantage in producing salads. Joe's opportunity cost of a salad is 1/5 of a smoothie, whereas Liz's opportunity cost of a salad is 1 smoothie.

Achieving the Gains from Trade

Liz and Joe run into each other one evening in a singles bar. After a few minutes of getting acquainted, Liz tells Joe about her amazing smoothie business. Her only problem, she tells Joe, is that she would like to produce more because potential customers leave when her lines get too long.

Joe is hesitant to risk spoiling his chances by telling Liz about his own struggling business, but he takes the risk. Joe explains to Liz that he spends 50 minutes of every hour making 5 smoothies and 10 minutes making 5 salads. Liz's eyes pop. "Have I got a deal for you!" she exclaims.

Here's the deal that Liz sketches on a paper napkin. Joe stops making smoothies and allocates all his time to producing salads; Liz stops making salads and allocates all her time to producing smoothies. That is, they both specialize in producing the good in which they have a comparative advantage. Together they produce 30 smoothies and 30 salads—see Table 2.3(b).

They then trade. Liz sells Joe 10 smoothies and Joe sells Liz 20 salads—the price of a smoothie is 2 salads—see Table 2.3(c).

After the trade, Joe has 10 salads—the 30 he produces minus the 20 he sells to Liz. He also has the 10 smoothies that he buys from Liz. So Joe now has increased the quantities of smoothies and salads that he can sell to his customers—see Table 2.3(d).

TABLE 2.3   Liz and Joe Gain from Trade

(a) Before trade	Liz	Joe
Smoothies	15	5
Salads	15	5

(b) Specialization	Liz	Joe
Smoothies	30	0
Salads	0	30

(c) Trade	Liz	Joe
Smoothies	sell 10	buy 10
Salads	buy 20	sell 20

(d) After trade	Liz	Joe
Smoothies	20	10
Salads	20	10

(e) Gains from trade	Liz	Joe
Smoothies	+5	+5
Salads	+5	+5

Liz has 20 smoothies—the 30 she produces minus the 10 she sells to Joe. She also has the 20 salads that she buys from Joe. Liz has increased the quantities of smoothies and salads that she can sell to her customers—see Table 2.3(d). Liz and Joe both gain 5 smoothies and 5 salads an hour—see Table 2.3(e).

To illustrate her idea, Liz grabs a fresh napkin and draws the graphs in Fig. 2.6. The blue *PPF* in part (a) shows Joe's production possibilities. Before trade, he is producing 5 smoothies and 5 salads an hour at point *A*. The blue *PPF* in part (b) shows Liz's production possibilities. Before trade, she is producing 15 smoothies and 15 salads an hour at point *A*.

Liz's proposal is that they each specialize in producing the good in which they have a comparative advantage. Joe produces 30 salads and no smoothies at point *B* on his *PPF*. Liz produces 30 smoothies and no salads at point *B* on her *PPF*.

Liz and Joe then trade smoothies and salads at a price of 2 salads per smoothie or 1/2 a smoothie per salad. Joe gets smoothies for 2 salads each, which is less than the 5 salads it costs him to produce a smoothie. Liz gets salads for 1/2 a smoothie each, which is less than the 1 smoothie that it costs her to produce a salad.

With trade, Joe has 10 smoothies and 10 salads at point *C*—a gain of 5 smoothies and 5 salads. Joe moves to a point *outside* his *PPF*.

With trade, Liz has 20 smoothies and 20 salads at point *C*—a gain of 5 smoothies and 5 salads. Liz moves to a point *outside* her *PPF*.

Despite Liz being more productive than Joe, both of them gain from specializing—producing the good in which they have a comparative advantage—and trading.

FIGURE 2.6   The Gains from Trade

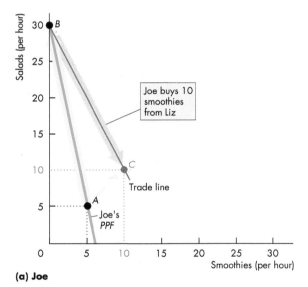

(a) Joe

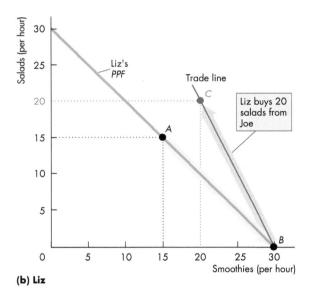

(b) Liz

Initially, Joe produces at point *A* on his *PPF* in part (a), and Liz produces at point *A* on her *PPF* in part (b). Joe's opportunity cost of producing a salad is less than Liz's, so Joe has a comparative advantage in producing salads. Liz's opportunity cost of producing a smoothie is less than Joe's, so Liz has a comparative advantage in producing smoothies.

If Joe specializes in making salads, he produces 30 salads and no smoothies at point *B* on his *PPF*. If Liz specializes

in making smoothies, she produces 30 smoothies and no salads at point *B* on her *PPF*. They exchange salads for smoothies along the red "Trade line." Liz buys salads from Joe for less than her opportunity cost of producing them. Joe buys smoothies from Liz for less than his opportunity cost of producing them. Each goes to point *C*—a point outside his or her *PPF*. With specialization and trade, Joe and Liz gain 5 smoothies and 5 salads each with no extra resources.

SUMMARY

Key Points

Production Possibilities and Opportunity Cost

(pp. 28–30)

- The production possibilities frontier is the boundary between production levels that are attainable and those that are not attainable when all the available resources are used to their limit.
- Production efficiency occurs at points on the production possibilities frontier.
- Along the production possibilities frontier, the opportunity cost of producing more of one good is the amount of the other good that must be given up.
- The opportunity cost of all goods increases as the production of the good increases.

Working Problems 1 to 3 will give you a better understanding of production possibilities and opportunity cost.

Using Resources Efficiently (pp. 31–33)

- Allocative efficiency occurs when goods and services are produced at the least possible cost and in the quantities that bring the greatest possible benefit.
- The marginal cost of a good is the opportunity cost of producing one more unit of it.
- The marginal benefit from a good is the benefit received from consuming one more unit of it and is measured by the willingness to pay for it.

- The marginal benefit of a good decreases as the amount of the good available increases.
- Resources are used efficiently when the marginal cost of each good is equal to its marginal benefit.

Working Problems 4 to 10 will give you a better understanding of the efficient use of resources.

Economic Growth (pp. 34–35)

- Economic growth, which is the expansion of production possibilities, results from capital accumulation and technological change.
- The opportunity cost of economic growth is forgone current consumption.
- The benefit of economic growth is increased future consumption.

Working Problem 11 will give you a better understanding of economic growth.

Gains from Trade (pp. 36–38)

- A person has a comparative advantage in producing a good if that person can produce the good at a lower opportunity cost than everyone else.
- People gain by specializing in the activity in which they have a comparative advantage and trading with others.

Working Problems 12 and 13 will give you a better understanding of the gains from trade.

Key Terms

Absolute advantage, 36
Allocative efficiency, 31
Capital accumulation, 34
Comparative advantage, 36
Economic growth, 34

Marginal benefit, 32
Marginal benefit curve, 32
Marginal cost, 31
Opportunity cost, 29
Preferences, 32

Production efficiency, 29
Production possibilities frontier, 28
Technological change, 34

STUDY PLAN PROBLEMS AND APPLICATIONS

myeconlab You can work Problems 1 to 19 in MyEconLab Chapter 2 Study Plan and get instant feedback.

Production Possibilities and Opportunity Cost

(Study Plan 2.1)

Use the following information to work Problems 1 to 3. Brazil produces ethanol from sugar, and the land used to grow sugar can be used to grow food crops. Suppose that Brazil's production possibilities for ethanol and food crops are as follows

Ethanol (barrels per day)		Food crops (tons per day)
70	and	0
64	and	1
54	and	2
40	and	3
22	and	4
0	and	5

1. a. Draw a graph of Brazil's PPF and explain how your graph illustrates scarcity.
   b. If Brazil produces 40 barrels of ethanol a day, how much food must it produce to achieve production efficiency?
   c. Why does Brazil face a tradeoff on its *PPF*?

2. a. If Brazil increases its production of ethanol from 40 barrels per day to 54 barrels per day, what is the opportunity cost of the additional ethanol?
   b. If Brazil increases its production of food crops from 2 tons per day to 3 tons per day, what is the opportunity cost of the additional food?
   c. What is the relationship between your answers to parts (a) and (b)?

3. Does Brazil face an increasing opportunity cost of ethanol? What feature of Brazil's *PPF* illustrates increasing opportunity cost?

Using Resources Efficiently (Study Plan 2.2)

Use the above table to work Problems 4 and 5.

4. Define marginal cost and calculate Brazil's marginal cost of producing a ton of food when the quantity produced is 2.5 tons per day.

5. Define marginal benefit, explain how it is measured, and explain why the data in the table does not enable you to calculate Brazil's marginal benefit from food.

6. Distinguish between *production efficiency* and *allocative efficiency*. Explain why many production possibilities achieve production efficiency but only one achieves allocative efficiency.

Use the following graphs to work Problems 7 to 10. Harry enjoys tennis but wants a high grade in his economics course. The graphs show his *PPF* for these two "goods" and his *MB* curve from tennis.

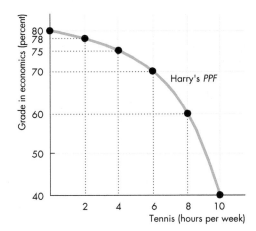

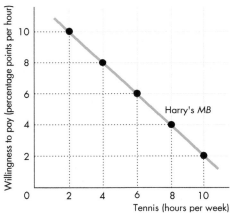

7. What is Harry's marginal cost of tennis if he plays for (i) 3 hours a week; (ii) 5 hours a week; and (iii) 7 hours a week?

8. a. If Harry uses his time to achieve allocative efficiency, what is his economics grade and how many hours of tennis does he play?
   b. Explain why Harry would be worse off getting a grade higher than your answer to part (a).

9. If Harry becomes a tennis superstar with big earnings from tennis, what happens to his *PPF*, *MB* curve, and his efficient time allocation?

10. If Harry suddenly finds high grades in economics easier to attain, what happens to his *PPF*, his *MB* curve, and his efficient time allocation?

Economic Growth (Study Plan 2.3)

11. A farm grows wheat and produces pork. The marginal cost of producing each of these products increases as more of it is produced.
    a. Make a graph that illustrates the farm's *PPF*.
    b. The farm adopts a new technology that allows it to use fewer resources to fatten pigs. Use your graph to illustrate the impact of the new technology on the farm's *PPF*.
    c. With the farm using the new technology described in part (b), has the opportunity cost of producing a ton of wheat increased, decreased, or remained the same? Explain and illustrate your answer.
    d. Is the farm more efficient with the new technology than it was with the old one? Why?

Gains from Trade (Study Plan 2.4)

12. In an hour, Sue can produce 40 caps or 4 jackets and Tessa can produce 80 caps or 4 jackets.
    a. Calculate Sue's opportunity cost of producing a cap.
    b. Calculate Tessa's opportunity cost of producing a cap.
    c. Who has a comparative advantage in producing caps?
    d. If Sue and Tessa specialize in producing the good in which each of them has a comparative advantage, and they trade 1 jacket for 15 caps, who gains from the specialization and trade?

13. Suppose that Tessa buys a new machine for making jackets that enables her to make 20 jackets an hour. (She can still make only 80 caps per hour.)
    a. Who now has a comparative advantage in producing jackets?
    b. Can Sue and Tessa still gain from trade?
    c. Would Sue and Tessa still be willing to trade 1 jacket for 15 caps? Explain your answer.

Economics in the News (Study Plan 2.N)

Use the following data to work Problems 14 to 16. Brazil produces ethanol from sugar at a cost of 83 cents per gallon. The United States produces ethanol from corn at a cost of $1.14 per gallon. Sugar grown on one acre of land produces twice the quantity of ethanol as the corn grown on an acre. The United States imports 5 percent of the ethanol it uses and produces the rest itself. Since 2003, U.S. ethanol production has more than doubled and U.S. corn production has increased by 45 percent.

14. a. Does Brazil or the United States have a comparative advantage in producing ethanol?
    b. Sketch the *PPF* for ethanol and other goods and services for the United States.
    c. Sketch the *PPF* for ethanol and other goods and services for Brazil.

15. a. Do you expect the opportunity cost of producing ethanol in the United States to have increased since 2003? Explain why.
    b. Do you think the United States has achieved production efficiency in its manufacture of ethanol? Explain why or why not.
    c. Do you think the United States has achieved allocative efficiency in its manufacture of ethanol? Explain why or why not.

16. Sketch a figure similar to Fig. 2.6 on p. 38 to show how both the United States and Brazil can gain from specialization and trade.

Use this news clip to work Problems 17 to 19.

Time For Tea

Americans are switching to loose-leaf tea for its health benefits. Tea could be grown in the United States, but picking tea leaves would be costly because it can only be done by workers and not by machine.

Source: *The Economist*, July 8, 2005

17. a. Sketch *PPF*s for the production of tea and other goods and services in India and in the United States.
    b. Sketch marginal cost curves for the production of tea in India and in the United States.

18. a. Sketch the marginal benefit curves for tea in the United States before and after Americans began to appreciate the health benefits of loose tea.
    b. Explain how the quantity of loose tea that achieves allocative efficiency has changed.
    c. Does the change in preferences toward tea affect the opportunity cost of producing tea?

19. Explain why the United States does not produce tea and instead imports it from India.

ADDITIONAL PROBLEMS AND APPLICATIONS

myeconlab You can work these problems in MyEconLab if assigned by your instructor.

Production Possibilities and Opportunity Cost

Use the following table to work Problems 20 to 21.
Suppose that Yucatan's production possibilities are

Food (pounds per month)		Sunscreen (gallons per month)
300	and	0
200	and	50
100	and	100
0	and	150

20. a. Draw a graph of Yucatan's *PPF* and explain how your graph illustrates a tradeoff.
    b. If Yucatan produces 150 pounds of food per month, how much sunscreen must it produce if it achieves production efficiency?
    c. What is Yucatan's opportunity cost of producing 1 pound of food?
    d. What is Yucatan's opportunity cost of producing 1 gallon of sunscreen?
    e. What is the relationship between your answers to parts (c) and (d)?

21. What feature of a *PPF* illustrates increasing opportunity cost? Explain why Yucatan's opportunity cost does or does not increase.

Using Resources Efficiently

22. In problem 20, what is the marginal cost of a pound of food in Yucatan when the quantity produced is 150 pounds per day? What is special about the marginal cost of food in Yucatan?

23. The table describes the preferences in Yucatan.

Sunscreen (gallons per month)	Willingness to pay (pounds of food per gallon)
25	3
75	2
125	1

    a. What is the marginal benefit from sunscreen and how is it measured?
    b. Draw a graph of Yucatan's marginal benefit from sunscreen.

Economic Growth

24. Capital accumulation and technological change bring economic growth, which means that the *PPF* keeps shifting outward: Production that was unattainable yesterday becomes attainable today; production that is unattainable today will become attainable tomorrow. Why doesn't this process of economic growth mean that scarcity is being defeated and will one day be gone?

Gains from Trade

Use the following data to work Problems 25 and 26.
Kim can produce 40 pies or 400 cakes an hour. Liam can produce 100 pies or 200 cakes an hour.

25. a. Calculate Kim's opportunity cost of a pie and Liam's opportunity cost of a pie.
    b. If each spends 30 minutes of each hour producing pies and 30 minutes producing cakes, how many pies and cakes does each produce?
    c. Who has a comparative advantage in producing pies? Who has a comparative advantage in producing cakes?

26. a. Draw a graph of Kim's *PPF* and Liam's *PPF*.
    b. On your graph, show the point at which each produces when they spend 30 minutes of each hour producing pies and 30 minutes producing cakes.
    c. On your graph, show what Kim produces and what does Liam produces when they specialize.
    d. When they specialize and trade, what are the total gains from trade?
    e. If Kim and Liam share the total gains equally, what trade takes place between them?

Economics in the News

27. **Malaria Eradication Back on the Table**
    In response to the Gates Malaria Forum in October 2007, countries are debating the pros and cons of eradication. Dr. Arata Kochi of the World Health Organization believes that with enough money malaria cases could be cut by 90 percent, but he believes that it would be very expensive to eliminate the remaining 10 percent of cases. He concluded that countries should not strive to eradicate malaria.
        Source: *The New York Times*, March 4, 2008
    a. Is Dr. Kochi talking about *production efficiency* or *allocative efficiency* or both?
    b. Make a graph with the percentage of malaria cases eliminated on the *x*-axis and the marginal cost and marginal benefit of driving down malaria cases on the *y*-axis. On your graph:
       (i) Draw a marginal cost curve that is consistent with Dr. Kochi's opinion.
       (ii) Draw a marginal benefit curve that is consistent with Dr. Kochi's opinion.

(iii) Identify the quantity of malaria eradicated that achieves allocative efficiency.

28. **Lots of Little Screens**

Inexpensive broadband access has created a generation of television producers for whom the Internet is their native medium. As they redirect the focus from TV to computers, cell phones, and iPods, the video market is developing into an open digital network.

Source: *The New York Times,* December 2, 2007

a. How has inexpensive broadband changed the production possibilities of video entertainment and other goods and services?

b. Sketch a *PPF* for video entertainment and other goods and services before broadband.

c. Show how the arrival of inexpensive broadband has changed the *PPF*.

d. Sketch a marginal benefit curve for video entertainment.

e. Show how the new generation of TV producers for whom the Internet is their native medium might have changed the marginal benefit from video entertainment.

f. Explain how the efficient quantity of video entertainment has changed.

Use the following information to work Problems 29 and 30.

Before the Civil War, the South traded with the North and with England. The South sold cotton and bought manufactured goods and food. During the war, one of President Lincoln's first actions was to blockade the ports and prevent this trade. The South increased its production of munitions and food.

29. In what did the South have a comparative advantage?

30. a. Draw a graph to illustrate production, consumption, and trade in the South before the Civil War.

b. Was the South consuming inside, on, or outside its *PPF*? Explain your answer.

c. Draw a graph to show the effects of the Civil War on consumption and production in the South.

d. Did the Civil War change any opportunity costs in the South? If so, did the opportunity cost of everything increase? Did the opportunity cost of any items decrease? Illustrate your answer with appropriate graphs.

Use the following information to work Problems 31 and 32.

He Shoots! He Scores! He Makes Movies!

NBA All-star Baron Davis and his school friend, Cash Warren, premiered their first movie *Made in America* at the Sundance Festival in January 2008. The movie, based on gang activity in South Central Los Angeles, received good reviews.

Source: *The New York Times,* February 24, 2008

31. a. Does Baron Davis have an absolute advantage in basketball and movie directing and is this the reason for his success in both activities?

b. Does Baron Davis have a comparative advantage in basketball or movie directing or both and is this the reason for his success in both activities?

32. a. Sketch a *PPF* between playing basketball and producing other goods and services for Baron Davis and for yourself.

b. How do you (and people like you) and Baron Davis (and people like him) gain from specialization and trade?

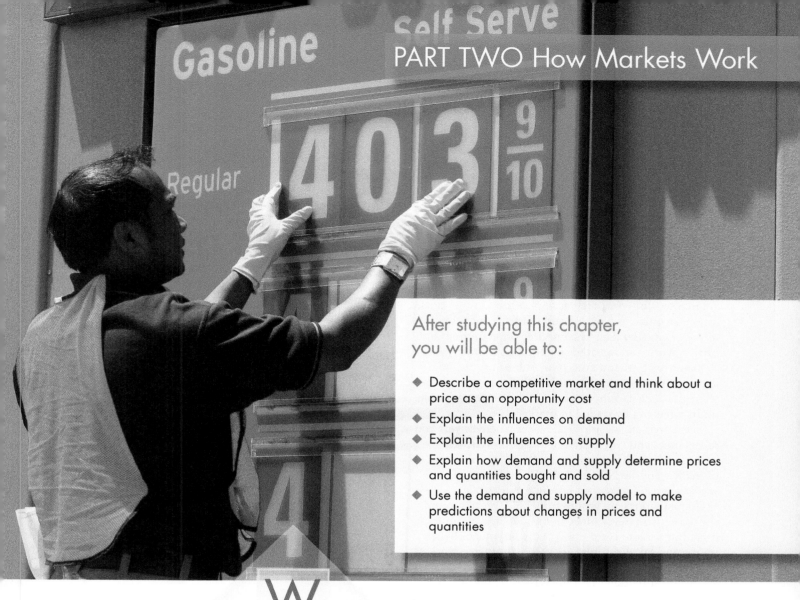

After studying this chapter,
you will be able to:

◆ Describe a competitive market and think about a
price as an opportunity cost

◆ Explain the influences on demand

◆ Explain the influences on supply

◆ Explain how demand and supply determine prices
and quantities bought and sold

◆ Use the demand and supply model to make
predictions about changes in prices and
quantities

3

DEMAND AND SUPPLY

What makes the price of oil double and the price of gasoline almost double in
just one year? Will these prices keep on rising? Are the oil companies taking
advantage of people? This chapter enables you to answer these and similar
questions about prices—prices that rise, prices that fall, and prices that
fluctuate.

You already know that economics is about the choices people make to cope
with scarcity and how those choices respond to incentives. Prices act as
incentives. You're going to see how people respond to prices and how prices
get determined by demand and supply. The demand and supply model that
you study in this chapter is the main tool of economics. It
helps us to answer the big economic question: What, how,
and for whom goods and services are produced?

At the end of the chapter, in *Reading Between the Lines*, we'll apply the
model to the market for coffee and explain why its price increased sharply in
2010 and why it was expected to rise again.

◆ Markets and Prices

When you need a new pair of running shoes, want a bagel and a latte, plan to upgrade your cell phone, or need to fly home for Thanksgiving, you must find a place where people sell those items or offer those services. The place in which you find them is a *market*. You learned that a market is any arrangement that enables buyers and sellers to get information and to do business with each other.

A market has two sides: buyers and sellers. There are markets for *goods* such as apples and hiking boots, for *services* such as haircuts and tennis lessons, for *factors of production* such as computer programmers and earthmovers, and for other manufactured *inputs* such as memory chips and auto parts. There are also markets for money such as Japanese yen and for financial securities such as Yahoo! stock. Only our imagination limits what can be traded in markets.

Some markets are physical places where buyers and sellers meet and where an auctioneer or a broker helps to determine the prices. Examples of this type of market are the New York Stock Exchange and the wholesale fish, meat, and produce markets.

Some markets are groups of people spread around the world who never meet and know little about each other but are connected through the Internet or by telephone and fax. Examples are the e-commerce markets and the currency markets.

But most markets are unorganized collections of buyers and sellers. You do most of your trading in this type of market. An example is the market for basketball shoes. The buyers in this $3 billion-a-year market are the 45 million Americans who play basketball (or who want to make a fashion statement). The sellers are the tens of thousands of retail sports equipment and footwear stores. Each buyer can visit several different stores, and each seller knows that the buyer has a choice of stores.

Markets vary in the intensity of competition that buyers and sellers face. In this chapter, we're going to study a **competitive market**—a market that has many buyers and many sellers, so no single buyer or seller can influence the price.

Producers offer items for sale only if the price is high enough to cover their opportunity cost. And consumers respond to changing opportunity cost by seeking cheaper alternatives to expensive items.

We are going to study how people respond to *prices* and the forces that determine prices. But to pursue these tasks, we need to understand the relationship between a price and an opportunity cost.

In everyday life, the *price* of an object is the number of dollars that must be given up in exchange for it. Economists refer to this price as the **money price**.

The *opportunity cost* of an action is the highest-valued alternative forgone. If, when you buy a cup of coffee, the highest-valued thing you forgo is some gum, then the opportunity cost of the coffee is the *quantity* of gum forgone. We can calculate the quantity of gum forgone from the money prices of the coffee and the gum.

If the money price of coffee is $1 a cup and the money price of gum is 50¢ a pack, then the opportunity cost of one cup of coffee is two packs of gum. To calculate this opportunity cost, we divide the price of a cup of coffee by the price of a pack of gum and find the *ratio* of one price to the other. The ratio of one price to another is called a **relative price**, and a *relative price is an opportunity cost*.

We can express the relative price of coffee in terms of gum or any other good. The normal way of expressing a relative price is in terms of a "basket" of all goods and services. To calculate this relative price, we divide the money price of a good by the money price of a "basket" of all goods (called a *price index*). The resulting relative price tells us the opportunity cost of the good in terms of how much of the "basket" we must give up to buy it.

The demand and supply model that we are about to study determines *relative prices*, and the word "price" means *relative* price. When we predict that a price will fall, we do not mean that its *money* price will fall—although it might. We mean that its *relative* price will fall. That is, its price will fall *relative* to the average price of other goods and services.

REVIEW QUIZ

1 What is the distinction between a money price and a relative price?
2 Explain why a relative price is an opportunity cost.
3 Think of examples of goods whose relative price has risen or fallen by a large amount.

You can work these questions in Study Plan 3.1 and get instant feedback.

Let's begin our study of demand and supply, starting with demand.

◆ Demand

If you demand something, then you

1. Want it,
2. Can afford it, and
3. Plan to buy it.

Wants are the unlimited desires or wishes that people have for goods and services. How many times have you thought that you would like something "if only you could afford it" or "if it weren't so expensive"? Scarcity guarantees that many—perhaps most—of our wants will never be satisfied. Demand reflects a decision about which wants to satisfy.

The **quantity demanded** of a good or service is the amount that consumers plan to buy during a given time period at a particular price. The quantity demanded is not necessarily the same as the quantity actually bought. Sometimes the quantity demanded exceeds the amount of goods available, so the quantity bought is less than the quantity demanded.

The quantity demanded is measured as an amount per unit of time. For example, suppose that you buy one cup of coffee a day. The quantity of coffee that you demand can be expressed as 1 cup per day, 7 cups per week, or 365 cups per year.

Many factors influence buying plans, and one of them is the price. We look first at the relationship between the quantity demanded of a good and its price. To study this relationship, we keep all other influences on buying plans the same and we ask: How, other things remaining the same, does the quantity demanded of a good change as its price changes?

The law of demand provides the answer.

The Law of Demand

The **law of demand** states

> Other things remaining the same, the higher the price of a good, the smaller is the quantity demanded; and the lower the price of a good, the greater is the quantity demanded.

Why does a higher price reduce the quantity demanded? For two reasons:

- Substitution effect
- Income effect

Substitution Effect When the price of a good rises, other things remaining the same, its *relative* price—its opportunity cost—rises. Although each good is unique, it has *substitutes*—other goods that can be used in its place. As the opportunity cost of a good rises, the incentive to economize on its use and switch to a substitute becomes stronger.

Income Effect When a price rises, other things remaining the same, the price rises *relative* to income. Faced with a higher price and an unchanged income, people cannot afford to buy all the things they previously bought. They must decrease the quantities demanded of at least some goods and services. Normally, the good whose price has increased will be one of the goods that people buy less of.

To see the substitution effect and the income effect at work, think about the effects of a change in the price of an energy bar. Several different goods are substitutes for an energy bar. For example, an energy drink could be consumed instead of an energy bar.

Suppose that an energy bar initially sells for $3 and then its price falls to $1.50. People now substitute energy bars for energy drinks—the substitution effect. And with a budget that now has some slack from the lower price of an energy bar, people buy even more energy bars—the income effect. The quantity of energy bars demanded increases for these two reasons.

Now suppose that an energy bar initially sells for $3 and then the price doubles to $6. People now buy fewer energy bars and more energy drinks—the substitution effect. And faced with a tighter budget, people buy even fewer energy bars—the income effect. The quantity of energy bars demanded decreases for these two reasons.

Demand Curve and Demand Schedule

You are now about to study one of the two most used curves in economics: the demand curve. You are also going to encounter one of the most critical distinctions: the distinction between *demand* and *quantity demanded*.

The term **demand** refers to the entire relationship between the price of a good and the quantity demanded of that good. Demand is illustrated by the demand curve and the demand schedule. The term *quantity demanded* refers to a point on a demand curve—the quantity demanded at a particular price.

Figure 3.1 shows the demand curve for energy bars. A **demand curve** shows the relationship between the quantity demanded of a good and its price when all other influences on consumers' planned purchases remain the same.

The table in Fig. 3.1 is the demand schedule for energy bars. A *demand schedule* lists the quantities demanded at each price when all the other influences on consumers' planned purchases remain the same. For example, if the price of a bar is 50¢, the quantity demanded is 22 million a week. If the price is $2.50, the quantity demanded is 5 million a week. The other rows of the table show the quantities demanded at prices of $1.00, $1.50, and $2.00.

We graph the demand schedule as a demand curve with the quantity demanded on the *x*-axis and the price on the *y*-axis. The points on the demand curve labeled *A* through *E* correspond to the rows of the demand schedule. For example, point *A* on the graph shows a quantity demanded of 22 million energy bars a week at a price of 50¢ a bar.

Willingness and Ability to Pay Another way of looking at the demand curve is as a willingness-and-ability-to-pay curve. The willingness and ability to pay is a measure of *marginal benefit*.

If a small quantity is available, the highest price that someone is willing and able to pay for one more unit is high. But as the quantity available increases, the marginal benefit of each additional unit falls and the highest price that someone is willing and able to pay also falls along the demand curve.

In Fig. 3.1, if only 5 million energy bars are available each week, the highest price that someone is willing to pay for the 5 millionth bar is $2.50. But if 22 million energy bars are available each week, someone is willing to pay 50¢ for the last bar bought.

A Change in Demand

When any factor that influences buying plans changes, other than the price of the good, there is a **change in demand**. Figure 3.2 illustrates an increase in demand. When demand increases, the demand curve shifts rightward and the quantity demanded at each price is greater. For example, at $2.50 a bar, the quantity demanded on the original (blue) demand curve is 5 million energy bars a week. On the new (red) demand curve, at $2.50 a bar, the quantity demanded is 15 million bars a week. Look closely at the numbers in the table and check that the quantity demanded at each price is greater.

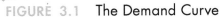

FIGURE 3.1   The Demand Curve

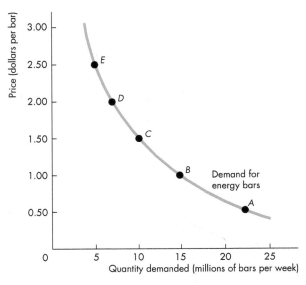

	Price (dollars per bar)	Quantity demanded (millions of bars per week)
A	0.50	22
B	1.00	15
C	1.50	10
D	2.00	7
E	2.50	5

The table shows a demand schedule for energy bars. At a price of 50¢ a bar, 22 million bars a week are demanded; at a price of $1.50 a bar, 10 million bars a week are demanded. The demand curve shows the relationship between quantity demanded and price, other things remaining the same. The demand curve slopes downward: As the price falls, the quantity demanded increases.

The demand curve can be read in two ways. For a given price, the demand curve tells us the quantity that people plan to buy. For example, at a price of $1.50 a bar, people plan to buy 10 million bars a week. For a given quantity, the demand curve tells us the maximum price that consumers are willing and able to pay for the last bar available. For example, the maximum price that consumers will pay for the 15 millionth bar is $1.00.

FIGURE 3.2 An Increase in Demand

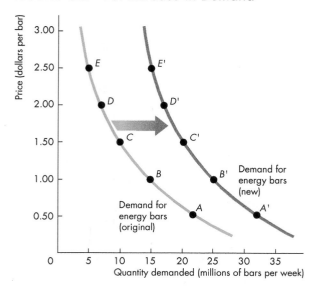

Original demand schedule Original income		New demand schedule New higher income		
Price (dollars per bar)	Quantity demanded (millions of bars per week)		Price (dollars per bar)	Quantity demanded (millions of bars per week)
A	0.50	22	A'	0.50	32
B	1.00	15	B'	1.00	25
C	1.50	10	C'	1.50	20
D	2.00	7	D'	2.00	17
E	2.50	5	E'	2.50	15

A change in any influence on buying plans other than the price of the good itself results in a new demand schedule and a shift of the demand curve. A change in income changes the demand for energy bars. At a price of $1.50 a bar, 10 million bars a week are demanded at the original income (row C of the table) and 20 million bars a week are demanded at the new higher income (row C'). A rise in income increases the demand for energy bars. The demand curve shifts *rightward*, as shown by the shift arrow and the resulting red curve.

X myeconlab animation

Six main factors bring changes in demand. They are changes in

- The prices of related goods
- Expected future prices
- Income
- Expected future income and credit
- Population
- Preferences

Prices of Related Goods The quantity of energy bars that consumers plan to buy depends in part on the prices of substitutes for energy bars. A **substitute** is a good that can be used in place of another good. For example, a bus ride is a substitute for a train ride; a hamburger is a substitute for a hot dog; and an energy drink is a substitute for an energy bar. If the price of a substitute for an energy bar rises, people buy less of the substitute and more energy bars. For example, if the price of an energy drink rises, people buy fewer energy drinks and more energy bars. The demand for energy bars increases.

The quantity of energy bars that people plan to buy also depends on the prices of complements with energy bars. A **complement** is a good that is used in conjunction with another good. Hamburgers and fries are complements, and so are energy bars and exercise. If the price of an hour at the gym falls, people buy more gym time *and more* energy bars.

Expected Future Prices If the expected future price of a good rises and if the good can be stored, the opportunity cost of obtaining the good for future use is lower today than it will be in the future when people expect the price to be higher. So people retime their purchases—they substitute over time. They buy more of the good now before its price is expected to rise (and less afterward), so the demand for the good today increases.

For example, suppose that a Florida frost damages the season's orange crop. You expect the price of orange juice to rise, so you fill your freezer with enough frozen juice to get you through the next six months. Your current demand for frozen orange juice has increased, and your future demand has decreased.

Similarly, if the expected future price of a good falls, the opportunity cost of buying the good today is high relative to what it is expected to be in the future. So again, people retime their purchases. They buy less of the good now before its price is expected to fall, so the demand for the good decreases today and increases in the future.

Computer prices are constantly falling, and this fact poses a dilemma. Will you buy a new computer now, in time for the start of the school year, or will you wait until the price has fallen some more? Because people expect computer prices to keep falling, the current demand for computers is less (and the future demand is greater) than it otherwise would be.

Income Consumers' income influences demand. When income increases, consumers buy more of most goods; and when income decreases, consumers buy less of most goods. Although an increase in income leads to an increase in the demand for *most* goods, it does not lead to an increase in the demand for *all* goods. A **normal good** is one for which demand increases as income increases. An **inferior good** is one for which demand decreases as income increases. As incomes increase, the demand for air travel (a normal good) increases and the demand for long-distance bus trips (an inferior good) decreases.

Expected Future Income and Credit When expected future income increases or credit becomes easier to get, demand for the good might increase now. For example, a salesperson gets the news that she will receive a big bonus at the end of the year, so she goes into debt and buys a new car right now, rather than wait until she receives the bonus.

Population Demand also depends on the size and the age structure of the population. The larger the population, the greater is the demand for all goods and services; the smaller the population, the smaller is the demand for all goods and services.

For example, the demand for parking spaces or movies or just about anything that you can imagine is much greater in New York City (population 7.5 million) than it is in Boise, Idaho (population 150,000).

Also, the larger the proportion of the population in a given age group, the greater is the demand for the goods and services used by that age group.

For example, during the 1990s, a decrease in the college-age population decreased the demand for college places. During those same years, the number of Americans aged 85 years and over increased by more than 1 million. As a result, the demand for nursing home services increased.

TABLE 3.1   The Demand for Energy Bars

The Law of Demand

The quantity of energy bars demanded

Decreases if:	Increases if:
■ The price of an energy bar rises	■ The price of an energy bar falls

Changes in Demand

The demand for energy bars

Decreases if:	Increases if:
■ The price of a substitute falls	■ The price of a substitute rises
■ The price of a complement rises	■ The price of a complement falls
■ The expected future price of an energy bar falls	■ The expected future price of an energy bar rises
■ Income falls*	■ Income rises*
■ Expected future income falls or credit becomes harder to get*	■ Expected future income rises or credit becomes easier to get*
■ The population decreases	■ The population increases

*An energy bar is a normal good.

Preferences Demand depends on preferences. *Preferences* determine the value that people place on each good and service. Preferences depend on such things as the weather, information, and fashion. For example, greater health and fitness awareness has shifted preferences in favor of energy bars, so the demand for energy bars has increased.

Table 3.1 summarizes the influences on demand and the direction of those influences.

A Change in the Quantity Demanded Versus a Change in Demand

Changes in the influences on buying plans bring either a change in the quantity demanded or a change in demand. Equivalently, they bring either a movement along the demand curve or a shift of the demand curve. The distinction between a change in the quantity demanded and a change in demand is the same as that between a movement along the demand curve and a shift of the demand curve.

A point on the demand curve shows the quantity demanded at a given price, so a movement along the demand curve shows a **change in the quantity demanded**. The entire demand curve shows demand, so a shift of the demand curve shows a *change in demand*. Figure 3.3 illustrates these distinctions.

Movement Along the Demand Curve If the price of the good changes but no other influence on buying plans changes, we illustrate the effect as a movement along the demand curve.

A fall in the price of a good increases the quantity demanded of it. In Fig. 3.3, we illustrate the effect of a fall in price as a movement down along the demand curve D_0.

A rise in the price of a good decreases the quantity demanded of it. In Fig. 3.3, we illustrate the effect of a rise in price as a movement up along the demand curve D_0.

A Shift of the Demand Curve If the price of a good remains constant but some other influence on buying plans changes, there is a change in demand for that good. We illustrate a change in demand as a shift of the demand curve. For example, if more people work out at the gym, consumers buy more energy bars regardless of the price of a bar. That is what a rightward shift of the demand curve shows—more energy bars are demanded at each price.

In Fig. 3.3, there is a *change in demand* and the demand curve shifts when any influence on buying plans changes, other than the price of the good. Demand *increases* and the demand curve *shifts rightward* (to the red demand curve D_1) if the price of a substitute rises, the price of a complement falls, the expected future price of the good rises, income increases (for a normal good), expected future income or credit increases, or the population increases. Demand *decreases* and the demand curve *shifts leftward* (to the red demand curve D_2) if the price of a substitute falls, the price of a complement rises, the expected future price of the good falls, income decreases (for a normal good), expected future income or credit decreases, or the population decreases. (For an inferior good, the effects of changes in income are in the opposite direction to those described above.)

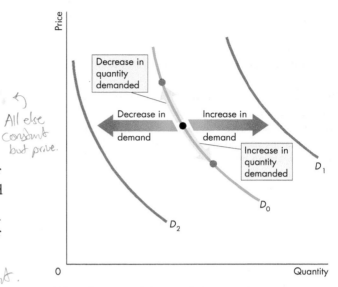

FIGURE 3.3   A Change in the Quantity Demanded Versus a Change in Demand

When the price of the good changes, there is a movement along the demand curve and *a change in the quantity demanded*, shown by the blue arrows on demand curve D_0. When any other influence on buying plans changes, there is a shift of the demand curve and a *change in demand*. An increase in demand shifts the demand curve rightward (from D_0 to D_1). A decrease in demand shifts the demand curve leftward (from D_0 to D_2).

myeconlab animation

REVIEW QUIZ

1 Define the quantity demanded of a good or service.
2 What is the law of demand and how do we illustrate it?
3 What does the demand curve tell us about the price that consumers are willing to pay?
4 List all the influences on buying plans that change demand, and for each influence, say whether it increases or decreases demand.
5 Why does demand not change when the price of a good changes with no change in the other influences on buying plans?

You can work these questions in Study Plan 3.2 and get instant feedback.    myeconlab

◆ Supply

If a firm supplies a good or service, the firm

1. Has the resources and technology to produce it,
2. Can profit from producing it, and
3. Plans to produce it and sell it.

A supply is more than just having the *resources* and the *technology* to produce something. *Resources and technology* are the constraints that limit what is possible.

Many useful things can be produced, but they are not produced unless it is profitable to do so. Supply reflects a decision about which technologically feasible items to produce.

The **quantity supplied** of a good or service is the amount that producers plan to sell during a given time period at a particular price. The quantity supplied is not necessarily the same amount as the quantity actually sold. Sometimes the quantity supplied is greater than the quantity demanded, so the quantity sold is less than the quantity supplied.

Like the quantity demanded, the quantity supplied is measured as an amount per unit of time. For example, suppose that GM produces 1,000 cars a day. The quantity of cars supplied by GM can be expressed as 1,000 a day, 7,000 a week, or 365,000 a year. Without the time dimension, we cannot tell whether a particular quantity is large or small.

Many factors influence selling plans, and again one of them is the price of the good. We look first at the relationship between the quantity supplied of a good and its price. Just as we did when we studied demand, to isolate the relationship between the quantity supplied of a good and its price, we keep all other influences on selling plans the same and ask: How does the quantity supplied of a good change as its price changes when other things remain the same?

The law of supply provides the answer.

The Law of Supply

The **law of supply** states:

> Other things remaining the same, the higher the price of a good, the greater is the quantity supplied; and the lower the price of a good, the smaller is the quantity supplied.

Why does a higher price increase the quantity supplied? It is because *marginal cost increases.* As the quantity produced of any good increases, the marginal cost of producing the good increases. (See Chapter 2, p. 31 to review marginal cost.)

It is never worth producing a good if the price received for the good does not at least cover the marginal cost of producing it. When the price of a good rises, other things remaining the same, producers are willing to incur a higher marginal cost, so they increase production. The higher price brings forth an increase in the quantity supplied.

Let's now illustrate the law of supply with a supply curve and a supply schedule.

Supply Curve and Supply Schedule

You are now going to study the second of the two most used curves in economics: the supply curve. You're also going to learn about the critical distinction between *supply* and *quantity supplied*.

The term **supply** refers to the entire relationship between the price of a good and the quantity supplied of it. Supply is illustrated by the supply curve and the supply schedule. The term *quantity supplied* refers to a point on a supply curve—the quantity supplied at a particular price.

Figure 3.4 shows the supply curve of energy bars. A **supply curve** shows the relationship between the quantity supplied of a good and its price when all other influences on producers' planned sales remain the same. The supply curve is a graph of a supply schedule.

The table in Fig. 3.4 sets out the supply schedule for energy bars. A *supply schedule* lists the quantities supplied at each price when all the other influences on producers' planned sales remain the same. For example, if the price of an energy bar is 50¢, the quantity supplied is zero—in row *A* of the table. If the price of an energy bar is $1.00, the quantity supplied is 6 million energy bars a week—in row *B*. The other rows of the table show the quantities supplied at prices of $1.50, $2.00, and $2.50.

To make a supply curve, we graph the quantity supplied on the *x*-axis and the price on the *y*-axis. The points on the supply curve labeled *A* through *E* correspond to the rows of the supply schedule. For example, point *A* on the graph shows a quantity supplied of zero at a price of 50¢ an energy bar. Point *E* shows a quantity supplied of 15 million bars at $2.50 an energy bar.

FIGURE 3.4 The Supply Curve

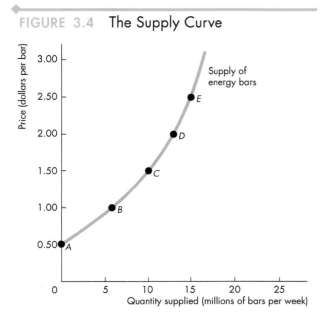

	Price (dollars per bar)	Quantity supplied (millions of bars per week)
A	0.50	0
B	1.00	6
C	1.50	10
D	2.00	13
E	2.50	15

The table shows the supply schedule of energy bars. For example, at a price of $1.00, 6 million bars a week are supplied; at a price of $2.50, 15 million bars a week are supplied. The supply curve shows the relationship between the quantity supplied and the price, other things remaining the same. The supply curve slopes upward: As the price of a good increases, the quantity supplied increases.

A supply curve can be read in two ways. For a given price, the supply curve tells us the quantity that producers plan to sell at that price. For example, at a price of $1.50 a bar, producers are planning to sell 10 million bars a week. For a given quantity, the supply curve tells us the minimum price at which producers are willing to sell one more bar. For example, if 15 million bars are produced each week, the lowest price at which a producer is willing to sell the 15 millionth bar is $2.50.

my**econ**lab   animation

Minimum Supply Price The supply curve can be interpreted as a minimum-supply-price curve—a curve that shows the lowest price at which someone is willing to sell. This lowest price is the *marginal cost.*

If a small quantity is produced, the lowest price at which someone is willing to sell one more unit is low. But as the quantity produced increases, the marginal cost of each additional unit rises, so the lowest price at which someone is willing to sell an additional unit rises along the supply curve.

In Fig. 3.4, if 15 million bars are produced each week, the lowest price at which someone is willing to sell the 15 millionth bar is $2.50. But if 10 million bars are produced each week, someone is willing to accept $1.50 for the last bar produced.

A Change in Supply

When any factor that influences selling plans other than the price of the good changes, there is a **change in supply**. Six main factors bring changes in supply. They are changes in

- The prices of factors of production
- The prices of related goods produced
- Expected future prices
- The number of suppliers
- Technology
- The state of nature

Prices of Factors of Production The prices of the factors of production used to produce a good influence its supply. To see this influence, think about the supply curve as a minimum-supply-price curve. If the price of a factor of production rises, the lowest price that a producer is willing to accept for that good rises, so supply decreases. For example, during 2008, as the price of jet fuel increased, the supply of air travel decreased. Similarly, a rise in the minimum wage decreases the supply of hamburgers.

Prices of Related Goods Produced The prices of related goods that firms produce influence supply. For example, if the price of energy gel rises, firms switch production from bars to gel. The supply of energy bars decreases. Energy bars and energy gel are *substitutes in production*—goods that can be produced by using the same resources. If the price of beef rises, the supply of cowhide increases. Beef and cowhide are *complements in production*—goods that must be produced together.

Expected Future Prices If the expected future price of a good rises, the return from selling the good in the future increases and is higher than it is today. So supply decreases today and increases in the future.

The Number of Suppliers The larger the number of firms that produce a good, the greater is the supply of the good. As new firms enter an industry, the supply in that industry increases. As firms leave an industry, the supply in that industry decreases.

Technology The term "technology" is used broadly to mean the way that factors of production are used to produce a good. A technology change occurs when a new method is discovered that lowers the cost of producing a good. For example, new methods used in the factories that produce computer chips have lowered the cost and increased the supply of chips.

The State of Nature The state of nature includes all the natural forces that influence production. It includes the state of the weather and, more broadly, the natural environment. Good weather can increase the supply of many agricultural products and bad weather can decrease their supply. Extreme natural events such as earthquakes, tornadoes, and hurricanes can also influence supply.

Figure 3.5 illustrates an increase in supply. When supply increases, the supply curve shifts rightward and the quantity supplied at each price is larger. For example, at $1.00 per bar, on the original (blue) supply curve, the quantity supplied is 6 million bars a week. On the new (red) supply curve, the quantity supplied is 15 million bars a week. Look closely at the numbers in the table in Fig. 3.5 and check that the quantity supplied is larger at each price.

Table 3.2 summarizes the influences on supply and the directions of those influences.

A Change in the Quantity Supplied Versus a Change in Supply

Changes in the influences on selling plans bring either a change in the quantity supplied or a change in supply. Equivalently, they bring either a movement along the supply curve or a shift of the supply curve.

A point on the supply curve shows the quantity supplied at a given price. A movement along the supply curve shows a **change in the quantity supplied**. The entire supply curve shows supply. A shift of the supply curve shows a *change in supply*.

FIGURE 3.5   **An Increase in Supply**

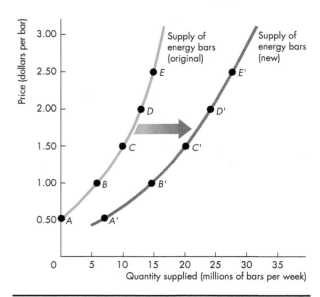

Original supply schedule Old technology			New supply schedule New technology		
	Price (dollars per bar)	**Quantity supplied (millions of bars per week)**		**Price (dollars per bar)**	**Quantity supplied (millions of bars per week)**
A	0.50	0	A'	0.50	7
B	1.00	6	B'	1.00	15
C	1.50	10	C'	1.50	20
D	2.00	13	D'	2.00	25
E	2.50	15	E'	2.50	27

A change in any influence on selling plans other than the price of the good itself results in a new supply schedule and a shift of the supply curve. For example, a new, cost-saving technology for producing energy bars changes the supply of energy bars. At a price of $1.50 a bar, 10 million bars a week are supplied when producers use the old technology (row C of the table) and 20 million energy bars a week are supplied when producers use the new technology (row C'). An advance in technology *increases* the supply of energy bars. The supply curve shifts *rightward*, as shown by the shift arrow and the resulting red curve.

 animation

Figure 3.6 illustrates and summarizes these distinctions. If the price of the good changes and other things remain the same, there is a *change in the quantity supplied* of that good. If the price of the good falls, the quantity supplied decreases and there is a movement down along the supply curve S_0. If the price of the good rises, the quantity supplied increases and there is a movement up along the supply curve S_0. When any other influence on selling plans changes, the supply curve shifts and there is a *change in supply*. If supply increases, the supply curve shifts rightward to S_1. If supply decreases, the supply curve shifts leftward to S_2.

TABLE 3.2   The Supply of Energy Bars

The Law of Supply

The quantity of energy bars supplied

Decreases if:	Increases if:
▪ The price of an energy bar falls	▪ The price of an energy bar rises

Changes in Supply

The supply of energy bars

Decreases if:	Increases if:
▪ The price of a factor of production used to produce energy bars rises	▪ The price of a factor of production used to produce energy bars falls
▪ The price of a substitute in production rises	▪ The price of a substitute in production falls
▪ The price of a complement in production falls	▪ The price of a complement in production rises
▪ The expected future price of an energy bar rises	▪ The expected future price of an energy bar falls
▪ The number of suppliers of bars decreases	▪ The number of suppliers of bars increases
▪ A technology change decreases energy bar production	▪ A technology change increases energy bar production
▪ A natural event decreases energy bar production	▪ A natural event increases energy bar production

FIGURE 3.6   A Change in the Quantity Supplied Versus a Change in Supply

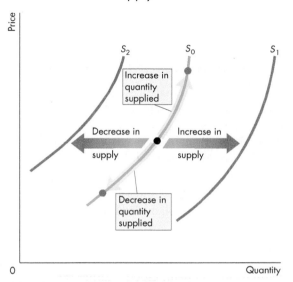

When the price of the good changes, there is a movement along the supply curve and *a change in the quantity supplied*, shown by the blue arrows on supply curve S_0. When any other influence on selling plans changes, there is a shift of the supply curve and a *change in supply*. An increase in supply shifts the supply curve rightward (from S_0 to S_1), and a decrease in supply shifts the supply curve leftward (from S_0 to S_2).

 animation

▸ REVIEW QUIZ

1 Define the quantity supplied of a good or service.
2 What is the law of supply and how do we illustrate it?
3 What does the supply curve tell us about the producer's minimum supply price?
4 List all the influences on selling plans, and for each influence, say whether it changes supply.
5 What happens to the quantity of cell phones supplied and the supply of cell phones if the price of a cell phone falls?

You can work these questions in Study Plan 3.3 and get instant feedback.   myeconlab

Now we're going to combine demand and supply and see how prices and quantities are determined.

◆ Market Equilibrium

We have seen that when the price of a good rises, the quantity demanded *decreases* and the quantity supplied *increases*. We are now going to see how the price adjusts to coordinate buying plans and selling plans and achieve an equilibrium in the market.

An *equilibrium* is a situation in which opposing forces balance each other. Equilibrium in a market occurs when the price balances buying plans and selling plans. The **equilibrium price** is the price at which the quantity demanded equals the quantity supplied. The **equilibrium quantity** is the quantity bought and sold at the equilibrium price. A market moves toward its equilibrium because

- Price regulates buying and selling plans.
- Price adjusts when plans don't match.

Price as a Regulator

The price of a good regulates the quantities demanded and supplied. If the price is too high, the quantity supplied exceeds the quantity demanded. If the price is too low, the quantity demanded exceeds the quantity supplied. There is one price at which the quantity demanded equals the quantity supplied. Let's work out what that price is.

Figure 3.7 shows the market for energy bars. The table shows the demand schedule (from Fig. 3.1) and the supply schedule (from Fig. 3.4). If the price is 50¢ a bar, the quantity demanded is 22 million bars a week but no bars are supplied. There is a shortage of 22 million bars a week. The final column of the table shows this shortage. At a price of $1.00 a bar, there is still a shortage but only of 9 million bars a week.

If the price is $2.50 a bar, the quantity supplied is 15 million bars a week but the quantity demanded is only 5 million. There is a surplus of 10 million bars a week.

The one price at which there is neither a shortage nor a surplus is $1.50 a bar. At that price, the quantity demanded equals the quantity supplied: 10 million bars a week. The equilibrium price is $1.50 a bar, and the equilibrium quantity is 10 million bars a week.

Figure 3.7 shows that the demand curve and the supply curve intersect at the equilibrium price of $1.50 a bar. At each price *above* $1.50 a bar, there is a surplus of bars. For example, at $2.00 a bar, the surplus is 6

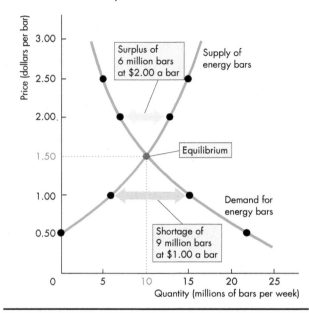

FIGURE 3.7   Equilibrium

Price (dollars per bar)	Quantity demanded	Quantity supplied	Shortage (−) or surplus (+)
	(millions of bars per week)		
0.50	22	0	−22
1.00	15	6	−9
1.50	10	10	0
2.00	7	13	+6
2.50	5	15	+10

The table lists the quantity demanded and the quantity supplied as well as the shortage or surplus of bars at each price. If the price is $1.00 a bar, 15 million bars a week are demanded and 6 million bars are supplied. There is a shortage of 9 million bars a week, and the price rises.

If the price is $2.00 a bar, 7 million bars a week are demanded and 13 million bars are supplied. There is a surplus of 6 million bars a week, and the price falls.

If the price is $1.50 a bar, 10 million bars a week are demanded and 10 million bars are supplied. There is neither a shortage nor a surplus, and the price does not change. The price at which the quantity demanded equals the quantity supplied is the equilibrium price, and 10 million bars a week is the equilibrium quantity.

million bars a week, as shown by the blue arrow. At each price *below* $1.50 a bar, there is a shortage of bars. For example, at $1.00 a bar, the shortage is 9 million bars a week, as shown by the red arrow.

Price Adjustments

You've seen that if the price is below equilibrium, there is a shortage and that if the price is above equilibrium, there is a surplus. But can we count on the price to change and eliminate a shortage or a surplus? We can, because such price changes are beneficial to both buyers and sellers. Let's see why the price changes when there is a shortage or a surplus.

A Shortage Forces the Price Up Suppose the price of an energy bar is $1. Consumers plan to buy 15 million bars a week, and producers plan to sell 6 million bars a week. Consumers can't force producers to sell more than they plan, so the quantity that is actually offered for sale is 6 million bars a week. In this situation, powerful forces operate to increase the price and move it toward the equilibrium price. Some producers, noticing lines of unsatisfied consumers, raise the price. Some producers increase their output. As producers push the price up, the price rises toward its equilibrium. The rising price reduces the shortage because it decreases the quantity demanded and increases the quantity supplied. When the price has increased to the point at which there is no longer a shortage, the forces moving the price stop operating and the price comes to rest at its equilibrium.

A Surplus Forces the Price Down Suppose the price of a bar is $2. Producers plan to sell 13 million bars a week, and consumers plan to buy 7 million bars a week. Producers cannot force consumers to buy more than they plan, so the quantity that is actually bought is 7 million bars a week. In this situation, powerful forces operate to lower the price and move it toward the equilibrium price. Some producers, unable to sell the quantities of energy bars they planned to sell, cut their prices. In addition, some producers scale back production. As producers cut the price, the price falls toward its equilibrium. The falling price decreases the surplus because it increases the quantity demanded and decreases the quantity supplied. When the price has fallen to the point at which there is no longer a surplus, the forces moving the price stop operating and the price comes to rest at its equilibrium.

The Best Deal Available for Buyers and Sellers
When the price is below equilibrium, it is forced upward. Why don't buyers resist the increase and refuse to buy at the higher price? The answer is because they value the good more highly than its current price and they can't satisfy their demand at the current price. In some markets—for example, the markets that operate on eBay—the buyers might even be the ones who force the price up by offering to pay a higher price.

When the price is above equilibrium, it is bid downward. Why don't sellers resist this decrease and refuse to sell at the lower price? The answer is because their minimum supply price is below the current price and they cannot sell all they would like to at the current price. Sellers willingly lower the price to gain market share.

At the price at which the quantity demanded and the quantity supplied are equal, neither buyers nor sellers can do business at a better price. Buyers pay the highest price they are willing to pay for the last unit bought, and sellers receive the lowest price at which they are willing to supply the last unit sold.

When people freely make offers to buy and sell and when demanders try to buy at the lowest possible price and suppliers try to sell at the highest possible price, the price at which trade takes place is the equilibrium price—the price at which the quantity demanded equals the quantity supplied. The price coordinates the plans of buyers and sellers, and no one has an incentive to change it.

REVIEW QUIZ

1 What is the equilibrium price of a good or service?
2 Over what range of prices does a shortage arise? What happens to the price when there is a shortage?
3 Over what range of prices does a surplus arise? What happens to the price when there is a surplus?
4 Why is the price at which the quantity demanded equals the quantity supplied the equilibrium price?
5 Why is the equilibrium price the best deal available for both buyers and sellers?

You can work these questions in Study Plan 3.4 and get instant feedback.

◆ Predicting Changes in Price and Quantity

The demand and supply model that we have just studied provides us with a powerful way of analyzing influences on prices and the quantities bought and sold. According to the model, a change in price stems from a change in demand, a change in supply, or a change in both demand and supply. Let's look first at the effects of a change in demand.

An Increase in Demand

If more people join health clubs, the demand for energy bars increases. The table in Fig. 3.8 shows the original and new demand schedules for energy bars as well as the supply schedule of energy bars.

The increase in demand creates a shortage at the original price and to eliminate the shortage, the price must rise.

Figure 3.8 shows what happens. The figure shows the original demand for and supply of energy bars. The original equilibrium price is $1.50 an energy bar, and the equilibrium quantity is 10 million energy bars a week. When demand increases, the demand curve shifts rightward. The equilibrium price rises to $2.50 an energy bar, and the quantity supplied increases to 15 million energy bars a week, as highlighted in the figure. There is an *increase in the quantity supplied* but *no change in supply*—a movement along, but no shift of, the supply curve.

A Decrease in Demand

We can reverse this change in demand. Start at a price of $2.50 a bar with 15 million energy bars a week being bought and sold, and then work out what happens if demand decreases to its original level. Such a decrease in demand might arise if people switch to energy gel (a substitute for energy bars). The decrease in demand shifts the demand curve leftward. The equilibrium price falls to $1.50 a bar, the quantity supplied decreases, and the equilibrium quantity decreases to 10 million bars a week.

We can now make our first two predictions:

1. When demand increases, the price rises and the quantity increases.

2. When demand decreases, the price falls and the quantity decreases.

FIGURE 3.8   The Effects of a Change in Demand

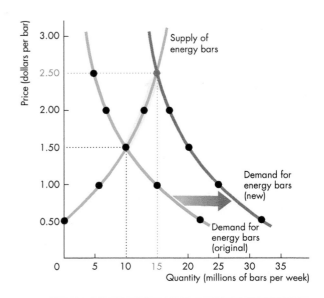

Price (dollars per bar)	Quantity demanded (millions of bars per week)		Quantity supplied (millions of bars per week)
	Original	New	
0.50	22	32	0
1.00	15	25	6
1.50	**10**	**20**	**10**
2.00	7	17	13
2.50	5	15	15

Initially, the demand for energy bars is the blue demand curve. The equilibrium price is $1.50 a bar, and the equilibrium quantity is 10 million bars a week. When more health-conscious people do more exercise, the demand for energy bars increases and the demand curve shifts rightward to become the red curve.

At $1.50 a bar, there is now a shortage of 10 million bars a week. The price of a bar rises to a new equilibrium of $2.50. As the price rises to $2.50, the quantity supplied increases—shown by the blue arrow on the supply curve—to the new equilibrium quantity of 15 million bars a week. Following an increase in demand, the quantity supplied increases but supply does not change—the supply curve does not shift.

 animation

Economics in Action
The Global Market for Crude Oil

The demand and supply model provides insights into all competitive markets. Here, we'll apply what you've learned about the effects of an increase in demand to the global market for crude oil.

Crude oil is like the life-blood of the global economy. It is used to fuel our cars, airplanes, trains, and buses, to generate electricity, and to produce a wide range of plastics. When the price of crude oil rises, the cost of transportation, power, and materials all increase.

In 2001, the price of a barrel of oil was $20 (using the value of money in 2010). In 2008, before the global financial crisis ended a long period of economic expansion, the price peaked at $127 a barrel.

While the price of oil was rising, the quantity of oil produced and consumed also increased. In 2001, the world produced 65 million barrels of oil a day. By 2008, that quantity was 72 million barrels.

Who or what has been raising the price of oil? Is it the action of greedy oil producers? Oil producers might be greedy, and some of them might be big enough to withhold supply and raise the price, but it wouldn't be in their self-interest to do so. The higher price would bring forth a greater quantity supplied from other producers and the profit of the producer limiting supply would fall.

Oil producers could try to cooperate and jointly withhold supply. The Organization of Petroleum Exporting Countries, OPEC, is such a group of producers. But OPEC doesn't control the *world* supply and its members' self-interest is to produce the quantities that give them the maximum attainable profit.

So even though the global oil market has some big players, they don't fix the price. Instead, the actions of thousands of buyers and sellers and the forces of demand and supply determine the price of oil.

So how have demand and supply changed?

Because both the price and the quantity have increased, the demand for oil must have increased. Supply might have changed too, but here we'll suppose that supply has remained the same.

The global demand for oil has increased for one major reason: World income has increased. The increase has been particularly large in the emerging economies of Brazil, China, and India. Increased world income has increased the demand for oil-using goods such as electricity, gasoline, and plastics, which in turn has increased the demand for oil.

The figure illustrates the effects of the increase in demand on the global oil market. The supply of oil remained constant along supply curve S. The demand for oil in 2001 was D_{2001}, so in 2001 the price was $20 a barrel and the quantity was 65 million barrels per day. The demand for oil increased and by 2008 it had reached D_{2008}. The price of oil increased to $127 a barrel and the quantity increased to 72 million barrels a day. The increase in the quantity is an *increase in the quantity supplied*, not an increase in supply.

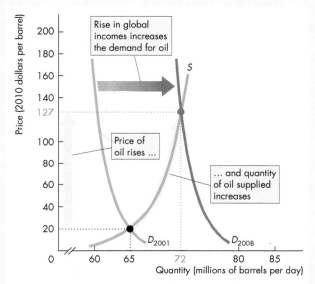

The Global Market for Crude Oil

An Increase in Supply

When Nestlé (the producer of PowerBar) and other energy bar producers switch to a new cost-saving technology, the supply of energy bars increases. Figure 3.9 shows the new supply schedule (the same one that was shown in Fig. 3.5). What are the new equilibrium price and quantity? The price falls to $1.00 a bar, and the quantity increases to 15 million bars a week. You can see why by looking at the quantities demanded and supplied at the old price of $1.50 a bar. The new quantity supplied at that price is 20 million bars a week, and there is a surplus. The price falls. Only when the price is $1.00 a bar does the quantity supplied equal the quantity demanded.

Figure 3.9 illustrates the effect of an increase in supply. It shows the demand curve for energy bars and the original and new supply curves. The initial equilibrium price is $1.50 a bar, and the equilibrium quantity is 10 million bars a week. When supply increases, the supply curve shifts rightward. The equilibrium price falls to $1.00 a bar, and the quantity demanded increases to 15 million bars a week, highlighted in the figure. There is an *increase in the quantity demanded* but *no change in demand*—a movement along, but no shift of, the demand curve.

A Decrease in Supply

Start out at a price of $1.00 a bar with 15 million bars a week being bought and sold. Then suppose that the cost of labor or raw materials rises and the supply of energy bars decreases. The decrease in supply shifts the supply curve leftward. The equilibrium price rises to $1.50 a bar, the quantity demanded decreases, and the equilibrium quantity decreases to 10 million bars a week.

We can now make two more predictions:

1. When supply increases, the price falls and the quantity increases.
2. When supply decreases, the price rises and the quantity decreases.

You've now seen what happens to the price and the quantity when either demand or supply changes while the other one remains unchanged. In real markets, both demand and supply can change together. When this happens, to predict the changes in price and quantity, we must combine the effects that you've just seen. That is your final task in this chapter.

FIGURE 3.9   The Effects of a Change in Supply

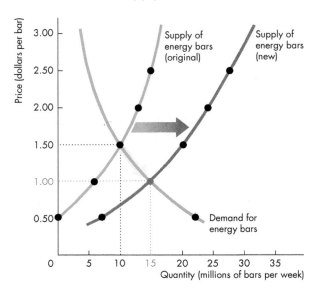

Price (dollars per bar)	Quantity demanded (millions of bars per week)	Quantity supplied (millions of bars per week)	
		Original	New
0.50	22	0	7
1.00	15	6	15
1.50	**10**	**10**	20
2.00	7	13	25
2.50	5	15	27

Initially, the supply of energy bars is shown by the blue supply curve. The equilibrium price is $1.50 a bar, and the equilibrium quantity is 10 million bars a week. When the new cost-saving technology is adopted, the supply of energy bars increases and the supply curve shifts rightward to become the red curve.

At $1.50 a bar, there is now a surplus of 10 million bars a week. The price of an energy bar falls to a new equilibrium of $1.00 a bar. As the price falls to $1.00, the quantity demanded increases—shown by the blue arrow on the demand curve—to the new equilibrium quantity of 15 million bars a week. Following an increase in supply, the quantity demanded increases but demand does not change—the demand curve does not shift.

myeconlab animation

Economics in Action
The Market for Strawberries

California produces 85 percent of the nation's strawberries and its crop, which starts to increase in March, is in top flight by April. During the winter months of January and February, Florida is the main strawberry producer.

In a normal year, the supplies from these two regions don't overlap much. As California's production steps up in March and April, Florida's production falls off. The result is a steady supply of strawberries and not much seasonal fluctuation in the price of strawberries.

But 2010 wasn't a normal year. Florida had exceptionally cold weather, which damaged the strawberry fields, lowered crop yields, and delayed the harvests. The result was unusually high strawberry prices.

With higher than normal prices, Florida farmers planted strawberry varieties that mature later than their normal crop and planned to harvest this fruit during the spring. Their plan worked perfectly and good growing conditions delivered a bumper crop by late March.

On the other side of the nation, while Florida was freezing, Southern California was drowning under unusually heavy rains. This wet weather put the strawberries to sleep and delayed their growth. But when the rains stopped and the temperature began to rise, California joined Florida with a super abundance of fruit.

With an abundance of strawberries, the price tumbled. Strawberry farmers in both regions couldn't hire enough labor to pick the super-sized crop, so some fruit was left in the fields to rot.

The figure explains what was happening in the market for strawberries.

Demand, shown by the demand curve, D, didn't change. In January, the failed Florida crop kept supply low and the supply curve was $S_{January}$. The price was high at $3.80 per pound and production was 5.0 million pounds per day.

In April, the bumper crops in both regions increased supply to S_{April}. This increase in supply lowered the price to $1.20 per pound and increased the quantity demanded—a movement along the demand curve—to 5.5 million pounds per day.

You can also see in the figure why farmers left fruit in the field to rot. At the January price of $3.80 a pound, farmers would have been paying top wages to hire the workers needed to pick fruit at the rate of 6.0 million pounds per day. This is the quantity on supply curve S_{April} at $3.80 a pound.

But with the fall in price to $1.20 a pound, growers were not able to earn a profit by picking more than 5.5 million pounds.

For some growers the price wasn't high enough to cover the cost of hiring labor, so they opened their fields to anyone who wanted to pick their own strawberries for free.

The events we've described here in the market for strawberries illustrate the effects of a change in supply with no change in demand.

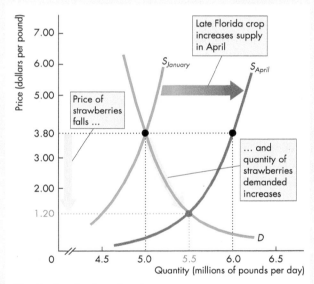

The Market for Strawberries

All the Possible Changes in Demand and Supply

Figure 3.10 brings together and summarizes the effects of all the possible changes in demand and supply. With what you've learned about the effects of a change in *either* demand or supply, you can predict what happens if *both* demand and supply change together. Let's begin by reviewing what you already know.

Change in Demand with No Change in Supply The first row of Fig. 3.10, parts (a), (b), and (c), summarizes the effects of a change in demand with no change in supply. In part (a), with no change in either demand or supply, neither the price nor the quantity changes. With an *increase* in demand and no change in supply in part (b), both the price and quantity increase. And with a *decrease* in demand and no change in supply in part (c), both the price and the quantity decrease.

Change in Supply with No Change in Demand The first column of Fig. 3.10, parts (a), (d), and (g), summarizes the effects of a change in supply with no change in demand. With an *increase* in supply and no change in demand in part (d), the price falls and quantity increases. And with a *decrease* in supply and no change in demand in part (g), the price rises and the quantity decreases.

Increase in Both Demand and Supply You've seen that an increase in demand raises the price and increases the quantity. And you've seen that an increase in supply lowers the price and increases the quantity. Fig. 3.10(e) combines these two changes. Because either an increase in demand or an increase in supply increases the quantity, the quantity also increases when both demand and supply increase. But the effect on the price is uncertain. An increase in demand raises the price and an increase in supply lowers the price, so we can't say whether the price will rise or fall when both demand and supply increase. We need to know the magnitudes of the changes in demand and supply to predict the effects on price. In the example in Fig. 3.10(e), the price does not change. But notice that if demand increases by slightly more than the amount shown in the figure, the price will rise. And if supply increases by slightly more than the amount shown in the figure, the price will fall.

Decrease in Both Demand and Supply Figure 3.10(i) shows the case in which demand and supply *both decrease*. For the same reasons as those we've just reviewed, when both demand and supply decrease, the quantity decreases, and again the direction of the price change is uncertain.

Decrease in Demand and Increase in Supply You've seen that a decrease in demand lowers the price and decreases the quantity. And you've seen that an increase in supply lowers the price and increases the quantity. Fig. 3.10(f) combines these two changes. Both the decrease in demand and the increase in supply lower the price, so the price falls. But a decrease in demand decreases the quantity and an increase in supply increases the quantity, so we can't predict the direction in which the quantity will change unless we know the magnitudes of the changes in demand and supply. In the example in Fig. 3.10(f), the quantity does not change. But notice that if demand decreases by slightly more than the amount shown in the figure, the quantity will decrease; if supply increases by slightly more than the amount shown in the figure, the quantity will increase.

Increase in Demand and Decrease in Supply Figure 3.10(h) shows the case in which demand increases and supply decreases. Now, the price rises, and again the direction of the quantity change is uncertain.

◢ REVIEW QUIZ

What is the effect on the price and quantity of MP3 players (such as the iPod) if

1 The price of a PC falls or the price of an MP3 download rises? (Draw the diagrams!)

2 More firms produce MP3 players or electronics workers' wages rise? (Draw the diagrams!)

3 Any two of the events in questions 1 and 2 occur together? (Draw the diagrams!)

You can work these questions in Study Plan 3.5 and get instant feedback.

◆ To complete your study of demand and supply, take a look at *Reading Between the Lines* on pp. 64–65, which explains why the price of coffee increased in 2010. Try to get into the habit of using the demand and supply model to understand the movements in prices in your everyday life.

FIGURE 3.10   The Effects of All the Possible Changes in Demand and Supply

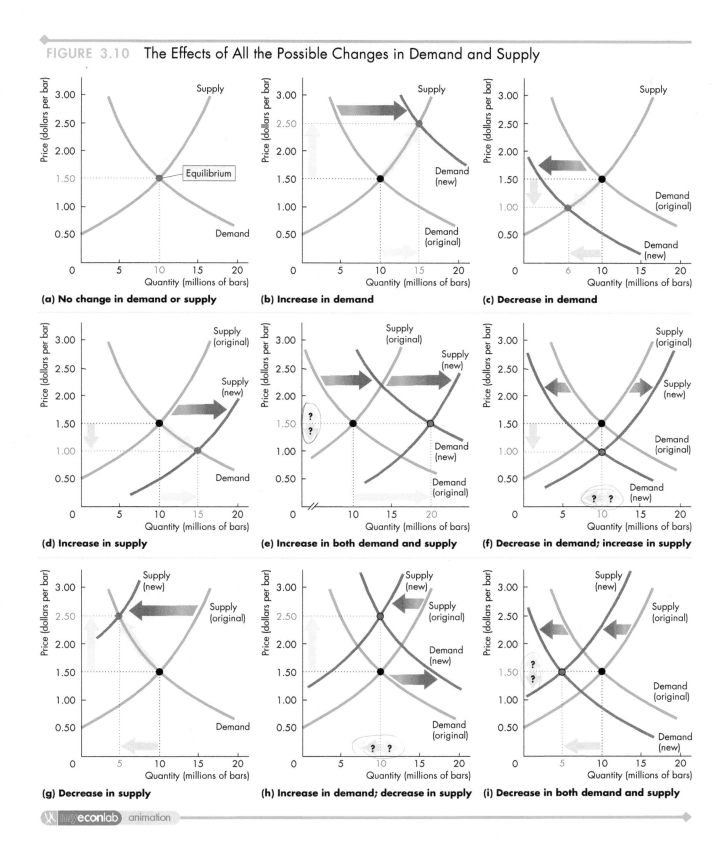

(a) No change in demand or supply

(b) Increase in demand

(c) Decrease in demand

(d) Increase in supply

(e) Increase in both demand and supply

(f) Decrease in demand; increase in supply

(g) Decrease in supply

(h) Increase in demand; decrease in supply

(i) Decrease in both demand and supply

Demand and Supply: The Price of Coffee

Coffee Surges on Poor Colombian Harvests

FT.com

July 30, 2010

Coffee prices hit a 12-year high on Friday on the back of low supplies of premium Arabica coffee from Colombia after a string of poor crops in the Latin American country.

The strong fundamental picture has also encouraged hedge funds to reverse their previous bearish views on coffee prices.

In New York, ICE September Arabica coffee jumped 3.2 percent to 178.75 cents per pound, the highest since February 1998. It traded later at 177.25 cents, up 6.8 percent on the week.

The London-based International Coffee Organization on Friday warned that the "current tight demand and supply situation" was "likely to persist in the near to medium term."

Coffee industry executives believe prices could rise toward 200 cents per pound in New York before the arrival of the new Brazilian crop later this year.

"Until October it is going to be tight on high quality coffee," said a senior executive at one of Europe's largest coffee roasters. He said: "The industry has been surprised by the scarcity of high quality beans."

Colombia coffee production, key for supplies of premium beans, last year plunged to a 33-year low of 7.8m bags, each of 60kg, down nearly a third from 11.1m bags in 2008, tightening supplies worldwide. ...

Excerpted from "Coffee Surges on Poor Colombian Harvests" by Javier Blas. *Financial Times*, July 30, 2010. Reprinted with permission.

ESSENCE OF THE STORY

- The price of premium Arabica coffee increased by 3.2 percent to almost 180 cents per pound in July 2010, the highest price since February 1998.

- A sequence of poor crops in Columbia cut the production of premium Arabica coffee to a 33-year low of 7.8 million 60 kilogram bags, down from 11.1 million bags in 2008.

- The International Coffee Organization said that the "current tight demand and supply situation" was "likely to persist in the near to medium term."

- Coffee industry executives say prices might approach 200 cents per pound before the arrival of the new Brazilian crop later this year.

- Hedge funds previously expected the price of coffee to fall but now expect it to rise further.

- This news article reports two sources of changes in supply and demand that changed the price of coffee.

- The first source of change is the sequence of poor harvests in Columbia. These events decreased the world supply of Arabica coffee. (Arabica is the type that Starbucks uses.)

- Before the reported events, the world production of Arabica was 120 million bags per year and its price was 174 cents per pound.

- The decrease in the Columbian harvest decreased world production to about 116 million bags, which is about 3 percent of world production.

- Figure 1 shows the situation before the poor Columbia harvests and the effects of those poor harvests. The demand curve is D and initially, the supply curve was S^0. The market equilibrium is at 120 million bags per year and a price of 174 cents per pound.

- The poor Columbian harvests decreased supply and the supply curve shifted leftward to S^1. The price increased to 180 cents per pound and the quantity decreased to 116 million bags.

- The second source of change influenced both supply and demand. It is a change in the expected future price of coffee.

- The hedge funds referred to in the news article are speculators that try to profit from buying at a low price and selling at a high price.

- With the supply of coffee expected to remain low, the price was expected to rise further—a rise in the expected future price of coffee.

- When the expected future price of coffee rises, some people want to buy more coffee (so they can sell it later)—an increase in the demand today. And some people offer less coffee for sale (so they can sell it later for a higher price)—a decrease in the supply today.

- Figure 2 shows the effects of these changes in the demand and supply today.

- Demand increased and the demand curve shifted from D^0 to D^1. Supply decreased and the supply curve shifted from S^1 to S^2.

- Because demand increases and supply decreases, the price rises. In this example, it rises to 200 cents per pound.

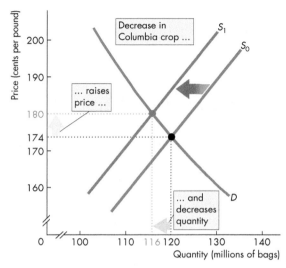

Figure 1 The effects of the Columbian crop

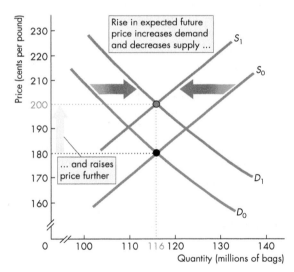

Figure 2 The effects of the expected future price

- Also, because demand increases and supply decreases, the change in the equilibrium quantity can go in either direction.

- In this example, the increase in demand equals the decrease in supply, so the equilibrium quantity remains constant at 116 million bags per year.

65

MATHEMATICAL NOTE

Demand, Supply, and Equilibrium

Demand Curve

The law of demand says that as the price of a good or service falls, the quantity demanded of that good or service increases. We can illustrate the law of demand by drawing a graph of the demand curve or writing down an equation. When the demand curve is a straight line, the following equation describes it:

$$P = a - bQ_D,$$

where P is the price and Q_D is the quantity demanded. The a and b are positive constants.

The demand equation tells us three things:

1. The price at which no one is willing to buy the good (Q_D is zero). That is, if the price is a, then the quantity demanded is zero. You can see the price a in Fig. 1. It is the price at which the demand curve hits the y-axis—what we call the demand curve's "y-intercept."

2. As the price falls, the quantity demanded increases. If Q_D is a positive number, then the price P must be less than a. As Q_D gets larger, the price P becomes smaller. That is, as the quantity increases, the maximum price that buyers are willing to pay for the last unit of the good falls.

3. The constant b tells us how fast the maximum price that someone is willing to pay for the good falls as the quantity increases. That is, the constant b tells us about the steepness of the demand curve. The equation tells us that the slope of the demand curve is $-b$.

Supply Curve

The law of supply says that as the price of a good or service rises, the quantity supplied of that good or service increases. We can illustrate the law of supply by drawing a graph of the supply curve or writing down an equation. When the supply curve is a straight line, the following equation describes it:

$$P = c + dQ_S,$$

where P is the price and Q_S is the quantity supplied. The c and d are positive constants.

The supply equation tells us three things:

1. The price at which sellers are not willing to supply the good (Q_S is zero). That is, if the price is c, then no one is willing to sell the good. You can see the price c in Fig. 2. It is the price at which the supply curve hits the y-axis—what we call the supply curve's "y-intercept."

2. As the price rises, the quantity supplied increases. If Q_S is a positive number, then the price P must be greater than c. As Q_S increases, the price P becomes larger. That is, as the quantity increases, the minimum price that sellers are willing to accept for the last unit rises.

3. The constant d tells us how fast the minimum price at which someone is willing to sell the good rises as the quantity increases. That is, the constant d tells us about the steepness of the supply curve. The equation tells us that the slope of the supply curve is d.

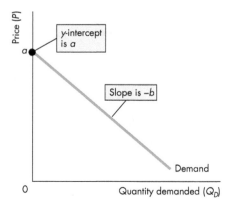

Figure 1 Demand curve

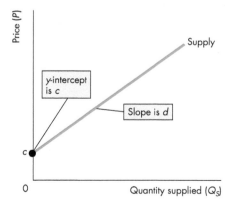

Figure 2 Supply curve

Market Equilibrium

Demand and supply determine market equilibrium. Figure 3 shows the equilibrium price (P^*) and equilibrium quantity (Q^*) at the intersection of the demand curve and the supply curve.

We can use the equations to find the equilibrium price and equilibrium quantity. The price of a good adjusts until the quantity demanded Q_D equals the quantity supplied Q_S. So at the equilibrium price (P^*) and equilibrium quantity (Q^*),

$$Q_D = Q_S = Q^*.$$

To find the equilibrium price and equilibrium quantity, substitute Q^* for Q_D in the demand equation and Q^* for Q_S in the supply equation. Then the price is the equilibrium price (P^*), which gives

$$P^* = a - bQ^*$$
$$P^* = c + dQ^*.$$

Notice that

$$a - bQ^* = c + dQ^*.$$

Now solve for Q^*:

$$a - c = bQ^* + dQ^*$$
$$a - c = (b + d)Q^*$$
$$Q^* = \frac{a - c}{b + d}.$$

To find the equilibrium price, (P^*), substitute for Q^* in either the demand equation or the supply equation.

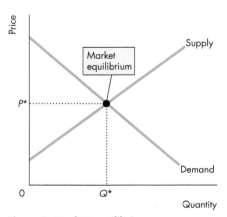

Price
Supply

Market
equilibrium

P^*

Demand

0   Q^*

Quantity

Figure 3 Market equilibrium

Using the demand equation, we have

$$P^* = a - b\left(\frac{a - c}{b + d}\right)$$
$$P^* = \frac{a(b + d) - b(a - c)}{b + d}$$
$$P^* = \frac{ad + bc}{b + d}.$$

Alternatively, using the supply equation, we have

$$P^* = c + d\left(\frac{a - c}{b + d}\right)$$
$$P^* = \frac{c(b + d) + d(a - c)}{b + d}$$
$$P^* = \frac{ad + bc}{b + d}.$$

An Example

The demand for ice-cream cones is

$$P = 800 - 2Q_D.$$

The supply of ice-cream cones is

$$P = 200 + 1Q_S.$$

The price of a cone is expressed in cents, and the quantities are expressed in cones per day.

To find the equilibrium price (P^*) and equilibrium quantity (Q^*), substitute Q^* for Q_D and Q_S and P^* for P. That is,

$$P^* = 800 - 2Q^*$$
$$P^* = 200 + 1Q^*.$$

Now solve for Q^*:

$$800 - 2Q^* = 200 + 1Q^*$$
$$600 = 3Q^*$$
$$Q^* = 200.$$

And

$$P^* = 800 - 2(200)$$
$$= 400.$$

The equilibrium price is $4 a cone, and the equilibrium quantity is 200 cones per day.

SUMMARY

Key Points

Markets and Prices (p. 46)

- A competitive market is one that has so many buyers and sellers that no single buyer or seller can influence the price.
- Opportunity cost is a relative price.
- Demand and supply determine relative prices.

Working Problem 1 will give you a better understanding of markets and prices.

Demand (pp. 47–51)

- Demand is the relationship between the quantity demanded of a good and its price when all other influences on buying plans remain the same.
- The higher the price of a good, other things remaining the same, the smaller is the quantity demanded—the law of demand.
- Demand depends on the prices of related goods (substitutes and complements), expected future prices, income, expected future income and credit, the population, and preferences.

Working Problems 2 to 5 will give you a better understanding of demand.

Supply (pp. 52–55)

- Supply is the relationship between the quantity supplied of a good and its price when all other influences on selling plans remain the same.
- The higher the price of a good, other things remaining the same, the greater is the quantity supplied—the law of supply.

- Supply depends on the prices of factors of production used to produce a good, the prices of related goods produced, expected future prices, the number of suppliers, technology, and the state of nature.

Working Problems 6 to 9 will give you a better understanding of supply.

Market Equilibrium (pp. 56–57)

- At the equilibrium price, the quantity demanded equals the quantity supplied.
- At any price above the equilibrium price, there is a surplus and the price falls.
- At any price below the equilibrium price, there is a shortage and the price rises.

Working Problems 10 and 11 will give you a better understanding of market equilibrium

Predicting Changes in Price and Quantity (pp. 58–63)

- An increase in demand brings a rise in the price and an increase in the quantity supplied. A decrease in demand brings a fall in the price and a decrease in the quantity supplied.
- An increase in supply brings a fall in the price and an increase in the quantity demanded. A decrease in supply brings a rise in the price and a decrease in the quantity demanded.
- An increase in demand and an increase in supply bring an increased quantity but an uncertain price change. An increase in demand and a decrease in supply bring a higher price but an uncertain change in quantity.

Working Problems 12 and 13 will give you a better understanding of predicting changes in price and quantity.

Key Terms

Change in demand, 48
Change in supply, 53
Change in the quantity
    demanded, 51
Change in the quantity supplied, 54
Competitive market, 46
Complement, 49
Demand, 47

Demand curve, 48
Equilibrium price, 56
Equilibrium quantity, 56
Inferior good, 50
Law of demand, 47
Law of supply, 52
Money price, 46
Normal good, 50

Quantity demanded, 47
Quantity supplied, 52
Relative price, 46
Substitute, 49
Supply, 52
Supply curve, 52

STUDY PLAN PROBLEMS AND APPLICATIONS

 You can work Problems 1 to 17 in MyEconLab Chapter 3 Study Plan and get instant feedback.

Markets and Prices (Study Plan 3.1)

1. William Gregg owned a mill in South Carolina. In December 1862, he placed a notice in the *Edgehill Advertiser* announcing his willingness to exchange cloth for food and other items. Here is an extract:

   1 yard of cloth for 1 pound of bacon
   2 yards of cloth for 1 pound of butter
   4 yards of cloth for 1 pound of wool
   8 yards of cloth for 1 bushel of salt

   a. What is the relative price of butter in terms of wool?

   b. If the money price of bacon was 20¢ a pound, what do you predict was the money price of butter?

   c. If the money price of bacon was 20¢ a pound and the money price of salt was $2.00 a bushel, do you think anyone would accept Mr. Gregg's offer of cloth for salt?

Demand (Study Plan 3.2)

2. The price of food increased during the past year.

   a. Explain why the law of demand applies to food just as it does to all other goods and services.

   b. Explain how the substitution effect influences food purchases and provide some examples of substitutions that people might make when the price of food rises and other things remain the same.

   c. Explain how the income effect influences food purchases and provide some examples of the income effect that might occur when the price of food rises and other things remain the same.

3. Place the following goods and services into pairs of likely substitutes and pairs of likely complements. (You may use an item in more than one pair.) The goods and services are

   coal, oil, natural gas, wheat, corn, rye, pasta, pizza, sausage, skateboard, roller blades, video game, laptop, iPod, cell phone, text message, email, phone call, voice mail

4. During 2010, the average income in China increased by 10 percent. Compared to 2009,

how do you expect the following would change:

   a. The demand for beef? Explain your answer.

   b. The demand for rice? Explain your answer.

5. In January 2010, the price of gasoline was $2.70 a gallon. By spring 2010, the price had increased to $3.00 a gallon. Assume that there were no changes in average income, population, or any other influence on buying plans. Explain how the rise in the price of gasoline would affect

   a. The demand for gasoline.

   b. The quantity of gasoline demanded.

Supply (Study Plan 3.3)

6. In 2008, the price of corn increased by 35 percent and some cotton farmers in Texas stopped growing cotton and started to grow corn.

   a. Does this fact illustrate the law of demand or the law of supply? Explain your answer.

   b. Why would a cotton farmer grow corn?

Use the following information to work Problems 7 to 9.

Dairies make low-fat milk from full-cream milk. In the process of making low-fat milk, the dairies produce cream, which is made into ice cream. In the market for low-fat milk, the following events occur one at a time:

   (i)   The wage rate of dairy workers rises.

   (ii) The price of cream rises.

   (iii) The price of low-fat milk rises.

   (iv) With the period of low rainfall extending, dairies raise their expected price of low-fat milk next year.

   (v)   With advice from health-care experts, dairy farmers decide to switch from producing full-cream milk to growing vegetables.

   (vi) A new technology lowers the cost of producing ice cream.

7. Explain the effect of each event on the supply of low-fat milk.

8. Use a graph to illustrate the effect of each event.

9. Does any event (or events) illustrate the law of supply?

Market Equilibrium (Study Plan 3.4)

10. "As more people buy computers, the demand for Internet service increases and the price of Internet service decreases. The fall in the price of Internet service decreases the supply of Internet service." Explain what is wrong with this statement.

11. The demand and supply schedules for gum are

Price (cents per pack)	Quantity demanded	Quantity supplied
	(millions of packs a week)	
20	180	60
40	140	100
60	100	140
80	60	180
100	20	220

   a. Draw a graph of the market for gum and mark in the equilibrium price and quantity.

   b. Suppose that the price of gum is 70¢ a pack. Describe the situation in the gum market and explain how the price adjusts.

   c. Suppose that the price of gum is 30¢ a pack. Describe the situation in the gum market and explain how the price adjusts.

Predicting Changes in Price and Quantity

(Study Plan 3.5)

12. The following events occur one at a time:
    (i)   The price of crude oil rises.
    (ii) The price of a car rises.
    (iii) All speed limits on highways are abolished.
    (iv) Robots cut car production costs.

    Which of these events will increase or decrease (state which occurs)
    a. The demand for gasoline?
    b. The supply of gasoline?
    c. The quantity of gasoline demanded?
    d. The quantity of gasoline supplied?

13. In Problem 11, a fire destroys some factories that produce gum and the quantity of gum supplied decreases by 40 million packs a week at each price.
    a. Explain what happens in the market for gum and draw a graph to illustrate the changes.
    b. If at the time the fire occurs there is an increase in the teenage population, which increases the quantity of gum demanded by 40 million packs a week at each price, what are the new equilibrium price and quantity of gum? Illustrate these changes on your graph.

Economics in the News (Study Plan 3.N)

14. **American to Cut Flights, Charge for Luggage**
    American Airlines announced yesterday that it will begin charging passengers $15 for their first piece of checked luggage, in addition to raising other fees and cutting domestic flights as it grapples with record-high fuel prices.
    Source: *Boston Herald*, May 22, 2008
    a. According to the news clip, what is the influence on the supply of American Airlines flights?
    b. Explain how supply changes.

15. **Of Gambling, Grannies, and Good Sense**
    Nevada has plenty of jobs for the over 50s and its elderly population is growing faster than that in other states.
    Source: *The Economist*, July 26, 2006
    Explain how grannies have influenced:
    a. The demand in some Las Vegas markets.
    b. The supply in other Las Vegas markets.

16. **Frigid Florida Winter is Bad News for Tomato Lovers**
    An unusually cold January in Florida destroyed entire fields of tomatoes and forced many farmers to delay their harvest. Florida's growers are shipping only a quarter of their usual 5 million pounds a week. The price has risen from $6.50 for a 25-pound box a year ago to $30 now.
    Source: *USA Today*, March 3, 2010
    a. Make a graph to illustrate the market for tomatoes in January 2009 and January 2010.
    b. On the graph, show how the events in the news clip influence the market for tomatoes.
    c. Why is the news "bad for tomato lovers"?

17. **Pump Prices on Pace to Top 2009 High by Weekend**
    The cost of filling up the car is rising as the crude oil price soars and pump prices may exceed the peak price of 2009.
    Source: *USA Today*, January 7, 2010
    a. Does demand for gasoline or the supply of gasoline or both change when the price of oil soars?
    b. Use a demand-supply graph to illustrate what happens to the equilibrium price of gasoline and the equilibrium quantity of gasoline bought when the price of oil soars.

ADDITIONAL PROBLEMS AND APPLICATIONS

 You can work these problems in MyEconLab if assigned by your instructor.

Markets and Prices

18. What features of the world market for crude oil make it a competitive market?
19. The money price of a textbook is $90 and the money price of the Wii game *Super Mario Galaxy* is $45.
    a. What is the opportunity cost of a textbook in terms of the Wii game?
    b. What is the relative price of the Wii game in terms of textbooks?

Demand

20. The price of gasoline has increased during the past year.
    a. Explain why the law of demand applies to gasoline just as it does to all other goods and services.
    b. Explain how the substitution effect influences gasoline purchases and provide some examples of substitutions that people might make when the price of gasoline rises and other things remain the same.
    c. Explain how the income effect influences gasoline purchases and provide some examples of the income effects that might occur when the price of gasoline rises and other things remain the same.
21. Think about the demand for the three game consoles: Xbox, PS3, and Wii. Explain the effect of the following events on the demand for Xbox games and the quantity of Xbox games demanded, other things remaining the same.
    a. The price of an Xbox falls.
    b. The prices of a PS3 and a Wii fall.
    c. The number of people writing and producing Xbox games increases.
    d. Consumers' incomes increase.
    e. Programmers who write code for Xbox games become more costly to hire.
    f. The expected future price of an Xbox game falls.
    g. A new game console that is a close substitute for Xbox comes onto the market.

Supply

22. Classify the following pairs of goods and services as substitutes in production, complements in production, or neither.
    a. Bottled water and health club memberships
    b. French fries and baked potatoes
    c. Leather purses and leather shoes
    d. Hybrids and SUVs
    e. Diet coke and regular coke
23. As the prices of homes fell across the United States in 2008, the number of homes offered for sale decreased.
    a. Does this fact illustrate the law of demand or the law of supply? Explain your answer.
    b. Why would home owners decide not to sell?
24. **G.M. Cuts Production for Quarter**
    General Motors cut its fourth-quarter production schedule by 10 percent because Ford Motor, Chrysler, and Toyota sales declined in August.
    Source: *The New York Times*, September 5, 2007

    Explain whether this news clip illustrates a change in the supply of cars or a change in the quantity supplied of cars.

Market Equilibrium

Use the following figure to work Problems 25 and 26.

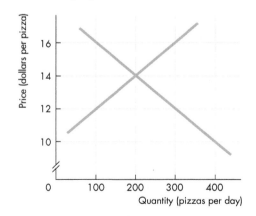

25. a. Label the curves. Which curve shows the willingness to pay for a pizza?
    b. If the price of a pizza is $16, is there a shortage or a surplus and does the price rise or fall?

c. Sellers want to receive the highest possible price, so why would they be willing to accept less than $16 a pizza?

26. a. If the price of a pizza is $12, is there a shortage or a surplus and does the price rise or fall?

b. Buyers want to pay the lowest possible price, so why would they be willing to pay more than $12 for a pizza?

27. The demand and supply schedules for potato chips are

Price (cents per bag)	Quantity demanded	Quantity supplied
	(millions of bags per week)	
50	160	130
60	150	140
70	140	150
80	130	160
90	120	170
100	110	180

a. Draw a graph of the potato chip market and mark in the equilibrium price and quantity.

b. If the price is 60¢ a bag, is there a shortage or a surplus, and how does the price adjust?

Predicting Changes in Price and Quantity

28. In Problem 27, a new dip increases the quantity of potato chips that people want to buy by 30 million bags per week at each price.
a. How does the demand and/or supply of chips change?
b. How does the price and quantity of chips change?

29. In Problem 27, if a virus destroys potato crops and the quantity of potato chips produced decreases by 40 million bags a week at each price, how does the supply of chips change?

30. If the virus in Problem 29 hits just as the new dip in Problem 28 comes onto the market, how does the price and quantity of chips change?

Economics in the News

31. After you have studied *Reading Between the Lines* on pp. 64–65 answer the following questions.
a. What happened to the price of coffee in 2010?
b. What substitutions do you expect might have been made to decrease the quantity of coffee demanded?
c. What influenced the demand for coffee in 2010 and what influenced the quantity of coffee demanded?
d. What influenced the supply of coffee during

2010 and how did the supply of coffee change?
e. How did the combination of the factors you have noted in parts (c) and (d) influence the price and quantity of coffee?
f. Was the change in quantity of coffee a change in the quantity demanded or a change in the quantity supplied?

32. **Strawberry Prices Drop as Late Harvest Hits Market**
Shoppers bought strawberries in March for $1.25 a pound rather than the $3.49 a pound they paid last year. With the price so low, some growers plowed over their strawberry plants to make way for spring melons; others froze their harvests and sold them to juice and jam makers.
   Source: *USA Today*, April 5, 2010
a. Explain how the market for strawberries would have changed if growers had not plowed in their plants but offered locals "you pick for free."
b. Describe the changes in demand and supply in the market for strawberry jam.

33. **"Popcorn Movie" Experience Gets Pricier**
Cinemas are raising the price of popcorn. Demand for field corn, which is used for animal feed, corn syrup, and ethanol, has increased and its price has exploded. That's caused some farmers to shift from growing popcorn to easier-to-grow field corn.
   Source: *USA Today*, May 24, 2008
Explain and illustrate graphically the events described in the news clip in the market for
a. Popcorn
b. Movie tickets

Use the following news clip to work Problems 34 and 35.

Sony's Blu-Ray Wins High-Definition War
Toshiba Corp. yesterday withdrew from the race to be the next-generation home movie format, leaving Sony Corp.'s Blu-ray technology the winner. The move could finally jump-start a high-definition home DVD market.
   Source: *The Washington Times*, February 20, 2008

34. a. How would you expect the price of a used Toshiba player on eBay to change? Will the price change result from a change in demand, supply, or both, and in which directions?
b. How would you expect the price of a Blu-ray player to change?

35. Explain how the market for Blu-ray format movies will change.

4

ELASTICITY

After studying this chapter,
you will be able to:

◆ Define, calculate, and explain the factors that influence
the price elasticity of demand

◆ Define, calculate, and explain the factors that influence
the cross elasticity of demand and the income elasticity
of demand

◆ Define, calculate, and explain the factors that influence
the elasticity of supply

W hat do you do when the price of gasoline soars to $3 a gallon? If you're
like most people, you complain a lot but keep on filling your tank and spending
more on gas. Would you react the same way to a rise in the price of tomatoes?
In the winter of 2010, a prolonged Florida frost wiped out most of the state's
tomato crop, driving the price of tomatoes to almost five times its normal level.
If faced with this price rise, do you keep buying the same quantity of tomatoes,
or do you find less costly substitutes?

How can we compare the effects of price changes on buying plans for
different goods such as gasoline and tomatoes?

This chapter introduces you to elasticity: a tool that addresses the
quantitative questions like the ones you've just considered and enables us to
compare the sensitivity of the quantity demanded to a change in price
regardless of the units in which the good is measured.

At the end of the chapter, in Reading Between the Lines, we'll use the
concepts of the elasticity of demand and the elasticity of supply to explain what
was happening in the market for fresh winter tomatoes from Florida during the
severe winter of 2010. But we'll begin by explaining elasticity in another
familiar setting: the market for pizza.

Price Elasticity of Demand

You know that when supply increases, the equilibrium price falls and the equilibrium quantity increases. But does the price fall by a large amount and the quantity increase by a little? Or does the price barely fall and the quantity increase by a large amount?

The answer depends on the responsiveness of the quantity demanded to a change in price. You can see why by studying Fig. 4.1, which shows two possible scenarios in a local pizza market. Figure 4.1(a) shows one scenario, and Fig. 4.1(b) shows the other.

In both cases, supply is initially S_0. In part (a), the demand for pizza is shown by the demand curve D_A. In part (b), the demand for pizza is shown by the demand curve D_B. Initially, in both cases, the price is $20 a pizza and the equilibrium quantity is 10 pizzas an hour.

Now a large pizza franchise opens up, and the supply of pizza increases. The supply curve shifts rightward to S_1. In case (a), the price falls by an enormous $15 to $5 a pizza, and the quantity increases by only 3 to 13 pizzas an hour. In contrast, in case (b), the price falls by only $5 to $15 a pizza and the quantity increases by 7 to 17 pizzas an hour.

The different outcomes arise from differing degrees of responsiveness of the quantity demanded to a change in price. But what do we mean by responsiveness? One possible answer is slope. The slope of demand curve D_A is steeper than the slope of demand curve D_B.

In this example, we can compare the slopes of the two demand curves, but we can't always make such a comparison. The reason is that the slope of a demand curve depends on the units in which we measure the price and quantity. And we often must compare the demand for different goods and services that are measured in unrelated units. For example, a pizza producer might want to compare the demand for pizza with the demand for soft drinks. Which quantity demanded is more responsive to a price change? This question can't be answered by comparing the slopes of two demand curves. The units of measurement of pizza and soft drinks are unrelated. The question can be answered with a measure of responsiveness that is independent of units of measurement. Elasticity is such a measure.

The **price elasticity of demand** is a units-free measure of the responsiveness of the quantity demanded of a good to a change in its price when all other influences on buying plans remain the same.

FIGURE 4.1   How a Change in Supply Changes Price and Quantity

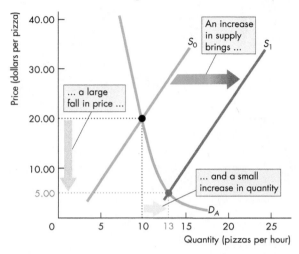

(a) Large price change and small quantity change

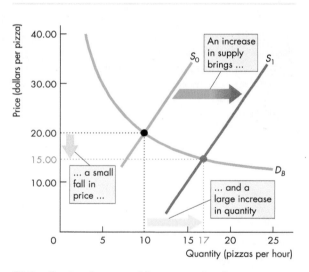

(b) Small price change and large quantity change

Initially, the price is $20 a pizza and the quantity sold is 10 pizzas an hour. Then supply increases from S_0 to S_1. In part (a), the price falls by $15 to $5 a pizza, and the quantity increases by 3 to 13 pizzas an hour. In part (b), the price falls by only $5 to $15 a pizza, and the quantity increases by 7 to 17 pizzas an hour. The price change is smaller and the quantity change is larger in case (b) than in case (a). The quantity demanded is more responsive to the change in the price in case (b) than in case (a).

myeconlab   animation

Calculating Price Elasticity of Demand

We calculate the *price elasticity of demand* by using the formula:

$$\text{Price elasticity of demand} = \frac{\text{Percentage change in quantity demanded}}{\text{Percentage change in price}}.$$

To calculate the price elasticity of demand for pizza, we need to know the quantity demanded of pizza at two different prices, when all other influences on buying plans remain the same.

Figure 4.2 zooms in on the demand curve for pizza and shows how the quantity demanded responds to a small change in price. Initially, the price is $20.50 a pizza and 9 pizzas an hour are demanded—the original point. The price then falls to $19.50 a pizza, and the quantity demanded increases to 11 pizzas an hour—the new point. When the price falls by $1 a pizza, the quantity demanded increases by 2 pizzas an hour.

To calculate the price elasticity of demand, we express the change in price as a percentage of the *average price* and the change in the quantity demanded as a percentage of the *average quantity*. By using the average price and average quantity, we calculate the elasticity at a point on the demand curve midway between the original point and the new point.

The original price is $20.50 and the new price is $19.50, so the price change is $1 and the average price is $20 a pizza. Call the percentage change in the price %ΔP, then

$$\%\Delta P = \Delta P/P_{ave} \times 100 = (\$1/\$20) \times 100 = 5\%.$$

The original quantity demanded is 9 pizzas and the new quantity demanded is 11 pizzas, so the quantity change is 2 pizzas and the average quantity demanded is 10 pizzas. Call the percentage change in the quantity demanded %ΔQ, then

$$\%\Delta Q = \Delta Q/Q_{ave} \times 100 = (2/10) \times 100 = 20\%.$$

The price elasticity of demand equals the percentage change in the quantity demanded (20 percent) divided by the percentage change in price (5 percent) and is 4. That is,

$$\begin{aligned}\text{Price elasticity of demand} &= \frac{\%\Delta Q}{\%\Delta P} \\ &= \frac{20\%}{5\%} = 4.\end{aligned}$$

FIGURE 4.2   Calculating the Elasticity of Demand

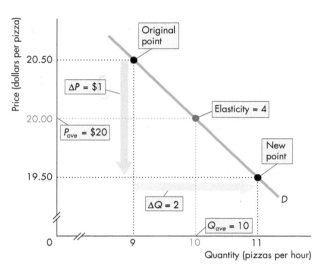

The elasticity of demand is calculated by using the formula:*

$$\begin{aligned}\text{Price elasticity of demand} &= \frac{\text{Percentage change in quantity demanded}}{\text{Percentage change in price}} \\ &= \frac{\%\Delta Q}{\%\Delta P} \\ &= \frac{\Delta Q/Q_{ave}}{\Delta P/P_{ave}} \\ &= \frac{2/10}{1/20} = 4.\end{aligned}$$

This calculation measures the elasticity at an average price of $20 a pizza and an average quantity of 10 pizzas an hour.

* In the formula, the Greek letter delta (Δ) stands for "change in" and %Δ stands for "percentage change in."

[myeconlab   animation]

Average Price and Quantity Notice that we use the *average* price and *average* quantity. We do this because it gives the most precise measurement of elasticity—at the midpoint between the original price and the new price. If the price falls from $20.50 to $19.50, the $1 price change is 4.9 percent of $20.50. The 2 pizza change in quantity is 22.2 percent of 9 pizzas, the original quantity. So if we use these numbers, the price elasticity of demand is 22.2 divided by 4.9, which equals 4.5. If the price rises from \$19.50 to \$20.50, the \$1 price change is 5.1 percent of \$19.50. The 2 pizza change in quantity is 18.2 percent of 11 pizzas, the original quantity. So if we use these numbers, the price elasticity of demand is 18.2 divided by 5.1, which equals 3.6.

By using percentages of the *average* price and *average* quantity, we get the same value for the elasticity regardless of whether the price falls from \$20.50 to \$19.50 or rises from \$19.50 to \$20.50.

Percentages and Proportions Elasticity is the ratio of two percentage changes, so when we divide one percentage change by another, the 100s cancel. A percentage change is a *proportionate* change multiplied by 100. The proportionate change in price is $\Delta P/P_{ave}$, and the proportionate change in quantity demanded is $\Delta Q/Q_{ave}$. So if we divide $\Delta Q/Q_{ave}$ by $\Delta P/P_{ave}$ we get the same answer as we get by using percentage changes.

A Units-Free Measure Now that you've calculated a price elasticity of demand, you can see why it is a *units-free measure*. Elasticity is a units-free measure because the percentage change in each variable is independent of the units in which the variable is measured. The ratio of the two percentages is a number without units.

Minus Sign and Elasticity When the price of a good *rises*, the quantity demanded *decreases*. Because a *positive* change in price brings a *negative* change in the quantity demanded, the price elasticity of demand is a negative number. But it is the magnitude, or *absolute value*, of the price elasticity of demand that tells us how responsive the quantity demanded is. So to compare price elasticities of demand, we use the magnitude of the elasticity and ignore the minus sign.

Inelastic and Elastic Demand

Figure 4.3 shows three demand curves that cover the entire range of possible elasticities of demand. In Fig. 4.3(a), the quantity demanded is constant regardless of the price. If the quantity demanded remains constant when the price changes, then the price elasticity of demand is zero and the good is said to have a **perfectly inelastic demand**. One good that has a very low price elasticity of demand (perhaps zero over some price range) is insulin. Insulin is of such importance to some diabetics that if the price rises or falls, they do not change the quantity they buy.

If the percentage change in the quantity demanded equals the percentage change in the price, then the price elasticity equals 1 and the good is said to have a **unit elastic demand**. The demand in Fig. 4.3(b) is an example of a unit elastic demand.

Between the cases shown in Fig. 4.3(a) and Fig. 4.3(b) is the general case in which the percentage change in the quantity demanded is less than the percentage change in the price. In this case, the price elasticity of demand is between zero and 1 and the good is said to have an **inelastic demand**. Food and shelter are examples of goods with inelastic demand.

FIGURE 4.3   Inelastic and Elastic Demand

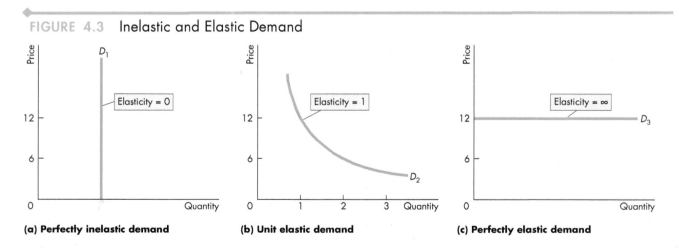

(a) Perfectly inelastic demand   **(b) Unit elastic demand**   **(c) Perfectly elastic demand**

Each demand illustrated here has a constant elasticity. The demand curve in part (a) illustrates the demand for a good that has a zero elasticity of demand. The demand curve in part (b) illustrates the demand for a good with a unit elasticity of demand. And the demand curve in part (c) illustrates the demand for a good with an infinite elasticity of demand.

myeconlab animation

If the quantity demanded changes by an infinitely large percentage in response to a tiny price change, then the price elasticity of demand is infinity and the good is said to have a **perfectly elastic demand**. Figure 4.3(c) shows a perfectly elastic demand. An example of a good that has a very high elasticity of demand (almost infinite) is a soft drink from two campus machines located side by side. If the two machines offer the same soft drinks for the same price, some people buy from one machine and some from the other. But if one machine's price is higher than the other's, by even a small amount, no one buys from the machine with the higher price. Drinks from the two machines are perfect substitutes. The demand for a good that has a perfect substitute is perfectly elastic.

Between the cases in Fig. 4.3(b) and Fig. 4.3(c) is the general case in which the percentage change in the quantity demanded exceeds the percentage change in price. In this case, the price elasticity of demand is greater than 1 and the good is said to have an **elastic demand**. Automobiles and furniture are examples of goods that have elastic demand.

Elasticity Along a Linear Demand Curve

Elasticity and slope are not the same. A linear demand curve has a constant slope but a varying elasticity. Let's see why.

The demand curve in Fig. 4.4 is linear. A $5 fall in the price brings an increase of 10 pizzas an hour no matter what the initial price and quantity.

Let's now calculate some elasticities along this demand curve.

At the midpoint of the demand curve, the price is $12.50 and the quantity is 25 pizzas per hour. When the price falls from $15 to $10 a pizza the quantity demanded increases from 20 to 30 pizzas an hour and the average price and average quantity are at the midpoint of the demand curve. So

$$\text{Price elasticity of demand} = \frac{10/25}{5/12.25}$$

$$= 1.$$

That is, at the midpoint of a linear demand curve, the price elasticity of demand is one.

At prices *above* the midpoint, demand is elastic. For example, when the price falls from $25 to $15 a pizza, the quantity demanded increases from zero to

20 pizzas an hour. The average price is $20 a pizza, and the average quantity is 10 pizzas. So

$$\text{Price elasticity of demand} = \frac{\Delta Q/Q_{ave}}{\Delta P/P_{ave}}$$

$$= \frac{20/10}{10/20}$$

$$= 4.$$

That is, the price elasticity of demand at an average price of $20 a pizza is 4.

At prices *below* the midpoint, demand is inelastic. For example, when the price falls from $10 a pizza to zero, the quantity demanded increases from 30 to 50 pizzas an hour. The average price is now $5 and the average quantity is 40 pizzas an hour. So

$$\text{Price elasticity of demand} = \frac{20/40}{10/5}$$

$$= 1/4.$$

That is, the price elasticity of demand at an average price of $5 a pizza is 1/4.

FIGURE 4.4   Elasticity Along a Linear Demand Curve

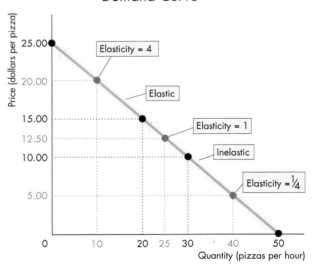

On a linear demand curve, demand is unit elastic at the midpoint (elasticity is 1), elastic above the midpoint, and inelastic below the midpoint.

Total Revenue and Elasticity

The **total revenue** from the sale of a good equals the price of the good multiplied by the quantity sold. When a price changes, total revenue also changes. But a cut in the price does not always decrease total revenue. The change in total revenue depends on the elasticity of demand in the following way:

- If demand is elastic, a 1 percent price cut increases the quantity sold by more than 1 percent and total revenue increases.

- If demand is inelastic, a 1 percent price cut increases the quantity sold by less than 1 percent and total revenue decreases.

- If demand is unit elastic, a 1 percent price cut increases the quantity sold by 1 percent and total revenue does not change.

In Fig. 4.5(a), over the price range from $25 to $12.50, demand is elastic. Over the price range from $12.50 to zero, demand is inelastic. At a price of $12.50, demand is unit elastic.

Figure 4.5(b) shows total revenue. At a price of $25, the quantity sold is zero, so total revenue is zero. At a price of zero, the quantity demanded is 50 pizzas an hour and total revenue is again zero. A price cut in the elastic range brings an increase in total revenue—the percentage increase in the quantity demanded is greater than the percentage decrease in price. A price cut in the inelastic range brings a decrease in total revenue—the percentage increase in the quantity demanded is less than the percentage decrease in price. At unit elasticity, total revenue is at a maximum.

Figure 4.5 shows how we can use this relationship between elasticity and total revenue to estimate elasticity using the total revenue test. The **total revenue test** is a method of estimating the price elasticity of demand by observing the change in total revenue that results from a change in the price, when all other influences on the quantity sold remain the same.

- If a price cut increases total revenue, demand is elastic.

- If a price cut decreases total revenue, demand is inelastic.

- If a price cut leaves total revenue unchanged, demand is unit elastic.

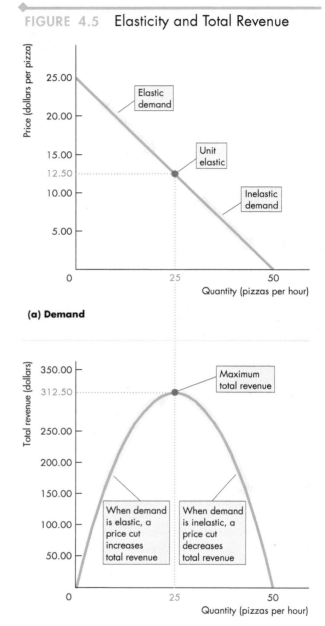

FIGURE 4.5   Elasticity and Total Revenue

(a) Demand

(b) Total revenue

When demand is elastic, in the price range from $25 to $12.50, a decrease in price (part a) brings an increase in total revenue (part b). When demand is inelastic, in the price range from $12.50 to zero, a decrease in price (part a) brings a decrease in total revenue (part b). When demand is unit elastic, at a price of $12.50 (part a), total revenue is at a maximum (part b).

myeconlab   animation

Your Expenditure and Your Elasticity

When a price changes, the change in your expenditure on the good depends on *your* elasticity of demand.

- If your demand is elastic, a 1 percent price cut increases the quantity you buy by more than 1 percent and your expenditure on the item increases.
- If your demand is inelastic, a 1 percent price cut increases the quantity you buy by less than 1 percent and your expenditure on the item decreases.
- If your demand is unit elastic, a 1 percent price cut increases the quantity you buy by 1 percent and your expenditure on the item does not change.

So if you spend more on an item when its price falls, your demand for that item is elastic; if you spend the same amount, your demand is unit elastic; and if you spend less, your demand is inelastic.

The Factors That Influence the Elasticity of Demand

The elasticity of demand for a good depends on

- The closeness of substitutes
- The proportion of income spent on the good
- The time elapsed since the price change

Closeness of Substitutes The closer the substitutes for a good or service, the more elastic is the demand for it. Oil from which we make gasoline has no close substitutes (imagine a steam-driven, coal-fueled car). So the demand for oil is inelastic. Plastics are close substitutes for metals, so the demand for metals is elastic.

The degree of substitutability depends on how narrowly (or broadly) we define a good. For example, a personal computer has no close substitutes, but a Dell PC is a close substitute for a Hewlett-Packard PC. So the elasticity of demand for personal computers is lower than the elasticity of demand for a Dell or a Hewlett-Packard.

In everyday language we call goods such as food and shelter *necessities* and goods such as exotic vacations *luxuries*. A necessity has poor substitutes and is crucial for our well-being. So a necessity generally has an inelastic demand. A luxury usually has many substitutes, one of which is not buying it. So a luxury generally has an elastic demand.

Proportion of Income Spent on the Good Other things remaining the same, the greater the proportion of income spent on a good, the more elastic (or less inelastic) is the demand for it.

Economics in Action
Elastic and Inelastic Demand

The real-world price elasticities of demand in the table range from 1.52 for metals, the item with the most elastic demand in the table, to 0.05 for oil, the item with the most inelastic demand in the table. The demand for food is also inelastic.

Oil and food, which have poor substitutes and inelastic demand, might be classified as necessities. Furniture and motor vehicles, which have good substitutes and elastic demand, might be classified as luxuries.

Price Elasticities of Demand

Good or Service	Elasticity
Elastic Demand	
Metals	1.52
Electrical engineering products	1.39
Mechanical engineering products	1.30
Furniture	1.26
Motor vehicles	1.14
Instrument engineering products	1.10
Professional services	1.09
Transportation services	1.03
Inelastic Demand	
Gas, electricity, and water	0.92
Chemicals	0.89
Drinks	0.78
Clothing	0.64
Tobacco	0.61
Banking and insurance services	0.56
Housing services	0.55
Agricultural and fish products	0.42
Books, magazines, and newspapers	0.34
Food	0.12
Oil	0.05

Sources of data: Ahsan Mansur and John Whalley, "Numerical Specification of Applied General Equilibrium Models: Estimation, Calibration, and Data," in *Applied General Equilibrium Analysis*, eds. Herbert E. Scarf and John B. Shoven (New York: Cambridge University Press, 1984), 109, and Henri Theil, Ching-Fan Chung, and James L. Seale, Jr., *Advances in Econometrics, Supplement I, 1989, International Evidence on Consumption Patterns* (Greenwich, Conn.: JAI Press Inc., 1989), and Geoffrey Heal, Columbia University, Web site.

Economics in Action

Price Elasticities of Demand for Food

The price elasticity of demand for food in the United States is estimated to be 0.12. This elasticity is an average over all types of food. The demand for most food items is inelastic, but there is a wide range of elasticities as the figure below shows for a range of fruits, vegetables, and meats.

The demand for grapes and beef is elastic. The demand for oranges is unit elastic. These food items have many good substitutes. Florida winter tomatoes have closer substitutes than tomatoes in general, so the demand for the Florida winter variety is more elastic (less inelastic) than the demand for tomatoes.

Carrots and cabbage, on which we spend a very small proportion of income, have an almost zero elastic demand.

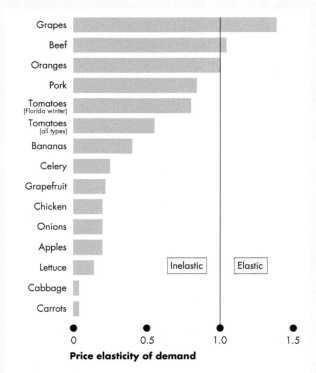

Price Elasticities of Demand for Food

Sources of data: Kuo S. Huang, *U.S. demand for food: A complete system of price and income effects* U.S. Dept. of Agriculture, Economic Research Service, Washington, DC, 1985 and J. Scott Shonkwiler and Robert D. Emerson, "Imports and the Supply of Winter Tomatoes: An Application of Rational Expectations", *American Journal of Agricultural Economics*, Vol. 64, No. 4 (Nov., 1982), pp. 634-641 and Kuo S. Huang, "A Further Look at Flexibilities and Elasticities", *American Journal of Agricultural Economics*, Vol. 76, No. 2 (May, 1994), pp. 313–317.

Think about your own elasticity of demand for chewing gum and housing. If the price of gum doubles, you consume almost as much as before. Your demand for gum is inelastic. If apartment rents double, you look for more students to share accommodation with you. Your demand for housing is not as inelastic as your demand for gum. Why the difference? Housing takes a large proportion of your budget, and gum takes only a tiny proportion. You don't like either price increase, but you hardly notice the higher price of gum, while the higher rent puts your budget under severe strain.

Time Elapsed Since Price Change The longer the time that has elapsed since a price change, the more elastic is demand. When the price of oil increased by 400 percent during the 1970s, people barely changed the quantity of oil and gasoline they bought. But gradually, as more efficient auto and airplane engines were developed, the quantity bought decreased. The demand for oil became more elastic as more time elapsed following the huge price hike.

REVIEW QUIZ

1 Why do we need a units-free measure of the responsiveness of the quantity demanded of a good or service to a change in its price?
2 Define the price elasticity of demand and show how it is calculated.
3 What is the total revenue test? Explain how it works.
4 What are the main influences on the elasticity of demand that make the demand for some goods elastic and the demand for other goods inelastic?
5 Why is the demand for a luxury generally more elastic (or less inelastic) than the demand for a necessity?

You can work these questions in Study Plan 4.1 and get instant feedback.

You've now completed your study of the *price* elasticity of demand. Two other elasticity concepts tell us about the effects of other influences on demand. Let's look at these other elasticities of demand.

◆ More Elasticities of Demand

Back at the pizzeria, you are trying to work out how a price rise by the burger shop next door will affect the demand for your pizza. You know that pizzas and burgers are substitutes. You also know that when the price of a substitute for pizza rises, the demand for pizza increases. But by how much?

You also know that pizza and soft drinks are complements. And you know that if the price of a complement of pizza rises, the demand for pizza decreases. So you wonder, by how much will a rise in the price of a soft drink decrease the demand for your pizza?

To answer these questions, you need to calculate the cross elasticity of demand. Let's examine this elasticity measure.

Cross Elasticity of Demand

We measure the influence of a change in the price of a substitute or complement by using the concept of the cross elasticity of demand. The **cross elasticity of demand** is a measure of the responsiveness of the demand for a good to a change in the price of a substitute or complement, other things remaining the same. We calculate the *cross elasticity of demand* by using the formula:

$$\text{Cross elasticity of demand} = \frac{\text{Percentage change in quantity demanded}}{\text{Percentage change in price of a substitute or complement}}.$$

The cross elasticity of demand can be positive or negative. It is *positive* for a *substitute* and *negative* for a *complement*.

Substitutes Suppose that the price of pizza is constant and people buy 9 pizzas an hour. Then the price of a burger rises from $1.50 to $2.50. No other influence on buying plans changes and the quantity of pizzas bought increases to 11 an hour.

The change in the quantity demanded is +2 pizzas—the new quantity, 11 pizzas, minus the original quantity, 9 pizzas. The average quantity is 10 pizzas. So the quantity of pizzas demanded increases by 20 percent. That is,

$$\Delta Q/Q_{ave} \times 100 = (+2/10) \times 100 = +20\%.$$

The change in the price of a burger, a substitute for pizza, is +$1—the new price, $2.50, minus the original price, $1.50. The average price is $2 a burger. So the price of a burger rises by 50 percent. That is,

$$\Delta P/P_{ave} \times 100 = (+\$1/\$2) \times 100 = +50\%.$$

So the cross elasticity of demand for pizza with respect to the price of a burger is

$$\frac{+20\%}{+50\%} = 0.4.$$

Figure 4.6 illustrates the cross elasticity of demand. Pizza and burgers are substitutes. Because they are substitutes, when the price of a burger rises, the demand for pizza increases. The demand curve for pizza shifts rightward from D_0 to D_1. Because a *rise* in the price of a burger brings an *increase* in the demand for pizza, the cross elasticity of demand for pizza with respect to the price of a burger is *positive*. Both the price and the quantity change in the same direction.

FIGURE 4.6   Cross Elasticity of Demand

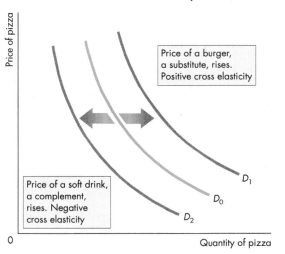

A burger is a *substitute* for pizza. When the price of a burger rises, the demand for pizza increases and the demand curve for pizza shifts rightward from D_0 to D_1. The cross elasticity of demand is *positive*.

A soft drink is a *complement* of pizza. When the price of a soft drink rises, the demand for pizza decreases and the demand curve for pizza shifts leftward from D_0 to D_2. The cross elasticity of demand is *negative*.

Ⓧ myeconlab animation

Complements Now suppose that the price of pizza is constant and 11 pizzas an hour are bought. Then the price of a soft drink rises from $1.50 to $2.50. No other influence on buying plans changes and the quantity of pizzas bought falls to 9 an hour.

The change in the quantity demanded is the opposite of what we've just calculated: The quantity of pizzas demanded decreases by 20 percent (−20%).

The change in the price of a soft drink, a complement of pizza, is the same as the percentage change in the price of a burger that we've just calculated. The price rises by 50 percent (+50%). So the cross elasticity of demand for pizza with respect to the price of a soft drink is

$$\frac{-20\%}{+50\%} = -0.4.$$

Because pizza and soft drinks are complements, when the price of a soft drink rises, the demand for pizza decreases. The demand curve for pizza shifts leftward from D_0 to D_2. Because a *rise* in the price of a soft drink brings a *decrease* in the demand for pizza, the cross elasticity of demand for pizza with respect to the price of a soft drink is *negative*. The price and quantity change in *opposite* directions.

The magnitude of the cross elasticity of demand determines how far the demand curve shifts. The larger the cross elasticity (absolute value), the greater is the change in demand and the larger is the shift in the demand curve.

If two items are close substitutes, such as two brands of spring water, the cross elasticity is large. If two items are close complements, such as movies and popcorn, the cross elasticity is large.

If two items are somewhat unrelated to each other, such as newspapers and orange juice, the cross elasticity is small—perhaps even zero.

Income Elasticity of Demand

Suppose the economy is expanding and people are enjoying rising incomes. This prosperity brings an increase in the demand for most types of goods and services. But by how much will the demand for pizza increase? The answer depends on the **income elasticity of demand**, which is a measure of the responsiveness of the demand for a good or service to a change in income, other things remaining the same.

The income elasticity of demand is calculated by using the formula:

$$\text{Income elasticity of demand} = \frac{\text{Percentage change in quantity demanded}}{\text{Percentage change in income}}.$$

Income elasticities of demand can be positive or negative and they fall into three interesting ranges:

- Greater than 1 (*normal* good, income elastic)
- Positive and less than 1 (*normal* good, income inelastic)
- Negative (*inferior* good)

Income Elastic Demand Suppose that the price of pizza is constant and 9 pizzas an hour are bought. Then incomes rise from $975 to $1,025 a week. No other influence on buying plans changes and the quantity of pizzas sold increases to 11 an hour.

The change in the quantity demanded is +2 pizzas. The average quantity is 10 pizzas, so the quantity demanded increases by 20 percent. The change in income is +$50 and the average income is $1,000, so incomes increase by 5 percent. The income elasticity of demand for pizza is

$$\frac{20\%}{5\%} = 4.$$

The demand for pizza is income elastic. The percentage increase in the quantity of pizza demanded exceeds the percentage increase in income. *When the demand for a good is income elastic, the percentage of income spent on that good increases as income increases.*

Income Inelastic Demand If the income elasticity of demand is positive but less than 1, demand is income inelastic. The percentage increase in the quantity demanded is positive but less than the percentage increase in income. *When the demand for a good is income inelastic, the percentage of income spent on that good decreases as income increases.*

Inferior Goods If the income elasticity of demand is negative, the good is an *inferior* good. The quantity demanded of an inferior good and the amount spent on it *decrease* when income increases. Goods in this category include small motorcycles, potatoes, and rice. Low-income consumers buy most of these goods.

Economics in Action
Necessities and Luxuries

The table shows estimates of some real-world income elasticities of demand. The demand for a necessity such as food or clothing is income inelastic, while the demand for a luxury such as transportation, which includes airline and foreign travel, is income elastic.

But what is a necessity and what is a luxury depends on the level of income. For people with a low income, food and clothing can be luxuries. So the level of income has a big effect on income elasticities of demand. The figure shows this effect on the income elasticity of demand for food in 10 countries. In countries with low incomes, such as Tanzania and India, the income elasticity of demand for food is high. In countries with high incomes, such as the United States, the income elasticity of

demand for food is low. That is, as income increases, the income elasticity of demand for food decreases. Low-income consumers spend a larger percentage of any increase in income on food than do high-income consumers.

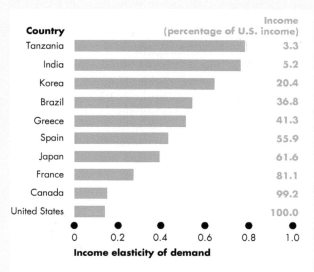

Country		Income (percentage of U.S. income)
Tanzania		3.3
India		5.2
Korea		20.4
Brazil		36.8
Greece		41.3
Spain		55.9
Japan		61.6
France		81.1
Canada		99.2
United States		100.0

Income elasticity of demand

Income Elasticities in 10 Countries

Some Real-World Income Elasticities of Demand

Income Elastic Demand

Airline travel	5.82
Movies	3.41
Foreign travel	3.08
Electricity	1.94
Restaurant meals	1.61
Local buses and trains	1.38
Haircuts	1.36
Automobiles	1.07

Income Inelastic Demand

Tobacco	0.86
Alcoholic drinks	0.62
Furniture	0.53
Clothing	0.51
Newspapers and magazines	0.38
Telephone	0.32
Food	0.14

Sources of data: H.S. Houthakker and Lester D. Taylor, Consumer Demand in the United States (Cambridge, Mass.: Harvard University Press, 1970), and Henri Theil, Ching-Fan Chung, and James L. Seale, Jr., Advances in Econometrics, Supplement 1, 1989, International Evidence on Consumption Patterns (Greenwich, Conn.: JAI Press, Inc., 1989).

 REVIEW QUIZ

1 What does the cross elasticity of demand measure?
2 What does the sign (positive versus negative) of the cross elasticity of demand tell us about the relationship between two goods?
3 What does the income elasticity of demand measure?
4 What does the sign (positive versus negative) of the income elasticity of demand tell us about a good?
5 Why does the level of income influence the magnitude of the income elasticity of demand?

You can work these questions in Study Plan 4.2 and get instant feedback.

You've now completed your study of the *cross elasticity* of demand and the *income elasticity* of demand. Let's look at the other side of the market and examine the elasticity of supply.

◆ Elasticity of Supply

You know that when demand increases, the equilibrium price rises and the equilibrium quantity increases. But does the price rise by a large amount and the quantity increase by a little? Or does the price barely rise and the quantity increase by a large amount?

The answer depends on the responsiveness of the quantity supplied to a change in price. You can see why by studying Fig. 4.7, which shows two possible scenarios in a local pizza market. Figure 4.7(a) shows one scenario, and Fig. 4.7(b) shows the other.

In both cases, demand is initially D_0. In part (a), supply is shown by the supply curve S_A. In part (b), supply is shown by the supply curve S_B. Initially, in both cases, the price is $20 a pizza and the equilibrium quantity is 10 pizzas an hour.

Now increases in incomes and population increase the demand for pizza. The demand curve shifts rightward to D_1. In case (a), the price rises by $10 to $30 a pizza, and the quantity increases by only 3 to 13 pizzas an hour. In contrast, in case (b), the price rises by only $1 to $21 a pizza, and the quantity increases by 10 to 20 pizzas an hour.

The different outcomes arise from differing degrees of responsiveness of the quantity supplied to a change in price. We measure the degree of responsiveness by using the concept of the elasticity of supply.

Calculating the Elasticity of Supply

The **elasticity of supply** measures the responsiveness of the quantity supplied to a change in the price of a good when all other influences on selling plans remain the same. It is calculated by using the formula:

$$\text{Elasticity of supply} = \frac{\text{Percentage change in quantity supplied}}{\text{Percentage change in price}}.$$

We use the same method that you learned when you studied the elasticity of demand. (Refer back to p. 85 to check this method.) Let's calculate the elasticity of supply along the supply curves in Fig. 4.7.

In Fig. 4.7(a), when the price rises from $20 to $30, the price rise is $10 and the average price is $25, so the price rises by 40 percent of the average price. The quantity increases from 10 to 13 pizzas an hour,

FIGURE 4.7   How a Change in Demand Changes Price and Quantity

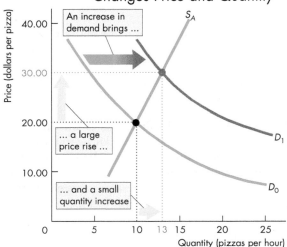

(a) Large price change and small quantity change

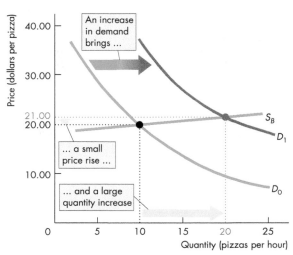

(b) Small price change and large quantity change

Initially, the price is $20 a pizza, and the quantity sold is 10 pizzas an hour. Then the demand for pizza increases. The demand curve shifts rightward to D_1. In part (a), the price rises by $10 to $30 a pizza, and the quantity increases by 3 to 13 pizzas an hour. In part (b), the price rises by only $1 to $21 a pizza, and the quantity increases by 10 to 20 pizzas an hour. The price change is smaller and the quantity change is larger in case (b) than in case (a). The quantity supplied is more responsive to a change in the price in case (b) than in case (a).

◆ myeconlab   animation ━━━◆

so the increase is 3 pizzas, the average quantity is 11.5 pizzas an hour, and the quantity increases by 26 percent. The elasticity of supply is equal to 26 percent divided by 40 percent, which equals 0.65.

In Fig. 4.7(b), when the price rises from $20 to $21, the price rise is $1 and the average price is $20.50, so the price rises by 4.9 percent of the average price. The quantity increases from 10 to 20 pizzas an hour, so the increase is 10 pizzas, the average quantity is 15 pizzas, and the quantity increases by 67 percent. The elasticity of supply is equal to 67 percent divided by 4.9 percent, which equals 13.67.

Figure 4.8 shows the range of elasticities of supply. If the quantity supplied is fixed regardless of the price, the supply curve is vertical and the elasticity of supply is zero. Supply is perfectly inelastic. This case is shown in Fig. 4.8(a). A special intermediate case occurs when the percentage change in price equals the percentage change in quantity. Supply is then unit elastic. This case is shown in Fig. 4.8(b). No matter how steep the supply curve is, if it is linear and passes through the origin, supply is unit elastic. If there is a price at which sellers are willing to offer any quantity for sale, the supply curve is horizontal and the elasticity of supply is infinite. Supply is perfectly elastic. This case is shown in Fig. 4.8(c).

The Factors That Influence the Elasticity of Supply

The elasticity of supply of a good depends on

- Resource substitution possibilities
- Time frame for the supply decision

Resource Substitution Possibilities Some goods and services can be produced only by using unique or rare productive resources. These items have a low, perhaps even a zero, elasticity of supply. Other goods and services can be produced by using commonly available resources that could be allocated to a wide variety of alternative tasks. Such items have a high elasticity of supply.

A Van Gogh painting is an example of a good with a vertical supply curve and a zero elasticity of supply. At the other extreme, wheat can be grown on land that is almost equally good for growing corn, so it is just as easy to grow wheat as corn. The opportunity cost of wheat in terms of forgone corn is almost constant. As a result, the supply curve of wheat is almost horizontal and its elasticity of supply is very large. Similarly, when a good is produced in many different countries (for example, sugar and beef), the supply of the good is highly elastic.

FIGURE 4.8   Inelastic and Elastic Supply

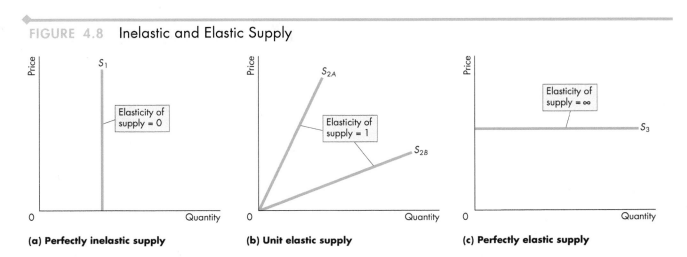

(a) Perfectly inelastic supply

(b) Unit elastic supply

(c) Perfectly elastic supply

Each supply illustrated here has a constant elasticity. The supply curve in part (a) illustrates the supply of a good that has a zero elasticity of supply. The supply curve in part (b) illustrates the supply of a good with a unit elasticity of supply. All linear supply curves that pass through the origin illustrate supplies that are unit elastic. The supply curve in part (c) illustrates the supply of a good with an infinite elasticity of supply.

The supply of most goods and services lies between these two extremes. The quantity produced can be increased but only by incurring a higher cost. If a higher price is offered, the quantity supplied increases. Such goods and services have an elasticity of supply between zero and infinity.

Time Frame for the Supply Decision To study the influence of the amount of time elapsed since a price change, we distinguish three time frames of supply:

- Momentary supply
- Short-run supply
- Long-run supply

Momentary Supply When the price of a good changes, the immediate response of the quantity supplied is determined by the *momentary supply* of that good.

Some goods, such as fruits and vegetables, have a perfectly inelastic momentary supply—a vertical supply curve. The quantities supplied depend on crop-planting decisions made earlier. In the case of oranges, for example, planting decisions have to be made many years in advance of the crop being available. Momentary supply is perfectly inelastic because, on a given day, no matter what the price of oranges, producers cannot change their output. They have picked, packed, and shipped their crop to market, and the quantity available for that day is fixed.

for crops

In contrast, some goods have a perfectly elastic momentary supply. Long-distance phone calls are an example. When many people simultaneously make a call, there is a big surge in the demand for telephone cables, computer switching, and satellite time. The quantity supplied increases, but the price remains constant. Long-distance carriers monitor fluctuations in demand and reroute calls to ensure that the quantity supplied equals the quantity demanded without changing the price.

for phone calls

Short-Run Supply The response of the quantity supplied to a price change when only *some* of the possible adjustments to production can be made is determined by *short-run supply*. Most goods have an inelastic short-run supply. To increase output in the short run, firms must work their labor force overtime and perhaps hire additional workers. To decrease their output in the short run, firms either lay off workers or reduce their hours of work. With the passage of time, firms can make more adjustments,

perhaps training additional workers or buying additional tools and other equipment.

For the orange grower, if the price of oranges falls, some pickers can be laid off and oranges left on the trees to rot. Or if the price of oranges rises, the grower can use more fertilizer and improved irrigation to increase the yields of their existing trees.

But an orange grower can't change the number of trees producing oranges in the short run.

Long-Run Supply The response of the quantity supplied to a price change after *all* the technologically possible ways of adjusting supply have been exploited is determined by *long-run supply*. For most goods and services, long-run supply is elastic and perhaps perfectly elastic.

For the orange grower, the long run is the time it takes new tree plantings to grow to full maturity—about 15 years. In some cases, the long-run adjustment occurs only after a completely new production plant has been built and workers have been trained to operate it—typically a process that might take several years.

REVIEW QUIZ

1 Why do we need a units-free measure of the responsiveness of the quantity supplied of a good or service to a change in its price?

2 Define the elasticity of supply and show how it is calculated.

3 What are the main influences on the elasticity of supply that make the supply of some goods elastic and the supply of other goods inelastic?

4 Provide examples of goods or services whose elasticities of supply are (a) zero, (b) greater than zero but less than infinity, and (c) infinity.

5 How does the time frame over which a supply decision is made influence the elasticity of supply? Explain your answer.

You can work these questions in Study Plan 4.3 and get instant feedback.

◆ You have now learned about the elasticities of demand and supply. Table 4.1 summarizes all the elasticities that you've met in this chapter. In the next chapter, we study the efficiency of competitive markets. But first study *Reading Between the Lines* on pp. 88–89, which puts the elasticity of demand to work and looks at the market for winter tomatoes.

TABLE 4.1   A Compact Glossary of Elasticities

Price Elasticities of Demand

A relationship is described as	When its magnitude is	Which means that
Perfectly elastic	Infinity	The smallest possible increase in price causes an infinitely large decrease in the quantity demanded*
Elastic	Less than infinity	The percentage decrease in the quantity demanded exceeds the percentage increase in price
Unit elastic	1	The percentage decrease in the quantity demanded equals the percentage increase in price
Inelastic	Less than 1 but greater than zero	The percentage decrease in the quantity demanded is less than the percentage increase in price
Perfectly inelastic	Zero	The quantity demanded is the same at all prices

Cross Elasticities of Demand

A relationship is described as	When its value is	Which means that
Close substitutes	Large	The smallest possible increase in the price of one good causes an infinitely large increase in the quantity demanded of the other good
Substitutes	Positive	If the price of one good increases, the quantity demanded of the other good also increases
Unrelated goods	Zero	If the price of one good increases, the quantity demanded of the other good remains the same
Complements	Negative	If the price of one good increases, the quantity demanded of the other good decreases

Income Elasticities of Demand

A relationship is described as	When its value is	Which means that
Income elastic (normal good)	Greater than 1	The percentage increase in the quantity demanded is greater than the percentage increase in income
Income inelastic (normal good)	Less than 1 but greater than zero	The percentage increase in the quantity demanded is greater than zero but less than the percentage increase in income
Negative (inferior good)	Less than zero	When income increases, quantity demanded decreases

Elasticities of Supply

A relationship is described as	When its magnitude is	Which means that
Perfectly elastic	Infinity	The smallest possible increase in price causes an infinitely large increase in the quantity supplied
Elastic	Less than infinity but greater than 1	The percentage increase in the quantity supplied exceeds the percentage increase in the price
Unit elastic	1	The percentage increase in the quantity supplied equals the percentage increase in the price
Inelastic	Greater than zero but less than 1	The percentage increase in the quantity supplied is less than the percentage increase in the price
Perfectly inelastic	Zero	The quantity supplied is the same at all prices

*In each description, the directions of change may be reversed. For example, in this case, the smallest possible *decrease* in price causes an infinitely large *increase* in the quantity demanded.

The Elasticities of Demand and Supply for Tomatoes

Frigid Florida Winter Is Bad News for Tomato Lovers

USA Today
March 5, 2010

ST. PETERSBURG, Fla. - A frigid Florida winter is taking its toll on your sandwich. The Sunshine State is the main U.S. source for fresh winter tomatoes, and its growers lost some 70 percent of their crop during January's prolonged cold snap. ...

The average wholesale price for a 25-pound box of tomatoes is now $30, up from $6.50 a year ago. Florida's growers would normally ship about 25 million pounds of tomatoes a week; right now, they're shipping less than a quarter of that, according to Reggie Brown of the Florida Tomato Grower's Exchange, a tomato farmer cooperative in Maitland. ...

And because high demand has driven up domestic prices, many wholesalers are buying from Mexico instead.

"We're obviously losing market share to Mexico, and there's always a price to pay to get the customer to get back into the Florida market," Brown said.

Florida is the only place where tomatoes are grown on a large scale in the United States during winter. California doesn't grow them until later in the year, and much of that state's crop is used for processed foods, such as ketchup, sauce, and juice. Other states grow tomatoes in greenhouses year-round, but Florida's winter tomato crop is by far the largest. ...

Some Wendy's restaurants posted signs saying tomatoes would only be provided upon request because of limited availability. ...

ESSENCE OF THE STORY

- Florida is the main U.S. source for fresh winter tomatoes.
- California tomatoes come to market later in the year and are mainly used for ketchup, sauce, and juice.
- Other states grow tomatoes in greenhouses year-round.
- In January 2010, a prolonged cold snap wiped out 70 percent of the Florida crop.
- The average wholesale price for a 25-pound box of tomatoes rose from $6.50 in January 2009 to $30 in January 2010.
- The quantity of tomatoes shipped decreased from a normal 25 million pounds per week to less than a quarter of that quantity.
- "High demand has driven up prices" and wholesalers are buying from Mexico.
- Some restaurants provided tomatoes only on request.

ECONOMIC ANALYSIS

- Using the information provided in this news article supplemented with an independent estimate of the price elasticity of demand, we can find the demand and supply curves in the market for winter tomatoes shown in Fig. 1.

- According to J. Scott Shonkwiler and Robert D. Emerson, two agricultural economists at the University of Florida, the price elasticity of demand for winter tomatoes is 0.8.

- A 1 percent rise in the price of these tomatoes brings a 0.8 percent decrease in the quantity demanded, other things remaining the same.

- According to the news article, in a normal period, the price of Florida winter tomatoes is $6.50 a box (25 pounds) and growers normally ship 25 million pounds a week.

- With the information just stated, we can determine the demand for winter tomatoes. It is the curve D in Figs. 1 and 2. This demand curve passes through the point that shows that 25 million pounds are demanded at a price of $6.50 a box. The elasticity of demand for winter tomatoes is 0.8.

- Figure 2 shows the calculation that confirms the price elasticity of demand is 0.8. When the price rises from $6.50 to $30 a box, as it did in January 2010, the quantity demanded decreases from 25 million to 8 million pounds. Use the numbers and the midpoint formula to confirm that the elasticity of demand is 0.8.

- Figures 1 and 3 show the supply of winter tomatoes. The news article says that Florida growers (the main producers of winter tomatoes) shipped less than a quarter of their normal 25 million pounds a week. So assume that they shipped 6 million pounds a week.

- Other growers (using greenhouses or in Mexico) make up the difference between what the Florida growers supply and the quantity demanded.

- The supply curve in normal times, S_0, must pass through the equilibrium point 25 million pounds and $6.50 a box.

- The supply curve in January 2010, S_1, must pass through the equilibrium point at that time of 8 million pounds and $30 a box. It also passes through the point 6 million pounds and $6.50 a box because that is the quantity that Florida growers would ship even if the price remained at $6.50 a box.

- We can calculate the elasticity of supply by using the numbers in Fig. 3 and the midpoint formula. The elasticity of supply is 0.22, which means that supply is inelastic.

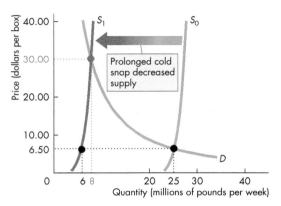

Figure 1   The market for winter tomatoes

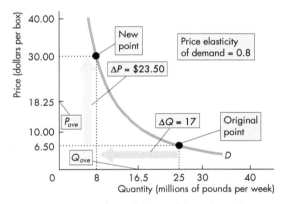

Figure 2   Price elasticity of demand for winter tomatoes

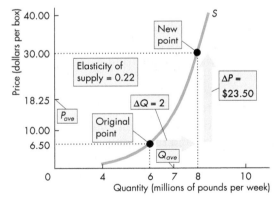

Figure 3   Price elasticity of supply of winter tomatoes

89

SUMMARY

Key Points

Price Elasticity of Demand (pp. 74–80)

- Elasticity is a measure of the responsiveness of the quantity demanded of a good to a change in its price, other things remaining the same.
- Price elasticity of demand equals the percentage change in the quantity demanded divided by the percentage change in the price.
- The larger the magnitude of the price elasticity of demand, the greater is the responsiveness of the quantity demanded to a given price change.
- If demand is elastic, a cut in price leads to an increase in total revenue. If demand is unit elastic, a cut in price leaves total revenue unchanged. And if demand is inelastic, a cut in price leads to a decrease in total revenue.
- Price elasticity of demand depends on how easily one good serves as a substitute for another, the proportion of income spent on the good, and the length of time elapsed since the price change.

Working Problems 1 to 8 will give you a better understanding of the price elasticity of demand.

More Elasticities of Demand (pp. 81–83)

- Cross elasticity of demand measures the responsiveness of the demand for one good to a change in the price of a substitute or a complement, other things remaining the same.
- The cross elasticity of demand with respect to the price of a substitute is positive. The cross elasticity of demand with respect to the price of a complement is negative.
- Income elasticity of demand measures the responsiveness of demand to a change in income, other things remaining the same. For a normal good, the income elasticity of demand is positive. For an inferior good, the income elasticity of demand is negative.

- When the income elasticity of demand is greater than 1 (income elastic), the percentage of income spent on the good increases as income increases.
- When the income elasticity of demand is less than 1 (income inelastic and inferior), the percentage of income spent on the good decreases as income increases.

Working Problems 9 to 16 will give you a better understanding of cross and income elasticities of demand.

Elasticity of Supply (pp. 84–86)

- Elasticity of supply measures the responsiveness of the quantity supplied of a good to a change in its price, other things remaining the same.
- The elasticity of supply is usually positive and ranges between zero (vertical supply curve) and infinity (horizontal supply curve).
- Supply decisions have three time frames: momentary, short run, and long run.
- Momentary supply refers to the response of the quantity supplied to a price change at the instant that the price changes.
- Short-run supply refers to the response of the quantity supplied to a price change after some of the technologically feasible adjustments in production have been made.
- Long-run supply refers to the response of the quantity supplied to a price change when all the technologically feasible adjustments in production have been made.

Working Problems 17 and 18 will give you a better understanding of the elasticity of supply.

Key Terms

Cross elasticity of demand, 81
Elastic demand, 77
Elasticity of supply, 84
Income elasticity of demand, 82

Inelastic demand, 76
Perfectly elastic demand, 77
Perfectly inelastic demand, 76
Price elasticity of demand, 74

Total revenue, 78
Total revenue test, 78
Unit elastic demand, 76

STUDY PLAN PROBLEMS AND APPLICATIONS

myeconlab You can work Problems 1 to 18 in MyEconLab Chapter 4 Study Plan and get instant feedback.

Price Elasticity of Demand (Study Plan 4.1)

1. Rain spoils the strawberry crop, the price rises from $4 to $6 a box, and the quantity demanded decreases from 1,000 to 600 boxes a week.
   a. Calculate the price elasticity of demand over this price range.
   b. Describe the demand for strawberries.

2. If the quantity of dental services demanded increases by 10 percent when the price of dental services falls by 10 percent, is the demand for dental services inelastic, elastic, or unit elastic?

3. The demand schedule for hotel rooms is

Price (dollars per night)	Quantity demanded (millions of rooms per night)
200	100
250	80
400	50
500	40
800	25

   a. What happens to total revenue when the price falls from $400 to $250 a night and from $250 to $200 a night?
   b. Is the demand for hotel rooms elastic, inelastic, or unit elastic?

4. The figure shows the demand for pens.

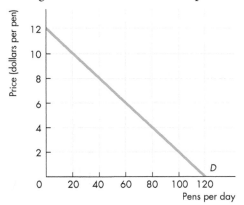

   Calculate the elasticity of demand when the price rises from $4 to $6 a pen. Over what price range is the demand for pens elastic?

5. In 2003, when music downloading first took off, Universal Music slashed the average price of a CD from $21 to $15. The company expected the price cut to boost the quantity of CDs sold by 30 percent, other things remaining the same.

a. What was Universal Music's estimate of the price elasticity of demand for CDs?
   b. If you were making the pricing decision at Universal Music, what would be your pricing decision? Explain your decision.

6. The demand for illegal drugs is inelastic. Much of the expenditure on illegal drugs comes from crime. Assuming these statements to be correct,
   a. How will a successful campaign that decreases the supply of drugs influence the price of illegal drugs and the amount spent on them?
   b. What will happen to the amount of crime?
   c. What is the most effective way of decreasing the quantity of illegal drugs bought and decreasing the amount of drug-related crime?

7. **The Grip of Gas**
   U.S. drivers are ranked as the least sensitive to changes in the price of gasoline. For example, if the price rose from $3 to $4 per gallon and stayed there for a year U.S. purchases of gasoline would fall only about 5 percent.
                   Source: *Slate*, September 27, 2005
   a. Calculate the price elasticity of demand for gasoline. Is the demand for gasoline elastic, unit elastic, or inelastic?
   b. Explain how the price rise from $3 to $4 a gallon changes the total revenue from gasoline sales.

8. **Spam Sales Rise as Food Costs Soar**
   Sales of Spam are rising as consumers realize that Spam and other lower-cost foods can be substituted for costlier cuts of meat as a way of controlling their already stretched food budgets.
                   Source: *AOL Money & Finance*, May 28, 2008
   a. Is Spam a normal good or inferior good? Explain.
   b. Would the income elasticity of demand for Spam be negative or positive? Explain.

More Elasticities of Demand (Study Plan 4.2)

9. If a 12 percent rise in the price of orange juice decreases the quantity of orange juice demanded by 22 percent and increases the quantity of apple juice demanded by 14 percent, calculate the
   a. Price elasticity of demand for orange juice.
   b. Cross elasticity of demand for apple juice with respect to the price of orange juice.

10. When Judy's income increased from $130 to $170 a week, she increased her demand for concert tickets by 15 percent and decreased her demand for bus rides by 10 percent. Calculate Judy's income elasticity of demand for (a) concert tickets and (b) bus rides.

11. If a 5 percent rise in the price of sushi increases the quantity of soy sauce demanded by 2 percent and decreases the quantity of sushi demanded by 1 percent, calculate the
    a. Price elasticity of demand for sushi.
    b. Cross elasticity of demand for soy sauce with respect to the price of sushi.

12. **Swelling Textbook Costs Have College Students Saying "Pass"**

    Textbook prices have doubled and risen faster than average prices for the past two decades. Sixty percent of students do not buy textbooks. Some students hunt for used copies and sell them back at the end of the semester; some buy online, which is often cheaper than the campus store; some use the library copy and wait till it's free; some share the book with a classmate.

    Source: *Washington Post*, January 23, 2006

    Explain what this news clip implies about
    a. The price elasticity of demand for college textbooks.
    b. The income elasticity of demand for college textbooks.
    c. The cross elasticity of demand for college textbooks from the campus bookstore with respect to the online price of a textbook.

Use the following information to work Problems 13 to 15.

As Gas Costs Soar, Buyers Flock to Small Cars

Faced with high gas prices, Americans are substituting smaller cars for SUVs. In April 2008, Toyota Yaris sales increased 46 percent and Ford Focus sales increased 32 percent from a year earlier. Sales of SUVs decreased by more than 25 percent in 2008 and Chevrolet Tahoe sales fell 35 percent. Full-size pickup sales decreased more than 15 percent in 2008 and Ford F-Series pickup sales decreased by 27 percent in April 2008. The effect of a downsized vehicle fleet on fuel consumption is unknown. In California, gasoline consumption decreased by 4 percent in January 2008 from a year earlier. The price of gasoline in January 2008 increased by about 30 percent from a year earlier.

    Source: *The New York Times*, May 2, 2009

13. Calculate the price elasticity of demand for gasoline in California.

14. Calculate the cross elasticity of demand for
    a. Toyota Yaris with respect to the price of gasoline.
    b. Ford Focus with respect to the price of gasoline.

15. Calculate the cross elasticity of demand for
    a. Chevrolet Tahoe with respect to the price of gasoline.
    b. A full-size pickup with respect to the price of gasoline.

16. **Home Depot Earnings Hammered**

    As gas and food prices increased and home prices slumped, people had less extra income to spend on home improvements. And the improvements that they made were on small inexpensive types of repairs and not major big-ticket items.

    Source: CNN, May 20, 2008

    a. What does this news clip imply about the income elasticity of demand for big-ticket home-improvement items?
    b. Would the income elasticity of demand be greater or less than 1? Explain.

Elasticity of Supply (Study Plan 4.3)

17. The table sets out the supply schedule of jeans.

Price (dollars per pair)	Quantity supplied (millions of pairs per year)
120	24
125	28
130	32
135	36

Calculate the elasticity of supply when

a. The price rises from $125 to $135 a pair.

b. The average price is $125 a pair.

18. **Study Ranks Honolulu Third Highest for "Unaffordable Housing"**

    A study ranks Honolulu number 3 in the world for the most unaffordable housing market in urban locations, behind Los Angeles and San Diego and is deemed "severely unaffordable." With significant constraints on the supply of land for residential development, housing inflation has resulted.

    Source: *Hawaii Reporter*, September 11, 2007

    a. Would the supply of housing in Honolulu be elastic or inelastic?

    b. Explain how the elasticity of supply plays an important role in influencing how rapidly housing prices in Honolulu rise.

ADDITIONAL PROBLEMS AND APPLICATIONS

 . You can work these problems in MyEconLab if assigned by your instructor.

Price Elasticity of Demand

19. With higher fuel costs, airlines raised their average fare from 75¢ to $1.25 per passenger mile and the number of passenger miles decreased from 2.5 million a day to 1.5 million a day.
    a. What is the price elasticity of demand for air travel over this price range?
    b. Describe the demand for air travel.

20. The figure shows the demand for DVD rentals.

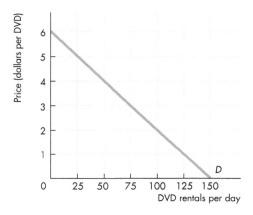

    a. Calculate the elasticity of demand when the price of a DVD rental rises from $3 to $5.
    b. At what price is the elasticity of demand for DVD rentals equal to 1?

Use the following table to work Problems 21 to 23.
The demand schedule for computer chips is

Price (dollars per chip)	Quantity demanded (millions of chips per year)
200	50
250	45
300	40
350	35
400	30

21. a. What happens to total revenue if the price falls from $400 to $350 a chip and from $350 to $300 a chip?
    b. At what price is total revenue at a maximum?

22. At an average price of $350, is the demand for chips elastic, inelastic, or unit elastic? Use the total revenue test to answer this question.

23. At $250 a chip, is the demand for chips elastic or inelastic? Use the total revenue test to answer this question.

24. Your price elasticity of demand for bananas is 4. If the price of bananas rises by 5 percent, what is
    a. The percentage change in the quantity of bananas you buy?
    b. The change in your expenditure on bananas?

25. **As Gasoline Prices Soar, Americans Slowly Adapt**

    As gas prices rose in March 2008, Americans drove 11 billion fewer miles than in March 2007. Realizing that prices are not going down, Americans are adapting to higher energy costs. Americans spend 3.7 percent of their disposable income on transportation fuels. How much we spend on gasoline depends on the choices we make: what car we drive, where we live, how much time we spend driving, and where we choose to go. For many people, higher energy costs mean fewer restaurant meals, deferred weekend outings with the kids, less air travel, and more time closer to home.
    Source: *International Herald Tribune*, May 23, 2008
    a. List and explain the elasticities of demand that are implicitly referred to in the news clip.
    b. Why, according to the news clip, is the demand for gasoline inelastic?

More Elasticities of Demand

Use this information to work Problems 26 and 27.
Economy Forces Many to Shorten Summer Vacation Plans
This year Americans are taking fewer exotic holidays by air and instead are visiting local scenic places by car. The global financial crisis has encouraged many Americans to cut their holiday budgets.
Source: *USA Today*, May 22, 2009

26. Given the prices of the two holidays, is the income elasticity of demand for exotic holidays positive or negative? Are exotic holidays a normal good or an inferior good? Are local holidays a normal good or an inferior good?

27. Are exotic holidays and local holidays substitutes? Explain your answer.

28. When Alex's income was $3,000, he bought 4 bagels and 12 donuts a month. Now his income is $5,000 and he buys 8 bagels and 6 donuts a month.

Calculate Alex's income elasticity of demand for
a. Bagels.
b. Donuts.

29. **Wal-Mart's Recession-Time Pet Project**
During the recession, Wal-Mart moved its pet food and supplies to in front of its other fast-growing business, baby products. Retail experts point out that kids and pets tend to be fairly recession-resistant businesses—even in a recession, dogs will be fed and kids will get their toys.
Source: CNN, May 13, 2008
a. What does this news clip imply about the income elasticity of demand for pet food and baby products?
b. Would the income elasticity of demand be greater or less than 1? Explain.

30. If a 5 percent fall in the price of chocolate sauce increases the quantity of chocolate sauce demanded by 10 percent and increases the quantity of ice cream demanded by 15 percent, calculate the
a. Price elasticity of demand for chocolate sauce.
b. Cross elasticity of demand for ice cream with respect to the price of chocolate sauce.

31. **Netflix to Offer Online Movie Viewing**
Online movie rental service Netflix has introduced a new feature to allow customers to watch movies and television series on their personal computers. Netflix competes with video rental retailer Blockbuster, which added an online rental service to the in-store rental service.
Source: CNN, January 16, 2007
a. How will online movie viewing influence the price elasticity of demand for in-store movie rentals?
b. Would the cross elasticity of demand for online movies and in-store movie rentals be negative or positive? Explain.
c. Would the cross elasticity of demand for online movies with respect to high-speed Internet service be negative or positive? Explain.

32. **To Love, Honor, and Save Money**
In a survey of caterers and event planners, nearly half of them said that they were seeing declines in wedding spending in response to the economic slowdown; 12% even reported wedding cancellations because of financial concerns.
Source: Time, June 2, 2008
a. Based upon this news clip, are wedding events a normal good or inferior good? Explain.

b. Are wedding events more a necessity or a luxury? Would the income elasticity of demand be greater than 1, less than 1, or equal to 1? Explain.

Elasticity of Supply

33. The supply schedule of long-distance phone calls is

Price (cents per minute)	Quantity supplied (millions of minutes per day)
10	200
20	400
30	600
40	800

Calculate the elasticity of supply when
a. The price falls from 40¢ to 30¢ a minute.
b. The average price is 20¢ a minute.

34. **Weak Coal Prices Hit China's Third-Largest Coal Miner**
The chairman of Yanzhou Coal Mining reported that the recession had decreased the demand for coal, with its sales falling by 11.9 percent to 7.92 million tons from 8.99 million tons a year earlier, despite a 10.6 percent cut in the price.
Source: Dow Jones, April 27, 2009
Calculate the price elasticity of supply of coal. Is the supply of coal elastic or inelastic?

Economics in the News

35. After you have studied *Reading Between the Lines* on pp. 88–89 answer the following questions.
a. Which demand is more price elastic and why: tomatoes in general or Florida winter tomatoes?
b. When cold weather destroyed the Florida crop and more tomatoes came from Mexico and greenhouses, what happened to the supply of tomatoes and the quantity of tomatoes supplied?
c. The news article says the "High demand has driven up prices and wholesalers are buying from Mexico." What does this statement mean? Did demand increase? Did it decrease? Is the news article correct?
d. Reggie Brown says "We're obviously losing market share to Mexico, and there's always a price to pay to get the customer to get back into the Florida market." What does he mean and what does that imply about the elasticity of demand for Florida tomatoes when the price rises and when the price falls?

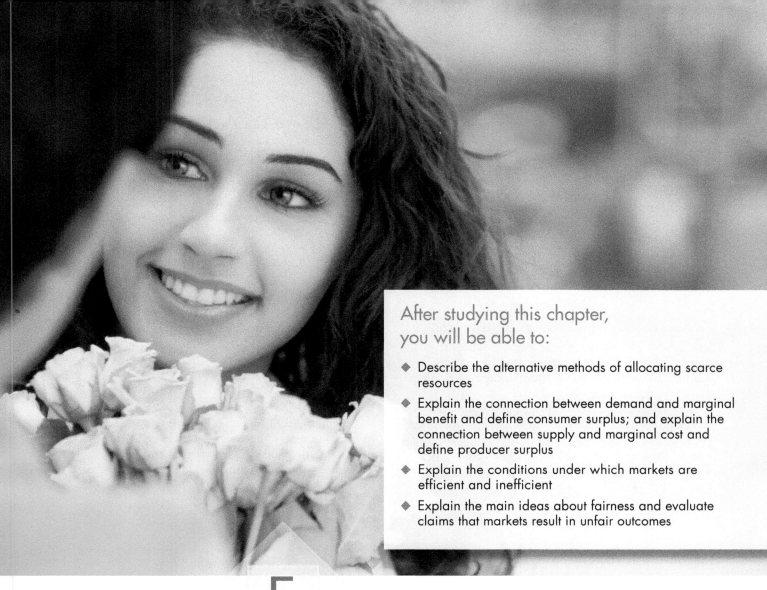

EFFICIENCY AND EQUITY

After studying this chapter,
you will be able to:

◆ Describe the alternative methods of allocating scarce resources

◆ Explain the connection between demand and marginal benefit and define consumer surplus; and explain the connection between supply and marginal cost and define producer surplus

◆ Explain the conditions under which markets are efficient and inefficient

◆ Explain the main ideas about fairness and evaluate claims that markets result in unfair outcomes

Every time you decide to buy something, whether it's an everyday pizza or a Valentine's Day rose, you express your view about how scarce resources should be used and you make choices in your *self-interest*. A pizza cook one block away and a Columbian rose grower 2,500 miles away make *their* self-interested choices about what to produce. Markets coordinate these self-interested choices. But do markets do a good job? Do they allocate resources between pizza and roses, and everything else, efficiently?

The market economy generates huge income inequality: *You* can afford to buy a pizza or give a rose, but they might be unaffordable luxuries for a pizza cook and a Columbian rose grower who supply them. Is this situation fair?

Efficiency and fairness (or equity) are the two dimensions of the *social interest*. So our central question in this chapter is: Do markets operate in the social interest?

Benefit, Cost, and Surplus

Resources are allocated efficiently and in the *social interest* when they are used in the ways that people value most highly. You saw in Chapter 2 that this outcome occurs when the quantities produced are at the point on the *PPF* at which marginal benefit equals marginal cost (see pp. 31–33). We're now going to see whether competitive markets produce the efficient quantities.

We begin on the demand side of a market.

Demand, Willingness to Pay, and Value

In everyday life, we talk about "getting value for money." When we use this expression, we are distinguishing between *value* and *price*. Value is what we get, and price is what we pay.

The value of one more unit of a good or service is its marginal benefit. We measure marginal benefit by the maximum price that is willingly paid for another unit of the good or service. But willingness to pay determines demand. *A demand curve is a marginal benefit curve.*

In Fig. 5.1(a), Lisa is willing to pay $1 for the 30th slice of pizza and $1 is her marginal benefit from that slice. In Fig. 5.1(b), Nick is willing to pay $1 for the 10th slice of pizza and $1 is his marginal benefit from that slice. But at what quantity is the market willing to pay $1 for the marginal slice? The answer is provided by the *market demand curve*.

Individual Demand and Market Demand

The relationship between the price of a good and the quantity demanded by one person is called *individual demand*. And the relationship between the price of a good and the quantity demanded by all buyers is called *market demand*.

The market demand curve is the horizontal sum of the individual demand curves and is formed by adding the quantities demanded by all the individuals at each price.

Figure 5.1(c) illustrates the market demand for pizza if Lisa and Nick are the only people in the market. Lisa's demand curve in part (a) and Nick's demand curve in part (b) sum horizontally to the market demand curve in part (c).

FIGURE 5.1   Individual Demand, Market Demand, and Marginal Social Benefit

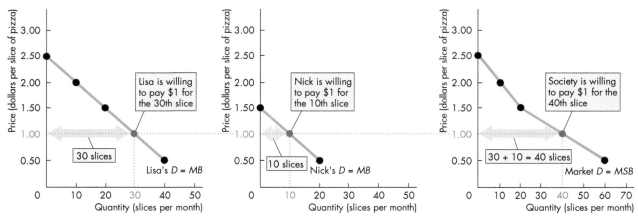

(a) Lisa's demand   **(b) Nick's demand**   **(c) Market demand**

At a price of $1 a slice, the quantity demanded by Lisa is 30 slices and the quantity demanded by Nick is 10 slices, so the quantity demanded by the market is 40 slices. Lisa's demand

curve in part (a) and Nick's demand curve in part (b) sum horizontally to the market demand curve in part (c). The market demand curve is the marginal social benefit (*MSB*) curve.

At a price of $1 a slice, Lisa demands 30 slices and Nick demands 10 slices, so the market quantity demanded at $1 a slice is 40 slices.

For Lisa and Nick, their demand curves are their marginal benefit curves. For society, the market demand curve is the marginal benefit curve. We call the marginal benefit to the entire society *marginal social benefit*. So the market demand curve is also the *marginal social benefit (MSB) curve*.

Consumer Surplus   *savings*

We don't always have to pay as much as we are willing to pay. We get a bargain. When people buy something for less than it is worth to them, they receive a consumer surplus. **Consumer surplus** is the excess of the benefit received from a good over the amount paid for it. We can calculate consumer surplus as the marginal benefit (or value) of a good minus its price, summed over the quantity bought.

Figure 5.2(a) shows Lisa's consumer surplus from pizza when the price is $1 a slice. At this price, she buys 30 slices a month because the 30th slice is worth exactly $1 to her. But Lisa is willing to pay $2 for the 10th slice, so her marginal benefit from this slice is

$1 more than she pays for it—she receives a surplus of $1 on the 10th slice.

Lisa's consumer surplus is the sum of the surpluses on *all of the slices she buys*. This sum is the area of the green triangle—the area below the demand curve and above the market price line. The area of this triangle is equal to its base (30 slices) multiplied by its height ($1.50) divided by 2, which is $22.50. The area of the blue rectangle in Fig. 5.2(a) shows what Lisa pays for 30 slices of pizza.

Figure 5.2(b) shows Nick's consumer surplus, and part (c) shows the consumer surplus for the market. The consumer surplus for the market is the sum of the consumer surpluses of Lisa and Nick.

All goods and services have decreasing marginal benefit, so people receive more benefit from their consumption than the amount they pay.

Supply and Marginal Cost

Your next task is to see how market supply reflects marginal cost. The connection between supply and cost closely parallels the related ideas about demand and benefit that you've just studied. Firms are in business to make a profit. To do so, they must sell

---

FIGURE 5.2   Demand and Consumer Surplus

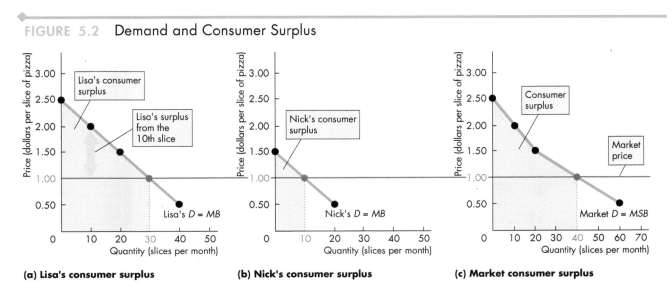

(a) Lisa's consumer surplus

(b) Nick's consumer surplus

(c) Market consumer surplus

Lisa is willing to pay $2.00 for her 10th slice of pizza in part (a). At a market price of $1 a slice, Lisa receives a surplus of $1 on the 10th slice. The green triangle shows her consumer surplus on the 30 slices she buys at $1 a slice.

The green triangle in part (b) shows Nick's consumer surplus on the 10 slices that he buys at $1 a slice. The green area in part (c) shows the consumer surplus for the market. The blue rectangles show the amounts spent on pizza.

their output for a price that exceeds the cost of production. Let's investigate the relationship between cost and price.

Supply, Cost, and Minimum Supply-Price

Firms make a profit when they receive more from the sale of a good or service than the cost of producing it. Just as consumers distinguish between value and price, so producers distinguish between *cost* and *price*. Cost is what a firm gives up when it produces a good or service and price is what a firm receives when it sells the good or service.

The cost of producing one more unit of a good or service is its marginal cost. Marginal cost is the minimum price that producers must receive to induce them to offer one more unit of a good or service for sale. But the minimum supply-price determines supply. *A supply curve is a marginal cost curve.*

In Fig. 5.3(a), Max is willing to produce the 100th pizza for $15, his marginal cost of that pizza. In Fig. 5.3(b), Mario is willing to produce the 50th pizza for $15, his marginal cost of that pizza.

What quantity is this market willing to produce for $15 a pizza? The answer is provided by the *market supply curve.*

Individual Supply and Market Supply

The relationship between the price of a good and the quantity supplied by one producer is called *individual supply*. And the relationship between the price of a good and the quantity supplied by all producers is called *market supply*.

The market supply curve is the horizontal sum of the individual supply curves and is formed by adding the quantities supplied by all the producers at each price.

Figure 5.3(c) illustrates the market supply of pizzas if Max and Mario are the only producers. Max's supply curve in part (a) and Mario's supply curve in part (b) sum horizontally to the market supply curve in part (c).

At a price of $15 a pizza, Max supplies 100 pizzas and Mario supplies 50 pizzas, so the quantity supplied by the market at $15 a pizza is 150 pizzas.

For Max and Mario, their supply curves are their marginal cost curves. For society, the market supply curve is the marginal cost curve. We call the society's marginal cost *marginal social cost*. So the market supply curve is also the *marginal social cost (MSC) curve.*

FIGURE 5.3   Individual Supply, Market Supply, and Marginal Social Cost

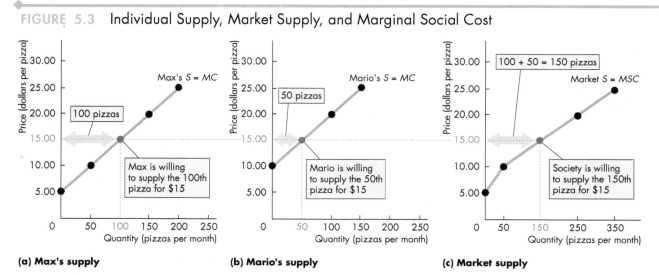

(a) Max's supply   **(b) Mario's supply**   **(c) Market supply**

At a price of $15 a pizza, the quantity supplied by Max is 100 pizzas and the quantity supplied by Mario is 50 pizzas, so the quantity supplied by the market is 150 pizzas. Max's

supply curve in part (a) and Mario's supply curve in part (b) sum horizontally to the market supply curve in part (c). The market supply curve is the marginal social cost (MSC) curve.

Producer Surplus

When price exceeds marginal cost, the firm receives a producer surplus. **Producer surplus** is the excess of the amount received from the sale of a good or service over the cost of producing it. It is calculated as the price received minus the marginal cost (or minimum supply-price), summed over the quantity sold.

Figure 5.4(a) shows Max's producer surplus from pizza when the price is $15 a pizza. At this price, he sells 100 pizzas a month because the 100th pizza costs him $15 to produce. But Max is willing to produce the 50th pizza for his marginal cost, which is $10, so he receives a surplus of $5 on this pizza.

Max's producer surplus is the sum of the surpluses on the pizzas he sells. This sum is the area of the blue triangle—the area below the market price and above the supply curve. The area of this triangle is equal to its base (100) multiplied by its height ($10) divided by 2, which is $500.

The red area below the supply curve in Fig. 5.4(a) shows what it costs Max to produce 100 pizzas.

The area of the blue triangle in Fig. 5.4(b) shows Mario's producer surplus and the blue area in Fig. 5.4(c) shows the producer surplus for the market.

The producer surplus for the market is the sum of the producer surpluses of Max and Mario.

Consumer surplus and producer surplus can be used to measure the efficiency of a market. Let's see how we can use these concepts to study the efficiency of a competitive market.

REVIEW QUIZ

1 What is the relationship between the marginal benefit, value, and demand?
2 What is the relationship between individual demand and market demand?
3 What is consumer surplus? How is it measured?
4 What is the relationship between the marginal cost, minimum supply-price, and supply?
5 What is the relationship between individual supply and market supply?
6 What is producer surplus? How is it measured?

You can work these questions in Study Plan 5.2 and get instant feedback.

FIGURE 5.4   Supply and Producer Surplus

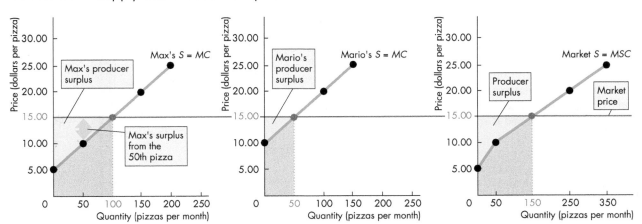

(a) Max's producer surplus   **(b) Mario's producer surplus**   **(c) Market producer surplus**

Max is willing to produce the 50th pizza for $10 in part (a). At a market price of $15 a pizza, Max gets a surplus of $5 on the 50th pizza. The blue triangle shows his producer surplus on the 100 pizzas he sells at $15 each. The blue triangle in part (b) shows Mario's producer surplus on the 50 pizzas that he sells at $15 each. The blue area in part (c) shows producer surplus for the market. The red areas show the cost of producing the pizzas sold.

myeconlab   animation

Is the Competitive Market Efficient?

Shortage.
Surplus

Figure 5.5(a) shows the market for pizza. The market forces that you studied in Chapter 3 (pp. 56–57) pull the pizza market to its equilibrium price of $15 a pizza and equilibrium quantity of 10,000 pizzas a day. Buyers enjoy a consumer surplus (green area) and sellers enjoy a producer surplus (blue area), but is this competitive equilibrium efficient?

Efficiency of Competitive Equilibrium

You've seen that the market demand curve for a good or service tells us the marginal social benefit from it. You've also seen that the market supply curve of a good or service tells us the marginal social cost of producing it.

Equilibrium in a competitive market occurs when the quantity demanded equals the quantity supplied at the intersection of the demand curve and the supply curve. At this intersection point, marginal social benefit on the demand curve equals marginal social cost on the supply curve. This equality is the condition for allocative efficiency. So in equilibrium, a competitive market achieves allocative efficiency.

Figure 5.5 illustrates the efficiency of competitive equilibrium. The demand curve and the supply curve intersect in part (a) and marginal social benefit equals marginal social cost in part (b).

If production is less than 10,000 pizzas a day, the marginal pizza is valued more highly than it costs to produce. If production exceeds 10,000 pizzas a day, the marginal pizza costs more to produce than the value that consumers place on it. Only when 10,000 pizzas a day are produced is the marginal pizza worth exactly what it costs.

The competitive market pushes the quantity of pizzas produced to its efficient level of 10,000 a day. If production is less than 10,000 pizzas a day, a shortage raises the price, which increases production. If production exceeds 10,000 pizzas a day, a surplus of pizzas lowers the price, which decreases production. So a competitive pizza market is efficient.

Figure 5.5(a) also shows the consumer surplus and producer surplus. The sum of consumer surplus and producer surplus is called **total surplus**. When the efficient quantity is produced, total surplus is maximized. Buyers and sellers acting in their self-interest end up promoting the social interest.

FIGURE 5.5   An Efficient Market for Pizza

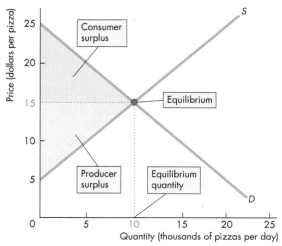

(a) Equilibrium and surpluses

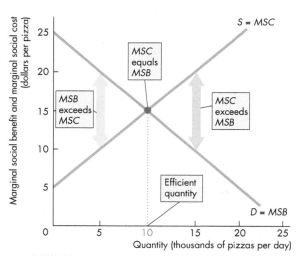

(b) Efficiency

Competitive equilibrium in part (a) occurs when the quantity demanded equals the quantity supplied. Resources are used efficiently in part (b) when marginal social benefit, *MSB*, equals marginal social cost, *MSC*. Total surplus, which is the sum of consumer surplus (the green triangle) and producer surplus (the blue triangle) is maximized.

The efficient quantity in part (b) is the same as the equilibrium quantity in part (a). The competitive pizza market produces the efficient quantity of pizzas.

 myeconlab animation

Economics in Action

The Invisible Hand

Writing in his *Wealth of Nations* in 1776, Adam Smith was the first to suggest that competitive markets send resources to the uses in which they have the highest value (see p. 51). Smith believed that each participant in a competitive market is "led by an invisible hand to promote an end [the efficient use of resources] which was no part of his intention."

You can see the invisible hand at work in the cartoon and in the world today.

Umbrella for Sale The cold drinks vendor has cold drinks and shade and he has a marginal cost and a minimum supply-price of each. The reader on the park bench has a marginal benefit and willingness to pay for each. The reader's marginal benefit from shade exceeds the vendor's marginal cost; but the vendor's marginal cost of a cold drink exceeds the reader's marginal benefit. They trade the umbrella. The vendor gets a producer surplus from selling the shade for more than its marginal cost, and the reader gets a consumer surplus from buying the shade for less than its marginal benefit. Both are better off and the umbrella has moved to its highest-valued use.

The Invisible Hand at Work Today The market economy relentlessly performs the activity illustrated in the cartoon to achieve an efficient allocation of resources.

A Florida frost cuts the supply of tomatoes. With fewer tomatoes available, the marginal social benefit increases. A shortage of tomatoes raises their price, so the market allocates the smaller quantity available to the people who value them most highly.

A new technology cuts the cost of producing a smart phone. With a lower production cost, the supply of smart phones increases and the price of a smart

phone falls. The lower price encourages an increase in the quantity demanded of this now less-costly tool. The marginal social benefit from a smart phone is brought to equality with its marginal social cost.

Market Failure

Markets do not always achieve an efficient outcome. We call a situation in which a market delivers an inefficient outcome one of **market failure**. Market failure can occur because too little of an item is produced (underproduction) or too much is produced (overproduction). We'll describe these two market failure outcomes and then see why they arise.

Underproduction In Fig. 5.6(a), the quantity of pizzas produced is 5,000 a day. At this quantity, consumers are willing to pay $20 for a pizza that costs only $10 to produce. By producing only 5,000 pizzas a day, total surplus is smaller than its maximum possible level. The quantity produced is inefficient—there is underproduction.

We measure the scale of inefficiency by **deadweight loss**, which is the decrease in total surplus that results

FIGURE 5.6 Underproduction and Overproduction

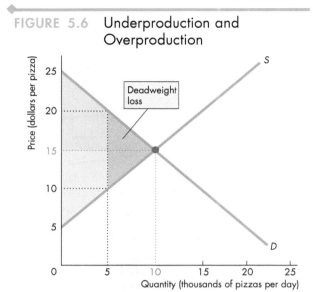

(a) Underproduction

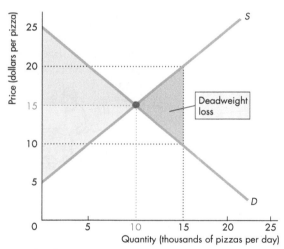

(b) Overproduction

If 5,000 pizzas a day are produced, in part (a), total surplus (the sum of the green and blue areas) is smaller than its maximum by the amount of the deadweight loss (the gray triangle). At all quantities below 10,000 pizzas a day, the benefit from one more pizza exceeds its cost.

If 15,000 pizzas a day are produced, in part (b), total surplus is also smaller than its maximum by the amount of the deadweight loss. At all quantities in excess of 10,000 pizzas a day, the cost of one more pizza exceeds its benefit.

ⓍⓂ myeconlab animation

from an inefficient level of production. The gray triangle in Fig. 5.6(a) shows the deadweight loss.

Overproduction In Fig. 5.6(b), the quantity of pizzas produced is 15,000 a day. At this quantity, consumers are willing to pay only $10 for a pizza that costs $20 to produce. By producing the 15,000th pizza, $10 of resources are wasted. Again, the gray triangle shows the deadweight loss, which reduces the total surplus to less than its maximum.

Inefficient production creates a deadweight loss that is borne by the entire society: It is a social loss.

Sources of Market Failure

Obstacles to efficiency that bring market failure and create deadweight losses are

- Price and quantity regulations
- Taxes and subsidies
- Externalities
- Public goods and common resources
- Monopoly
- High transactions costs

Price and Quantity Regulations *Price regulations* that put a cap on the rent a landlord is permitted to charge and laws that require employers to pay a minimum wage sometimes block the price adjustments that balance the quantity demanded and the quantity supplied and lead to underproduction. *Quantity regulations* that limit the amount that a farm is permitted to produce also lead to underproduction.

Taxes and Subsidies   *Tax ↓demand ↓supply* *Taxes* increase the prices paid by buyers and lower the prices received by sellers. So taxes decrease the quantity produced and lead to underproduction. *Subsidies*, which are payments by the government to producers, decrease the prices paid by buyers and increase the prices received by sellers. So subsidies increase the quantity produced and lead to overproduction. *Subsidies ↑demand ↑supply*

Externalities An *externality* is a cost or a benefit that affects someone other than the seller or the buyer. An *external cost* arises when an electric utility burns coal and emits carbon dioxide. The utility doesn't consider the cost of climate change when it decides how much power to produce. The result is overproduction. An *external benefit* arises when an apartment owner installs a smoke detector and decreases her neighbor's fire risk. She doesn't consider the benefit to her neighbor when she decides how many detectors to install. The result is underproduction.

Public Goods and Common Resources A *public good* is a good or service that is consumed simultaneously by everyone even if they don't pay for it. National defense is an example. Competitive markets would underproduce national defense because it is in each person's interest to free ride on everyone else and avoid paying for her or his share of such a good.

A *common resource* is owned by no one but is available to be used by everyone. Atlantic salmon is an example. It is in everyone's self-interest to ignore the costs they impose on others when they decide how much of a common resource to use. The result is that the resource is overused.

Monopoly A *monopoly* is a firm that is the sole provider of a good or service. Local water supply and cable television are supplied by firms that are monopolies. The monopoly's self-interest is to maximize its profit. Because the monopoly has no competitors, it can set the price to achieve its self-interested goal. To achieve its goal, a monopoly produces too little and charges too high a price. It leads to underproduction.

High Transactions Costs When you go to Starbucks, you pay for more than the coffee. You pay your share of the cost of the barrista's time, the espresso maker, and the decor. When you buy your first apartment, you will pay for more than the apartment. You will buy the services of a realtor and a lawyer. Economists call the costs of the services that enable a market to bring buyers and sellers together **transactions costs**.

It is costly to operate *any* market so to use market price to allocate resources, it must be worth bearing the transactions costs. Some markets are too costly to operate. For example, it is too costly to operate a market in time slots on a local tennis court. Instead of a market, the court uses first-come, first-served: You hang around until the court becomes vacant and "pay" with your waiting time. When transactions costs are high, the market might underproduce.

You now know the conditions under which resource allocation is efficient. You've seen how a competitive market can be efficient, and you've seen some obstacles to efficiency. Can alternative allocation methods improve on the market?

Alternatives to the Market

When a market is inefficient, can one of the alternative nonmarket methods that we described at the beginning of this chapter do a better job? Sometimes it can.

Often, majority rule might be used in an attempt to improve the allocation of resources. But majority rule has its own shortcomings. A group that pursues the self-interest of its members can become the majority. For example, a price or quantity regulation that creates inefficiency is almost always the result of a self-interested group becoming the majority and imposing costs on the minority. Also, with majority rule, votes must be translated into actions by bureaucrats who have their own agendas based on their self-interest.

Managers in firms issue commands and avoid the transactions costs that they would incur if they went to a market every time they needed a job done.

First-come, first-served works best in some situations. Think about the scene at a busy ATM. Instead of waiting in line people might trade places at a "market" price. But someone would need to ensure that trades were honored. At a busy ATM, first-come, first-served is the most efficient arrangement.

There is no one efficient mechanism that allocates all resources efficiently. But markets, when supplemented by other mechanisms such as majority rule, command systems, and first-come, first-served, do an amazingly good job.

REVIEW QUIZ

1 Do competitive markets use resources efficiently? Explain why or why not.
2 What is deadweight loss and under what conditions does it occur?
3 What are the obstacles to achieving an efficient allocation of resources in the market economy?

You can work these questions in Study Plan 5.3 and get instant feedback.

Is an efficient allocation of resources also a fair allocation? Does the competitive market provide people with fair incomes for their work? Do people always pay a fair price for the things they buy? Don't we need the government to step into some competitive markets to prevent the price from rising too high or falling too low? Let's now study these questions.

◆ Is the Competitive Market Fair?

When a natural disaster strikes, such as a severe winter storm or a hurricane, the prices of many essential items jump. The reason prices jump is that the demand and willingness to pay for these items has increased, but the supply has not changed. So the higher prices achieve an efficient allocation of scarce resources. News reports of these price hikes almost never talk about efficiency. Instead, they talk about equity or fairness. The claim that is often made is that it is unfair for profit-seeking dealers to cheat the victims of natural disaster.

Similarly, when low-skilled people work for a wage that is below what most would regard as a "living wage," the media and politicians talk of employers taking unfair advantage of their workers.

How do we decide whether something is fair or unfair? You know when you *think* something is unfair, but how do you *know*? What are the *principles* of fairness?

Philosophers have tried for centuries to answer this question. Economists have offered their answers too. But before we look at the proposed answers, you should know that there is no universally agreed upon answer.

Economists agree about efficiency. That is, they agree that it makes sense to make the economic pie as large as possible and to produce it at the lowest possible cost. But they do not agree about equity. That is, they do not agree about what are fair shares of the economic pie for all the people who make it. The reason is that ideas about fairness are not exclusively economic ideas. They touch on politics, ethics, and religion. Nevertheless, economists have thought about these issues and have a contribution to make. Let's examine the views of economists on this topic.

To think about fairness, think of economic life as a game—a serious game. All ideas about fairness can be divided into two broad groups. They are

- It's not fair if the *result* isn't fair.
- It's not fair if the *rules* aren't fair.

It's Not Fair If the *Result* Isn't Fair

The earliest efforts to establish a principle of fairness were based on the view that the result is what matters. The general idea was that it is unfair if people's incomes are too unequal. For example, it is unfair

that a bank president earns millions of dollars a year while a bank teller earns only thousands of dollars. It is unfair that a store owner makes a larger profit and her customers pay higher prices in the aftermath of a winter storm.

During the nineteenth century, economists thought they had made the incredible discovery: Efficiency requires equality of incomes. To make the economic pie as large as possible, it must be cut into equal pieces, one for each person. This idea turns out to be wrong. But there is a lesson in the reason that it is wrong, so this idea is worth a closer look.

Utilitarianism The nineteenth-century idea that only equality brings efficiency is called *utilitarianism*. **Utilitarianism** is a principle that states that we should strive to achieve "the greatest happiness for the greatest number." The people who developed this idea were known as utilitarians. They included the most eminent thinkers, such as Jeremy Bentham and John Stuart Mill.

Utilitarians argued that to achieve "the greatest happiness for the greatest number," income must be transferred from the rich to the poor up to the point of complete equality—to the point at which there are no rich and no poor.

They reasoned in the following way: First, everyone has the same basic wants and a similar capacity to enjoy life. Second, the greater a person's income, the smaller is the marginal benefit of a dollar. The millionth dollar spent by a rich person brings a smaller marginal benefit to that person than the marginal benefit that the thousandth dollar spent brings to a poorer person. So by transferring a dollar from the millionaire to the poorer person, more is gained than is lost. The two people added together are better off.

Figure 5.7 illustrates this utilitarian idea. Tom and Jerry have the same marginal benefit curve, *MB*. (Marginal benefit is measured on the same scale of 1 to 3 for both Tom and Jerry.) Tom is at point *A*. He earns $5,000 a year, and his marginal benefit from a dollar is 3 units. Jerry is at point *B*. He earns $45,000 a year, and his marginal benefit from a dollar is 1 unit. If a dollar is transferred from Jerry to Tom, Jerry loses 1 unit of marginal benefit and Tom gains 3 units. So together, Tom and Jerry are better off—they are sharing the economic pie more efficiently. If a second dollar is transferred, the same thing happens: Tom gains more than Jerry loses. And the same is true for every dollar transferred until they both reach point *C*. At point *C*, Tom and Jerry have $25,000

FIGURE 5.7 Utilitarian Fairness

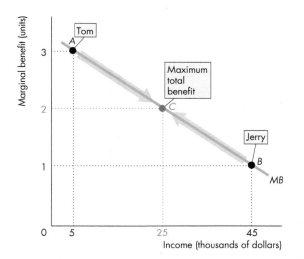

Tom earns $5,000 and has 3 units of marginal benefit at point A. Jerry earns $45,000 and has 1 unit of marginal benefit at point B. If income is transferred from Jerry to Tom, Jerry's loss is less than Tom's gain. Only when each of them has $25,000 and 2 units of marginal benefit (at point C) can the sum of their total benefit increase no further.

each and a marginal benefit of 2 units. Now they are sharing the economic pie in the most efficient way. It brings the greatest happiness to Tom and Jerry.

The Big Tradeoff One big problem with the utilitarian ideal of complete equality is that it ignores the costs of making income transfers. Recognizing the costs of making income transfers leads to what is called the **big tradeoff**, which is a tradeoff between efficiency and fairness.

The big tradeoff is based on the following facts. Income can be transferred from people with high incomes to people with low incomes only by taxing the high incomes. Taxing people's income from employment makes them work less. It results in the quantity of labor being less than the efficient quantity. Taxing people's income from capital makes them save less. It results in the quantity of capital being less than the efficient quantity. With smaller quantities of both labor and capital, the quantity of goods and services produced is less than the efficient quantity. The economic pie shrinks.

The tradeoff is between the size of the economic pie and the degree of equality with which it is shared. The greater the amount of income redistribution through income taxes, the greater is the inefficiency—the smaller is the economic pie.

There is a second source of inefficiency. A dollar taken from a rich person does not end up as a dollar in the hands of a poorer person. Some of the dollar is spent on administration of the tax and transfer system. The cost of tax-collecting agencies, such as the Internal Revenue Service (IRS), and welfare-administering agencies, such as the Centers for Medicare and Medicaid, must be paid with some of the taxes collected. Also, taxpayers hire accountants, auditors, and lawyers to help them ensure that they pay the correct amount of taxes. These activities use skilled labor and capital resources that could otherwise be used to produce goods and services that people value.

When all these costs are taken into account, taking a dollar from a rich person does not give a dollar to a poor person. It is possible that with high taxes, people with low incomes might end up being worse off. Suppose, for example, that highly taxed entrepreneurs decide to work less hard and shut down some of their businesses. Low-income workers get fired and must seek other, perhaps even lower-paid, work.

Today, because of the big tradeoff, no one says that fairness requires equality of incomes.

Make the Poorest as Well Off as Possible A new solution to the big-tradeoff problem was proposed by philosopher John Rawls in a classic book entitled *A Theory of Justice*, published in 1971. Rawls says that, taking all the costs of income transfers into account, the fair distribution of the economic pie is the one that makes the poorest person as well off as possible. The incomes of rich people should be taxed, and after paying the costs of administering the tax and transfer system, what is left should be transferred to the poor. But the taxes must not be so high that they make the economic pie shrink to the point at which the poorest person ends up with a smaller piece. A bigger share of a smaller pie can be less than a smaller share of a bigger pie. The goal is to make the piece enjoyed by the poorest person as big as possible. Most likely, this piece will not be an equal share.

The "fair results" idea requires a change in the results after the game is over. Some economists say that these changes are themselves unfair and propose a different way of thinking about fairness.

It's Not Fair If the *Rules* Aren't Fair

The idea that it's not fair if the rules aren't fair is based on a fundamental principle that seems to be hardwired into the human brain: the symmetry principle. The **symmetry principle** is the requirement that people in similar situations be treated similarly. It is the moral principle that lies at the center of all the big religions and that says, in some form or other, "Behave toward other people in the way you expect them to behave toward you."

In economic life, this principle translates into *equality of opportunity*. But equality of opportunity to do what? This question is answered by the philosopher Robert Nozick in a book entitled *Anarchy, State, and Utopia*, published in 1974.

Nozick argues that the idea of fairness as an outcome or result cannot work and that fairness must be based on the fairness of the rules. He suggests that fairness obeys two rules:

1. The state must enforce laws that establish and protect private property.
2. Private property may be transferred from one person to another only by voluntary exchange.

The first rule says that everything that is valuable must be owned by individuals and that the state must ensure that theft is prevented. The second rule says that the only legitimate way a person can acquire property is to buy it in exchange for something else that the person owns. If these rules, which are the only fair rules, are followed, then the result is fair. It doesn't matter how unequally the economic pie is shared, provided that the pie is made by people, each one of whom voluntarily provides services in exchange for the share of the pie offered in compensation.

These rules satisfy the symmetry principle. If these rules are not followed, the symmetry principle is broken. You can see these facts by imagining a world in which the laws are not followed.

First, suppose that some resources or goods are not owned. They are common property. Then everyone is free to participate in a grab to use them. The strongest will prevail. But when the strongest prevails, the strongest effectively *owns* the resources or goods in question and prevents others from enjoying them.

Second, suppose that we do not insist on voluntary exchange for transferring ownership of resources from one person to another. The alternative is *involuntary* transfer. In simple language, the alternative is theft.

Both of these situations violate the symmetry principle. Only the strong acquire what they want. The weak end up with only the resources and goods that the strong don't want.

In a majority-rule political system, the strong are those in the majority or those with enough resources to influence opinion and achieve a majority.

In contrast, if the two rules of fairness are followed, everyone, strong and weak, is treated in a similar way. All individuals are free to use their resources and human skills to create things that are valued by themselves and others and to exchange the fruits of their efforts with all others. This set of arrangements is the only one that obeys the symmetry principle.

Fairness and Efficiency If private property rights are enforced and if voluntary exchange takes place in a competitive market, resources will be allocated efficiently if there are no

1. Price and quantity regulations
2. Taxes and subsidies
3. Externalities
4. Public goods and common resources
5. Monopolies
6. High transactions costs

And according to the Nozick rules, the resulting distribution of income and wealth will be fair. Let's study an example to check the claim that if resources are allocated efficiently, they are also allocated fairly.

Case Study: A Water Shortage in a Natural Disaster

An earthquake has broken the pipes that deliver drinking water to a city. Bottled water is available, but there is no tap water. What is the fair way to allocate the bottled water?

Market Price Suppose that if the water is allocated by market price, the price jumps to $8 a bottle—five times its normal price. At this price, the people who own water can make a large profit by selling it. People who are willing and able to pay $8 a bottle get the water. And because most people can't afford the $8 price, they end up either without water or consuming just a few drops a day.

You can see that the water is being used efficiently. There is a fixed amount available, some people are willing to pay $8 to get a bottle, and the water goes to those people. The people who own and sell water receive a large producer surplus and total surplus is maximized.

In the rules view, the outcome is fair. No one is denied the water they are willing to pay for. In the results view, the outcome would most likely be regarded as unfair. The lucky owners of water make a killing, and the poorest end up the thirstiest.

Nonmarket Methods Suppose that by a majority vote, the citizens decide that the government will buy all the water, pay for it with a tax, and use one of the nonmarket methods to allocate the water to the citizens. The possibilities now are

Command Someone decides who is the most deserving and needy. Perhaps everyone is given an equal share. Or perhaps government officials and their families end up with most of the water.

Contest Bottles of water are prizes that go to those who are best at a particular contest.

First-come, first-served Water goes to the first off the mark or to those who place the lowest value on their time and can afford to wait in line.

Lottery Water goes to those in luck.

Personal characteristics Water goes to those with the "right" characteristics. Perhaps the old, the young, or pregnant women get the water.

Except by chance, none of these methods delivers an allocation of water that is either fair or efficient. It is unfair in the rules view because the distribution involves involuntary transfers of resources among citizens. It is unfair in the results view because the poorest don't end up being made as well off as possible.

The allocation is inefficient for two reasons. First, resources have been used to operate the allocation scheme. Second, some people are willing to pay for more water than the quantity they have been allocated and others have been allocated more water than they are willing to pay for.

The second source of inefficiency can be overcome if, after the nonmarket allocation, people are permitted to trade water at its market price. Those who value the water they have at less than the market price sell, and people who are willing to pay the market price to obtain more water buy. Those who value the water most highly are the ones who consume it.

Market Price with Taxes Another approach is to allocate the scarce water using the market price but then to alter the redistribution of buying power by taxing the sellers and providing benefits to the poor.

Suppose water owners are taxed on each bottle sold and the revenue from these taxes is given to the poorest people. People are then free, starting from this new distribution of buying power, to trade water at the market price.

Because the owners of water are taxed on what they sell, they have a weaker incentive to offer water for sale and the supply decreases. The equilibrium price rises to more than $8 a bottle. There is now a deadweight loss in the market for water—similar to the loss that arises from underproduction on pp. 101–102. (We study the effects of a tax and show its inefficiency in Chapter 6 on pp. 117–122.)

So the tax is inefficient. In the rules view, the tax is also unfair because it forces the owners of water to make a transfer to others. In the results view, the outcome might be regarded as being fair.

This brief case study illustrates the complexity of ideas about fairness. Economists have a clear criterion of efficiency but no comparably clear criterion of fairness. Most economists regard Nozick as being too extreme and want a fair tax system, but there is no consensus about what a fair tax system looks like.

REVIEW QUIZ

1 What are the two big approaches to thinking about fairness?
2 What is the utilitarian idea of fairness and what is wrong with it?
3 Explain the big tradeoff. What idea of fairness has been developed to deal with it?
4 What is the idea of fairness based on fair rules?

You can work these questions in Study Plan 5.4 and get instant feedback.

◆ You've now studied efficiency and equity (fairness), the two biggest issues that run through the whole of economics. At many points throughout this book—and in your life—you will return to and use the ideas you've learned in this chapter. We start in the next chapter where we study some sources of *in*efficiency and *un*fairness.

SUMMARY

Key Points

Benefit, Cost, and Surplus (pp. 96–99)

- The maximum price willingly paid is marginal benefit, so a demand curve is also a marginal benefit curve.
- The market demand curve is the horizontal sum of the individual demand curves and is the marginal social benefit curve.
- Value is what people are *willing to* pay; price is what people *must* pay.
- Consumer surplus is the excess of the benefit received from a good or service over the amount paid for it.
- The minimum supply-price is marginal cost, so a supply curve is also a marginal cost curve.
- The market supply curve is the horizontal sum of the individual supply curves and is the marginal social cost curve.
- Cost is what producers pay; price is what producers receive.
- Producer surplus is the excess of the amount received from the sale of a good or service over the cost of producing it.

Working Study Plan Problems 3 to 10 will give you a better understanding of benefit, cost, and surplus.

Is the Competitive Market Efficient? (pp. 100–103)

- In a competitive equilibrium, marginal social benefit equals marginal social cost and resource allocation is efficient.
- Buyers and sellers acting in their self-interest end up promoting the social interest.
- Total surplus, consumer surplus plus producer surplus, is maximized.
- Producing less than or more than the efficient quantity creates deadweight loss.
- Price and quantity regulations; taxes and subsidies; externalities; public goods and common resources; monopoly; and high transactions costs can lead to market failure.

Working Study Plan Problems 11 to 13 will give you a better understanding of the efficiency of competitive markets.

Is the Competitive Market Fair? (pp. 104–107)

- Ideas about fairness can be divided into two groups: fair *results* and fair *rules*.
- Fair-results ideas require income transfers from the rich to the poor.
- Fair-rules ideas require property rights and voluntary exchange.

Working Study Plan Problems 14 and 15 will give you a better understanding of the fairness of competitive markets.

Key Terms

Big tradeoff, 105
Consumer surplus, 97
Deadweight loss, 101

Market failure, 101
Producer surplus, 99
Symmetry principle, 106

Total surplus, 100
Transactions costs, 103
Utilitarianism, 104

STUDY PLAN PROBLEMS AND APPLICATIONS

Resource Allocation Methods (Study Plan 5.1)

Use the following information to work Problems 1 and 2.

At Chez Panisse, the restaurant in Berkeley that is credited with having created California cuisine, reservations are essential. At Mandarin Dynasty, a restaurant near the University of California San Diego, reservations are recommended. At Eli Cannon's, a restaurant in Middletown, Connecticut, reservations are not accepted.

1. a. Describe the method of allocating scarce table resources at these three restaurants.
   b. Why do you think restaurants have different reservations policies?

2. Why do you think restaurants don't use the market price to allocate their tables?

Benefit, Cost, and Surplus (Study Plan 5.2)

Use the following table to work Problems 3 to 5.

The table gives the demand schedules for train travel for the only buyers in the market, Ann, Beth, and Cy.

Price	Quantity demanded (miles)		
(dollars per mile)	Ann	Beth	Cy
3	30	25	20
4	25	20	15
5	20	15	10
6	15	10	5
7	10	5	0
8	5	0	0
9	0	0	0

3. a. Construct the market demand schedule.
   b. What are the maximum price that Ann, Beth, and Cy are willing to pay to travel 20 miles? Why?

4. a. What is the marginal social benefit when the total distance travelled is 60 miles?
   b. What is the marginal private benefit for each person when they travel a total distance of 60 miles and how many miles does each of the people travel?

5. a. What is each traveler's consumer surplus when the price is $4 a mile?

b. What is the market consumer surplus when the price is $4 a mile?

Use the following table to work Problems 6 to 8.

The table gives the supply schedules of hot air balloon rides for the only sellers in the market, Xavier, Yasmin, and Zack.

Price	Quantity supplied (rides per week)		
(dollars per ride)	Xavier	Yasmin	Zack
100	30	25	20
90	25	20	15
80	20	15	10
70	15	10	5
60	10	5	0
50	5	0	0
40	0	0	0

6. a. Construct the market supply schedule.
   b. What are the minimum prices that Xavier, Yasmin, and Zack are willing to accept to supply 20 rides? Why?

7. a. What is the marginal social cost when the total number of rides is 30?
   b. What is the marginal cost for each supplier when the total number of rides is 30 and how many rides does each of the firms supply?

8. When the price is $70 a ride,
   a. What is each firm's producer surplus?
   b. What is the market producer surplus?

Use the following news clip to work Problems 9 and 10.

eBay Saves Billions for Bidders

If you think you would save money by bidding on eBay auctions, you would likely be right. Two Maryland researchers calculated the difference between the actual purchase price paid for auction items and the top price bidders stated they were willing to pay. They found that the difference averaged at least $4 per auction.

Source: *Information Week*, January 28, 2008

9. What method is used to allocate goods on eBay? How does the allocation method used by eBay auctions influence consumer surplus?

10. a. Can an eBay auction give the seller a surplus?

b. On a graph show the consumer surplus and producer surplus from an eBay auction.

Is the Competitive Market Efficient? (Study Plan 5.3)

11. The figure illustrates the competitive market for cell phones.

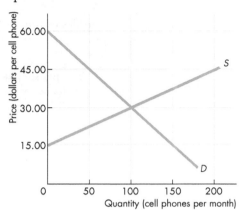

a. What are the equilibrium price and equilibrium quantity of cell phones?

b. Shade in and label the consumer surplus at the competitive equilibrium.

c. Shade in and label the producer surplus at the competitive equilibrium.

d. Calculate total surplus at the competitive equilibrium.

e. Is the competitive market for cell phones efficient?

12. The table gives the demand and supply schedules for sunscreen.

Price	Quantity demanded	Quantity supplied
(dollars per bottle)	(bottles per day)	
0	400	0
5	300	100
10	200	200
15	100	300
20	0	400

Sunscreen factories are required to limit production to 100 bottles a day.

a. What is the maximum price that consumers are willing to pay for the 100th bottle?

b. What is the minimum price that producers are willing to accept for the 100th bottle?

c. Describe the situation in this market.

13. Explain why each restaurant in Problem 1 might be using an efficient allocation method.

Is the Competitive Market Fair? (Study Plan 5.4)

14. Explain why the allocation method used by each restaurant in Problem 1 is fair or not fair.

15. In Problem 12, how can the 100 bottles available be allocated to beach-goers? Which possible methods would be fair and which would be unfair?

Economics in the News (Study Plan 5.N)

16. **The World's Largest Tulip and Flower Market**

Every day 20 million tulips, roses, and other cut flowers are auctioned at the Dutch market called *The Bloemenveiling*. Each day 55,000 Dutch auctions take place, matching buyers and sellers.

Source: Tulip-Bulbs.com

A Dutch auction is one in which the auctioneer starts by announcing the highest price. If no one offers to buy the flowers, the auctioneer lowers the price until a buyer is found.

a. What method is used to allocate flowers at the Bloemenveiling?

b. How does a Dutch flower auction influence consumer surplus and producer surplus?

c. Are the flower auctions at the Bloemenveiling efficient?

17. **Wii Sells Out Across Japan**

After a two-month TV-ad blitz for Wii in Japan, demand was expected to be much higher than supply. Yodobashi Camera was selling Wii games on a first-come, first-served basis. Eager customers showed up early and those who tried to join the line after 6 or 7 a.m. were turned away—many rushed off to the smaller stores that were holding raffles to decide who got a Wii.

Source: *Gamespot News*, December 1, 2006

a. Why was the quantity demanded of Wii expected to exceed the quantity supplied?

b. Did Nintendo produce the efficient quantity of Wii? Explain.

c. Can you think of reasons why Nintendo might want to underproduce and leave the market with fewer Wii than people want to buy?

d. What are the two methods of resource allocation described in the news clip? Is either method of allocating Wii efficient?

e. What do you think some of the people who managed to buy a Wii did with it?

f. Explain which is the fairer method of allocating the Wii: the market price or the two methods described in the news clip.

Raise The Minimum Wage

For 7.3 Million Americans

After studying this chapter,
you will be able to:

◆ Explain how rent ceilings create housing shortages and inefficiency

◆ Explain how minimum wage laws create unemployment and inefficiency

◆ Explain the effects of a tax

◆ Explain the effects of production quotas and subsidies on production, costs, and prices

◆ Explain how markets for illegal goods work

6

GOVERNMENT ACTIONS
IN MARKETS

In New York City, where the average weekly wage rate is $1,000, it costs $3,500 a month to rent an average two-bedroom apartment. Can governments cap rents to help renters live in affordable housing? Or instead, can governments make housing more affordable by raising incomes with minimum wage laws?

Taxes put the hand of government in almost every pocket and market. You probably think that you pay more than your fair share of taxes. But who actually pays and who benefits when a tax is cut: buyers or sellers?

In markets for farm products, governments intervene with the opposite of a tax: a subsidy. Sometimes, governments limit the quantities that farms may produce. Do subsidies and production limits help to make markets efficient?

◆ A Housing Market with a Rent Ceiling

We spend more of our income on housing than on any other good or service, so it isn't surprising that rents can be a political issue. When rents are high, or when they jump by a large amount, renters might lobby the government for limits on rents.

A government regulation that makes it illegal to charge a price higher than a specified level is called a **price ceiling** or **price cap**.

The effects of a price ceiling on a market depend crucially on whether the ceiling is imposed at a level that is above or below the equilibrium price.

A price ceiling set *above the equilibrium price* has no effect. The reason is that the price ceiling does not constrain the market forces. The force of the law and the market forces are not in conflict. But a price ceiling *below the equilibrium price* has powerful effects on a market. The reason is that the price ceiling attempts to prevent the price from regulating the quantities demanded and supplied. The force of the law and the market forces are in conflict.

When a price ceiling is applied to a housing market, it is called a **rent ceiling**. A rent ceiling set below the equilibrium rent creates

- A housing shortage
- Increased search activity
- A black market

A Housing Shortage

At the equilibrium price, the quantity demanded equals the quantity supplied. In a housing market, when the rent is at the equilibrium level, the quantity of housing supplied equals the quantity of housing demanded and there is neither a shortage nor a surplus of housing.

But at a rent set below the equilibrium rent, the quantity of housing demanded exceeds the quantity of housing supplied—there is a shortage. So if a rent ceiling is set below the equilibrium rent, there will be a shortage of housing.

When there is a shortage, the quantity available is the quantity supplied and somehow, this quantity must be allocated among the frustrated demanders. One way in which this allocation occurs is through increased search activity.

Increased Search Activity

The time spent looking for someone with whom to do business is called **search activity**. We spend some time in search activity almost every time we make a purchase. When you're shopping for the latest hot new cell phone, and you know four stores that stock it, how do you find which store has the best deal? You spend a few minutes on the Internet, checking out the various prices. In some markets, such as the housing market, people spend a lot of time checking the alternatives available before making a choice.

When a price is regulated and there is a shortage, search activity increases. In the case of a rent-controlled housing market, frustrated would-be renters scan the newspapers, not only for housing ads but also for death notices! Any information about newly available housing is useful, and apartment seekers race to be first on the scene when news of a possible supplier breaks.

The *opportunity cost* of a good is equal not only to its price but also to the value of the search time spent finding the good. So the opportunity cost of housing is equal to the rent (a regulated price) plus the time and other resources spent searching for the restricted quantity available. Search activity is costly. It uses time and other resources, such as phone calls, automobiles, and gasoline that could have been used in other productive ways.

A rent ceiling controls only the rent portion of the cost of housing. The cost of increased search activity might end up making the full cost of housing *higher* than it would be without a rent ceiling.

A Black Market

A rent ceiling also encourages illegal trading in a **black market**, an illegal market in which the equilibrium price exceeds the price ceiling. Black markets occur in rent-controlled housing and many other markets. For example, scalpers run black markets in tickets for big sporting events and rock concerts.

When a rent ceiling is in force, frustrated renters and landlords constantly seek ways of increasing rents. One common way is for a new tenant to pay a high price for worthless fittings, such as charging $2,000 for threadbare drapes. Another is for the tenant to pay an exorbitant price for new locks and keys—called "key money."

The level of a black market rent depends on how tightly the rent ceiling is enforced. With loose enforcement, the black market rent is close to the unregulated rent. But with strict enforcement, the black market rent is equal to the maximum price that a renter is willing to pay.

Figure 6.1 illustrates the effects of a rent ceiling. The demand curve for housing is *D* and the supply curve is *S*. A rent ceiling is imposed at $800 a month. Rents that exceed $800 a month are in the gray-shaded illegal region in the figure. You can see that the equilibrium rent, where the demand and supply curves intersect, is in the illegal region.

At a rent of $800 a month, the quantity of housing supplied is 60,000 units and the quantity demanded is 100,000 units. So with a rent of $800 a month, there is a shortage of 40,000 units of housing.

To rent the 60,000th unit, someone is willing to pay $1,200 a month. They might pay this amount by incurring search costs that bring the total cost of housing to $1,200 a month, or they might pay a black market price of $1,200 a month. Either way, they end up incurring a cost that exceeds what the equilibrium rent would be in an unregulated market.

Inefficiency of a Rent Ceiling

A rent ceiling set below the equilibrium rent results in an inefficient underproduction of housing services. The *marginal social benefit* of housing exceeds its *marginal social cost* and a deadweight loss shrinks the producer surplus and consumer surplus (Chapter 5, pp. 100–102).

Figure 6.2 shows this inefficiency. The rent ceiling ($800 per month) is below the equilibrium rent ($1,000 per month) and the quantity of housing supplied (60,000 units) is less than the efficient quantity (80,000 units).

Because the quantity of housing supplied (the quantity available) is less than the efficient quantity, there is a deadweight loss, shown by the gray triangle. Producer surplus shrinks to the blue triangle and consumer surplus shrinks to the green triangle. The red rectangle represents the potential loss from increased search activity. This loss is borne by consumers and the full loss from the rent ceiling is the sum of the deadweight loss and the increased cost of search.

FIGURE 6.1   A Rent Ceiling

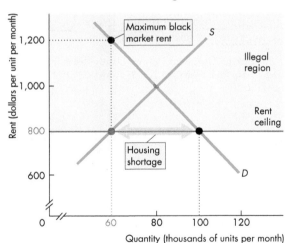

A rent above the rent ceiling of $800 a month is illegal (in the gray-shaded illegal region). At a rent of $800 a month, the quantity of housing supplied is 60,000 units. Frustrated renters spend time searching for housing and they make deals with landlords in a black market. Someone is willing to pay $1,200 a month for the 60,000th unit.

FIGURE 6.2   The Inefficiency of a Rent Ceiling

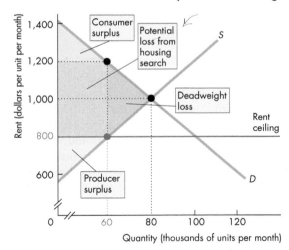

Without a rent ceiling, the market produces an efficient 80,000 units of housing at a rent of $1,000 a month. A rent ceiling of $800 a month decreases the quantity of housing supplied to 60,000 units. Producer surplus and consumer surplus shrink and a deadweight loss arises. The red rectangle represents the cost of resources used in increased search activity. The full loss from the rent ceiling equals the sum of the red rectangle and gray triangle.

Are Rent Ceilings Fair?

Rent ceilings might be inefficient, but don't they achieve a fairer allocation of scarce housing? Let's explore this question.

Chapter 5 (pp. 104–106) reviews two key ideas about fairness. According to the *fair rules* view, anything that blocks voluntary exchange is unfair, so rent ceilings are unfair. But according to the *fair result* view, a fair outcome is one that benefits the less well off. So according to this view, the fairest outcome is the one that allocates scarce housing to the poorest. To see whether rent ceilings help to achieve a fairer outcome in this sense, we need to consider how the market allocates scarce housing resources in the face of a rent ceiling.

Blocking rent adjustments doesn't eliminate scarcity. Rather, because it decreases the quantity of housing available, it creates an even bigger challenge for the housing market. Somehow, the market must ration a smaller quantity of housing and allocate that housing among the people who demand it.

When the rent is not permitted to allocate scarce housing, what other mechanisms are available, and are *they* fair? Some possible mechanisms are

- A lottery
- First-come, first-served
- Discrimination

A lottery allocates housing to those who are lucky, not to those who are poor. First-come, first-served (a method used to allocate housing in England after World War II) allocates housing to those who have the greatest foresight and who get their names on a list first, not to the poorest. Discrimination allocates scarce housing based on the views and self-interest of the owner of the housing. In the case of public housing, what counts is the self-interest of the bureaucracy that administers the allocation.

In principle, self-interested owners and bureaucrats could allocate housing to satisfy some criterion of fairness, but they are not likely to do so. Discrimination based on friendship, family ties, and criteria such as race, ethnicity, or sex is more likely to enter the equation. We might make such discrimination illegal, but we cannot prevent it from occurring.

It is hard, then, to make a case for rent ceilings on the basis of fairness. When rent adjustments are blocked, other methods of allocating scarce housing resources operate that do not produce a fair outcome.

Economics in Action
Rent Control Winners: The Rich and Famous

New York, San Francisco, London, and Paris, four of the world's great cities, have rent ceilings in some part of their housing markets. Boston had rent ceilings for many years but abolished them in 1997. Many other U.S. cities do not have, and have never had, rent ceilings. Among them are Atlanta, Baltimore, Chicago, Dallas, Philadelphia, Phoenix, and Seattle.

To see the effects of rent ceilings in practice we can compare the housing markets in cities with ceilings with those without ceilings. We learn two main lessons from such a comparison.

First, rent ceilings definitely create a housing shortage. Second, they do lower the rents for some but raise them for others.

A survey[*] conducted in 1997 showed that the rents of housing units *actually available for rent* were 2.5 times the average of all rents in New York, but equal to the average rent in Philadelphia. The winners from rent ceilings are the families that have lived in a city for a long time. In New York, these families include some rich and famous ones. The voting power of the winners keeps the rent ceilings in place. Mobile newcomers are the losers in a city with rent ceilings.

The bottom line is that in principle and in practice, rent ceilings are inefficient and unfair.

---

[*] William Tucker, "How Rent Control Drives Out Affordable Housing," Cato Policy Analysis No. 274, May 21, 1997, Cato Institute.

REVIEW QUIZ

1 What is a rent ceiling and what are its effects if it is set above the equilibrium rent?
2 What are the effects of a rent ceiling that is set below the equilibrium rent?
3 How are scarce housing resources allocated when a rent ceiling is in place?
4 Why does a rent ceiling create an inefficient and unfair outcome in the housing market?

You can work these questions in Study Plan 6.1 and get instant feedback.

You now know how a price ceiling (rent ceiling) works. Next, we'll learn about the effects of a price floor by studying a minimum wage in a labor market.

A Labor Market with a Minimum Wage

For each one of us, the labor market is the market that influences the jobs we get and the wages we earn. Firms decide how much labor to demand, and the lower the wage rate, the greater is the quantity of labor demanded. Households decide how much labor to supply, and the higher the wage rate, the greater is the quantity of labor supplied. The wage rate adjusts to make the quantity of labor demanded equal to the quantity supplied.

When wage rates are low, or when they fail to keep up with rising prices, labor unions might turn to governments and lobby for a higher wage rate.

A government imposed regulation that makes it illegal to charge a price lower than a specified level is called a **price floor**.

The effects of a price floor on a market depend crucially on whether the floor is imposed at a level that is above or below the equilibrium price.

A price floor set *below the equilibrium price* has no effect. The reason is that the price floor does not constrain the market forces. The force of the law and the market forces are not in conflict. But a price floor *above the equilibrium price* has powerful effects on a market. The reason is that the price floor attempts to prevent the price from regulating the quantities demanded and supplied. The force of the law and the market forces are in conflict.

When a price floor is applied to a labor market, it is called a **minimum wage**. A minimum wage imposed at a level that is above the equilibrium wage creates unemployment. Let's look at the effects of a minimum wage.

Minimum Wage Brings Unemployment

At the equilibrium price, the quantity demanded equals the quantity supplied. In a labor market, when the wage rate is at the equilibrium level, the quantity of labor supplied equals the quantity of labor demanded: There is neither a shortage of labor nor a surplus of labor.

But at a wage rate above the equilibrium wage, the quantity of labor supplied exceeds the quantity of labor demanded—there is a surplus of labor. So when a minimum wage is set above the equilibrium wage, there is a surplus of labor. The demand for labor determines the level of employment, and the surplus of labor is unemployed.

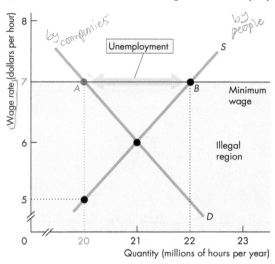

FIGURE 6.3   Minimum Wage and Unemployment

The minimum wage rate is set at $7 an hour. Any wage rate below $7 an hour is illegal (in the gray-shaded illegal region). At the minimum wage of $7 an hour, 20 million hours are hired but 22 million hours are available. Unemployment—*AB*—of 2 million hours a year is created. With only 20 million hours demanded, someone is willing to supply the 20 millionth hour for $5.

myeconlab   animation

Figure 6.3 illustrates the effect of the minimum wage on unemployment. The demand for labor curve is *D* and the supply of labor curve is *S*. The horizontal red line shows the minimum wage set at $7 an hour. A wage rate below this level is illegal, in the gray-shaded illegal region of the figure. At the minimum wage rate, 20 million hours of labor are demanded (point *A*) and 22 million hours of labor are supplied (point *B*), so 2 million hours of available labor are unemployed.

With only 20 million hours demanded, someone is willing to supply that 20 millionth hour for $5. Frustrated unemployed workers spend time and other resources searching for hard-to-find jobs.

Inefficiency of a Minimum Wage

In the labor market, the supply curve measures the marginal social cost of labor to workers. This cost is leisure forgone. The demand curve measures the marginal social benefit from labor. This benefit is the value of the goods and services produced. An unregulated labor market allocates the economy's scarce labor resources to the jobs in which they are valued most highly. The market is efficient.

The minimum wage frustrates the market mechanism and results in unemployment and increased job search. At the quantity of labor employed, the marginal social benefit of labor exceeds its marginal social cost and a deadweight loss shrinks the firms' surplus and the workers' surplus.

Figure 6.4 shows this inefficiency. The minimum wage ($7 an hour) is above the equilibrium wage ($6 an hour) and the quantity of labor demanded and employed (20 million hours) is less than the efficient quantity (21 million hours).

Because the quantity of labor employed is less than the efficient quantity, there is a deadweight loss, shown by the gray triangle. The firms' surplus shrinks to the blue triangle and the workers' surplus shrinks to the green triangle. The red rectangle shows the potential loss from increased job search, which is borne by workers. The full loss from the minimum wage is the sum of the deadweight loss and the increased cost of job search.

FIGURE 6.4   The Inefficiency of a
             Minimum Wage

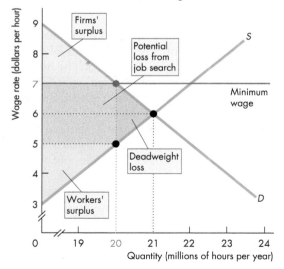

A minimum wage decreases employment. Firms' surplus (blue area) and workers' surplus (green area) shrink and a deadweight loss (gray area) arises. Job search increases and the red area shows the loss from this activity.

myeconlab animation

Economics in Action
Unscrambling Cause and Effect of the Minimum Wage

In the United States, the federal government's Fair Labor Standards Act sets the minimum wage, which has fluctuated between 35 percent and 50 percent of the average wage, and in 2010 was $7.25 an hour. Most states have minimum wages that exceed the federal minimum.

Does the minimum wage result in unemployment, and if so, how much unemployment does it create? The consensus answer is that a 10 percent rise in the minimum wage decreases teenage employment by between 1 and 3 percent.

This consensus answer has been challenged by David Card of the University of California at Berkeley and Alan Krueger of Princeton University.

Card and Krueger say that increases in the minimum wage have *increased* teenage employment and *decreased* unemployment.

From their study of minimum wages in California, New Jersey, and Texas, Card and Krueger say that the employment rate of low-income workers increased following an increase in the minimum wage. They argue that a higher wage *increases* employment by making workers become more conscientious and productive

Is the Minimum Wage Fair?

The minimum wage is unfair on both views of fairness: It delivers an unfair *result* and imposes an unfair *rule*.

The *result* is unfair because only those people who have jobs and keep them benefit from the minimum wage. The unemployed end up worse off than they would be with no minimum wage. Some of those who search for jobs and find them end up worse off because of the increased cost of job search they incur. Also those who find jobs aren't always the least well off. When the wage rate doesn't allocate labor, other mechanisms determine who finds a job. One such mechanism is discrimination, which is yet another source of unfairness.

The minimum wage imposes an unfair *rule* because it blocks voluntary exchange. Firms are willing to hire more labor and people are willing to work more, but they are not permitted by the minimum wage law to do so.

and less likely to quit, which lowers unproductive labor turnover. They also argue that a higher wage rate makes managers seek ways to increase labor productivity.

Most economists are skeptical about Card and Krueger's argument. Why, economists ask, don't firms freely pay wage rates above the equilibrium wage to encourage more productive work habits? Also, they point to other explanations for the employment responses that Card and Krueger found.

According to Daniel Hamermesh of the University of Texas at Austin, Card and Krueger got the timing wrong. Hamermesh says that firms cut employment *before* the minimum wage is increased in anticipation of the increase. If he is correct, looking for the effects of an increase *after* it has occurred misses its main effects.

Finis Welch of Texas A&M University and Kevin Murphy of the University of Chicago say the employment effects that Card and Krueger found are caused by regional differences in economic growth, not by changes in the minimum wage.

One effect of the minimum wage is an increase in the quantity of labor supplied. If this effect occurs, it might show up as an increase in the number of people who quit school to look for work before completing high school. Some economists say that this response does occur.

REVIEW QUIZ

1 What is a minimum wage and what are its effects if it is set above the equilibrium wage?
2 What are the effects of a minimum wage set below the equilibrium wage?
3 Explain how scarce jobs are allocated when a minimum wage is in place.
4 Explain why a minimum wage creates an inefficient allocation of labor resources.
5 Explain why a minimum wage is unfair.

You can work these questions in Study Plan 6.2 and get instant feedback.

Next we're going to study a more widespread government action in markets: taxes. We'll see how taxes change prices and quantities. You will discover the surprising fact that while the government can impose a tax, it can't decide who will pay the tax! You will also see that a tax creates a deadweight loss.

◆ Taxes

Everything you earn and almost everything you buy is taxed. Income taxes and Social Security taxes are deducted from your earnings and sales taxes are added to the bill when you buy something. Employers also pay a Social Security tax for their workers, and producers of tobacco products, alcoholic drinks, and gasoline pay a tax every time they sell something.

Who *really* pays these taxes? Because the income tax and Social Security tax are deducted from your pay, and the sales tax is added to the prices that you pay, isn't it obvious that *you* pay these taxes? And isn't it equally obvious that your employer pays the employer's contribution to the Social Security tax and that tobacco producers pay the tax on cigarettes?

You're going to discover that it isn't obvious who *really* pays a tax and that lawmakers don't make that decision. We begin with a definition of tax incidence.

Tax Incidence

Tax incidence is the division of the burden of a tax between buyers and sellers. When the government imposes a tax on the sale of a good*, the price paid by buyers might rise by the full amount of the tax, by a lesser amount, or not at all. If the price paid by buyers rises by the full amount of the tax, then the burden of the tax falls entirely on buyers—the buyers pay the tax. If the price paid by buyers rises by a lesser amount than the tax, then the burden of the tax falls partly on buyers and partly on sellers. And if the price paid by buyers doesn't change at all, then the burden of the tax falls entirely on sellers.

Tax incidence does not depend on the tax law. The law might impose a tax on sellers or on buyers, but the outcome is the same in either case. To see why, let's look at the tax on cigarettes in New York City.

A Tax on Sellers

On July 1, 2002, Mayor Bloomberg put a tax of $1.50 a pack on cigarettes sold in New York City. To work out the effects of this tax on the sellers of cigarettes, we begin by examining the effects on demand and supply in the market for cigarettes.

---

* These propositions also apply to services and factors of production (land, labor, capital).

Tax on seller decrease supply.
Tax on buyer decrease demand.

In Fig. 6.5, the demand curve is *D*, and the supply curve is *S*. With no tax, the equilibrium price is $3 per pack and 350 million packs a year are bought and sold.

A tax on sellers is like an increase in cost, so it decreases supply. To determine the position of the new supply curve, we add the tax to the minimum price that sellers are willing to accept for each quantity sold. You can see that without the tax, sellers are willing to offer 350 million packs a year for $3 a pack. So with a $1.50 tax, they will offer 350 million packs a year only if the price is $4.50 a pack. The supply curve shifts to the red curve labeled *S + tax on sellers*.

Equilibrium occurs where the new supply curve intersects the demand curve at 325 million packs a year. The price paid by buyers rises by $1 to $4 a pack. And the price received by sellers falls by 50¢ to $2.50 a pack. So buyers pay $1 of the tax and sellers pay the other 50¢.

A Tax on Buyers

Suppose that instead of taxing sellers, New York City taxes cigarette buyers $1.50 a pack.

A tax on buyers lowers the amount they are willing to pay sellers, so it decreases demand and shifts the demand curve leftward. To determine the position of this new demand curve, we subtract the tax from the maximum price that buyers are willing to pay for each quantity bought. You can see, in Fig. 6.6, that without the tax, buyers are willing to buy 350 million packs a year for $3 a pack. So with a $1.50 tax, they are willing to buy 350 million packs a year only if the price including the tax is $3 a pack, which means that they're willing to pay sellers only $1.50 a pack. The demand curve shifts to become the red curve labeled *D – tax on buyers*.

Equilibrium occurs where the new demand curve intersects the supply curve at a quantity of 325 million packs a year. The price received by sellers is $2.50 a pack, and the price paid by buyers is $4.

Equivalence of Tax on Buyers and Sellers

You can see that the tax on buyers in Fig. 6.6 has the same effects as the tax on sellers in Fig. 6.5. In both cases, the equilibrium quantity decreases to 325 million packs a year, the price paid by buyers rises to $4 a pack, and the price received by sellers falls to $2.50 a pack. Buyers pay $1 of the $1.50 tax, and sellers pay the other 50¢ of the tax.

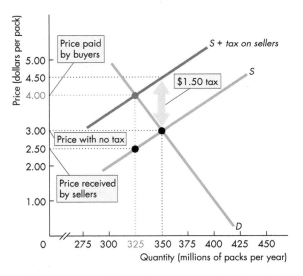

FIGURE 6.5   A Tax on Sellers

With no tax, 350 million packs a year are bought and sold at $3 a pack. A tax on sellers of $1.50 a pack shifts the supply curve from *S* to *S + tax on sellers*. The equilibrium quantity decreases to 325 million packs a year, the price paid by buyers rises to $4 a pack, and the price received by sellers falls to $2.50 a pack. The tax raises the price paid by buyers by less than the tax and lowers the price received by sellers, so buyers and sellers share the burden of the tax.

Can We Share the Burden Equally? Suppose that Mayor Bloomberg wants the burden of the cigarette tax to fall equally on buyers and sellers and declares that a 75¢ tax be imposed on each. Is the burden of the tax then shared equally?

You can see that it is not. The tax is still $1.50 a pack. You've seen that the tax has the same effect regardless of whether it is imposed on sellers or buyers. So imposing half the tax on sellers and half on buyers is like an average of the two cases you've just examined. (Draw the demand-supply graph and work out what happens in this case. The demand curve shifts downward by 75¢ and the supply curve shifts upward by 75¢. The new equilibrium quantity is still 325 million packs a year. Buyers pay $4 a pack, of which 75¢ is tax. Sellers receive $3.25 from buyers, but pay a 75¢ tax, so sellers net $2.50 a pack.)

When a transaction is taxed, there are two prices: the price paid by buyers, which includes the tax; and the price received by sellers, which excludes the tax.

FIGURE 6.6   A Tax on Buyers

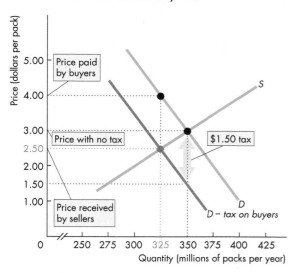

With no tax, 350 million packs a year are bought and sold at $3 a pack. A tax on buyers of $1.50 a pack shifts the demand curve from D to D – tax on buyers. The equilibrium quantity decreases to 325 million packs a year, the price paid by buyers rises to $4 a pack, and the price received by sellers falls to $2.50 a pack. The tax raises the price paid by buyers by less than the tax and lowers the price received by sellers, so buyers and sellers share the burden of the tax.

myeconlab animation

Buyers respond to the price that *includes* the tax and sellers respond to the price that *excludes* the tax.

A tax is like a wedge between the price buyers pay and the price sellers receive. The size of the wedge determines the effects of the tax, not the side of the market on which the government imposes the tax.

The Social Security Tax The Social Security tax is an example of a tax that Congress imposes equally on both buyers and sellers. But the principles you've just learned apply to this tax too. The market for labor, not Congress, decides how the burden of the Social Security tax is divided between firms and workers.

In the New York City cigarette tax example, buyers bear twice the burden of the tax borne by sellers. In special cases, either buyers or sellers bear the entire burden. The division of the burden of a tax between buyers and sellers depends on the elasticities of demand and supply, as you will now see.

Tax Incidence and Elasticity of Demand

The division of the tax between buyers and sellers depends in part on the elasticity of demand. There are two extreme cases:

- Perfectly inelastic demand—buyers pay.
- Perfectly elastic demand—sellers pay.

Perfectly Inelastic Demand Figure 6.7 shows the market for insulin, a vital daily medication for those with diabetes. Demand is perfectly inelastic at 100,000 doses a day, regardless of the price, as shown by the vertical demand curve D. That is, a diabetic would sacrifice all other goods and services rather than not consume the insulin dose that provides good health. The supply curve of insulin is S. With no tax, the price is $2 a dose and the quantity is 100,000 doses a day.

If insulin is taxed at 20¢ a dose, we must add the tax to the minimum price at which drug companies are willing to sell insulin. The result is the new supply curve S + *tax*. The price rises to $2.20 a dose, but the quantity does not change. Buyers pay the entire tax of 20¢ a dose.

FIGURE 6.7   Tax with Perfectly Inelastic Demand

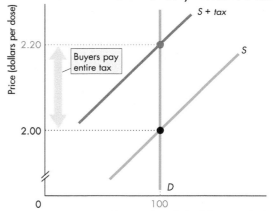

In this market for insulin, demand is perfectly inelastic. With no tax, the price is $2 a dose and the quantity is 100,000 doses a day. A tax of 20¢ a dose shifts the supply curve to S + *tax*. The price rises to $2.20 a dose, but the quantity bought does not change. Buyers pay the entire tax.

myeconlab animation

Perfectly Elastic Demand Figure 6.8 shows the market for pink marker pens. Demand is perfectly elastic at $1 a pen, as shown by the horizontal demand curve D. If pink pens are less expensive than the other colors, everyone uses pink. If pink pens are more expensive than other colors, no one uses pink. The supply curve is S. With no tax, the price of a pink pen is $1 and the quantity is 4,000 pens a week.

Suppose that the government imposes a tax of 10¢ a pen on pink marker pens but not on other colors. The new supply curve is S + *tax*. The price remains at $1 a pen, and the quantity decreases to 1,000 pink pens a week. The 10¢ tax leaves the price paid by buyers unchanged but lowers the amount received by sellers by the full amount of the tax. Sellers pay the entire tax of 10¢ a pink pen.

We've seen that when demand is perfectly inelastic, buyers pay the entire tax and when demand is perfectly elastic, sellers pay the entire tax. In the usual case, demand is neither perfectly inelastic nor perfectly elastic and the tax is split between buyers and sellers. But the division depends on the elasticity of demand: The more inelastic the demand, the larger is the amount of the tax paid by buyers.

FIGURE 6.8   Tax with Perfectly Elastic Demand

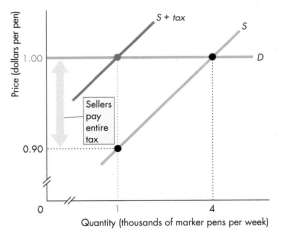

In this market for pink pens, demand is perfectly elastic. With no tax, the price of a pen is $1 and the quantity is 4,000 pens a week. A tax of 10¢ a pink pen shifts the supply curve to S + *tax*. The price remains at $1 a pen, and the quantity of pink pens sold decreases to 1,000 a week. Sellers pay the entire tax.

Tax Incidence and Elasticity of Supply

The division of the tax between buyers and sellers also depends, in part, on the elasticity of supply. Again, there are two extreme cases:

- Perfectly inelastic supply—sellers pay.
- Perfectly elastic supply—buyers pay.

Perfectly Inelastic Supply Figure 6.9(a) shows the market for water from a mineral spring that flows at a constant rate that can't be controlled. Supply is perfectly inelastic at 100,000 bottles a week, as shown by the supply curve S. The demand curve for the water from this spring is D. With no tax, the price is 50¢ a bottle and the quantity is 100,000 bottles.

Suppose this spring water is taxed at 5¢ a bottle. The supply curve does not change because the spring owners still produce 100,000 bottles a week, even though the price they receive falls. But buyers are willing to buy the 100,000 bottles only if the price is 50¢ a bottle, so the price remains at 50¢ a bottle. The tax reduces the price received by sellers to 45¢ a bottle, and sellers pay the entire tax.

Perfectly Elastic Supply Figure 6.9(b) shows the market for sand from which computer-chip makers extract silicon. Supply of this sand is perfectly elastic at a price of 10¢ a pound, as shown by the supply curve S. The demand curve for sand is D. With no tax, the price is 10¢ a pound and 5,000 pounds a week are bought.

If this sand is taxed at 1¢ a pound, we must add the tax to the minimum supply-price. Sellers are now willing to offer any quantity at 11¢ a pound along the curve S + *tax*. A new equilibrium is determined where the new supply curve intersects the demand curve: at a price of 11¢ a pound and a quantity of 3,000 pounds a week. The tax has increased the price buyers pay by the full amount of the tax—1¢ a pound—and has decreased the quantity sold. Buyers pay the entire tax.

We've seen that when supply is perfectly inelastic, sellers pay the entire tax, and when supply is perfectly elastic, buyers pay the entire tax. In the usual case, supply is neither perfectly inelastic nor perfectly elastic and the tax is split between buyers and sellers. But how the tax is split depends on the elasticity of supply: The more elastic the supply, the larger is the amount of the tax paid by buyers.

FIGURE 6.9   Tax and the Elasticity of Supply

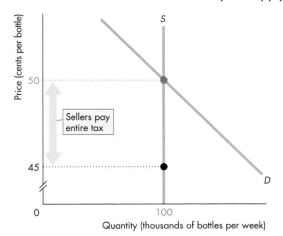

(a) Perfectly inelastic supply

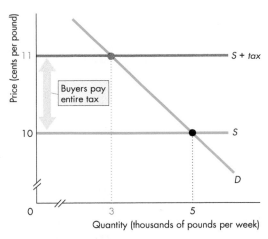

(b) Perfectly elastic supply

Part (a) shows the market for water from a mineral spring. Supply is perfectly inelastic. With no tax, the price is 50¢ a bottle. With a tax of 5¢ a bottle, the price remains at 50¢ a bottle. The number of bottles bought remains the same, but the price received by sellers decreases to 45¢ a bottle. Sellers pay the entire tax.

Part (b) shows the market for sand. Supply is perfectly elastic. With no tax, the price is 10¢ a pound. A tax of 1¢ a pound increases the minimum supply-price to 11¢ a pound. The supply curve shifts to *S + tax*. The price increases to 11¢ a pound. Buyers pay the entire tax.

myeconlab animation

Taxes and Efficiency

A tax drives a wedge between the buying price and the selling price and results in inefficient underproduction. The price buyers pay is also the buyers' willingness to pay, which measures *marginal social benefit*. The price sellers receive is also the sellers' minimum supply-price, which equals *marginal social cost*.

A tax makes marginal social benefit exceed marginal social cost, shrinks the producer surplus and consumer surplus, and creates a deadweight loss.

Figure 6.10 shows the inefficiency of a tax on MP3 players. The demand curve, *D*, shows marginal social benefit, and the supply curve, *S*, shows marginal social cost. Without a tax, the market produces the efficient quantity (5,000 players a week).

With a tax, the sellers' minimum supply-price rises by the amount of the tax and the supply curve shifts to *S + tax*. This supply curve does *not* show marginal social cost. The tax component isn't a *social* cost of

FIGURE 6.10   Taxes and Efficiency

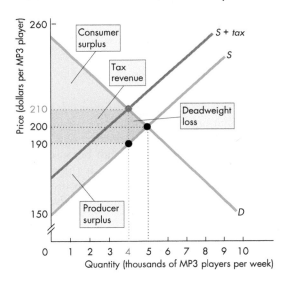

With no tax, 5,000 players a week are produced. With a $20 tax, the buyers' price rises to $210, the sellers' price falls to $190, and the quantity decreases to 4,000 players a week. Consumer surplus shrinks to the green area, and the producer surplus shrinks to the blue area. Part of the loss of consumer surplus and producer surplus goes to the government as tax revenue (the purple area) and part becomes a deadweight loss (the gray area).

myeconlab animation

production. It is a transfer of resources to the government. At the new equilibrium quantity (4,000 players a week), both consumer surplus and producer surplus shrink. Part of each surplus goes to the government in tax revenue—the purple area; part becomes a deadweight loss—the gray area.

Only in the extreme cases of perfectly inelastic demand and perfectly inelastic supply does a tax not change the quantity bought and sold so that no deadweight loss arises.

Taxes and Fairness

We've examined the incidence and the efficiency of taxes. But when political leaders debate tax issues, it is fairness, not incidence and efficiency, that gets the most attention. Democrats complain that Republican tax cuts are unfair because they give the benefits of lower taxes to the rich. Republicans counter that it is fair that the rich get most of the tax cuts because they pay most of the taxes. No easy answers are available to the questions about the fairness of taxes.

Economists have proposed two conflicting principles of fairness to apply to a tax system:

- The benefits principle
- The ability-to-pay principle

The Benefits Principle The *benefits principle* is the proposition that people should pay taxes equal to the benefits they receive from the services provided by government. This arrangement is fair because it means that those who benefit most pay the most taxes. It makes tax payments and the consumption of government-provided services similar to private consumption expenditures.

The benefits principle can justify high fuel taxes to pay for freeways, high taxes on alcoholic beverages and tobacco products to pay for public health-care services, and high rates of income tax on high incomes to pay for the benefits from law and order and from living in a secure environment, from which the rich might benefit more than the poor.

The Ability-to-Pay Principle The *ability-to-pay principle* is the proposition that people should pay taxes according to how easily they can bear the burden of the tax. A rich person can more easily bear the burden than a poor person can, so the ability-to-pay principle can reinforce the benefits principle to justify high rates of income tax on high incomes.

Economics in Action
Workers and Consumers Pay the Most Tax

Because the elasticity of the supply of labor is low and the elasticity of demand for labor is high, workers pay most of the personal income taxes and most of the Social Security taxes. Because the elasticities of demand for alcohol, tobacco, and gasoline are low and the elasticities of supply are high, the burden of these taxes (excise taxes) falls more heavily on buyers than on sellers.

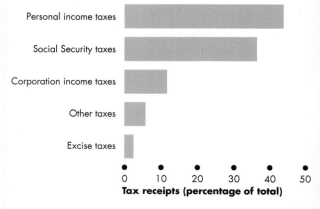

U.S. Taxes

Source of data: Budget of the United States Government, Fiscal Year 2011, Historical Tables, Table 2.2.

REVIEW QUIZ

1. How does the elasticity of demand influence the incidence of a tax, the tax revenue, and the deadweight loss?
2. How does the elasticity of supply influence the incidence of a tax, the quantity bought, the tax revenue, and the deadweight loss?
3. Why is a tax inefficient?
4. When would a tax be efficient?
5. What are the two principles of fairness that are applied to tax systems?

You can work these questions in Study Plan 6.3 and get instant feedback.

Your next task is to study production quotas and subsidies, tools that are used to influence the markets for farm products.

Production Quotas and Subsidies

An early or late frost, a hot dry summer, and a wet spring present just a few of the challenges that fill the lives of farmers with uncertainty and sometimes with economic hardship. Fluctuations in the weather bring fluctuations in farm output and prices and sometimes leave farmers with low incomes. To help farmers avoid low prices and low incomes, governments intervene in the markets for farm products.

Price floors that work a bit like the minimum wage that you've already studied might be used. But as you've seen, this type of government action creates a surplus and is inefficient. These same conclusions apply to the effects of a price floor for farm products.

Governments often use two other methods of intervention in the markets for farm products:

- Production quotas
- Subsidies

Production Quotas

In the markets for sugarbeets, tobacco leaf, and cotton (among others), governments have, from time to time, imposed production quotas. A **production quota** is an upper limit to the quantity of a good that may be produced in a specified period. To discover the effects of a production quota, let's look at what a quota does to the market for sugarbeets.

Suppose that the growers of sugarbeets want to limit total production to get a higher price. They persuade the government to introduce a production quota on sugarbeets.

The effect of the production quota depends on whether it is set below or above the equilibrium quantity. If the government introduced a production quota above the equilibrium quantity, nothing would change because sugarbeet growers would already be producing less than the quota. But a production quota set *below the equilibrium quantity* has big effects, which are

- A decrease in supply
- A rise in price
- A decrease in marginal cost
- Inefficient underproduction
- An incentive to cheat and overproduce
  Figure 6.11 illustrates these effects.

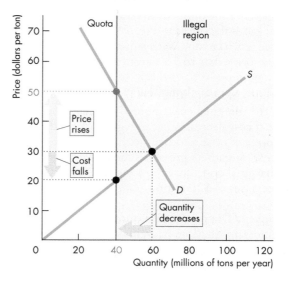

FIGURE 6.11   The Effects of a Production Quota

With no quota, growers produce 60 million tons a year and the price is $30 a ton. A production quota of 40 million tons a year restricts total production to that amount. The quantity produced decreases to 40 million tons a year, the price rises to $50 a ton, and the farmers' marginal cost falls to $20 a ton. Because marginal social cost (on the supply curve) is less than marginal social benefit (on the demand curve), a deadweight loss arises from the underproduction.

 myeconlab animation

A Decrease in Supply A production quota on sugarbeets decreases the supply of sugarbeets. Each grower is assigned a production limit that is less than the amount that would be produced—and supplied—without the quota. The total of the growers' limits equals the quota, and any production in excess of the quota is illegal.

The quantity supplied becomes the amount permitted by the production quota, and this quantity is fixed. The supply of sugarbeets becomes perfectly inelastic at the quantity permitted under the quota.

In Fig. 6.11, with no quota, growers would produce 60 million tons of sugarbeets a year—the market equilibrium quantity. With a production quota set at 40 million tons a year, the gray-shaded area shows the illegal region. As in the case of price ceilings and price floors, market forces and political forces are in conflict in this illegal region.

The vertical red line labeled "Quota" becomes the supply curve of sugarbeets at prices above $20 a ton.

A Rise in Price The production quota raises the price of sugarbeets. When the government sets a production quota, it leaves market forces free to determine the price. Because the quota decreases the supply of sugarbeets, it raises the price. In Fig. 6.11, with no quota, the price is $30 a ton. With a quota of 40 million tons, the price rises to $50 a ton.

A Decrease in Marginal Cost The production quota lowers the marginal cost of growing sugarbeets. Marginal cost decreases because growers produce less and stop using the resources with the highest marginal cost. Sugarbeet growers slide down their supply (and marginal cost) curves. In Fig. 6.11, marginal cost decreases to $20 a ton.

Inefficiency The production quota results in inefficient underproduction. Marginal social benefit at the quantity produced is equal to the market price, which has increased. Marginal social cost at the quantity produced has decreased and is less than the market price. So marginal social benefit exceeds marginal social cost and a deadweight loss arises.

An Incentive to Cheat and Overproduce The production quota creates an incentive for growers to cheat and produce more than their individual production limit. With the quota, the price exceeds marginal cost, so the grower can get a larger profit by producing one more unit. Of course, if all growers produce more than their assigned limit, the production quota becomes ineffective, and the price falls to the equilibrium (no quota) price.

To make the production quota effective, growers must set up a monitoring system to ensure that no one cheats and overproduces. But it is costly to set up and operate a monitoring system and it is difficult to detect and punish producers who violate their quotas.

Because of the difficulty of operating a quota, producers often lobby governments to establish a quota and provide the monitoring and punishment systems that make it work.

Subsidies

In the United States, the producers of peanuts, sugarbeets, milk, wheat, and many other farm products receive subsidies. A **subsidy** is a payment made by the government to a producer. A large and controversial Farm Bill passed by Congress in 2008 renewed and extended a wide range of subsidies.

The effects of a subsidy are similar to the effects of a tax but they go in the opposite directions. These effects are

- An increase in supply
- A fall in price and increase in quantity produced
- An increase in marginal cost
- Payments by government to farmers
- Inefficient overproduction

Figure 6.12 illustrates the effects of a subsidy to peanut farmers.

An Increase in Supply In Fig. 6.12, with no subsidy, the demand curve D and the supply curve S determine the price of peanuts at $40 a ton and the quantity of peanuts at 40 million tons a year.

Suppose that the government introduces a subsidy of $20 a ton to peanut farmers. A subsidy is like a negative tax. A tax is equivalent to an increase in cost, so a subsidy is equivalent to a decrease in cost. The subsidy brings an increase in supply.

To determine the position of the new supply curve, we subtract the subsidy from the farmers' minimum supply-price. In Fig. 6.12, with no subsidy, farmers are willing to offer 40 million tons a year at a price of $40 a ton. With a subsidy of $20 a ton, they will offer 40 million tons a year if the price is as low as $20 a ton. The supply curve shifts to the red curve labeled $S - subsidy$.

A Fall in Price and Increase in Quantity Produced The subsidy lowers the price of peanuts and increases the quantity produced. In Fig. 6.12, equilibrium occurs where the new supply curve intersects the demand curve at a price of $30 a ton and a quantity of 60 million tons a year.

An Increase in Marginal Cost The subsidy lowers the price paid by consumers but increases the marginal cost of producing peanuts. Marginal cost increases because farmers grow more peanuts, which means that they must begin to use some resources that are less ideal for growing peanuts. Peanut farmers slide up their supply (and marginal cost) curves. In Fig. 6.12, marginal cost increases to $50 a ton.

Payments by Government to Farmers The government pays a subsidy to peanut farmers on each ton of peanuts produced. In this example, farmers increase production to 60 million tons a year and receive a

FIGURE 6.12 The Effects of a Subsidy

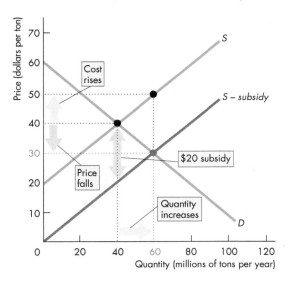

With no subsidy, farmers produce 40 million tons a year at $40 a ton. A subsidy of $20 a ton shifts the supply curve rightward to S – subsidy. The equilibrium quantity increases to 60 million tons a year, the price falls to $30 a ton, and the price plus the subsidy received by farmers rises to $50 a ton. In the new equilibrium, marginal social cost (on the supply curve) exceeds marginal social benefit (on the demand curve) and the subsidy results in inefficient overproduction.

 myeconlab animation

subsidy of $20 a ton. So peanut farmers receive payments from the government that total $1,200 million a year.

Inefficient Overproduction The subsidy results in inefficient overproduction. At the quantity produced with the subsidy, marginal social benefit is equal to the market price, which has fallen. Marginal social cost has increased and it exceeds the market price. Because marginal social cost exceeds marginal social benefit, the increased production brings inefficiency.

Subsidies spill over to the rest of the world. Because a subsidy lowers the domestic market price, subsidized farmers will offer some of their output for sale on the world market. The increase in supply on the world market lowers the price in the rest of the world. Faced with lower prices, farmers in other countries decrease production and receive smaller revenues.

Economics in Action
Rich High-Cost Farmers the Winners

Farm subsidies are a major obstacle to achieving an efficient use of resources in the global markets for farm products and are a source of tension between the United States, Europe, and developing nations.

The United States and the European Union are the world's two largest and richest economies. They also pay their farmers the biggest subsidies, which create inefficient overproduction of food in these rich economies.

At the same time, U.S. and European subsidies make it more difficult for farmers in the developing nations of Africa, Asia, and Central and South America to compete in global food markets. Farmers in these countries can often produce at a lower opportunity cost than the U.S. and European farmers.

Two rich countries, Australia and New Zealand, have stopped subsidizing farmers. The result has been an improvement in the efficiency of farming in these countries. New Zealand is so efficient at producing lamb and dairy products that it has been called the Saudi Arabia of milk (an analogy with Saudi Arabia's huge oil reserve and production.)

International opposition to U.S. and European farm subsidies is strong. Opposition to farm subsidies inside the United States and Europe is growing, but it isn't as strong as the pro-farm lobby, so don't expect an early end to these subsidies.

REVIEW QUIZ

1 Summarize the effects of a production quota on the market price and the quantity produced.
2 Explain why a production quota is inefficient.
3 Explain why a voluntary production quota is difficult to operate.
4 Summarize the effects of a subsidy on the market price and the quantity produced.
5 Explain why a subsidy is inefficient.

You can work these questions in Study Plan 6.4 and get instant feedback.    myeconlab

Governments intervene in some markets by making it illegal to trade in a good. Let's now see how these markets work.

SUMMARY

Key Points

A Housing Market with a Rent Ceiling (pp. 112–114)

- A rent ceiling that is set above the equilibrium rent has no effect.
- A rent ceiling that is set below the equilibrium rent creates a housing shortage, increased search activity, and a black market.
- A rent ceiling that is set below the equilibrium rent is inefficient and unfair.

Working Problems 1 to 6 will give you a better understanding of a housing market with a rent ceiling.

A Labor Market with a Minimum Wage (pp. 115–117)

- A minimum wage set below the equilibrium wage rate has no effect.
- A minimum wage set above the equilibrium wage rate creates unemployment and increases the amount of time people spend searching for a job.
- A minimum wage set above the equilibrium wage rate is inefficient, unfair, and hits low-skilled young people hardest.

Working Problems 7 to 12 will give you a better understanding of a labor market with a minimum wage.

Taxes (pp. 117–122)

- A tax raises the price paid by buyers, but usually by less than the tax.
- The elasticity of demand and the elasticity of supply determine the share of a tax paid by buyers and sellers.
- The less elastic the demand or the more elastic the supply, the larger is the share of the tax paid by buyers.
- If demand is perfectly elastic or supply is perfectly inelastic, sellers pay the entire tax. And if demand is perfectly inelastic or supply is perfectly elastic, buyers pay the entire tax.

Working Problems 13 to 15 will give you a better understanding of taxes.

Production Quotas and Subsidies (pp. 123–125)

- A production quota leads to inefficient underproduction, which raises the price.
- A subsidy is like a negative tax. It lowers the price, increases the cost of production, and leads to inefficient overproduction.

Working Problems 16 and 17 will give you a better understanding of production quotas and subsidies.

Key Terms

Black market, 112
Minimum wage, 115
Price cap, 112
Price ceiling, 112

Price floor, 115
Production quota, 123
Rent ceiling, 112
Search activity, 112

Subsidy, 124
Tax incidence, 117

STUDY PLAN PROBLEMS AND APPLICATIONS

myeconlab You can work Problems 1 to 17 in MyEconLab Chapter 6 Study Plan and get instant feedback.

A Housing Market with a Rent Ceiling (Study Plan 6.1)

Use the following graph of the market for rental housing in Townsville to work Problems 1 and 2.

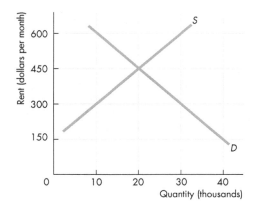

1. a. What are the equilibrium rent and equilibrium quantity of rental housing?
    b. If a rent ceiling is set at $600 a month, what is the quantity of housing rented and what is the shortage of housing?

2. If a rent ceiling is set at $300 a month, what is the quantity of housing rented, the shortage of housing, and the maximum price that someone is willing to pay for the last unit of housing available?

Use the following news clip to work Problems 3 to 6.

Capping Gasoline Prices

As gasoline prices rise, many people are calling for price caps, but price caps generate a distorted reflection of reality, which leads buyers and suppliers to act in ways inconsistent with the price cap. By masking reality, price caps only make matters worse.

Source: *Pittsburgh Tribune-Review*,
September 12, 2005

Suppose that a price ceiling is set below the equilibrium price of gasoline.

3. How does the price cap influence the quantity of gasoline supplied and the quantity demanded?
4. How does the price cap influence
    a. The quantity of gasoline sold and the shortage or surplus of gasoline?
    b. The maximum price that someone is willing to pay for the last gallon of gasoline available on a black market?

5. Draw a graph to illustrate the effects of a price ceiling set below the equilibrium price in the market for gasoline.
6. Explain the various ways in which a price ceiling on gasoline that is set below the equilibrium price would make buyers and sellers of gasoline better off or worse off. What would happen to total surplus and deadweight loss in this market?

A Labor Market with a Minimum Wage

(Study Plan 6.2)

Use the following data to work Problems 7 to 9.
The table gives the demand and supply schedules of teenage labor.

Wage rate (dollars per hour)	Quantity demanded	Quantity supplied
	(hours per month)	
4	3,000	1,000
5	2,500	1,500
6	2,000	2,000
7	1,500	2,500
8	1,000	3,000

7. Calculate the equilibrium wage rate, the number of hours worked, and the quantity of unemployment.
8. If a minimum wage for teenagers is set at $5 an hour, how many hours do they work and how many hours of teenage labor are unemployed?
9. If a minimum wage for teenagers is set at $7 an hour,
    a. How many hours do teenagers work and how many hours are unemployed?
    b. Demand for teenage labor increases by 500 hours a month. What is the wage rate paid to teenagers and how many hours of teenage labor are unemployed?

Use the following news clip to work Problems 10 to 12.

India Steps Up Pressure for Minimum Wage for Its Workers in the Gulf

Oil-rich countries in the [Persian] Gulf, already confronted by strong labor protests, are facing renewed pressure from India to pay minimum wages for unskilled workers. With five million immigrant workers in the region, India is trying to win better conditions for their citizens.

Source: *International Herald Tribune*,
March 27, 2008

Suppose that the Gulf countries paid a minimum wage above the equilibrium wage to Indian workers.

10. How would the market for labor be affected in the Gulf countries? Draw a supply and demand graph to illustrate your answer.

11. How would the market for labor be affected in India? Draw a supply and demand graph to illustrate your answer. [Be careful: the minimum wage is in the Gulf countries, not in India.]

12. Would migrant Indian workers be better off or worse off or unaffected by this minimum wage?

Taxes (Study Plan 6.3)

13. The table gives the demand and supply schedules for chocolate brownies.

Price (cents per brownie)	Quantity demanded	Quantity supplied
	(millions per day)	
50	5	3
60	4	4
70	3	5
80	2	6
90	1	7

a. If brownies are not taxed, what is the price of a brownie and how many are bought?

b. If sellers are taxed 20¢ a brownie, what is the price? How many are sold? Who pays the tax?

c. If buyers are taxed 20¢ a brownie, what is the price? How many are bought? Who pays the tax?

14. **Luxury Tax Heavier Burden on Working Class, it Would Seem**

The Omnibus Budget Reconciliation Act of 1990 included a stern tax on "luxury items." In 1990 the Joint Committee on Taxation projected that the 1991 revenue yield from the luxury taxes would be $31 million. The actual yield was $16.6 million. Why? Because —surprise!—the taxation changed behavior.

Source: *The Topeka Capital-Journal*, October 29, 1999

a. Would buyers or sellers of "luxury items" pay more of the luxury tax?

b. Explain why the luxury tax generated far less tax revenue than was originally anticipated.

15. **How to Take a Gas Holiday**

High fuel prices will probably keep Americans closer to home this summer, despite the gas-tax "holiday" that would shave 18¢ off every gallon.

Source: *Time*, May 19, 2008

Would the price of gasoline that consumers pay fall by 18¢ a gallon? How would consumer surplus change? Explain your answers.

Production Quotas and Subsidies (Study Plan 6.4)

Use the following data to work Problems 16 and 17.

The demand and supply schedules for rice are

Price (dollars per box)	Quantity demanded	Quantity supplied
	(boxes per week)	
1.20	3,000	1,500
1.30	2,750	2,000
1.40	2,500	2,500
1.50	2,250	3,000
1.60	2,000	3,500

16. Calculate the price, the marginal cost of rice, and the quantity produced if the government sets a production quota of 2,000 boxes a week.

17. Calculate the price, the marginal cost of rice, and the quantity produced if the government introduces a subsidy of $0.30 a box.

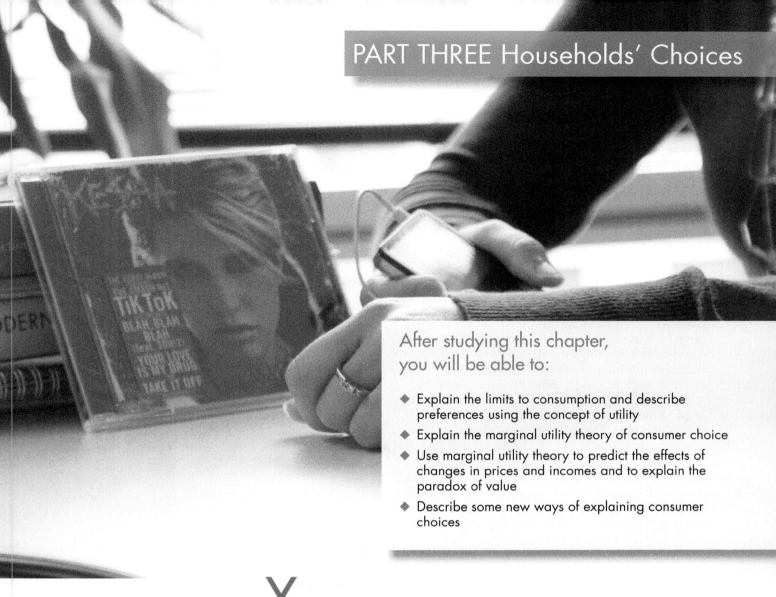

After studying this chapter,
you will be able to:

◆ Explain the limits to consumption and describe preferences using the concept of utility

◆ Explain the marginal utility theory of consumer choice

◆ Use marginal utility theory to predict the effects of changes in prices and incomes and to explain the paradox of value

◆ Describe some new ways of explaining consumer choices

7

UTILITY AND DEMAND

You want Ke$ha's album *Animal*. Will you buy the CD version from Amazon for $11.88, or will you download it from the iTunes store for $7.99? Some people choose a physical CD, others a download. What determines our choices as buyers of recorded music? Also, how much better off are we because we can download an album for less than $10 and some songs for less than $1?

You know that diamonds are expensive and water is cheap. Doesn't that seem odd? Why do we place a higher value on useless diamonds than on essential-to-life water? You can think of many other examples of this paradox. For example, paramedics who save peoples lives get paid a tiny fraction of what a National Hockey League player earns. Do we really place less value on the people who take care of the injured and the sick than we place on those who provide us with entertaining hockey games?

Consumption Choices

The choices that you make as a buyer of goods and services—your consumption choices—are influenced by many factors. We can summarize them under two broad headings:

■ Consumption possibilities
■ Preferences

Consumption Possibilities

Consumption choices are limited by income and by prices. A household has a given amount of income to spend and cannot influence the prices of the goods and services it buys. A household's **budget line** describes the limits to its consumption choices.

Let's look at Lisa's budget line.* Lisa has an income of $40 a month to spend. She buys two goods: movies and soda. The price of a movie is $8, and the price of soda is $4 a case.

Figure 7.1 shows alternative combinations of movies and soda that Lisa can afford. In row A, she sees no movies and buys 10 cases of soda. In row F, she sees 5 movies and buys no soda. Both of these combinations of movies and soda exhaust the $40 available. Check that the combination of movies and soda in each of the other rows also exhausts Lisa's $40 of income. The numbers in the table and the points A through F in the graph describe Lisa's consumption possibilities.

Divisible and Indivisible Goods Some goods—called divisible goods—can be bought in any quantity desired. Examples are gasoline and electricity. We can best understand household choice if we suppose that all goods and services are divisible. For example, Lisa can see half a movie a month on average by seeing one movie every two months. When we think of goods as being divisible, the consumption possibilities are not only the points A through F shown in Fig. 7.1, but also all the intermediate points that form the line running from A to F. This line is Lisa's budget line.

Affordable and Unaffordable Quantities Lisa's budget line is a constraint on her choices. It marks the boundary between what is affordable and what is unaffordable. She can afford any point on the line and inside it. She cannot afford any point outside the line. The constraint on her consumption depends on the prices and her income, and the constraint changes when the price of a good or her income changes. To see how, we use a budget equation.

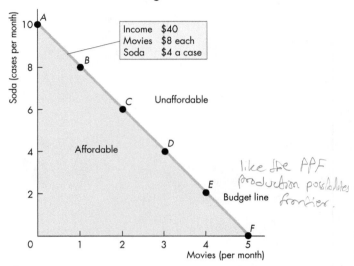

FIGURE 7.1   The Budget Line

Income $40
Movies $8 each
Soda $4 a case

like the PPF production possibilities frontier.

Consumption possibility	Movies (per month)	Soda (cases per month)
A	0	10
B	1	8
C	2	6
D	3	4
E	4	2
F	5	0

Lisa's budget line shows the boundary between what she can and cannot afford. The rows of the table list Lisa's affordable combinations of movies and soda when her income is $40, the price of soda is $4 a case, and the price of a movie is $8. For example, row A tells us that Lisa spends all of her $40 income when she buys 10 cases of soda and sees no movies. The figure graphs Lisa's budget line. Points A through F in the graph represent the rows of the table. For divisible goods, the budget line is the continuous line AF. To calculate the equation for Lisa's budget line, start with expenditure equal to income:

$$\$4Q_S + \$8Q_M = \$40.$$

Divide by $4 to obtain

$$Q_S + 2Q_M = 10.$$

Subtract $2Q_M$ from both sides to obtain

$$Q_S = 10 - 2Q_M.$$

Budget Equation

We can describe the budget line by using a *budget equation*. The budget equation starts with the fact that

$$\text{Expenditure} = \text{Income}.$$

Expenditure is equal to the sum of the price of each good multiplied by the quantity bought. For Lisa,

$$\text{Expenditure} = (\text{Price of soda} \times \text{Quantity of soda})$$
$$+ (\text{Price of movie} \times \text{Quantity of movies}).$$

Call the price of soda P_S, the quantity of soda Q_S, the price of a movie P_M, the quantity of movies Q_M, and income Y. We can now write Lisa's budget equation as

$$P_S Q_S + P_M Q_M = Y.$$

Or, using the prices Lisa faces, $4 a case of soda and $8 a movie, and Lisa's income, $40, we get

$$\$4 Q_S + \$8 Q_M = \$40.$$

Lisa can choose any quantities of soda (Q_S) and movies (Q_M) that satisfy this equation. To find the relationship between these quantities, divide both sides of the equation by the price of soda (P_S) to get

$$Q_S + \frac{P_M}{P_S} \times Q_M = \frac{Y}{P_S}.$$

Now subtract the term (P_M/P_S) × Q_M from both sides of this equation to get

$$Q_S = \frac{Y}{P_S} - \frac{P_M}{P_S} \times Q_M.$$

[handwritten: y-intercept] [handwritten: slope]

For Lisa, income (Y) is $40, the price of a movie (P_M) is $8, and the price of soda (P_S) is $4 a case. So Lisa must choose the quantities of movies and soda to satisfy the equation

$$Q_S = \frac{\$40}{\$4} - \frac{\$8}{\$4} \times Q_M,$$

or

$$Q_S = 10 - 2Q_M.$$

To interpret the equation, look at the budget line in Fig. 7.1 and check that the equation delivers that budget line. First, set Q_M equal to zero. The budget equation tells us that Q_S, the quantity of soda, is Y/P_S, which is 10 cases. This combination of Q_M and Q_S is the one shown in row *A* of the table in Fig. 7.1. Next set Q_M equal to 5. Q_S now equals zero (row *F* of the table). Check that you can derive the other rows.

The budget equation contains two variables chosen by the household (Q_M and Q_S) and two variables that the household takes as given (Y/P_S and P_M/P_S). Let's look more closely at these variables.

Real Income A household's **real income** is its income expressed as a quantity of goods that the household can afford to buy. Expressed in terms of soda, Lisa's real income is Y/P_S. This quantity is the maximum quantity of soda that she can buy. It is equal to her money income divided by the price of soda. Lisa's money income is $40 and the price of soda is $4 a case, so her real income in terms of soda is 10 cases, which is shown in Fig. 7.1 as the point at which the budget line intersects the y-axis.

Relative Price A **relative price** is the price of one good divided by the price of another good. In Lisa's budget equation, the variable P_M/P_S is the relative price of a movie in terms of soda. For Lisa, P_M is $8 a movie and P_S is $4 a case, so P_M/P_S is equal to 2 cases of soda per movie. That is, to see 1 movie, Lisa must give up 2 cases of soda.

[handwritten: x - axis / y - axis]

You've just calculated Lisa's opportunity cost of seeing a movie. Recall that the opportunity cost of an action is the best alternative forgone. For Lisa to see 1 more movie a month, she must forgo 2 cases of soda. You've also calculated Lisa's opportunity cost of soda. For Lisa to buy 2 more cases of soda a month, she must forgo seeing 1 movie. So her opportunity cost of 2 cases of soda is 1 movie.

The relative price of a movie in terms of soda is the magnitude of the slope of Lisa's budget line. To calculate the slope of the budget line, recall the formula for slope (see the Chapter 1 Appendix): Slope equals the change in the variable measured on the y-axis divided by the change in the variable measured on the x-axis as we move along the line. In Lisa's case (Fig. 7.1), the variable measured on the y-axis is the quantity of soda and the variable measured on the x-axis is the quantity of movies. Along Lisa's budget line, as soda decreases from 10 to 0 cases, movies increase from 0 to 5. So the magnitude of the slope of the budget line is 10 cases divided by 5 movies, or 2 cases of soda per movie. The magnitude of this slope is exactly the same as the relative price we've just calculated. It is also the opportunity cost of a movie.

A Change in Prices When prices change, so does the budget line. The lower the price of the good measured on the x-axis, other things remaining the same, the flatter is the budget line. For example, if the price of a movie falls from $8 to $4, real income in terms of soda does not change but the

FIGURE 7.2   Changes in Prices and Income

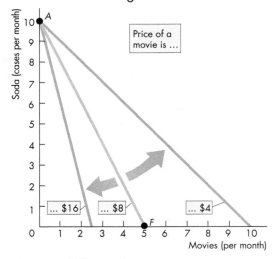

(a) A change in price

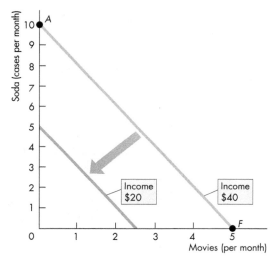

(b) A change in income

In part (a), the price of a movie changes. A fall in the price from $8 to $4 rotates the budget line outward and makes it flatter. A rise in the price from $8 to $16 rotates the budget line inward and makes it steeper.

In part (b), income falls from $40 to $20 while the prices of movies and soda remain the same. The budget line shifts leftward, but its slope does not change.

myeconlab animation

relative price of a movie falls. The budget line rotates outward and becomes flatter, as Fig. 7.2(a) illustrates. The higher the price of the good measured on the *x*-axis, other things remaining the same, the steeper is the budget line. For example, if the price of a movie rises from $8 to $16, the relative price of a movie increases. The budget line rotates inward and becomes steeper, as Fig. 7.2(a) illustrates.

A Change in Income A change in money income changes real income but does not change the relative price. The budget line shifts, but its slope does not change. An increase in money income increases real income and shifts the budget line rightward. A decrease in money income decreases real income and shifts the budget line leftward.

Figure 7.2(b) shows the effect of a change in money income on Lisa's budget line. The initial budget line when Lisa's income is $40 is the same as in Fig. 7.1. The new budget line shows how much Lisa can buy if her income falls to $20 a month. The two budget lines have the same slope because the relative price is the same. The new budget line is closer to the origin because Lisa's real income has decreased.

REVIEW QUIZ

1 What does a household's budget line show?
2 How does the relative price and a household's real income influence its budget line?
3 If a household has an income of $40 and buys only bus rides at $2 each and magazines at $4 each, what is the equation of the household's budget line?
4 If the price of one good changes, what happens to the relative price and the slope of the household's budget line?
5 If a household's money income changes and prices do not change, what happens to the household's real income and budget line?

You can work these questions in Study Plan 7.1 and get instant feedback.

Preferences

Lisa's income and the prices that she faces limit her consumption choices, but she still has lots of choice. The choice that she makes depends on her **preferences**—a description of her likes and dislikes.

You saw one way that economists use to describe preferences in Chapter 2 (p. 32), the concept of *marginal benefit* and the *marginal benefit curve*. But you also saw in Chapter 5 (p. 96) that a marginal benefit curve is also a demand curve. The goal of a theory of consumer choice is to derive the demand curve from a deeper account of how consumers make their buying plans. That is, we want to *explain what determines demand and marginal benefit.*

To achieve this goal, we need a deeper way of describing preferences. One approach to this problem uses the idea of utility, and defines **utility** as the benefit or satisfaction that a person gets from the consumption of goods and services. We distinguish two utility concepts:

- Total utility
- Marginal utility

Total Utility The total benefit that a person gets from the consumption of all the different goods and services is called **total utility**. Total utility depends on the level of consumption—more consumption generally gives more total utility.

To illustrate the concept of total utility, think about Lisa's choices. We tell Lisa that we want to measure her utility from movies and soda. We can use any scale that we wish to measure her total utility and we give her two starting points: (1) We will call the total utility from no movies and no soda zero utility; and (2) We will call the total utility she gets from seeing 1 movie a month 50 units.

We then ask Lisa to tell us, using the same scale, how much she would like 2 movies, and more, up to 10 movies a month. We also ask her to tell us, on the same scale, how much she would like 1 case of soda a month, 2 cases, and more, up to 10 cases a month.

In Table 7.1, the columns headed "Total utility" show Lisa's answers. Looking at those numbers, you can say a lot about how much Lisa likes soda and movies. She says that 1 case of soda gives her 75 units of utility—50 percent more than the utility that she gets from seeing 1 movie. You can also see that her total utility from soda climbs more slowly than her total utility from movies. This difference turns on the second utility concept: *marginal utility.*

TABLE 7.1   Lisa's Utility from Movies and Soda

Movies			Soda		
Quantity (per month)	Total utility	Marginal utility	Cases (per month)	Total utility	Marginal utility
0	0		0	0	
		 50			 75
1	50		1	75	
		 40			 48
2	90		2	123	
		 32			 36
3	122		3	159	
		 28			 24
4	150		4	183	
		 26			 22
5	176		5	205	
		 24			 20
6	200		6	225	
		 22			 13
7	222		7	238	
		 20			 10
8	242		8	248	
		 17			 7
9	259		9	255	
		 16			 5
10	275		10	260	

Marginal Utility We define **marginal utility** as the *change* in total utility that results from a one-unit increase in the quantity of a good consumed.

In Table 7.1, the columns headed "Marginal utility" show Lisa's marginal utility from movies and soda. You can see that if Lisa increases the soda she buys from 1 to 2 cases a month, her total utility from soda increases from 75 units to 123 units. For Lisa, the marginal utility from the second case each month is 48 units (123 − 75).

The marginal utility numbers appear midway between the quantities of soda because it is the *change* in the quantity she buys from 1 to 2 cases that produces the marginal utility of 48 units.

Marginal utility is *positive,* but it *diminishes* as the quantity of a good consumed increases.

Positive Marginal Utility All the things that people enjoy and want more of have a positive marginal utility. Some objects and activities can generate negative marginal utility—and lower total utility. Two examples are hard labor and polluted air. But all the goods and services that people value and that we are thinking about here have positive marginal utility: Total utility increases as the quantity consumed increases.

Diminishing Marginal Utility As Lisa sees more movies, her total utility from movies increases but her marginal utility from movies decreases. Similarly, as she

FIGURE 7.3   Total Utility and Marginal Utility

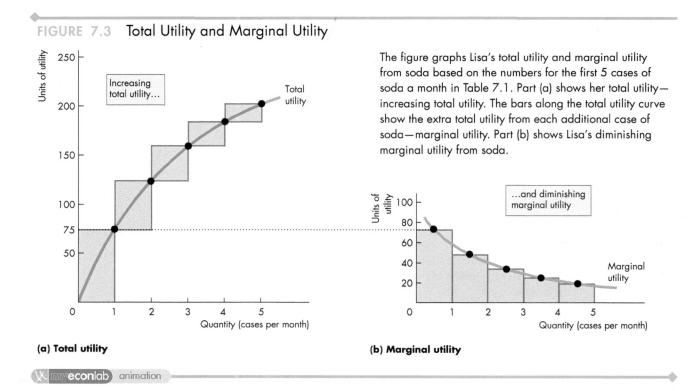

(a) Total utility

(b) Marginal utility

The figure graphs Lisa's total utility and marginal utility from soda based on the numbers for the first 5 cases of soda a month in Table 7.1. Part (a) shows her total utility—increasing total utility. The bars along the total utility curve show the extra total utility from each additional case of soda—marginal utility. Part (b) shows Lisa's diminishing marginal utility from soda.

 myeconlab animation

consumes more soda, her total utility from soda increases but her marginal utility from soda decreases.

The tendency for marginal utility to decrease as the consumption of a good increases is so general and universal that we give it the status of a *principle*—the principle of **diminishing marginal utility**.

You can see Lisa's diminishing marginal utility by calculating a few numbers. Her marginal utility from soda decreases from 75 units from the first case to 48 units from the second case and to 36 units from the third. Her marginal utility from movies decreases from 50 units for the first movie to 40 units for the second and 32 units for the third. Lisa's marginal utility diminishes as she buys more of each good.

Your Diminishing Marginal Utility You've been studying all day and into the evening, and you've been too busy finishing an assignment to shop for soda. A friend drops by with a can of soda. The utility you get from that soda is the marginal utility from your first soda of the day—from *one* can. On another day you've been on a soda binge. You've been working on an assignment, but you've guzzled 10 cans of soda while doing so, and are now totally wired. You are happy enough to have one more can, but the thrill that you get from it is not very large. It is the marginal utility from the *eleventh* can in a day.

Graphing Lisa's Utility Schedules Figure 7.2(a) illustrates Lisa's total utility from soda. The more soda Lisa consumes in a month, the more total utility she gets. Her total utility curve slopes upward.

Figure 7.2(b) illustrates Lisa's marginal utility from soda. It is a graph of the marginal utility numbers in Table 7.1. This graph shows Lisa's diminishing marginal utility from soda. Her marginal utility curve slopes downward as she consumes more soda.

We've described Lisa's consumption possibilities and preferences. Your next task is to see how Lisa chooses what to consume.

REVIEW QUIZ

1 Explain how a consumer's income and the prices of goods limit consumption possibilities.
2 What is utility and how do we use the concept of utility to describe a consumer's preferences?
3 What is the distinction between total utility and marginal utility?
4 What is the key assumption about marginal utility?

You can work these questions in Study Plan 7.1 and get instant feedback.

◆ Utility-Maximizing Choice

Consumers want to get the most utility possible from their limited resources. They make the choice that maximizes utility. To discover this choice, we combine the constraint imposed by the budget and the consumer's preferences and find the point on the budget line that gives the consumer the maximum attainable utility. Let's find Lisa's utility-maximizing choice.

A Spreadsheet Solution

Lisa's most direct way of finding the quantities of movies and soda that maximize her utility is to make a table in a spreadsheet with the information and calculations shown in Table 7.2. Let's see what that table tells us.

Find the Just-Affordable Combinations Table 7.2 shows the combinations of movies and soda that Lisa can afford and that exhaust her $40 income. For example, in row A, Lisa buys only soda and at $4 a case she can buy 10 cases. In row B, Lisa sees 1 movie and buys 8 cases of soda. She spends $8 on the movie. At $4 a case, she spends $32 on soda and can buy 8 cases. The combination in row B just exhausts her $40. The combinations shown in the table are the same as those plotted on her budget line in Fig. 7.1.

We noted that the budget line shows that Lisa can also afford any combination *inside* the budget line. The quantities in those combinations would be smaller than the ones shown in Table 7.2 and they do not exhaust her $40. But smaller quantities don't maximize her utility. Why? The marginal utilities of movies and soda are positive, so the more of each that Lisa buys, the more total utility she gets.

Find the Total Utility for Each Just-Affordable Combination Table 7.2 shows the total utility that Lisa gets from the just-affordable quantities of movies and soda. The second and third columns show the numbers for movies and fourth and fifth columns show those for soda. The center column adds the total utility from movies to the total utility from soda. This number, the total utility from movies *and* soda, is what Lisa wants to maximize.

In row A of the table, Lisa sees no movies and buys 10 cases of soda. She gets no utility from movies and 260 units of utility from soda. Her total utility from movies and soda (the center column) is 260 units.

TABLE 7.2   Lisa's Utility-Maximizing Choice

	Movies $8		Total utility from movies and soda	Soda $4	
	Quantity (per month)	Total utility		Total utility	Cases (per month)
A	0	0	260	260	10
B	1	50	298	248	8
C	2	90	315	225	6
D	3	122	305	183	4
E	4	150	273	123	2
F	5	176	176	0	0

In row C of the table, Lisa sees 2 movies and buys 6 cases of soda. She gets 90 units of utility from movies and 225 units of utility from soda. Her total utility from movies and soda is 315 units. This combination of movies and soda maximizes Lisa's total utility. That is, given the prices of movies and soda, Lisa's best choice when she has $40 to spend is to see 2 movies and buy 6 cases of soda.

If Lisa sees 1 movie, she can buy 8 cases of soda, but she gets only 298 units of total utility—17 units less than the maximum attainable. If she sees 3 movies, she can buy only 4 cases of soda. She gets 305 units of total utility—10 units less than the maximum attainable.

Consumer Equilibrium We've just described Lisa's consumer equilibrium. A **consumer equilibrium** is a situation in which a consumer has allocated all of his or her available income in the way that maximizes his or her total utility, given the prices of goods and services. Lisa's consumer equilibrium is 2 movies and 6 cases of soda.

To find Lisa's consumer equilibrium, we did something that an economist might do but that a consumer is not likely to do: We measured her total utility from all the affordable combinations of movies and soda and then, by inspection of the numbers, selected the combination that gives the highest total utility. There is a more natural way of finding a consumer's equilibrium—a way that uses the idea that choices are made at the margin, as you first met in Chapter 1. Let's look at this approach.

Choosing at the Margin

When you go shopping you don't do utility calculations. But you do decide how to allocate your budget, and you do so in a way that you think is best for you. If you could make yourself better off by spending a few more dollars on an extra unit of one item and the same number of dollars less on something else, you would make that change. So, when you've allocated your budget in the best possible way, you can't make yourself better off by spending more on one item and less on others.

Marginal Utility per Dollar Economists interpret your best possible choice by using the idea of marginal utility per dollar. *Marginal utility* is the increase in total utility that results from consuming *one more unit* of a good. **Marginal utility per dollar** is the *marginal utility* from a good that results from spending *one more dollar* on it.

The distinction between these two marginal concepts is clearest for a good that is infinitely divisible, such as gasoline. You can buy gasoline by the smallest fraction of a gallon and literally choose to spend one more or one less dollar at the pump. The increase in total utility that results from spending one more dollar at the pump is the marginal utility per dollar from gasoline. When you buy a movie ticket or a case of soda, you must spend your dollars in bigger lumps. To buy our marginal movie ticket or case of soda, you must spend the price of one unit and your total utility increases by the marginal utility from that item. So to calculate the marginal utility per dollar for movies (or soda), we must divide marginal utility from the good by its price.

Call the marginal utility from movies MU_M and the price of a movie P_M. Then the *marginal utility per dollar from movies* is

$$MU_M/P_M.$$

Call the marginal utility from soda MU_S and the price of a case of soda P_S. Then the *marginal utility per dollar from soda* is

$$MU_S/P_S.$$

By comparing the marginal utility per dollar from all the goods that a person buys, we can determine whether the budget has been allocated in the way that maximizes total utility.

Let's see how we use the marginal utility per dollar to define a utility-maximizing rule.

Utility-Maximizing Rule A consumer's total utility is maximized by following the rule:

- Spend all the available income
- Equalize the marginal utility per dollar for all goods

Spend All the Available Income Because more consumption brings more utility, only those choices that exhaust income can maximize utility. For Lisa, combinations of movies and soda that leave her with money to spend don't give her as much total utility as those that exhaust her $40 per month income.

Equalize the Marginal Utility per Dollar The basic idea behind this rule is to move dollars from good A to good B if doing so increases the utility from good A by more than it decreases the utility from good B. Such a utility-increasing move is possible if the marginal utility per dollar from good A exceeds that from good B.

But buying more of good A decreases its marginal utility. And buying less of good B increases its marginal utility. So by moving dollars from good A to good B, total utility rises, but the gap between the marginal utilities per dollar gets smaller.

As long as the gap exists—as long as the marginal utility per dollar from good A exceeds that from good B—total utility can be increased by spending more on A and less on B. But when enough dollars have been moved from B to A to make the two marginal utilities per dollar equal, total utility cannot be increased further. Total utility is maximized.

Lisa's Marginal Calculation Let's apply the basic idea to Lisa. To calculate Lisa's marginal utility per dollar, we divide her marginal utility numbers for each quantity of each good by the price of the good. The table in Fig. 7.3 shows these calculations for Lisa, and the graph illustrates the situation on Lisa's budget line. The rows of the table are three of her affordable combinations of movies and soda.

Too Much Soda and Too Few Movies In row B, Lisa sees 1 movie a month and consumes 8 cases of soda a month. Her marginal utility from seeing 1 movie a month is 50 units. Because the price of a movie is $8, Lisa's marginal utility per dollar from movies is 50 units divided by $8, or 6.25 units of utility per dollar.

Lisa's marginal utility from soda when she consumes 8 cases of soda a month is 10 units. Because the price of soda is $4 a case, Lisa's marginal utility per dollar from soda is 10 units divided by $4, or 2.50 units of utility per dollar.

When Lisa sees 1 movie and consumes 8 cases of soda a month, her marginal utility per dollar from soda is *less than* her marginal utility per dollar from movies. That is,

$$MU_S/P_S < MU_M/P_M.$$

If Lisa spent an extra dollar on movies and a dollar less on soda, her total utility would increase. She would get 6.25 units from the extra dollar spent on movies and lose 2.50 units from the dollar less spent on soda. Her total utility would increase by 3.75 units (6.25 − 2.50).

Too Little Soda and Too Many Movies In row *D*, Lisa sees 3 movies a month and consumes 4 cases of soda. Her marginal utility from seeing the third movie a month is 32 units. At a price of $8 a movie, Lisa's marginal utility per dollar from movies is 32 units divided by $8, or 4 units of utility per dollar.

Lisa's marginal utility from soda when she buys 4 cases a month is 24 units. At a price of $4 a case, Lisa's marginal utility per dollar from soda is 24 units divided by $4, or 6 units of utility per dollar.

When Lisa sees 3 movies and consumes 4 cases of soda a month, her marginal utility from soda *exceeds* her marginal utility from movies. That is,

$$MU_S/P_S > MU_M/P_M.$$

If Lisa spent an extra dollar on soda and a dollar less on movies, her total utility would increase. She would get 6 units from the extra dollar spent on soda and she would lose 4 units from the dollar less spent on movies. Her total utility would increase by 2 units (6 − 4).

Utility-Maximizing Movies and Soda In Fig. 7.4, if Lisa moves from row *B* to row *C*, she increases the movies she sees from 1 to 2 a month and decreases the soda she consumes from 8 to 6 cases a month. Her marginal utility per dollar from movies falls to 5 and her marginal utility per dollar from soda rises to 5.

Similarly, if Lisa moves from row *D* to row *C*, she decreases the movies she sees from 3 to 2 a month and increases the soda she consumes from 4 to 6 cases a month. Her marginal utility per dollar from movies rises to 5 and her marginal utility per dollar from soda falls to 5.

When Lisa sees 2 movies and consumes 6 cases of soda a month, her marginal utility per dollar from soda *equals* her marginal utility per dollar from

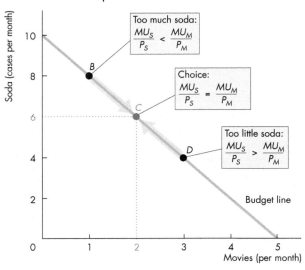

FIGURE 7.4 Equalizing Marginal Utilities per Dollar

	Movies ($8 each)			Soda ($4 per case)		
	Quantity	Marginal utility	Marginal utility per dollar	Cases	Marginal utility	Marginal utility per dollar
B	1	50	6.25	8	10	2.50
C	2	40	5.00	6	20	5.00
D	3	32	4.00	4	24	6.00

The graph shows Lisa's budget line and identifies three points on it. The rows of the table describe these points.

At point *B* (row *B*), with 1 movie and 8 cases of soda, Lisa's marginal utility per dollar from soda is less than that from movies: Buy less soda and see more movies.

At point *D* (row *D*), with 3 movies and 4 cases of soda, Lisa's marginal utility per dollar from soda is greater than that from movies: Buy more soda and see fewer movies.

At point *C* (row *C*), with 2 movies and 6 cases of soda, Lisa's marginal utility per dollar from soda is equal to that from movies: Lisa's utility is maximized.

myeconlab   animation

movies. That is,

$$MU_S/P_S = MU_M/P_M.$$

Lisa can't move from this allocation of her budget without making herself worse off.

The Power of Marginal Analysis

The method we've just used to find Lisa's utility-maximizing choice of movies and soda is an example of the power of marginal analysis. Lisa doesn't need a computer and a spreadsheet program to maximize utility. She can achieve this goal by comparing the marginal gain from having more of one good with the marginal loss from having less of another good.

The rule that she follows is simple: If the marginal utility per dollar from movies exceeds the marginal utility per dollar from soda, see more movies and buy less soda; if the marginal utility per dollar from soda exceeds the marginal utility per dollar from movies, buy more soda and see fewer movies.

More generally, if the marginal gain from an action exceeds the marginal loss, take the action. You will meet this principle time and again in your study of economics, and you will find yourself using it when you make your own economic choices, especially when you must make big decisions.

Revealing Preferences

When we introduced the idea of utility, we arbitrarily chose 50 units as Lisa's total utility from 1 movie, and we pretended that we asked Lisa to tell us how many units of utility she got from different quantities of soda and movies.

You're now about to discover that we don't need to ask Lisa to tell us her preferences. We can figure them out for ourselves by observing what she buys at various prices.

Also, the units in which we measure Lisa's preferences don't matter. Any arbitrary units will work. In this respect, utility is like temperature. Predictions about the freezing point of water don't depend on the temperature scale; and predictions about a household's consumption choice don't depend on the units of utility.

Lisa's Preferences In maximizing total utility by making the marginal utility per dollar equal for all goods, the units in which utility is measured do not matter.

You've seen that when Lisa maximizes her total utility, her marginal utility per dollar from soda, MU_S/P_S, equals her marginal utility per dollar from movies, MU_M/P_M. That is,

$$MU_S/P_S = MU_M/P_M.$$

Multiply both sides of this equation by the price of soda, P_S, to obtain

$$MU_S = MU_M \times (P_S/P_M).$$

This equation says that the marginal utility from soda, MU_S, is equal to the marginal utility from movies, MU_M, multiplied by the ratio of the price of soda, P_S, to the price of a movie, P_M.

The ratio P_S/P_M is the relative price of soda in terms of movies: It is the number of movies that must be forgone to get 1 case of soda. It is also the opportunity cost of soda. (See Chapter 2, p. 29 and Chapter 3, p. 46.)

For Lisa, when P_M = $8 and P_S = $4 we observe that in a month she goes to the movies twice and buys 6 cases of soda. So we know that her MU_S from 6 cases of soda equals her MU_M from 2 movies multiplied by $4/$8 or 0.5. That is, for Lisa, the marginal utility from 6 cases of soda equals one-half of the marginal utility from 2 movies.

If we observe the choices that Lisa makes at more prices, we can find more rows in her utility schedule. By her choices, Lisa reveals her preferences.

Units of Utility Don't Matter Lisa's marginal utility from 2 movies is a half of her marginal utility from 6 cases of soda. So if the marginal utility from the second movie is 40 units, then the marginal utility from the sixth case of soda is 20 units. But if we call the marginal utility from the second movie 50 units, then the marginal utility from the sixth case of soda is 25 units. The units of utility are arbitrary.

◢ REVIEW QUIZ

1 Why does a consumer spend the entire budget?
2 What is the marginal utility per dollar and how is it calculated?
3 What two conditions are met when a consumer is maximizing utility?
4 Explain why equalizing the marginal utility per dollar for all goods maximizes utility.

You can work these questions in Study Plan 7.2 and get instant feedback.

You now understand the marginal utility theory of consumer choices. Your next task is to see what the theory predicts.

◆ Predictions of Marginal Utility Theory

We're now going to use marginal utility theory to make some predictions. You will see that marginal utility theory predicts the law of demand. The theory also predicts that a fall in the price of a substitute of a good decreases the demand for the good and that for a normal good, a rise in income increases demand. All these effects, which in Chapter 3 we simply assumed, are predictions of marginal utility theory.

To derive these predictions, we will study the effects of three events:

■ A fall in the price of a movie
■ A rise in the price of soda
■ A rise in income

A Fall in the Price of a Movie

With the price of a movie at $8 and the price of soda at $4, Lisa is maximizing utility by seeing 2 movies and buying 6 cases of soda each month. Then, with no change in her $40 income and no change in the price of soda, the price of a movie falls from $8 to $4. How does Lisa change her buying plans?

Finding the New Quantities of Movies and Soda
You can find the effect of a fall in the price of a movie on the quantities of movies and soda that Lisa buys in a three-step calculation.

1. Determine the just-affordable combinations of movies and soda at the new prices.

2. Calculate the new marginal utilities per dollar from the good whose price has changed.

3. Determine the quantities of movies and soda that make their marginal utilities per dollar equal.

Affordable Combinations The lower price of a movie means that Lisa can afford more movies or more soda. Table 7.3 shows her new affordable combinations. In row *A*, if she continues to see 2 movies a month, she can now afford 8 cases of soda and in row *B*, if she continues to buy 6 cases of soda, she can now afford 4 movies. Lisa can afford any of the combinations shown in the rows of Table 7.3.

The next step is to find her new marginal utilities per dollar from movies.

New Marginal Utilities per Dollar from Movies A person's preferences don't change just because a price has changed. With no change in her preferences, Lisa's marginal utilities in Table 7.3 are the same as those in Table 7.1. But because the price of a movie has changed, the marginal utility *per dollar* from movies changes. In fact, with a halving of the price of a movie from $8 to $4, the marginal utility per dollar from movies has doubled.

The numbers in Table 7.3 show Lisa's new marginal utility per dollar from movies for each quantity of movies. The table also shows Lisa's marginal utility per dollar from soda for each quantity.

Equalizing the Marginal Utilities per Dollar You can see that if Lisa continues to see 2 movies a month and buy 6 cases of soda, her marginal utility per dollar from movies (row *A*) is 10 units and her marginal utility per dollar from soda (row *B*) is 5 units. Lisa is buying too much soda and too few movies. If she spends a dollar more on movies and a dollar less on soda, her total utility increases by 5 units (10 − 5).

If Lisa continues to buy 6 cases of soda and decreases the number of movies to 4 (row *B*), her

---

◆ TABLE 7.3   How a Change in the Price of Movies Affects Lisa's Choices

	Movies ($4 each)			Soda ($4 per case)		
	Quantity	Marginal utility	Marginal utility per dollar	Cases	Marginal utility	Marginal utility per dollar
	0	0		10	5	1.25
	1	50	12.50	9	7	1.75
A	2	40	**10.00**	8	10	2.50
	3	32	8.00	7	13	3.25
B	4	28	7.00	**6**	20	**5.00**
	5	26	6.50	5	22	5.50
C	6	24	6.00	4	24	6.00
	7	22	5.50	3	36	9.00
	8	20	5.00	2	48	12.00
	9	17	4.25	1	75	18.75
	10	16	4.00	0	0	

marginal utility per dollar from movies falls to 7 units, but her marginal utility per dollar from soda is 5 units. Lisa is still buying too much soda and seeing too few movies. If she spends a dollar more on movies and a dollar less on soda, her total utility increases by 2 units (7 − 5).

But if Lisa sees 6 movies and buys 4 cases of soda a month (row *C*), her marginal utility per dollar from movies (6 units) equals her marginal utility per dollar from soda and she is maximizing utility. If Lisa moves from this allocation of her budget in either direction, her total utility decreases.

Lisa's increased purchases of movies results from a substitution effect—she substitutes the now lower-priced movies for soda—and an income effect—she can afford more movies.

A Change in the Quantity Demanded Lisa's increase in the quantity of movies that she sees is a change in the quantity demanded. It is the change in the quantity of movies that she plans to see each month when the price of a movie changes and all other influences on buying plans remain the same. We illustrate a change in the quantity demanded by a movement along a demand curve.

Figure 7.5(a) shows Lisa's demand curve for movies. When the price of a movie is $8, Lisa sees 2 movies a month. When the price of a movie falls to $4, she sees 6 movies a month. Lisa moves downward along her demand curve for movies.

The demand curve traces the quantities that maximize utility at each price, with all other influences remaining the same. You can also see that utility-maximizing choices generate a downward-sloping demand curve. Utility maximization with diminishing marginal utility implies the law of demand.

A Change in Demand The decrease in the quantity of soda that Lisa buys is the change in the quantity of soda that she plans to buy at a given price of soda when the price of a movie changes. It is a change in her demand for soda. We illustrate a change in demand by a shift of a demand curve.

Figure 7.5(b) shows Lisa's demand curve for soda. The price of soda is fixed at $4 a case. When the price of a movie is $8, Lisa buys 6 cases of soda on demand curve D_0. When the price of a movie falls to $4, Lisa buys 4 cases of soda on demand curve D_1. The fall in the price of a movie decreases Lisa's demand for soda. Her demand curve for soda shifts leftward. For Lisa, soda and movies are substitutes.

FIGURE 7.5   A Fall in the Price of a Movie

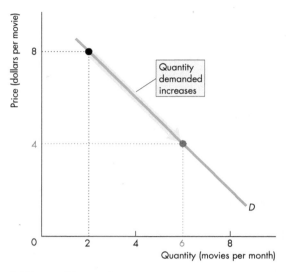

(a) Demand for movies

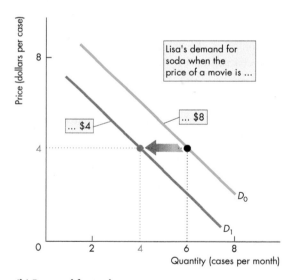

(b) Demand for soda

When the price of a movie falls and the price of soda remains the same, the quantity of movies demanded by Lisa increases, and in part (a), Lisa moves along her demand curve for movies. Also, when the price of a movie falls, Lisa's demand for soda decreases, and in part (b), her demand curve for soda shifts leftward. For Lisa, soda and movies are substitutes.

myeconlab animation

A Rise in the Price of Soda

Now suppose that with the price of a movie at $4, the price of soda rises from $4 to $8 a case. How does this price change influence Lisa's buying plans? We find the answer by repeating the three-step calculation with the new price of soda.

Table 7.4 shows Lisa's new affordable combinations. In row *A*, if she continues to buy 4 cases of soda a month she can afford to see only 2 movies; and in row *B*, if she continues to see 6 movies a month, she can afford only 2 cases of soda.

Table 7.4 show Lisa's marginal utility per dollar from soda for each quantity of soda when the price is $8 a case. The table also shows Lisa's marginal utility per dollar from movies for each quantity.

If Lisa continues to buy 4 cases of soda (row *A*), her marginal utility per dollar from soda is 3. But she must cut the movies she sees to 2, which increases her marginal utility per dollar from movies to 10. Lisa is buying too much soda and too few movies. If she spends a dollar less on soda and a dollar more on movies, her utility increases by 7 units (10 − 3) .

But if Lisa sees 6 movies a month and cuts her soda to 2 cases (row *B*), her marginal utility per dollar from movies (6 units) equals her marginal utility per dollar from soda. She is maximizing utility.

Lisa's decreased purchases of soda results from an income effect—she can afford fewer cases and she buys fewer cases. But she continues to buy the same quantity of movies.

Lisa's Demand for Soda

Now that we've calculated the effect of a change in the price of soda on Lisa's buying plans when income and the price of movies remain the same, we have found two points on her demand curve for soda: When the price of soda is $4 a case, Lisa buys 4 cases a month; and when the price of soda is $8 a case, she buys 2 cases a month.

Figure 7.6 shows these points on Lisa's demand curve for soda. It also shows the change in the quantity of soda demanded when the price of soda rises and all other influences on Lisa's buying plans remain the same.

In this example, Lisa continues to buy the same quantity of movies, but this outcome does not always occur. It is a consequence of Lisa's preferences. With different marginal utilities, she might have decreased or increased the quantity of movies that she sees when the price of soda changes.

You've seen that marginal utility theory predicts the law of demand—the way in which the quantity demanded of a good changes when its price changes. Next, we'll see how marginal utility theory predicts the effect of a change in income on demand.

TABLE 7.4   How a Change in the Price of
            Soda Affects Lisa's Choices

	Movies ($4 each)			Soda ($8 per case)		
	Quantity	Marginal utility	Marginal utility per dollar	Cases	Marginal utility	Marginal utility per dollar
	0	0		5	22	2.75
A	2	40	10.00	**4**	24	**3.00**
	4	28	7.00	3	36	4.50
B	6	24	6.00	2	48	6.00
	8	20	5.00	1	75	9.38
	10	16	4.00	0	0	

FIGURE 7.6   A Rise in the Price of Soda

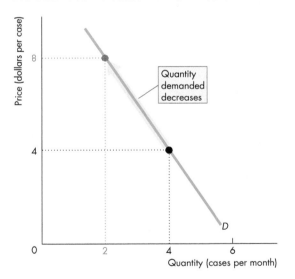

When the price of soda rises and the price of a movie and Lisa's income remain the same, the quantity of soda demanded by Lisa decreases. Lisa moves along her demand curve for soda.

A Rise in Income

Suppose that Lisa's income increases from $40 to $56 a month and that the price of a movie is $4 and the price of soda is $4 a case. With these prices and with an income of $40 a month, Lisa sees 6 movies and buys 4 cases of soda a month (Table 7.3). How does the increase in Lisa's income from $40 to $56 change her buying plans?

Table 7.5 shows the calculations needed to answer this question. If Lisa continues to see 6 movies a month, she can now afford to buy 8 cases of soda (row A); if she continues to buy 4 cases of soda, she can now afford to see 10 movies (row C).

In row A, Lisa's marginal utility per dollar from movies is greater than her marginal utility per dollar from soda. She is buying too much soda and too few movies. In row C, Lisa's marginal utility per dollar from movies is less than her marginal utility per dollar from soda. She is buying too little soda and too many movies. But in row B, when Lisa sees 8 movies a month and buys 6 cases of soda, her marginal utility per dollar from movies equals that from soda. She is maximizing utility.

Figure 7.7 shows the effects of the rise in Lisa's income on her demand curves for movies and soda. The price of each good is $4. When Lisa's income

TABLE 7.5   Lisa's Choices with an Income of $56 a Month

	Movies ($4 each)			Soda ($4 per case)		
	Quantity	Marginal utility	Marginal utility per dollar	Cases	Marginal utility	Marginal utility per dollar
	4	28	7.00	10	5	1.25
	5	26	6.50	9	7	1.75
A	6	24	**6.00**	8	10	2.50
	7	22	5.50	7	13	3.25
B	8	20	5.00	6	20	5.00
	9	17	4.25	5	22	5.50
C	10	16	4.00	4	24	**6.00**

rises to $56 a month, she sees 2 more movies and buys 2 more cases of soda. Her demand curves for both movies and soda shift rightward—her demand for both movies and soda increases. With a larger income, the consumer always buys more of a *normal* good. For Lisa, movies and soda are normal goods.

FIGURE 7.7   The Effects of a Rise in Income

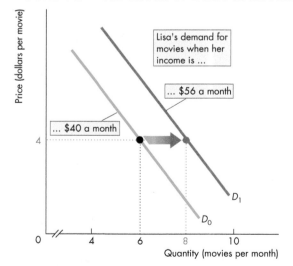

(a) Demand for movies

When Lisa's income increases, her demand for movies and her demand for soda increase. Lisa's demand curves for

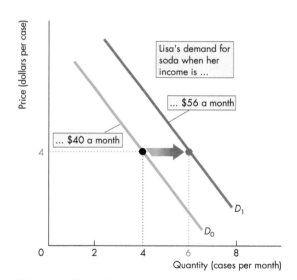

(b) Demand for soda

movies, in part (a), and for soda, in part (b), shift rightward. For Lisa, movies and soda are normal goods.

The Paradox of Value

The price of water is low and the price of a diamond is high, but water is essential to life while diamonds are used mostly for decoration. How can valuable water be so cheap while a relatively useless diamond is so expensive? This so-called *paradox of value* has puzzled philosophers for centuries. Not until the theory of marginal utility had been developed could anyone give a satisfactory answer.

The Paradox Resolved The paradox is resolved by distinguishing between *total* utility and *marginal* utility. The total utility that we get from water is enormous. But remember, the more we consume of something, the smaller is its marginal utility.

We use so much water that its marginal utility—the benefit we get from one more glass of water or another 30 seconds in the shower—diminishes to a small value.

Diamonds, on the other hand, have a small total utility relative to water, but because we buy few diamonds, they have a high marginal utility.

When a household has maximized its total utility, it has allocated its income in the way that makes the marginal utility per dollar equal for all goods. That is, the marginal utility from a good divided by the price of the good is equal for all goods.

This equality of marginal utilities per dollar holds true for diamonds and water: Diamonds have a high price and a high marginal utility. Water has a low price and a low marginal utility. When the high marginal utility from diamonds is divided by the high price of a diamond, the result is a number that equals the low marginal utility from water divided by the low price of water. The marginal utility per dollar is the same for diamonds and water.

Value and Consumer Surplus Another way to think about the paradox of value and illustrate how it is resolved uses *consumer surplus*. Figure 7.8 explains the paradox of value by using this idea. The supply of water in part (a) is perfectly elastic at price P_W, so the quantity of water consumed is Q_W and the large green area shows the consumer surplus from water. The supply of diamonds in part (b) is perfectly inelastic at the quantity Q_D, so the price of a diamond is P_D and the small green area shows the consumer surplus from diamonds. Water is cheap, but brings a large consumer surplus; diamonds are expensive, but bring a small consumer surplus.

FIGURE 7.8   The Paradox of Value

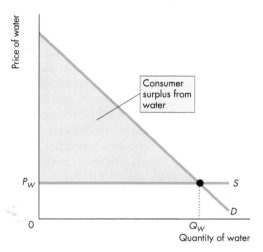

(a) Water

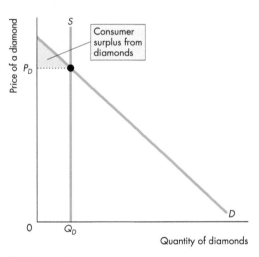

(b) Diamonds

Part (a) shows the demand for and supply of water. Supply is perfectly elastic at the price P_W. At this price, the quantity of water consumed is Q_W and the large green triangle shows consumer surplus. Part (b) shows the demand for and supply of diamonds. Supply is perfectly inelastic at the quantity Q_D. At this quantity, the price of a diamond is P_D and the small green triangle shows consumer surplus. Water is valuable—has a large consumer surplus—but cheap. Diamonds are less valuable than water—have a smaller consumer surplus—but are expensive.

Temperature: An Analogy

Utility is similar to temperature—both are abstract concepts. You can't *observe* temperature. You can observe water turning to steam if it is hot enough or turning to ice if it is cold enough. You can also construct an instrument—a thermometer—that can help you to predict when such changes will occur. We call the scale on the thermometer *temperature* and we call the units of temperature *degrees*. But like the units of utility, these degree units are arbitrary. We can use Celsius units or Fahrenheit units or some other units.

The concept of utility helps us to make predictions about consumption choices in much the same way that the concept of temperature helps us to make predictions about physical phenomena.

Admittedly, marginal utility theory does not enable us to predict how buying plans change with the same precision that a thermometer enables us to predict when water will turn to ice or steam. But the theory provides important insights into buying plans and has some powerful implications. It helps us to understand why people buy more of a good or service when its price falls and why people buy more of most goods when their incomes increase. It also resolves the paradox of value.

We're going to end this chapter by looking at some new ways of studying individual economic choices and consumer behavior.

REVIEW QUIZ

1 When the price of a good falls and the prices of other goods and a consumer's income remain the same, explain what happens to the consumption of the good whose price has fallen and to the consumption of other goods.

2 Elaborate on your answer to the previous question by using demand curves. For which good does demand change and for which good does the quantity demanded change?

3 If a consumer's income increases and if all goods are normal goods, explain how the quantity bought of each good changes.

4 What is the paradox of value and how is the paradox resolved?

5 What are the similarities between utility and temperature?

You can work these questions in Study Plan 7.3 and get instant feedback. myeconlab

Economics in Action

Maximizing Utility from Recorded Music

In 2007, Americans spent $10 billion on recorded music, down from $14 billion in 2000. But the combined quantity of discs and downloads bought increased from 1 billion in 2000 to 1.8 billion in 2007 and the average price of a unit of recorded music fell from $14 to $5.50.

The average price fell because the mix of formats bought changed dramatically. In 2000, we bought 940 million CDs; in 2007, we bought only 500 million CDs and downloaded 1.2 billion music files.

Figure 1 shows the longer history of the changing formats of recorded music.

The music that we buy isn't just one good—it is several goods. Singles and albums are different goods; downloads and discs are different goods; and downloads to a computer and downloads to a cell phone are different goods. There are five major categories and the table shows the quantities of each that we bought in 2007 (excluding DVDs and cassettes).

Format	Singles	Albums
	(millions in 2007)	
Disc	3	500
Download	800	40
Mobile	400	–

Source of data: Recording Industry Association of America.

Most people buy all their music in digital form, but many still buy physical CDs and some people buy both downloads and CDs.

We get utility from the singles and albums that we buy, and the more songs and albums we have, the more utility we get. But our marginal utility from songs and albums decreases as the quantity that we own increases.

We also get utility from convenience. A song that we can buy with a mouse click and play with the spin of a wheel is more convenient both to buy and to use than a song on a CD. The convenience of songs downloaded over the Internet means that, song for song, we get more utility from a song downloaded than we get from a song on a physical CD.

But most albums are still played at home on a CD player. So for most people, a physical CD is a more convenient medium for delivering an album. Album for album, people on average get more utility from a CD than from a download.

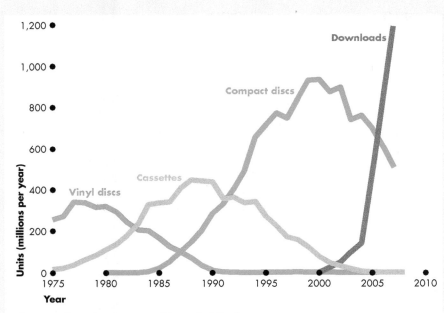

Figure 1 Changing Formats of Recorded Music
Graph from www.swivel.com.

In the 1970s, recorded music came on vinyl discs. Cassettes gradually replaced vinyl, then compact discs (CDs) gradually replaced cassettes, and today, digital files downloaded to computers and mobile devices are replacing physical CDs.

When we decide how many singles and albums to download and how many to buy on CD, we compare the marginal utility per dollar from each type of music in each format. We make the marginal utility per dollar from each type of music in each format equal, as the equations below show.

The market for single downloads has created an enormous consumer surplus. The table shows that the quantity of single downloads demanded at 99 cents each was 800 million in 2007, and the quantity of singles on a disc demanded at $4.75 a disc was 3 million in 2007. If we assume that $4.75 is the most that anyone would pay for a single download (probably an underestimate), the demand curve for single downloads is that shown in Fig. 2.

With the price of a single download at $0.99, consumer surplus (the area of the green triangle in Fig. 2) is $1.5 billion.

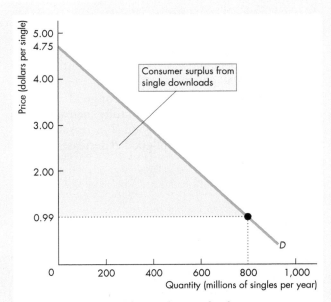

Figure 2 The Demand for Single Downloads

$$\frac{MU_{single\ downloads}}{P_{single\ downloads}} = \frac{MU_{album\ downloads}}{P_{album\ downloads}} = \frac{MU_{physical\ singles}}{P_{physical\ singles}} = \frac{MU_{physical\ albums}}{P_{physical\ albums}} = \frac{MU_{mobile}}{P_{mobile}}$$

$$\frac{MU_{single\ downloads}}{\$0.99} = \frac{MU_{album\ downloads}}{\$10} = \frac{MU_{physical\ singles}}{\$4.75} = \frac{MU_{physical\ albums}}{\$15} = \frac{MU_{mobile}}{\$2.50}$$

SUMMARY

Key Points

Consumption Possibilities (pp. 130–134)

- The budget line is the boundary between what a household can and cannot afford, given its income and the prices of goods.
- The point at which the budget line intersects the *y*-axis is the household's real income in terms of the good measured on that axis.
- The magnitude of the slope of the budget line is the relative price of the good measured on the *x*-axis in terms of the good measured on the *y*-axis.
- A change in the price of one good changes the slope of the budget line. A change in income shifts the budget line but does not change its slope.

Working Problems 1 to 10 will give you a better understanding of consumption possibilities.

Utility-Maximizing Choice (pp. 135–138)

- A consumer's objective is to maximize total utility.
- Total utility is maximized when all the available income is spent and when the marginal utility per dollar from all goods is equal.
- If the marginal utility per dollar for good *A* exceeds that for good *B*, total utility increases if the quantity purchased of good *A* increases and the quantity purchased of good *B* decreases.

Working Problems 11 to 16 will give you a better understanding of a consumer's utility-maximizing choice.

Predictions of Marginal Utility Theory (pp. 139–145)

- Marginal utility theory predicts the law of demand. That is, other things remaining the same, the higher the price of a good, the smaller is the quantity demanded of that good.
- Marginal utility theory also predicts that, other things remaining the same, an increase in the consumer's income increases the demand for a normal good.
- Marginal utility theory resolves the paradox of value.
- Total value is *total* utility or consumer surplus. But price is related to *marginal* utility.
- Water, which we consume in large amounts, has a high total utility and a large consumer surplus, but the price of water is low and the marginal utility from water is low.
- Diamonds, which we buy in small quantities, have a low total utility and a small consumer surplus, but the price of a diamond is high and the marginal utility from diamonds is high.

Working Problems 17 to 26 will give you a better understanding of the predictions of marginal utility theory.

Key Terms

Budget line, 130
Consumer equilibrium, 135
Diminishing marginal utility, 134

Marginal utility, 133
Marginal utility per dollar, 136
Preferences, 133

Total utility, 133
Utility, 133

STUDY PLAN PROBLEMS AND APPLICATIONS

 You can work Problems 1 to 26 in MyEconLab Chapter 7 Study Plan and get instant feedback.

Consumption Possibilities (Study Plan 7.1)

Use the following information to work Problems 1 to 4.

Sara's income is $12 a week. The price of popcorn is $3 a bag, and the price of a smoothie is $3.

1. Calculate Sara's real income in terms of smoothies. Calculate her real income in terms of popcorn.
2. What is the relative price of smoothies in terms of popcorn? What is the opportunity cost of a smoothie?
3. Calculate the equation for Sara's budget line (with bags of popcorn on the left side).
4. Draw a graph of Sara's budget line with the quantity of smoothies on the *x*-axis. What is the slope of Sara's budget line? What determines its value?

Use the following information to work Problems 5 to 8.

Sara's income falls from $12 to $9 a week, while the price of popcorn is unchanged at $3 a bag and the price of a smoothie is unchanged at $3.

5. What is the effect of the fall in Sara's income on her real income in terms of smoothies?
6. What is the effect of the fall in Sara's income on her real income in terms of popcorn?
7. What is the effect of the fall in Sara's income on the relative price of a smoothie in terms of popcorn?
8. What is the slope of Sara's new budget line if it is drawn with smoothies on the *x*-axis?

Use the following information to work Problems 9 and 10.

Sara's income is $12 a week. The price of popcorn rises from $3 to $6 a bag, and the price of a smoothie is unchanged at $3.

9. What is the effect of the rise in the price of popcorn on Sara's real income in terms of smoothies and her real income in terms of popcorn?
10. What is the effect of the rise in the price of popcorn on the relative price of a smoothie in terms of popcorn? What is the slope of Sara's new budget line if it is drawn with smoothies on the *x*-axis?

Utility-Maximizing Choice (Study Plan 7.2)

11. Make a table that shows the various combinations of hours spent windsurfing and snorkeling that Max can afford.
12. In your table in Problem 11, add two columns and list Max's marginal utility per dollar from windsurfing and from snorkeling.
13. a. How many hours does Max windsurf and how many hours does he snorkel to maximize his utility?
    b. If Max spent a dollar more on windsurfing and a dollar less on snorkeling than in part (a), by how much would his total utility change?
    c. If Max spent a dollar less on windsurfing and a dollar more on snorkeling than in part (a), by how much would his total utility change?
14. Explain why, if Max equalized the marginal utility per hour from windsurfing and from snorkeling, he would *not* maximize his utility.
15. **Schools Get a Lesson in Lunch Line Economics**
    Sharp rises in the cost of milk, grain, and fresh fruits and vegetables are hitting cafeterias across the country, forcing cash-strapped schools to raise prices or serve more economical dishes. For example, Fairfax schools serve oranges —14¢ each—instead of grapes, which are 25¢ a serving.
    Source: *The Washington Post*, April 14, 2008
    Assume that a Fairfax school has a $14 daily fruit budget.
    a. How many oranges a day can the school afford to serve if it serves no grapes? How many servings of grapes can the school afford each day if it serves no oranges?
    b. If the school provides 50 oranges a day and maximizes utility, how many servings of grapes does it provide? If the marginal utility from an orange is 14 units, what is the marginal utility from a serving of grapes?
16. **Can Money Buy Happiness?**
    Whoever said money can't buy happiness isn't spending it right. There must be some connection, but once your basic human needs are met, does more money buy more happiness? An increase in income from $20,000 a year to

$50,000 makes you twice as likely to be happy, but the payoff from more than $90,000 is slight.

Source: CNN, July 18, 2006

a. What does the fundamental assumption of marginal utility theory suggest about the connection between money and happiness?

b. Explain why this news clip is consistent with marginal utility theory.

Predictions of Marginal Utility Theory

(Study Plan 7.3)

Use the following news clip to work Problems 17 to 21.

17. Max is offered a special deal: The price of renting windsurfing equipment is cut to $5 an hour. How many hours does Max spend windsurfing and how many hours does he spend snorkeling?

18. Draw Max's demand curve for rented windsurfing equipment. Over the price range from $5 to $10 an hour, is Max's demand for windsurfing equipment elastic or inelastic?

19. How does Max's demand for snorkeling equipment change when the price of windsurfing equipment falls? What is Max's cross elasticity of demand for snorkeling with respect to the price of windsurfing? Are windsurfing and snorkeling substitutes or complements for Max?

20. If Max's income increases from $35 to $55 a day, how does his demand for rented windsurfing equipment change? Is windsurfing a normal good or an inferior good for Max? Explain.

21. If Max's income increases from $35 to $55 a day, how does his demand for rented snorkeling equipment change? Is snorkeling a normal good or an inferior good for Max? Explain.

Use the following news clip to work Problems 22 and 23.

Compared to Other Liquids, Gasoline is Cheap

In 2008, when gasoline hit $4 a gallon, motorists complained, but they didn't complain about $1.59 for a 20-oz Gatorade and $18 for 16 mL of HP ink.

Source: *The New York Times*, May 27, 2008

The prices per gallon are $10.17 for Gatorade and $4,294.58 for printer ink.

22. a. What does marginal utility theory predict about the marginal utility per dollar from gasoline, Gatorade, and printer ink?

b. What do the prices per gallon tell you about the marginal utility from a gallon of gasoline, Gatorade, and printer ink?

23. a. What do the prices per unit reported in the news clip tell you about the marginal utility from a gallon of gasoline, a 20-oz bottle of Gatorade, and a cartridge of printer ink?

b. How can the paradox of value be used to explain why the fluids listed in the news clip might be less valuable than gasoline, yet far more expensive?

Use the following news clip to work Problems 24 to 26.

Exclusive Status: It's in The Bag; $52,500 Purses. 24 Worldwide. 1 in Washington.

Forget your Coach purse. Put away your Kate Spade. Even Hermes's famous Birkin bag seems positively discount. The Louis Vuitton Tribute Patchwork is this summer's ultimate status bag, ringing in at $52,500, and the company is offering only five for sale in North America and 24 worldwide.

Source: *The Washington Post*, August 21, 2007

24. Use marginal utility theory to explain the facts reported in the news clip.

25. If Louis Vuitton offered 500 Tribute Patchwork bags in North America and 2,400 worldwide, what do you predict would happen to the price that buyers would be willing to pay and what would happen to the consumer surplus?

26. If the Tribute Patchwork bag is copied and thousands are sold illegally, what do you predict would happen to the price that buyers would be willing to pay for a genuine bag and what would happen to the consumer surplus?

8

POSSIBILITIES, PREFERENCES, AND CHOICES

After studying this chapter,
you will be able to:

◆ Describe a household's budget line and show how it changes when prices or income change

◆ Use indifference curves to map preferences and explain the principle of diminishing marginal rate of substitution

◆ Predict the effects of changes in prices and income on consumption choices

You buy your music online and play it on an iPod. And as the prices of a music download and an iPod have tumbled, the volume of downloads and sales of iPods have skyrocketed.

The price of a DVD rental has also fallen and we're renting ever more of them. But we're also going to movie theaters in ever-greater numbers. Why are we going to the movies more when it is so cheap and easy to rent a DVD?

The price of electronic books—e-books—and electronic readers such as Amazon's Kindle are also falling. But most students continue to buy printed textbooks and in the entire $24-billion book market, e-books contribute only 1.3 percent of the total revenue.

Why have downloading music and watching movies on DVD become so popular while downloading e-books has made only a tiny inroad into the overall market for books?

In this chapter, we're going to study a model of choice that answers questions like the ones just posed. We'll use this model to explain the choices we make about movies, and at the end of the chapter in *Reading Between the Lines*, to explain why e-books are only slowly replacing printed books.

Preferences and Indifference Curves

You are going to discover a very cool idea: that of drawing a map of a person's preferences. A preference map is based on the intuitively appealing idea that people can sort all the possible combinations of goods into three groups: preferred, not preferred, and indifferent. To make this idea more concrete, let's ask Lisa to tell us how she ranks various combinations of movies and soda.

Figure 8.1 shows part of Lisa's answer. She tells us that she currently sees 2 movies and buys 6 cases of soda a month at point C. She then lists all the combinations of movies and soda that she says are just as acceptable to her as her current situation. When we plot these combinations of movies and soda, we get the green curve in Fig. 8.1(a). This curve is the key element in a preference map and is called an indifference curve.

An **indifference curve** is a line that shows combinations of goods among which a consumer is *indifferent*. The indifference curve in Fig. 8.1(a) tells us that Lisa is just as happy to see 2 movies and buy 6 cases of soda a month at point C as she is to have the combination of movies and soda at point G or at any other point along the curve.

Lisa also says that she prefers all the combinations of movies and soda above the indifference curve in Fig. 8.1(a)—the yellow area—to those on the indifference curve. And she prefers any combination on the indifference curve to any combination in the gray area below the indifference curve.

The indifference curve in Fig. 8.1(a) is just one of a whole family of such curves. This indifference curve appears again in Fig. 8.1(b), labeled I_1. The curves labeled I_0 and I_2 are two other indifference curves. Lisa prefers any point on indifference curve I_2 to any point on indifference curve I_1, and she prefers any point on I_1 to any point on I_0. We refer to I_2 as being a higher indifference curve than I_1 and I_1 as being higher than I_0.

A preference map is a series of indifference curves that resemble the contour lines on a map. By looking at the shape of the contour lines on a map, we can draw conclusions about the terrain. Similarly, by looking at the shape of the indifference curves, we can draw conclusions about a person's preferences.

Let's learn how to "read" a preference map.

FIGURE 8.1   A Preference Map

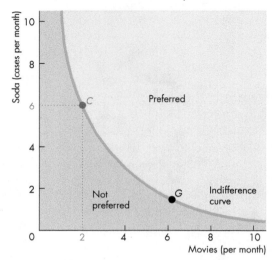

(a) An indifference curve

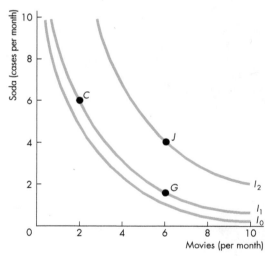

(b) Lisa's preference map

Part (a) shows one of Lisa's indifference curves. She is indifferent between point C (with 2 movies and 6 cases of soda) and all other points on the green indifference curve, such as G. She prefers points above the indifference curve (in the yellow area) to points on it, and she prefers points on the indifference curve to points below it (in the gray area).

Part (b) shows three of the indifference curves—I_0, I_1, and I_2—in Lisa's preference map. She prefers point J to point C or G, and she prefers all the points on I_2 to those on I_1.

Marginal Rate of Substitution

The **marginal rate of substitution** (*MRS*) is the rate at which a person will give up good *y* (the good measured on the *y*-axis) to get an additional unit of good *x* (the good measured on the *x*-axis) while remaining indifferent (remaining on the same indifference curve). The magnitude of the slope of an indifference curve measures the marginal rate of substitution.

■ If the indifference curve is *steep*, the marginal rate of substitution is *high*. The person is willing to give up a large quantity of good *y* to get an additional unit of good *x* while remaining indifferent.

■ If the indifference curve is *flat*, the marginal rate of substitution is *low*. The person is willing to give up a small amount of good *y* to get an additional unit of good *x* while remaining indifferent.

Figure 8.2 shows you how to calculate the marginal rate of substitution.

At point *C* on indifference curve I_1, Lisa buys 6 cases of soda and sees 2 movies. Her marginal rate of substitution is the magnitude of the slope of the indifference curve at point *C*. To measure this magnitude, place a straight line against, or tangent to, the indifference curve at point *C*. Along that line, as the quantity of soda decreases by 10 cases, the number of movies increases by 5—or 2 cases per movie. At point *C*, Lisa is willing to give up soda for movies at the rate of 2 cases per movie—a marginal rate of substitution of 2.

At point *G* on indifference curve I_1, Lisa buys 1.5 cases of soda and sees 6 movies. Her marginal rate of substitution is measured by the slope of the indifference curve at point *G*. That slope is the same as the slope of the tangent to the indifference curve at point *G*. Now, as the quantity of soda decreases by 4.5 cases, the number of movies increases by 9—or 1/2 case per movie. At point *G*, Lisa is willing to give up soda for movies at the rate of 1/2 case per movie—a marginal rate of substitution of 1/2.

As Lisa sees more movies and buys less soda, her marginal rate of substitution diminishes. Diminishing marginal rate of substitution is the key assumption about preferences. A **diminishing marginal rate of substitution** is a general tendency for a person to be willing to give up less of good *y* to get one more unit of good *x*, while at the same time remaining indifferent as the quantity of *x* increases. In Lisa's case, she is less willing to give up soda to see one more movie as the number of movies she sees increases.

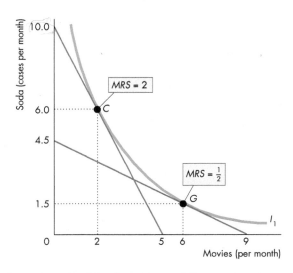

FIGURE 8.2   The Marginal Rate of Substitution

The magnitude of the slope of an indifference curve is called the marginal rate of substitution (MRS). The red line at point *C* tells us that Lisa is willing to give up 10 cases of soda to see 5 movies. Her marginal rate of substitution at point *C* is 10 divided by 5, which equals 2. The red line at point *G* tells us that Lisa is willing to give up 4.5 cases of soda to see 9 movies. Her marginal rate of substitution at point *G* is 4.5 divided by 9, which equals 1/2.

myeconlab animation

Your Diminishing Marginal Rate of Substitution

Think about your own diminishing marginal rate of substitution. Imagine that in a week, you drink 10 cases of soda and see no movies. Most likely, you are willing to give up a lot of soda so that you can see just 1 movie. But now imagine that in a week, you buy 1 case of soda and see 6 movies. Most likely, you will now not be willing to give up much soda to see a seventh movie. As a general rule, the greater the number of movies you see, the smaller is the quantity of soda you are willing to give up to see one additional movie.

The shape of a person's indifference curves incorporates the principle of the diminishing marginal rate of substitution because the curves are bowed toward the origin. The tightness of the bend of an indifference curve tells us how willing a person is to substitute one good for another while remaining indifferent. Let's look at some examples that make this point clear.

Degree of Substitutability

Most of us would not regard movies and soda as being *close* substitutes, but they are substitutes. No matter how much you love soda, some increase in the number of movies you see will compensate you for being deprived of a can of soda. Similarly, no matter how much you love going to the movies, some number of cans of soda will compensate you for being deprived of seeing one movie. A person's indifference curves for movies and soda might look something like those for most ordinary goods and services shown in Fig. 8.3(a).

Close Substitutes Some goods substitute so easily for each other that most of us do not even notice which we are consuming. The different brands of marker pens and pencils are examples. Most people don't care which brand of these items they use or where they buy them. A marker pen from the campus bookstore is just as good as one from the local grocery store. You would be willing to forgo a pen from the campus store if you could get one more pen from the local grocery store. When two goods are perfect substitutes, their indifference curves are straight lines that slope downward, as Fig. 8.3(b) illustrates. The marginal rate of substitution is constant.

Complements Some goods do not substitute for each other at all. Instead, they are complements. The complements in Fig. 8.3(c) are left and right running shoes. Indifference curves of perfect complements are L-shaped. One left running shoe and one right running shoe are as good as one left shoe and two right shoes. Having two of each is preferred to having one of each, but having two of one and one of the other is no better than having one of each.

The extreme cases of perfect substitutes and perfect complements shown here don't often happen in reality, but they do illustrate that the shape of the indifference curve shows the degree of substitutability between two goods. The closer the two goods are to perfect substitutes, the closer the marginal rate of substitution is to being constant (a straight line), rather than diminishing (a curved line). Indifference

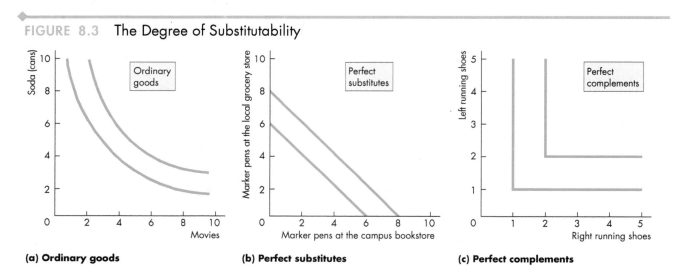

FIGURE 8.3   The Degree of Substitutability

(a) Ordinary goods   **(b) Perfect substitutes**   **(c) Perfect complements**

The shape of the indifference curves reveals the degree of substitutability between two goods. Part (a) shows the indifference curves for two ordinary goods: movies and soda. To drink less soda and remain indifferent, one must see more movies. The number of movies that compensates for a reduction in soda increases as less soda is consumed. Part (b) shows the indifference curves for two perfect substitutes. For the consumer to remain indifferent, one fewer marker pen from the local grocery store must be replaced by one extra marker pen from the campus bookstore. Part (c) shows two perfect complements—goods that cannot be substituted for each other at all. Having two left running shoes with one right running shoe is no better than having one of each. But having two of each is preferred to having one of each.

"With the pork I'd recommend an Alsatian white or a Coke."

© The New Yorker Collection 1988
Robert Weber from cartoonbank.com. All Rights Reserved.

curves for poor substitutes are tightly curved and lie between the shapes of those shown in Figs. 8.3(a) and 8.3(c).

As you can see in the cartoon, according to the waiter's preferences, Coke and Alsatian white wine are perfect substitutes and each is a complement of pork. We hope the customers agree with him.

REVIEW QUIZ

1 What is an indifference curve and how does a preference map show preferences?
2 Why does an indifference curve slope downward and why is it bowed toward the origin?
3 What do we call the magnitude of the slope of an indifference curve?
4 What is the key assumption about a consumer's marginal rate of substitution?

You can work these questions in Study Plan 8.1 and get instant feedback.

The two components of the model of household choice are now in place: the budget line and the preference map. We will now use these components to work out a household's choice and to predict how choices change when prices and income change.

◆ Predicting Consumer Choices

We are now going to predict the quantities of movies and soda that Lisa chooses to buy. We're also going to see how these quantities change when a price changes or when Lisa's income changes. Finally, we're going to see how the *substitution effect* and the *income effect*, two ideas that you met in Chapter 3 (see p. 47), guarantee that for a normal good, the demand curve slopes downward.

Best Affordable Choice

When Lisa makes her best affordable choice of movies and soda, she spends all her income and is on her highest attainable indifference curve. Figure 8.4 illustrates this choice: The indifference curves are from Fig. 8.1(b). Lisa's best affordable choice is 2 movies and 6 cases of soda at point C—the *best affordable point*.

FIGURE 8.4   The Best Affordable Choice

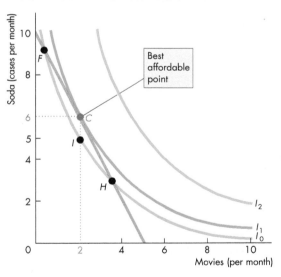

Lisa's best affordable choice is at point C, the point on her budget line and on her highest attainable indifference curve. At point C, Lisa's marginal rate of substitution between movies and soda (the magnitude of the slope of the indifference curve I_1) equals the relative price of movies and soda (the slope of the budget line).

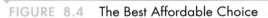 animation

On the Budget Line The best affordable point is on the budget line. For every point inside the budget line, such as point I, there are points on the budget line that Lisa prefers. For example, she prefers all the points on the budget line between F and H to point I, so she chooses a point on the budget line.

On the Highest Attainable Indifference Curve Every point on the budget line lies on an indifference curve. For example, points F and H lie on the indifference curve I_0. By moving along her budget line from either F or H toward C, Lisa reaches points on ever-higher indifference curves that she prefers to points F or H. When Lisa gets to point C, she is on the highest attainable indifference curve.

Marginal Rate of Substitution Equals Relative Price
At point C, Lisa's marginal rate of substitution between movies and soda (the magnitude of the slope of the indifference curve) is equal to the relative price of movies and soda (the magnitude of the slope of the budget line). Lisa's willingness to pay for a movie equals her opportunity cost of a movie.

Let's now see how Lisa's choices change when a price changes.

A Change in Price

The effect of a change in the price of a good on the quantity of the good consumed is called the **price effect**. We will use Fig. 8.5(a) to work out the price effect of a fall in the price of a movie. We start with the price of a movie at $8, the price of soda at $4 a case, and Lisa's income at $40 a month. In this situation, she buys 6 cases of soda and sees 2 movies a month at point C.

Now suppose that the price of a movie falls to $4. With a lower price of a movie, the budget line rotates outward and becomes flatter. The new budget line is the darker orange one in Fig. 8.5(a). For a refresher on how a price change affects the budget line.

Lisa's best affordable point is now point J, where she sees 6 movies and drinks 4 cases of soda. Lisa drinks less soda and watches more movies now that movies are cheaper. She cuts her soda purchases from 6 to 4 cases and increases the number of movies she sees from 2 to 6 a month. When the price of a movie falls and the price of soda and her income remain constant, Lisa substitutes movies for soda.

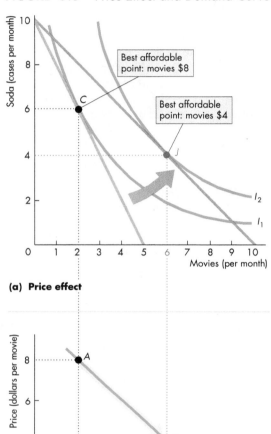

FIGURE 8.5   Price Effect and Demand Curve

(a) Price effect

(b) Demand curve

Initially, Lisa's best affordable point is C in part (a). If the price of a movie falls from $8 to $4, Lisa's best affordable point is J. The move from C to J is the price effect.

At a price of $8 a movie, Lisa sees 2 movies a month, at point A in part (b). At a price of $4 a movie, she sees 6 movies a month, at point B. Lisa's demand curve for movies traces out her best affordable quantity of movies as the price of a movie varies.

myeconlab   animation

Economics in Action

Best Affordable Choice of Movies and DVDs

Between 2005 and 2010, box-office receipts increased by more than 20 percent. During that same period, the average price of a movie ticket increased by 6 percent. So most of the increase in box-office receipts occurred because people went to the movies more often.

Why is movie-going booming? One answer is that the consumer's experience has improved. Movies in 3-D such as *Avatar* and *Alice in Wonderland* play much better on the big screen than at home. Also, movie theaters are able to charge a higher price for 3-D films, which further boosts receipts. But there is another answer, and at first thought an unlikely one: Events in the market for DVD rentals have impacted going to the movies. To see why, let's look at the recent history of the DVD rentals market.

Back in 2005, Blockbuster was the main player and the price of a DVD rental was around $4 a night. Redbox was a fledgling. It had started a year earlier with just 140 kiosks in selected McDonald's restaurants. But Redbox expanded rapidly and by 2007 had as many outlets as Blockbuster. In February 2008, Redbox rented 100 million DVDs at a price of $1 a night.

The easy access to DVDs at $1 a night transformed the markets for movie watching and the figure shows why.

A student has a budget of $40 a month to allocate to movies. To keep the story clear, we'll suppose that it cost $8 to go to a movie in both 2005 and 2010. The price of a DVD rental in 2005 was $4, so the student's budget line is the one that runs from 5 movies on the *y*-axis to 10 DVD rentals on the *x*-axis.

The student's best affordable point is 2 movies and 6 rentals a month.

In 2010, the price of a rental falls to $1 a night but the price of a movie ticket remains at $8. So the budget line rotates outward. The student's best affordable point is now at 3 movies and 16 rentals a month. (This student loves movies!)

Many other things changed between 2005 and 2010 that influenced the markets for movies and DVD rentals, but the fall in the price of a DVD rental was the biggest influence.

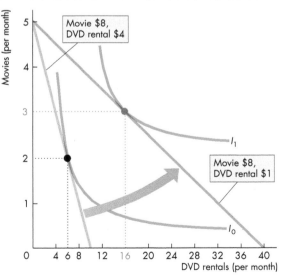

Best Affordable Movies and DVD Rentals

The Demand Curve In Chapter 3, we asserted that the demand curve slopes downward. We can now derive a demand curve from a consumer's budget line and indifference curves. By doing so, we can see that the law of demand and the downward-sloping demand curve are consequences of a consumer's choosing her or his best affordable combination of goods.

To derive Lisa's demand curve for movies, lower the price of a movie and find her best affordable point at different prices. We've just done this for two movie prices in Fig. 8.5(a). Figure 8.5(b) highlights these two prices and two points that lie on Lisa's demand curve for movies. When the price of a movie is $8, Lisa sees 2 movies a month at point *A*. When the price falls to $4, she increases the number of movies she sees to 6 a month at point *B*. The demand curve is made up of these two points plus all the other points that tell us Lisa's best affordable quantity of movies at each movie price, with the price of soda and Lisa's income remaining the same. As you can see, Lisa's demand curve for movies slopes downward—the lower the price of a movie, the more movies she sees. This is the law of demand.

Next, let's see how Lisa changes her purchases of movies and soda when her income changes.

A Change in Income

The effect of a change in income on buying plans is called the **income effect**. Let's work out the income effect by examining how buying plans change when income changes and prices remain constant. Figure 8.6 shows the income effect when Lisa's income falls. With an income of $40, the price of a movie at $4, and the price of soda at $4 a case, Lisa's best affordable point is *J*—she buys 6 movies and 4 cases of soda. If her income falls to $28, her best affordable point is *K*—she sees 4 movies and buys 3 cases of soda. When Lisa's income falls, she buys less of both goods. Movies and soda are normal goods.

The Demand Curve and the Income Effect A change in income leads to a shift in the demand curve, as shown in Fig. 8.6(b). With an income of $40, Lisa's demand curve for movies is D_0, the same as in Fig. 8.5(b). But when her income falls to $28, she plans to see fewer movies at each price, so her demand curve shifts leftward to D_1.

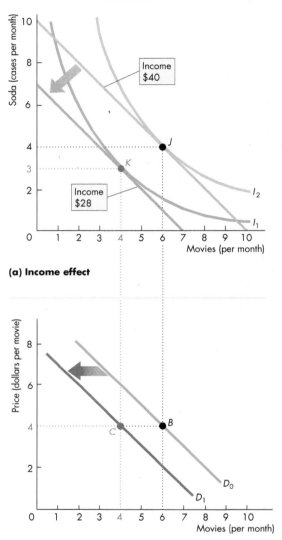

FIGURE 8.6   Income Effect and Change in Demand

(a) Income effect

(b) Demand curve for movies

A change in income shifts the budget line, changes the best affordable point, and changes demand.

In part (a), when Lisa's income decreases from $40 to $28, she sees fewer movies and buys less soda.

In part (b), when Lisa's income is $40, her demand curve for movies is D_0. When Lisa's income falls to $28, her demand curve for movies shifts leftward to D_1. For Lisa, going to the movies is a normal good. Her demand for movies decreases because she now sees fewer movies at each price.

myeconlab animation

Substitution Effect and Income Effect

For a normal good, a fall in its price *always* increases the quantity bought. We can prove this assertion by dividing the price effect into two parts:

- Substitution effect
- Income effect

Figure 8.7(a) shows the price effect and Figs. 8.7(b) and 8.7(c) show the two parts into which we separate the price effect.

Substitution Effect The **substitution effect** is the effect of a change in price on the quantity bought when the consumer (hypothetically) remains indifferent between the original situation and the new one. To work out Lisa's substitution effect when the price of a movie falls, we must lower her income by enough to keep her on the same indifference curve as before.

Figure 8.7(a) shows the price effect of a fall in the price of a movie from $8 to $4. The number of movies increases from 2 to 6 a month. When the price falls, suppose (hypothetically) that we cut Lisa's income to $28. What's special about $28? It is the

income that is just enough, at the new price of a movie, to keep Lisa's best affordable point on the same indifference curve (I_1) as her original point C. Lisa's budget line is now the medium orange line in Fig. 8.7(b). With the lower price of a movie and a smaller income, Lisa's best affordable point is K. The move from C to K along indifference curve I_1 is the substitution effect of the price change. The substitution effect of the fall in the price of a movie is an increase in the quantity of movies from 2 to 4. The direction of the substitution effect never varies: When the relative price of a good falls, the consumer substitutes more of that good for the other good.

Income Effect To calculate the substitution effect, we gave Lisa a $12 pay cut. To calculate the income effect, we give Lisa back her $12. The $12 increase in income shifts Lisa's budget line outward, as shown in Fig. 8.7(c). The slope of the budget line does not change because both prices remain the same. This change in Lisa's budget line is similar to the one illustrated in Fig. 8.6. As Lisa's budget line shifts outward, her consumption possibilities expand and her best affordable

FIGURE 8.7   Substitution Effect and Income Effect

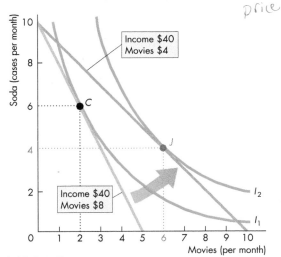

(a) Price effect

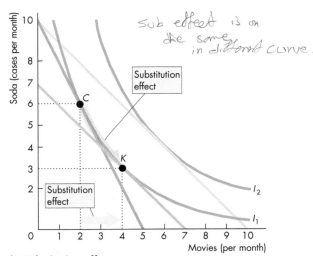

(b) Substitution effect

When the price of a movie falls from $8 to $4, Lisa moves from point C to point J in part (a). The price effect is an increase in the number of movies from 2 to 6 a month. This price effect is separated into a substitution effect in part (b) and an income effect in part (c).

To isolate the substitution effect, we confront Lisa with the new price but keep her on her original indifference curve, I_1. The substitution effect is the move from C to K along indifference curve I_1—an increase from 2 to 4 movies a month.

myeconlab   animation

point becomes *J* on indifference curve I_2. The move from *K* to *J* is the income effect of the price change.

As Lisa's income increases, she sees more movies. For Lisa, a movie is a normal good. For a normal good, the income effect *reinforces* the substitution effect. Because the two effects work in the same direction, we can be sure that the demand curve slopes downward. But some goods are inferior goods. What can we say about the demand for an inferior good?

Inferior Goods Recall that an *inferior good* is a good for which *demand decreases* when *income increases*. For an inferior good, the income effect is negative, which means that a lower price does not inevitably lead to an increase in the quantity demanded. The substitution effect of a fall in the price increases the quantity demanded, but the negative income effect works in the opposite direction and offsets the substitution effect to some degree. The key question is to what degree.

If the negative income effect *equals* the positive substitution effect, a fall in price leaves the quantity bought the same. When a fall in price leaves the quantity demanded unchanged, the demand curve is vertical and demand is perfectly inelastic.

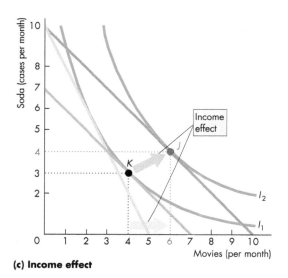

(c) Income effect

To isolate the income effect, we confront Lisa with the new price of movies but increase her income so that she can move from the original indifference curve, I_1, to the new one, I_2. The income effect is the move from *K* to *J*—an increase from 4 to 6 movies a month.

If the negative income effect *is smaller than* the positive substitution effect, a fall in price increases the quantity bought and the demand curve still slopes downward like that for a normal good. But the demand for an inferior good might be less elastic than that for a normal good.

If the negative income effect *exceeds* the positive substitution effect, a fall in the price *decreases* the quantity bought and the demand curve *slopes upward*. This case does not appear to occur in the real world.

You can apply the indifference curve model that you've studied in this chapter to explain the changes in the way we buy recorded music, see movies, and make all our other consumption choices. We allocate our budgets to make our best affordable choices. Changes in prices and incomes change our best affordable choices and change consumption patterns.

REVIEW QUIZ

1 When a consumer chooses the combination of goods and services to buy, what is she or he trying to achieve?
2 Explain the conditions that are met when a consumer has found the best affordable combination of goods to buy. (Use the terms budget line, marginal rate of substitution, and relative price in your explanation.)
3 If the price of a normal good falls, what happens to the quantity demanded of that good?
4 Into what two effects can we divide the effect of a price change?
5 For a normal good, does the income effect reinforce the substitution effect or does it partly offset the substitution effect?

You can work these questions in Study Plan 8.2 and get instant feedback.

Reading Between the Lines on pp. 159–160 shows you how the theory of household choice explains why e-books are taking off, and how people chose whether to buy their books in electronic or paper format.

In the chapters that follow, we study the choices that firms make in their pursuit of profit and how those choices determine the supply of goods and services and the demand for productive resources.

Paper Books Versus e-Books

Amazon.com E-Book Sales Exceed Hardcovers for First Time

http://www.bloomberg.com
July 19, 2010

Amazon.com Inc., the largest Internet retailer, said growth in sales of its Kindle digAmazon.com Inc., the largest Internet retailer, said growth in sales of its Kindle digital reader accelerated every month in the second quarter and that it's selling more electronic books than hardcover editions.

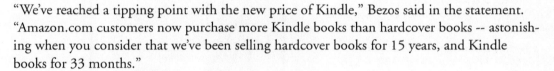

The pace of Kindle sales also has tripled since the company cut the price to $189 from $259, Amazon.com Chief Executive Officer Jeff Bezos said in a statement. ...Amazon.com sold more than triple the number of Kindle books in the first half of the year as it did in the same period last year, Seattle-based Amazon.com said. More than 81 percent of its 630,000 electronic books are $9.99 or less.

"We've reached a tipping point with the new price of Kindle," Bezos said in the statement. "Amazon.com customers now purchase more Kindle books than hardcover books -- astonishing when you consider that we've been selling hardcover books for 15 years, and Kindle books for 33 months."

...In the past three months, Amazon.com has sold 143 Kindle books for every 100 hardcover books, the company said. In July, sales of e-books accelerated to 180 sold for every 100 hardcover versions. Kindle book sales this year have also exceeded broader e-book sales growth, pegged by the Association of American Publishers at 207 percent through May, Amazon.com said.

ESSENCE OF THE STORY

- During the three months ended June 30, 2010, Amazon sold 143 Kindle e-books for every 100 hardcover paper books.

- The Kindle store lists 630,000 eBooks, and 80 percent of them are priced at less than $10.

- Amazon has cut the price of its Kindle reader from $259 to $189 and the quantity sold has tripled.

- The quantity sold might explode if the Kindle was cheaper still.

- Print books and e-books are substitutes.

- For most people, though, e-books and print books are extremely poor substitutes.

- For a committed print-book lover, no quantity of e-books can compensate for a print book—the marginal rate of substitution between print books and e-books is zero.

- Beth is a print-book lover and Fig. 1 shows her indifference curves for print books and e-books.

- With print books on the x-axis, Beth's indifference curves are steep. They tell us that Beth is willing to forgo a large number of e-books to get one more print book.

- Beth's annual book budget is $340. The price of an e-book reader is $190 (the current price of the Kindle reader is $189). The price of an e-book is $10 and the price of a print book is $20.

- We'll assume that an e-book reader has only a one-year life. (Buyers know they will want the next-generation, improved reader next year.)

- The orange line is Beth's budget line if she buys a reader. She can afford 15 e-books if she buys no print books [$190 + (15 × $10) = $340] and along this line, by forgoing 2 e-books she can buy 1 print book.

- If Beth doesn't buy an e-book reader, she buys no e-books and can afford 17 print books ($340 ÷ $20 = 17). The red dot shows this affordable point.

- The red dot is also the best affordable choice because this choice gets her onto her highest attainable indifference curve, I_2.

- Andy differs from Beth: He thinks that print books and e-books are perfect substitutes. But he also likes music and buys albums. Figure 2 shows Andy's indifference curves for books (all types) and albums.

- Andy's annual budget for albums and books is $550. The price of an album is $10 and the prices of an e-book reader, an e-book, and a print book are the same as those that Beth faces.

- Figure 2 shows Andy's two budget lines: one if he buys only e-books and albums and another if he buys only print books and albums.

- If Andy buys e-books, he must spend $190 on a reader, which leaves him with $360 for albums and e-books. If he buys 10 e-books, he can afford 25 albums [(10 x $10) + (26 x $10) = $360].

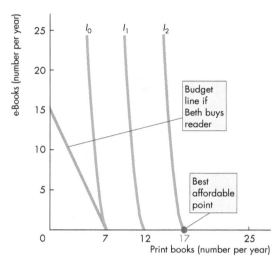

Figure 1 Print books versus e-books for a print-book lover

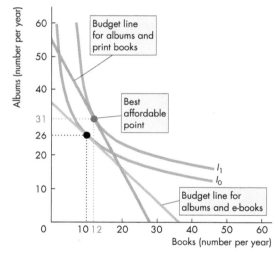

Figure 2 Books versus albums

- If Andy buys print books and albums, he can afford 12 print books and 22 albums [(12 × $20) + (31 × $10) = $550].

- Andy's best affordable choice is 12 print books and 31 albums.

- So even Andy, who thinks that e-books and print books are perfect substitutes, doesn't buy e-books. But he probably would if he had a larger budget.

SUMMARY

Key Points

Preferences and Indifference Curves (pp. 150–153)

- A consumer's preferences can be represented by indifference curves. The consumer is indifferent among all the combinations of goods that lie on an indifference curve.
- A consumer prefers any point above an indifference curve to any point on it and prefers any point on an indifference curve to any point below it.
- The magnitude of the slope of an indifference curve is called the marginal rate of substitution.
- The marginal rate of substitution diminishes as consumption of the good measured on the *y*-axis decreases and consumption of the good measured on the *x*-axis increases.

Working Problems 1 to 5 will give you a better understanding of preferences and indifference curves.

Predicting Consumer Choices (pp. 153–158)

- A household consumes at its best affordable point. This point is on the budget line and on the highest attainable indifference curve and has a marginal rate of substitution equal to relative price.
- The effect of a price change (the price effect) can be divided into a substitution effect and an income effect.
- The substitution effect is the effect of a change in price on the quantity bought when the consumer (hypothetically) remains indifferent between the original choice and the new choice.
- The substitution effect always results in an increase in consumption of the good whose relative price has fallen.
- The income effect is the effect of a change in income on consumption.
- For a normal good, the income effect reinforces the substitution effect. For an inferior good, the income effect works in the opposite direction to the substitution effect.

Working Problems 6 to 10 will give you a better understanding of predicting consumer choices.

Key Terms

Diminishing marginal rate of substitution, 151
Income effect, 156

Indifference curve, 150
Marginal rate of substitution, 151
Price effect, 154

Substitution effect, 157

STUDY PLAN PROBLEMS AND APPLICATIONS

myeconlab You can work Problems 1 to 12 in MyEconLab Chapter 8 Study Plan and get instant feedback.

Preferences and Indifference Curves (Study Plan 8.1)

1. Draw figures that show your indifference curves for the following pairs of goods:
   - Right gloves and left gloves
   - Coca-Cola and Pepsi
   - Tylenol and acetaminophen (the generic form of Tylenol)
   - Desktop computers and laptop computers
   - Strawberries and ice cream

   For each pair, are the goods perfect substitutes, perfect complements, substitutes, complements, or unrelated?

2. Discuss the shape of the indifference curve for each of the following pairs of goods:
   - Orange juice and smoothies
   - Baseballs and baseball bats
   - Left running shoe and right running shoe
   - Eyeglasses and contact lenses

   Explain the relationship between the shape of the indifference curve and the marginal rate of substitution as the quantities of the two goods change.

Use the following news clip to work Problems 3 and 4.

The Year in Medicine

Sudafed, used by allergy sufferers, contains as the active ingredient pseudoephedrine, which is widely used to make home-made methamphetamine. Allergy sufferers looking to buy Sudafed, must now show photo ID, and sign a logbook. The most common alternative, phenylephrine, isn't as effective as pseudoephedrine.

Source: *Time*, December 4, 2006

3. Sketch an indifference curve for Sudafed and phenylephrine that is consistent with this news clip. On your graph, identify combinations that allergy sufferers prefer, do not prefer, and are indifferent among.

4. Explain how the marginal rate of substitution changes as an allergy sufferer increases the consumption of Sudafed.

Use the following news clip to work Problems 5 and 6.

Gas Prices to Stunt Memorial Day Travel

With high gas prices, 12% of the people surveyed say that they have cancelled their Memorial Day

road trip and 11% will take a shorter trip near home. That may save consumers some money, but it will also likely hurt service stations, which will sell less gas and fewer snacks and hurt roadside hotels, which will have fewer rooms used and serve fewer casual meals.

Source: *MarketWatch*, May 22, 2008

5. Describe the degree of substitutability between Memorial Day trips and other trip-related goods and services and sketch a consumer's preference map that illustrates your description.

Predicting Consumer Choices (Study Plan 8.2)

6. a. Sketch a consumer's preference map between Memorial Day trips and other goods and services. Draw a consumer's budget line prior to the rise in the price of gasoline and mark the consumer's best affordable point.
   b. On your graph, show how the best affordable point changes when the price of gasoline rises.

Use the following information to work Problems 7 and 8.

Pam has chosen her best affordable combination of cookies and granola bars. She spends all of her weekly income on 30 cookies at $1 each and 5 granola bars at $2 each. Next week, people expect the price of a cookie to fall to 50¢ and the price of a granola bar to rise to $5.

7. a. Will Pam be able to buy and want to buy 30 cookies and 5 granola bars next week?
   b. Which situation does Pam prefer: cookies at $1 and granola bars at $2 or cookies at 50¢ and granola bars at $5?

8. a. If Pam changes how she spends her weekly income, will she buy more or fewer cookies and more or fewer granola bars?
   b. When the prices change next week, will there be an income effect, a substitution effect, or both at work?

Use the following information to work Problems 9 and 10.

Boom Time For "Gently Used" Clothes

Most retailers are blaming the economy for their poor sales, but one store chain that sells used name-brand children's clothes, toys, and furniture is boldly declaring that an economic downturn can actually be a boon for its business. Last year, the company took in $20 million in sales, up 5% from the previous year. Sales are already up 5% this year.

Source: CNN, April 17, 2008

9. a. According to the news clip, is used clothing a normal good or an inferior good?
    b. If the price of used clothing falls and income remains the same, explain how the quantity of used clothing bought changes.
    c. If the price of used clothing falls and income remains the same, describe the substitution effect and the income effect that occur.

10. a. Use a graph to illustrate a family's indifference curves for used clothing and other goods and services.
    b. In your graph in part (a), draw two budget lines to show the effect of a fall in income on the quantity of used clothing purchased.

Economics in the News (Study Plan 8.N)

Use the following information to work Problems 11 and 12.

Gas Prices Send Surge of Travelers to Mass Transit

With the price of gas approaching $4 a gallon, more commuters are abandoning their cars and taking the train or bus. It's very clear that a significant portion of the increase in transit use is directly caused by people who are looking for alternatives to paying $3.50 a gallon for gas. Some cities with long-established public transit systems, like New York and Boston, have seen increases in ridership of 5 percent, but the biggest surges—of 10 to 15 percent over last year—are occurring in many metropolitan areas in the Southwest where the driving culture is strongest and bus and rail lines are more limited.

Source: *The New York Times*, May 10, 2008

11. a. Sketch a graph of a preference map and a budget line to illustrate the best affordable combination of gasoline and public transit.
    b. On your graph in part (a), show the effect of a rise in the price of gasoline on the quantities of gasoline and public transit services purchased.

12. If the gas price rise has been similar in all regions, compare the marginal rates of substitution in the Northeast and the Southwest. Explain how you have inferred the different marginal rates of substitution from the information in the news clip.

ADDITIONAL PROBLEMS AND APPLICATIONS

 These problems are available in MyEconLab if assigned by your instructor.

Preferences and Indifference Curves

Use the following information to work Problems 13 and 15.

Rashid buys only books and CDs and the figure shows his preference map.

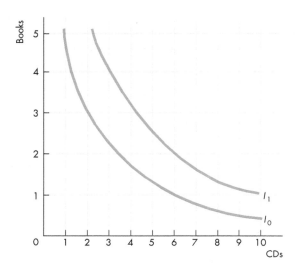

13. a. If Rashid chooses 3 books and 2 CDs, what is his marginal rate of substitution?
    b. If Rashid chooses 2 books and 6 CDs, what is his marginal rate of substitution?

14. Do Rashid's indifference curves display diminishing marginal rate of substitution? Explain why or why not.

15. **You May Be Paid More (or Less) Than You Think**

    It's so hard to put a price on happiness, isn't it? But if you've ever had to choose between a job you like and a better-paying one that you like less, you probably wished some economist would tell you how much job satisfaction is worth. Trust in management is by far the biggest component to consider. Say you get a new boss and your trust in management goes up a bit (say, up 1 point on a 10-point scale). That's like getting a 36 percent pay raise. In

other words, that increased level of trust will boost your level of overall satisfaction in life by about the same amount as a 36 percent raise would.

Source: CNN, March 29, 2006

a. Measure trust in management on a 10-point scale, measure pay on the same 10-point scale, and think of them as two goods. Sketch an indifference curve (with trust on the *x*-axis) that is consistent with the news clip.

b. What is the marginal rate of substitution between trust in management and pay according to this news clip?

c. What does the news clip imply about the principle of diminishing marginal rate of substitution? Is that implication likely to be correct?

Predicting Consumer Choices

Use the following information to work Problems 16 and 17.

Jim has made his best affordable choice of muffins and coffee. He spends all of his income on 10 muffins at $1 each and 20 cups of coffee at $2 each. Now the price of a muffin rises to $1.50 and the price of coffee falls to $1.75 a cup.

16. a. Will Jim now be able and want to buy 10 muffins and 20 coffees?

b. Which situation does Jim prefer: muffins at $1 and coffee at $2 a cup or muffins at $1.50 and coffee at $1.75 a cup?

17. a. If Jim changes the quantities that he buys, will he buy more or fewer muffins and more or less coffee?

b. When the prices change, will there be an income effect, a substitution effect, or both at work?

Use the following information to work Problems 18 to 20.

Sara's income is $12 a week. The price of popcorn is $3 a bag, and the price of cola is $1.50 a can. The figure shows Sara's preference map for popcorn and cola.

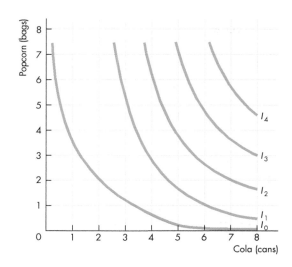

18. What quantities of popcorn and cola does Sara buy? What is Sara's marginal rate of substitution at the point at which she consumes?

19. Suppose that the price of cola rises to $3.00 a can and the price of popcorn and Sara's income remain the same. What quantities of cola and popcorn does Sara now buy? What are two points on Sara's demand curve for cola? Draw Sara's demand curve.

20. Suppose that the price of cola rises to $3.00 a can and the price of popcorn and Sara's income remain the same.
    a. What is the substitution effect of this price change and what is the income effect of the price change?
    b. Is cola a normal good or an inferior good? Explain.

Economics in the News

21. After you have studied *Reading Between the Lines* on pp. 159–160 answer the following questions.
    a. How do you buy books?
    b. Sketch your budget line for books and other goods.
    c. Sketch your indifference curves for books and other goods.
    d. Explain why Andy would buy e-books if the price of a reader fell to $100.

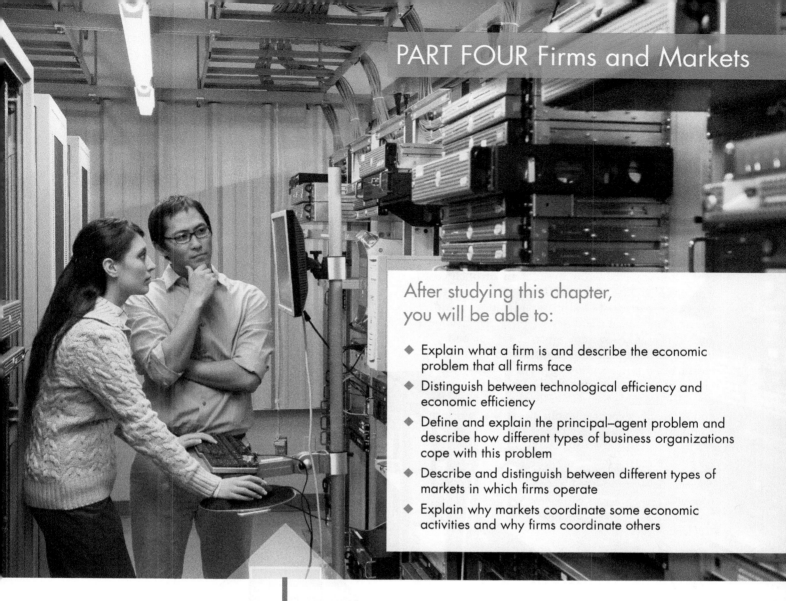

After studying this chapter,
you will be able to:

- Explain what a firm is and describe the economic problem that all firms face
- Distinguish between technological efficiency and economic efficiency
- Define and explain the principal–agent problem and describe how different types of business organizations cope with this problem
- Describe and distinguish between different types of markets in which firms operate
- Explain why markets coordinate some economic activities and why firms coordinate others

9
PROFIT, OUTPUT, AND COSTS

In the fall of 1990, a British scientist named Tim Berners-Lee invented the World Wide Web. This remarkable idea paved the way for the creation of thousands of profitable businesses that include Facebook and Twitter, Apple, Microsoft, Google, and Yahoo!.

Some of these successful dot.com firms sell goods and others sell services. But many firms, especially those that you can name, don't *make* the things they sell: They *buy* them from other firms. For example, Apple doesn't make the iPhone. Intel makes its memory chip and Foxconn, a firm in Taiwan, assembles its components. Why doesn't Apple make the iPhone? How do firms decide what to make themselves and what to buy from other firms?

How do Facebook, Twitter, Apple, Microsoft, Google, Intel, Foxconn, and the millions of other firms make their business decisions?

167

◆ Economic Profit vs. Accounting Profit

The goal of any firm is to maximize profit, the difference between revenue and costs. Because the definition of an economic cost includes more than just monetary costs, we need to distinguish between two different measures of profit: accounting profit and economic profit. **Accounting profit** can be defined as the difference between revenues and explicit costs, where explicit costs refer to a firm's monetary or "out-of-pocket" expenses. On the other hand, **economic profit** is defined as the difference between revenues and economic costs. Remember, economic costs include both explicit (nonsunk) costs *and* implicit costs. As a result, accounting profit generally will be greater than economic profit. To see the difference, consider the table below that lists annual revenues and monetary expenses (explicit costs) for a printing company.

Annual Sales Revenue		$4,000,000
Wage costs of labor	$1,500,000	
Paper expense	$500,000	
Rental payments for printers	$350,000	
Rental payments for office space	$150,000	
Total Costs		$2,500,000
Profit		$1,500,000

Based on these numbers, the printing company is earning $1,500,000 more in revenues than it is paying out in expenses--$1,500,000 in accounting profit. But this example includes only the explicit monetary expenses of production and none of the implicit costs of production. There are monetary costs included for labor (wages), land (office space), and capital (printers), but what about the cost of the owner's entrepreneurship resource?

The profit earned in the business is the reward to the printing company owner, but just because the owner earns this monetary profit doesn't mean owning the printing company is the best choice for this entrepreneur. Presumably, the owner of the printing company has other options available for his or her labor and entrepreneurial services. For example, what if the printing company owner's best alternative to owning the printing company is working as an advertising executive for a local business at an annual salary of $800,000? By choosing to own the printing company, the owner of the printing company is sacrificing that $800,000 salary he or she would earn as an advertising executive. Even though this $800,000 is not paid by the owner of the printing company, it is still an opportunity the owner is sacrificing and must be included as an economic cost of production. The table of revenues and costs changes to the following:

Annual Sales Revenue		$4,000,000
Wage costs of labor	$1,500,000	
Paper expense	$500,000	
Rental payments for printers	$350,000	
Rental payments for office space	$150,000	
Forgone Salary as Advertising Executive	$800,000	
Total Costs		$3,300,000
Profit		$700,000

Notice that the printing company owner is still earning a positive economic profit of $700,000, even after including the opportunity cost of entrepreneurship. Anytime economic profit is positive, revenues are large enough to pay off all the economic costs and still leave some surplus. In other words, the revenues made in this business are greater than the opportunity costs, so the printing company owner is earning more by using resources in this business than he or she could in the best alternative.

Accounting profit focuses only on the firm's ability to pay off its expenses. When accounting profit is positive, the firm is earning enough to pay its bills. However, that does not imply that the firm is earning the highest level of profit it could. Economic profit identifies whether a firm is earning more or less than it could earn if the firm's resources were used elsewhere.

When economic profits are positive, firms recognize that the industry offers the best return for use of their resources and are attracted to that industry. However, if revenues are not high enough to pay off all the economic costs of a business, economic profit will be negative. When economic profit is negative, the resources being used in an industry would have a higher value if they were moved to their best alternatives. In other words, opportunity costs are greater than revenues. With negative economic profits, firms have an incentive to leave an industry, as they recognize that their resources have higher value elsewhere.

If economic profit is zero, a firm's resources are earning revenues exactly equal to their opportunity costs. When a firm's resources are earning the same value they would earn in their best alternative, we say a firm is earning **normal profit**. In that case, a firm is receiving no more and no less than what it would earn if the firm moved its resources to their best alternative uses. There is no incentive for a firm to leave an industry when it is earning normal profit, and there is no incentive for new firms to enter the industry either. In the table above, if the owner of the printing company could earn $1,500,000 as an advertising executive (instead of the $800,000), total economic costs would rise from $3,300,000 to $4,000,000. Now total economic costs equal total revenues, and economic profit is zero. This does not mean the printing company owner should get out of the printing business though. The printing company owner is making an accounting profit of $1,500,000 ($4,000,000 in revenues minus $2,500,000 in accounting costs), and that accounting profit is the same amount of money the owner would have if he or she worked as an advertising executive instead. The owner would be indifferent between making $1,500,000 in accounting profit as a printing company owner and making $1,500,000 as an advertising executive. Because the best alternative has the same value as the current use of resources, the firm cannot leave this market and do any better somewhere else. When the firm earns zero economic profit, the firm is earning a "normal" profit.

◆ More Implicit Costs and Benefits

In the example above, rental expenses for printers ($350,000) and office space ($150,000) are included. But what if the company already owned its own printers or its own building? In that case, there are no explicit expenses associated with those rental payments for those resources. You don't have to pay rent on a building or piece of equipment you already own. It may appear then that $500,000 of cost disappears and profit increases by $500,000. However, we know that the true cost of a resource doesn't include just what you pay for it.

The true cost, or economic cost, of a resource is its opportunity cost—the value of the best alternative. Even though the company owns its own printers and its building, using the printers and the building as part of the printing business means those resources are not available for other potential uses. Printers, for example, could be rented out to other companies or sold to other companies. The economic cost of using those printers would be the value the owner of the printing company would receive in the best alternative use of those printers.

For example, if printers can be rented out for $350,000 (the same price the company in the above example would have to pay to rent them), then the economic cost of using those printers in the printing company is still $350,000 (the value of the best alternative to owning the printers).

The same is true for the building. If the company owns the building, it is not a "free" resource. There is still an economic cost of using the building, even if there is no explicit cost. The economic cost of using the building in the printing business would be the value of its best alternative—the value of income that could be earned from renting or selling the building to another business, for example.

Just as economists include implicit costs in the economic costs of operating a business, there may be some *implicit benefit* to running a business that an accountant would not consider. For example, many entrepreneurs see value in being able to set their own work schedules without having to answer to anyone else. In that case, even if the difference between revenues and economic costs is negative, the printing company owner may decide to continue owning the printing company simply because there is enough intrinsic value to "being your own boss" that it is worthwhile to continue operating the business. The goal of measuring economic profit is to uncover the most valuable use of resources. The concept of economic profit should also include these "implicit benefits" as part of the value of running a company in addition to the monetary revenues.

Because implicit benefits and implicit costs are determined by an individual entrepreneur's alternatives and preferences, the economic profit earned from a business can vary with each entrepreneur. To simplify this, we will focus simply on revenue earned by a company as the benefit to running a business. However, you should keep in mind that true economic profit would include an individual entrepreneur's implicit benefits as well. When we refer to the costs of production from now on, we will include all the relevant explicit (nonsunk) costs and implicit costs so that the "cost of production" will refer to the "economic cost of production."

◆ Markets and the Competitive Environment

The markets in which firms operate vary a great deal. Some are highly competitive, and profits in these markets are hard to come by. Some appear to be almost free from competition, and firms in these markets earn large profits. Some markets are dominated by fierce advertising campaigns in which each firm seeks to persuade buyers that it has the best products. And some markets display the character of a strategic game.

Economists identify four market types:

1. Perfect competition
2. Monopolistic competition
3. Oligopoly
4. Monopoly

Perfect competition arises when there are many firms, each selling an identical product, many buyers, and no restrictions on the entry of new firms into the industry. The many firms and buyers are all well informed about the prices of the products of each firm in the industry. The worldwide markets for corn, rice, and other grain crops are examples of perfect competition.

Monopolistic competition is a market structure in which a large number of firms compete by making similar but slightly different products. Making a product slightly different from the product of a competing firm is called **product differentiation**. Product differentiation gives a firm in monopolistic competition an element of market power. The firm is the sole producer of the particular version of the good in question. For example, in the market for pizzas, hundreds of firms make their own version of the perfect pizza. Each of these firms is the sole producer of a particular brand. Differentiated products are not necessarily different products. What matters is that consumers perceive them to be different. For example, different brands of potato chips and ketchup might be almost identical but be perceived by consumers to be different.

Oligopoly is a market structure in which a small number of firms compete. Computer software, airplane manufacture, and international air transportation are examples of oligopolistic industries. Oligopolies might produce almost identical products, such as the colas produced by Coke and Pepsi. Or they might produce differentiated products such as Boeing and Airbus aircraft.

Monopoly arises when there is one firm, which produces a good or service that has no close substitutes and in which the firm is protected by a barrier preventing the entry of new firms. In some places, the phone, gas, electricity, cable television, and water suppliers are local monopolies—monopolies restricted to a given location. Microsoft Corporation, the software developer that created Windows and Vista, is an example of a global monopoly.

Perfect competition is the most extreme form of competition. Monopoly is the most extreme absence of competition. The other two market types fall between these extremes.

Many factors must be taken into account to determine which market structure describes a particular real-world market. One of these factors is the extent to which a small number of firms dominates the market. To measure this feature of markets, economists use indexes called measures of concentration. Let's look at these measures.

Measures of Concentration

Economists use two measures of concentration:

- The four-firm concentration ratio
- The Herfindahl-Hirschman Index

The Four-Firm Concentration Ratio The **four-firm concentration ratio** is the percentage of the value of sales accounted for by the four largest firms in an industry. The range of the concentration ratio is from almost zero for perfect competition to 100 percent for monopoly. This ratio is the main measure used to assess market structure.

Table 9.1 shows two calculations of the four-firm concentration ratio: one for tire makers and one for printers. In this example, 14 firms produce tires. The largest four have 80 percent of the sales, so the four-firm concentration ratio is 80 percent. In the printing industry, with 1,004 firms, the largest four firms have only 0.5 percent of the sales, so the four-firm concentration ratio is 0.5 percent.

A low concentration ratio indicates a high degree of competition, and a high concentration ratio indicates an absence of competition. A monopoly has a concentration ratio of 100 percent—the largest (and only) firm has 100 percent of the sales. A four-firm concentration ratio that exceeds 60 percent is regarded as an indication of a market that is highly concentrated and dominated by a few firms in an oligopoly. A ratio of less than 60 percent is regarded as an indication of a competitive market.

The Herfindahl-Hirschman Index The **Herfindahl-Hirschman Index**—also called the HHI—is the square of the percentage market share of each firm summed over the largest 50 firms (or summed over all the firms if there are fewer than 50) in a market. For example, if there are four firms in a market and the market shares of the firms are 50 percent, 25 percent, 15 percent, and 10 percent, the Herfindahl-Hirschman Index is

$$HHI = 50^2 + 25^2 + 15^2 + 10^2 = 3,450.$$

TABLE 9.1   Calculating the Four-Firm Concentration Ratio

Tire makers		Printers	
Firm	**Sales** (millions of dollars)	**Firm**	**Sales** (millions of dollars)
Top, Inc.	200	Fran's	2.5
ABC, Inc.	250	Ned's	2.0
Big, Inc.	150	Tom's	1.8
XYZ, Inc.	100	Jill's	1.7
Largest 4 firms	700	Largest 4 firms	8.0
Other 10 firms	175	Other 1,000 firms	1,592.0
Industry	875	Industry	1,600.0

Four-firm concentration ratios:

Tire makers: $\frac{700}{875} \times 100 = 80$ percent

Printers: $\frac{8}{1,600} \times 100 = 0.5$ percent

Economics in Action

Concentration in the U.S. Economy

The U.S. Department of Commerce calculates and publishes data showing concentration ratios and the HHI for each industry in the United States. The bars in the figure show the four-firm concentration ratio and the number at the end of each bar is the HHI.

Chewing gum is one of the most concentrated industries. William Wrigley Jr. Company of Chicago employs 16,000 people and sells $5 billion worth of gum a year. It does have some competitors but they have a very small market share.

Household laundry equipment, light bulbs, breakfast cereal, and motor vehicles are highly concentrated industries. They are oligopolies.

Pet food, cookies and crackers, computers, and soft drinks are moderately concentrated industries. They are examples of monopolistic competition.

Ice cream, milk, clothing, concrete blocks and bricks, and commercial printing industries have low concentration measures and are highly competitive.

Concentration measures are useful indicators of the degree of competition in a market, but they must be supplemented by other information to determine the structure of the market.

Newspapers and automobiles are examples of how the concentration measures give a misleading reading of the degree of competition. Most newspapers are local. They serve a single city or even smaller area. So despite the low concentration measure, newspapers are concentrated in their own local areas. Automobiles are traded internationally and foreign cars are freely imported into the United States. Despite the high U.S. concentration measure, the automobile industry is competitive.

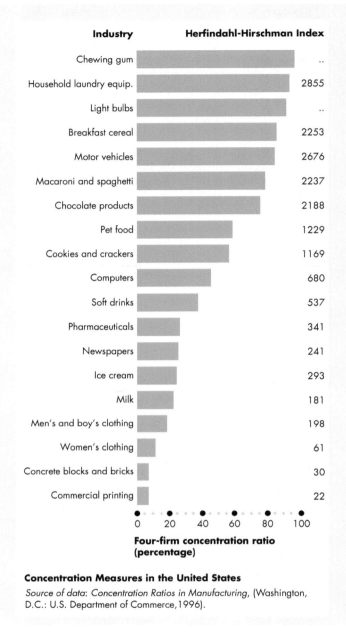

Concentration Measures in the United States

Source of data: Concentration Ratios in Manufacturing, (Washington, D.C.: U.S. Department of Commerce, 1996).

In perfect competition, the HHI is small. For example, if each of the largest 50 firms in an industry has a market share of 0.1 percent, then the HHI is $0.1^2 \times 50 = 0.5$. In a monopoly, the HHI is 10,000. The firm has 100 percent of the market: $100^2 = 10,000$.

The HHI became a popular measure of the degree of competition during the 1980s, when the Justice Department used it to classify markets. A market in which the HHI is less than 1,000 is regarded as being competitive. A market in which the HHI lies between 1,000 and 1,800 is regarded as being moderately competitive. But a market in which the HHI exceeds 1,800 is regarded as being uncompetitive. The Justice Department scrutinizes any merger of firms in a market in which the HHI exceeds 1,000 and is likely to challenge a merger if the HHI exceeds 1,800.

TABLE 9.2   Market Structure

Characteristics	Perfect competition	Monopolistic competition	Oligopoly	Monopoly
Number of firms in industry	Many	Many	Few	One
Product	Identical	Differentiated	Either identical or differentiated	No close substitutes
Barriers to entry	None	None	Moderate	High
Firm's control over price	None	Some	Considerable	Considerable or regulated
Concentration ratio	0	Low	High	100
HHI (approx. ranges)	Less than 100	101 to 999	More than 1,000	10,000
Examples	Wheat, corn	Food, clothing	Computer chips	Local water supply

Limitations of a Concentration Measure

The three main limitations of using only concentration measures as determinants of market structure are their failure to take proper account of

- The geographical scope of the market
- Barriers to entry and firm turnover
- The correspondence between a market and an industry

Geographical Scope of Market Concentration measures take a national view of the market. Many goods are sold in a *national* market, but some are sold in a *regional* market and some in a *global* one. The concentration measures for newspapers are low, indicating competition, but in most cities the newspaper industry is highly concentrated. The concentration measures for automobiles is high, indicating little competition, but the biggest three U.S. car makers compete with foreign car makers in a highly competitive global market.

Barriers to Entry and Firm Turnover Some markets are highly concentrated but entry is easy and the turnover of firms is large. For example, small towns have few restaurants, but no restrictions hinder a new restaurant from opening and many attempt to do so.

Also, a market with only a few firms might be competitive because of *potential entry*. The few firms in a market face competition from the many potential firms that will enter the market if economic profit opportunities arise.

Market and Industry Correspondence To calculate concentration ratios, the Department of Commerce classifies each firm as being in a particular industry. But markets do not always correspond closely to industries for three reasons.

First, markets are often narrower than industries. For example, the pharmaceutical industry, which has a low concentration ratio, operates in many separate markets for individual products—for example, measles vaccine and AIDS-fighting drugs. These drugs do not compete with each other, so this industry, which looks competitive, includes firms that are monopolies (or near monopolies) in markets for individual drugs.

Second, most firms make several products. For example, Westinghouse makes electrical equipment and, among other things, gas-fired incinerators and plywood. So this one firm operates in at least three separate markets, but the Department of Commerce classifies Westinghouse as being in the electrical goods and equipment industry. The fact that Westinghouse competes with other producers of plywood does not

Economics in Action
A Competitive Environment

How competitive are markets in the United States? Do most U.S. firms operate in competitive markets, in monopolistic competition, in oligopoly, or in monopoly markets?

The data needed to answer these questions are hard to get. The last attempt to answer the questions, in a study by William G. Shepherd, an economics professor at the University of Massachusetts at Amherst, covered the years from 1939 to 1980. The figure shows what he discovered.

In 1980, three quarters of the value of goods and services bought and sold in the United States was traded in markets that are essentially competitive—markets that have almost perfect competition or monopolistic competition. Monopoly and the dominance of a single firm accounted for about 5 percent of sales. Oligopoly, which is found mainly in manufacturing, accounted for about 18 percent of sales.

Over the period studied, the U.S. economy became increasingly competitive. The percentage of output sold by firms operating in competitive markets (blue bars) has expanded most, and has shrunk most in oligopoly markets (red bars).

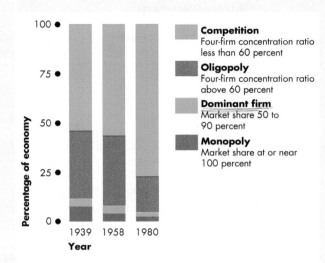

The Market Structure of the U.S. Economy

William G. Shepherd, "Causes of Increased Competition in the U.S. Economy, 1939–1980," *Review of Economics and Statistics*, 64:4 (November, 1982), pp. 613–626. © 1982 by the President and Fellows of Harvard College. Reprinted with permission.

But also during the past decades, the U.S. economy has become much more exposed to competition from the rest of the world. The data used by William G. Shepherd don't capture this international competition, so the data probably understate the degree of true competition in the U.S. economy.

show up in the concentration numbers for the plywood market.

Third, firms switch from one market to another depending on profit opportunities. For example, Motorola, which today produces cellular telephones and other communications products, has diversified from being a TV and computer chip maker. Motorola no longer produces TVs. Publishers of newspapers, magazines, and textbooks are today rapidly diversifying into Internet and multimedia products. These switches among markets show that there is much scope for entering and exiting a market, and so measures of concentration have limited usefulness.

Despite their limitations, concentration measures do provide a basis for determining the degree of competition in a market when they are combined with information about the geographical scope of the market, barriers to entry, and the extent to which large, multiproduct firms straddle a variety of markets.

REVIEW QUIZ

1 What are the four market types? Explain the distinguishing characteristics of each.

2 What are the two measures of concentration? Explain how each measure is calculated.

3 Under what conditions do the measures of concentration give a good indication of the degree of competition in a market?

4 Is our economy competitive? Is it becoming more competitive or less competitive?

You can work these questions in Study Plan 9.1 and get instant feedback.

You now know the variety of market types and how we identify them. Our final question in this chapter is: What determines the things that firms decide to buy from other firms rather than produce for themselves?

◆ Decision Time Frames

People who operate firms make many decisions, and all of their decisions are aimed at achieving one overriding goal: maximum attainable profit. But not all decisions are equally critical. Some decisions are big ones. Once made, they are costly (or impossible) to reverse. If such a decision turns out to be incorrect, it might lead to the failure of the firm. Other decisions are small. They are easily changed. If one of these decisions turns out to be incorrect, the firm can change its actions and survive.

The biggest decision that an entrepreneur makes is in what industry to establish a firm. For most entrepreneurs, their background knowledge and interests drive this decision. But the decision also depends on profit prospects—on the expectation that total revenue will exceed total cost.

Cindy has already decided to set up Campus Sweaters. She has also decided the most effective method of organizing the firm. But she has not decided the quantity to produce, the factors of production to hire, or the price to charge for sweaters.

Decisions about the quantity to produce and the price to charge depend on the type of market in which the firm operates. Perfect competition, monopolistic competition, oligopoly, and monopoly all confront the firm with their own special problems. Decisions about *how* to produce a given output do not depend on the type of market in which the firm operates. *All* types of firms in *all* types of markets make similar decisions about how to produce.

The actions that a firm can take to influence the relationship between output and cost depend on how soon the firm wants to act. A firm that plans to change its output rate tomorrow has fewer options than one that plans to change its output rate six months or six years from now.

To study the relationship between a firm's output decision and its costs, we distinguish between two decision time frames:

- The short run
- The long run

The Short Run

The **short run** is a time frame in which the quantity of at least one factor of production is fixed. For most firms, capital, land, and entrepreneurship are fixed factors of production and labor is the variable factor of production. We call the fixed factors of production the firm's *plant*: In the short run, a firm's plant is fixed.

For Campus Sweaters, the fixed plant is its factory building and its knitting machines. For an electric power utility, the fixed plant is its buildings, generators, computers, and control systems.

To increase output in the short run, a firm must increase the quantity of a variable factor of production, which is usually labor. So to produce more output, Campus Sweaters must hire more labor and operate its knitting machines for more hours a day. Similarly, an electric power utility must hire more labor and operate its generators for more hours a day.

Short-run decisions are easily reversed. The firm can increase or decrease its output in the short run by increasing or decreasing the amount of labor it hires.

The Long Run

The **long run** is a time frame in which the quantities of *all* factors of production can be varied. That is, the long run is a period in which the firm can change its *plant*.

To increase output in the long run, a firm can change its plant as well as the quantity of labor it hires. Campus Sweaters can decide whether to install more knitting machines, use a new type of machine, reorganize its management, or hire more labor. Long-run decisions are *not* easily reversed. Once a plant decision is made, the firm usually must live with it for some time. To emphasize this fact, we call the past expenditure on a plant that has no resale value a **sunk cost**. A sunk cost is irrelevant to the firm's current decisions. The only costs that influence its current decisions are the short-run cost of changing its labor inputs and the long-run cost of changing its plant.

REVIEW QUIZ

1 Distinguish between the short run and the long run.
2 Why is a sunk cost irrelevant to a firm's current decisions?

You can work these questions in Study Plan 9.2 and get instant feedback.

We're going to study costs in the short run and the long run. We begin with the short run and describe a firm's technology constraint.

◆ Short-Run Technology Constraint

To increase output in the short run, a firm must increase the quantity of labor employed. We describe the relationship between output and the quantity of labor employed by using three related concepts:

1. Total product
2. Marginal product
3. Average product

These product concepts can be illustrated either by product schedules or by product curves. Let's look first at the product schedules.

Product Schedules

Table 9.3 shows some data that describe Campus Sweaters' total product, marginal product, and average product. The numbers tell us how the quantity of sweaters produced increases as Campus Sweaters employs more workers. The numbers also tell us about the productivity of the labor that Campus Sweaters employs.

Focus first on the columns headed "Labor" and "Total product." **Total product** is the maximum output that a given quantity of labor can produce. You can see from the numbers in these columns that as Campus Sweaters employs more labor, total product increases. For example, when 1 worker is employed, total product is 4 sweaters a day, and when 2 workers are employed, total product is 10 sweaters a day. Each increase in employment increases total product.

The **marginal product** of labor is the increase in total product that results from a one-unit increase in the quantity of labor employed, with all other inputs remaining the same. For example, in Table 9.3, when Campus Sweaters increases employment from 2 to 3 workers and does not change its capital, the marginal product of the third worker is 3 sweaters—total product increases from 10 to 13 sweaters.

Average product tells how productive workers are on average. The **average product** of labor is equal to total product divided by the quantity of labor employed. For example, in Table 9.3, the average product of 3 workers is 4.33 sweaters per worker—13 sweaters a day divided by 3 workers.

If you look closely at the numbers in Table 9.3, you can see some patterns. As Campus Sweaters hires more labor, marginal product increases initially, and

$MP = \Delta Q / \Delta L$

TABLE 9.3 Total Product, Marginal Product, and Average Product

	Labor (workers per day)	Total product (sweaters per day)	Marginal product (sweaters per additional worker)	Average product (sweaters per worker)
A	0	0		
			4	
B	1	4		4.00
			6	
C	2	10		5.00
			3	
D	3	13		4.33
			2	
E	4	15		3.75
			1	
F	5	16		3.20

Total product is the total amount produced. Marginal product is the change in total product that results from a one-unit increase in labor. For example, when labor increases from 2 to 3 workers a day (row C to row D), total product increases from 10 to 13 sweaters a day. The marginal product of going from 2 to 3 workers is 3 sweaters. Average product is total product divided by the quantity of labor employed. For example, the average product of 3 workers is 4.33 sweaters per worker (13 sweaters a day divided by 3 workers).

then begins to decrease. For example, marginal product increases from 4 sweaters a day for the first worker to 6 sweaters a day for the second worker and then decreases to 3 sweaters a day for the third worker. Average product also increases at first and then decreases. You can see the relationships between the quantity of labor hired and the three product concepts more clearly by looking at the product curves.

Product Curves

The product curves are graphs of the relationships between employment and the three product concepts you've just studied. They show how total product, marginal product, and average product change as employment changes. They also show the relationships among the three concepts. Let's look at the product curves.

Total Product Curve

Figure 9.1 shows Campus Sweaters' total product curve, *TP*, which is a graph of the total product schedule. Points *A* through *F* correspond to rows *A* through *F* in Table 9.1. To graph the entire total product curve, we vary labor by hours rather than whole days.

Notice the shape of the total product curve. As employment increases from zero to 1 worker a day, the curve becomes steeper. Then, as employment increases to 3, 4, and 5 workers a day, the curve becomes less steep.

The total product curve is similar to the *production possibilities frontier* (explained in Chapter 2). It separates the attainable output levels from those that are unattainable. All the points that lie above the curve are unattainable. Points that lie below the curve, in the orange area, are attainable, but they are inefficient—they use more labor than is necessary to produce a given output. Only the points *on* the total product curve are technologically efficient.

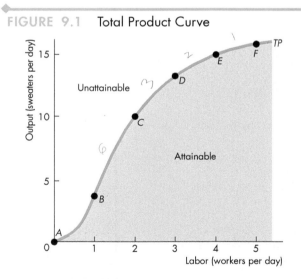

FIGURE 9.1   Total Product Curve

The total product curve, *TP*, is based on the data in Table 9.1. The total product curve shows how the quantity of sweaters produced changes as the quantity of labor employed changes. For example, 2 workers can produce 10 sweaters a day (point *C*). Points *A* through *F* on the curve correspond to the rows of Table 9.1. The total product curve separates attainable outputs from unattainable outputs. Points below the *TP* curve are inefficient.

myeconlab   animation

Marginal Product Curve

Figure 9.2 shows Campus Sweaters' marginal product of labor. Part (a) reproduces the total product curve from Fig. 9.1 and part (b) shows the marginal product curve, *MP*.

In part (a), the orange bars illustrate the marginal product of labor. The height of a bar measures marginal product. Marginal product is also measured by the slope of the total product curve. Recall that the slope of a curve is the change in the value of the variable measured on the *y*-axis—output—divided by the change in the variable measured on the *x*-axis—labor—as we move along the curve. A one-unit increase in labor, from 2 to 3 workers, increases output from 10 to 13 sweaters, so the slope from point *C* to point *D* is 3 sweaters per additional worker, the same as the marginal product we've just calculated.

Again varying the amount of labor in the smallest units possible, we can draw the marginal product curve shown in Fig. 9.2(b). The *height* of this curve measures the *slope* of the total product curve at a point. Part (a) shows that an increase in employment from 2 to 3 workers increases output from 10 to 13 sweaters (an increase of 3). The increase in output of 3 sweaters appears on the *y*-axis of part (b) as the marginal product of going from 2 to 3 workers. We plot that marginal product at the midpoint between 2 and 3 workers. Notice that the marginal product shown in Fig. 9.2(b) reaches a peak at 1.5 workers, and at that point, marginal product is 6 sweaters per additional worker. The peak occurs at 1.5 workers because the total product curve is steepest when employment increases from 1 worker to 2 workers.

The total product and marginal product curves differ across firms and types of goods. GM's product curves are different from those of PennPower, whose curves in turn are different from those of Campus Sweaters. But the shapes of the product curves are similar because almost every production process has two features:

- Increasing marginal returns initially
- Diminishing marginal returns eventually

Increasing Marginal Returns Increasing marginal returns occur when the marginal product of an additional worker exceeds the marginal product of the previous worker. Increasing marginal returns arise from increased specialization and division of labor in the production process.

FIGURE 9.2   Total Product and Marginal Product

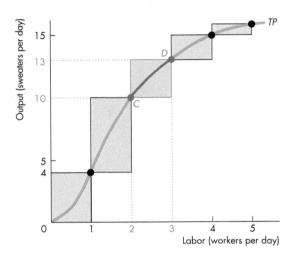

(a) Total product

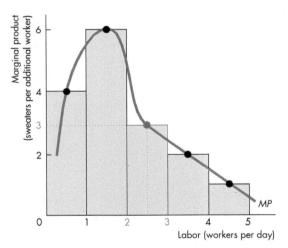

(b) Marginal product

Marginal product is illustrated by the orange bars. For example, when labor increases from 2 to 3 workers a day, marginal product is the orange bar whose height is 3 sweaters. (Marginal product is shown midway between the quantities of labor to emphasize that marginal product results from *changing* the quantity of labor.) The steeper the slope of the total product curve (*TP*) in part (a), the larger is marginal product (*MP*) in part (b). Marginal product increases to a maximum (in this example when 1.5 workers a day are employed) and then declines—diminishing marginal product.

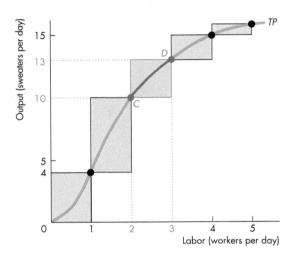 myeconlab animation

For example, if Campus Sweaters employs one worker, that person must learn all the aspects of sweater production: running the knitting machines, fixing breakdowns, packaging and mailing sweaters, buying and checking the type and color of the wool. All these tasks must be performed by that one person.

If Campus Sweaters hires a second person, the two workers can specialize in different parts of the production process and can produce more than twice as much as one worker. The marginal product of the second worker is greater than the marginal product of the first worker. Marginal returns are increasing.

Diminishing Marginal Returns Most production processes experience increasing marginal returns initially, but all production processes eventually reach a point of *diminishing* marginal returns. **Diminishing marginal returns** occur when the marginal product of an additional worker is less than the marginal product of the previous worker.

Diminishing marginal returns arise from the fact that more and more workers are using the same capital and working in the same space. As more workers are added, there is less and less for the additional workers to do that is productive. For example, if Campus Sweaters hires a third worker, output increases but not by as much as it did when it hired the second worker. In this case, after two workers are hired, all the gains from specialization and the division of labor have been exhausted. By hiring a third worker, the factory produces more sweaters, but the equipment is being operated closer to its limits. There are even times when the third worker has nothing to do because the machines are running without the need for further attention. Hiring more and more workers continues to increase output but by successively smaller amounts. Marginal returns are diminishing. This phenomenon is such a pervasive one that it is called a "law"—the law of diminishing returns. The **law of diminishing returns** states that

As a firm uses more of a variable factor of production with a given quantity of the fixed factor of production, the marginal product of the variable factor eventually diminishes.

You are going to return to the law of diminishing returns when we study a firm's costs, but before we do that, let's look at the average product of labor and the average product curve.

Average Product Curve

Figure 9.3 illustrates Campus Sweaters' average product of labor and shows the relationship between average product and marginal product. Points *B* through *F* on the average product curve *AP* correspond to those same rows in Table 9.1. Average product increases from 1 to 2 workers (its maximum value at point *C*) but then decreases as yet more workers are employed. Notice also that average product is largest when average product and marginal product are equal. That is, the marginal product curve cuts the average product curve at the point of maximum average product. For the number of workers at which marginal product exceeds average product, average product is *increasing*. For the number of workers at which marginal product is less than average product, average product is *decreasing*.

The relationship between the average product and marginal product is a general feature of the relationship between the average and marginal values of any variable—even your grades.

FIGURE 9.3   Average Product $AP_L = Q/L$

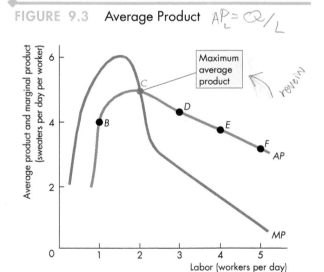

The figure shows the average product of labor and the connection between average product and marginal product. With 1 worker, marginal product exceeds average product, so average product is increasing. With 2 workers, marginal product equals average product, so average product is at its maximum. With more than 2 workers, marginal product is less than average product, so average product is decreasing.

 animation

Economics in Action
How to Pull Up Your Average

Do you want to pull up your average grade? Then make sure that your grade this semester is better than your current average! This semester is your marginal semester. If your marginal grade exceeds your average grade (like the second semester in the figure), your average will rise. If your marginal grade equals your average grade (like the third semester in the figure), your average won't change. If your marginal grade is below your average grade (like the fourth semester in the figure), your average will fall.

The relationship between your marginal and average grades is exactly the same as that between marginal product and average product.

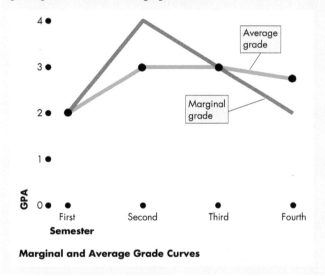

Marginal and Average Grade Curves

REVIEW QUIZ

1 Explain how the marginal product and average product of labor change as the labor employed increases (a) initially and (b) eventually.
2 What is the law of diminishing returns? Why does marginal product eventually diminish?
3 Explain the relationship between marginal product and average product.

You can work these questions in Study Plan 9.3 and get instant feedback.   **myeconlab**

Campus Sweaters' product curves influence its costs, as you are now going to see.

◆ Short-Run Cost

To produce more output in the short run, a firm must employ more labor, which means that it must increase its costs. We describe the relationship between output and cost by using three cost concepts:

- Total cost
- Marginal cost
- Average cost

Total Cost

A firm's **total cost** (TC) is the cost of *all* the factors of production it uses. We separate total cost into total *fixed* cost and total *variable* cost.

Total fixed cost (TFC) is the cost of the firm's fixed factors. For Campus Sweaters, total fixed cost includes the cost of renting knitting machines and *normal profit*, which is the opportunity cost of Cindy's entrepreneurship. The quantities of fixed factors don't change as output changes, so total fixed cost is the same at all outputs.

Total variable cost (TVC) is the cost of the firm's variable factors. For Campus Sweaters, labor is the variable factor, so this component of cost is its wage bill. Total variable cost changes as output changes.

Total cost is the sum of total fixed cost and total variable cost. That is,

$$TC = TFC + TVC.$$

The table in Fig. 9.4 shows total costs. Campus Sweaters rents one knitting machine for $25 a day, so its TFC is $25. To produce sweaters, the firm hires labor, which costs $25 a day. TVC is the number of workers multiplied by $25. For example, to produce 13 sweaters a day, in row D, the firm hires 3 workers and TVC is $75. TC is the sum of TFC and TVC, so to produce 13 sweaters a day, TC is $100. Check the calculations in the other rows of the table.

Figure 9.4 shows Campus Sweaters' total cost curves, which graph total cost against output. The green TFC curve is horizontal because total fixed cost ($25 a day) does not change when output changes. The purple TVC curve and the blue TC curve both slope upward because to increase output, more labor must be employed, which increases total variable cost. Total fixed cost equals the vertical distance between the TVC and TC curves.

Let's now look at a firm's marginal cost.

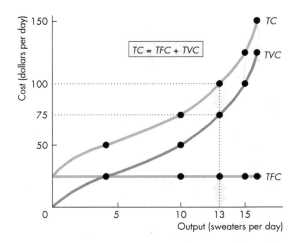

FIGURE 9.4   Total Cost Curves

$$TC = TFC + TVC$$

Labor (workers per day)	Output (sweaters per day)	Total fixed cost (*TFC*)	Total variable cost (*TVC*)	Total cost (*TC*)
		(dollars per day)		
A 0	0	25	0	25
B 1	4	25	25	50
C 2	10	25	50	75
D 3	**13**	**25**	**75**	**100**
E 4	15	25	100	125
F 5	16	25	125	150

Campus Sweaters rents a knitting machine for $25 a day, so this cost is the firm's total fixed cost. The firm hires workers at a wage rate of $25 a day, and this cost is its total variable cost. For example, in row D, Campus Sweaters employs 3 workers and its total variable cost is 3 × $25, which equals $75. Total cost is the sum of total fixed cost and total variable cost. For example, when Campus Sweaters employs 3 workers, total cost is $100—total fixed cost of $25 plus total variable cost of $75.

The graph shows Campus Sweaters' total cost curves. Total fixed cost is constant—the TFC curve is a horizontal line. Total variable cost increases as output increases, so the TVC curve and the TC curve increase as output increases. The vertical distance between the TC curve and the TVC curve equals total fixed cost, as illustrated by the two arrows.

 myeconlab animation

Marginal Cost

$MC = \Delta VC / Q$

$= (wage \times \Delta L) / \Delta Q = \dfrac{wage}{MP_L}$

Figure 9.4 shows that total variable cost and total cost increase at a decreasing rate at small outputs but eventually, as output increases, total variable cost and total cost increase at an increasing rate. To understand this pattern in the change in total cost as output increases, we need to use the concept of *marginal cost*.

A firm's **marginal cost** is the increase in total cost that results from a one-unit increase in output. We calculate marginal cost as the increase in total cost divided by the increase in output. The table in Fig. 9.5 shows this calculation. When, for example, output increases from 10 sweaters to 13 sweaters, total cost increases from $75 to $100. The change in output is 3 sweaters, and the change in total cost is $25. The marginal cost of one of those 3 sweaters is ($25 ÷ 3), which equals $8.33.

Figure 9.5 graphs the marginal cost data in the table as the red marginal cost curve, *MC*. This curve is U-shaped because when Campus Sweaters hires a second worker, marginal cost decreases, but when it hires a third, a fourth, and a fifth worker, marginal cost successively increases.

At small outputs, marginal cost decreases as output increases because of greater specialization and the division of labor. But as output increases further, marginal cost eventually increases because of the *law of diminishing returns*. The law of diminishing returns means that the output produced by each additional worker is successively smaller. To produce an additional unit of output, ever more workers are required, and the cost of producing the additional unit of output—marginal cost—must eventually increase.

Marginal cost tells us how total cost changes as output increases. The final cost concept tells us what it costs, on average, to produce a unit of output. Let's now look at Campus Sweaters' average costs.

Average Cost

Three average costs of production are

1. Average fixed cost
2. Average variable cost
3. Average total cost

$AVC = TVC / Q$

$= (wage \times L) / Q$

$wage / AP_L$

Average fixed cost (*AFC*) is total fixed cost per unit of output. **Average variable cost** (*AVC*) is total variable cost per unit of output. **Average total cost** (*ATC*) is total cost per unit of output. The average cost con-

cepts are calculated from the total cost concepts as follows:

$$TC = TFC + TVC.$$

Divide each total cost term by the quantity produced, *Q*, to get

$$\frac{TC}{Q} = \frac{TFC}{Q} + \frac{TVC}{Q},$$

(fixed)

or

$$ATC = AFC + AVC.$$

The table in Fig. 9.5 shows the calculation of average total cost. For example, in row *C*, output is 10 sweaters. Average fixed cost is ($25 ÷ 10), which equals $2.50, average variable cost is ($50 ÷ 10), which equals $5.00, and average total cost is ($75 ÷ 10), which equals $7.50. Note that average total cost is equal to average fixed cost ($2.50) plus average variable cost ($5.00).

Figure 9.5 shows the average cost curves. The green average fixed cost curve (*AFC*) slopes downward. As output increases, the same constant total fixed cost is spread over a larger output. The blue average total cost curve (*ATC*) and the purple average variable cost curve (*AVC*) are U-shaped. The vertical distance between the average total cost and average variable cost curves is equal to average fixed cost—as indicated by the two arrows. That distance shrinks as output increases because average fixed cost declines with increasing output.

Marginal Cost and Average Cost

The marginal cost curve (*MC*) intersects the average variable cost curve and the average total cost curve *at their minimum points*. When marginal cost is less than average cost, average cost is decreasing, and when marginal cost exceeds average cost, average cost is increasing. This relationship holds for both the *ATC* curve and the *AVC* curve. It is another example of the relationship you saw in Fig. 9.5 for average product and marginal product and in your average and marginal grades.

Why the Average Total Cost Curve Is U-Shaped

Average total cost is the sum of average fixed cost and average variable cost, so the shape of the *ATC* curve

*AVC reaches a minimum at a lower level
of output than ATC.
Distance between ATC and AVC is AFC
and AFC is falling as output expand*

FIGURE 9.5   Marginal Cost and Average Costs

$AVC_{min} < ATC_{min}$

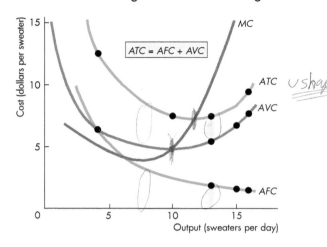

ATC = AFC + AVC

ATC *Ushaped*

Marginal cost is calculated as the change in total cost divided by the change in output. When output increases from 4 to 10 sweaters, an increase of 6 sweaters, total cost increases by $25. Marginal cost is $25 ÷ 6, which is $4.17.

Each average cost concept is calculated by dividing the related total cost by output. When 10 sweaters are produced, AFC is $2.50 ($25 ÷ 10), AVC is $5 ($50 ÷ 10), and ATC is $7.50 ($75 ÷ 10).

The graph shows that the MC curve is U-shaped and intersects the AVC curve and the ATC curve at their minimum points. The average fixed cost curve (AFC) is downward sloping. The ATC curve and AVC curve are U-shaped. The vertical distance between the ATC curve and the AVC curve is equal to average fixed cost, as illustrated by the two arrows.

	Labor (workers per day)	Output (sweaters per day)	Total fixed cost (TFC)	Total variable cost (TVC)	Total cost (TC)	Marginal cost (MC) (dollars per additional sweater)	Average fixed cost (AFC)	Average variable cost (AVC)	Average total cost (ATC)
			(dollars per day)				(dollars per sweater)		
A	0	0	25	0	25		—	—	—
						...... 6.25			
B	1	4	25	25	50		6.25	6.25	12.50
						...... 4.17			
C	2	10	25	50	75		2.50	5.00	7.50
						...... 8.33			
D	3	13	25	75	100		1.92	5.77	7.69
						......12.50			
E	4	15	25	100	125		1.67	6.67	8.33
						......25.00			
F	5	16	25	125	150		1.56	7.81	9.38

MP
]G
AVC
ΔVC / MP

myeconlab animation

combines the shapes of the AFC and AVC curves. The U shape of the ATC curve arises from the influence of two opposing forces:

1. Spreading total fixed cost over a larger output
2. Eventually diminishing returns

When output increases, the firm spreads its total fixed cost over a larger output and so its average fixed cost decreases—its AFC curve slopes downward.

Diminishing returns means that as output increases, ever-larger amounts of labor are needed to produce an additional unit of output. So as output increases, average variable cost decreases initially but

eventually increases, and the AVC curve slopes upward. The AVC curve is U shaped.

The shape of the ATC curve combines these two effects. Initially, as output increases, both average fixed cost and average variable cost decrease, so average total cost decreases. The ATC curve slopes downward.

But as output increases further and diminishing returns set in, average variable cost starts to increase. With average fixed cost decreasing more quickly than average variable cost is increasing, the ATC curve continues to slope downward. Eventually, average variable cost starts to increase more quickly than average fixed cost decreases, so average total cost starts to increase. The ATC curve slopes upward.

Cost Curves and Product Curves

The technology that a firm uses determines its costs. Figure 9.6 shows the links between the firm's product curves and its cost curves. The upper graph shows the average product curve, *AP*, and the marginal product curve, *MP*—like those in Fig. 9.3. The lower graph shows the average variable cost curve, *AVC*, and the marginal cost curve, *MC*—like those in Fig. 9.5.

As labor increases up to 1.5 workers a day (upper graph), output increases to 6.5 sweaters a day (lower graph). Marginal product and average product rise and marginal cost and average variable cost fall. At the point of maximum marginal product, marginal cost is at a minimum.

As labor increases from 1.5 workers to 2 workers a day, (upper graph) output increases from 6.5 sweaters to 10 sweaters a day (lower graph). Marginal product falls and marginal cost rises, but average product continues to rise and average variable cost continues to fall. At the point of maximum average product, average variable cost is at a minimum. As labor increases further, output increases. Average product diminishes and average variable cost increases.

Shifts in the Cost Curves

The position of a firm's short-run cost curves depends on two factors:

- Technology
- Prices of factors of production

Technology A technological change that increases productivity increases the marginal product and average product of labor. With a better technology, the same factors of production can produce more output, so the technological advance lowers the costs of production and shifts the cost curves downward.

For example, advances in robot production techniques have increased productivity in the automobile industry. As a result, the product curves of Chrysler, Ford, and GM have shifted upward and their cost curves have shifted downward. But the relationships between their product curves and cost curves have not changed. The curves are still linked in the way shown in Fig. 9.6.

Often, as in the case of robots producing cars, a technological advance results in a firm using more capital, a fixed factor, and less labor, a variable factor.

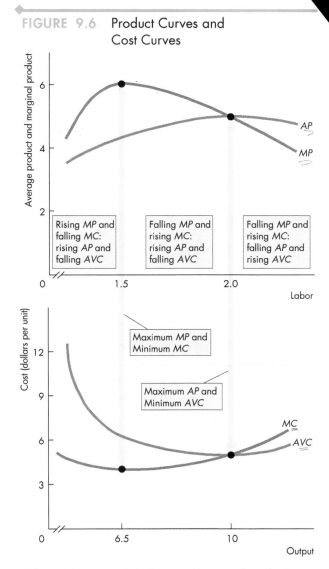

FIGURE 9.6 Product Curves and Cost Curves

A firm's *MP* curve is linked to its *MC* curve. If, as the firm increases its labor from 0 to 1.5 workers a day, the firm's marginal product rises, its marginal cost falls. If marginal product is at a maximum, marginal cost is at a minimum. If, as the firm hires more labor, its marginal product diminishes, its marginal cost rises.

A firm's *AP* curve is linked to its *AVC* curve. If, as the firm increases its labor to 2 workers a day, its average product rises, its average variable cost falls. If average product is at a maximum, average variable cost is at a minimum. If, as the firm hires more labor, its average product diminishes, its average variable cost rises.

... pact Glossary of Costs

	Symbol	Definition	Equation
...st		Cost that is independent of the output level; cost of a fixed factor of production	
Variable cost		Cost that varies with the output level; cost of a variable factor of production	
Total fixed cost	TFC	Cost of the fixed factors of production	
Total variable cost	TVC	Cost of the variable factors of production	
Total cost	TC	Cost of all factors of production	$TC = TFC + TVC$
Output (total product)	TP	Total quantity produced (output Q)	
Marginal cost	MC	Change in total cost resulting from a one-unit increase in total product	$MC = \Delta TC \div \Delta Q$
Average fixed cost	AFC	Total fixed cost per unit of output	$AFC = TFC \div Q$
Average variable cost	AVC	Total variable cost per unit of output	$AVC = TVC \div Q$
Average total cost	ATC	Total cost per unit of output	$ATC = AFC + AVC$

Another example is the use of ATMs by banks to dispense cash. ATMs, which are fixed capital, have replaced tellers, which are variable labor. Such a technological change decreases total cost but increases fixed costs and decreases variable cost. This change in the mix of fixed cost and variable cost means that at small outputs, average total cost might increase, while at large outputs, average total cost decreases.

Prices of Factors of Production An increase in the price of a factor of production increases the firm's costs and shifts its cost curves. How the curves shift depends on which factor price changes.

An increase in rent or some other component of *fixed* cost shifts the *TFC* and *AFC* curves upward and shifts the *TC* curve upward but leaves the *AVC* and *TVC* curves and the *MC* curve unchanged. For example, if the interest expense paid by a trucking company increases, the fixed cost of transportation services increases.

An increase in wages, gasoline, or another component of *variable* cost shifts the *TVC* and *AVC* curves upward and shifts the *MC* curve upward but leaves the *AFC* and *TFC* curves unchanged. For example, if

truck drivers' wages or the price of gasoline increases, the variable cost and marginal cost of transportation services increase.

You've now completed your study of short-run costs. All the concepts that you've met are summarized in a compact glossary in Table 9.4.

REVIEW QUIZ

1 What relationships do a firm's short-run cost curves show?

2 How does marginal cost change as output increases (a) initially and (b) eventually?

3 What does the law of diminishing returns imply for the shape of the marginal cost curve?

4 What is the shape of the *AFC* curve and why does it have this shape?

5 What are the shapes of the *AVC* curve and the *ATC* curve and why do they have these shapes?

You can work these questions in Study Plan 9.4 and get instant feedback.

Long-Run Cost

We are now going to study the firm's long-run costs. In the long run, a firm can vary both the quantity of labor and the quantity of capital, so in the long run, all the firm's costs are variable.

The behavior of long-run cost depends on the firm's *production function*, which is the relationship between the maximum output attainable and the quantities of both labor and capital.

The Production Function

Table 9.5 shows Campus Sweaters' production function. The table lists total product schedules for four different quantities of capital. The quantity of capital identifies the plant size. The numbers for plant 1 are for a factory with 1 knitting machine—the case we've just studied. The other three plants have 2, 3, and 4 machines. If Campus Sweaters uses plant 2 with 2 knitting machines, the various amounts of labor can produce the outputs shown in the second column of the table. The other two columns show the outputs of yet larger quantities of capital. Each column of the table could be graphed as a total product curve for each plant.

Diminishing Returns Diminishing returns occur with each of the four plant sizes as the quantity of labor increases. You can check that fact by calculating the marginal product of labor in each of the plants with 2, 3, and 4 machines. With each plant size, as the firm increases the quantity of labor employed, the marginal product of labor (eventually) diminishes.

Diminishing Marginal Product of Capital
Diminishing returns also occur with each quantity of labor as the quantity of capital increases. You can check that fact by calculating the marginal product of capital at a given quantity of labor. The *marginal product of capital* is the change in total product divided by the change in capital when the quantity of labor is constant—equivalently, the change in output resulting from a one-unit increase in the quantity of capital. For example, if Campus Sweaters has 3 workers and increases its capital from 1 machine to 2 machines, output increases from 13 to 18 sweaters a day. The marginal product of the second machine is 5 sweaters a day. If Campus Sweaters continues to employ 3 workers

TABLE 9.5   The Production Function

Labor (workers per day)	Output (sweaters per day)			
	Plant 1	Plant 2	Plant 3	Plant 4
1	4	10	13	15
2	10	15	18	20
3	13	18	22	24
4	15	20	24	26
5	16	21	25	27
Knitting machines (number)	1	2	3	4

The table shows the total product data for four quantities of capital (plant sizes). The greater the plant size, the larger is the output produced by any given quantity of labor. For a given plant size, the marginal product of labor diminishes as more labor is employed. For a given quantity of labor, the marginal product of capital diminishes as the quantity of capital used increases.

and increases the number of machines from 2 to 3, output increases from 18 to 22 sweaters a day. The marginal product of the third machine is 4 sweaters a day, down from 5 sweaters a day for the second machine.

Let's now see what the production function implies for long-run costs.

Short-Run Cost and Long-Run Cost

As before, Campus Sweaters can hire workers for $25 a day and rent knitting machines for $25 a day. Using these factor prices and the data in Table 9.5, we can calculate the average total cost and graph the *ATC* curves for factories with 1, 2, 3, and 4 knitting machines. We've already studied the costs of a factory with 1 machine in Figs. 9.4 and 9.5. In Fig. 9.7, the average total cost curve for that case is ATC_1. Figure 9.7 also shows the average total cost curve for a factory with 2 machines, ATC_2, with 3 machines, ATC_3, and with 4 machines, ATC_4.

You can see, in Fig. 9.7, that the plant size has a big effect on the firm's average total cost.

FIGURE 9.7   Short-Run Costs of Four Different Plants

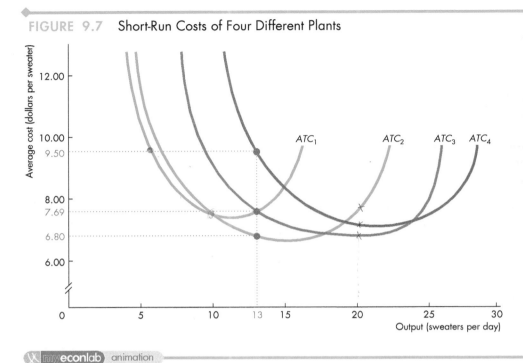

The figure shows short-run average total cost curves for four different quantities of capital at Campus Sweaters. The firm can produce 13 sweaters a day with 1 knitting machine on ATC_1 or with 3 knitting machines on ATC_3 for an average cost of $7.69 a sweater. The firm can produce 13 sweaters a day by using 2 machines on ATC_2 for $6.80 a sweater or by using 4 machines on ATC_4 for $9.50 a sweater.

If the firm produces 13 sweaters a day, the least-cost method of production, *the long-run method*, is with 2 machines on ATC_2.

In Fig. 9.7, two things stand out:

1. Each short-run ATC curve is U-shaped.
2. For each short-run ATC curve, the larger the plant, the greater is the output at which average total cost is at a minimum.

Each short-run ATC curve is U-shaped because, as the quantity of labor increases, its marginal product initially increases and then diminishes. This pattern in the marginal product of labor, which we examined in some detail for the plant with 1 knitting machine on pp. 177–178, occurs at all plant sizes.

The minimum average total cost for a larger plant occurs at a greater output than it does for a smaller plant because the larger plant has a higher total fixed cost and therefore, for any given output, a higher average fixed cost.

Which short-run ATC curve a firm operates on depends on the plant it has. In the long run, the firm can choose its plant and the plant it chooses is the one that enables it to produce its planned output at the lowest average total cost.

To see why, suppose that Campus Sweaters plans to produce 13 sweaters a day. In Fig. 9.7, with 1 machine, the average total cost curve is ATC_1 and the

average total cost of 13 sweaters a day is $7.69 a sweater. With 2 machines, on ATC_2, average total cost is $6.80 a sweater. With 3 machines, on ATC_3, average total cost is $7.69 a sweater, the same as with 1 machine. Finally, with 4 machines, on ATC_4, average total cost is $9.50 a sweater.

The economically efficient plant for producing a given output is the one that has the lowest average total cost. For Campus Sweaters, the economically efficient plant to use to produce 13 sweaters a day is the one with 2 machines.

In the long run, Cindy chooses the plant that minimizes average total cost. When a firm is producing a given output at the least possible cost, it is operating on its *long-run average cost curve*.

The **long-run average cost curve** is the relationship between the lowest attainable average total cost and output when the firm can change both the plant it uses and the quantity of labor it employs.

The long-run average cost curve is a planning curve. It tells the firm the plant and the quantity of labor to use at each output to minimize average cost. Once the firm chooses a plant, the firm operates on the short-run cost curves that apply to that plant.

The Long-Run Average Cost Curve

Figure 9.8 shows how a long-run average cost curve is derived. The long-run average cost curve *LRAC* consists of pieces of the four short-run *ATC* curves. For outputs up to 10 sweaters a day, average total cost is the lowest on ATC_1. For outputs between 10 and 18 sweaters a day, average total cost is the lowest on ATC_2. For outputs between 18 and 24 sweaters a day, average total cost is the lowest on ATC_3. And for outputs in excess of 24 sweaters a day, average total cost is the lowest on ATC_4. The piece of each *ATC* curve with the lowest average total cost is highlighted in dark blue in Fig. 9.8. This dark blue scallop-shaped curve made up of the pieces of the four *ATC* curves is the *LRAC* curve.

Economies and Diseconomies of Scale

Economies of scale are features of a firm's technology that make average total cost *fall* as output increases. When economies of scale are present, the *LRAC* curve slopes downward. In Fig. 9.8, Campus Sweaters has economies of scale for outputs up to 15 sweaters a day.

Greater specialization of both labor and capital is the main source of economies of scale. For example, if

GM produces 100 cars a week, each worker must perform many different tasks and the capital must be general-purpose machines and tools. But if GM produces 10,000 cars a week, each worker specializes in a small number of tasks, uses task-specific tools, and becomes highly proficient.

Diseconomies of scale are features of a firm's technology that make average total cost *rise* as output increases. When diseconomies of scale are present, the *LRAC* curve slopes upward. In Fig. 9.8, Campus Sweaters experiences diseconomies of scale at outputs greater than 15 sweaters a day.

The challenge of managing a large enterprise is the main source of diseconomies of scale.

Constant returns to scale are features of a firm's technology that keep average total cost constant as output increases. When constant returns to scale are present, the *LRAC* curve is horizontal.

Economies of Scale at Campus Sweaters The economies of scale and diseconomies of scale at Campus Sweaters arise from the firm's production function in Table 9.3. With 1 machine and 1 worker, the firm produces 4 sweaters a day. With 2 machines and 2 workers, total cost doubles but out-

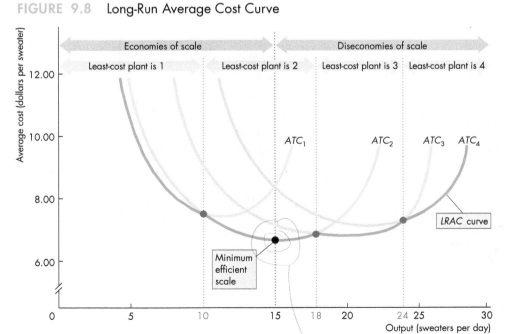

FIGURE 9.8   Long-Run Average Cost Curve

The long-run average cost curve traces the lowest attainable *ATC* when both labor and capital change. The green arrows highlight the output range over which each plant achieves the lowest *ATC*. Within each range, to change the quantity produced, the firm changes the quantity of labor it employs.

Along the *LRAC* curve, economies of scale occur if average cost falls as output increases; diseconomies of scale occur if average cost rises as output increases. Minimum efficient scale is the output at which average cost is lowest, 15 sweaters a day.

Economics in Action
Produce More to Cut Cost

Why do GM, Ford, and the other automakers have expensive equipment lying around that isn't fully used? You can answer this question with what you've learned in this chapter.

The basic answer is that auto production enjoys economies of scale. A larger output rate brings a lower long-run average cost—the firm's $LRAC$ curve slopes downward.

An auto producer's average total cost curves look like those in the figure. To produce 20 vehicles an hour, the firm installs the plant with the short-run average total cost curve ATC_1. The average cost of producing a vehicle is $20,000.

Producing 20 vehicles an hour doesn't use the plant at its lowest possible average total cost. If the firm could sell enough cars for it to produce 40 vehicles an hour, the firm could use its current plant and produce at an average cost of $15,000 a vehicle.

But if the firm planned to produce 40 vehicles an hour, it would not stick with its current plant. The firm would install a bigger plant with the short-run average total cost curve ATC_2, and produce 40 vehicles an hour for $10,000 a car.

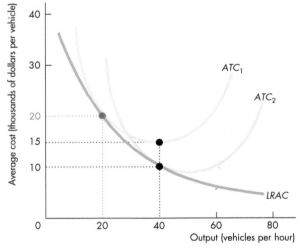

Automobile Plant Average Cost Curves

put more than doubles to 15 sweaters a day, so average cost decreases and Campus Sweaters experiences economies of scale. With 4 machines and 4 workers, total cost doubles again but output less than doubles to 26 sweaters a day, so average cost increases and the firm experiences diseconomies of scale.

Minimum Efficient Scale A firm's **minimum efficient scale** is the *smallest* output at which long-run average cost reaches its lowest level. At Campus Sweaters, the minimum efficient scale is 15 sweaters a day.

The minimum efficient scale plays a role in determining market structure. In a market in which the minimum efficient scale is small relative to market demand, the market has room for many firms, and the market is competitive. In a market in which the minimum efficient scale is large relative to market demand, only a small number of firms, and possibly only one firm, can make a profit and the market is either an oligopoly or monopoly. We will return to this idea in the next three chapters.

REVIEW QUIZ

1 What does a firm's production function show and how is it related to a total product curve?
2 Does the law of diminishing returns apply to capital as well as labor? Explain why or why not.
3 What does a firm's $LRAC$ curve show? How is it related to the firm's short-run ATC curves?
4 What are economies of scale and diseconomies of scale? How do they arise? What do they imply for the shape of the $LRAC$ curve?
5 What is a firm's minimum efficient scale?

You can work these questions in Study Plan 9.4 and get instant feedback.

SUMMARY

Key Points

Markets and the Competitive Environment

(pp. 170–174)

- In perfect competition, many sellers offer an identical product to many buyers and entry is free.
- In monopolistic competition, many sellers offer slightly different products to many buyers and entry is free.
- In oligopoly, a small number of sellers compete and barriers to entry limit the number of firms.
- In monopoly, one firm produces an item that has no close substitutes and the firm is protected by a barrier to entry that prevents the entry of competitors.

Working Problems 9 and 10 will give you a better understanding of markets and the competitive environment.

Decision Time Frames (p. 175)

- In the short run, the quantity of at least one factor of production is fixed and the quantities of the other factors of production can be varied.
- In the long run, the quantities of all factors of production can be varied.

Working Problems 1 and 2 will give you a better understanding of a firm's decision time frames.

Short-Run Technology Constraint (pp. 176–179)

- A total product curve shows the quantity a firm can produce with a given quantity of capital and different quantities of labor.
- Initially, the marginal product of labor increases as the quantity of labor increases, because of increased specialization and the division of labor.

- Eventually, marginal product diminishes because an increasing quantity of labor must share a fixed quantity of capital—the law of diminishing returns.
- Initially, average product increases as the quantity of labor increases, but eventually average product diminishes.

Working Problems 3 to 8 will give you a better understanding of a firm's short-run technology constraint.

Short-Run Cost (pp. 180–184)

- As output increases, total fixed cost is constant, and total variable cost and total cost increase.
- As output increases, average fixed cost decreases and average variable cost, average total cost, and marginal cost decrease at low outputs and increase at high outputs. These cost curves are U-shaped.

Working Problems 9 to 14 will give you a better understanding of a firm's short-run cost.

Long-Run Cost (pp. 185–188)

- A firm has a set of short-run cost curves for each different plant. For each output, the firm has one least-cost plant. The larger the output, the larger is the plant that will minimize average total cost.
- The long-run average cost curve traces out the lowest attainable average total cost at each output when both capital and labor inputs can be varied.
- With economies of scale, the long-run average cost curve slopes downward. With diseconomies of scale, the long-run average cost curve slopes upward.

Working Problems 15 to 20 will give you a better understanding of a firm's long-run cost.

Key Terms

Average fixed cost, 181
Average product, 176
Average total cost, 181
Average variable cost, 181
Constant returns to scale, 187
Diminishing marginal returns, 178
Diseconomies of scale, 187
Economic profit, 168
Economies of scale, 187
Four-firm concentration ratio, 171

Herfindahl-Hirschman Index, 171
Law of diminishing returns, 178
Long run, 175
Long-run average cost curve, 186
Marginal cost, 181
Marginal product, 176
Minimum efficient scale, 188
Monopolistic competition, 170
Monopoly, 171
Normal profit, 169

Oligopoly, 170
Perfect competition, 170
Product differentiation, 170
Short run, 175
Sunk cost, 175
Total cost, 180
Total fixed cost, 180
Total product, 176
Total variable cost, 180

STUDY PLAN PROBLEMS AND APPLICATIONS

myeconlab   You can work Problems 1 to 22 in MyEconLab Chapter 9 Study Plan and get instant feedback.

The Firm and Its Economic Problem (Study Plan 9.1)

1. One year ago, Jack and Jill set up a vinegar-bottling firm (called JJVB). Use the following information to calculate JJVB's opportunity cost of production during its first year of operation:
   - Jack and Jill put $50,000 of their own money into the firm.
   - They bought equipment for $30,000.
   - They hired one employee to help them for an annual wage of $20,000.
   - Jack gave up his previous job, at which he earned $30,000, and spent all his time working for JJVB.
   - Jill kept her old job, which paid $30 an hour, but gave up 10 hours of leisure each week (for 50 weeks) to work for JJVB.
   - JJVB bought $10,000 of goods and services from other firms.
   - The market value of the equipment at the end of the year was $28,000.
   - Jack and Jill have a $100,000 home loan on which they pay interest of 6 percent a year.

2. Joe, who has no skills, no job experience, and no alternative employment, runs a shoeshine stand at the airport. Operators of other shoeshine stands earn $10,000 a year. Joe pays rent to the airport of $2,000 a year, and his total revenue from shining shoes is $15,000 a year. Joe spent $1,000 on a chair, polish, and brushes, using his credit card to buy them. The interest on a credit card balance is 20 percent a year. At the end of the year, Joe was offered $500 for his business and all its equipment. Calculate Joe's opportunity cost of production and his economic profit.

Technological and Economic Efficiency (Study Plan 9.2)

3. Alternative ways of laundering 100 shirts are

Method	Labor (hours)	Capital (machines)
A	1	10
B	5	8
C	20	4
D	50	1

a. Which methods are technologically efficient?

b. Which method is economically efficient if the

hourly wage rate and the implicit rental rate of capital are as follows:
(i)   Wage rate $1, rental rate $100?
(ii) Wage rate $5, rental rate $50?
(iii) Wage rate $50, rental rate $5?

4. **John Deere's Farm Team**
   Deere opened up the Pune [India] center in 2001. Deere's move was unexpected: Deere is known for its heavy-duty farm equipment and big construction gear whereas many of India's 300 million farmers still use oxen-pulled plows.

   Source: *Fortune*, April 14, 2008

   a. Why do many Indian farmers still use oxen-pulled plows? Are they efficient or inefficient? Explain.

   b. How might making John Deere farm equipment available to Indian farmers change the technology constraint they face?

Markets and the Competitive Environment
(Study Plan 9.4)

5. Sales of the firms in the tattoo industry are

Firm	Sales (dollars per year)
Bright Spots	450
Freckles	325
Love Galore	250
Native Birds	200
Other 15 firms	800

Calculate the four-firm concentration ratio. What is the structure of the tattoo industry?

6. **GameStop Racks Up the Points**
   No retailer has more cachet among gamers than GameStop. For now, only Wal-Mart has a larger market share—21.3% last year. GameStop's share was 21.1% last year, and may well overtake Wal-Mart this year. But if new women gamers prefer shopping at Target to GameStop, Wal-Mart and Target might erode GameStop's market share.

   Source: *Fortune*, June 9, 2008

   a. According to the news clip, what is the structure of the U.S. retail video-game market?

   b. Estimate a range for the four-firm concentration ratio and the HHI for the game market in the United States based on the information provided in this news clip.

Economics in the News (Study Plan 9.N)

7. Lego, the Danish toymaker, incurred economic losses in 2003 and 2004. Lego faced competition from low-cost copiers of its products and a fall in demand. In 2004, to restore profits, Lego fired 3,500 of its 8,000 workers; closed factories in Switzerland and the United States; opened factories in Eastern Europe and Mexico; and introduced performance-based pay for its managers. Lego returned to profit in 2005.

> Based on **Picking Up the Pieces**,
> *The Economist*, October 28, 2006

   a. Describe the problems that Lego faced in 2003 and 2004, using the concepts of the three types of constraints that all firms face.

   b. Which of the actions that Lego took to restore profits addressed an inefficiency? How did Lego seek to achieve economic efficiency?

   c. Which of Lego's actions addressed an information and organization problem? How did Lego change the way in which it coped with the principal–agent problem?

   d. In what type of market does Lego operate?

The Firm and Its Economic Problem

Use the following information to work Problems 8 and 9.

Lee is a computer programmer who earned $35,000 in 2009. But on January 1, 2010, Lee opened a body board manufacturing business. At the end of the first year of operation, he submitted the following information to his accountant:

- He stopped renting out his cottage for $3,500 a year and used it as his factory. The market value of the cottage increased from $70,000 to $71,000.
- He spent $50,000 on materials, phone, etc.
- He leased machines for $10,000 a year.
- He paid $15,000 in wages.
- He used $10,000 from his savings account, which earns 5 percent a year interest.
- He borrowed $40,000 at 10 percent a year.
- He sold $160,000 worth of body boards.
- Normal profit is $25,000 a year.

8. Calculate Lee's opportunity cost of production and his economic profit.

9. Lee's accountant recorded the depreciation on his cottage during 2010 as $7,000. According to the accountant, what profit did Lee make?

10. In 2009, Toni taught music and earned $20,000. She also earned $4,000 by renting out her basement. On January 1, 2010, she quit teaching, stopped renting out her basement, and began to use it as the office for her new Web site design business. She took $2,000 from her savings account to buy a computer. During 2010, she paid $1,500 for the lease of a Web server and $1,750 for high-speed Internet service. She received a total revenue from Web site designing of $45,000 and earned interest at 5 percent a year on her savings account balance. Normal profit is $55,000 a year. At the end of 2010, Toni could have sold her computer for $500. Calculate Toni's opportunity cost of production and her economic profit in 2010.

11. **The Colvin Interview: Chrysler**
    The key driver of profitability will be that the focus of the company isn't on profitability. Our focus is on the customer. If we can find a way to give customers what they want better than anybody else, then what can stop us?

> Source: *Fortune*, April 14, 2008

   a. In spite of what Chrysler's vice chairman and co-president claims, why is Chrysler's focus actually on profitability?

   b. What would happen to Chrysler if it didn't focus on maximizing profit, but instead focused its production and pricing decisions to "give customers what they want"?

12. **Must Watches**
    Stocks too volatile? Bonds too boring? Then try an alternative investment—one you can wear on your wrist. … [The] typical return on a watch over five to ten years is roughly 10%. [One could] do better in an index fund, but … what other investment is so wearable?

> Source: *Fortune*, April 14, 2008

   a. What is the cost of buying a watch?

   b. What is the opportunity cost of owning a watch?

   c. Does owning a watch create an economic profit opportunity?

Technological and Economic Efficiency

Use the following information to work Problems 13 and 14.

Four methods of completing a tax return and the time taken by each method are: with a PC, 1 hour; with a pocket calculator, 12 hours; with a pocket calculator and paper and pencil, 12 hours; and with a pencil and paper, 16 hours. The PC and its software cost $1,000, the pocket calculator costs $10, and the pencil and paper cost $1.

13. Which, if any, of the methods is technologically efficient?

14. Which method is economically efficient if the wage rate is
    (i) $5 an hour?
    (ii) $50 an hour?
    (iii) $500 an hour?

15. **A Medical Sensation**

    Hospitals are buying da Vinci surgical robots. Surgeons, sitting comfortably at a da Vinci console, can use various robotic attachments to perform even the most complex procedures.

    Source: *Fortune*, April 28, 2008

    a. Assume that performing a surgery with a surgical robot requires fewer surgeons and nurses. Is using the surgical robot technologically efficient?

    b. What additional information would you need to be able to say that switching to surgical robots is economically efficient for a hospital?

Information and Organization

16. Wal-Mart has more than 3,700 stores, more than one million employees, and total revenues of close to a quarter of a trillion dollars in the United States alone. Sarah Frey-Talley runs the family-owned Frey Farms in Illinois and supplies Wal-Mart with pumpkins and other fresh produce.

    a. How does Wal-Mart coordinate its activities? Is it likely to use mainly a command system or also to use incentive systems? Explain.

    b. How do you think Sarah Frey-Talley coordinates the activities of Frey Farms? Is she likely to use mainly a command system or also to use incentive systems? Explain.

    c. Describe, compare, and contrast the principal–agent problems faced by Wal-Mart and Frey Farms. How might these firms cope with their principal–agent problems?

17. **Where Does Google Go Next?**

    Google gives its engineers one day a week to work on whatever project they want. A couple of colleagues did what many of the young geniuses do at Google: They came up with a cool idea. At Google, you often end up with a laissez-faire mess instead of resource allocation.

    Source: *Fortune*, May 26, 2008

    a. Describe Google's method of organizing production with their software engineers.

    b. What are the potential gains and opportunity costs associated with this method?

Markets and the Competitive Environment

18. Market shares of chocolate makers are

Firm	Market share (percent)
Mayfair, Inc.	15
Bond, Inc.	10
Magic, Inc.	20
All Natural, Inc.	15
Truffles, Inc.	25
Gold, Inc.	15

    a. Calculate the Herfindahl-Hirschman Index.

    b. What is the structure of the chocolate industry?

Produce or Outsource? Firms and Markets

Use the following information to work Problems 19 to 21.

Two leading design firms, Astro Studios of San Francisco and Hers Experimental Design Laboratory, Inc. of Osaka, Japan, worked with Microsoft to design the Xbox 360 video game console. IBM, ATI, and SiS designed the Xbox 360's hardware. Three firms—Flextronics, Wistron, and Celestica—manufacture the Xbox 360 at their plants in China and Taiwan.

19. Describe the roles of market coordination and coordination by firms in the design, manufacture, and marketing of the Xbox 360.

20. a. Why do you think Microsoft works with a large number of other firms, rather than performing all the required tasks itself?

    b. What are the roles of transactions costs, economies of scale, economies of scope, and economies of team production in the design, manufacture, and marketing of the Xbox?

21. Why do you think the Xbox is designed in the United States and Japan but built in China?

Economics in the News

22. **Long Reviled, Merit Pay Gains Among Teachers**
School districts in many states experiment with plans that compensate teachers partly based on classroom performance, rather than their years on the job and coursework completed. Working with mentors to improve their instruction and getting bonuses for raising student achievement encourages efforts to raise teaching quality.

Source: *The New York Times*, June 18, 2007

How does "merit pay" attempt to cope with the principal–agent problem in public education?

After studying this chapter, you will be able to:

◆ Define perfect competition

◆ Explain how a firm makes its output decision and why it sometimes shuts down temporarily and lays off its workers

◆ Explain how price and output are determined in a perfectly competitive market

◆ Explain why firms enter and leave a competitive market and the consequences of entry and exit

◆ Predict the effects of a change in demand and of a technological advance

◆ Explain why perfect competition is efficient

10

PERFECT COMPETITION

An Iowa corn farmer must make many decisions, but figuring out the price to charge for his corn is not one of them. Corn farmers must accept the price determined by supply and demand. The producers of most crops—among them wheat, rice, soybean, sugarbeet, and coffee—must also accept the prices that markets determine.

During the booming economic conditions of 2006 and 2007, crop prices and production soared. Then, following the global financial crisis of 2008 prices sagged, but for many crops production kept rising.

What are the forces that brought these changes in prices and production in the world's markets for farm products?

We're going to answer this question by studying competitive markets and building a model of a market in which competition is as fierce and extreme as possible. We call this situation *perfect* competition.

In *Reading Between the Lines* at the end of the chapter, we'll apply the model to the global market for corn and see how changes in demand and fortunate weather bring changes in prices and quantities produced in this key global agricultural market.

◆ What Is Perfect Competition?

The firms that you study in this chapter face the force of raw competition. We call this extreme form of competition perfect competition. **Perfect competition** is a market in which

- Many firms sell identical products to many buyers.
- There are no restrictions on entry into the market.
- Established firms have no advantage over new ones.
- Sellers and buyers are well informed about prices.

Farming, fishing, wood pulping and paper milling, the manufacture of paper cups and shopping bags, grocery and fresh flower retailing, photo finishing, lawn services, plumbing, painting, dry cleaning, and laundry services are all examples of highly competitive industries.

How Perfect Competition Arises

Perfect competition arises if the minimum efficient scale of a single producer is small relative to the market demand for the good or service. In this situation, there is room in the market for many firms. A firm's *minimum efficient scale* is the smallest output at which long-run average cost reaches its lowest level. (See Chapter 9, p. 188.)

In perfect competition, each firm produces a good that has no unique characteristics, so consumers don't care which firm's good they buy.

Price Takers

Firms in perfect competition are price takers. A **price taker** is a firm that cannot influence the market price because its production is an insignificant part of the total market.

Imagine that you are a wheat farmer in Kansas. You have a thousand acres planted—which sounds like a lot. But compared to the millions of acres in Colorado, Oklahoma, Texas, Nebraska, and the Dakotas, as well as the millions more in Canada, Argentina, Australia, and Ukraine, your thousand acres are a drop in the ocean. Nothing makes your wheat any better than any other farmer's, and all the buyers of wheat know the price at which they can do business.

If the market price of wheat is $4 a bushel, then that is the highest price you can get for your wheat. Ask for $4.10 and no one will buy from you. Offer it for $3.90 and you'll be sold out in a flash and have given away 10¢ a bushel. You take the market price.

Economic Profit and Revenue

A firm's goal is to maximize *economic profit*, which is equal to total revenue minus total cost. Total cost is the *opportunity cost* of production, which includes *normal profit*.

A firm's **total revenue** equals the price of its output multiplied by the number of units of output sold (price × quantity). **Marginal revenue** is the change in total revenue that results from a one-unit increase in the quantity sold. Marginal revenue is calculated by dividing the change in total revenue by the change in the quantity sold.

Figure 10.1 illustrates these revenue concepts. In part (a), the market demand curve, D, and market supply curve, S, determine the market price. The market price is $25 a sweater. Campus Sweaters is just one of many producers of sweaters, so the best it can do is to sell its sweaters for $25 each.

Total Revenue Total revenue is equal to the price multiplied by the quantity sold. In the table in Fig. 10.1, if Campus Sweaters sells 9 sweaters, its total revenue is $225 (9 × $25).

Figure 10.1(b) shows the firm's total revenue curve (TR), which graphs the relationship between total revenue and the quantity sold. At point A on the TR curve, the firm sells 9 sweaters and has a total revenue of $225. Because each additional sweater sold brings in a constant amount—$25—the total revenue curve is an upward-sloping straight line.

Marginal Revenue Marginal revenue is the change in total revenue that results from a one-unit increase in quantity sold. In the table in Fig. 10.1, when the quantity sold increases from 8 to 9 sweaters, total revenue increases from $200 to $225, so marginal revenue is $25 a sweater.

Because the firm in perfect competition is a price taker, the change in total revenue that results from a one-unit increase in the quantity sold equals the market price. *In perfect competition, the firm's marginal revenue equals the market price.* Figure 10.1(c) shows the firm's marginal revenue curve (MR) as the horizontal line at the market price.

Demand for the Firm's Product The firm can sell any quantity it chooses at the market price. So the demand curve for the firm's product is a horizontal line at the market price, the same as the firm's marginal revenue curve.

FIGURE 10.1   Demand, Price, and Revenue in Perfect Competition

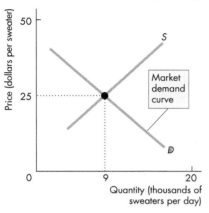
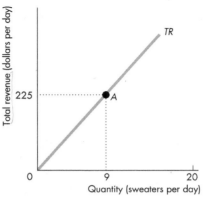
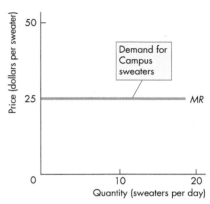

(a) Sweater market   **(b) Campus Sweaters' total revenue**   **(c) Campus Sweaters' marginal revenue**

Quantity sold (Q) (sweaters per day)	Price (P) (dollars per sweater)	Total revenue (TR = P × Q) (dollars)	Marginal revenue (MR = ΔTR/ΔQ) (dollars per additional sweater)
8	25	200	
			 25
9	25	225	
			 25
10	25	250	. . . .

In part (a), market demand and market supply determine the market price (and quantity). Part (b) shows the firm's total revenue curve (*TR*). Point *A* corresponds to the second row of the table—Campus Sweaters sells 9 sweaters at $25 a sweater, so total revenue is $225. Part (c) shows the firm's marginal revenue curve (*MR*). This curve is also the demand curve for the firm's sweaters. The demand for sweaters from Campus Sweaters is perfectly elastic at the market price of $25 a sweater.

 animation

A horizontal demand curve illustrates a perfectly elastic demand, so the demand for the firm's product is perfectly elastic. A sweater from Campus Sweaters is a *perfect substitute* for a sweater from any other factory. But the *market* demand for sweaters is *not* perfectly elastic: Its elasticity depends on the substitutability of sweaters for other goods and services.

The Firm's Decisions

The goal of the competitive firm is to maximize economic profit, given the constraints it faces. To achieve its goal, a firm must decide

1. How to produce at minimum cost
2. What quantity to produce
3. Whether to enter or exit a market

You've already seen how a firm makes the first decision. It does so by operating with the plant that minimizes long-run average cost—by being on its

long-run average cost curve. We'll now see how the firm makes the other two decisions. We start by looking at the firm's output decision.

REVIEW QUIZ

1 Why is a firm in perfect competition a price taker?
2 In perfect competition, what is the relationship between the demand for the firm's output and the market demand?
3 In perfect competition, why is a firm's marginal revenue curve also the demand curve for the firm's output?
4 What decisions must a firm make to maximize profit?

You can work these questions in Study Plan 10.1 and get instant feedback.

◆ The Firm's Output Decision

A firm's cost curves (total cost, average cost, and marginal cost) describe the relationship between its output and costs (see pp. 180–184). And a firm's revenue curves (total revenue and marginal revenue) describe the relationship between its output and revenue (p. 197). From the firm's cost curves and revenue curves, we can find the output that maximizes the firm's economic profit.

Figure 10.2 shows how to do this for Campus Sweaters. The table lists the firm's total revenue and total cost at different outputs, and part (a) of the figure shows the firm's total revenue curve, *TR*, and total cost curve, *TC*. These curves are graphs of numbers in the first three columns of the table.

Economic profit equals total revenue minus total cost. The fourth column of the table in Fig. 10.2 shows the economic profit made by Campus Sweaters, and part (b) of the figure graphs these numbers as its economic profit curve, *EP*.

Campus Sweaters maximizes its economic profit by producing 9 sweaters a day: Total revenue is $225, total cost is $183, and economic profit is $42. No other output rate achieves a larger profit.

At outputs of less than 4 sweaters and more than 12 sweaters a day, the Campus Sweaters would incur an economic loss. At either 4 or 12 sweaters a day, the Campus Sweaters would make zero economic profit, called a *break-even point*.

FIGURE 10.2   Total Revenue, Total Cost, and Economic Profit

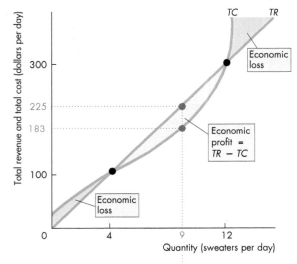

(a) Revenue and cost

(b) Economic profit and loss

Quantity (Q) (sweaters per day)	Total revenue (TR) (dollars)	Total cost (TC) (dollars)	Economic profit (TR − TC) (dollars)
0	0	22	–22
1	25	45	–20
2	50	66	–16
3	75	85	–10
4	100	100	0
5	125	114	11
6	150	126	24
7	175	141	34
8	200	160	40
9	225	183	42
10	250	210	40
11	275	245	30
12	300	300	0
13	325	360	–35

The table lists Campus Sweaters' total revenue, total cost, and economic profit. Part (a) graphs the total revenue and total cost curves and part (b) graphs economic profit.

Campus Sweaters makes maximum economic profit, $42 a day ($225 – $183), when it produces 9 sweaters a day. At outputs of 4 sweaters and 12 sweaters a day, Campus Sweaters makes zero economic profit—these are break-even points. At outputs less than 4 sweaters and greater than 12 sweaters a day, Campus Sweaters incurs an economic loss.

Marginal Analysis and the Supply Decision

Another way to find the profit-maximizing output is to use marginal analysis, which compares marginal revenue, *MR*, with marginal cost, *MC*. As output increases, the firm's marginal revenue is constant but its marginal cost eventually increases.

If marginal revenue exceeds marginal cost (*MR* > *MC*), then the revenue from selling one more unit exceeds the cost of producing it and an increase in output increases economic profit. If marginal revenue is less than marginal cost (*MR* < *MC*), then the revenue from selling one more unit is less than the cost of producing that unit and a *decrease* in output *increases* economic profit. If marginal revenue equals marginal cost (*MR* = *MC*), then the revenue from selling one more unit equals the cost incurred to produce that unit. Economic profit is maximized and either an increase or a decrease in output decreases economic profit.

Figure 10.3 illustrates these propositions. If Campus Sweaters increases its output from 8 sweaters to 9 sweaters a day, marginal revenue ($25) exceeds marginal cost ($23), so by producing the 9th sweater economic profit increases by $2 from $40 to $42 a day. The blue area in the figure shows the increase in economic profit when the firm increases production from 8 to 9 sweaters per day.

If Campus Sweaters increases its output from 9 sweaters to 10 sweaters a day, marginal revenue ($25) is less than marginal cost ($27), so by producing the 10th sweater, economic profit decreases. The last column of the table shows that economic profit decreases from $42 to $40 a day. The red area in the figure shows the economic loss that arises from increasing production from 9 to 10 sweaters a day.

Campus Sweaters maximizes economic profit by producing 9 sweaters a day, the quantity at which marginal revenue equals marginal cost.

A firm's profit-maximizing output is its quantity supplied at the market price. The quantity supplied at a price of $25 a sweater is 9 sweaters a day. If the price were higher than $25 a sweater, the firm would increase production. If the price were lower than $25 a sweater, the firm would decrease production. These profit-maximizing responses to different market prices are the foundation of the law of supply:

Other things remaining the same, the higher the market price of a good, the greater is the quantity supplied of that good.

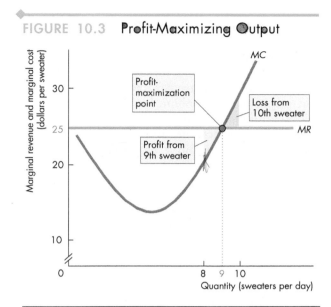

FIGURE 10.3 Profit-Maximizing Output

Quantity (Q) (sweaters per day)	Total revenue (TR) (dollars)	Marginal revenue (MR) (dollars per additional sweater)	Total cost (TC) (dollars)	Marginal cost (MC) (dollars per additional sweater)	Economic profit (TR − TC) (dollars)
7	175		141		34
		 25		 19	
8	200		160		40
		 25		 23	
9	225		183		42
		 25		 27	
10	250		210		40
		 25		 35	
11	275		245		30

The firm maximizes profit by producing the output at which marginal revenue equals marginal cost and marginal cost is increasing. The table and figure show that marginal cost equals marginal revenue and economic profit is maximized when Campus Sweaters produces 9 sweaters a day.

The table shows that if Campus Sweaters increases output from 8 to 9 sweaters, marginal cost is $23, which is less than the marginal revenue of $25. If output increases from 9 to 10 sweaters, marginal cost is $27, which exceeds the marginal revenue of $25. If marginal revenue exceeds marginal cost, an increase in output increases economic profit. If marginal revenue is less than marginal cost, an increase in output decreases economic profit. If marginal revenue equals marginal cost, economic profit is maximized.

Temporary Shutdown Decision

You've seen that a firm maximizes profit by producing the quantity at which marginal revenue (price) equals marginal cost. But suppose that at this quantity, price is less than average total cost. In this case, the firm incurs an economic loss. Maximum profit is a loss (a minimum loss). What does the firm do?

If the firm expects the loss to be permanent, it goes out of business. But if it expects the loss to be temporary, the firm must decide whether to shut down temporarily and produce no output, or to keep producing. To make this decision, the firm compares the loss from shutting down with the loss from producing and takes the action that minimizes its loss.

Loss Comparisons A firm's economic loss equals total fixed cost, *TFC*, plus total variable cost minus total revenue. Total variable cost equals average variable cost, *AVC*, multiplied by the quantity produced, *Q*, and total revenue equals price, *P*, multiplied by the quantity *Q*. So

$$\text{Economic loss} = TFC + (AVC - P) \times Q.$$

If the firm shuts down, it produces no output ($Q = 0$). The firm has no variable costs and no revenue but it must pay its fixed costs, so its economic loss equals total fixed cost.

If the firm produces, then in addition to its fixed costs, it incurs variable costs. But it also receives revenue. Its economic loss equals total fixed cost—the loss when shut down—plus total variable cost minus total revenue. If total variable cost exceeds total revenue, this loss exceeds total fixed cost and the firm shuts down. Equivalently, if average variable cost *exceeds* price, this loss exceeds total fixed cost and the firm *shuts down*.

The Shutdown Point A firm's **shutdown point** is the price and quantity at which it is indifferent between producing and shutting down. The shutdown point occurs at the price and the quantity at which average variable cost is a minimum. At the shutdown point, the firm is minimizing its loss and its loss equals total fixed cost. If the price falls below minimum average variable cost, the firm shuts down temporarily and continues to incur a loss equal to total fixed cost. At prices above minimum average variable cost but below average total cost, the firm produces the loss-minimizing output and incurs a loss, but a loss that is less than total fixed cost.

Figure 10.4 illustrates the firm's shutdown decision and the shutdown point that we've just described for Campus Sweaters.

The firm's average variable cost curve is *AVC* and the marginal cost curve is *MC*. Average variable cost has a minimum of $17 a sweater when output is 7 sweaters a day. The *MC* curve intersects the *AVC* curve at its minimum. (We explained this relationship between marginal cost and average cost in Chapter 9; see pp. 181–182.)

The figure shows the marginal revenue curve *MR* when the price is $17 a sweater, a price equal to minimum average variable cost.

Marginal revenue equals marginal cost at 7 sweaters a day, so this quantity maximizes economic profit (minimizes economic loss). The *ATC* curve shows that the firm's average total cost of producing 7 sweaters a day is $20.14 a sweater. The firm incurs a loss equal to $3.14 a sweater on 7 sweaters a day, so its loss is $22 a day, which equals total fixed cost.

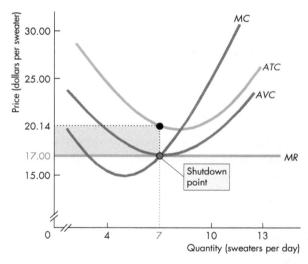

FIGURE 10.4   The Shutdown Decision

The shutdown point is at minimum average variable cost. At a price below minimum average variable cost, the firm shuts down and produces no output. At a price equal to minimum average variable cost, the firm is indifferent between shutting down and producing no output or producing the output at minimum average variable cost. Either way, the firm minimizes its economic loss and incurs a loss equal to total fixed cost.

myeconlab animation

The Firm's Supply Curve

A perfectly competitive firm's supply curve shows how its profit-maximizing output varies as the market price varies, other things remaining the same. The supply curve is derived from the firm's marginal cost curve and average variable cost curves. Figure 10.5 illustrates the derivation of the supply curve.

When the price *exceeds* minimum average variable cost (more than $17), the firm maximizes profit by producing the output at which marginal cost equals price. If the price rises, the firm increases its output—it moves up along its marginal cost curve.

When the price is *less than* minimum average variable cost (less than $17 a sweater), the firm maximizes profit by temporarily shutting down and producing no output. The firm produces zero output at all prices below minimum average variable cost.

When the price *equals* minimum average variable cost, the firm maximizes profit *either* by temporarily shutting down and producing no output *or* by producing the output at which average variable cost is a minimum—the shutdown point, *T.* The firm never produces a quantity between zero and the quantity at the shutdown point *T* (a quantity greater than zero and less than 7 sweaters a day).

The firm's supply curve in Fig. 10.5(b) runs along the *y*-axis from a price of zero to a price equal to minimum average variable cost, jumps to point *T,* and then, as the price rises above minimum average variable cost, follows the marginal cost curve.

REVIEW QUIZ

1 Why does a firm in perfect competition produce the quantity at which marginal cost equals price?

2 What is the lowest price at which a firm produces an output? Explain why.

3 What is the relationship between a firm's supply curve, its marginal cost curve, and its average variable cost curve?

You can work these questions in Study Plan 10.2 and get instant feedback.

So far, we've studied a single firm in isolation. We've seen that the firm's profit-maximizing decision depends on the market price, which it takes as given. How is the market price determined? Let's find out.

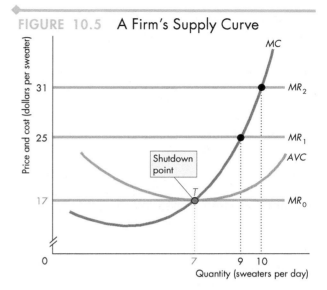

FIGURE 10.5   A Firm's Supply Curve

(a) Marginal cost and average variable cost

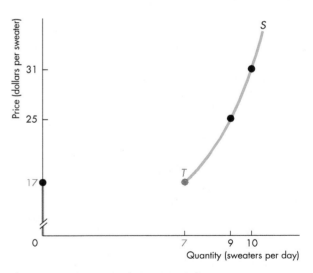

(b) Campus Sweaters' short-run supply curve

Part (a) shows the firm's profit-maximizing output at various market prices. At $25 a sweater, it produces 9 sweaters, and at $17 a sweater, it produces 7 sweaters. At all prices below $17 a sweater, Campus Sweaters produces nothing. Its shutdown point is *T.* Part (b) shows the firm's supply curve—the quantity of sweaters it produces at each price. Its supply curve is made up of the marginal cost curve at all prices above minimum average variable cost and the vertical axis at all prices below minimum average variable cost.

myeconlab animation

◆ Output, Price, and Profit in the Short Run

To determine the price and quantity in a perfectly competitive market, we need to know how market demand and market supply interact. We start by studying a perfectly competitive market in the short run. The short run is a situation in which the number of firms is fixed.

Market Supply in the Short Run

The **short-run market supply curve** shows the quantity supplied by all the firms in the market at each price when each firm's plant and the number of firms remain the same.

You've seen how an individual firm's supply curve is determined. The market supply curve is derived from the individual supply curves. The quantity supplied by the market at a given price is the sum of the quantities supplied by all the firms in the market at that price.

Figure 10.6 shows the supply curve for the competitive sweater market. In this example, the market consists of 1,000 firms exactly like Campus Sweaters. At each price, the quantity supplied by the market is 1,000 times the quantity supplied by a single firm.

The table in Fig. 10.6 shows the firm's and the market's supply schedules and how the market supply curve is constructed. At prices below $17 a sweater, every firm in the market shuts down; the quantity supplied by the market is zero. At $17 a sweater, each firm is indifferent between shutting down and producing nothing or operating and producing 7 sweaters a day. Some firms will shut down, and others will supply 7 sweaters a day. The quantity supplied by each firm is *either* 0 or 7 sweaters, and the quantity supplied by the market is *between* 0 (all firms shut down) and 7,000 (all firms produce 7 sweaters a day each).

The market supply curve is a graph of the market supply schedules and the points on the supply curve A through D represent the rows of the table.

To construct the market supply curve, we sum the quantities supplied by all the firms at each price. Each of the 1,000 firms in the market has a supply schedule like Campus Sweaters. At prices below $17 a sweater, the market supply curve runs along the *y*-axis. At $17 a sweater, the market supply curve is horizontal—supply is perfectly elastic. As the price

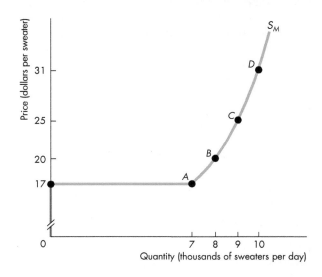

FIGURE 10.6   Short-Run Market Supply Curve

	Price (dollars per sweater)	Quantity supplied by Campus Sweaters (sweaters per day)	Quantity supplied by market (sweaters per day)
A	17	0 or 7	0 to 7,000
B	20	8	8,000
C	25	9	9,000
D	31	10	10,000

The market supply schedule is the sum of the supply schedules of all the individual firms. A market that consists of 1,000 identical firms has a supply schedule similar to that of one firm, but the quantity supplied by the market is 1,000 times as large as that of the one firm (see the table). The market supply curve is S_M. Points A, B, C, and D correspond to the rows of the table. At the shutdown price of $17 a sweater, each firm produces either 0 or 7 sweaters a day and the quantity supplied by the market is between 0 and 7,000 sweaters a day. The market supply is perfectly elastic at the shutdown price.

myeconlab   animation

rises above $17 a sweater, each firm increases its quantity supplied and the quantity supplied by the market increases by 1,000 times that of one firm.

Short-Run Equilibrium

Market demand and short-run market supply determine the market price and market output. Figure 10.7(a) shows a short-run equilibrium. The short-run supply curve, S, is the same as S_M in Fig. 10.6. If the market demand curve is D_1, the market price is $20 a sweater. Each firm takes this price as given and produces its profit-maximizing output, which is 8 sweaters a day. Because the market has 1,000 identical firms, the market output is 8,000 sweaters a day.

A Change in Demand

Changes in demand bring changes to short-run market equilibrium. Figure 10.7 shows these changes.

If demand increases and the demand curve shifts rightward to D_2, the market price rises to $25 a sweater. At this price, each firm maximizes profit by increasing its output to 9 sweaters a day. The market output increases to 9,000 sweaters a day.

If demand decreases and the demand curve shifts leftward to D_3, the market price falls to $17. At this price, each firm maximizes profit by decreasing its output. If each firm produces 7 sweaters a day, the market output decreases to 7,000 sweaters a day.

If the demand curve shifts farther leftward than D_3, the market price remains at $17 a sweater because the market supply curve is horizontal at that price. Some firms continue to produce 7 sweaters a day, and others temporarily shut down. Firms are indifferent between these two activities, and whichever they choose, they incur an economic loss equal to total fixed cost. The number of firms continuing to produce is just enough to satisfy the market demand at a price of $17 a sweater.

Profits and Losses in the Short Run

In short-run equilibrium, although the firm produces the profit-maximizing output, it does not necessarily end up making an economic profit. It might do so, but it might alternatively break even or incur an economic loss. Economic profit (or loss) per sweater is price, P, minus average total cost, ATC. So economic profit (or loss) is $(P - ATC) \times Q$. If price

FIGURE 10.7   Short-Run Equilibrium

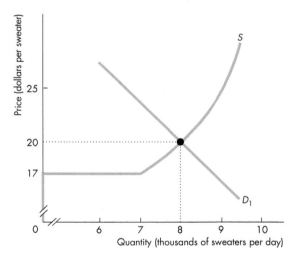

(a) Equilibrium

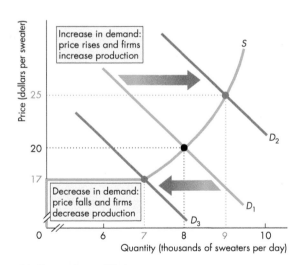

(b) Change in equilibrium

In part (a), the market supply curve is S and the market demand curve is D_1. The market price is $20 a sweater. At this price, each firm produces 8 sweaters a day and the market produces 8,000 sweaters a day.

In part (b), if the market demand increases to D_2, the

price rises to $25 a sweater. Each firm produces 9 sweaters a day and market output is 9,000 sweaters. If market demand decreases to D_3, the price falls to $17 a sweater and each firm decreases its output. If each firm produces 7 sweaters a day, the market output is 7,000 sweaters a day.

equals average total cost, a firm breaks even—the entrepreneur makes normal profit. If price exceeds average total cost, a firm makes an economic profit. If price is less than average total cost, a firm incurs an economic loss. Figure 10.8 shows these three possible short-run profit outcomes for Campus Sweaters. These outcomes correspond to the three different levels of market demand that we've just examined.

Three Possible Short-Run Outcomes

Figure 10.8(a) corresponds to the situation in Fig. 10.7(a) where the market demand is D_1. The equilibrium price of a sweater is $20 and the firm produces 8 sweaters a day. Average total cost is $20 a sweater. Price equals average total cost (ATC), so the firm breaks even (makes zero economic profit).

Figure 10.8(b) corresponds to the situation in Fig. 10.7(b) where the market demand is D_2. The equilibrium price of a sweater is $25 and the firm produces 9 sweaters a day. Here, price exceeds average total cost, so the firm makes an economic profit. Its economic profit is $42 a day, which equals $4.67 per sweater ($25.00 − $20.33) multiplied by 9, the

profit-maximizing number of sweaters produced. The blue rectangle shows this economic profit. The height of that rectangle is profit per sweater, $4.67, and the length is the quantity of sweaters produced, 9 a day. So the area of the rectangle is economic profit of $42 a day.

Figure 10.8(c) corresponds to the situation in Fig. 10.7(b) where the market demand is D_3. The equilibrium price of a sweater is $17. Here, the price is less than average total cost, so the firm incurs an economic loss. Price and marginal revenue are $17 a sweater, and the profit-maximizing (in this case, loss-minimizing) output is 7 sweaters a day. Total revenue is $119 a day (7 × $17). Average total cost is $20.14 a sweater, so the economic loss is $3.14 per sweater ($20.14 − $17.00). This loss per sweater multiplied by the number of sweaters is $22. The red rectangle shows this economic loss. The height of that rectangle is economic loss per sweater, $3.14, and the length is the quantity of sweaters produced, 7 a day. So the area of the rectangle is the firm's economic loss of $22 a day. If the price dips below $17 a sweater, the firm temporarily shuts down and incurs an economic loss equal to total fixed cost.

FIGURE 10.8   Three Short-Run Outcomes for the Firm

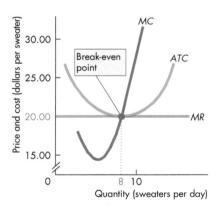

(a) Break even

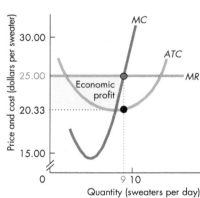

(b) Economic profit

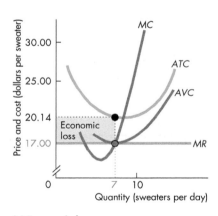

(c) Economic loss

In the short run, the firm might break even (make zero economic profit), make an economic profit, or incur an economic loss. In part (a), the price equals minimum average total cost. At the profit-maximizing output, the firm breaks even and makes zero economic profit. In part (b), the market price is $25 a sweater. At the profit-maximizing output,

the price exceeds average total cost and the firm makes an economic profit equal to the area of the blue rectangle. In part (c), the market price is $17 a sweater. At the profit-maximizing output, the price is below minimum average total cost and the firm incurs an economic loss equal to the area of the red rectangle.

Economics in Action

Production Cutback and Temporary Shutdown

The high price of gasoline and anxiety about unemployment and future incomes brought a decrease in the demand for luxury goods including high-end motorcycles such as Harley-Davidsons.

Harley-Davidson's profit-maximizing response to the decrease in demand was to cut production and lay off workers. Some of the production cuts and layoffs were temporary and some were permanent.

Harley-Davidson's bike production plant in York County, Pennsylvania, was temporarily shut down in the summer of 2008 because total revenue was insufficient to cover total variable cost.

The firm also permanently cut its workforce by 300 people. This permanent cut was like that at Campus Sweaters when the market demand for sweaters decreased from D_1 to D_3 in Fig. 10.7(b).

◈ REVIEW QUIZ

1 How do we derive the short-run market supply curve in perfect competition?
2 In perfect competition, when market demand increases, explain how the price of the good and the output and profit of each firm changes in the short run.
3 In perfect competition, when market demand decreases, explain how the price of the good and the output and profit of each firm changes in the short run.

You can work these questions in Study Plan 10.3 and get instant feedback.

◆ Output, Price, and Profit in the Long Run

In short-run equilibrium, a firm might make an economic profit, incur an economic loss, or break even. Although each of these three situations is a short-run equilibrium, only one of them is a long-run equilibrium. The reason is that in the long run, firms can enter or exit the market.

Entry and Exit

Entry occurs in a market when new firms come into the market and the number of firms increases. Exit occurs when existing firms leave a market and the number of firms decreases.

Firms respond to economic profit and economic loss by either entering or exiting a market. New firms enter a market in which existing firms are making an economic profit. Firms exit a market in which they are incurring an economic loss. Temporary economic profit and temporary economic loss don't trigger entry and exit. It's the prospect of persistent economic profit or loss that triggers entry and exit.

Entry and exit change the market supply, which influences the market price, the quantity produced by each firm, and its economic profit (or loss).

If firms enter a market, supply increases and the market supply curve shifts rightward. The increase in supply lowers the market price and eventually eliminates economic profit. When economic profit reaches zero, entry stops.

If firms exit a market, supply decreases and the market supply curve shifts leftward. The market price rises and economic loss decreases. Eventually, economic loss is eliminated and exit stops.

To summarize:

- New firms enter a market in which existing firms are making an economic profit.
- As new firms enter a market, the market price falls and the economic profit of each firm decreases.
- Firms exit a market in which they are incurring an economic loss.
- As firms leave a market, the market price rises and the economic loss incurred by the remaining firms decreases.
- Entry and exit stop when firms make zero economic profit.

A Closer Look at Entry

The sweater market has 800 firms with cost curves like those in Fig. 10.9(a). The market demand curve is D, the market supply curve is S_1, and the price is $25 a sweater in Fig. 10.9(b). Each firm produces 9 sweaters a day and makes an economic profit.

This economic profit is a signal for new firms to enter the market. As entry takes place, supply increases and the market supply curve shifts rightward toward S^*. As supply increases with no change in demand, the market price gradually falls from $25 to $20 a sweater. At this lower price, each firm makes zero economic profit and entry stops.

Entry results in an increase in market output, but each firm's output *decreases*. Because the price falls, each firm moves down its supply curve and produces less. Because the number of firms increases, the market produces more.

A Closer Look at Exit

The sweater market has 1,200 firms with cost curves like those in Fig. 10.9(a). The market demand curve is D, the market supply curve is S_2, and the price is $17 a sweater in Fig. 10.9(b). Each firm produces 7 sweaters a day and incurs an economic loss.

This economic loss is a signal for firms to exit the market. As exit takes place, supply decreases and the market supply curve shifts leftward toward S^*. As supply decreases with no change in demand, the market price gradually rises from $17 to $20 a sweater. At this higher price, losses are eliminated, each firm makes zero economic profit, and exit stops.

Exit results in a decrease in market output, but each firm's output *increases*. Because the price rises, each firm moves up its supply curve and produces more. Because the number of firms decreases, the market produces less.

FIGURE 10.9   Entry, Exit, and Long-Run Equilibrium

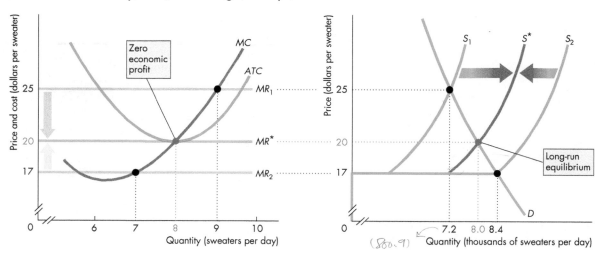

(a) Campus Sweaters

(b) The sweater market

Each firm has cost curves like those of Campus Sweaters in part (a). The market demand curve is D in part (b).

When the market supply curve in part (b) is S_1, the price is $25 a sweater. In part (a), each firm produces 9 sweaters a day and makes an economic profit. Profit triggers the entry of new firms and as new firms enter, the market supply curve shifts rightward, from S_1 toward S^*. The price falls from $25 to $20 a sweater, and the quantity produced increases from 7,200 to 8,000 sweaters. Each firm's output decreases to 8

sweaters a day and economic profit falls to zero.

When the market supply curve is S_2, the price is $17 a sweater. In part (a), each firm produces 7 sweaters a day and incurs an economic loss. Loss triggers exit and as firms exit, the market supply curve shifts leftward, from S_2 toward S^*. The price rises from $17 to $20 a sweater, and the quantity produced decreases from 8,400 to 8,000 sweaters. Each firm's output increases from 7 to 8 sweaters a day and economic profit rises to zero.

Economics in Action

Entry and Exit

An example of entry and falling prices occurred during the 1980s and 1990s in the personal computer market. When IBM introduced its first PC in 1981, IBM had little competition. The price was $7,000 (about $16,850 in today's money) and IBM made a large economic profit selling the new machine.

Observing IBM's huge success, new firms such as Gateway, NEC, Dell, and a host of others entered the market with machines that were technologically identical to IBM's. In fact, they were so similar that they came to be called "clones." The massive wave of entry into the personal computer market increased the market supply and lowered the price. The economic profit for all firms decreased.

Today, a $400 computer is vastly more powerful than its 1981 ancestor that cost 42 times as much.

The same PC market that saw entry during the 1980s and 1990s has seen some exit more recently. In 2001, IBM, the firm that first launched the PC, announced that it was exiting the market. The intense competition from Gateway, NEC, Dell, and others that entered the market following IBM's lead has lowered the price and eliminated the economic profit. So IBM now concentrates on servers and other parts of the computer market.

IBM exited the PC market because it was incurring economic losses. Its exit decreased market supply and made it possible for the remaining firms in the market to make zero economic profit.

International Harvester, a manufacturer of farm equipment, provides another example of exit. For decades, people associated the name "International Harvester" with tractors, combines, and other farm machines. But International Harvester wasn't the only maker of farm equipment. The market became intensely competitive, and the firm began to incur economic losses. Now the firm has a new name, Navistar International, and it doesn't make tractors any more. After years of economic losses and shrinking revenues, it got out of the farm-machine business in 1985 and started to make trucks.

International Harvester exited because it was incurring an economic loss. Its exit decreased supply and made it possible for the remaining firms in the market to break even.

Long-Run Equilibrium

You've now seen how economic profit induces entry, which in turn eliminates the profit. You've also seen how economic loss induces exit, which in turn eliminates the loss.

When economic profit and economic loss have been eliminated and entry and exit have stopped, a competitive market is in *long-run equilibrium.*

You've seen how a competitive market adjusts toward its long-run equilibrium. But a competitive market is rarely *in* a state of long-run equilibrium. Instead, it is constantly and restlessly evolving toward long-run equilibrium. The reason is that the market is constantly bombarded with events that change the constraints that firms face.

Markets are constantly adjusting to keep up with changes in tastes, which change demand, and changes in technology, which change costs.

In the next sections, we're going to see how a competitive market reacts to changing tastes and technology and how it guides resources to their highest-valued use.

 REVIEW QUIZ

1   What triggers entry in a competitive market? Describe the process that ends further entry.
2   What triggers exit in a competitive market? Describe the process that ends further exit.

You can work these questions in Study Plan 10.4 and get instant feedback.

◆ Changing Tastes and Advancing Technology

Increased awareness of the health hazards of smoking has decreased the demand for tobacco products. The development of inexpensive automobile and air transportation during the 1990s decreased the demand for long-distance trains and buses. Solid-state electronics has decreased the demand for TV and radio repair. The development of good-quality inexpensive clothing has decreased the demand for sewing machines. What happens in a competitive market when there is a permanent decrease in the demand for its product?

Microwave food preparation has increased the demand for paper, glass, and plastic cooking utensils and for plastic wrap. The Internet has increased the demand for personal computers and the widespread use of computers has increased the demand for high-speed connections and music downloads. What happens in a competitive market when the demand for its output increases?

Advances in technology are constantly lowering the costs of production. New biotechnologies have dramatically lowered the costs of producing many food and pharmaceutical products. New electronic technologies have lowered the cost of producing just about every good and service. What happens in a competitive market for a good when technological change lowers its production costs?

Let's use the theory of perfect competition to answer these questions.

A Permanent Change in Demand

Figure 10.10(a) shows a competitive market that initially is in long-run equilibrium. The demand curve is D_0, the supply curve is S_0, the market price is P_0, and market output is Q_0. Figure 10.10(b) shows a single firm in this initial long-run equilibrium. The firm produces q_0 and makes zero economic profit.

Now suppose that demand decreases and the demand curve shifts leftward to D_1, as shown in Fig. 10.10(a). The market price falls to P_1, and the quantity supplied by the market decreases from Q_0 to Q_1 as the market moves down along its short-run supply curve S_0. Figure 10.10(b) shows the situation facing a firm. The market price is now below the firm's minimum average total cost, so the firm incurs an eco-

nomic loss. But to minimize its loss, the firm adjusts its output to keep marginal cost equal to price. At a price of P_1, each firm produces an output of q_1.

The market is now in short-run equilibrium but not long-run equilibrium. It is in short-run equilibrium because each firm is maximizing profit; it is not in long-run equilibrium because each firm is incurring an economic loss—its average total cost exceeds the price.

The economic loss is a signal for some firms to exit the market. As they do so, short-run market supply decreases and the market supply curve gradually shifts leftward. As market supply decreases, the price rises. At each higher price, a firm's profit-maximizing output is greater, so the firms remaining in the market increase their output as the price rises. Each firm moves up along its marginal cost or supply curve in Fig. 10.10(b). That is, as some firms exit the market, market output decreases but the output of the firms that remain in the market increases.

Eventually, enough firms have exited the market for the market supply curve to have shifted to S_1 in Fig. 10.10(a). The market price has returned to its original level, P_0. At this price, the firms remaining in the market produce q_0, the same quantity that they produced before the decrease in demand. Because firms are now making zero economic profit, no firm has an incentive to enter or exit the market. The market supply curve remains at S_1, and market output is Q_2. The market is again in long-run equilibrium.

The difference between the initial long-run equilibrium and the final long-run equilibrium is the number of firms in the market. A permanent decrease in demand has decreased the number of firms. Each firm remaining in the market produces the same output in the new long-run equilibrium as it did initially and makes zero economic profit. In the process of moving from the initial equilibrium to the new one, firms incur economic losses.

We've just worked out how a competitive market responds to a permanent *decrease* in demand. A permanent increase in demand triggers a similar response, except in the opposite direction. The increase in demand brings a higher price, economic profit, and entry. Entry increases market supply and eventually lowers the price to its original level and economic profit to zero.

The demand for Internet service increased permanently during the 1990s and huge profit opportunities arose in this market. The result was a massive rate

FIGURE 10.10   A Decrease in Demand

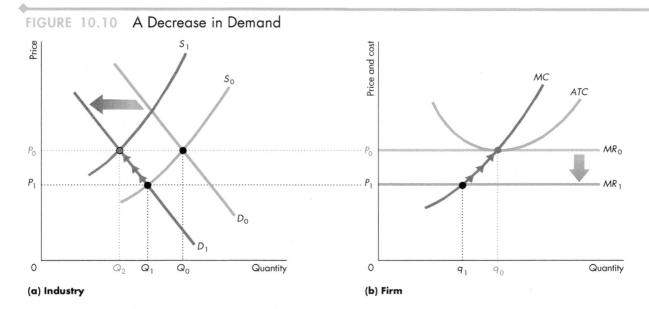

(a) Industry

(b) Firm

A market starts out in long-run competitive equilibrium. Part (a) shows the market demand curve D_0, the market supply curve S_0, the market price P_0, and the equilibrium quantity Q_0. Each firm sells its output at the price P_0, so its marginal revenue curve is MR_0 in part (b). Each firm produces q_0 and makes zero economic profit.

Market demand decreases permanently from D_0 to D_1 in part (a) and the market price falls to P_1. Each firm decreases its output to q_1 in part (b), and the market output

decreases to Q_1 in part (a). Firms now incur economic losses. Some firms exit the market, and as they do so, the market supply curve gradually shifts leftward, from S_0 toward S_1. This shift gradually raises the market price from P_1 back to P_0. While the price is below P_0, firms incur economic losses and some firms exit the market. Once the price has returned to P_0, each firm makes zero economic profit and has no incentive to exit. Each firm produces q_0, and the market output is Q_2.

myeconlab animation

of entry of Internet service providers. The process of competition and change in the Internet service market is similar to what we have just studied but with an increase in demand rather than a decrease in demand.

We've now studied the effects of a permanent change in demand for a good. In doing so, we began and ended in a long-run equilibrium and examined the process that takes a market from one equilibrium to another. It is this process, not the equilibrium points, that describes the real world.

One feature of the predictions that we have just generated seems odd: In the long run, regardless of whether demand increases or decreases, the market price returns to its original level. Is this outcome inevitable? In fact, it is not. It is possible for the equilibrium market price in the long run to remain the same, rise, or fall.

External Economies and Diseconomies

The change in the long-run equilibrium price depends on external economies and external diseconomies. **External economies** are factors beyond the control of an individual firm that lower the firm's costs as the *market* output increases. **External diseconomies** are factors outside the control of a firm that raise the firm's costs as the *market* output increases. With no external economies or external diseconomies, a firm's costs remain constant as the market output changes.

Figure 10.11 illustrates these three cases and introduces a new supply concept: the long-run market supply curve.

A **long-run market supply curve** shows how the quantity supplied in a market varies as the market price varies after all the possible adjustments have been made, including changes in each firm's plant and the number of firms in the market.

Figure 10.11(a) shows the case we have just studied—no external economies or diseconomies. The long-run market supply curve (LS_A) is perfectly elastic. In this case, a permanent increase in demand from D_0 to D_1 has no effect on the price in the long run. The increase in demand brings a temporary increase in price to P_S and in the short run the quantity increases from Q_0 to Q_S. Entry increases short-run supply from S_0 to S_1, which lowers the price from P_S back to P_0 and increases the quantity to Q_1.

Figure 10.11(b) shows the case of external diseconomies. The long-run market supply curve (LS_B) slopes upward. A permanent increase in demand from D_0 to D_1 increases the price in both the short run and the long run. The increase in demand brings a temporary increase in price to P_S and in the short run the quantity increases from Q_0 to Q_S. Entry increases short-run supply from S_0 to S_2, which lowers the price from P_S to P_2 and increases the quantity to Q_2.

One source of external diseconomies is congestion. The airline market provides a good example. With bigger airline market output, congestion at both airports and in the air increases, resulting in longer delays and extra waiting time for passengers and airplanes. These external diseconomies mean that as the output of air transportation services increases (in the absence of technological advances), average cost increases. As a result, the long-run market supply curve is upward sloping. A permanent increase in demand brings an increase in quantity and a rise in the price. (Markets with external diseconomies might nonetheless have a falling price because technological advances shift the long-run supply curve downward.)

Figure 10.11(c) shows the case of external economies. The long-run market supply curve (LS_C) slopes downward. A permanent increase in demand from D_0 to D_1 increases the price in the short run and lowers it in the long run. Again, the increase in demand brings a temporary increase in price to P_S and in the short run the quantity increases from Q_0 to Q_S. Entry increases short-run supply from S_0 to S_3, which lowers the price to P_3 and increases the quantity to Q_3.

An example of external economies is the growth of specialist support services for a market as it expands.

FIGURE 10.11   Long-Run Changes in Price and Quantity

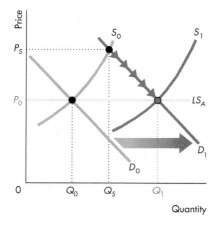

(a) Constant-cost industry

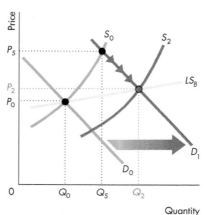

(b) Increasing-cost industry

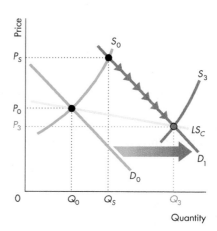

(c) Decreasing-cost industry

Three possible changes in price and quantity occur in the long run. When demand increases from D_0 to D_1, entry occurs and the market supply curve shifts rightward from S_0 to S_1. In part (a), the long-run market supply curve, LS_A, is horizontal. The quantity increases from Q_0 to Q_1, and the price remains constant at P_0.

In part (b), the long-run market supply curve is LS_B; the price rises to P_2, and the quantity increases to Q_2. This case occurs in industries with external diseconomies. In part (c), the long-run market supply curve is LS_C; the price falls to P_3, and the quantity increases to Q_3. This case occurs in a market with external economies.

As farm output increased in the nineteenth and early twentieth centuries, the services available to farmers expanded. New firms specialized in the development and marketing of farm machinery and fertilizers. As a result, average farm costs decreased. Farms enjoyed the benefits of external economies. As a consequence, as the demand for farm products increased, the output increased but the price fell.

Over the long term, the prices of many goods and services have fallen, not because of external economies but because of technological change. Let's now study this influence on a competitive market.

Technological Change

Industries are constantly discovering lower-cost techniques of production. Most cost-saving production techniques cannot be implemented, however, without investing in new plant and equipment. As a consequence, it takes time for a technological advance to spread through a market. Some firms whose plants are on the verge of being replaced will be quick to adopt the new technology, while other firms whose plants have recently been replaced will continue to operate with an old technology until they can no longer cover their average variable cost. Once average variable cost cannot be covered, a firm will scrap even a relatively new plant (embodying an old technology) in favor of a plant with a new technology.

New technology allows firms to produce at a lower cost. As a result, as firms adopt a new technology, their cost curves shift downward. With lower costs, firms are willing to supply a given quantity at a lower price or, equivalently, they are willing to supply a larger quantity at a given price. In other words, market supply increases, and the market supply curve shifts rightward. With a given demand, the quantity produced increases and the price falls.

Two forces are at work in a market undergoing technological change. Firms that adopt the new technology make an economic profit, so there is entry by new-technology firms. Firms that stick with the old technology incur economic losses. They either exit the market or switch to the new technology.

As old-technology firms disappear and new-technology firms enter, the price falls and the quantity produced increases. Eventually, the market arrives at a long-run equilibrium in which all the firms use the new technology and make a zero economic profit. Because in the long run competition eliminates economic profit, technological change brings only temporary gains to producers. But the lower prices and better products that technological advances bring are permanent gains for consumers.

The process that we've just described is one in which some firms experience economic profits and others experience economic losses. It is a period of dynamic change in a market. Some firms do well, and others do badly. Often, the process has a geographical dimension—the expanding new-technology firms bring prosperity to what was once the boondocks, and traditional industrial regions decline. Sometimes, the new-technology firms are in a foreign country, while the old-technology firms are in the domestic economy. The information revolution of the 1990s produced many examples of changes like these. Commercial banking, which was traditionally concentrated in New York, San Francisco, and other large cities now flourishes in Charlotte, North Carolina, which has become the nation's number three commercial banking city. Television shows and movies, traditionally made in Los Angeles and New York, are now made in large numbers in Orlando.

Technological advances are not confined to the information and entertainment industries. Even food production is undergoing a major technological change because of genetic engineering.

REVIEW QUIZ

1 Describe the course of events in a competitive market following a permanent decrease in demand. What happens to output, price, and economic profit in the short run and in the long run?

2 Describe the course of events in a competitive market following a permanent increase in demand. What happens to output, price, and economic profit in the short run and in the long run?

3 Describe the course of events in a competitive market following the adoption of a new technology. What happens to output, price, and economic profit in the short run and in the long run?

You can work these questions in Study Plan 10.5 and get instant feedback.

We've seen how a competitive market operates in the short run and the long run, but is a competitive market efficient?

◆ Competition and Efficiency

A competitive market can achieve an efficient use of resources. You first studied efficiency in Chapter 2. Then in Chapter 5, using only the concepts of demand, supply, consumer surplus, and producer surplus, you saw how a competitive market achieves efficiency. Now that you have learned what lies behind the demand and supply curves of a competitive market, you can gain a deeper understanding of the efficiency of a competitive market.

Efficient Use of Resources

Recall that resource use is efficient when we produce the goods and services that people value most highly (see Chapter 2, pp. 31–33, and Chapter 5, p. 96). If someone can become better off without anyone else becoming worse off, resources are *not* being used efficiently. For example, suppose we produce a computer that no one wants and no one will ever use and, at the same time, some people are clamoring for more video games. If we produce fewer computers and reallocate the unused resources to produce more video games, some people will become better off and no one will be worse off. So the initial resource allocation was inefficient.

In the more technical language that you have learned, resource use is efficient when marginal social benefit equals marginal social cost. In the computer and video games example, the marginal social benefit of a video game exceeds its marginal social cost; the marginal social cost of a computer exceeds its marginal social benefit. So by producing fewer computers and more video games, we move resources toward a higher-valued use.

Choices, Equilibrium, and Efficiency

We can use what you have learned about the decisions made by consumers and competitive firms and market equilibrium to describe an efficient use of resources.

Choices Consumers allocate their budgets to get the most value possible out of them. We derive a consumer's demand curve by finding how the best budget allocation changes as the price of a good changes. So consumers get the most value out of their resources at all points along their demand curves. If the people who consume a good or service are the

only ones who benefit from it, then the market demand curve measures the benefit to the entire society and is the marginal social benefit curve.

Competitive firms produce the quantity that maximizes profit. We derive the firm's supply curve by finding the profit-maximizing quantity at each price. So firms get the most value out of their resources at all points along their supply curves. If the firms that produce a good or service bear all the costs of producing it, then the market supply curve measures the marginal cost to the entire society and the market supply curve is the marginal social cost curve.

Equilibrium and Efficiency Resources are used efficiently when marginal social benefit equals marginal social cost. Competitive equilibrium achieves this efficient outcome because, with no externalities, price equals marginal social benefit for consumers, and price equals marginal social cost for producers.

The gains from trade are the sum of consumer surplus and producer surplus. The gains from trade for consumers are measured by *consumer surplus*, which is the area below the demand curve and above the price paid. (See Chapter 5, p. 97.) The gains from trade for producers are measured by *producer surplus*, which is the area above the supply curve and below the price received. (See Chapter 5, p. 99.) The total gains from trade equals total surplus —the sum of consumer surplus and producer surplus. When the market for a good or service is in equilibrium, the gains from trade are maximized.

Illustrating an Efficient Allocation Figure 10.12 illustrates the efficiency of perfect competition in long-run equilibrium. Part (a) shows the individual firm, and part (b) shows the market. The equilibrium market price is P^*. At that price, each firm makes zero economic profit and each firm has the plant that enables it to produce at the lowest possible average total cost. Consumers are as well off as possible because the good cannot be produced at a lower cost and the price equals that least possible cost.

In part (b), consumers get the most out of their resources at all points on the market demand curve, $D = MSB$. Consumer surplus is the green area. Producers get the most out of their resources at all points on the market supply curve, $S = MSC$. Producer surplus is the blue area. Resources are used efficiently at the quantity Q^* and price P^*. At this point, marginal social benefit equals marginal social

FIGURE 10.12   Efficiency of Perfect Competition

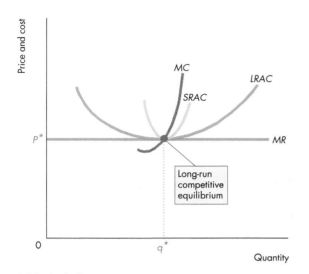

(a) A single firm

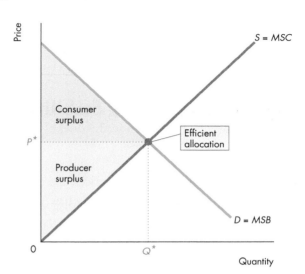

(b) A market

Demand, *D*, and supply, *S*, determine the equilibrium price, *P**. A firm in perfect competition in part (a) produces *q** at the lowest possible long-run average total cost. In part (b), consumers have made the best available choices and are

on the market demand curve, and firms are producing at least cost and are on the market supply curve. With no externalities, marginal social benefit equals marginal social cost, so resources are used efficiently at the quantity *Q**.

 animation

---

cost, and total surplus (the sum of producer surplus and consumer surplus) is maximized.

When firms in perfect competition are away from long-run equilibrium, either entry or exit is taking place and the market is moving toward the situation depicted in Fig. 10.12. But the market is still efficient. As long as marginal social benefit (on the market demand curve) equals marginal social cost (on the market supply curve), the market is efficient. But it is only in long-run equilibrium that consumers pay the lowest possible price.

You've now completed your study of perfect competition. *Reading Between the Lines* on pp. 214–215 gives you an opportunity to use what you have learned to understand events in the global market for corn during the past few years.

Although many markets approximate the model of perfect competition, many do not. In Chapter 11, we study markets at the opposite extreme of market power: monopoly. Then we'll study markets that lie between perfect competition and monopoly. In

REVIEW QUIZ

1 State the conditions that must be met for resources to be allocated efficiently.
2 Describe the choices that consumers make and explain why consumers are efficient on the market demand curve.
3 Describe the choices that producers make and explain why producers are efficient on the market supply curve.
4 Explain why resources are used efficiently in a competitive market.

You can work these questions in Study Plan 10.6 and get instant feedback.

Chapter 12 we study monopolistic competition and in Chapter 13 we study oligopoly. When you have completed this study, you'll have a tool kit that will enable you to understand the variety of real-world markets.

Perfect Competition in Corn

Bumper Harvests Bring Stability

http://www.ft.com
June 1, 2010

There is no better fertilizer than high prices, the old farming adage goes. Trends in agriculture appear to be proving this resoundingly true.

The spike in prices that caused the first global food crisis in 30 years in 2007–08 has led to large increases in production of foods such as corn and wheat. Farmers have responded to higher prices. ...

The U.S. Department of Agriculture said ..."Higher prices, and thus expanded acreage, in combination with favorable weather, have helped production expand sharply."

Global corn production will hit 835m metric tons in the 2010–11 season, its highest ever level, the USDA forecasts. ... That is likely to lead to a period of relatively stable prices. ...

While prices for the main food and feed grain crops—corn, wheat, and soybeans—are likely to remain steady and low in the next year or so, that does not mean a repeat of the food crisis is impossible. ...

One argument against that view holds that technological gains in response to the crisis have boosted productivity, making farmers more able to deal with increasing consumption.

Some crops, such as corn, saw record yields in the 2009–10 season and the USDA is predicting high yields for next year as well.

But analysts ascribe the gains in productivity more to fortunate weather conditions than a revolution in farming technology. ...

ESSENCE OF THE STORY

- In 2010–11, global corn production will reach its highest ever level at 835 million metric tons.
- High prices in 2007–08 led to large increases in the acreage of corn and wheat.
- Favorable weather also helped to increase production of these crops.
- Prices for corn, wheat, and soybeans will likely remain low next year, but a future price rise might occur.
- A revolution in farming technology would increase production without raising costs and prices.
- The current gain in productivity is most likely the result of fortunate weather and likely to be temporary.

- The global market for corn is competitive and the model of perfect competition shows how that market works.

- During 2006 through 2008, increases in demand brought a rising price and an increase in the quantity of corn supplied.

- In 2009 and 2010, good weather conditions brought an increase in the supply of corn and the quantity of corn increased further but its price fell.

- Figure 1 illustrates these events in the market for corn and Fig. 2 their effects on an individual farm.

- From 2006 through 2008, the supply curve of corn was S_0 in Fig. 1. The demand for corn increased and by 2008, the demand curve was D. The price of corn in 2008 was $310 per metric ton and 800 million metric tons were produced.

- In 2008, the farm faced a marginal revenue curve MR_0 and had average total cost curve ATC_0 and marginal cost curve MC_0 in Fig. 2.

- The farm maximized profit by producing 8,000 metric tons and (we will assume) made zero economic profit.

- In 2009 and 2010, good weather conditions increased the supply of corn. By 2010–11, the supply curve had shifted rightward to S_1. The price fell to $230 per metric ton and production increased to 835 million metric tons.

- Back on the farm in Fig. 2, the lower price decreased marginal revenue and the MR curve shifted downward to MR_1.

- But the fortunate weather increased farm productivity and lowered the cost of producing corn. The average total cost curve shifted downward to ATC_1 and the marginal cost curve shifted downward to MC_1.

- The combination of the lower price and lower costs might leave the farm with an economic profit. In Fig. 2 we're assuming that the farm again made zero economic profit.

- If farms did make a positive (or negative) economic profit, entry (or exit) would eventually return them to a zero economic profit position like that shown in Fig. 2.

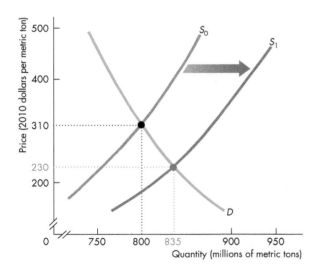

Figure 1 The market for corn

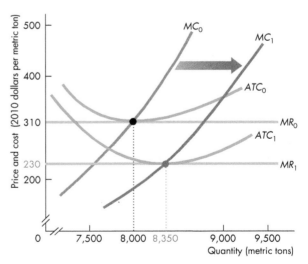

Figure 2 A corn farmer

SUMMARY

Key Points

What Is Perfect Competition? (pp. 196–197)

- In perfect competition, many firms sell identical products to many buyers; there are no restrictions on entry; sellers and buyers are well informed about prices.
- A perfectly competitive firm is a price taker.
- A perfectly competitive firm's marginal revenue always equals the market price.

Working Problems 1 to 3 will give you a better understanding of perfect competition.

The Firm's Output Decision (pp. 198–201)

- The firm produces the output at which marginal revenue (price) equals marginal cost.
- In short-run equilibrium, a firm can make an economic profit, incur an economic loss, or break even.
- If price is less than minimum average variable cost, the firm temporarily shuts down.
- At prices below minimum average variable cost, a firm's supply curve runs along the y-axis; at prices above minimum average variable cost, a firm's supply curve is its marginal cost curve.

Working Problems 4 to 7 will give you a better understanding of a firm's output decision.

Output, Price, and Profit in the Short Run
(pp. 202–205)

- The market supply curve shows the sum of the quantities supplied by each firm at each price.
- Market demand and market supply determine price.
- A firm might make a positive economic profit, a zero economic profit, or incur an economic loss.

Working Problems 8 and 9 will give you a better understanding of output, price, and profit in the short run.

Output, Price, and Profit in the Long Run
(pp. 205–207)

- Economic profit induces entry and economic loss induces exit.
- Entry increases supply and lowers price and profit. Exit decreases supply and raises price and profit.
- In long-run equilibrium, economic profit is zero. There is no entry or exit.

Working Problems 10 and 11 will give you a better understanding of output, price, and profit in the long run.

Changing Tastes and Advancing Technology
(pp. 208–211)

- A permanent decrease in demand leads to a smaller market output and a smaller number of firms. A permanent increase in demand leads to a larger market output and a larger number of firms.
- The long-run effect of a change in demand on price depends on whether there are external economies (the price falls) or external diseconomies (the price rises) or neither (the price remains constant).
- New technologies increase supply and in the long run lower the price and increase the quantity.

Working Problems 12 to 16 will give you a better understanding of changing tastes and advancing technologies.

Competition and Efficiency (pp. 212–213)

- Resources are used efficiently when we produce goods and services in the quantities that people value most highly.
- Perfect competition achieves an efficient allocation. In long-run equilibrium, consumers pay the lowest possible price and marginal social benefit equals marginal social cost.

Working Problems 17 and 18 will give you a better understanding of competition and efficiency.

Key Terms

External diseconomies, 209
External economies, 209
Long-run market supply curve, 209

Marginal revenue, 196
Perfect competition, 196
Price taker, 196

Short-run market supply curve, 202
Shutdown point, 200
Total revenue, 196

STUDY PLAN PROBLEMS AND APPLICATIONS

 You can work Problems 1 to 18 in MyEconLab Chapter 10 Study Plan and get instant feedback.

What Is Perfect Competition? (Study Plan 10.1)

Use the following information to work Problems 1 to 3.

Lin's makes fortune cookies that are identical to those made by dozens of other firms, and there is free entry in the fortune cookie market. Buyers and sellers are well informed about prices.

1. In what type of market does Lin's operate? What determines the price of fortune cookies and what determines Lin's marginal revenue from fortune cookies?

2. a. If fortune cookies sell for $10 a box and Lin's offers its cookies for sale at $10.50 a box, how many boxes does it sell?
   b. If fortune cookies sell for $10 a box and Lin's offers its cookies for sale at $9.50 a box, how many boxes does it sell?

3. What is the elasticity of demand for Lin's fortune cookies and how does it differ from the elasticity of the market demand for fortune cookies?

The Firm's Output Decision (Study Plan 10.2)

Use the following table to work Problems 4 to 6. Pat's Pizza Kitchen is a price taker. Its costs are

Output (pizzas per hour)	Total cost (dollars per hour)
0	10
1	21
2	30
3	41
4	54
5	69

4. Calculate Pat's profit-maximizing output and economic profit if the market price is
   (i) $14 a pizza.
   (ii) $12 a pizza.
   (iii) $10 a pizza.

5. What is Pat's shutdown point and what is Pat's economic profit if it shuts down temporarily?

6. Derive Pat's supply curve.

7. The market for paper is perfectly competitive and there are 1,000 firms that produce paper. The table sets out the market demand schedule for paper.

Price (dollars per box)	Quantity demanded (thousands of boxes per week)
3.65	500
5.20	450
6.80	400
8.40	350
10.00	300
11.60	250
13.20	200

Each producer of paper has the following costs when it uses its least-cost plant:

Output (boxes per week)	Marginal cost (dollars per additional box)	Average variable cost (dollars per box)	Average total cost (dollars per box)
200	6.40	7.80	12.80
250	7.00	7.00	11.00
300	7.65	7.10	10.43
350	8.40	7.20	10.06
400	10.00	7.50	10.00
450	12.40	8.00	10.22
500	20.70	9.00	11.00

a. What is the market price of paper?
b. What is the market's output?
c. What is the output produced by each firm?
d. What is the economic profit made or economic loss incurred by each firm?

Output, Price, and Profit in the Short Run
(Study Plan 10.3)

8. In Problem 7, as more and more computer users read documents online rather than print them, the market demand for paper decreases and in the short run the demand schedule becomes

Price (dollars per box)	Quantity demanded (thousands of boxes per week)
2.95	500
4.13	450
5.30	400
6.48	350
7.65	300
8.83	250
10.00	200
11.18	150

If each firm producing paper has the costs set out in Problem 7, what is the market price and the economic profit or loss of each firm in the short run?

9. **Fuel Prices Could Squeeze Cheap Flights**

   Airlines are having difficulty keeping prices low, especially as fuel prices keep rising. Airlines have raised fares to make up for the fuel costs. American Airlines increased its fuel surcharge by $20 a roundtrip, which Delta, United Airlines, and Continental matched.

   Source: CNN, June 12, 2008

   a. Explain how an increase in fuel prices might cause an airline to change its output (number of flights) in the short run.

   b. Draw a graph to show the increase in fuel prices on an airline's output in the short run.

   c. Explain why an airline might incur an economic loss in the short run as fuel prices rise.

Output, Price, and Profit in the Long Run

(Study Plan 10.4)

10. The pizza market is perfectly competitive, and all pizza producers have the same costs as Pat's Pizza Kitchen in Problem 4.

    a. At what price will some firms exit the pizza market in the long run?

    b. At what price will firms enter the pizza market in the long run?

11. In Problem 7, in the long run,

    a. Do firms have an incentive to enter or exit the paper market?

    b. If firms do enter or exit the market, explain how the economic profit or loss of the remaining paper producers will change.

    c. What is the long-run equilibrium market price and the quantity of paper produced? What is the number of firms in the market?

Changing Tastes and Advancing Technology

(Study Plan 10.5)

12. If in the long run, the market demand for paper remains the same as in Problem 8,

    a. What is the long-run equilibrium price of paper, the market output, and the economic profit or loss of each firm?

    b. Does this market experience external economies, external diseconomies, or constant cost? Illustrate by drawing the long-run supply curve.

Use the following news clip to work Problems 13 and 14.

Coors Brewing Expanding Plant

Coors Brewing Co. of Golden will expand its Virginia packaging plant at a cost of $24 million. The addition will accommodate a new production line, which will bottle beer faster. Coors Brewing employs 470 people at its Virginia plant. The expanded packaging line will add another eight jobs.

Source: *Denver Business Journal*, January 6, 2006

13. a. How will Coors' expansion change its marginal cost curve and short-run supply curve?

    b. What does this expansion decision imply about the point on Coors' *LRAC* curve at which the firm was before the expansion?

14. a. If other breweries follow the lead of Coors, what will happen to the market price of beer?

    b. How will the adjustment that you have described in part (a) influence the economic profit of Coors and other beer producers?

15. Explain and illustrate graphically how the growing world population is influencing the world market for wheat and a representative individual wheat farmer.

16. Explain and illustrate graphically how the diaper service market has been affected by the decrease in the North American birth rate and the development of disposable diapers.

Competition and Efficiency (Study Plan 10.6)

17. In a perfectly competitive market in long-run equilibrium, can consumer surplus be increased? Can producer surplus be increased? Can a consumer become better off by making a substitution away from this market?

18. **Never Pay Retail Again**

    Not only has scouring the Web for the best possible price become standard protocol before buying a big-ticket item, but more consumers are employing creative strategies for scoring hot deals. Comparison shopping, haggling and swapping discount codes are all becoming mainstream marks of savvy shoppers. Online shoppers can check a comparison service like Price Grabber before making a purchase.

    Source: CNN, May 30, 2008

    a. Explain the effect of the Internet on the degree of competition in the market.

    b. Explain how the Internet influences market efficiency.

ADDITIONAL PROBLEMS AND APPLICATIONS

 myeconlab You can work these problems in MyEconLab if assigned by your instructor.

What Is Perfect Competition?

Use the following news clip to work Problems 19 to 21.

Money in the Tank

Two gas stations stand on opposite sides of the road: Rutter's Farm Store and Sheetz gas station. Rutter's doesn't even have to look across the highway to know when Sheetz changes its price for a gallon of gas. When Sheetz raises the price, Rutter's pumps are busy. When Sheetz lowers prices, there's not a car in sight. Both gas stations survive but each has no control over the price.

Source: *The Mining Journal*, May 24, 2008

19. In what type of market do these gas stations operate? What determines the price of gasoline and the marginal revenue from gasoline?

20. Describe the elasticity of demand that each of these gas stations faces.

21. Why does each of these gas stations have so little control over the price of the gasoline it sells?

The Firm's Output Decision

22. The figure shows the costs of Quick Copy, one of many copy shops near campus.

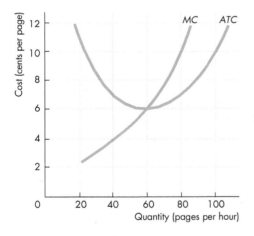

If the market price of copying is 10¢ a page, calculate Quick Copy's

a. Profit-maximizing output.

b. Economic profit.

23. The market for smoothies is perfectly competitive. The following table sets out the market demand schedule.

Price (dollars per smoothie)	Quantity demanded (smoothies per hour)
1.90	1,000
2.00	950
2.20	800
2.91	700
4.25	550
5.25	400
5.50	300

Each of the 100 producers of smoothies has the following costs when it uses its least-cost plant:

Output (smoothies per hour)	Marginal cost (dollars per additional smoothie)	Average variable cost	Average total cost
		(dollars per smoothie)	
3	2.50	4.00	7.33
4	2.20	3.53	6.03
5	1.90	3.24	5.24
6	2.00	3.00	4.67
7	2.91	2.91	4.34
8	4.25	3.00	4.25
9	8.00	3.33	4.44

a. What is the market price of a smoothie?

b. What is the market quantity of smoothies?

c. How many smoothies does each firm sell?

d. What is the economic profit made or economic loss incurred by each firm?

24. **Cadillac Plant Shuts Down Temporarily, Future Uncertain**

Delta Truss in Cadillac [Michigan] is shutting down and temporarily discontinuing truss production. Workers fear this temporary shutdown will become permanent, but the firm announced that it anticipates that production will resume when the spring business begins.

Source: *9&10 News*, February 18, 2008

a. Explain how the shutdown decision will affect Delta Truss' *TFC*, *TVC*, and *TC*.

b. Under what conditions would this shutdown decision maximize Delta Truss' economic profit (or minimize its loss)?

c. Under what conditions will Delta Truss start producing again?

Output, Price, and Profit in the Short Run

25. **Big Drops in Prices for Crops Make It Tough Down on the Farm**

    Grain prices have fallen roughly 50 percent from earlier this year. With better-than-expected crop yields, world grain production this year will rise 5 percent from 2007 to a record high.

    Source: *USA Today*, October 23, 2008

    Why did grain prices fall in 2008? Draw a graph to show that short-run effect on an individual farmer's economic profit.

Output, Price, and Profit in the Long Run

26. In Problem 23, do firms enter or exit the market in the long run? What is the market price and the equilibrium quantity in the long run?

27. In Problem 24, under what conditions will Delta Truss exit the market?

28. **Exxon Mobil Selling All Its Retail Gas Stations**

    Exxon Mobil is not alone among Big Oil exiting the retail gas business, a market where profits have gotten tougher as crude oil prices have risen. Gas station owners say they're struggling to turn a profit because while wholesale gasoline prices have risen sharply, they've been unable to raise pump prices fast enough to keep pace.

    Source: *Houston Chronicle*, June 12, 2008

    a. Is Exxon Mobil making a shutdown or exit decision in the retail gasoline market?

    b. Under what conditions will this decision maximize Exxon Mobil's economic profit?

    c. How might Exxon Mobil's decision affect the economic profit of other gasoline retailers?

Changing Tastes and Advancing Technology

29. **Another DVD Format, but It's Cheaper**

    New Medium Enterprises claims the quality of its new system, HD VMD, is equal to Blu-ray's but it costs only $199—cheaper than the $300 cost of a Blu-ray player. Chairman of the Blu-ray Disc Association says New Medium will fail because it believes that Blu-ray technology will always be more expensive. But mass production will cut the cost of a Blu-ray player to $90.

    Source: *The New York Times*, March 10, 2008

    a. Explain how technological change in Blu-ray production might support the prediction of lower prices in the long run. Illustrate your explanation with a graph.

    b. Even if Blu-ray prices do drop to $90 in the long run, why might the HD VMD still end up being less expensive at that time?

Competition and Efficiency

30. In a perfectly competitive market, each firm maximizes its profit by choosing only the quantity to produce. Regardless of whether the firm makes an economic profit or incurs an economic loss, the short-run equilibrium is efficient. Is the statement true? Explain why or why not.

Economics in the News

31. After you have studied *Reading Between the Lines* on pp. 214–215 answer the following questions.

    a. What are the features of the global market for corn that make it competitive?

    b. If the increase in production during 2009 and 2010 was due entirely to good weather, what will happen to the price and quantity produced when normal weather returns?

    c. What will happen to an individual farmer's marginal revenue, marginal cost, average total cost, and economic profit if the events in part (b) occur?

    d. If the increase in production during 2009 and 2010 was due mainly to a revolution in farm technology, what will happen to the price and quantity produced when normal weather returns?

32. **Cell Phone Sales Hit 1 Billion Mark**

    More than 1.15 billion mobile phones were sold worldwide in 2007, a 16 percent increase in a year. Emerging markets, especially China and India, provided much of the growth as many people bought their first phone. Carolina Milanesi, research director for mobile devices at Gartner, reported that in mature markets, such as Japan and Western Europe, consumers' appetite for feature-laden phones was met with new models packed with TV tuners, global positioning satellite functions, touch screens, and cameras.

    Source: *CNET News*, February 27, 2008

    a. Explain the effects of the increase in global demand for cell phones on the market for cell phones and on an individual cell-phone producer in the short run.

    b. Draw a graph to illustrate your explanation in part (a).

    c. Explain the long-run effects of the increase in global demand for cell phones on the market for cell phones.

    d. What factors will determine whether the price of cell phones will rise, fall, or stay the same in the new long-run equilibrium?

After studying this chapter,
you will be able to:

◆ Explain how monopoly arises and distinguish
between single-price monopoly and price-
discriminating monopoly

◆ Explain how a single-price monopoly determines its
output and price

◆ Compare the performance and efficiency of
single-price monopoly and competition

◆ Explain how price discrimination increases profit

◆ Explain how monopoly regulation influences output,
price, economic profit, and efficiency

11

MONOPOLY

Microsoft, Google, and eBay are dominant players in the markets they serve.
Because most PCs use Windows, programmers write most applications for this
operating system, which attracts more users. Because most Web searchers use
Google, most advertisers use it too, which attracts more searchers. Because
most online auction buyers use eBay, most online sellers do too, which attracts
more buyers. Each of these firms benefits from a phenomenon called a network
externality, which makes it hard for other firms to break into their markets.

Microsoft, Google, and eBay are obviously not like firms in perfect
competition. How does their behavior compare with perfectly competitive
firms? Do they charge prices that are too high and that damage the interests of
consumers? What benefits do they bring?

In this chapter, we study markets in which the firm can influence the price.
We also compare the performance of the firm in such a market with that in a
competitive market and examine whether monopoly is as efficient as
competition. In *Reading Between the Lines* at the end of the chapter, we'll look
at a claim by Consumer Watchdog, a California consumer protection
organization, that Google abuses its market power and should be scrutinized
by the Justice Department using the antitrust laws.

◆ Monopoly and How It Arises

A **monopoly** is a market with a single firm that produces a good or service for which no close substitute exists and that is protected by a barrier that prevents other firms from selling that good or service.

How Monopoly Arises

Monopoly arises for two key reasons:

- No close substitute
- Barrier to entry

No Close Substitute If a good has a close substitute, even though only one firm produces it, that firm effectively faces competition from the producers of the substitute. A monopoly sells a good or service that has no good substitute. Tap water and bottled water are close substitutes for drinking, but tap water has no effective substitute for showering or washing a car and a local public utility that supplies tap water is a monopoly.

Barrier to Entry A constraint that protects a firm from potential competitors is called a **barrier to entry**. The three types of barrier to entry are

- Natural
- Ownership
- Legal

Natural Barrier to Entry A natural barrier to entry creates a **natural monopoly**: a market in which economies of scale enable one firm to supply the entire market at the lowest possible cost. The firms that deliver gas, water, and electricity to our homes are examples of natural monopoly.

In Fig. 11.1 the market demand curve for electric power is *D*, and the long-run average cost curve is *LRAC*. Economies of scale prevail over the entire length of the *LRAC* curve.

One firm can produce 4 million kilowatt-hours at 5 cents a kilowatt-hour. At this price, the quantity demanded is 4 million kilowatt-hours. So if the price was 5 cents, one firm could supply the entire market.

If two firms shared the market equally, it would cost each of them 10 cents a kilowatt-hour to produce a total of 4 million kilowatt-hours.

In conditions like those shown in Fig. 11.1, one firm can supply the entire market at a lower cost than

FIGURE 11.1   Natural Monopoly

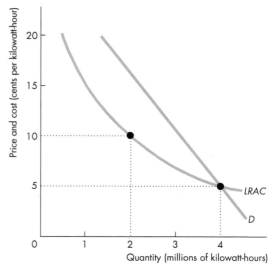

The market demand curve for electric power is *D*, and the long-run average cost curve is *LRAC*. Economies of scale exist over the entire *LRAC* curve. One firm can distribute 4 million kilowatt-hours at a cost of 5 cents a kilowatt-hour. This same total output costs 10 cents a kilowatt-hour with two firms. One firm can meet the market demand at a lower cost than two or more firms can. The market is a natural monopoly.

two or more firms can. The market is a natural monopoly.

Ownership Barrier to Entry An ownership barrier to entry occurs if one firm owns a significant portion of a key resource. An example of this type of monopoly occurred during the last century when De Beers controlled up to 90 percent of the world's supply of diamonds. (Today, its share is only 65 percent.)

Legal Barrier to Entry A legal barrier to entry creates a **legal monopoly**: a market in which competition and entry are restricted by the granting of a public franchise, government license, patent, or copyright.

A *public franchise* is an exclusive right granted to a firm to supply a good or service. An example is the U.S. Postal Service, which has the exclusive right to carry first-class mail. A *government license* controls entry into particular occupations, professions, and industries. Examples of this type of barrier to entry occur in medicine, law, dentistry, schoolteaching, architecture, and many other professional services. Licensing does not always create a monopoly, but it does restrict competition.

A *patent* is an exclusive right granted to the inventor of a product or service. A *copyright* is an exclusive right granted to the author or composer of a literary, musical, dramatic, or artistic work. Patents and copyrights are valid for a limited time period that varies from country to country. In the United States, a patent is valid for 20 years. Patents encourage the *invention* of new products and production methods. They also stimulate *innovation*—the use of new inventions—by encouraging inventors to publicize their discoveries and offer them for use under license. Patents have stimulated innovations in areas as diverse as soybean seeds, pharmaceuticals, memory chips, and video games.

Economics in Action
Information-Age Monopolies

Information-age technologies have created four big natural monopolies. These firms have large plant costs but almost zero marginal cost, so they experience economies of scale.

Microsoft has captured 90 percent of the personal computer operating system market with Windows and 73 percent of the Web browser market with Internet Explorer. eBay has captured 85 percent of the consumer-to-consumer Internet auction market and Google has 78 percent of the search engine market.

New technologies also destroy monopoly. FedEx, UPS, the fax machine, and e-mail have weakened the monopoly of the U.S. Postal Service; and the satellite dish has weakened the monopoly of cable television companies.

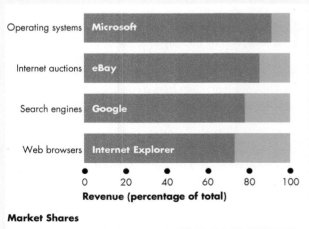

Market Shares

Monopoly Price-Setting Strategies

A major difference between monopoly and competition is that a monopoly sets its own price. In doing so, the monopoly faces a market constraint: To sell a larger quantity, the monopoly must set a lower price. There are two monopoly situations that create two pricing strategies:

- Single price
- Price discrimination

Single Price A **single-price monopoly** is a firm that must sell each unit of its output for the same price to all its customers. De Beers sells diamonds (of a given size and quality) for the same price to all its customers. If it tried to sell at a low price to some customers and at a higher price to others, only the low-price customers would buy from De Beers. Others would buy from De Beers' low-price customers. De Beers is a *single-price* monopoly.

Price Discrimination When a firm practices **price discrimination**, it sells different units of a good or service for different prices. Many firms price discriminate. Microsoft sells its Windows and Office software at different prices to different buyers. Computer manufacturers who install the software on new machines, students and teachers, governments, and businesses all pay different prices. Pizza producers offer a second pizza for a lower price than the first one. These are examples of *price discrimination*.

When a firm price discriminates, it looks as though it is doing its customers a favor. In fact, it is charging the highest possible price for each unit sold and making the largest possible profit.

 REVIEW QUIZ

1 How does monopoly arise?
2 How does a natural monopoly differ from a legal monopoly?
3 Distinguish between a price-discriminating monopoly and a single-price monopoly.

You can work these questions in Study Plan 11.1 and get instant feedback.

We start with a single-price monopoly and see how it makes its decisions about the quantity to produce and the price to charge to maximize its profit.

◆ A Single-Price Monopoly's Output and Price Decision

To understand how a single-price monopoly makes its output and price decision, we must first study the link between price and marginal revenue.

Price and Marginal Revenue

Because in a monopoly there is only one firm, the demand curve facing the firm is the market demand curve. Let's look at Bobbie's Barbershop, the sole supplier of haircuts in Cairo, Nebraska. The table in Fig. 11.2 shows the market demand schedule. At a price of $20, Bobbie sells no haircuts. The lower the price, the more haircuts per hour she can sell. For example, at $12, consumers demand 4 haircuts per hour (row *E*).

Total revenue (*TR*) is the price (*P*) multiplied by the quantity sold (*Q*). For example, in row *D*, Bobbie sells 3 haircuts at $14 each, so total revenue is $42. *Marginal revenue* (*MR*) is the change in total revenue (Δ*TR*) resulting from a one-unit increase in the quantity sold. For example, if the price falls from $16 (row *C*) to $14 (row *D*), the quantity sold increases from 2 to 3 haircuts. Total revenue increases from $32 to $42, so the change in total revenue is $10. Because the quantity sold increases by 1 haircut, marginal revenue equals the change in total revenue and is $10. Marginal revenue is placed between the two rows to emphasize that marginal revenue relates to the *change* in the quantity sold.

Figure 11.2 shows the market demand curve and marginal revenue curve (*MR*) and also illustrates the calculation we've just made. Notice that at each level of output, marginal revenue is less than price—the marginal revenue curve lies below the demand curve. Why is marginal revenue *less* than price? It is because when the price is lowered to sell one more unit, two opposing forces affect total revenue. The lower price results in a revenue loss, and the increased quantity sold results in a revenue gain. For example, at a price of $16, Bobbie sells 2 haircuts (point *C*). If she lowers the price to $14, she sells 3 haircuts and has a revenue gain of $14 on the third haircut. But she now receives only $14 on the first two haircuts—$2 less than before. As a result, she loses $4 of revenue on the first 2 haircuts. To calculate marginal revenue, she must deduct this amount from the revenue gain of $14. So her marginal revenue is $10, which is less than the price.

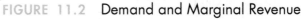

FIGURE 11.2   Demand and Marginal Revenue

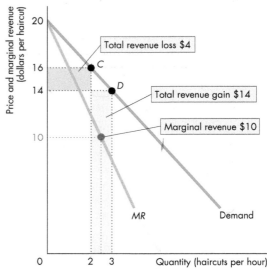

	Price (P) (dollars per haircut)	Quantity demanded (Q) (haircuts per hour)	Total revenue (TR = P × Q) (dollars)	Marginal revenue (MR = ΔTR/ΔQ) (dollars per haircut)
A	20	0	0	
				18
B	18	1	18	
				14
C	16	2	32	
				10
D	14	3	42	
				6
E	12	4	48	
				2
F	10	5	50	

The table shows the demand schedule. Total revenue (*TR*) is price multiplied by quantity sold. For example, in row *C*, the price is $16 a haircut, Bobbie sells 2 haircuts, and total revenue is $32. Marginal revenue (*MR*) is the change in total revenue that results from a one-unit increase in the quantity sold. For example, when the price falls from $16 to $14 a haircut, the quantity sold increases from 2 to 3, an increase of 1 haircut, and total revenue increases by $10. Marginal revenue is $10. The demand curve and the marginal revenue curve, *MR*, are based on the numbers in the table and illustrate the calculation of marginal revenue when the price falls from $16 to $14 a haircut.

myeconlab animation

Marginal Revenue and Elasticity

A single-price monopoly's marginal revenue is related to the *elasticity of demand* for its good. The demand for a good can be *elastic* (the elasticity is greater than 1), *inelastic* (the elasticity is less than 1), or *unit elastic* (the elasticity is equal to 1). Demand is *elastic* if a 1 percent fall in the price brings a greater than 1 percent increase in the quantity demanded. Demand is *inelastic* if a 1 percent fall in the price brings a less than 1 percent increase in the quantity demanded. Demand is *unit elastic* if a 1 percent fall in the price brings a 1 percent increase in the quantity demanded. (See Chapter 4, pp. 74–76.)

If demand is elastic, a fall in the price brings an increase in total revenue—the revenue gain from the increase in quantity sold outweighs the revenue loss from the lower price—and marginal revenue is *positive*. If demand is inelastic, a fall in the price brings a decrease in total revenue—the revenue gain from the increase in quantity sold is outweighed by the revenue loss from the lower price—and marginal revenue is *negative*. If demand is unit elastic, total revenue does not change—the revenue gain from the increase in the quantity sold offsets the revenue loss from the lower price—and marginal revenue is *zero*. (See Chapter 4, p. 78.)

Figure 11.3 illustrates the relationship between marginal revenue, total revenue, and elasticity. As the price gradually falls from $20 to $10 a haircut, the quantity demanded increases from 0 to 5 haircuts an hour. Over this output range, marginal revenue is positive in part (a), total revenue increases in part (b), and the demand for haircuts is elastic. As the price falls from $10 to $0 a haircut, the quantity of haircuts demanded increases from 5 to 10 an hour. Over this output range, marginal revenue is negative in part (a), total revenue decreases in part (b), and the demand for haircuts is inelastic. When the price is $10 a haircut, marginal revenue is zero in part (a), total revenue is at a maximum in part (b), and the demand for haircuts is unit elastic.

In Monopoly, Demand Is Always Elastic The relationship between marginal revenue and elasticity of demand that you've just discovered implies that a profit-maximizing monopoly never produces an output in the inelastic range of the market demand curve. If it did so, it could charge a higher price, produce a smaller quantity, and increase its profit. Let's now look at a monopoly's price and output decision.

FIGURE 11.3   Marginal Revenue and Elasticity

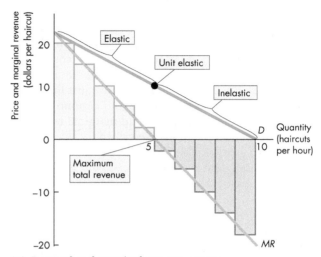

(a) Demand and marginal revenue curves

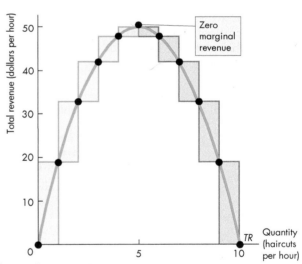

(b) Total revenue curve

In part (a), the demand curve is *D* and the marginal revenue curve is *MR*. In part (b), the total revenue curve is *TR*. Over the range 0 to 5 haircuts an hour, a price cut increases total revenue, so marginal revenue is positive—as shown by the blue bars. Demand is elastic. Over the range 5 to 10 haircuts an hour, a price cut decreases total revenue, so marginal revenue is negative—as shown by the red bars. Demand is inelastic. At 5 haircuts an hour, total revenue is maximized and marginal revenue is zero. Demand is unit elastic.

myeconlab animation

Price and Output Decision

A monopoly sets its price and output at the levels that maximize economic profit. To determine this price and output level, we need to study the behavior of both cost and revenue as output varies. A monopoly faces the same types of technology and cost constraints as a competitive firm, so its costs (total cost, average cost, and marginal cost) behave just like those of a firm in perfect competition. And a monopoly's revenues (total revenue, price, and marginal revenue) behave in the way we've just described.

Table 11.1 provides information about Bobbie's costs, revenues, and economic profit, and Fig. 11.4 shows the same information graphically.

Maximizing Economic Profit You can see in Table 11.1 and Fig. 11.4(a) that total cost (*TC*) and total revenue (*TR*) both rise as output increases, but *TC* rises at an increasing rate and *TR* rises at a decreasing rate. Economic profit, which equals *TR* minus *TC*, increases at small output levels, reaches a maximum, and then decreases. The maximum profit ($12) occurs when Bobbie sells 3 haircuts for $14 each. If she sells 2 haircuts for $16 each or 4 haircuts for $12 each, her economic profit will be only $8.

Marginal Revenue Equals Marginal Cost You can see Bobbie's marginal revenue (*MR*) and marginal cost (*MC*) in Table 11.1 and Fig. 11.4(b).

When Bobbie increases output from 2 to 3 haircuts, *MR* is $10 and *MC* is $6. *MR* exceeds *MC* by $4 and Bobbie's profit increases by that amount. If Bobbie increases output yet further, from 3 to 4 haircuts, *MR* is $6 and *MC* is $10. In this case, *MC* exceeds *MR* by $4, so profit decreases by that amount. When *MR* exceeds *MC*, profit increases if output increases. When *MC* exceeds *MR*, profit increases if output *decreases*. When *MC* equals *MR*, profit is maximized.

Figure 11.4(b) shows the maximum profit as price (on the demand curve *D*) minus average total cost (on the *ATC* curve) multiplied by the quantity produced—the blue rectangle.

Maximum Price the Market Will Bear Unlike a firm in perfect competition, a monopoly influences the price of what it sells. But a monopoly doesn't set the price at the maximum *possible* price. At the maximum possible price, the firm would be able to sell only one unit of output, which in general is less than the profit-maximizing quantity. Rather, a monopoly produces the profit-maximizing quantity and sells that quantity for the highest price it can get.

TABLE 11.1   A Monopoly's Output and Price Decision

Price (P) (dollars per haircut)	Quantity demanded (Q) (haircuts per hour)	Total revenue (TR = P × Q) (dollars)	Marginal revenue (MR = ΔTR/ΔQ) (dollars per haircut)	Total cost (TC) (dollars)	Marginal cost (MC = ΔTC/ΔQ) (dollars per haircut)	Profit (TR − TC) (dollars)
20	0	0		20		−20
			18		1	
18	1	18		21		−3
			14		3	
16	2	32		24		+8
			10		6	
14	3	42		30		+12
			6		10	
12	4	48		40		+8
			2		15	
10	5	50		55		−5

This table gives the information needed to find the profit-maximizing output and price. Total revenue (*TR*) equals price multiplied by the quantity sold. Profit equals total revenue minus total cost (*TC*). Profit is maximized when 3 haircuts are sold at a price of $14 each. Total revenue is $42, total cost is $30, and economic profit is $12 ($42 − $30).

FIGURE 11.4   A Monopoly's Output and Price

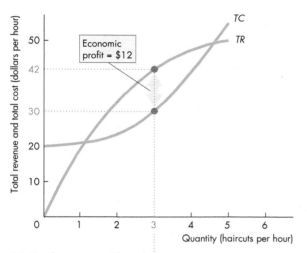

(a) Total revenue and total cost curves

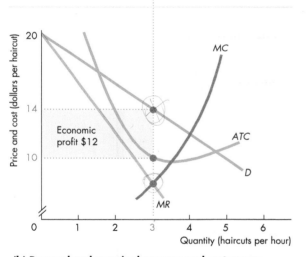

(b) Demand and marginal revenue and cost curves

In part (a), economic profit is the vertical distance equal to total revenue (*TR*) minus total cost (*TC*) and it is maximized at 3 haircuts an hour. In part (b), economic profit is maximized when marginal cost (*MC*) equals marginal revenue (*MR*). The profit-maximizing output is 3 haircuts an hour. The price is determined by the demand curve (*D*) and is $14 a haircut. The average total cost of a haircut is $10, so economic profit, the blue rectangle, is $12—the profit per haircut ($4) multiplied by 3 haircuts.

All firms maximize profit by producing the output at which marginal revenue equals marginal cost. For a competitive firm, price equals marginal revenue, so price also equals marginal cost. For a monopoly, price exceeds marginal revenue, so price also exceeds marginal cost.

A monopoly charges a price that exceeds marginal cost, but does it always make an economic profit? In Fig. 11.4(b), Bobbie produces 3 haircuts an hour. Her average total cost is $10 (on the *ATC* curve) and her price is $14 (on the *D* curve), so her profit per haircut is $4 ($14 minus $10). Bobbie's economic profit is shown by the area of the blue rectangle, which equals the profit per haircut ($4) multiplied by the number of haircuts (3), for a total of $12.

If firms in a perfectly competitive market make a positive economic profit, new firms enter. That does *not* happen in monopoly. Barriers to entry prevent new firms from entering the market, so a monopoly can make a positive economic profit and might continue to do so indefinitely. Sometimes that economic profit is large, as in the international diamond business.

Bobbie makes a positive economic profit. But suppose that Bobbie's landlord increases the rent on her salon. If Bobbie pays an additional $12 an hour for rent, her fixed cost increases by $12 an hour. Her marginal cost and marginal revenue don't change, so her profit-maximizing output remains at 3 haircuts an hour. Her profit decreases by $12 an hour to zero. If Bobbie's salon rent increases by more than $12 an hour, she incurs an economic loss. If this situation were permanent, Bobbie would go out of business.

REVIEW QUIZ

1 What is the relationship between marginal cost and marginal revenue when a single-price monopoly maximizes profit?

2 How does a single-price monopoly determine the price it will charge its customers?

3 What is the relationship between price, marginal revenue, and marginal cost when a single-price monopoly is maximizing profit?

4 Why can a monopoly make a positive economic profit even in the long run?

You can work these questions in Study Plan 11.2 and get instant feedback.

◆ Single-Price Monopoly and Competition Compared

Imagine a market that is made up of many small firms operating in perfect competition. Then imagine that a single firm buys out all these small firms and creates a monopoly.

What will happen in this market? Will the price rise or fall? Will the quantity produced increase or decrease? Will economic profit increase or decrease? Will either the original competitive situation or the new monopoly situation be efficient?

These are the questions we're now going to answer. First, we look at the effects of monopoly on the price and quantity produced. Then we turn to the questions about efficiency.

Comparing Price and Output

Figure 11.5 shows the market we'll study. The market demand curve is D. The demand curve is the same regardless of how the industry is organized. But the supply side and the equilibrium are different in monopoly and competition. First, let's look at the case of perfect competition.

Perfect Competition Initially, with many small perfectly competitive firms in the market, the market supply curve is S. This supply curve is obtained by summing the supply curves of all the individual firms in the market.

In perfect competition, equilibrium occurs where the supply curve and the demand curve intersect. The price is P_C, and the quantity produced by the industry is Q_C. Each firm takes the price P_C and maximizes its profit by producing the output at which its own marginal cost equals the price. Because each firm is a small part of the total industry, there is no incentive for any firm to try to manipulate the price by varying its output.

Monopoly Now suppose that this industry is taken over by a single firm. Consumers do not change, so the market demand curve remains the same as in the case of perfect competition. But now the monopoly recognizes this demand curve as a constraint on the price at which it can sell its output. The monopoly's marginal revenue curve is MR.

The monopoly maximizes profit by producing the quantity at which marginal revenue equals marginal cost. To find the monopoly's marginal cost curve, first

recall that in perfect competition, the market supply curve is the sum of the supply curves of the firms in the industry. Also recall that each firm's supply curve is its marginal cost curve (see Chapter 10, p. 201). So when the market is taken over by a single firm, the competitive market's supply curve becomes the monopoly's marginal cost curve. To remind you of this fact, the supply curve is also labeled MC.

The output at which marginal revenue equals marginal cost is Q_M. This output is smaller than the competitive output Q_C. And the monopoly charges the price P_M, which is higher than P_C. We have established that

Compared to a perfectly competitive market, a single-price monopoly produces a smaller output and charges a higher price.

We've seen how the output and price of a monopoly compare with those in a competitive market. Let's now compare the efficiency of the two types of market.

FIGURE 11.5   Monopoly's Smaller Output and Higher Price

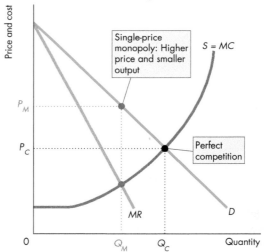

A competitive market produces the quantity Q_C at price P_C. A single-price monopoly produces the quantity Q_M at which marginal revenue equals marginal cost and sells that quantity for the price P_M. Compared to perfect competition, a single-price monopoly produces a smaller output and charges a higher price.

myeconlab   animation

Efficiency Comparison

Perfect competition (with no externalities) is efficient. Figure 11.6(a) illustrates the efficiency of perfect competition and serves as a benchmark against which to measure the inefficiency of monopoly. Along the demand curve and marginal social benefit curve ($D = MSB$), consumers are efficient. Along the supply curve and marginal social cost curve ($S = MSC$), producers are efficient. In competitive equilibrium, the price is P_C, the quantity is Q_C, and marginal social benefit equals marginal social cost.

Consumer surplus is the green triangle under the demand curve and above the equilibrium price (see Chapter 5, p. 97). *Producer surplus* is the blue area above the supply curve and below the equilibrium price (see Chapter 5, p. 99). Total surplus (consumer surplus and producer surplus) is maximized.

Also, in long-run competitive equilibrium, entry and exit ensure that each firm produces its output at the minimum possible long-run average cost.

To summarize: At the competitive equilibrium, marginal social benefit equals marginal social cost; total surplus is maximized; firms produce at the lowest possible long-run average cost; and resource use is efficient.

Figure 11.6(b) illustrates the inefficiency of monopoly and the sources of that inefficiency. A monopoly produces Q_M and sells its output for P_M. The smaller output and higher price drive a wedge between marginal social benefit and marginal social cost and create a *deadweight loss*. The gray triangle shows the deadweight loss and its magnitude is a measure of the inefficiency of monopoly.

Consumer surplus shrinks for two reasons. First, consumers lose by having to pay more for the good. This loss to consumers is a gain for monopoly and increases the producer surplus. Second, consumers lose by getting less of the good, and this loss is part of the deadweight loss.

Although the monopoly gains from a higher price, it loses some producer surplus because it produces a smaller output. That loss is another part of the deadweight loss.

A monopoly produces a smaller output than perfect competition and faces no competition, so it does not produce at the lowest possible long-run average cost. As a result, monopoly damages the consumer interest in three ways: A monopoly produces less, increases the cost of production, and raises the price by more than the increased cost of production.

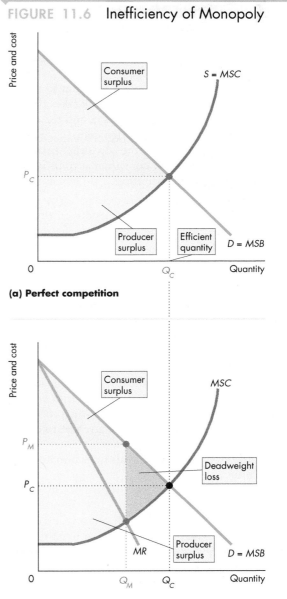

FIGURE 11.6   Inefficiency of Monopoly

(a) Perfect competition

(b) Monopoly

In perfect competition in part (a), output is Q_C and the price is P_C. Marginal social benefit (MSB) equals marginal social cost (MSC); total surplus, the sum of consumer surplus (the green triangle) and producer surplus (the blue area), is maximized; and in the long run, firms produce at the lowest possible average cost. Monopoly in part (b) produces Q_M and raises the price to P_M. Consumer surplus shrinks, the monopoly gains, and a deadweight loss (the gray triangle) arises.

myeconlab   animation

Redistribution of Surpluses

You've seen that monopoly is inefficient because marginal social benefit exceeds marginal social cost and there is deadweight loss—a social loss. But monopoly also brings a *redistribution* of surpluses.

Some of the lost consumer surplus goes to the monopoly. In Fig. 11.6, the monopoly takes the difference between the higher price, P_M, and the competitive price, P_C, on the quantity sold, Q_M. So the monopoly takes that part of the consumer surplus. This portion of the loss of consumer surplus is not a loss to society. It is redistribution from consumers to the monopoly producer.

Rent Seeking

You've seen that monopoly creates a deadweight loss and is inefficient. But the social cost of monopoly can exceed the deadweight loss because of an activity called rent seeking. Any surplus—consumer surplus, producer surplus, or economic profit—is called **economic rent**. The pursuit of wealth by capturing economic rent is called **rent seeking**.

You've seen that a monopoly makes its economic profit by diverting part of consumer surplus to itself—by converting consumer surplus into economic profit. So the pursuit of economic profit by a monopoly is rent seeking. It is the attempt to capture consumer surplus.

Rent seekers pursue their goals in two main ways. They might

- Buy a monopoly
- Create a monopoly

Buy a Monopoly To rent seek by buying a monopoly, a person searches for a monopoly that is for sale at a lower price than the monopoly's economic profit. Trading of taxicab licenses is an example of this type of rent seeking. In some cities, taxicabs are regulated. The city restricts both the fares and the number of taxis that can operate so that operating a taxi results in economic profit. A person who wants to operate a taxi must buy a license from someone who already has one. People rationally devote time and effort to seeking out profitable monopoly businesses to buy. In the process, they use up scarce resources that could otherwise have been used to produce goods and services. The value of this lost production is part of the social cost of monopoly. The amount paid for a monopoly is not a social cost because the payment is just a transfer of an existing producer surplus from the buyer to the seller.

Create a Monopoly Rent seeking by creating a monopoly is mainly a political activity. It takes the form of lobbying and trying to influence the political process. Such influence might be sought by making campaign contributions in exchange for legislative support or by indirectly seeking to influence political outcomes through publicity in the media or more direct contacts with politicians and bureaucrats. An example of a monopoly created in this way is the government-imposed restrictions on the quantities of textiles that may be imported into the United States. Another is a regulation that limits the number of oranges that may be sold in the United States. These are regulations that restrict output and increase price.

This type of rent seeking is a costly activity that uses up scarce resources. Taken together, firms spend billions of dollars lobbying Congress, state legislators, and local officials in the pursuit of licenses and laws that create barriers to entry and establish a monopoly.

Rent-Seeking Equilibrium

Barriers to entry create monopoly. But there is no barrier to entry into rent seeking. Rent seeking is like perfect competition. If an economic profit is available, a new rent seeker will try to get some of it. And competition among rent seekers pushes up the price that must be paid for a monopoly, to the point at which the rent seeker makes zero economic profit by operating the monopoly. For example, competition for the right to operate a taxi in New York City leads to a price of more than $100,000 for a taxi license, which is sufficiently high to eliminate the economic profit made by a taxi operator.

Figure 11.7 shows a rent-seeking equilibrium. The cost of rent seeking is a fixed cost that must be added to a monopoly's other costs. Rent seeking and rent-seeking costs increase to the point at which no economic profit is made. The average total cost curve, which includes the fixed cost of rent seeking, shifts upward until it just touches the demand curve. Economic profit is zero. It has been lost in rent seeking.

Consumer surplus is unaffected, but the deadweight loss from monopoly is larger. The deadweight loss now includes the original deadweight loss triangle plus the lost producer surplus, shown by the enlarged gray area in Fig. 11.7.

FIGURE 11.7   Rent-Seeking Equilibrium

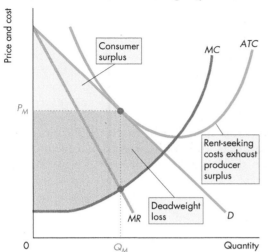

With competitive rent seeking, a monopoly uses all its economic profit to maintain its monopoly. The firm's rent-seeking costs are fixed costs. They add to total fixed cost and to average total cost. The *ATC* curve shifts upward until, at the profit-maximizing price, the firm breaks even.

 animation

---

◢ REVIEW QUIZ

1 Why does a single-price monopoly produce a smaller output and charge more than the price that would prevail if the market were perfectly competitive?
2 How does a monopoly transfer consumer surplus to itself?
3 Why is a single-price monopoly inefficient?
4 What is rent seeking and how does it influence the inefficiency of monopoly?

You can work these questions in Study Plan 11.3 and get instant feedback.

So far, we've considered only a single-price monopoly. But many monopolies do not operate with a single price. Instead, they price discriminate. Let's now see how a price-discriminating monopoly works.

◆ Price Discrimination

You encounter *price discrimination*—selling a good or service at a number of different prices—when you travel, go to the movies, get your hair cut, buy pizza, or visit an art museum or theme park. Many of the firms that price discriminate are not monopolies, but monopolies price discriminate when they can do so.

To be able to price discriminate, a firm must be able to identify and separate different buyer types and sell a product that cannot be resold.

Not all price *differences* are price *discrimination*. Some goods that are similar have different prices because they have different costs of production. For example, the price per ounce of cereal is lower if you buy your cereal in a big box than if you buy individual serving size boxes. This price difference reflects a cost difference and is not price discrimination.

At first sight, price discrimination appears to be inconsistent with profit maximization. Why would a movie theater allow children to see movies at a discount? Why would a hairdresser charge students and senior citizens less? Aren't these firms losing profit by being nice to their customers?

Capturing Consumer Surplus

Price discrimination captures consumer surplus and converts it into economic profit. It does so by getting buyers to pay a price as close as possible to the maximum willingness to pay.

Firms price discriminate in two broad ways. They discriminate:

- Among groups of buyers
- Among units of a good

Discriminating Among Groups of Buyers People differ in the value they place on a good—their marginal benefit and willingness to pay. Some of these differences are correlated with features such as age, employment status, and other easily distinguished characteristics. When such a correlation is present, firms can profit by price discriminating among the different groups of buyers.

For example, a face-to-face sales meeting with a customer might bring a large and profitable order. So for salespeople and other business travelers, the marginal benefit from a trip is large and the price that such a traveler is willing to pay for a trip is high. In contrast, for a vacation traveler, any of several different trips and even no vacation trip are options. So for vacation travelers, the marginal benefit of a trip is small and the price that such a traveler is willing to pay for a trip is low. Because business travelers are willing to pay more than vacation travelers are, it is possible for an airline to profit by price discriminating between these two groups.

Discriminating Among Units of a Good Everyone experiences diminishing marginal benefit and has a downward-sloping demand curve. For this reason, if all the units of the good are sold for a single price, buyers end up with a consumer surplus equal to the value they get from each unit of the good minus the price paid for it.

A firm that price discriminates by charging a buyer one price for a single item and a lower price for a second or third item can capture some of the consumer surplus. Buy one pizza and get a second one free (or for a low price) is an example of this type of price discrimination.

(Note that some discounts for bulk arise from lower costs of production for greater bulk. In these cases, such discounts are not price discrimination.)

Let's see how price discriminating increases economic profit.

Profiting by Price Discriminating

Global Airlines has a monopoly on an exotic route. Figure 11.8 shows the market demand curve (*D*) for travel on this route. It also shows Global Airline's marginal revenue curve (*MR*), marginal cost curve (*MC*), and average total cost curve (*ATC*).

As a single-price monopoly, Global maximizes profit by producing the quantity at which *MR* equals *MC*, which is 8,000 trips a year, and charging $1,200 per trip. At this quantity, average total cost is $600 per trip, economic profit is $600 a trip, and Global's economic profit is $4.8 million a year, shown by the blue rectangle. Global's customers enjoy a consumer surplus shown by the green triangle.

Global is struck by the fact that many of its customers are business travelers, and it suspects they are willing to pay more than $1,200 a trip. Global does some market research, which reveals that some business travelers are willing to pay as much as $1,800 a trip. Also, these customers frequently change their travel plans at the last minute. Another group of business travelers is willing to pay $1,600. These

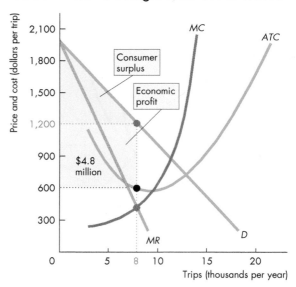

FIGURE 11.8   A Single Price of Air Travel

Global Airlines has a monopoly on an air route. The market demand curve is *D*. Global Airline's marginal revenue curve is *MR*, its marginal cost curve is *MC*, and its average total cost curve is *ATC*. As a single-price monopoly, Global maximizes profit by selling 8,000 trips a year at $1,200 a trip. Its profit is $4.8 million a year—the blue rectangle. Global's customers enjoy a consumer surplus—the green triangle.

myeconlab animation

customers know a week ahead when they will travel, and they never want to stay over a weekend. Yet another group would pay up to $1,400. These travelers know two weeks ahead when they will travel and also don't want to stay away over a weekend.

Global announces a new fare schedule: no restrictions, $1,800; 7-day advance purchase, nonrefundable, $1,600; 14-day advance purchase, nonrefundable, $1,400; 14-day advance purchase, must stay over a weekend, $1,200.

Figure 11.9 shows the outcome with this new fare structure and also shows why Global is pleased with its new fares. It sells 2,000 seats at each of its four prices. Global's economic profit increases by the dark blue steps. Its economic profit is now its original $4.8 million a year plus an additional $2.4 million from its new higher fares. Consumer surplus shrinks to the sum of the smaller green areas.

FIGURE 11.9   Price Discrimination

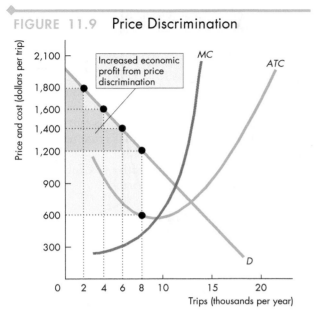

Global revises its fare structure: no restrictions at $1,800, 7-day advance purchase at $1,600, 14-day advance purchase at $1,400, and must stay over a weekend at $1,200. Global sells 2,000 trips at each of its four new fares. Its economic profit increases by $2.4 million a year to $7.2 million a year, which is shown by the original blue rectangle plus the dark blue steps. Global's customers' consumer surplus shrinks.

Perfect Price Discrimination

Perfect price discrimination occurs if a firm is able to sell each unit of output for the highest price anyone is willing to pay for it. In such a case, the entire consumer surplus is eliminated and captured by the producer. To practice perfect price discrimination, a firm must be creative and come up with a host of prices and special conditions, each one of which appeals to a tiny segment of the market.

With perfect price discrimination, something special happens to marginal revenue—the market demand curve becomes the marginal revenue curve. The reason is that when the price is cut to sell a larger quantity, the firm sells only the marginal unit at the lower price. All the other units continue to be sold for the highest price that each buyer is willing to pay. So for the perfect price discriminator, marginal revenue *equals* price and the demand curve becomes the marginal revenue curve.

With marginal revenue equal to price, Global can obtain even greater profit by increasing output up to the point at which price (and marginal revenue) is equal to marginal cost.

So Global seeks new travelers who will not pay as much as $1,200 a trip but who will pay more than marginal cost. Global offers a variety of vacation specials at different low fares that appeal only to new travelers. Existing customers continue to pay the higher fares. With all these fares and specials, Global increases sales, extracts the entire consumer surplus, and maximizes economic profit.

Figure 11.10 shows the outcome with perfect price discrimination. The fares paid by the original travelers extract the entire consumer surplus from this group. The new fares between $900 and $1,200 attract 3,000 additional travelers and take their entire consumer surplus also. Global now makes an economic profit of more than $9 million.

FIGURE 11.10   Perfect Price Discrimination

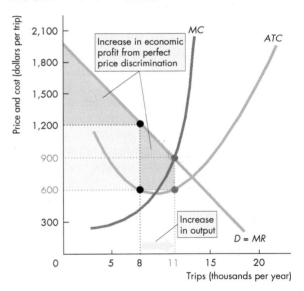

Dozens of fares discriminate among many different types of business traveler, and many new low fares with restrictions appeal to vacation travelers. With perfect price discrimination, the market demand curve becomes Global's marginal revenue curve. Economic profit is maximized when the lowest price equals marginal cost. Global sells 11,000 trips and makes an economic profit of more than $9 million a year.

Efficiency and Rent Seeking with Price Discrimination

With perfect price discrimination, output increases to the point at which price equals marginal cost—where the marginal cost curve intersects the market demand curve (see Fig. 11.10). This output is identical to that of perfect competition. Perfect price discrimination pushes consumer surplus to zero but increases the monopoly's producer surplus to equal the total surplus in perfect competition. With perfect price discrimination, deadweight loss is zero, so perfect price discrimination achieves efficiency.

> The more perfectly the monopoly can price discriminate, the closer its output is to the competitive output and the more efficient is the outcome.

But there are two differences between perfect competition and perfect price discrimination. First, the distribution of the total surplus is different. It is shared by consumers and producers in perfect competition, while the producer gets it all with perfect price discrimination. Second, because the producer grabs all the surplus, rent seeking becomes profitable.

People use resources in pursuit of economic rent, and the bigger the rents, the more resources get used in pursuing them. With free entry into rent seeking, the long-run equilibrium outcome is that rent seekers use up the entire producer surplus.

Real-world airlines are as creative as Global Airlines, as you can see in the cartoon!

Would it bother you to hear how little I paid for this flight?

From William Hamilton, "Voodoo Economics," © 1992 by The Chronicle Publishing Company, p.3. Reprinted with permission of Chronicle Books.

Economics in Action
Attempting Perfect Price Discrimination

If you want to spend a day at Disney World in Orlando, it will cost you $75.62. You can spend a second (consecutive) day for an extra $72.42. A third day will cost you $68.17. But for a fourth day, you'll pay only $9.59 and for a fifth day, $3.20. For more days all the way up to 10, you'll pay only $2.12 a day.

The Disney Corporation hopes that it has read your willingness to pay correctly and not left you with too much consumer surplus. Disney figures though that after three days, your marginal benefit is crashing.

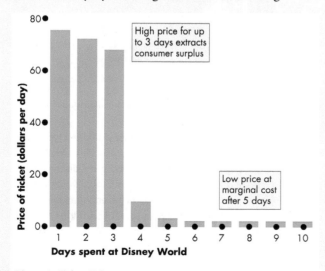

Disney's Ticket Prices

REVIEW QUIZ

1 What is price discrimination and how is it used to increase a monopoly's profit?
2 Explain how consumer surplus changes when a monopoly price discriminates.
3 Explain how consumer surplus, economic profit, and output change when a monopoly perfectly price discriminates.
4 What are some of the ways that real-world airlines price discriminate?

You've seen that monopoly is profitable for the monopoly but costly for consumers. It results in inefficiency. Because of these features of monopoly, it is subject to policy debate and regulation. We'll now study the key monopoly policy issues.

◆ Monopoly Regulation

Natural monopoly presents a dilemma. With economies of scale, it produces at the lowest possible cost. But with market power, it has an incentive to raise the price above the competitive price and produce too little—to operate in the self-interest of the monopolist and not in the social interest.

Regulation—rules administered by a government agency to influence prices, quantities, entry, and other aspects of economic activity in a firm or industry—is a possible solution to this dilemma.

To implement regulation, the government establishes agencies to oversee and enforce the rules. For example, the Surface Transportation Board regulates prices on interstate railroads, some trucking and bus lines, and water and oil pipelines. By the 1970s, almost a quarter of the nation's output was produced by regulated industries (far more than just natural monopolies) and a process of deregulation began.

Deregulation is the process of removing regulation of prices, quantities, entry, and other aspects of economic activity in a firm or industry. During the past 30 years, deregulation has occurred in domestic air transportation, telephone service, interstate trucking, and banking and financial services. Cable TV was deregulated in 1984, re-regulated in 1992, and deregulated again in 1996.

Regulation is a possible solution to the dilemma presented by natural monopoly but not a guaranteed solution. There are two theories about how regulation actually works: *the social interest theory* and the *capture theory*.

The **social interest theory** is that the political and regulatory process relentlessly seeks out inefficiency and introduces regulation that eliminates deadweight loss and allocates resources efficiently.

The **capture theory** is that regulation serves the self-interest of the producer, who captures the regulator and maximizes economic profit. Regulation that benefits the producer but creates a deadweight loss gets adopted because the producer's gain is large and visible while each individual consumer's loss is small and invisible. No individual consumer has an incentive to oppose the regulation but the producer has a big incentive to lobby for it.

We're going to examine efficient regulation that serves the social interest and see why it is not a simple matter to design and implement such regulation.

Efficient Regulation of a Natural Monopoly

A cable TV company is a *natural monopoly*—it can supply the entire market at a lower price than two or more competing firms can. Cox Communications, based in Atlanta, provides cable TV to households in 20 states. The firm has invested heavily in satellite receiving dishes, cables, and control equipment and so has large fixed costs. These fixed costs are part of the firm's average total cost. Its average total cost decreases as the number of households served increases because the fixed cost is spread over a larger number of households.

Unregulated, Cox produces the quantity that maximizes profit. Like all single-price monopolies, the profit-maximizing quantity is less than the efficient quantity, and underproduction results in a deadweight loss.

How can Cox be regulated to produce the efficient quantity of cable TV service? The answer is by being regulated to set its price equal to marginal cost, known as the **marginal cost pricing rule**. The quantity demanded at a price equal to marginal cost is the efficient quantity—the quantity at which marginal benefit equals marginal cost.

Figure 11.11 illustrates the marginal cost pricing rule. The demand curve for cable TV is *D*. Cox's marginal cost curve is *MC*. That marginal cost curve is (assumed to be) horizontal at $10 per household per month—that is, the cost of providing each additional household with a month of cable programming is $10. The efficient outcome occurs if the price is regulated at $10 per household per month with 10 million households served.

But there is a problem: At the efficient output, average total cost exceeds marginal cost, so a firm that uses marginal cost pricing incurs an economic loss. A cable TV company that is required to use a marginal cost pricing rule will not stay in business for long. How can the firm cover its costs and, at the same time, obey a marginal cost pricing rule?

There are two possible ways of enabling the firm to cover its costs: price discrimination and a two-part price (called a *two-part tariff*).

For example, Verizon offers plans at a fixed monthly price that give access to the cell-phone network and unlimited free calls. The price of a call (zero) equals Verizon's marginal cost of a call. Similarly, a cable TV operator can charge a one-time connection fee that covers its fixed cost and then charge a monthly fee equal to marginal cost.

FIGURE 11.11   Regulating a Natural Monopoly

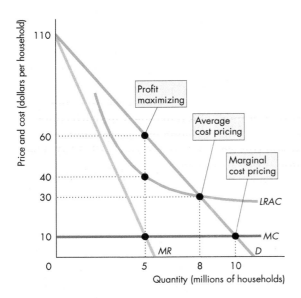

A natural monopoly cable TV supplier faces the demand curve *D*. The firm's marginal cost is constant at $10 per household per month, as shown by the curve labeled *MC*. The long-run average cost curve is *LRAC*.

Unregulated, as a profit-maximizer, the firm serves 5 million households at a price of $60 a month. An efficient marginal cost pricing rule sets the price at $10 a month. The monopoly serves 10 million households and incurs an economic loss. A second-best average cost pricing rule sets the price at $30 a month. The monopoly serves 8 million households and earns zero economic profit.

Second-Best Regulation of a Natural Monopoly

A natural monopoly cannot always be regulated to achieve an efficient outcome. Two possible ways of enabling a regulated monopoly to avoid an economic loss are

- Average cost pricing
- Government subsidy

Average Cost Pricing The **average cost pricing rule** sets price equal to average total cost. With this rule the firm produces the quantity at which the average total cost curve cuts the demand curve. This rule results in the firm making zero economic profit— breaking even. But because for a natural monopoly average total cost exceeds marginal cost, the quantity produced is less than the efficient quantity and a deadweight loss arises.

Figure 11.11 illustrates the average cost pricing rule. The price is $30 a month and 8 million households get cable TV.

Government Subsidy A government subsidy is a direct payment to the firm equal to its economic loss. To pay a subsidy, the government must raise the revenue by taxing some other activity. You saw in Chapter 6 that taxes themselves generate deadweight loss.

And the Second-Best Is ... Which is the better option, average cost pricing or marginal cost pricing with a government subsidy? The answer depends on the relative magnitudes of the two deadweight losses. Average cost pricing generates a deadweight loss in the market served by the natural monopoly. A subsidy generates deadweight losses in the markets for the items that are taxed to pay for the subsidy. The smaller deadweight loss is the second-best solution to regulating a natural monopoly. Making this calculation in practice is too difficult and average cost pricing is generally preferred to a subsidy.

Implementing average cost pricing presents the regulator with a challenge because it is not possible to be sure what a firm's costs are. So regulators use one of two practical rules:

- Rate of return regulation
- Price cap regulation

Rate of Return Regulation Under **rate of return regulation**, a firm must justify its price by showing that its return on capital doesn't exceed a specified target rate. This type of regulation can end up serving the self-interest of the firm rather than the social interest. The firm's managers have an incentive to inflate costs by spending on items such as private jets, free baseball tickets (disguised as public relations expenses), and lavish entertainment. Managers also have an incentive to use more capital than the efficient amount. The rate of return on capital is regulated but not the total return on capital, and the greater the amount of capital, the greater is the total return.

Price Cap Regulation For the reason that we've just examined, rate of return regulation is increasingly being replaced by price cap regulation. A **price cap regulation** is a price ceiling—a rule that specifies the highest price the firm is permitted to set. This type of regulation gives a firm an incentive to operate efficiently and keep costs under control. Price cap regulation has become common for the electricity and telecommunications industries and is replacing rate of return regulation.

To see how a price cap works, let's suppose that the cable TV operator is subject to this type of regulation. Figure 11.12 shows that without regulation, the firm maximizes profit by serving 5 million households and charging a price of $60 a month. If a price cap is set at $30 a month, the firm is permitted to sell

any quantity it chooses at that price or at a lower price. At 5 million households, the firm now incurs an economic loss. It can decrease the loss by increasing output to 8 million households. To increase output above 8 million households, the firm would have to lower the price and again it would incur a loss. So the profit-maximizing quantity is 8 million households—the same as with average cost pricing.

Notice that a price cap lowers the price and increases output. This outcome is in sharp contrast to the effect of a price ceiling in a competitive market that you studied in Chapter 6 (pp. 112–114). The reason is that in a monopoly, the unregulated equilibrium output is less than the competitive equilibrium output, and the price cap regulation replicates the conditions of a competitive market.

In Fig. 11.12, the price cap delivers average cost pricing. In practice, the regulator might set the cap too high. For this reason, price cap regulation is often combined with *earnings sharing regulation*—a regulation that requires firms to make refunds to customers when profits rise above a target level.

FIGURE 11.12   Price Cap Regulation

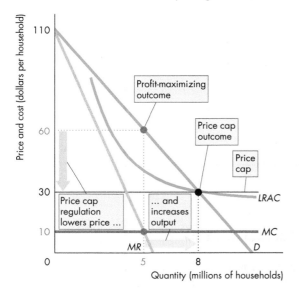

A natural monopoly cable TV supplier faces the demand curve *D*. The firm's marginal cost is constant at $10 per household per month, as shown by the curve labeled *MC*. The long-run average cost curve is *LRAC*.

Unregulated, the firm serves 5 million households at a price of $60 a month. A price cap sets the maximum price at $30 a month. The firm has an incentive to minimize cost and serve the quantity of households that demand service at the price cap. The price cap regulation lowers the price and increases the quantity.

myeconlab animation

REVIEW QUIZ

1 What is the pricing rule that achieves an efficient outcome for a regulated monopoly? What is the problem with this rule?

2 What is the average cost pricing rule? Why is it not an efficient way of regulating monopoly?

3 What is a price cap? Why might it be a more effective way of regulating monopoly than rate of return regulation?

4 Compare the consumer surplus, producer surplus, and deadweight loss that arise from average cost pricing with those that arise from profit-maximization pricing and marginal cost pricing.

You can work these questions in Study Plan 11.5 and get instant feedback.

You've now completed your study of monopoly. *Reading Between the Lines* on pp. 238–239 looks at Google's dominant position in the market for Internet search advertising.

In the next chapter, we study markets that lie between the extremes of perfect competition and monopoly and that blend elements of the two.

Is Google Misusing Monopoly Power?

Data Show Google Abuses Search Role, Group Contends

http://www.sfgate.com
June 3, 2010

Consumer Watchdog continues to push its case that Google Inc.'s behavior necessitates antitrust scrutiny, releasing a report Wednesday that alleges that the company is abusing its dominance in online search to direct users to its own services.

The study, which will be sent to U.S. and European antitrust regulators, cites online traffic data that the Santa Monica group claims shows the Mountain View Internet giant seized large portions of market share in areas like online maps, video and comparison shopping after its search engine began highlighting links to its products in results.

Google called the report's methodology and premise flawed and said its practices are designed to benefit users.

"Our goal is to give users the info they're seeking as quickly as possible," a spokesman said in a statement. "Sometimes that means showing a map, a streaming audio link, or an answer to a question at the top of the page if we think that's what users want. We strive to deliver what we think is the most relevant result from a variety of content types, and if we're not giving users the information they want then other sources of information are always one click away."

Google doubled its market share in online video to nearly 80 percent since 2007, the year in which the company began returning high or prominent links to videos from its YouTube subsidiary in search results, according to the report by Consumer Watchdog's Inside Google project.

…

ESSENCE OF THE STORY

- Consumer Watchdog says that Google should be scrutinized by U.S. and European antitrust regulators because it is abusing its dominant position in online search by directing users to its own services.

- The claim is that Google has grown a large market share in online maps, video, and comparison shopping because its search engine highlights links to these products in search results.

- Google says its goal is to give users the information they are seeking, in the format required, as quickly as possible.

- Google's market share in online video has doubled to nearly 80 percent since 2007 when it began returning links to YouTube videos.

- Google began selling advertisements associated with search keywords in 2000.

- Google sells keywords based on a combination of willingness-to-pay and the number of clicks an advertisement receives, with bids starting at 5 cents per click.

- Google has steadily improved its search engine and refined and simplified its interface with both searchers and advertisers to make searches more powerful and advertising more effective.

- Figure 1 shows Google's extraordinary success in terms of its revenue, cost, and profit.

- Google could have provided a basic search engine with none of the features of today's Google.

- If Google had followed this strategy, people seeking information would have used other search engines and advertisers would have been willing to pay low prices for Google ads.

- Google would have faced the market described in Fig. 2 and earned a small economic profit.

- Instead, Google improved its search and the effectiveness of advertising. The demand for Google ads increased.

- By selling keywords to the highest bidder, Google is able to achieve perfect price discrimination.

- Figure 3 shows the consequences of Google's successful strategy. With perfect price discrimination, Google's producer surplus is maximized. Google produces the efficient quantity of search and advertising by accepting ads as long as price exceeds marginal cost.

- Google does not appear to be acting against the social interest: There is no antitrust case to answer.

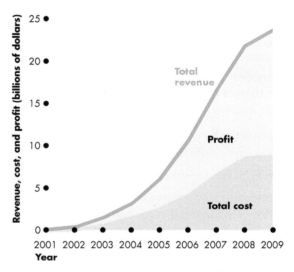

Figure 1 Google's revenue, cost, and profit

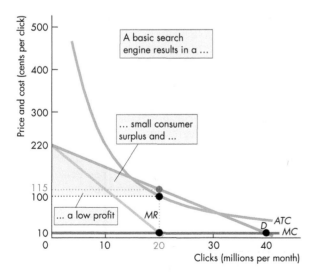

Figure 2 Basic search engine

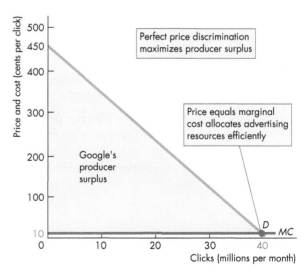

Figure 3 Google with AdWords and other features

239

SUMMARY

Key Points

Monopoly and How It Arises (pp. 222–223)

- A monopoly is a market with a single supplier of a good or service that has no close substitutes and in which barriers to entry prevent competition.
- Barriers to entry may be legal (public franchise, license, patent, copyright), firm owns control of a resource, or natural (created by economies of scale).
- A monopoly might be able to price discriminate when there is no resale possibility.
- Where resale is possible, a firm charges one price.

Working Problems 1 to 4 will give you a better understanding of monopoly and how it arises.

A Single-Price Monopoly's Output and Price Decision (pp. 224–227)

- A monopoly's demand curve is the market demand curve and a single-price monopoly's marginal revenue is less than price.
- A monopoly maximizes profit by producing the output at which marginal revenue equals marginal cost and by charging the maximum price that consumers are willing to pay for that output.

Working Problems 5 to 9 will give you a better understanding of a single-price monopoly's output and price.

Single-Price Monopoly and Competition Compared (pp. 228–231)

- A single-price monopoly charges a higher price and produces a smaller quantity than a perfectly competitive market.
- A single-price monopoly restricts output and creates a deadweight loss.

- The total loss that arises from monopoly equals the deadweight loss plus the cost of the resources devoted to rent seeking.

Working Problems 10 to 12 will give you a better understanding of the comparison of single-price monopoly and perfect competition.

Price Discrimination (pp. 231–234)

- Price discrimination converts consumer surplus into economic profit.
- Perfect price discrimination extracts the entire consumer surplus; each unit is sold for the maximum price that each consumer is willing to pay; the quantity produced is the efficient quantity.
- Rent seeking with perfect price discrimination might eliminate the entire consumer surplus and producer surplus.

Working Problems 13 to 16 will give you a better understanding of price discrimination.

Monopoly Regulation (pp. 235–237)

- Monopoly regulation might serve the social interest or the interest of the monopoly (the monopoly captures the regulator).
- Price equal to marginal cost achieves efficiency but results in economic loss.
- Price equal to average cost enables the firm to cover its cost but is inefficient.
- Rate of return regulation creates incentives for inefficient production and inflated cost.
- Price cap regulation with earnings sharing regulation can achieve a more efficient outcome than rate of return regulation.

Working Problems 17 to 19 will give you a better understanding of monopoly regulation.

Key Terms

Average cost pricing rule, 236	Marginal cost pricing rule, 235	Rate of return regulation, 236
Barrier to entry, 222	Monopoly, 222	Regulation, 235
Capture theory, 235	Natural monopoly, 222	Rent seeking, 230
Deregulation, 235	Perfect price discrimination, 233	Single-price monopoly, 223
Economic rent, 230	Price cap regulation, 237	Social interest theory, 235
Legal monopoly, 222	Price discrimination, 223	

STUDY PLAN PROBLEMS AND APPLICATIONS

myeconlab You can work problems 1 to 19 in MyEconLab Chapter 11 Study Plan and get instant feedback.

Monopoly and How It Arises (Study Plan 11.1)

Use the following information to work Problems 1 to 3.

The United States Postal Service has a monopoly on non-urgent First Class Mail and the exclusive right to put mail in private mailboxes. Pfizer Inc. makes LIPITOR, a prescription drug that lowers cholesterol. Cox Communications is the sole provider of cable television service in some parts of San Diego.

1. a. What are the substitutes, if any, for the goods and services described above?
   b. What are the barriers to entry, if any, that protect these three firms from competition?

2. Which of these three firms, if any, is a natural monopoly? Explain your answer and draw a graph to illustrate it.

3. a. Which of these three firms, if any, is a legal monopoly? Explain your answer.
   b. Which of these three firms are most likely to be able to profit from price discrimination and which are most likely to sell their good or service for a single price?

4. **Barbie's Revenge: Brawl over Doll Is Heading to Trial**

   Four years ago, Mattel Inc. exhorted its executives to help save Barbie from a new doll clique called the Bratz. With its market share dropping at a "chilling rate," Barbie needed to be more "aggressive, revolutionary, and ruthless." Mattel has gone to court and is trying to seize ownership of the Bratz line, which Mattel accuses of stealing the idea for the pouty-lipped dolls with the big heads.

   Source: *The Wall Street Journal*, May 23, 2008

   a. Before Bratz entered the market, what type of monopoly did Mattel Inc. possess in the market for "the pouty-lipped dolls with the big heads"?
   b. What is the barrier to entry that Mattel might argue should protect it from competition in the market for Barbie dolls?
   c. Explain how the entry of Bratz dolls might be expected to change the demand for Barbie dolls.

A Single-Price Monopoly's Output and Price Decision

(Study Plan 11.2)

Use the following table to work Problems 5 to 8.
Minnie's Mineral Springs, a single-price monopoly, faces the market demand schedule:

Price (dollars per bottle)	Quantity demanded (bottles per hour)
10	0
8	1
6	2
4	3
2	4
0	5

5. a. Calculate Minnie's total revenue schedule.
   b. Calculate its marginal revenue schedule.

6. a. Draw a graph of the market demand curve and Minnie's marginal revenue curve.
   b. Why is Minnie's marginal revenue less than the price?

7. a. At what price is Minnie's total revenue maximized?
   b. Over what range of prices is the demand for water from Minnie's Mineral Springs elastic?

8. Why will Minnie not produce a quantity at which the market demand for water is inelastic?

9. Minnie's Mineral Springs faces the market demand schedule in Problem 5 and has the following total cost schedule:

Quantity produced (bottles per hour)	Total cost (dollars)
0	1
1	3
2	7
3	13
4	21
5	31

   a. Calculate Minnie's profit-maximizing output and price.
   b. Calculate the economic profit.

Single-Price Monopoly and Competition Compared
(Study Plan 11.3)

Use the following news clip to work Problems 10 to 12.

Zoloft Faces Patent Expiration

Pfizer's antidepressant Zoloft, with $3.3 billion in 2005 sales, loses patent protection on June 30. When a brand name drug loses its patent, both the price of the drug and the dollar value of its sales each tend to drop 80 percent over the next year, as competition opens to a host of generic drugmakers. The real winners are the patients and the insurers, who pay much lower prices. The Food and Drug Administration insists that generics work identically to brand-names.

Source: CNN, June 15, 2006

10. a. Assume that Pfizer has a monopoly in the antidepressant market and that Pfizer cannot price discriminate. Use a graph to illustrate the market price and quantity of Zoloft sold.

b. On your graph, identify consumer surplus, producer surplus, and deadweight loss.

11. How might you justify protecting Pfizer from competition with a legal barrier to entry?

12. a. Explain how the market for an antidepressant drug changes when a patent expires.

b. Draw a graph to illustrate how the expiration of the Zoloft patent will change the price and quantity in the market for antidepressants.

c. Explain how consumer surplus, producer surplus, and deadweight loss change with the expiration of the Zoloft patent.

Price Discrimination (Study Plan 11.4)

Use the following news clip to work Problems 13 and 14.

The Saturday-Night Stay Requirement Is on Its Final Approach

The Saturday-night stay—the requirement that airlines instituted to ensure that business travelers pay an outrageous airfare if he or she wants to go home for the weekend—has gone the way of the dodo bird. Experts agree that low-fare carriers, such as Southwest, are the primary reason major airlines are adopting more consumer-friendly fare structures, which include the elimination of the Saturday-night stay, the introduction of one-way and walk-up fares, and the general restructuring of fares.

Source: *Los Angeles Times*, August 15, 2004

13. Explain why the opportunity for price discrimination exists for air travel. How does an airline profit from price discrimination?

14. Describe the change in price discrimination in the market for air travel when discount airlines entered the market and explain the effect of discount airlines on the price and the quantity of air travel.

Use the following information to work Problems 15 and 16.

La Bella Pizza can produce a pizza for a marginal cost of $2. Its standard price is $15 a pizza. It offers a second pizza for $5. It also distributes coupons that give a $5 rebate on a standard-priced pizza.

15. How can La Bella Pizza make a larger economic profit with this range of prices than it could if it sold every pizza for $15? Use a graph to illustrate your answer.

16. How might La Bella Pizza make even more economic profit? Would La Bella Pizza then be more efficient than it would be if it charged $15 for each pizza?

Monopoly Regulation (Study Plan 11.5)

Use the following information to work Problems 17 to 19.

The figure shows a situation similar to that of Calypso U.S. Pipeline, a firm that operates a natural gas distribution system in the United States. Calypso is a natural monopoly that cannot price discriminate.

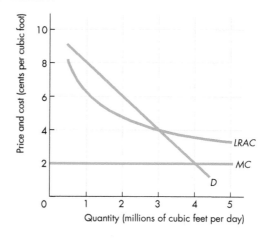

What quantity will Calypso produce, what price will it charge, what is the total surplus, and what is the deadweight loss if Calypso is

17. An unregulated profit-maximizing firm?

18. Regulated to make zero economic profit?

19. Regulated to be efficient?

ADDITIONAL PROBLEMS AND APPLICATIONS

myeconlab You can work these problems in MyEconLab if assigned by your instructor.

Monopoly and How It Arises

Use the following list, which gives some information about seven firms, to answer Problems 20 and 21.

- Coca-Cola cuts its price below that of Pepsi-Cola in an attempt to increase its market share.
- A single firm, protected by a barrier to entry, produces a personal service that has no close substitutes.
- A barrier to entry exists, but the good has some close substitutes.
- A firm offers discounts to students and seniors.
- A firm can sell any quantity it chooses at the going price.
- The government issues Nike an exclusive license to produce golf balls.
- A firm experiences economies of scale even when it produces the quantity that meets the entire market demand.

20. In which of the seven cases might monopoly arise?

21. Which of the seven cases are natural monopolies and which are legal monopolies? Which can price discriminate, which cannot, and why?

A Single-Price Monopoly's Output and Price Decision

Use the following information to work Problems 22 to 26.

Hot Air Balloon Rides is a single-price monopoly. Columns 1 and 2 of the table set out the market demand schedule and columns 2 and 3 set out the total cost schedule:

Price (dollars per ride)	Quantity demanded (rides per month)	Total cost (dollars per month)
220	0	80
200	1	160
180	2	260
160	3	380
140	4	520
120	5	680

22. Construct Hot Air's total revenue and marginal revenue schedules.

23. Draw a graph of the market demand curve and Hot Air's marginal revenue curve.

24. Find Hot Air's profit-maximizing output and price and calculate the firm's economic profit.

25. If the government imposes a tax on Hot Air's profit, how do its output and price change?

26. If instead of taxing Hot Air's profit, the government imposes a sales tax on balloon rides of $30 a ride, what are the new profit-maximizing quantity, price, and economic profit?

27. The figure illustrates the situation facing the publisher of the only newspaper containing local news in an isolated community.

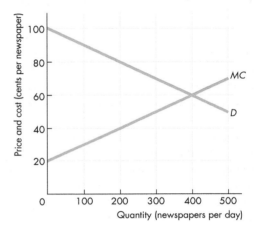

a. On the graph, mark the profit-maximizing quantity and price and the publisher's total revenue per day.

b. At the price charged, is the demand for this newspaper elastic or inelastic? Why?

Single-Price Monopoly and Competition Compared

28. Show on the graph in Problem 27 the consumer surplus from newspapers and the deadweight loss created by the monopoly. Explain why this market might encourage rent seeking.

29. If the newspaper market in Problem 27 were perfectly competitive, what would be the quantity, price, consumer surplus, and producer surplus? Mark each on the graph.

30. **Telecoms Look to Grow by Acquisition**
Multibillion-dollar telecommunications mergers show how global cellular powerhouses are scouting for growth in emerging economies while consolidating in their own, crowded backyards. France Télécom offered to buy TeliaSonera, a Swedish-Finnish telecommunications operator, but

within hours, TeliaSonera rejected the offer as too low. Analysts said higher bids—either from France Télécom or others—could persuade TeliaSonera to accept a deal. In the United States, Verizon Wireless agreed to buy Alltel for $28.1 billion—a deal that would make the company the biggest mobile phone operator in the United States. A combination of France Télécom and TeliaSonera would create the world's fourth-largest mobile operator, smaller only than China Mobile, Vodafone, and Telefónica of Spain.

Source: *International Herald Tribune*,
June 5, 2008

a. Explain the rent-seeking behavior of global telecommunications companies.

b. Explain how mergers may affect the efficiency of the telecommunications market.

Price Discrimination

31. **AT&T Moves Away from Unlimited-Data Pricing**

AT&T said it will eliminate its $30 unlimited data plan as the crush of data use from the iPhone has hurt call quality. AT&T is introducing new plans costing $15 a month for 200 megabytes of data traffic or $25 a month for 2 gigabytes. AT&T says those who exceed 2 gigabytes of usage will pay $10 a month for each additional gigabyte. AT&T hopes that these plans will attract more customers.

Source: *The Wall Street Journal*, June 2, 2010

a. Explain why AT&T's new plans might be price discrimination.

b. Draw a graph to illustrate the original plan and the new plans.

Monopoly Regulation

32. **iSurrender**

Getting your hands on a new iPhone means signing a two-year AT&T contract. Some markets, because of the costs of being a player, tend toward either a single firm or a small number of firms. Everyone hoped the wireless market would be different. A telephone monopoly has been the norm for most of American telecommunication history, except for what may turn out to have been a brief experimental period from 1984 through 2012 or so. It may be that telephone monopolies in America are a national tradition.

Source: *Slate*, June 10, 2008

a. How does AT&T being the exclusive provider of wireless service for the iPhone influence the wireless telecommunication market?

b. Explain why the wireless market may "tend toward either a single firm or a small number of firms." Why might this justify allowing a regulated monopoly to exist in this market?

Economics in the News

33. After you have studied *Reading Between the Lines* on pp. 316 – 317 answer the following questions.

a. Why does Consumer Watchdog say that Google needs to be investigated? Do you agree? Explain why or why not.

b. Explain why it would be inefficient to regulate Google to make it charge the same price per keyword click to all advertisers.

c. Explain why selling keywords to the highest bidder can lead to an efficient allocation of advertising resources.

34. **F.C.C. Planning Rules to Open Cable Market**

The Federal Communications Commission (F.C.C.) is setting new regulations to open the cable television market to independent programmers and rival video services. The new rules will make it easier for small independent programmers to lease access to cable channels and the size of the nation's largest cable companies will be capped at 30 percent of the market.

Source: *The New York Times*,
November 10, 2007

a. What barriers to entry exist in the cable television market?

b. Are high cable prices evidence of monopoly power?

c. Draw a graph to illustrate the effects of the F.C.C.'s new regulations on the price, quantity, total surplus, and deadweight loss.

35. **Antitrust Inquiry Launched into Intel**

Intel, the world's largest chipmaker, holds 80 percent of the microprocessor market. Advanced Micro Devices complains that Intel stifles competition, but Intel says that the 42.4 percent fall in prices between 2000 and 2007 shows that this industry is fiercely competitive.

Source: *The Washington Post*, June 7, 2008

a. Is Intel a monopoly in the chip market?

b. Evaluate the argument made by Intel that the fall in prices "shows that this industry is fiercely competitive."

After studying this chapter,
you will be able to:

◆ Define and identify monopolistic competition

◆ Explain how a firm in monopolistic competition
determines its price and output in the short run
and the long run

◆ Explain why advertising costs are high and why
firms use brand names in a monopolistically
competitive industry

12

MONOPOLISTIC COMPETITION

The online shoe store shoebuy.com lists athletic shoes made by 56 different producers in 40 different categories and priced between $25 and $850. Shoebuy offers 1,401 different types of athletic shoes for women and 1,757 different types for men. Because there are many different types of athletic shoes, the market for them isn't perfectly competitive. Athletic shoe producers compete, but each has a monopoly on its own special kind of shoe.

Most of the things that you buy are like athletic shoes—they come in many different types. Pizza and cell phones are two more striking examples.

The model of monopolistic competition that is explained in this chapter helps us to understand the competition that we see every day in the markets for athletic shoes, pizza, cell phones, and for most other consumer goods and services.

This chapter blends the models in the two preceding chapters on perfect competition and monopoly sto create the model of monopolistic competition. To get the most out of this chapter, you will have studied the two preceding ones.

Reading Between the Lines, at the end of this chapter, applies the monopolistic competition model to the market for smart phones and the entry of other firms in that market following the success of the Apple iPhone.

◆ What Is Monopolistic Competition?

You have studied perfect competition, in which a large number of firms produce at the lowest possible cost, make zero economic profit, and are efficient. You've also studied monopoly, in which a single firm restricts output, produces at a higher cost and price than in perfect competition, and is inefficient.

Most real-world markets are competitive but not perfectly competitive, because firms in these markets have some power to set their prices, as monopolies do. We call this type of market *monopolistic competition*.

Monopolistic competition is a market structure in which

- A large number of firms compete.
- Each firm produces a differentiated product.
- Firms compete on product quality, price, and marketing.
- Firms are free to enter and exit the industry.

Large Number of Firms

In monopolistic competition, as in perfect competition, the industry consists of a large number of firms. The presence of a large number of firms has three implications for the firms in the industry.

Small Market Share In monopolistic competition, each firm supplies a small part of the total industry output. Consequently, each firm has only limited power to influence the price of its product. Each firm's price can deviate from the average price of other firms by only a relatively small amount.

Ignore Other Firms A firm in monopolistic competition must be sensitive to the average market price of the product, but the firm does not pay attention to any one individual competitor. Because all the firms are relatively small, no one firm can dictate market conditions, and so no one firm's actions directly affect the actions of the other firms.

Collusion Impossible Firms in monopolistic competition would like to be able to conspire to fix a higher price—called *collusion*. But because the number of firms in monopolistic competition is large, coordination is difficult and collusion is not possible.

Product Differentiation

A firm practices **product differentiation** if it makes a product that is slightly different from the products of competing firms. A differentiated product is one that is a close substitute but not a perfect substitute for the products of the other firms. Some people are willing to pay more for one variety of the product, so when its price rises, the quantity demanded of that variety decreases, but it does not (necessarily) decrease to zero. For example, Adidas, Asics, Diadora, Etonic, Fila, New Balance, Nike, Puma, and Reebok all make differentiated running shoes. If the price of Adidas running shoes rises and the prices of the other shoes remain constant, Adidas sells fewer shoes and the other producers sell more. But Adidas shoes don't disappear unless the price rises by a large enough amount.

Competing on Quality, Price, and Marketing

Product differentiation enables a firm to compete with other firms in three areas: product quality, price, and marketing.

Quality The quality of a product is the physical attributes that make it different from the products of other firms. Quality includes design, reliability, the service provided to the buyer, and the buyer's ease of access to the product. Quality lies on a spectrum that runs from high to low. Some firms—such as Dell Computer Corp.—offer high-quality products. They are well designed and reliable, and the customer receives quick and efficient service. Other firms offer a lower-quality product that is poorly designed, that might not work perfectly, and that is not supported by effective customer service.

Price Because of product differentiation, a firm in monopolistic competition faces a downward-sloping demand curve. So, like a monopoly, the firm can set both its price and its output. But there is a tradeoff between the product's quality and price. A firm that makes a high-quality product can charge a higher price than a firm that makes a low-quality product.

Marketing Because of product differentiation, a firm in monopolistic competition must market its product. Marketing takes two main forms: advertising and packaging. A firm that produces a high-quality product wants to sell it for a suitably high price. To be able to do so, it must advertise and package its product in a way that convinces buyers that they are getting the higher quality for which they are paying a higher price. For example, pharmaceutical companies advertise and package their brand-name drugs to persuade buyers that these items are superior to the lower-priced generic alternatives. Similarly, a low-quality producer uses advertising and packaging to persuade buyers that although the quality is low, the low price more than compensates for this fact.

Entry and Exit

Monopolistic competition has no barriers to prevent new firms from entering the industry in the long run. Consequently, a firm in monopolistic competition cannot make an economic profit in the long run. When existing firms make an economic profit, new firms enter the industry. This entry lowers prices and eventually eliminates economic profit. When firms incur economic losses, some firms leave the industry in the long run. This exit increases prices and eventually eliminates the economic loss.

In long-run equilibrium, firms neither enter nor leave the industry and the firms in the industry make zero economic profit.

Examples of Monopolistic Competition

The box below shows 10 industries that are good examples of monopolistic competition. These industries have a large number of firms (shown in parentheses after the name of the industry). In the market for audio and video equipment, the largest 4 firms produce only 30 percent of the industry's total sales and the largest 20 firms produce 75 percent of total sales. The number on the right is the Herfindahl-Hirschman Index. Producers of clothing, jewelry, computers, and sporting goods operate in monopolistic competition.

REVIEW QUIZ

1   What are the distinguishing characteristics of monopolistic competition?
2   How do firms in monopolistic competition compete?
3   Provide some examples of industries near your school that operate in monopolistic competition (excluding those in the figure below).

You can work these questions in Study Plan 12.1 and get instant feedback.   myeconlab

Economics in Action

Monopolistic Competition Today

These ten industries operate in monopolistic competition. The number of firms in the industry is shown in parentheses after the name of the industry. The red bars show the percentage of industry sales by the largest 4 firms. The green bars show the percentage of industry sales by the next 4 largest firms, and the blue bars show the percentage of industry sales by the next 12 largest firms. So the entire length of the combined red, green, and blue bars shows the percentage of industry sales by the largest 20 firms. The Herfindahl-Hirschman Index is shown on the right.

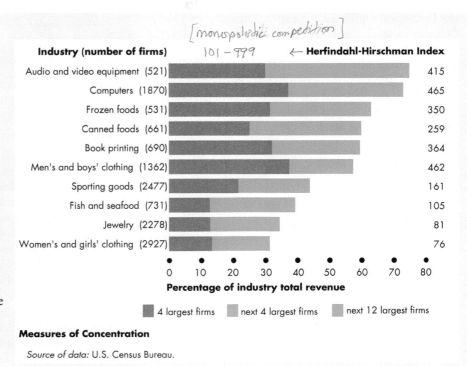

[monopolistic competition]
101 – 999

Industry (number of firms)	← Herfindahl-Hirschman Index
Audio and video equipment (521)	415
Computers (1870)	465
Frozen foods (531)	350
Canned foods (661)	259
Book printing (690)	364
Men's and boys' clothing (1362)	462
Sporting goods (2477)	161
Fish and seafood (731)	105
Jewelry (2278)	81
Women's and girls' clothing (2927)	76

Percentage of industry total revenue

■ 4 largest firms   ■ next 4 largest firms   ■ next 12 largest firms

Measures of Concentration

Source of data: U.S. Census Bureau.

Price and Output in Monopolistic Competition

Suppose you've been hired by VF Corporation, the firm that owns Nautica Clothing Corporation, to manage the production and marketing of Nautica jackets. Think about the decisions that you must make at Nautica. First, you must decide on the design and quality of jackets and on your marketing program. Second, you must decide on the quantity of jackets to produce and the price at which to sell them.

We'll suppose that Nautica has already made its decisions about design, quality, and marketing and now we'll concentrate on the output and pricing decision. We'll study quality and marketing decisions in the next section.

For a given quality of jackets and marketing activity, Nautica faces given costs and market conditions. Given its costs and the demand for its jackets, how does Nautica decide the quantity of jackets to produce and the price at which to sell them?

The Firm's Short-Run Output and Price Decision

In the short run, a firm in monopolistic competition makes its output and price decision just like a monopoly firm does. Figure 12.1 illustrates this decision for Nautica jackets.

The demand curve for Nautica jackets is D. This demand curve tells us the quantity of Nautica jackets demanded at each price, given the prices of other jackets. It is not the demand curve for jackets in general.

The MR curve shows the marginal revenue curve associated with the demand curve for Nautica jackets. It is derived just like the marginal revenue curve of a single-price monopoly that you studied in Chapter 11.

The ATC curve and the MC curve show the average total cost and the marginal cost of producing Nautica jackets.

Nautica's goal is to maximize its economic profit. To do so, it produces the output at which marginal revenue equals marginal cost. In Fig. 12.1, this output is 125 jackets a day. Nautica charges the price that buyers are willing to pay for this quantity, which is determined by the demand curve. This price is $75 per jacket. When Nautica produces 125 jackets a day, its average total cost is $25 per jacket and it makes an economic profit of $6,250 a day ($50 per jacket mul-

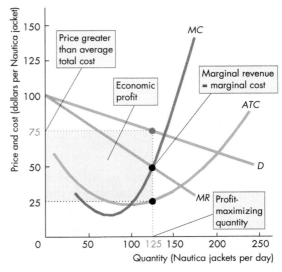

FIGURE 12.1   Economic Profit in the Short Run

Nautica maximizes profit by producing the quantity at which marginal revenue equals marginal cost,125 jackets a day, and charging the price of $75 a jacket. This price exceeds the average total cost of $25 a jacket, so the firm makes an economic profit of $50 a jacket. The blue rectangle illustrates economic profit, which equals $6,250 a day ($50 a jacket multiplied by 125 jackets a day).

tiplied by 125 jackets a day). The blue rectangle shows Nautica's economic profit.

Profit Maximizing Might Be Loss Minimizing

Figure 12.1 shows that Nautica is making a large economic profit. But such an outcome is not inevitable. A firm might face a level of demand for its product that is too low for it to make an economic profit.

Excite@Home was such a firm. Offering high-speed Internet service over the same cable that provides television, Excite@Home hoped to capture a large share of the Internet portal market in competition with AOL, MSN, and a host of other providers.

Figure 12.2 illustrates the situation facing Excite@Home in 2001. The demand curve for its portal service is D, the marginal revenue curve is MR, the average total cost curve is ATC, and the marginal cost curve is MC. Excite@Home maximized profit—

FIGURE 12.2   Economic Loss in the Short Run

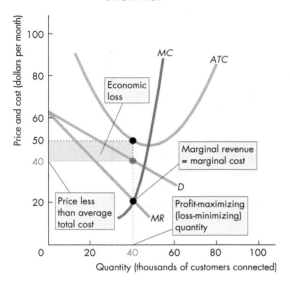

Profit is maximized where marginal revenue equals marginal cost. The loss-minimizing quantity is 40,000 customers. The price of $40 a month is less than the average total cost of $50 a month, so the firm incurs an economic loss of $10 a customer. The red rectangle illustrates economic loss, which equals $400,000 a month ($10 a customer multiplied by 40,000 customers).

myeconlab animation

equivalently, it minimized its loss—by producing the output at which marginal revenue equals marginal cost. In Fig. 12.2, this output is 40,000 customers. Excite@Home charged the price that buyers were willing to pay for this quantity, which was determined by the demand curve and which was $40 a month. With 40,000 customers, Excite@Home's average total cost was $50 per customer, so it incurred an economic loss of $400,000 a month ($10 a customer multiplied by 40,000 customers). The red rectangle shows Excite@Home's economic loss.

So far, the firm in monopolistic competition looks like a single-price monopoly. It produces the quantity at which marginal revenue equals marginal cost and then charges the price that buyers are willing to pay for that quantity, as determined by the demand curve. The key difference between monopoly and monopolistic competition lies in what happens next when firms either make an economic profit or incur an economic loss.

Long Run: Zero Economic Profit

A firm like Excite@Home is not going to incur an economic loss for long. Eventually, it goes out of business. Also, there is no restriction on entry into monopolistic competition, so if firms in an industry are making economic profit, other firms have an incentive to enter that industry.

As the Gap and other firms start to make jackets similar to those made by Nautica, the demand for Nautica jackets decreases. The demand curve for Nautica jackets and the marginal revenue curve shift leftward. As these curves shift leftward, the profit-maximizing quantity and price fall.

Figure 12.3 shows the long-run equilibrium. The demand curve for Nautica jackets and the marginal revenue curve have shifted leftward. The firm produces 75 jackets a day and sells them for $25 each. At this output level, average total cost is also $25 per jacket.

FIGURE 12.3   Output and Price in the Long Run

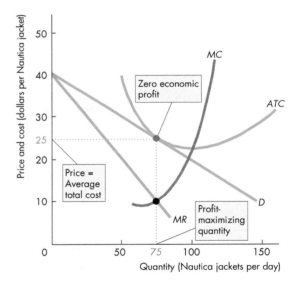

Economic profit encourages entry, which decreases the demand for each firm's product. When the demand curve touches the ATC curve at the quantity at which MR equals MC, the market is in long-run equilibrium. The output that maximizes profit is 75 jackets a day, and the price is $25 per jacket. Average total cost is also $25 per jacket, so economic profit is zero.

myeconlab animation

So Nautica is making zero economic profit on its jackets. When all the firms in the industry are making zero economic profit, there is no incentive for new firms to enter.

If demand is so low relative to costs that firms incur economic losses, exit will occur. As firms leave an industry, the demand for the products of the remaining firms increases and their demand curves shift rightward. The exit process ends when all the firms in the industry are making zero economic profit.

Monopolistic Competition and Perfect Competition

Figure 12.4 compares monopolistic competition and perfect competition and highlights two key differences between them:

- Excess capacity
- Markup

Excess Capacity A firm has **excess capacity** if it produces below its **efficient scale**, which is the quantity at which average total cost is a minimum—the quantity at the bottom of the U-shaped *ATC* curve. In Fig. 12.4, the efficient scale is 100 jackets a day. Nautica in part (a) produces 75 Nautica jackets a day and has *excess capacity* of 25 jackets a day. But if all jackets are alike and are produced by firms in perfect competition, each firm in part (b) produces 100 jackets a day, which is the efficient scale. Average total cost is the lowest possible only in *perfect* competition.

You can see the excess capacity in monopolistic competition all around you. Family restaurants (except for the truly outstanding ones) almost always have some empty tables. You can always get a pizza delivered in less than 30 minutes. It is rare that every pump at a gas station is in use with customers waiting in line. There are always many real estate agents ready to help find or sell a home. These industries are examples of monopolistic competition. The firms

FIGURE 12.4   Excess Capacity and Markup

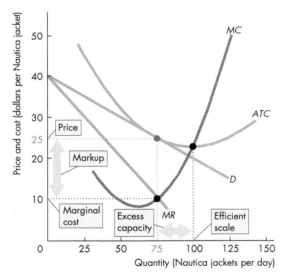

(a) Monopolistic competition

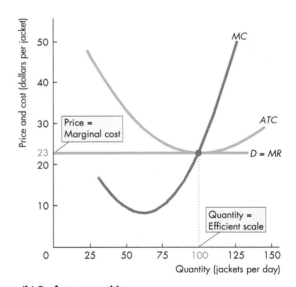

(b) Perfect competition

The efficient scale is 100 jackets a day. In monopolistic competition in the long run, because the firm faces a downward-sloping demand curve for its product, the quantity produced is less than the efficient scale and the firm has excess capacity. Price exceeds marginal cost by the amount of the markup.

In contrast, because in perfect competition the demand for each firm's product is perfectly elastic, the quantity produced in the long run equals the efficient scale and price equals marginal cost. The firm produces at the least possible cost and there is no markup.

have excess capacity. They could sell more by cutting their prices, but they would then incur losses.

Markup A firm's **markup** is the amount by which price exceeds marginal cost. Figure 12.4(a) shows Nautica's markup. In perfect competition, price always equals marginal cost and there is no markup. Figure 12.4(b) shows this case. In monopolistic competition, buyers pay a higher price than in perfect competition and also pay more than marginal cost.

Is Monopolistic Competition Efficient?

Resources are used efficiently when marginal social benefit equals marginal social cost. Price equals marginal social benefit and the firm's marginal cost equals marginal social cost (assuming there are no external benefits or costs). So if the price of a Nautica jacket exceeds the marginal cost of producing it, the quantity of Nautica jackets produced is less than the efficient quantity. And you've just seen that in long-run equilibrium in monopolistic competition, price *does* exceed marginal cost. So is the quantity produced in monopolistic competition less than the efficient quantity?

Making the Relevant Comparison Two economists meet in the street, and one asks the other, "How is your husband?" The quick reply is "Compared to what?" This bit of economic wit illustrates a key point: Before we can conclude that something needs fixing, we must check out the available alternatives.

The markup that drives a gap between price and marginal cost in monopolistic competition arises from product differentiation. It is because Nautica jackets are not quite the same as jackets from Banana Republic, CK, Diesel, DKNY, Earl Jackets, Gap, Levi's, Ralph Lauren, or any of the other dozens of producers of jackets that the demand for Nautica jackets is not perfectly elastic. The only way in which the demand for jackets from Nautica might be perfectly elastic is if there is only one kind of jacket and all firms make it. In this situation, Nautica jackets are indistinguishable from all other jackets. They don't even have identifying labels.

If there was only one kind of jacket, the total benefit of jackets would almost certainly be less than it is with variety. People value variety—not only because it enables each person to select what he or she likes best but also because it provides an external benefit. Most of us enjoy seeing variety in the choices of oth-

ers. Contrast a scene from the China of the 1960s, when everyone wore a Mao tunic, with the China of today, where everyone wears the clothes of their own choosing. Or contrast a scene from the Germany of the 1930s, when almost everyone who could afford a car owned a first-generation Volkswagen Beetle, with the world of today with its enormous variety of styles and types of automobiles.

If people value variety, why don't we see infinite variety? The answer is that variety is costly. Each different variety of any product must be designed, and then customers must be informed about it. These initial costs of design and marketing—called setup costs—mean that some varieties that are too close to others already available are just not worth creating.

The Bottom Line Product variety is both valued and costly. The efficient degree of product variety is the one for which the marginal social benefit of product variety equals its marginal social cost. The loss that arises because the quantity produced is less than the efficient quantity is offset by the gain that arises from having a greater degree of product variety. So compared to the alternative—product uniformity—monopolistic competition might be efficient.

REVIEW QUIZ

1 How does a firm in monopolistic competition decide how much to produce and at what price to offer its product for sale?

2 Why can a firm in monopolistic competition make an economic profit only in the short run?

3 Why do firms in monopolistic competition operate with excess capacity?

4 Why is there a price markup over marginal cost in monopolistic competition?

5 Is monopolistic competition efficient?

You can work these questions in Study Plan 12.2 and get instant feedback.

You've seen how the firm in monopolistic competition determines its output and price in both the short run and the long run when it produces a given product and undertakes a *given* marketing effort. But how does the firm choose its product quality and marketing effort? We'll now study these decisions.

◆ Product Development and Marketing

When Nautica made its price and output decision that we've just studied, it had already made its product quality and marketing decisions. We're now going to look at these decisions and see how they influence the firm's output, price, and economic profit.

Innovation and Product Development

The prospect of new firms entering the industry keeps firms in monopolistic competition on their toes! To enjoy economic profits, they must continually seek ways of keeping one step ahead of imitators—other firms who imitate the success of profitable firms.

One major way of trying to maintain economic profit is for a firm to seek out new products that will provide it with a competitive edge, even if only temporarily. A firm that introduces a new and differentiated product faces a demand that is less elastic and is able to increase its price and make an economic profit. Eventually, imitators will make close substitutes for the innovative product and compete away the economic profit arising from an initial advantage. So to restore economic profit, the firm must again innovate.

Profit-Maximizing Product Innovation The decision to innovate and develop a new or improved product is based on the same type of profit-maximizing calculation that you've already studied.

Innovation and product development are costly activities, but they also bring in additional revenues. The firm must balance the cost and revenue at the margin.

The marginal dollar spent on developing a new or improved product is the marginal cost of product development. The marginal dollar that the new or improved product earns for the firm is the marginal revenue of product development. At a low level of product development, the marginal revenue from a better product exceeds the marginal cost. At a high level of product development, the marginal cost of a better product exceeds the marginal revenue.

When the marginal cost and marginal revenue of product development are equal, the firm is undertaking the profit-maximizing amount of product development.

Efficiency and Product Innovation Is the profit-maximizing amount of product innovation also the efficient amount? Efficiency is achieved if the marginal social benefit of a new and improved product equals its marginal social cost.

The marginal social benefit of an innovation is the increase in price that consumers are willing to pay for it. The marginal social cost is the amount that the firm must pay to make the innovation. Profit is maximized when marginal *revenue* equals marginal cost. But in monopolistic competition, marginal revenue is less than price, so product innovation is probably not pushed to its efficient level.

Monopolistic competition brings many product innovations that cost little to implement and are purely cosmetic, such as new and improved packaging or a new scent in laundry powder. And even when there is a genuine improved product, it is never as good as what the consumer is willing to pay for. For example, "The Legend of Zelda: Twilight Princess" is regarded as an almost perfect and very cool game, but users complain that it isn't quite perfect. It is a game whose features generate a marginal revenue equal to the marginal cost of creating them.

Advertising

A firm with a differentiated product needs to ensure that its customers know how its product is different from the competition. A firm also might attempt to create a consumer perception that its product is different from its competitors, even when that difference is small. Firms use advertising and packaging to achieve this goal.

Advertising Expenditures Firms in monopolistic competition incur huge costs to ensure that buyers appreciate and value the differences between their own products and those of their competitors. So a large proportion of the price that we pay for a good covers the cost of selling it, and this proportion is increasing. Advertising in newspapers and magazines and on radio, television, and the Internet is the main selling cost. But it is not the only one. Selling costs include the cost of shopping malls that look like movie sets, glossy catalogs and brochures, and the salaries, airfares, and hotel bills of salespeople.

Advertising expenditures affect the profits of firms in two ways: They increase costs, and they change demand. Let's look at these effects.

Economics in Action

The Cost of Selling a Pair of Shoes

When you buy a pair of running shoes that cost you $70, you're paying $9 for the materials from which the shoes are made, $2.75 for the services of the Malaysian worker who made the shoes, and $5.25 for the production and transportation services of a manufacturing firm in Asia and a shipping company. These numbers total $17. You pay $3 to the U.S. government in import duty. So we've now accounted for a total of $20. Where did the other $50 go? It is the cost of advertising, retailing, and other sales and distribution services.

The selling costs associated with running shoes are not unusual. Almost everything that you buy includes a selling cost component that exceeds one half of the total cost. Your clothing, food, electronic items, DVDs, magazines, and even your textbooks cost more to sell than they cost to manufacture.

Advertising costs are only a part, and often a small part, of total selling costs. For example, Nike spends about $4 on advertising per pair of running shoes sold.

For the U.S. economy as a whole, there are some 20,000 advertising agencies, which employ more than 200,000 people and have sales of $45 billion. These numbers are only part of the total cost of advertising because firms have their own internal advertising departments, the costs of which we can only guess.

But the biggest part of selling costs is not the cost of advertising. It is the cost of retailing services. The retailer's selling costs (and economic profit) are often as much as 50 percent of the price you pay.

| Raw materials $9 | Production costs $8 | Import duty $3 | Selling costs $50 |

Selling Costs and Total Cost Selling costs are fixed costs and they increase the firm's total cost. So like the fixed cost of producing a good, advertising costs per unit decrease as the quantity produced increases.

Figure 12.5 shows how selling costs change a firm's average total cost. The blue curve shows the average total cost of production. The red curve shows the firm's average total cost of production plus advertising. The height of the red area between the two curves shows the average fixed cost of advertising. The *total* cost of advertising is fixed. But the *average* cost of advertising decreases as output increases.

Figure 12.5 shows that if advertising increases the quantity sold by a large enough amount, it can lower average total cost. For example, if the quantity sold increases from 25 jackets a day with no advertising to 100 jackets a day with advertising, average total cost falls from $60 to $40 a jacket. The reason is that although the *total* fixed cost has increased, the greater fixed cost is spread over a greater output, so average total cost decreases.

FIGURE 12.5   Selling Costs and Total Cost

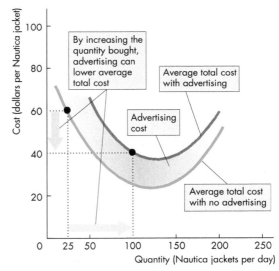

Selling costs such as the cost of advertising are fixed costs. When added to the average total cost of production, selling costs increase average total cost by a greater amount at small outputs than at large outputs. If advertising enables sales to increase from 25 jackets a day to 100 jackets a day, average total cost *falls* from $60 to $40 a jacket.

myeconlab   animation

Selling Costs and Demand Advertising and other selling efforts change the demand for a firm's product. But how? Does demand increase or does it decrease? The most natural answer is that advertising increases demand. By informing people about the quality of its products or by persuading people to switch from the products of other firms, a firm might expect to increase the demand for its own products.

But all firms in monopolistic competition advertise, and all seek to persuade customers that they have the best deal. If advertising enables a firm to survive, the number of firms in the market might increase. And to the extent that the number of firms does increase, advertising *decreases* the demand faced by any one firm. It also makes the demand for any one firm's product more elastic. So advertising can end up not only lowering average total cost but also lowering the markup and the price.

Figure 12.6 illustrates this possible effect of advertising. In part (a), with no advertising, the demand for Nautica jackets is not very elastic. Profit is maxi-

mized at 75 jackets per day, and the markup is large. In part (b), advertising, which is a fixed cost, increases average total cost from ATC_0 to ATC_1 but leaves marginal cost unchanged at MC. Demand becomes much more elastic, the profit-maximizing quantity increases, and the markup shrinks.

Using Advertising to Signal Quality

Some advertising, like the Ashton Kutcher Nikon Coolpix ads on television or the huge number of dollars that Coke and Pepsi spend, seems hard to understand. There doesn't seem to be any concrete information about a camera in an actor's glistening smile. And surely everyone knows about Coke and Pepsi. What is the gain from pouring millions of dollars into advertising these well-known colas?

One answer is that advertising is a signal to the consumer of a high-quality product. A **signal** is an action taken by an informed person (or firm) to send a message to uninformed people. Think about two colas:

FIGURE 12.6   Advertising and the Markup

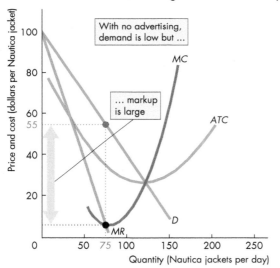

(a) No firms advertise

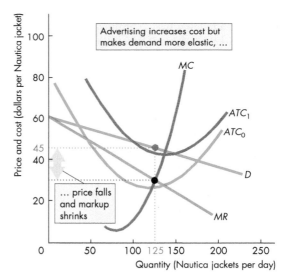

(b) All firms advertise

If no firms advertise, demand for each firm's product is low and not very elastic. The profit-maximizing output is small, the markup is large, and the price is high.

Advertising increases average total cost and shifts the ATC curve upward from ATC_0 to ATC_1. If all firms advertise, the demand for each firm's product becomes more elastic. Output increases, the price falls, and the markup shrinks.

Coke and Oke. Oke knows that its cola is not very good and that its taste varies a lot depending on which cheap batch of unsold cola it happens to buy each week. So Oke knows that while it could get a lot of people to try Oke by advertising, they would all quickly discover what a poor product it is and switch back to the cola they bought before. Coke, in contrast, knows that its product has a high-quality consistent taste and that once consumers have tried it, there is a good chance they'll never drink anything else. On the basis of this reasoning, Oke doesn't advertise but Coke does. And Coke spends a lot of money to make a big splash.

Cola drinkers who see Coke's splashy ads know that the firm would not spend so much money advertising if its product were not truly good. So consumers reason that Coke is indeed a really good product. The flashy expensive ad has signaled that Coke is really good without saying anything about Coke.

Notice that if advertising is a signal, it doesn't need any specific product information. It just needs to be expensive and hard to miss. That's what a lot of advertising looks like. So the signaling theory of advertising predicts much of the advertising that we see.

Brand Names

Many firms create and spend a lot of money promoting a brand name. Why? What benefit does a brand name bring to justify the sometimes high cost of establishing it?

The basic answer is that a brand name provides information to consumers about the quality of a product, and is an incentive to the producer to achieve a high and consistent quality standard.

To see how a brand name helps the consumer, think about how you use brand names to get information about quality. You're on a road trip, and it is time to find a place to spend the night. You see roadside advertisements for Holiday Inn, Joe's Motel, and Annie's Driver's Stop. You know about Holiday Inn because you've stayed in it before. You've also seen their advertisements and know what to expect. You have no information at all about Joe's and Annie's. They might be better than the lodgings you do know about, but without that knowledge, you're not going to try them. You use the brand name as information and stay at Holiday Inn.

This same story explains why a brand name provides an incentive to achieve high and consistent quality. Because no one would know whether Joe's and Annie's were offering a high standard of service, they

have no incentive to do so. But equally, because everyone expects a given standard of service from Holiday Inn, a failure to meet a customer's expectation would almost surely lose that customer to a competitor. So Holiday Inn has a strong incentive to deliver what it promises in the advertising that creates its brand name.

Efficiency of Advertising and Brand Names

To the extent that advertising and brand names provide consumers with information about the precise nature of product differences and about product quality, they benefit the consumer and enable a better product choice to be made. But the opportunity cost of the additional information must be weighed against the gain to the consumer.

The final verdict on the efficiency of monopolistic competition is ambiguous. In some cases, the gains from extra product variety unquestionably offset the selling costs and the extra cost arising from excess capacity. The tremendous varieties of books and magazines, clothing, food, and drinks are examples of such gains. It is less easy to see the gains from being able to buy a brand-name drug that has a chemical composition identical to that of a generic alternative, but many people do willingly pay more for the brand-name alternative.

 REVIEW QUIZ

1 How, other than by adjusting price, do firms in monopolistic competition compete?
2 Why might product innovation and development be efficient and why might it be inefficient?
3 How do selling costs influence a firm's cost curves and its average total cost?
4 How does advertising influence demand?
5 Are advertising and brand names efficient?

You can work these questions in Study Plan 12.3 and get instant feedback.

Monopolistic competition is one of the most common market structures that you encounter in your daily life. *Reading Between the Lines* on pp. 256–257 applies the model of monopolistic competition to the market for smart phones and shows why you can expect continual innovation and the introduction of new phones from Apple and other producers of smart phones.

Product Differentiation and Entry in the Market for Smart Phones

Apple Sues Rival HTC as Phone Competition Rises

http://seattletimes.nwsource.com
March 2, 2010

As Apple Inc.'s iPhone faces stiffer competition in the lucrative market for smart phones, the company is going after one of its main rivals with patent lawsuits claiming theft of touch screen technology and other features.

The complaints, which Apple filed Tuesday, cover a slew of models made by Taiwanese phone maker HTC Corp., including the Nexus One, G1, and myTouch 3G—all using the free, rival Android mobile operating software from Google Inc. Non-Android phones include HTC's Touch series.

But consumers shouldn't worry about buying or using any of those phones. Patent cases can take months or years to resolve—sometimes longer than the life of these phones—and agreements over licensing and royalty payments often emerge.

Still, it shows Apple's get-tough strategy as significant competitors emerge.

"We can sit by and watch competitors steal our patented inventions, or we can do something about it," Apple CEO Steve Jobs said in a statement. "We've decided to do something about it."...

Since the iPhone's debut, Apple has had a lock on much of the smart phone market, alongside Research In Motion Ltd., which makes the popular BlackBerry devices.

However, over the last year or so, more competition has emerged from such phone makers as HTC and Motorola Inc., which are rolling out smart phones that use Google's Android software. Not only do these phones appeal to consumers, but they also work on numerous wireless networks, unlike the iPhone, which is still limited in the United States to AT&T Inc. ...

ESSENCE OF THE STORY

- The iPhone faces stiff competition in the market for smart phones.

- Apple is bringing patent lawsuits against HTC Corp., one of its main rivals, claiming theft of touch screen technology.

- The smart phones produced by HTC Corp. include the Nexus One, G1, and myTouch 3G.

- Resolving patent cases can take longer than the life of the product.

- Apple and Research In Motion Ltd., which makes the BlackBerry, have the largest share of the smart phone market.

- More competition is coming from phone makers HTC, Motorola Inc., and others.

- Apple sold its first iPhone in 2007 and brought the more powerful 3G version to market in 2008.

- By creating a substantially differentiated product, Apple was able to generate a great deal of interest in smart phones throughout the world.

- In the first weekend, Apple sold 1 million of the 3G iPhone.

- But within a month of the launch of the 3G iPhone, many competing but differentiated devices were on the market.

- The monopolistic competition model explains what is happening in the smart phone market.

- Figure 1 shows the market for Apple's iPhone in its first month. (The numbers are assumptions.)

- Because Apple's iPhone differs from its competitors and has features that users value, the demand curve, D, and marginal revenue curve, MR, provide a large short-run profit opportunity.

- The marginal cost curve is MC and the average total cost curve is ATC. Apple maximizes its economic profit by producing the quantity at which marginal revenue equals marginal cost, which in this example is 3 million iPhones a month.

- This quantity of iPhones can be sold for $200 each.

- The blue rectangle shows Apple's economic profit.

- Because this market is profitable, entry takes place. HTC, Motorola, and others (such as Research in Motion, LG, Nokia, and Samsung) enter the smart phone market.

- Figure 2 shows the the consequences of entry.

- The demand for the iPhone decreases as the market is shared with the other phones.

- Apple's profit-maximizing price for the iPhone falls, and in the long run, economic profit is eliminated.

- With zero economic profit, Apple has an incentive to develop an even better differentiated phone and start the cycle described here again, making an economic profit in a new phone in the short run.

- The iPhone 4, announced in June 2010, was Apple's response to the entry described in the news article.

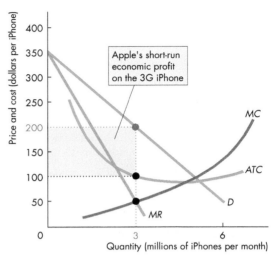

Figure 1 Economic profit in the short run

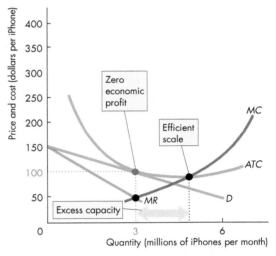

Figure 2 Zero economic profit in the long run

257

SUMMARY

Key Points

What Is Monopolistic Competition? (pp. 246–247)

- Monopolistic competition occurs when a large number of firms compete with each other on product quality, price, and marketing.

Working Problems 1 and 2 will give you a better understanding of what monopolistic competition is.

Price and Output in Monopolistic Competition

(pp. 248–251)

- Each firm in monopolistic competition faces a downward-sloping demand curve and produces the profit-maximizing quantity.
- Entry and exit result in zero economic profit and excess capacity in long-run equilibrium.

Working Problems 3 to 12 will give you a better understanding of price and output in monopolistic competition.

Product Development and Marketing (pp. 252–255)

- Firms in monopolistic competition innovate and develop new products.
- Advertising expenditures increase total cost, but average total cost might fall if the quantity sold increases by enough.
- Advertising expenditures might increase demand, but demand might decrease if competition increases.
- Whether monopolistic competition is inefficient depends on the value we place on product variety.

Working Problems 13 to 18 will give you a better understanding of product development and marketing.

Key Terms

Efficient scale, 250

Excess capacity, 250

Markup, 251

Monopolistic competition, 246

Product differentiation, 246

Signal, 254

STUDY PLAN PROBLEMS AND APPLICATIONS

 myeconlab You can work Problems 1 to 19 in MyEconLab Chapter 12 Study Plan and get instant feedback.

What Is Monopolistic Competition? (Study Plan 12.1)

1. Which of the following items are sold by firms in monopolistic competition? Explain your selections.
   - Cable television service
   - Wheat
   - Athletic shoes
   - Soda
   - Toothbrushes
   - Ready-mix concrete

2. The four-firm concentration ratio for audio equipment makers is 30 and for electric lamp makers it is 89. The HHI for audio equipment makers it is 415 and for electric lamp makers it is 2,850. Which of these markets is an example of monopolistic competition?

Price and Output in Monopolistic Competition

(Study Plan 12.2)

Use the following information to work Problems 3 and 4.

Sara is a dot.com entrepreneur who has established a Web site at which people can design and buy sweatshirts. Sara pays $1,000 a week for her Web server and Internet connection. The sweatshirts that her customers design are made to order by another firm, and Sara pays this firm $20 a sweatshirt. Sara has no other costs. The table sets out the demand schedule for Sara's sweatshirts.

Price (dollars per sweatshirt)	Quantity demanded (sweatshirts per week)
0	100
20	80
40	60
60	40
80	20
100	0

3. Calculate Sara's profit-maximizing output, price, and economic profit.

4. a. Do you expect other firms to enter the Web sweatshirt business and compete with Sara?
   b. What happens to the demand for Sara's sweatshirts in the long run? What happens to Sara's economic profit in the long run?

Use the following figure, which shows the situation facing a producer of running shoes, to work Problems 5 to 10.

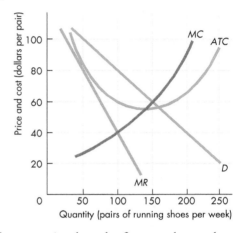

5. What quantity does the firm produce, what price does it charge, and what is its economic profit or economic loss?

6. In the long run, how does the number of firms producing running shoes change?

7. In the long run, how does the price of running shoes and the quantity the firm produces change? What happens to the market output?

8. Does the firm have excess capacity in the long run? If the firm has excess capacity in the long run, why doesn't it decrease its capacity?

9. In the long run, compare the price of a pair of running shoes and the marginal cost of producing the pair.

10. Is the market for running shoes efficient or inefficient in the long run? Explain your answer.

11. **Wake Up and Smell the Coffee**

    Every change that Starbucks made over the past few years—automated espresso machines, pre-ground coffee, drive-throughs, fewer soft chairs and less carpeting—was made for a reason: to smooth operations or boost sales. Those may have been the right choices at the time, but together they ultimately diluted the coffee-centric experience. By 2008, Starbucks experienced a drop in traffic as customers complained that in pursuing rapid growth, the company has strayed too far from its roots. Starbucks will once again grind beans in its stores for drip coffee, give free drip refills, and provide two hours of wi-fi. The company will roll out its new sleek, low-rise espresso machine that makes baristas more visible.

Source: *Time*, April 7, 2008

a. Explain how Starbucks' past attempts to maximize profits ended up eroding product differentiation.

b. Explain how Starbucks' new plan intends to increase economic profit.

12. **The Shoe That Won't Quit**

I finally decided to take the plunge and buy a pair of Uggs, but when I got around to shopping for my Uggs, the style that I wanted was sold out. The scarcity factor was not a glitch in the supply chain, but rather a carefully calibrated strategy by Ugg's parent Deckers Outdoor that is one of the big reasons behind the brand's success. Deckers tightly controls distribution to ensure that supply does not outstrip demand. If Deckers ever opened up the supply of Uggs to meet demand, sales would shoot up like a rocket, but they'd come back down just as fast.

Source: *Fortune*, June 5, 2008

a. Explain why Deckers intentionally restricts the quantity of Uggs that the firm sells.

b. Draw a graph to illustrate how Deckers maximizes the economic profit from Uggs.

Product Development and Marketing (Study Plan 12.3)

Use the following information to work Problems 13 to 16.

Suppose that Tommy Hilfiger's marginal cost of a jacket is a constant $100 and the total fixed cost at one of its stores is $2,000 a day. This store sells 20 jackets a day, which is its profit-maximizing number of jackets. Then the stores nearby start to advertise their jackets. The Tommy Hilfiger store now spends $2,000 a day advertising its jackets, and its profit-maximizing number of jackets sold jumps to 50 a day.

13. a. What is this store's average total cost of a jacket sold before the advertising begins?

b. What is this store's average total cost of a jacket sold after the advertising begins?

14. a. Can you say what happens to the price of a Tommy Hilfiger jacket? Why or why not?

b. Can you say what happens to Tommy's markup? Why or why not?

c. Can you say what happens to Tommy's economic profit? Why or why not?

15. How might Tommy Hilfiger use advertising as a signal? How is a signal sent and how does it work?

16. How does having a brand name help Tommy Hilfiger to increase its economic profit?

Use the following news clip to work Problems 17 and 18.

Food's Next Billion-Dollar Brand?

While it's not the biggest brand in margarine, Smart Balance has an edge on its rivals in that it's made with a patented blend of vegetable and fruit oils that has been shown to help improve consumers' cholesterol levels. Smart Balance sales have skyrocketed while overall sales for margarine have stagnated. It remains to be seen if Smart Balance's healthy message and high price will resound with consumers.

Source: *Fortune*, June 4, 2008

17. How do you expect advertising and the Smart Balance brand name will affect Smart Balance's ability to make a positive economic profit?

18. Are long-run economic profits a possibility for Smart Balance? In long-run equilibrium, will Smart Balance have excess capacity or a markup?

Economics in the News (Study Plan 12.N)

19. **Computer Makers Prepare to Stake Bigger Claim in Phones**

Emboldened by Apple's success with its iPhone, many PC makers and chip companies are charging into the mobile-phone business, promising new devices that can pack the horsepower of standard computers into palm-size packages—devices that handle the full glory of the Internet, power two-way video conferences, and stream high-definition movies to your TV. It is a development that spells serious competition for established cell-phone makers and phone companies.

Source: *The New York Times*, March 15, 2009

a. Draw a graph of the cost curves and revenue curves of a cell-phone company that makes a positive economic profit in the short run.

b. If cell-phone companies start to include the popular features introduced by PC makers, explain how this decision will affect their profit in the short run.

c. What do you expect to happen to the cell-phone company's economic profit in the long run, given the information in the news clip?

d. Draw a graph to illustrate your answer to part (c).

ADDITIONAL PROBLEMS AND APPLICATIONS

myeconlab You can work these problems in MyEconLab if assigned by your instructor.

What Is Monopolistic Competition?

20. Which of the following items are sold by firms in monopolistic competition? Explain your selection.
    - Orange juice
    - Canned soup
    - PCs
    - Chewing gum
    - Breakfast cereals
    - Corn

21. The HHI for automobiles is 2,350, for sporting goods it is 161, for batteries it is 2,883, and for jewelry it is 81. Which of these markets is an example of monopolistic competition?

Price and Output in Monopolistic Competition

Use the following information to work Problems 22 and 23.

Lorie teaches singing. Her fixed costs are $1,000 a month, and it costs her $50 of labor to give one class. The table shows the demand schedule for Lorie's singing lessons.

Price (dollars per lesson)	Quantity demanded (lessons per month)
0	250
50	200
100	150
150	100
200	50
250	0

22. Calculate Lorie's profit-maximizing output, price, and economic profit.

23. a. Do you expect other firms to enter the singing lesson business and compete with Lorie?

    b. What happens to the demand for Lorie's lessons in the long run? What happens to Lorie's economic profit in the long run?

Use the following figure, which shows the situation facing Mike's Bikes, a producer of mountain bikes, to work Problems 24 to 28. The demand and costs of other mountain bike producers are similar to those of Mike's Bikes.

24. What quantity does the firm produce and what is its price? Calculate the firm's economic profit or economic loss.

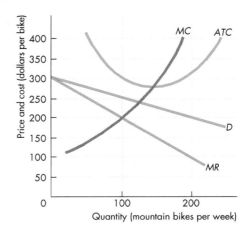

25. What will happen to the number of firms producing mountain bikes in the long run?

26. a. How will the price of a mountain bike and the number of bikes produced by Mike's Bikes change in the long run?

    b. How will the quantity of mountain bikes produced by all firms change in the long run?

27. Is there any way for Mike's Bikes to avoid having excess capacity in the long run?

28. Is the market for mountain bikes efficient or inefficient in the long run? Explain your answer.

Use the following news clip to work Problems 29 and 30.

Groceries for the Gourmet Palate

No food, it seems, is safe from being repackaged to look like an upscale product. Samuel Adams' $120 Utopias, in a ridiculous copper-covered 24-oz. bottle meant to resemble an old-fashioned brew kettle, is barely beer. It's not carbonated like a Bud, but aged in oak barrels like scotch. It has a vintage year, like a Bordeaux, is light, complex, and free of any alcohol sting, despite having six times as much alcohol content as a regular can of brew.

Source: *Time*, April 14, 2008

29. a. Explain how Samuel Adams has differentiated its Utopias to compete with other beer brands in terms of quality, price, and marketing.

    b. Predict whether Samuel Adams produces at, above, or below the efficient scale in the short run.

30. a. Predict whether the $120 price tag on the Utopias is at, above, or below marginal cost:

(i) In the short run.

(ii) In the long run.

   b. Do you think that Samuel Adams Utopias makes the market for beer inefficient?

Use the following news clip to work Problems 31 and 32.

Swinging for Female Golfers

One of the hottest areas of innovation is in clubs for women, who now make up nearly a quarter of the 24 million golfers in the United States. Callaway and Nike, two of the leading golf-equipment manufacturers, recently released new clubs designed specifically for women.

                Source: *Time*, April 21, 2008

31. a. How are Callaway and Nike attempting to maintain economic profit?

   b. Draw a graph to illustrate the cost curves and revenue curves of Callaway or Nike in the market for golf clubs for women.

   c. Show on your graph in part (b) the short-run economic profit.

32. a. Explain why the economic profit that Callaway and Nike make on golf clubs for women is likely to be temporary.

   b. Draw a graph to illustrate the cost curves and revenue curves of Callaway or Nike in the market for golf clubs for women in the long run. Mark the firm's excess capacity.

Product Development and Marketing

Use the following information to work Problems 33 to 35.

Bianca bakes delicious cookies. Her total fixed cost is $40 a day, and her average variable cost is $1 a bag. Few people know about Bianca's Cookies, and she is maximizing her profit by selling 10 bags a day for $5 a bag. Bianca thinks that if she spends $50 a day on advertising, she can increase her market share and sell 25 bags a day for $5 a bag.

33. If Bianca's advertising works as she expects, can she increase her economic profit by advertising?

34. If Bianca advertises, will her average total cost increase or decrease at the quantity produced?

35. If Bianca advertises, will she continue to sell her cookies for $5 a bag or will she change her price?

Use the following news clip to work Problems 36 and 37.

A Thirst for More Champagne

Champagne exports have tripled in the past 20 years. That poses a problem for northern France, where the bubbly hails from—not enough grapes. So French authorities have unveiled a plan to extend the official Champagne grape-growing zone to cover 40 new villages. This revision has provoked debate. The change will take several years to become effective. In the meantime the vineyard owners whose land values will jump markedly if the changes are finalized certainly have reason to raise a glass.

                Source: *Fortune*, May 12, 2008

36. a. Why is France so strict about designating the vineyards that can use the Champagne label?

   b. Explain who most likely opposes this plan.

37. Assuming that vineyards in these 40 villages are producing the same quality of grapes with or without this plan, why will their land values "jump markedly" if this plan is approved?

38. **Under Armour's Big Step Up**

Under Armour, the red-hot athletic-apparel brand, has joined Nike, Adidas, and New Balance as a major player in the market for athletic footwear. Under Armour plans to revive the long-dead cross-training category. But will young athletes really spend $100 for a cross training shoe to lift weights in?

                Source: *Time*, May 26, 2008

What factors influence Under Armour's ability to make an economic profit in the cross-training shoe market?

Economics in the News

39. After you have studied *Reading Between the Lines* on pp. 256–257 answer the following questions.

   a. Describe the cost curves (*MC* and *ATC*) and the marginal revenue and demand curves for the iPhone when Apple first introduced it.

   b. How do you think the creation of the iPhone influenced the demand for older generation cell phones?

   c. Explain the effects of the introduction of the 3G iPhone on HTC and other firms in the market for smart phones.

   d. Draw a graph to illustrate your answer to part (c).

   e. Explain the effect on Apple of the decisions by BlackBerry and HTC to bring their own smart phones to market.

   f. Draw a graph to illustrate your answer to part (e).

   g. Do you think the smart phone market is efficient? Explain your answer.

   h. Do you predict that producers of smart phones have excess capacity? Explain your answer.

13

OLIGOPOLY

After studying this chapter,
you will be able to:

◆ Define and identify oligopoly

◆ Use game theory to explain how price and output are
determined in oligopoly

◆ Use game theory to explain other strategic decisions

◆ Describe the antitrust laws that regulate oligopoly

The chip in your laptop was made by either Intel or Advanced Micro Devices;
the battery in your TV remote is most likely a Duracell or Energizer; if you use a
high-tech razor, it is either a Gillette or a Schick; and if you take a long-
distance trip by air, you will fly in an airplane made by either Boeing or the
European firm Airbus. In the markets for computer chips, batteries, high-tech
razors, and big airplanes, two producers compete for market share in the
pursuit of maximum profit. Many other markets have only a small number of
firms. Among them are the markets for light bulbs, breakfast cereals, and major
appliances.

How does a market work when only a handful of firms compete? Is the
market efficient like perfect competition with the firms operating in the social
interest? Or is the market inefficient like monopoly with the firms restricting
output to increase profit?

To answer these questions, we need to understand the models of oligopoly.
These models use game theory, which the chapter explains.

What Is Oligopoly?

Oligopoly, like monopolistic competition, lies between perfect competition and monopoly. The firms in oligopoly might produce an identical product and compete only on price, or they might produce a differentiated product and compete on price, product quality, and marketing. **Oligopoly** is a market structure in which

- Natural or legal barriers prevent the entry of new firms.
- A small number of firms compete.

Barriers to Entry

Natural or legal barriers to entry can create oligopoly. You saw in Chapter 11 how economies of scale and demand form a natural barrier to entry that can create a *natural monopoly*. These same factors can create a *natural oligopoly*.

Figure 13.1 illustrates two natural oligopolies. The demand curve, D (in both parts of the figure), shows the demand for taxi rides in a town. If the average

total cost curve of a taxi company is ATC_1 in part (a), the market is a natural **duopoly**—an oligopoly market with two firms. You can probably see some examples of duopoly where you live. Some cities have only two taxi companies, two car rental firms, two copy centers, or two college bookstores.

The lowest price at which the firm would remain in business is $10 a ride. At that price, the quantity of rides demanded is 60 a day, the quantity that can be provided by just two firms. There is no room in this market for three firms. But if there were only one firm, it would make an economic profit and a second firm would enter to take some of the business and economic profit.

If the average total cost curve of a taxi company is ATC_2 in part (b), the efficient scale of one firm is 20 rides a day. This market is large enough for three firms.

A legal oligopoly arises when a legal barrier to entry protects the small number of firms in a market. A city might license two taxi firms or two bus companies, for example, even though the combination of demand and economies of scale leaves room for more than two firms.

FIGURE 13.1   Natural Oligopoly

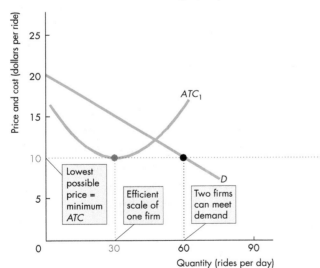

(a) Natural duopoly

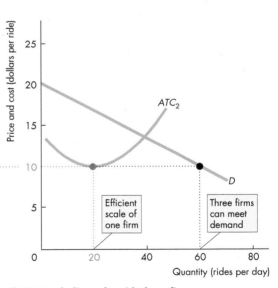

(b) Natural oligopoly with three firms

The lowest possible price is $10 a ride, which is the minimum average total cost. When a firm produces 30 rides a day, the efficient scale, two firms can satisfy the market demand. This natural oligopoly has two firms—a natural duopoly.

When the efficient scale of one firm is 20 rides per day, three firms can satisfy the market demand at the lowest possible price. This natural oligopoly has three firms.

Small Number of Firms

Because barriers to entry exist, oligopoly consists of a small number of firms, each of which has a large share of the market. Such firms are interdependent, and they face a temptation to cooperate to increase their joint economic profit.

Interdependence With a small number of firms in a market, each firm's actions influence the profits of all the other firms. When Penny Stafford opened her coffee shop in Bellevue, Washington, a nearby Starbucks coffee shop took a hit. Within days, Starbucks began to attract Penny's customers with enticing offers and lower prices. Starbucks survived but Penny eventually went out of business. Penny Stafford and Starbucks were interdependent.

Temptation to Cooperate When a small number of firms share a market, they can increase their profits by forming a cartel and acting like a monopoly. A **cartel** is a group of firms acting together—colluding—to limit output, raise price, and increase economic profit. Cartels are illegal, but they do operate in some markets. But for reasons that you'll discover in this chapter, cartels tend to break down.

Examples of Oligopoly

The box below shows some examples of oligopoly. The dividing line between oligopoly and monopolistic competition is hard to pin down. As a practical matter, we identify oligopoly by looking at concentration ratios, the Herfindahl-Hirschman Index, and information about the geographical scope of the market and barriers to entry. The HHI that divides oligopoly from monopolistic competition is generally taken to be 1,000. An HHI below 1,000 is usually an example of monopolistic competition, and a market in which the HHI exceeds 1,000 is usually an example of oligopoly.

REVIEW QUIZ

1   What are the two distinguishing characteristics of oligopoly?
2   Why are firms in oligopoly interdependent?
3   Why do firms in oligopoly face a temptation to collude?
4   Can you think of some examples of oligopolies that you buy from?

You can work these questions in Study Plan 13.1 and get instant feedback.

Economics in Action
Oligopoly Today

These markets are oligopolies. Although in some of them, the number of firms (in parentheses) is large, the share of the market held by the 4 largest firms (the red bars) is close to 100 percent.

The most concentrated markets—cigarettes, glass bottles and jars, washing machines and dryers, and batteries, are dominated by just one or two firms.

If you want to buy a battery for your TV remote or toothbrush, you'll find it hard to avoid buying a Duracell or an Energizer.

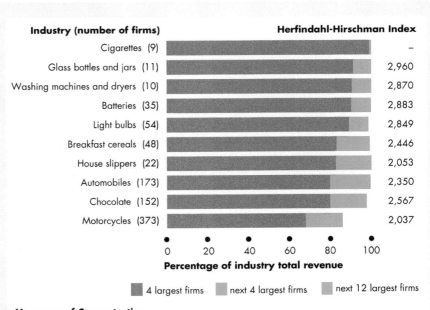

Industry (number of firms)	Herfindahl-Hirschman Index
Cigarettes (9)	–
Glass bottles and jars (11)	2,960
Washing machines and dryers (10)	2,870
Batteries (35)	2,883
Light bulbs (54)	2,849
Breakfast cereals (48)	2,446
House slippers (22)	2,053
Automobiles (173)	2,350
Chocolate (152)	2,567
Motorcycles (373)	2,037

Percentage of industry total revenue

■ 4 largest firms   ■ next 4 largest firms   ■ next 12 largest firms

Measures of Concentration

Source of data: U.S. Census Bureau.

◆ Oligopoly Games

Economists think about oligopoly as a game between two or a few players, and to study oligopoly markets they use game theory. **Game theory** is a set of tools for studying *strategic behavior*—behavior that takes into account the expected behavior of others and the recognition of mutual interdependence. Game theory was invented by John von Neumann in 1937 and extended by von Neumann and Oskar Morgenstern in 1944. Today, it is one of the major research fields in economics.

Game theory seeks to understand oligopoly as well as other forms of economic, political, social, and even biological rivalries by using a method of analysis specifically designed to understand games of all types, including the familiar games of everyday life. To lay the foundation for studying oligopoly games, we first think about the features that all games share.

What Is a Game?

What is a game? At first thought, the question seems silly. After all, there are many different games. There are ball games and parlor games, games of chance and games of skill. But what is it about all these different activities that makes them games? What do all these games have in common? All games share four common features:

- Rules
- Strategies
- Payoffs
- Outcome

We're going to look at these features of games by playing at a game called "the prisoners' dilemma." The prisoners' dilemma game displays the essential features of many games, including oligopoly games, and it gives a good illustration of how game theory works and generates predictions.

The Prisoners' Dilemma ✳*Interesting*

Art and Bob have been caught red-handed stealing a car. Facing airtight cases, they will receive a sentence of two years each for their crime. During his interviews with the two prisoners, the district attorney begins to suspect that he has stumbled on the two people who were responsible for a multimillion-dollar bank robbery some months earlier. But this is just a suspicion. He has no evidence on which he can

convict them of the greater crime unless he can get them to confess. But how can he extract a confession? The answer is by making the prisoners play a game. The district attorney makes the prisoners play the following game.

Rules Each prisoner (player) is placed in a separate room and cannot communicate with the other prisoner. Each is told that he is suspected of having carried out the bank robbery and that

If both of them confess to the larger crime, each will receive a sentence of 3 years for both crimes.

If he alone confesses and his accomplice does not, he will receive only a 1-year sentence while his accomplice will receive a 10-year sentence.

Strategies In game theory, **strategies** are all the possible actions of each player. Art and Bob each have two possible actions:

1. Confess to the bank robbery.
2. Deny having committed the bank robbery.

Because there are two players, each with two strategies, there are four possible outcomes:

1. Both confess.
2. Both deny.
3. Art confesses and Bob denies.
4. Bob confesses and Art denies.

Payoffs Each prisoner can work out his *payoff* in each of these situations, and we can tabulate the four possible payoffs for each of the prisoners in what is called a payoff matrix for the game. A **payoff matrix** is a table that shows the payoffs for every possible action by each player for every possible action by each other player.

Table 13.1 shows a payoff matrix for Art and Bob. The squares show the payoffs for each prisoner—the red triangle in each square shows Art's and the blue triangle shows Bob's. If both prisoners confess (top left), each gets a prison term of 3 years. If Bob confesses but Art denies (top right), Art gets a 10-year sentence and Bob gets a 1-year sentence. If Art confesses and Bob denies (bottom left), Art gets a 1-year sentence and Bob gets a 10-year sentence. Finally, if both of them deny (bottom right), neither can be convicted of the bank robbery charge but both are sentenced for the car theft—a 2-year sentence.

Outcome The choices of both players determine the outcome of the game. To predict that outcome, we use an equilibrium idea proposed by John Nash of Princeton University (who received the Nobel Prize for Economic Science in 1994 and was the subject of the 2001 movie *A Beautiful Mind*). In **Nash equilibrium**, player *A* takes the best possible action given the action of player *B* and player *B* takes the best possible action given the action of player *A*.

In the case of the prisoners' dilemma, the Nash equilibrium occurs when Art makes his best choice given Bob's choice and when Bob makes his best choice given Art's choice.

To find the Nash equilibrium, we compare all the possible outcomes associated with each choice and eliminate those that are dominated—that are not as good as some other choice. Let's find the Nash equilibrium for the prisoners' dilemma game.

Finding the Nash Equilibrium Look at the situation from Art's point of view. If Bob confesses (top row), Art's best action is to confess because in that case, he is sentenced to 3 years rather than 10 years. If Bob denies (bottom row), Art's best action is still to confess because in that case he receives 1 year rather than 2 years. So Art's best action is to confess.

Now look at the situation from Bob's point of view. If Art confesses (left column), Bob's best action is to confess because in that case, he is sentenced to 3 years rather than 10 years. If Art denies (right column), Bob's best action is still to confess because in that case, he receives 1 year rather than 2 years. So Bob's best action is to confess.

Because each player's best action is to confess, each does confess, each goes to jail for 3 years, and the district attorney has solved the bank robbery. This is the Nash equilibrium of the game.

The Nash equilibrium for the prisoners' dilemma is called a **dominant-strategy equilibrium**, which is an equilibrium in which the best strategy of each player is to cheat (confess) *regardless of the strategy of the other player.*

The Dilemma The dilemma arises as each prisoner contemplates the consequences of his decision and puts himself in the place of his accomplice. Each knows that it would be best if both denied. But each also knows that if he denies it is in the best interest of the other to confess. So each considers whether to deny and rely on his accomplice to deny or to confess

TABLE 13.1   Prisoners' Dilemma Payoff Matrix

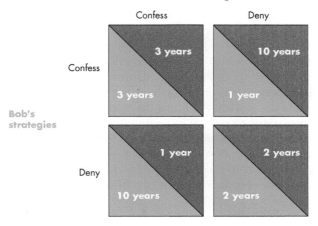

Each square shows the payoffs for the two players, Art and Bob, for each possible pair of actions. In each square, the red triangle shows Art's payoff and the blue triangle shows Bob's. For example, if both confess, the payoffs are in the top left square. The equilibrium of the game is for both players to confess and each gets a 3-year sentence.

hoping that his accomplice denies but expecting him to confess. The dilemma leads to the equilibrium of the game.

A Bad Outcome For the prisoners, the equilibrium of the game, with each confessing, is not the best outcome. If neither of them confesses, each gets only 2 years for the lesser crime. Isn't there some way in which this better outcome can be achieved? It seems that there is not, because the players cannot communicate with each other. Each player can put himself in the other player's place, and so each player can figure out that there is a best strategy for each of them. The prisoners are indeed in a dilemma. Each knows that he can serve 2 years *only* if he can trust the other to deny. But each prisoner also knows that it is *not* in the best interest of the other to deny. So each prisoner knows that he must confess, thereby delivering a bad outcome for both.

The firms in an oligopoly are in a similar situation to Art and Bob in the prisoners' dilemma game. Let's see how we can use this game to understand oligopoly.

An Oligopoly Price-Fixing Game

We can use game theory and a game like the prisoners' dilemma to understand price fixing, price wars, and other aspects of the behavior of firms in oligopoly. We'll begin with a price-fixing game.

To understand price fixing, we're going to study the special case of duopoly—an oligopoly with two firms. Duopoly is easier to study than oligopoly with three or more firms, and it captures the essence of all oligopoly situations. Somehow, the two firms must share the market. And how they share it depends on the actions of each. We're going to describe the costs of the two firms and the market demand for the item they produce. We're then going to see how game theory helps us to predict the prices charged and the quantities produced by the two firms in a duopoly.

Cost and Demand Conditions Two firms, Trick and Gear, produce switchgears. They have identical costs. Figure 13.2(a) shows their average total cost curve (*ATC*) and marginal cost curve (*MC*). Figure 13.2(b) shows the market demand curve for switchgears (*D*). The two firms produce identical switchgears, so one firm's switchgear is a perfect substitute for the other's, and the market price of each firm's product is identical. The quantity demanded depends on that price—the higher the price, the smaller is the quantity demanded.

This industry is a natural duopoly. Two firms can produce this good at a lower cost than either one firm or three firms can. For each firm, average total cost is at its minimum when production is 3,000 units a week. When price equals minimum average total cost, the total quantity demanded is 6,000 units a week, and two firms can just produce that quantity.

Collusion We'll suppose that Trick and Gear enter into a collusive agreement. A **collusive agreement** is an agreement between two (or more) producers to form a cartel to restrict output, raise the price, and increase profits. Such an agreement is illegal in the United States and is undertaken in secret. The strategies that firms in a cartel can pursue are to

- Comply
- Cheat

A firm that complies carries out the agreement. A firm that cheats breaks the agreement to its own benefit and to the cost of the other firm.

Because each firm has two strategies, there are four possible combinations of actions for the firms:

1. Both firms comply.
2. Both firms cheat.
3. Trick complies and Gear cheats.
4. Gear complies and Trick cheats.

FIGURE 13.2   Costs and Demand

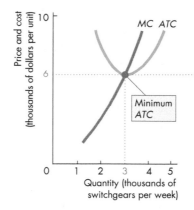

(a) Individual firm

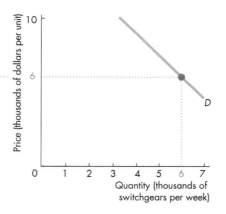

(b) Industry

The average total cost curve for each firm is *ATC*, and the marginal cost curve is *MC* (part a). Minimum average total cost is $6,000 a unit, and it occurs at a production of 3,000 units a week.

Part (b) shows the market demand curve. At a price of $6,000, the quantity demanded is 6,000 units per week. The two firms can produce this output at the lowest possible average cost. If the market had one firm, it would be profitable for another to enter. If the market had three firms, one would exit. There is room for only two firms in this industry. It is a natural duopoly.

Colluding to Maximize Profits Let's work out the payoffs to the two firms if they collude to make the maximum profit for the cartel by acting like a monopoly. The calculations that the two firms perform are the same calculations that a monopoly performs. (You can refresh your memory of these calculations by looking at Chapter 11, pp. 226–227.) The only thing that the firms in duopoly must do beyond what a monopoly does is to agree on how much of the total output each of them will produce.

Figure 13.3 shows the price and quantity that maximize industry profit for the duopoly. Part (a) shows the situation for each firm, and part (b) shows the situation for the industry as a whole. The curve labeled MR is the industry marginal revenue curve. This marginal revenue curve is like that of a single-price monopoly (Chapter 11, p. 224). The curve labeled MC_I is the industry marginal cost curve if each firm produces the same quantity of output. This curve is constructed by adding together the outputs of the two firms at each level of marginal cost. Because the two firms are the same size, at each level of marginal cost, the industry output is twice the output of one firm. The curve MC_I in part (b) is twice as far to the right as the curve MC in part (a).

To maximize industry profit, the firms in the duopoly agree to restrict output to the rate that makes the industry marginal cost and marginal revenue equal. That output rate, as shown in part (b), is 4,000 units a week. The demand curve shows that the

highest price for which the 4,000 switchgears can be sold is $9,000 each. Trick and Gear agree to charge this price.

To hold the price at $9,000 a unit, production must be 4,000 units a week. So Trick and Gear must agree on output rates for each of them that total 4,000 units a week. Let's suppose that they agree to split the market equally so that each firm produces 2,000 switchgears a week. Because the firms are identical, this division is the most likely.

The average total cost (ATC) of producing 2,000 switchgears a week is $8,000, so the profit per unit is $1,000 and economic profit is $2 million (2,000 units × $1,000 per unit). The economic profit of each firm is represented by the blue rectangle in Fig. 13.3(a).

We have just described one possible outcome for a duopoly game: The two firms collude to produce the monopoly profit-maximizing output and divide that output equally between themselves. From the industry point of view, this solution is identical to a monopoly. A duopoly that operates in this way is indistinguishable from a monopoly. The economic profit that is made by a monopoly is the maximum total profit that can be made by the duopoly when the firms collude.

But with price greater than marginal cost, either firm might think of trying to increase profit by cheating on the agreement and producing more than the agreed amount. Let's see what happens if one of the firms does cheat in this way.

FIGURE 13.3 **Colluding to Make Monopoly Profits**

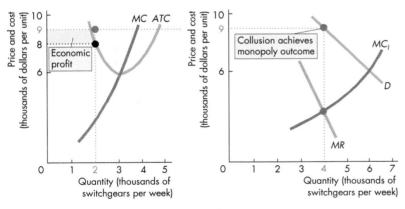

(a) Individual firm

(b) Industry

The industry marginal cost curve, MC_I in part (b), is the horizontal sum of the two firms' marginal cost curves, MC in part (a). The industry marginal revenue curve is MR. To maximize profit, the firms produce 4,000 units a week (the quantity at which marginal revenue equals marginal cost). They sell that output for $9,000 a unit. Each firm produces 2,000 units a week. Average total cost is $8,000 a unit, so each firm makes an economic profit of $2 million (blue rectangle)—2,000 units multiplied by $1,000 profit a unit.

One Firm Cheats on a Collusive Agreement To set the stage for cheating on their agreement, Trick convinces Gear that demand has decreased and that it cannot sell 2,000 units a week. Trick tells Gear that it plans to cut its price so that it can sell the agreed 2,000 units each week. Because the two firms produce an identical product, Gear matches Trick's price cut but still produces only 2,000 units a week.

In fact, there has been no decrease in demand. Trick plans to increase output, which it knows will lower the price, and Trick wants to ensure that Gear's output remains at the agreed level.

Figure 13.4 illustrates the consequences of Trick's cheating. Part (a) shows Gear (the complier); part (b) shows Trick (the cheat); and part (c) shows the industry as a whole. Suppose that Trick increases output to 3,000 units a week. If Gear sticks to the agreement to produce only 2,000 units a week, total output is now 5,000 a week, and given demand in part (c), the price falls to $7,500 a unit.

Gear continues to produce 2,000 units a week at a cost of $8,000 a unit and incurs a loss of $500 a unit, or $1 million a week. This economic loss is shown by the red rectangle in part (a). Trick produces 3,000 units a week at a cost of $6,000 a unit. With a price of $7,500, Trick makes a profit of $1,500 a unit and therefore an economic profit of $4.5 million. This economic profit is the blue rectangle in part (b).

We've now described a second possible outcome for the duopoly game: One of the firms cheats on the collusive agreement. In this case, the industry output is larger than the monopoly output and the industry price is lower than the monopoly price. The total economic profit made by the industry is also smaller than the monopoly's economic profit. Trick (the cheat) makes an economic profit of $4.5 million, and Gear (the complier) incurs an economic loss of $1 million. The industry makes an economic profit of $3.5 million. This industry profit is $0.5 million less than the economic profit that a monopoly would make, but it is distributed unevenly. Trick makes a bigger economic profit than it would under the collusive agreement, while Gear incurs an economic loss.

A similar outcome would arise if Gear cheated and Trick complied with the agreement. The industry profit and price would be the same, but in this case, Gear (the cheat) would make an economic profit of $4.5 million and Trick (the complier) would incur an economic loss of $1 million.

Let's next see what happens if both firms cheat.

FIGURE 13.4   One Firm Cheats

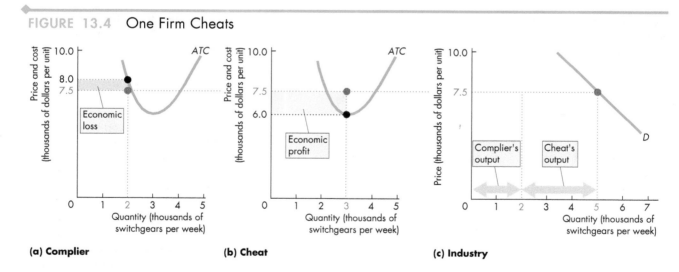

(a) Complier   **(b) Cheat**   **(c) Industry**

One firm, shown in part (a), complies with the agreement and produces 2,000 units. The other firm, shown in part (b), cheats on the agreement and increases its output to 3,000 units a week. Given the market demand curve, shown in part (c), and with a total production of 5,000 units a week,

the price falls to $7,500 a unit. At this price, the complier in part (a) incurs an economic loss of $1 million ($500 per unit × 2,000 units), shown by the red rectangle. In part (b), the cheat makes an economic profit of $4.5 million ($1,500 per unit × 3,000 units), shown by the blue rectangle.

Both Firms Cheat Suppose that both firms cheat and that each firm behaves like the cheating firm that we have just analyzed. Each tells the other that it is unable to sell its output at the going price and that it plans to cut its price. But because both firms cheat, each will propose a successively lower price. As long as price exceeds marginal cost, each firm has an incentive to increase its production—to cheat. Only when price equals marginal cost is there no further incentive to cheat. This situation arises when the price has reached $6,000. At this price, marginal cost equals price. Also, price equals minimum average total cost. At a price less than $6,000, each firm incurs an economic loss. At a price of $6,000, each firm covers all its costs and makes zero economic profit. Also, at a price of $6,000, each firm wants to produce 3,000 units a week, so the industry output is 6,000 units a week. Given the demand conditions, 6,000 units can be sold at a price of $6,000 each.

Figure 13.5 illustrates the situation just described. Each firm, in part (a), produces 3,000 units a week, and its average total cost is a minimum ($6,000 per unit). The market as a whole, in part (b), operates at the point at which the market demand curve (*D*) intersects the industry marginal cost curve (*MC₁*). Each firm has lowered its price and increased its output to try to gain an advantage over the other firm. Each has pushed this process as far as it can without incurring an economic loss.

We have now described a third possible outcome of this duopoly game: Both firms cheat. If both firms

cheat on the collusive agreement, the output of each firm is 3,000 units a week and the price is $6,000 a unit. Each firm makes zero economic profit.

The Payoff Matrix Now that we have described the strategies and payoffs in the duopoly game, we can summarize the strategies and the payoffs in the form of the game's payoff matrix. Then we can find the Nash equilibrium.

Table 13.2 sets out the payoff matrix for this game. It is constructed in the same way as the payoff matrix for the prisoners' dilemma in Table 13.1. The squares show the payoffs for the two firms—Gear and Trick. In this case, the payoffs are profits. (For the prisoners' dilemma, the payoffs were losses.)

The table shows that if both firms cheat (top left), they achieve the perfectly competitive outcome— each firm makes zero economic profit. If both firms comply (bottom right), the industry makes the monopoly profit and each firm makes an economic profit of $2 million. The top right and bottom left squares show the payoff if one firm cheats while the other complies. The firm that cheats makes an economic profit of $4.5 million, and the one that complies incurs a loss of $1 million.

Nash Equilibrium in the Duopolists' Dilemma The duopolists have a dilemma like the prisoners' dilemma. Do they comply or cheat? To answer this question, we must find the Nash equilibrium.

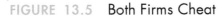

FIGURE 13.5   Both Firms Cheat

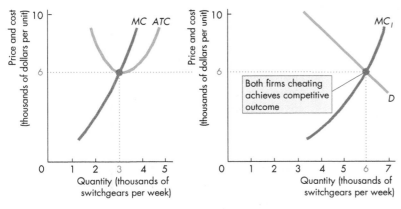

(a) Individual firm   (b) Industry

If both firms cheat by increasing production, the collusive agreement collapses. The limit to the collapse is the competitive equilibrium. Neither firm will cut its price below $6,000 (minimum average total cost) because to do so will result in losses. In part (a), each firm produces 3,000 units a week at an average total cost of $6,000. In part (b), with a total production of 6,000 units, the price falls to $6,000. Each firm now makes zero economic profit. This output and price are the ones that would prevail in a competitive industry.

TABLE 13.2　Duopoly Payoff Matrix

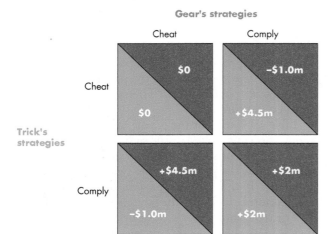

Gear's strategies

	Cheat	Comply
Cheat	$0 / $0	−$1.0m / +$4.5m
Comply	+$4.5m / −$1.0m	+$2m / +$2m

Trick's strategies

Each square shows the payoffs from a pair of actions. For example, if both firms comply with the collusive agreement, the payoffs are recorded in the bottom right square. The red triangle shows Gear's payoff, and the blue triangle shows Trick's. In Nash equilibrium, both firms cheat.

Look at things from Gear's point of view. Gear reasons as follows: Suppose that Trick cheats. If I comply, I will incur an economic loss of $1 million. If I also cheat, I will make zero economic profit. Zero is better than *minus* $1 million, so I'm better off if I cheat. Now suppose Trick complies. If I cheat, I will make an economic profit of $4.5 million, and if I comply, I will make an economic profit of $2 million. A $4.5 million profit is better than a $2 million profit, so I'm better off if I cheat. So regardless of whether Trick cheats or complies, it pays Gear to cheat. Cheating is Gear's best strategy.

Trick comes to the same conclusion as Gear because the two firms face an identical situation. So both firms cheat. The Nash equilibrium of the duopoly game is that both firms cheat. And although the industry has only two firms, they charge the same price and produce the same quantity as those in a competitive industry. Also, as in perfect competition, each firm makes zero economic profit.

This conclusion is not general and will not always arise. We'll see why not by looking first at some other games that are like the prisoners' dilemma. Then we'll broaden the types of games we consider.

Other Oligopoly Games

Firms in oligopoly must decide whether to mount expensive advertising campaigns; whether to modify their product; whether to make their product more reliable and more durable; whether to price discriminate and, if so, among which groups of customers and to what degree; whether to undertake a large research and development (R&D) effort aimed at lowering production costs; and whether to enter or leave an industry.

All of these choices can be analyzed as games that are similar to the one that we've just studied. Let's look at one example: an R&D game.

Economics in Action
An R&D Game in the Market for Diapers

Disposable diapers have been around for a bit more than 40 years. Procter & Gamble (which has a 40 percent market share with Pampers) and Kimberly-Clark (which has a 33 percent market share with Huggies) have always been the market leaders.

When the disposable diaper was first introduced, it had to be cost-effective in competition with reusable, laundered diapers. A costly research and development effort resulted in the development of machines that could make disposable diapers at a low enough cost to achieve that initial competitive edge. But new firms tried to get into the business and take market share away from the two industry leaders, and the industry leaders themselves battled each other to maintain or increase their own market shares.

During the early 1990s, Kimberly-Clark was the first to introduce Velcro closures. And in 1996, Procter & Gamble was the first to introduce "breathable" diapers.

The key to success in this industry (as in any other) is to design a product that people value highly relative to the cost of producing it. The firm that creates the most highly valued product and also develops the least-cost technology for producing it gains a competitive edge, undercutting the rest of the market, increasing its market share, and increasing its profit.

But the R&D that must be undertaken to improve product quality and cut cost is itself costly. So the cost of R&D must be deducted from the profit resulting from the increased market share that lower costs achieve. If no firm does R&D, every firm can be better off, but if one firm initiates the R&D activity, all must follow.

Table 13.3 illustrates the dilemma (with hypothetical numbers) for the R&D game that Kimberly-Clark and Procter & Gamble play. Each firm has two strategies: Spend $25 million a year on R&D or spend nothing on R&D. If neither firm spends on R&D, they make a joint profit of $100 million: $30 million for Kimberly-Clark and $70 million for Procter & Gamble (bottom right of the payoff matrix). If each firm conducts R&D, market shares are maintained but each firm's profit is lower by the amount spent on R&D (top left square of the payoff matrix). If Kimberly-Clark pays for R&D but Procter & Gamble does not, Kimberly-Clark gains a large part of Procter & Gamble's market. Kimberly-Clark profits, and Procter & Gamble loses (top right square of the payoff matrix). Finally, if Procter & Gamble conducts R&D and Kimberly-Clark does not, Procter & Gamble gains market share from Kimberly-Clark, increasing its profit, while Kimberly-Clark incurs a loss (bottom left square).

TABLE 13.3   Pampers Versus Huggies:
An R&D Game

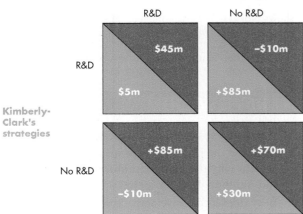

If both firms undertake R&D, their payoffs are those shown in the top left square. If neither firm undertakes R&D, their payoffs are in the bottom right square. When one firm undertakes R&D and the other one does not, their payoffs are in the top right and bottom left squares. The red triangle shows Procter & Gamble's payoff, and the blue triangle shows Kimberly-Clark's. The Nash equilibrium for this game is for both firms to undertake R&D. The structure of this game is the same as that of the prisoners' dilemma.

Confronted with the payoff matrix in Table 13.3, the two firms calculate their best strategies. Kimberly-Clark reasons as follows: If Procter & Gamble does not undertake R&D, we will make $85 million if we do and $30 million if we do not; so it pays us to conduct R&D. If Procter & Gamble conducts R&D, we will lose $10 million if we don't and make $5 million if we do. Again, R&D pays off. So conducting R&D is the best strategy for Kimberly-Clark. It pays, regardless of Procter & Gamble's decision.

Procter & Gamble reasons similarly: If Kimberly-Clark does not undertake R&D, we will make $70 million if we follow suit and $85 million if we conduct R&D. It therefore pays to conduct R&D. If Kimberly-Clark does undertake R&D, we will make $45 million by doing the same and lose $10 million by not doing R&D. Again, it pays us to conduct R&D. So for Procter & Gamble, R&D is also the best strategy.

Because R&D is the best strategy for both players, it is the Nash equilibrium. The outcome of this game is that both firms conduct R&D. They make less profit than they would if they could collude to achieve the cooperative outcome of no R&D.

The real-world situation has more players than Kimberly-Clark and Procter & Gamble. A large number of other firms share a small portion of the market, all of them ready to eat into the market share of Procter & Gamble and Kimberly-Clark. So the R&D efforts by these two firms not only serve the purpose of maintaining shares in their own battle but also help to keep barriers to entry high enough to preserve their joint market share.

The Disappearing Invisible Hand

All the games that we've studied are versions of the prisoners' dilemma. The essence of that game lies in the structure of its payoffs. The worst possible outcome for each player arises from cooperating when the other player cheats. The best possible outcome, for each player to cooperate, is not a Nash equilibrium because it is in neither player's *self-interest* to cooperate if the other one cooperates. It is this failure to achieve the best outcome for both players—the best social outcome if the two players are the entire economy—that led John Nash to claim (as he was portrayed as doing in the movie *A Beautiful Mind*) that he had challenged Adam Smith's idea that we are always guided, as if by an invisible hand, to promote the social interest when we are pursuing our self-interest.

A Game of Chicken

The Nash equilibrium for the prisoners' dilemma is unique: both players cheat (confess). Not all games have a unique equilibrium, and one that doesn't is a game called "chicken."

An Example of the Game of Chicken A graphic, if disturbing, version of "chicken" has two cars racing toward each other. The first driver to swerve and avoid a crash is the "chicken." The payoffs are a big loss for both if no one "chickens out;" zero for both if both "chicken out;" and zero for the chicken and a gain for the one who stays the course. If player 1 swerves, player 2's best strategy is to stay the course; and if player 1 stays the course, player 2's best strategy is to swerve.

An Economic Example of Chicken An economic game of chicken can arise when R&D creates a new technology that cannot be kept secret or patented, so both firms benefit from the R&D of either firm. The chicken in this case is the firm that does the R&D.

Suppose, for example, that either Apple or Nokia spends $9 million developing a new touch-screen technology that both would end up being able to use regardless of which of them developed it.

Table 13.4 illustrates a payoff matrix for the game that Apple and Nokia play. Each firm has two strategies: Do the R&D ("chicken out") or do not do the R&D. Each entry shows the additional profit (the profit from the new technology minus the cost of the research), given the strategies adopted.

If neither firm does the R&D, each makes zero additional profit. If both firms conduct the R&D, each firm makes an additional $5 million. If one of the firms does the R&D ("chickens out"), the chicken makes $1 million and the other firm makes $10 million. Confronted with these payoffs the two firms calculate their best strategies. Nokia is better off doing R&D if Apple does no R&D. Apple is better off doing R&D if Nokia does no R&D. There are two Nash equilibrium outcomes: Only one of them does the R&D, but we can't predict which one.

You can see that an outcome with no firm doing R&D isn't a Nash equilibrium because one firm would be better off doing it. Also both firms doing R&D isn't a Nash equilibrium because one firm would be better off *not* doing it. To decide *which* firm does the R&D, the firms might toss a coin, called a mixed strategy.

TABLE 13.4   An R&D Game of Chicken

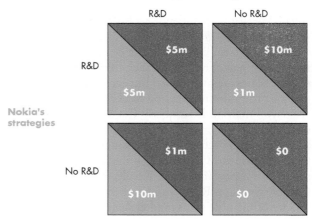

If neither firm does the R&D, their payoffs are in the bottom right square. When one firm "chickens out" and does the R&D while the other does no R&D, their payoffs are in the top right and bottom left squares. When both "chicken out" and do the R&D, the payoffs are in the top left square. The red triangle shows Apple's payoff, and the blue triangle shows Nokia's. The equilibrium for this R&D game of chicken is for only one firm to undertake the R&D. We cannot tell which firm will do the R&D and which will not.

REVIEW QUIZ

1 What are the common features of all games?
2 Describe the prisoners' dilemma game and explain why the Nash equilibrium delivers a bad outcome for both players.
3 Why does a collusive agreement to restrict output and raise price create a game like the prisoners' dilemma?
4 What creates an incentive for firms in a collusive agreement to cheat and increase production?
5 What is the equilibrium strategy for each firm in a duopolists' dilemma and why do the firms not succeed in colluding to raise the price and profits?
6 Describe two structures of payoffs for an R&D game and contrast the prisoners' dilemma and the chicken game.

You can work these questions in Study Plan 13.2 and get instant feedback.

Repeated Games and Sequential Games

The games that we've studied are played just once. In contrast, many real-world games are played repeatedly. This feature of games turns out to enable real-world duopolists to cooperate, collude, and make a monopoly profit.

Another feature of the games that we've studied is that the players move simultaneously. But in many real-world situations, one player moves first and then the other moves—the play is sequential rather than simultaneous. This feature of real-world games creates a large number of possible outcomes.

We're now going to examine these two aspects of strategic decision-making.

A Repeated Duopoly Game

If two firms play a game repeatedly, one firm has the opportunity to penalize the other for previous "bad" behavior. If Gear cheats this week, perhaps Trick will cheat next week. Before Gear cheats this week, won't it consider the possibility that Trick will cheat next week? What is the equilibrium of this game?

Actually, there is more than one possibility. One is the Nash equilibrium that we have just analyzed. Both players cheat, and each makes zero economic profit forever. In such a situation, it will never pay one of the players to start complying unilaterally because to do so would result in a loss for that player and a profit for the other. But a **cooperative equilibrium** in which the players make and share the monopoly profit is possible.

A cooperative equilibrium might occur if cheating is punished. There are two extremes of punishment. The smallest penalty is called "tit for tat." A *tit-for-tat strategy* is one in which a player cooperates in the current period if the other player cooperated in the previous period, but cheats in the current period if the other player cheated in the previous period. The most severe form of punishment is called a trigger strategy. A *trigger strategy* is one in which a player cooperates if the other player cooperates but plays the Nash equilibrium strategy forever thereafter if the other player cheats.

In the duopoly game between Gear and Trick, a tit-for-tat strategy keeps both players cooperating and making monopoly profits. Let's see why with an example.

Table 13.5 shows the economic profit that Trick and Gear will make over a number of periods under two alternative sequences of events: colluding and cheating with a tit-for-tat response by the other firm.

If both firms stick to the collusive agreement in period 1, each makes an economic profit of $2 million. Suppose that Trick contemplates cheating in period 1. The cheating produces a quick $4.5 million economic profit and inflicts a $1 million economic loss on Gear. But a cheat in period 1 produces a response from Gear in period 2. If Trick wants to get back into a profit-making situation, it must return to the agreement in period 2 even though it knows that Gear will punish it for cheating in period 1. So in period 2, Gear punishes Trick and Trick cooperates. Gear now makes an economic profit of $4.5 million, and Trick incurs an economic loss of $1 million. Adding up the profits over two periods of play, Trick would have made more profit by cooperating—$4 million compared with $3.5 million.

What is true for Trick is also true for Gear. Because each firm makes a larger profit by sticking with the collusive agreement, both firms do so and the monopoly price, quantity, and profit prevail.

In reality, whether a cartel works like a one-play game or a repeated game depends primarily on the

TABLE 13.5 Cheating with Punishment

Period of play	Collude		Cheat with tit-for-tat	
	Trick's profit	Gear's profit	Trick's profit	Gear's profit
	(millions of dollars)		(millions of dollars)	
1	2	2	4.5	−1.0
2	2	2	−1.0	4.5
3	2	2	2.0	2.0
4	.	.	.	.

If duopolists repeatedly collude, each makes a profit of $2 million per period of play. If one player cheats in period 1, the other player plays a tit-for-tat strategy and cheats in period 2. The profit from cheating can be made for only one period and must be paid for in the next period by incurring a loss. Over two periods of play, the best that a duopolist can achieve by cheating is a profit of $3.5 million, compared to an economic profit of $4 million by colluding.

number of players and the ease of detecting and punishing cheating. The larger the number of players, the harder it is to maintain a cartel.

Games and Price Wars

A repeated duopoly game can help us understand real-world behavior and, in particular, price wars. Some price wars can be interpreted as the implementation of a tit-for-tat strategy. But the game is a bit more complicated than the one we've looked at because the players are uncertain about the demand for the product.

Playing a tit-for-tat strategy, firms have an incentive to stick to the monopoly price. But fluctuations in demand lead to fluctuations in the monopoly price, and sometimes, when the price changes, it might seem to one of the firms that the price has fallen because the other has cheated. In this case, a price war will break out. The price war will end only when each firm is satisfied that the other is ready to cooperate again. There will be cycles of price wars and the restoration of collusive agreements. Fluctuations in the world price of oil might be interpreted in this way.

Some price wars arise from the entry of a small number of firms into an industry that had previously been a monopoly. Although the industry has a small number of firms, the firms are in a prisoners' dilemma and they cannot impose effective penalties for price cutting. The behavior of prices and outputs in the computer chip industry during 1995 and 1996 can be explained in this way. Until 1995, the market for Pentium chips for IBM-compatible computers was dominated by one firm, Intel Corporation, which was able to make maximum economic profit by producing the quantity of chips at which marginal cost equaled marginal revenue. The price of Intel's chips was set to ensure that the quantity demanded equaled the quantity produced. Then in 1995 and 1996, with the entry of a small number of new firms, the industry became an oligopoly. If the firms had maintained Intel's price and shared the market, together they could have made economic profits equal to Intel's profit. But the firms were in a prisoners' dilemma, so prices fell toward the competitive level.

Let's now study a sequential game. There are many such games, and the one we'll examine is among the simplest. It has an interesting implication and it will give you the flavor of this type of game. The sequential game that we'll study is an entry game in a contestable market.

A Sequential Entry Game in a Contestable Market

If two firms play a sequential game, one firm makes a decision at the first stage of the game and the other makes a decision at the second stage.

We're going to study a sequential game in a **contestable market**—a market in which firms can enter and leave so easily that firms in the market face competition from *potential* entrants. Examples of contestable markets are routes served by airlines and by barge companies that operate on the major waterways. These markets are contestable because firms could enter if an opportunity for economic profit arose and could exit with no penalty if the opportunity for economic profit disappeared.

If the Herfindahl-Hirschman Index (p. 171) is used to determine the degree of competition, a contestable market appears to be uncompetitive. But a contestable market can behave as if it were perfectly competitive. To see why, let's look at an entry game for a contestable air route.

A Contestable Air Route

Agile Air is the only firm operating on a particular route. Demand and cost conditions are such that there is room for only one airline to operate. Wanabe Inc. is another airline that could offer services on the route.

We describe the structure of a sequential game by using a *game tree* like that in Fig. 13.6. At the first stage, Agile Air must set a price. Once the price is set and advertised, Agile can't change it. That is, once set, Agile's price is fixed and Agile can't react to Wanabe's entry decision. Agile can set its price at either the monopoly level or the competitive level.

At the second stage, Wanabe must decide whether to enter or to stay out. Customers have no loyalty (there are no frequent-flyer programs) and they buy from the lowest-price firm. So if Wanabe enters, it sets a price just below Agile's and takes all the business.

Figure 13.6 shows the payoffs from the various decisions (Agile's in the red triangles and Wanabe's in the blue triangles).

To decide on its price, Agile's CEO reasons as follows: Suppose that Agile sets the monopoly price. If Wanabe enters, it earns 90 (think of all payoff numbers as thousands of dollars). If Wanabe stays out, it earns nothing. So Wanabe will enter. In this case Agile will lose 50.

Now suppose that Agile sets the competitive price. If Wanabe stays out, it earns nothing, and if it enters,

FIGURE 13.6   Agile Versus Wanabe: A Sequential Entry Game in a Contestable Market

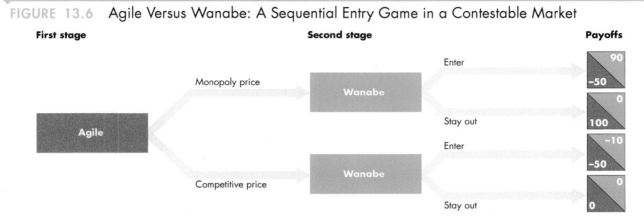

First stage

Second stage

Payoffs

Agile

Monopoly price

Wanabe

Enter — 90 / −50

Stay out — 0 / 100

Competitive price

Wanabe

Enter — −10 / −50

Stay out — 0 / 0

If Agile sets the monopoly price, Wanabe makes 90 (thousand dollars) by entering and earns nothing by staying out. So if Agile sets the monopoly price, Wanabe enters.

If Agile sets the competitive price, Wanabe earns nothing if it stays out and incurs a loss if it enters. So if Agile sets the competitive price, Wanabe stays out.

 myeconlab   animation

it loses 10, so Wanabe will stay out. In this case, Agile will make zero economic profit.

Agile's best strategy is to set its price at the competitive level and make zero economic profit. The option of earning 100 by setting the monopoly price with Wanabe staying out is not available to Agile. If Agile sets the monopoly price, Wanabe enters, undercuts Agile, and takes all the business.

In this example, Agile sets its price at the competitive level and makes zero economic profit. A less costly strategy, called **limit pricing**, sets the price at the highest level that inflicts a loss on the entrant. Any loss is big enough to deter entry, so it is not always necessary to set the price as low as the competitive price. In the example of Agile and Wanabe, at the competitive price, Wanabe incurs a loss of 10 if it enters. A smaller loss would still keep Wanabe out.

This game is interesting because it points to the possibility of a monopoly behaving like a competitive industry and serving the social interest without regulation. But the result is not general and depends on one crucial feature of the setup of the game: At the second stage, Agile is locked in to the price set at the first stage.

If Agile could change its price in the second stage, it would want to set the monopoly price if Wanabe stayed out—100 with the monopoly price beats zero with the competitive price. But Wanabe can figure out what Agile would do, so the price set at the first stage

has no effect on Wanabe. Agile sets the monopoly price and Wanabe might either stay out or enter.

We've looked at two of the many possible repeated and sequential games, and you've seen how these types of games can provide insights into the complex forces that determine prices and profits.

REVIEW QUIZ

1 If a prisoners' dilemma game is played repeatedly, what punishment strategies might the players employ and how does playing the game repeatedly change the equilibrium?

2 If a market is contestable, how does the equilibrium differ from that of a monopoly?

You can work these questions in Study Plan 13.3 and get instant feedback.    myeconlab

So far, we've studied oligopoly with unregulated market power. Firms like Trick and Gear are free to collude to maximize their profit with no concern for the consumer or the law.

But when firms collude to achieve the monopoly outcome, they also have the same effects on efficiency and the social interest as monopoly. Profit is made at the expense of consumer surplus and a deadweight loss arises. Your next task is to see how U.S. antitrust law limits market power.

SUMMARY

Key Points

What Is Oligopoly? (pp. 264–265)

- Oligopoly is a market in which a small number of firms compete.

Working Problems 1 to 3 will give you a better understanding of what oligopoly is.

Oligopoly Games (pp. 266–274)

- Oligopoly is studied by using game theory, which is a method of analyzing strategic behavior.
- In a prisoners' dilemma game, two prisoners acting in their own self-interest harm their joint interest.
- An oligopoly (duopoly) price-fixing game is a prisoners' dilemma in which the firms might collude or cheat.

- In Nash equilibrium, both firms cheat and output and price are the same as in perfect competition.
- Firms' decisions about advertising and R&D can be studied by using game theory.

Working Problems 4 to 7 will give you a better understanding of oligopoly games.

Repeated Games and Sequential Games (pp. 275–277)

- In a repeated game, a punishment strategy can produce a cooperative equilibrium in which price and output are the same as in a monopoly.
- In a sequential contestable market game, a small number of firms can behave like firms in perfect competition.

Working Problem 8 will give you a better understanding of repeated and sequential games.

Key Terms

Cartel, 265
Collusive agreement, 268
Contestable market, 276
Cooperative equilibrium, 275

Dominant-strategy equilibrium, 267
Duopoly, 264
Game theory, 266
Limit pricing, 277

Nash equilibrium, 267
Oligopoly, 264
Payoff matrix, 266
Strategies, 266

STUDY PLAN PROBLEMS AND APPLICATIONS

 You can work Problems 1 to 8 in MyEconLab Chapter 13 Study Plan and get instant feedback.

What Is Oligopoly? (Study Plan 13.1)

1. Two firms make most of the chips that power a PC: Intel and Advanced Micro Devices. What makes the market for PC chips a duopoly? Sketch the market demand curve and cost curves that describe the situation in this market and that prevent other firms from entering.

2. **Sparks Fly for Energizer**

   Energizer is gaining market share against competitor Duracell and its profit is rising despite the sharp rise in the price of zinc, a key battery ingredient.

   Source: www.businessweek.com, August 2007

   In what type of market are batteries sold? Explain your answer.

3. **Oil City**

   In the late 1990s, Reliance spent $6 billion to build a world-class oil refinery at Jamnagar, India. Now Reliance is more than doubling the size of the facility, which will make it the world's biggest producer of gasoline —1.2 million gallons of gasoline per day, or about 5% of global capacity. Reliance plans to sell the gasoline in the United States and Europe where it's too expensive and politically difficult to build new refineries. The bulked-up Jamnagar will be able to move the market and Singapore traders expect a drop in fuel prices as soon as it's going at full steam.

   Source: *Fortune*, April 28, 2008

   a. Explain why the news clip claims that the global market for gasoline is not perfectly competitive.

   b. What barriers to entry might limit competition in this market and give a firm such as Reliance power to influence the market price?

Oligopoly Games (Study Plan 13.2)

4. Consider a game with two players who cannot communicate, and in which each player is asked a question. The players can answer the question honestly or lie. If both answer honestly, each receives $100. If one player answers honestly and the other lies, the liar receives $500 and the honest player gets nothing. If both lie, then each receives $50.

   a. Describe the strategies and payoffs of this game.

   b. Construct the payoff matrix.

   c. What is the equilibrium of this game?

   d. Compare this game to the prisoners' dilemma. Are the two games similar or different? Explain.

Use the following information to work Problems 5 and 6.

Soapy Inc. and Suddies Inc. are the only producers of soap powder. They collude and agree to share the market equally. If neither firm cheats on the agreement, each makes $1 million profit. If either firm cheats, the cheat makes a profit of $1.5 million, while the complier incurs a loss of $0.5 million. If both cheat, they break even. Neither firm can monitor the other's actions.

5. a. What are the strategies in this game?

   b. Construct the payoff matrix for this game.

6. a. What is the equilibrium of this game if it is played only once?

   b. Is the equilibrium a dominant-strategy equilibrium? Explain.

7. **The World's Largest Airline**

   On May 3, 2010, United Airlines and Continental Airlines announced a $3 billion merger that would create the world's biggest airline. The deal was completed in a remarkably short three weeks, and would give the airlines the muscle to fend off low-cost rivals at home and to take on foreign carriers abroad. For consumers, the merger could eventually result in higher prices although the new company does not intend to raise fares. One of the rationales for airline mergers is to cut capacity.

   Source: *The New York Times*, June 7, 2010

   a. Explain how this airline merger might increase air travel prices.

   b. Explain how this airline merger might lower air travel production costs.

   c. Explain how cost savings arising from a cut in capacity might get passed on to travelers and might boost producers' profits. Which do you predict will happen from this airline merger and why?

Repeated Games and Sequential Games

(Study Plan 13.3)

8. If Soapy Inc. and Suddies Inc., repeatedly play the duopoly game that has the payoffs described in Problem 5, on each round of play:
   a. What now are the strategies that each firm might adopt?

   b. Can the firms adopt a strategy that gives the game a cooperative equilibrium?
   c. Would one firm still be tempted to cheat in a cooperative equilibrium? Explain your answer.

After studying this chapter,
you will be able to:

◆ Explain why some choices are *public* choices and
  how these choices are made in the political marketplace

◆ Explain how the free-rider problem arises and how
  the quantity of public goods is determined

◆ Explain why mixed goods with external benefits lead
  to inefficient underproduction and how public production, subsidies, and vouchers can achieve allocative
  efficiency

14

PUBLIC GOODS

Fighting a California wildfire, screening passengers at an airport, providing
good schools and colleges, defending the nation's borders and interests
around the globe, policing neighborhoods and highways, operating courts and
a legal system: Governments are involved in all these activities. But why? Why
does government provide some goods and services and not others? Why don't
we leave it to private firms to provide and sell *all* goods and services? Do
governments overprovide or underprovide—provide too much or too little?
These are the questions we study in this chapter.

We begin by classifying goods and services and explaining the economic
theory of why and how governments intervene in markets, or even replace
them. We apply this theory to the provision of public services. Two such
public services are education and health care. You will see how the political
marketplace provides these services.

In *Reading Between the Lines* at the end of the chapter, we look at some of
the strengths and weaknesses of the 2010 Affordable Care Act.

What is a Public Good?

To see what makes a good a *public* good, we distinguish two features of all goods: the extent to which people can be *excluded* from consuming them and the extent to which one person's consumption *rivals* the consumption of others.

Excludable A good is **excludable** if it is possible to prevent someone from enjoying its benefits. Brink's security services, East Point Seafood's fish, and a U2 concert are examples. People must pay to benefit from them.

A good is **nonexcludable** if it is impossible (or extremely costly) to prevent anyone from benefiting from it. The services of the LAPD, fish in the Pacific Ocean, and a concert on network television are examples. When an LAPD cruiser enforces the speed limit, everyone on the highway benefits; anyone with a boat can fish in the ocean; and anyone with a TV can watch a network broadcast.

Rival A good is **rival** if one person's use of it decreases the quantity available for someone else. A Brink's truck can't deliver cash to two banks at the same time. A fish can be consumed only once.

A good is **nonrival** if one person's use of it does not decrease the quantity available for someone else. The services of the LAPD and a concert on network television are nonrival. One person's benefit doesn't lower the benefit of others.

A Fourfold Classification

Figure 14.2 classifies goods, services, and resources into four types.

Private Goods A **private good** is both rival and excludable. A can of Coke and a fish on East Point Seafood's farm are examples of private goods.

Public Goods A **public good** is both nonrival and nonexcludable. A public good simultaneously benefits everyone, and no one can be excluded from its benefits. National defense is the best example of a public good.

Common Resources A **common resource** is rival and nonexcludable. A unit of a common resource can be used only once, but no one can be prevented from using what is available. Ocean fish are a common resource. They are rival because a fish taken by one person isn't available for anyone else, and they are

FIGURE 14.2   Fourfold Classification of Goods

	Private goods	Common resources
Rival	Food and drink Car House	Fish in ocean Atmosphere National parks
	Natural monopoly goods	**Public goods**
Nonrival	Internet Cable television Bridge or tunnel	National defense The law Air traffic control
	Excludable	Nonexcludable

A private good is one for which consumption is rival and from which consumers can be excluded. A public good is one for which consumption is nonrival and from which it is impossible to exclude a consumer. A common resource is one that is rival but nonexcludable. A good that is nonrival but excludable is produced by a natural monopoly.

 myeconlab animation

nonexcludable because it is difficult to prevent people from catching them.

Natural Monopoly Goods A **natural monopoly good** is nonrival and excludable. When buyers can be excluded if they don't pay but the good is nonrival, marginal cost is zero. The fixed cost of producing such a good is usually high so economies of scale exist over the entire range of output for which there is a demand (see p. 222). An iTunes song and cable television are examples of natural monopoly goods.

Mixed Goods and Externalities

Some goods don't fit neatly into the four-fold classification of Fig. 14.2. They are mixed goods. A **mixed good** is a private good the production or consumption of which creates an externality. An **externality** is a cost (external cost) or a benefit (external benefit) that arises from the production or consumption of a private good and that falls on someone other than its producer or consumer. A **negative externality** imposes a cost and a **positive externality** provides a benefit.

We'll look at some examples of mixed goods with externalities and study those with positive externalities later in this chapter and those with negative externalities in Chapter 15.

Economics in Action
Is a Lighthouse a Public Good?

Built on Little Brewster Island in 1716 to guide ships into and out of the Boston Harbor, Boston Lighthouse was the first light station in North America.

For two centuries, economists used the lighthouse as an example of a public good. No one can be prevented from seeing its warning light—*nonexcludable*—and one person seeing its light doesn't prevent someone else from doing so too—*nonrival.*

Ronald Coase, who won the 1991 Nobel Prize for ideas he first developed when he was an undergraduate at the London School of Economics, discovered that before the nineteenth century, lighthouses in England were built and operated by private corporations that earned profits by charging tolls on ships docking at nearby ports. A ship that refused to pay the lighthouse toll was *excluded* from the port.

So the benefit arising from the services of a lighthouse is *excludable.* Because the services provided by a lighthouse are nonrival but excludable, a lighthouse is an example of a natural monopoly good and not a public good.

Mixed Goods with External Benefits Two of the things that have the greatest impact on your welfare, your education and health care, are mixed goods with external benefits.

Think about a flu vaccination. It is *excludable* because it would be possible to sell vaccinations and exclude those not willing to pay from benefiting from them. A flu vaccination is also *rival* because providing one person with a vaccination means one fewer available for everyone else. A flu vaccination is a private good, but it creates an externality.

If you decide to get a flu vaccination, you benefit from a lower risk of getting infected in the coming flu season. But if you avoid the flu, your neighbor who didn't get vaccinated has a better chance of avoiding it too. A flu vaccination brings a benefit to others, so it is a *mixed good* with an external benefit.

The external benefit of a flu vaccination is like a public good. It is nonexcludable because everyone with whom you come into contact benefits. You can't selectively benefit only your friends! And it is nonrival—protecting one person from the flu does not diminish the protection for others.

Your education is another example of a mixed good with external benefits. If all education was organized by private schools and universities, those not willing or able to pay would be excluded, and one person's place in a class would rival another's. So education is a private good.

But your being educated brings benefits to others. It brings benefits to your friends who enjoy your sharp, educated wit and it brings benefits to the community in which you live because well-educated people with a strong sense of fellowship and responsibility toward others make good neighbors. These external benefits are like a public good. You can't selectively decide who benefits from your good neighborliness and one person's enjoyment of your good behavior doesn't rival someone else's. So education is a mixed good with an external benefit.

Mixed Goods with External Costs Mixed goods with external costs have become a huge political issue in recent years. The main ones are electricity and transportation (road, rail, and air) produced by burning hydrocarbon fuels—coal, oil, and natural gas.

Electricity and transportation are excludable and rival—they are private goods. But when you use electricity or travel by car, bus, train, or airplane, carbon dioxide and other chemicals pour into the atmosphere. This consequence of consuming a private good creates an external cost and is a public bad. (A "bad" is the opposite of a good.) No one can be excluded from bearing the external cost and one person's discomfort doesn't rival another's. Electricity and transportation are mixed goods with external costs.

Other private goods that generate external costs include logging and the clearing of forests, which destroy the habitat of wildlife and influence the amount of carbon dioxide in the atmosphere; smoking cigarettes in a confined space, which imposes a health risk on others; and driving under the influence of alcohol, which increases the risk of accident and injury for others.

Inefficiencies that Require Public Choices

Public goods, mixed goods, common resources, and natural monopoly goods all create inefficiency problems that require public choices. Public choices must be made to

- Provide public goods and mixed goods
- Conserve common resources
- Regulate natural monopoly

Provide Public Goods and Mixed Goods Because no one can be excluded from enjoying the benefits of a public good, no one has an incentive to pay for their share of it. Even people with a social conscience have no incentive to pay because one person's enjoyment of a public good doesn't lower the enjoyment of others—it is nonrival.

If private firms tried to produce and sell public goods to consumers, they wouldn't remain in business for very long. The market economy would fail to deliver the efficient quantity of those goods. For example, there would be too little national defense, police services and law enforcement, courts and judges, storm-water and sewage disposal services.

important

Mixed goods pose a less extreme problem. The market economy would underprovide mixed goods with external benefits because their producers and consumers don't take the external benefits into account when they make their own choices. The market economy would overprovide mixed goods with

external costs because their producers and consumers don't take the external costs into account when they make their own choices.

Conserve Common Resources Because no one can be excluded from enjoying the benefits of a common resource, no one has an incentive to pay for their share of it or to conserve it for future enjoyment.

If boat owners are left to catch as much Southern Bluefin tuna as they wish, the stock will deplete and eventually the species will vanish. The market economy would overproduce tuna while stocks lasted and then underproduce as stocks ran out.

This problem, called the *tragedy of the commons*, requires public choices to limit the overuse and eventual destruction of common resources.

Regulate Natural Monopoly When people can be excluded from enjoying the benefits of a good if they don't pay for it, and when the good is nonrival, the marginal cost of producing it is zero. A natural monopoly can produce such a good at the lowest cost. But as Chapter 11 explains, when one firm serves a market, that firm maximizes profit by producing too little of the good.

You studied the regulation of natural monopoly in Chapter 11. This chapter and the next one study the other two public choices that must be made. In this chapter, we'll focus on the underprovision of public goods and mixed goods with external benefits. Chapter 15 studies mixed goods with external costs and conserving common resources.

REVIEW QUIZ

1 List three main reasons why governments exist.
2 Describe the political marketplace. Who demands, who supplies, and what is the political equilibrium?
3 Distinguish among public goods, private goods, common resources, natural monopoly goods, and mixed goods.
4 What are the problems that arise from public goods, common resources, natural monopoly goods, and mixed goods?

You can work these questions in Study Plan 14.1 and get instant feedback.

Providing Public Goods

Why do governments provide firefighting services? Why don't the people of California buy brush fire-fighting services from Firestorm, a private firm that competes for our dollars in the marketplace in the same way that McDonalds does? The answer is that firefighting is a public good. It is nonexcludable and nonrival and it has a free-rider problem.

The Free-Rider Problem

A free rider enjoys the benefits of a good or service without paying for it. Because a public good is provided for everyone to use and no one can be excluded from its benefits, no one has an incentive to pay his or her share of the cost. Everyone has an incentive to free ride. The **free-rider problem** is that the economy would provide an inefficiently small quantity of a public good. Marginal social benefit from the public good would exceed its marginal social cost and a deadweight loss would arise.

Let's look at the marginal social benefit and marginal social cost of a public good.

Marginal Social Benefit from a Public Good

Lisa and Max (the only people in a society) value fire-fighting airplanes. Figure 14.3(a) and 14.3(b) graph their marginal benefits from the airplanes as MB_L for Lisa and MB_M for Max. The marginal benefit from a public good (like that from a private good) diminishes as the quantity of the good increases.

Figure 14.3(c) shows the marginal *social* benefit curve, *MSB*. Because everyone gets the same quantity of a public good, its marginal social benefit curve is the sum of the marginal benefits of all the individuals at each *quantity*—it is the *vertical* sum of the individual marginal benefit curves. So the curve *MSB* is the marginal social benefit curve for the economy made up of Lisa and Max. For each airplane, Lisa's marginal benefit is added to Max's marginal benefit.

Contrast the *MSB* curve for a public good with that of a private good. To obtain the economy's *MSB* curve for a private good, we sum the *quantities demanded* by all the individuals at each *price*—we sum the individual marginal benefit curves *horizontally* (see Chapter 5, p. 96).

FIGURE 14.3 Benefits of a Public Good

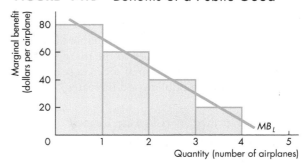

(a) Lisa's marginal benefit

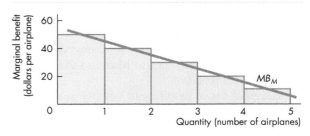

(b) Max's marginal benefit

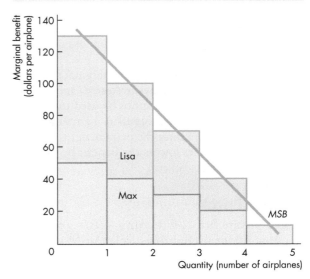

(c) Economy's marginal social benefit

The marginal social benefit at each quantity of the public good is the sum of the marginal benefits of all individuals. The marginal benefit curves are MB_L for Lisa and MB_M for Max. The economy's marginal social benefit curve is *MSB*.

 animation

Marginal Social Cost of a Public Good

The marginal social cost of a public good is determined in exactly the same way as that of a private good—see Chapter 5, p. 98. The principle of increasing marginal cost applies to the marginal cost of a public good, so the marginal social cost ~~decreases~~ *increases* as the quantity of the public good increases.

Efficient Quantity of a Public Good

To determine the efficient quantity of a public good, we use the principles that you learned in Chapter 5. The efficient quantity is that at which marginal social benefit equals marginal social cost.

Figure 14.4 shows the marginal social benefit curve, *MSB*, and the marginal social cost curve, *MSC*, for firefighting airplanes. (We'll now think of society as consisting of Lisa and Max and the other 39 million Californians.)

If marginal social benefit exceeds marginal social cost, as it does with 2 airplanes, resources can be used more efficiently by increasing the number of airplanes. The extra benefit exceeds the extra cost. If marginal social cost exceeds marginal social benefit, as it does with 4 airplanes, resources can be used more efficiently by decreasing the number of airplanes. The cost saving exceeds the loss of benefit.

If marginal social benefit equals marginal social cost, as it does with 3 airplanes, resources are allocated efficiently. Resources cannot be used more efficiently because to provide more than 3 airplanes increases cost by more than the extra benefit, and to provide fewer airplanes lowers the benefit by more than the cost saving.

Inefficient Private Provision

Could a private firm—Firestorm—deliver the efficient quantity of firefighting airplanes? Most likely it couldn't, because no one would have an incentive to buy his or her share of the airplanes. Everyone would reason as follows: The number of airplanes provided by Firestorm is not affected by my decision to pay my share or not. But my own private consumption will be greater if I free ride and do not pay my share of the cost of the airplanes. If I don't pay, I enjoy the same level of fire protection and I can buy more private goods. I will spend my money on private goods and free ride on fire protection. Such reasoning is the free-rider problem. If

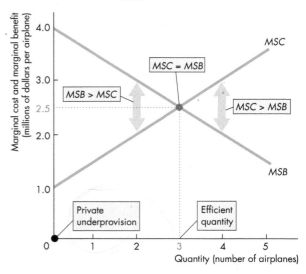

FIGURE 14.4   The Efficient Quantity of a Public Good

With fewer than 3 airplanes, marginal social benefit, *MSB*, exceeds marginal social cost, *MSC*. With more than 3 airplanes, *MSC* exceeds *MSB*. Only with 3 airplanes is *MSC* equal to *MSB* and the number of airplanes is efficient.

myeconlab   animation

everyone reasons the same way, Firestorm has no revenue and so provides no airplanes. Because the efficient number of airplanes is 3, private provision is inefficient.

◆ Providing Mixed Goods with External Benefits

Most of the goods and services provided by governments are *mixed* goods, not *public* goods. Two of the largest mixed goods with external benefits are education and health care. We're going to look at how governments operate ~~in such s.~~ We're also going to look at possible improvements on the current arrangements in these markets.

To keep our explanation clear, we'll focus first on the market for college education. We'll then apply the lessons we learn to the market for health care.

We begin our study of the provision of mixed goods by distinguishing between private benefits and social benefits.

Private Benefits and Social Benefits

A *private benefit* is a benefit that the consumer of a good or service receives. For example, expanded job opportunities and a higher income are private benefits of a college education.

Marginal benefit is the benefit from an *additional unit* of a good or service. So **marginal private benefit** (*MB*) is the benefit that the consumer of a good or service receives from an additional unit of it. When one additional student attends college, the benefit that student receives is the marginal private benefit from college education.

The *external benefit* from a good or service is the benefit that someone other than the consumer of the good or service receives. College graduates generate many external benefits. On average, they are better citizens, have lower crime rates, and are more tolerant of the views of others. They enable the success of high quality newspapers and television channels, music, theater, and other organized social activities that bring benefits to many other people.

A **marginal external benefit** is the benefit from an additional unit of a good or service that people *other than its consumer* enjoy. The benefit that your friends and neighbors get from your college education is the marginal external benefit of your college education.

Marginal social benefit (*MSB*) is the marginal benefit enjoyed by society—by the consumer of a good or service (marginal private benefit) and by others (the marginal external benefit). That is,

$$MSB = MB + \text{Marginal external benefit.}$$

Figure 14.7 shows an example of the relationship between marginal private benefit, marginal external benefit, and marginal social benefit. The marginal benefit curve, *MB*, describes the marginal private benefit enjoyed by the people who receive a college education. Marginal private benefit decreases as the number of students enrolled in college increases.

In the example in Fig. 14.7, when 15 million students enroll in college, the marginal external benefit is $15,000 per student per year . The marginal social benefit curve, *MSB*, is the sum of marginal private benefit and marginal external benefit at each number of students. For example, when 15 million students a year enroll in college, the marginal private benefit is $10,000 per student and the marginal external benefit is $15,000 per student, so the marginal social benefit is $25,000 per student.

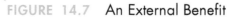

FIGURE 14.7   An External Benefit

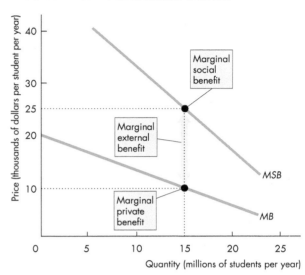

The *MB* curve shows the marginal private benefit enjoyed by the people who receive a college education. The *MSB* curve shows the sum of marginal private benefit and marginal external benefit. When 15 million students attend college, the marginal private benefit is $10,000 per student, the marginal external benefit is $15,000 per student, and the marginal social benefit is $25,000 per student.

myeconlab   animation

When people make schooling decisions, they ignore its external benefits and consider only its private benefits. So if education were provided by private schools that charged full-cost tuition, there would be too few college graduates.

Figure 14.8 illustrates this private underprovision. The supply curve is the marginal social cost curve, *S = MSC*. The demand curve is the marginal *private* benefit curve, *D = MB*. Market equilibrium occurs at a tuition of $15,000 per student per year and 7.5 million students per year. At this equilibrium, the marginal social benefit of $38,000 per student exceeds the marginal social cost by $23,000 per student. Too few students are enrolled in college. The efficient number is 15 million per year, where marginal social benefit equals marginal social cost. The gray triangle shows the deadweight loss created.

To get closer to producing the efficient quantity of a mixed good with an external benefit, we make public choices, through governments, to modify the market outcome.

FIGURE 14.8   Inefficiency with an External Benefit

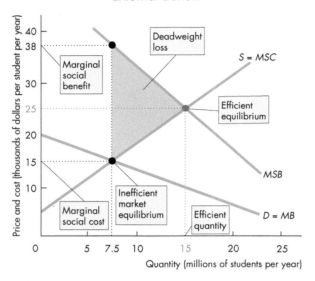

FIGURE 14.9   An Efficient Outcome with an External Benefit

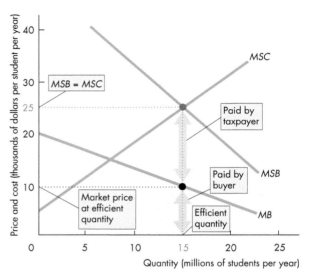

The market demand curve is the marginal private benefit curve, D = MB. The supply curve is the marginal social cost curve, S = MSC. Market equilibrium at a tuition of $15,000 a year and 7.5 million students is inefficient because marginal social benefit exceeds marginal social cost. The efficient quantity is 15 million students. A deadweight loss arises (gray triangle) because too few students enroll in college.

The efficient number of college students is 15 million, where marginal social benefit equals marginal social cost. With the demand and marginal private benefit curve, D = MB, the price at which the efficient number will enrol is $10,000 per year. If students pay this price, the taxpayer must somehow pay the rest, which equals the marginal external cost at the efficient quantity—$15,000 per student per year.

Government Actions in the Market for a Mixed Good with External Benefits

To encourage more students to enroll in college — to achieve an efficient quantity of college education—students must be confronted with a lower market price and the taxpayer must somehow pay for the costs not covered by what the student pays.

Figure 14.9 illustrates an efficient outcome. With marginal social cost curve MSC and marginal social benefit curve MSB, the efficient number of college students is 15,000. The marginal *private* benefit curve MB, tells us that 15,000 students will enroll only if the tuition is $10,000 per year. But the marginal social cost of 15,000 students is $25,000 per year. To enable the marginal social cost to be paid,

taxpayers must pay the balance of $15,000 per student per year.

Four devices that governments can use to achieve a more efficient allocation of resources in the presence of external benefits are

- Public production
- Private subsidies
- Vouchers

Public Production With **public production,** a good or service is produced by a public authority that receives its revenue from the government. The education ser-vices produced by state universities and colleges and public schools are examples of public production.

provision :— provide, supply

In the example in Fig. 14.9, efficient public production occurs if public colleges receive funds from government equal to $15,000 per student per year, charge tuition of $10,000 per student per year, and enrol 15 million students.

Private Subsidies A **subsidy** is a payment that the government makes to private producers. By making the subsidy depend on the level of output, the government can induce private decision-makers to consider external benefits when they make their choices.

In the example in Fig. 14.9, efficient private provision would occur if private colleges received a government subsidy of $15,000 per student per year. This subsidy reduces the colleges' costs and would make their marginal cost equal to $10,000 per student at the efficient quantity. Tuition of $10,000 would cover this cost, and the subsidy of $15,000 per student would cover the balance of the cost.

Vouchers A **voucher** is a token that the government provides to households, which they can use to buy specified goods or services. Food stamps are examples of vouchers. The vouchers (food stamps) can be spent only on food and are designed to improve the diet and health of extremely poor families.

School vouchers have been advocated as a means of improving the quality of education and are used in Washington D.C. A school voucher allows parents to choose the school their children will attend and to use the voucher to pay part of the cost. The school cashes the vouchers to pay its bills. A voucher could be provided to a college student in a similar way, and although technically not a voucher, a federal Pell Grant has a similar effect.

Because vouchers can be spent only on a specified item, they increase the willingness to pay for that item and so increase the demand for it.

Efficient provision of college education occurs if the government provides a voucher to each student with a value equal to the marginal external benefit at the efficient number of students. In the example in Fig. 14.9, the efficient number of students is 15 million and the voucher is valued at $15,000 per student. Each student pays $10,000 tuition and gives the college a $15,000 voucher. The colleges receive $25,000 per student, which equals their marginal cost.

Bureaucratic Inefficiency and Government Failure

You've seen three government actions that achieve an efficient provision of a mixed good with an external benefit. In each case, if the government estimates the marginal external benefit correctly and makes marginal social benefit equal to marginal social cost, the outcome is efficient.

Does the comparison that we've just made mean that pubic provision, subsidized private provision, and vouchers are equivalent? It does not. And the reason lies in something that you've already encountered in your study of public goods earlier in this chapter—the behavior of bureaucrats combined with rational ignorance that leads to government failure.

The Problem with Public Production Public colleges (and schools) are operated by a bureaucracy and are subject to the same problems as the provision of public goods. If bureaucrats seek to maximize their budgets, the outcome might be inefficient.

But *overprovision* of colleges (and schools) doesn't seem to be a problem. Just the opposite: People complain about *underprovision*—about inadequate public colleges and schools. The probable reason is that there is another type of bureaucratic budget maximization: budget padding and waste.

Bureaucrats often incur costs that exceed the minimum efficient cost. They might hire more assistants than the number needed to do their work efficiently; give themselves sumptuous offices; get generous expense allowances; build schools in the wrong places where land costs are too high.

Economists have studied the possibility that education bureaucrats pad their budgets by comparing the production costs of private and public colleges and schools. They have found that the costs per student of public schools are of the order of *three times* the costs of comparable private schools.

Problems with Private Subsidies Subsidizing private producers might overcome some of the problems created by public production. A private producer has an incentive to produce at minimum cost and avoid the budget padding of a bureaucratic producer. But two problems arise with private subsidies.

First, the subsidy budget must be allocated by a bureau. A national, state, or local department of education must lobby for its own budget and allocate this budget between school subsidies and its own administration costs. To the extent that the bureaucrats succeed in maximizing their own adminstration budget, they siphon off resources from schools and a problem similar to that of public production arises.

Second, it is in the self-interest of subsidized producers to maximize their subsidy. These producers might even spend some of the subsidy they receive lobbying for an even bigger one.

So neither public production nor subsidized private provision are likely to achieve an efficient allocation of resources in the face of external benefits.

Are Vouchers the Solution? Vouchers have four advantages over the other two approaches:

1. Vouchers can be used with public production, private provision, or competition between the two.
2. Governments can set the value of vouchers and the total voucher budget to overcome bureaucratic overprovision and budget padding.
3. Vouchers spread the public contribution thinly across millions of consumers, so no one consumer has an interest in wasting part of the value received in lobbying for overprovision.
4. By giving the buying power to the final consumer, producers must compete for business and provide a high standard of service at the lowest attainable cost.

For these four reasons, vouchers are popular with economists. But they are controversial and opposed by most education administrators and teachers.

In *The Economics of School Choice*, a book edited by Caroline M. Hoxby, economists study the effect of school choice on student achievement and school productivity and show how vouchers can be designed to achieve their goals while avoiding their potential pitfalls. Caroline Hoxby is confident that she can design a voucher that best achieves any educational and school performance objective.

Economics in Action
Delivering Health Care Efficiently

Americans spend 17 percent of income—$8,000 per person per year—on health care, which is more than double the average of other rich countries. And the cost is projected to rise as the population ages and the "baby boom" generation retires. Despite this enormous expenditure, until the passage of the 2010 Affordable Care Act, 47 million people had no health insurance and a further 25 million had too little insurance.

Of those who do have health insurance nearly 40 million are covered by the government's Medicare and Medicaid programs. These programs are in effect an open-ended commitment of public funds to the health care of the aged (Medicare) and those too poor to buy private health care (Medicaid). In 2035, when those born in 1955 turn 80, benefits under these programs will cost an estimated $50,000 per person per year. Benefits on these programs alone will cost more than 18 percent of the value of the nation's total production.

You can see that health care in the United States faces two problems: *underprovision* because private choices don't value all the external benefits; and *over expenditure* because private health-care producers decide how much to produce and then collect fees for their services from the government.

Health-Care Services

Health care is another example of a mixed good with external benefits. The external benefits from health care include avoiding infectious diseases, living and working with healthy neighbors, and for many people, just living in a society in which poor, sick people have access to affordable health care.

An additional problem arises in the case of health care: People with the biggest health problems are the elderly and the poor, who are least able to afford health care.

Because of its special features, no country just leaves the delivery of health care to the private market economy. In almost all countries, health care is provided at a zero price, or very low price, and doctors and other health-care professionals and the hospitals in which they work receive most (and in some cases all) their incomes from government.

The Obama Affordable Care Act addresses the first of these problems by requiring everyone to be insured and by creating a new Pre-Existing Condition Insurance Plan financed partly by the government.

But the act does little to address the problem of over-expenditure, and this problem is extremely serious. It is so serious that without massive change, the present open-ended health-care programs will bankrupt the United States.

Other countries contain health-care costs by limiting the budget and the number of physicians and hospital beds and by rationing services with long wait-times for treatment. This "solution" is inefficient because some people would be willing to pay more than the cost (marginal benefit exceeds marginal cost) and it is unfair (some people are better at playing the system than others and are able to jump the line).

A more effective solution to both the problem of coverage and access and the problem of over-expenditure has been suggested by Laurence Kotlikoff, an economics professor at Boston University. His proposal uses health-care vouchers to ensure universal coverage and a cap on total expenditure. His *Medicare Part C for all* is summarized in the ten-point plan in the next column.

This solution can deliver health care efficiently, distribute public funds among individuals based on their health status, and cap total expenditure.

Professor Laurence J. Kotlikoff of Boston University; author of *The Healthcare Fix* and creator of *Medicare Part C for all*.

1. Everyone is covered.
2. Every American gets a health-plan voucher.
3. Those with higher expected health-care costs receive bigger vouchers.
4. Can change health plan annually.
5. Government defines basic policy each year.
6. Basic policy covers drugs, home health care, and nursing home care.
7. Plans must cover basic policy.
8. Plans compete for participants.
9. Annual voucher budget is fixed as a percentage of the value of total production.
10. Medicare and employer-based health insurance tax breaks are eliminated.

In the United States, most health-care services are produced by private doctors and hospitals that receive their incomes from both governments and private health insurance companies. The health insurance companies in turn receive their income from employers and individual contributors.

Economics in Action (above) describes some of the features of health-care delivery in the United States and explains why it faces two serious problems, only one of which has been addressed by the Affordable Care Act of 2010.

Again, vouchers—health-care vouchers—are a crucial component of a program capable of achieving an efficient quantity and distribution of health-care services across individuals.

◆ *Reading Between the Lines* on pp. 292–293 looks at the effects of the 2010 Act and some of the problems that it brings.

REVIEW QUIZ

1 What is special about education and health care that makes them mixed goods with external benefits?

2 Why would the market economy produce too little education and health care?

3 How might public production, private subsidies, and vouchers achieve an efficient provision of a mixed good with external benefits?

4 What are the key differences among public production, private subsidies, and vouchers?

5 Why do economists generally favor vouchers rather than public production or subsidies to achieve an efficient outcome?

You can work these questions in Study Plan 14.3 and get instant feedback.

Reforming Health Care

Protective Net for All Residents; Q&A Legislation Details

Financial Times
March 22, 2010

What would the U.S. health-care bill do?

Offer or subsidise health-care coverage for 32m people, a tenth of the population, who are uninsured; mandate that every U.S. and legal resident receive minimal coverage.

Beginning in 2014, people who are out of work, self-employed, or working for companies that do not offer insurance could buy coverage from "health exchanges" in which private insurers would offer different kinds of plans.

About 19m people would be eligible for financial subsidies to help pay for insurance. If individuals refused to buy insurance coverage, they would be subject to a tax penalty.

How much would it cost and who is paying for it?

The non-partisan Congressional Budget Office estimates the bill would cost $940 billion over 10 years. This is expected to be paid for through tax on the wealthy and health-related industries, including a tax on so-called "Cadillac" insurance plans that would raise $32 billion over 10 years. The bill would also create a Medicare (the healthcare scheme for the elderly) commission that would have power to impose steep cuts in payments. Individuals making more than $200,000 a year, or couples making more than $250,000 a year, would pay higher taxes on Medicare and face a new 3.8 percent tax on dividends, interest, and other unearned income. The tax would take effect in January 2013. The CBO estimates the health-care bill would reduce the U.S. deficit by $138 billion over 10 years. ...

ESSENCE OF THE STORY

- Over the first ten years, health-care reform will cost $940 billion.

- Coverage will expand to 32 million American who are currently uninsured.

- New taxes will pay for the plan and cut the budget deficit.

- Medicaid will expand to cover about 19 million low-income people.

- Insurance companies will not be able to deny coverage for preexisting conditions.

- Except for some low-income families, everyone will be required to buy health insurance and will face penalties if they refuse to do so.

- Health care in the United States faces two problems: 1) *Underprovision* because private choices leave too many families and individuals without health insurance; 2) *Over expenditure* on public programs because the government pays for the quantity that patients demand and doctors supply.

- The health-care reform of 2010 (the Patient Protection and Affordable Care Act of 2010) addresses the first problem. It expands the scope of government provision of health care by covering more families and individuals and by improving the health-care insurance of those already covered. (The news article describes some of the details of the Act.)

- The 2010 Act notes the problem of cost containment but does little to address the main source of over expenditure: Medicare and Medicaid.

- Medicare and Medicaid remain and Medicaid will be expanded to cover more people.

- Figure 1 shows how Medicare and Medicaid overprovide services to those covered by the programs. The quantity is the quantity demanded by patients and supplied by doctors at a zero (or almost zero) price.

- Because the price is zero, marginal benefit, *MB*, is also zero.

- Doctors and hospitals negotiate fees with the government that equal marginal cost, which also equals marginal social cost, *MSC*.

- Marginal social cost, shown by the *MSC* curve, exceeds the (zero) marginal benefit. In this example, *MSC* is $25 at the quantity provided.

- Medicare and Medicaid services would be provided efficiently if marginal social cost, *MSC* equalled marginal social benefit, *MSB*.

- With overprovision, a deadweight loss arises shown by the gray triangle.

- Expenditure on Medicare and Medicaid equals the fee per unit of service multiplied by the quantity provided, and Fig. 2 illustrates this expenditure.

- The white rectangle shows what expenditure would be on the efficient quantity. The purple area shows the over expenditure. Total expenditure is the sum of these areas and equals $25 × 30 million.

- As the population gets older and as treatment techniques become more sophisticated and more conditions can be treated, the *MB* curve shifts rightward.

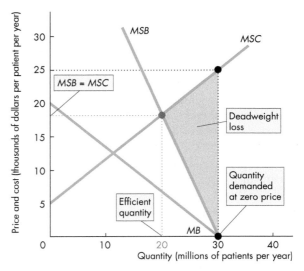

Figure 1 Overprovision of Medicare and Medicaid

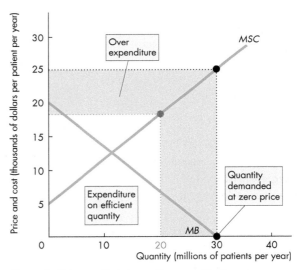

Figure 2 Uncontrolled expenditure on Medicare and Medicaid

- The quantity of health-care services provided by Medicare and Medicaid increases and the expenditure on these programs grows.

- A health-care voucher program like that explained on pp. 290–291 is one way (and possibly the only effective way) of achieving an efficient provision of Medicare and Medicaid and of containing their cost.

293

SUMMARY

Key Points

Providing Public Goods (pp. 285–286)

- Because a public good is a good or service that is *nonrival* and *nonexcludable*, it creates a *free-rider* problem: No one has an incentive to pay their share of the cost of providing a public good.
- The efficient level of provision of a public good is that at which marginal social benefit equals marginal social cost.
- Competition between political parties can lead to the efficient scale of provision of a public good.
- Bureaucrats who maximize their budgets and voters who are rationally ignorant can lead to the inefficient overprovision of a public good—government failure.

Working Problems 7 to 15 will give you a better understanding of providing public goods.

Providing Mixed Goods with External Benefits (pp. 286–291)

- Mixed goods provide external benefits—benefits that are received by people other than the consumer of a good or service.
- Marginal social benefit equals marginal private benefit plus marginal external benefit.
- External benefits arise from education and health care.
- Vouchers provided to households can achieve a more efficient provision of education and health care than public production or subsidies to private producers.

Working Problems 16 to 20 will give you a better understanding of providing mixed goods with external benefits.

Key Terms

Common resource, 282
Excludable, 282
Externality, 282
Free-rider problem, 285
Marginal external benefit, 287
Marginal private benefit, 287
Marginal social benefit, 287

Mixed good, 282
Natural monopoly good, 282
Negative externality, 282
Nonexcludable, 282
Nonrival, 282
Postive externality, 282
Private good, 282

Public good, 282
Public production, 289
Rival, 282
Subsidy, 289
Voucher, 289

STUDY PLAN PROBLEMS AND APPLICATIONS

myeconlab You can work Problems 1 to 20 in MyEconLab Chapter 14 Study Plan and get instant feedback.

Public Choices (Study Plan 14.1)

1. Classify each of the following items as excludable, nonexcludable, rival, or nonrival.
   - A Big Mac
   - Brooklyn Bridge
   - A view of the Statue of Liberty
   - A tsunami warning system

2. Classify each of the following items as a public good, a private good, a natural monopoly good, or a common resource.
   - Highway control services
   - City sidewalks
   - U.S. Postal Service
   - FedEx courier service

3. Classify the following services for computer owners with an Internet connection as rival, nonrival, excludable, or nonexcludable:
   - eBay
   - A mouse
   - A Twitter page
   - MyEconLab Web site

4. Classify each of the following items as a public good, a private good, a mixed good, or a common resource:
   - Firefighting services
   - A courtside seat at the U.S. Open (tennis)
   - A well-stocked buffet that promises the most bang for your buck
   - The Mississippi River

5. Explain which of the following events creates an external benefit or an external cost:
   - A huge noisy crowd gathers outside the lecture room
   - Your neighbor grows beautiful flowers on his apartment deck.
   - A fire alarm goes off accidently in the middle of a lecture.
   - Your instructor offers a free tutorial after class.

6. **Wind Farm Off Cape Cod Clears Hurdle**

   The nation's first offshore wind farm with 130 turbines will be built 5 miles off the coast. Wind turbines are noisy, stand 440 feet tall, can be seen from the coast, and will produce power for 75 percent of nearby homes.

   Source: *The New York Times*, January 16, 2009

   List the externalities created by this wind farm.

Providing Public Goods (Study Plan 14.2)

7. For each of the following goods, explain whether there is a free-rider problem. If there is no such problem, how is it avoided?
   - July 4th fireworks display
   - Interstate 81 in Virginia
   - Wireless Internet access in hotels
   - The public library in your city

8. The table sets out the marginal benefits that Terri and Sue receive from police officers on duty on the college campus:

Police officers on duty (number per night)	Marginal benefit Terri	Sue
	(dollars per police officer)	
1	18	22
2	14	18
3	10	14
4	6	10
5	2	6

   a. If the police officers are provided by the city government, is the presence of the police on-campus a private good or a public good?

   b. Suppose that Terri and Sue are the only students on the campus at night. Draw a graph to show the marginal social benefit from on-campus police officers on duty at night.

9. For each of the following goods and services, explain whether there is a free-rider problem. If there is no such problem, how is it avoided?
   - National hurricane warning system
   - Ambulance service
   - Road safety signs
   - The U.S. Coast Guard

10. **Vaccination Dodgers**

    Doctors struggle to eradicate polio worldwide, but one of the biggest problems is persuading parents to vaccinate their children. Since the discovery of the vaccine, polio has been eliminated from Europe and the law requires everyone to be vaccinated. People who refuse to be vaccinated are "free riders."

    Source: *USA Today*, March 12, 2008

    Explain why someone who has not opted out on medical or religious grounds and refuses to be vaccinated is a "free rider."

Use the following figure to work Problems 11 to 13. The figure provides information about a waste disposal system that a city of 1 million people is considering installing.

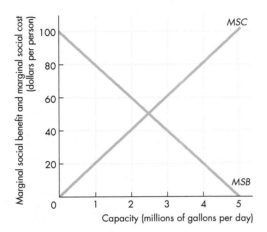

11. What is the efficient capacity of the waste disposal system? How much will each person have to pay in taxes for the city to install the efficient capacity?
12. What is the political equilibrium if voters are well informed?
13. What is the political equilibrium if voters are rationally ignorant and bureaucrats achieve the highest attainable budget?

Use the data on a mosquito control program in the following table to work Problems 14 and 15.

Quantity (square miles sprayed per day)	Marginal social cost	Marginal social benefit
	(thousands of dollars per day)	
1	2	10
2	4	8
3	6	6
4	8	4
5	10	2

14. What quantity of spraying would a private mosquito control program provide? What is the efficient quantity of spraying? In a single-issue election on the quantity of spraying, what quantity would the winner of the election provide?
15. If the government sets up a Department of Mosquito Control and appoints a bureaucrat to run it, would mosquito spraying most likely be underprovided, overprovided, or provided at the efficient quantity?

Providing Mixed Goods with External Benefits

(Study Plan 14.3)

Use the following figure, which shows the marginal private benefit from college education, to work Problems 16 to 19. The marginal cost of a college education is a constant $6,000 per student per year. The marginal external benefit from a college education is a constant $4,000 per student per year.

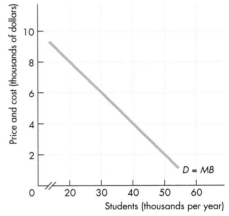

16. What is the efficient number of students? If all colleges are private, how many people enroll in college and what is the tuition?
17. If the government decides to provide public colleges, what tuition will these colleges charge to achieve the efficient number of students? How much will taxpayers have to pay?
18. If the government decides to subsidize private colleges, what subsidy will achieve the efficient number of college students?
19. If the government offers vouchers to those who enroll at a college and no subsidy, what is the value of the voucher that will achieve the efficient number of students?
20. **Tuition Hikes, not Loan Access, Should Frighten Students**

    The real danger during a recession is a hike in tuition, not a cut in student loans. In past recessions, states have cut funding for colleges and increased tuition. The Cato Institute says a better policy would be for states to maintain the subsidies to colleges and increase their deficits.

    Source: *USA Today*, October 22, 2008

    If government cuts the subsidy to colleges, why will tuition rise and the number of students enrolled decrease? Why is it a better policy for government to maintain the subsidy to colleges?

ADDITIONAL PROBLEMS AND APPLICATIONS

myeconlab You can work these problems in MyEconLab if assigned by your instructor.

Public Choices

21. Classify each of the following items as excludable, nonexcludable, rival, or nonrival.
    - Firefighting service
    - A Starbucks coffee
    - A view of the Liberty Bell
    - The Appalachian Trail
    - A google search

22. Classify each of the following items as a public good, a private good, a natural monopoly good, a common resource, or a mixed good.
    - Measles vaccinations
    - Tuna in the Pacific Ocean
    - Air service in the United States
    - Local storm-water system

23. Consider each of the following activities or events and say for each one whether it creates an externality. If so, say whether it creates an external benefit or external cost and whether the externality arises from production or consumption.
    - Airplanes take off from LaGuardia Airport during the U.S. Open tennis tournament, which is taking place nearby.
    - A sunset over the Pacific Ocean
    - An increase in the number of people who are studying for graduate degrees
    - A person wears strong perfume to class.

24. Classify each of the following goods as a private good, a public good, or a mixed good and say whether it creates an external benefit, external cost, or neither.
    - Chewing gum
    - The Santa Monica freeway at peak travel time
    - The New York City subway
    - A skateboard
    - The Santa Monica beach

Providing Public Goods

Use the following news clip to work Problems 25 and 26.

"Free Riders" Must be Part of Health Debate

President Obama insists that "the reason people don't have health insurance isn't because they don't want it, it's because they can't afford it." There are 47 million uninsured people in the United States. Of these, 16 percent earn more than $75,000 a year and 15 percent earn between $50,000 and $75,000 a year. About 16 percent of those who received "free" medical care in 2004 had incomes at least four times the federal poverty level.

Source: *Los Angeles Times*, March 4, 2008

25. Explain why government-subsidized health-care services can create a free-rider problem.

26. Explain the evidence the news clip presents to contradict the argument that "the reason people don't have health insurance isn't because they don't want it, it's because they can't afford it."

27. The table sets out the marginal benefits that Sam and Nick receive from the town's street lighting:

Number of street lights	Marginal benefit	
	Sam	Nick
	(dollars per street light)	
1	10	12
2	8	9
3	6	6
4	4	3
5	2	0

   a. Is the town's street lighting a private good or a public good?

   b. Suppose that Sam and Nick are the only residents of the town. Draw a graph to show the marginal social benefit from the town's street lighting.

28. What is the principle of diminishing marginal benefit? In Problem 27, does Sam's, Nick's or the society's marginal benefit diminish faster?

Use the following news clip to work Problems 29 and 30.

A Bridge Too Far Gone

The gas taxes paid for much of America's post-war freeway system. Now motorists pay about one-third in gas taxes to drive a mile as they did in the 1960s. Yet raising such taxes is politically tricky. This would matter less if private cash was flooding into infrastructure, or if new ways were being found to control demand. Neither is happening, and private companies building toll roads brings howls of outrage.

Source: *The Economist*, August 9, 2007

29. Why is it "politically tricky" to raise gas taxes to finance infrastructure?

30. What in this news clip points to a distinction between public *production* of a public good and public *provision*? Give examples of three public goods that are *produced* by private firms but *provided* by government and paid for with taxes.

15

ECONOMICS OF THE ENVIRONMENT

We burn huge quantities of fossil fuels—coal, natural gas, and oil—that cause acid rain and global warming. We dump toxic waste into rivers, lakes, and oceans. These environmental issues are simultaneously everybody's problem and nobody's problem. How can we take account of the damage that we cause others every time we turn on our heating or air-conditioning systems?

More and more people with ever-increasing incomes demand ever-greater quantities of most goods and services. One item that we demand more and more of is fish grown wild in the ocean. The fish stocks of the world's oceans are not owned by anyone. They are common resources and everyone is free to use them. But we are overusing our fish stocks and bringing some species to extinction. Must the price of fish inevitably keep rising? What can be done to conserve the world's fish stocks?

In this chapter, we study the problems that arise because many of our actions impose costs on other people in ways that we do not take into account when we make our own economic choices. We focus on two big issues—air pollution and overfishing. In *Reading Between the Lines* at the end of the chapter, we look at the effects of a carbon tax designed to lower carbon emissions and address global warming and climate change.

◆ Negative Externality: Pollution

Can each individual be relied upon to make decisions that influence the Earth's carbon-dioxide concentration in the social interest? Must governments change the incentives we face so that our self-interested choices are also in the social interest? How can governments change incentives? These questions about climate change that we posed here involve *external costs* and this chapter answers them.

This chapter also studies another environmental problem that requires public choices: the overuse and sometimes the depletion of renewable natural resources.

We first study the external costs of pollution and begin with a quick review of the production activities that pollute our environment.

Sources of Pollution

Economic activity pollutes air, water, and land, and these individual areas of pollution interact through the ecosystem. The three biggest sources of pollution are road transportation, electricity generation, and industrial processes.

A common belief is that our advanced industrial economy is creating ever more pollution. But for many pollutants, in the rich countries that include

the United States, pollution is less serious today that it was in earlier years (see *Economics in Action* below for a description of the trends in air pollution).

Effects of Pollution

While the facts about the sources and trends in air pollution are not in doubt, there is disagreement about the effects of air pollution. The least controversial is acid rain caused by sulphur dioxide and nitrogen oxide emissions from coal- and oil-fired generators of power stations. Acid rain begins with air pollution, and it leads to water pollution and damages vegetation.

More than 180 others airborne substances (suspended particulates) such as lead from leaded gasoline have been identified, which in sufficiently large concentrations, are believed to cause cancer and other life-threatening conditions.

Many scientists believe that carbon dioxide emissions are a major cause of global warming and climate change.

The effects of pollution mean that production and consumption decisions impose costs that are not taken fully into account when decisions are made. You are now going to see how economists analyse these decisions and solve the pollution problem.

Economics in Action
U.S. Air Pollution Trends: Cleaner and Safer

The figure shows the percentage changes in the concentrations of six air pollutants between 1990 and 2008 and their economic sources. All of these pollutants decreased.

These reductions in air pollution are more impressive when they are seen against the trends in economic activity. Between 1990 and 2008, total production in the United States increased by 66 percent, vehicle miles traveled increased by 40 percent, and the population increased by 20 percent.

The Clean Air Act has brought regulations that cut emissions of carbon monoxide, volatile organic compounds, oxides of nitrogen, sulfur dioxide and particulate matter to around a half of their 1990 levels. And economic actions that you will learn about in this chapter almost eliminated lead from highways and industrial processes.

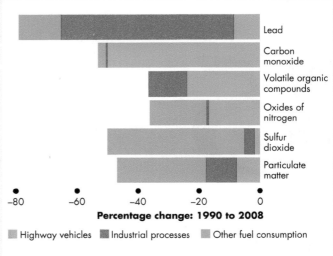

Six Air Pollutants and their Economic Sources

Source of data: Latest Findings on National Air Quality: Status and Trends through 2008, United States Environmental Protection Agency, http://www.epa.gov/air/airtrends/2010/report/airpollution.pdf

Private Cost and Social Cost of Pollution

To study the economics of the external costs that arise from pollution, we distinguish between the private cost and the social cost of production.

A *private cost* of production is a cost that is borne by the producer of a good or service. *Marginal cost* is the cost of producing an *additional unit* of a good or service. So **marginal private cost** (*MC*) is the cost of producing an additional unit of a good or service that is borne by its producer.

An *external cost* is a cost of producing a good or service that is *not* borne by the producer but borne by other people. A **marginal external cost** is the cost of producing an additional unit of a good or service that falls on people other than the producer.

Marginal social cost (*MSC*) is the marginal cost incurred by the producer and by everyone else on whom the cost falls—by society. It is the sum of marginal private cost and marginal external cost. That is,

$$MSC = MC + \text{Marginal external cost.}$$

We express costs in dollars, but we must always remember that a cost is an opportunity cost—something real, such as clean air or a clean river, is given up to get something.

Valuing an External Cost Economists use market prices to put a dollar value on the cost of pollution. For example, suppose that there are two similar rivers, one polluted and the other clean. Five hundred identical homes are built along the side of each river. The homes on the clean river rent for $2,500 a month, and those on the polluted river rent for $1,500 a month. If the pollution is the only detectable difference between the two rivers and the two locations, the rent decrease of $1,000 per month is the cost of the pollution. With 500 homes on the polluted river, the external cost of pollution is $500,000 a month.

External Cost and Output Figure 15.1 shows an example of the relationship between output and cost in a chemical industry that pollutes. The marginal cost curve, *MC*, describes the marginal private cost borne by the firms that produce the chemical. Marginal cost increases as the quantity of chemical produced increases.

If the firms dump waste into a river, they impose an external cost on other users of the river. We will assume that the marginal external cost increases with the amount of the chemical produced.

The marginal social cost curve, *MSC*, is found by adding the marginal external cost to the marginal private cost. So a point on the *MSC* curve shows the sum of the marginal private cost of producing a given output and marginal external cost created.

For example, when the chemical industry produces 4,000 tons of chemical a month, its marginal private cost is $100 a ton and the marginal external cost is $125 a ton, so the marginal social cost is $225 a ton.

In Fig. 15.1, when the quantity of chemical produced increases, the amount of pollution increases and the external cost of pollution increases.

Figure 15.1 shows the relationship between the quantity of chemical produced and the cost of the pollution it creates, but it doesn't tell us how much pollution the chemical industry creates. That quantity depends on the quantity of the chemical produced, which depends on supply and demand in the market for the chemical. We now look at that market.

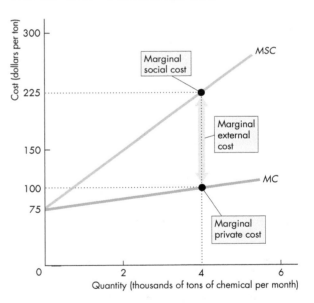

FIGURE 15.1   An External Cost

The *MC* curve shows the marginal private cost borne by the factories that produce a chemical. The *MSC* curve shows the sum of marginal private cost and marginal external cost. When output is 4,000 tons of chemical a month, marginal private cost is $100 a ton, marginal external cost is $125 a ton, and marginal social cost is $225 a ton.

Production and Pollution: How Much?

When an industry is unregulated and free to pollute, the amount of pollution it creates depends on the market equilibrium price and quantity of the good produced. In Fig. 15.2, the demand curve for a pollution-creating chemical is *D*. This curve also measures the marginal social benefit, *MSB*, from the chemical. The supply curve of the chemical is *S*. This curve also measures the producers' marginal private cost, *MC*. The supply curve is the marginal private cost curve because when firms make their production and supply decisions, they consider only the costs that they will bear. Market equilibrium occurs at a price of $100 a ton and 4,000 tons of chemical a month.

This equilibrium is inefficient. You learned in Chapter 5 that the allocation of resources is efficient when marginal social benefit equals marginal social cost. But we must count *all* the costs—private and external—when we compare marginal social benefit and marginal social cost. So with an external cost, the allocation is efficient when marginal social benefit equals marginal *social* cost. This outcome occurs when the quantity of chemical produced is 2,000 tons a month. The unregulated market overproduces by 2,000 tons of chemical a month and creates a deadweight loss shown by the gray triangle.

How can the people who live by the polluted river get the chemical factories to decrease their output of chemical and create less pollution? If some method can be found to achieve this outcome, everyone—the owners of the chemical factories and the residents of the riverside homes—can gain. Let's explore some solutions.

Property Rights

Sometimes it is possible to reduce the inefficiency arising from an external cost by establishing a property right where one does not currently exist. **Property rights** are legally established titles to the ownership, use, and disposal of factors of production and goods and services that are enforceable in the courts.

Suppose that the chemical factories own the river and the 500 homes alongside it. The rent that people are willing to pay depends on the amount of pollution. Using the earlier example, people are willing to pay $2,500 a month to live alongside a pollution-free river but only $1,500 a month to live with the pollution created by 4,000 tons of chemical a month. If the factories produce this quantity, they lose $1,000 a month for each home for a total of $500,000 a month. The chem-

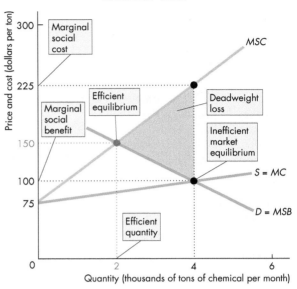

FIGURE 15.2 Inefficiency with an External Cost

The market supply curve is the factories' marginal private cost curve, *S = MC*. The market demand curve is the marginal social benefit curve, *D = MSB*. The market equilibrium occurs at a price of $100 a ton and 4,000 tons of chemical a month This market outcome is inefficient because marginal social cost exceeds marginal social benefit. The efficient quantity of chemical is 2,000 tons a month. The gray triangle shows the deadweight loss created by the pollution.

myeconlab   animation

ical factories are now confronted with the cost of their pollution—forgone rent from the people who live by the river.

Figure 15.3 illustrates the outcome by using the same example as in Fig. 15.2. With property rights in place, the *MC* curve no longer measures all the costs that the factories face in producing the chemical. It excludes the pollution costs that they must now bear. The *MSC* curve now becomes the factories' marginal private cost curve *MC*. The factories bear all the costs, so the market supply curve based on all the costs is the curve labeled *S = MC = MSC*.

Market equilibrium now occurs at a price of $150 a ton and 2,000 tons of chemical a month. This outcome is efficient. The factories still produce some pollution, but it is the efficient quantity.

FIGURE 15.3 Property Rights Achieve an Efficient Outcome

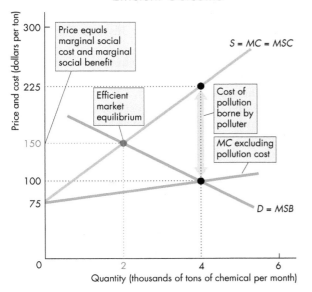

With property rights, the marginal cost curve that excludes pollution costs shows only part of the producers' marginal cost. The marginal cost of producing the chemical now includes the cost of pollution—the external cost. So the producers' supply curve is $S = MC = MSC$. The market equilibrium now occurs at a price of $150 a ton and 2,000 tons of chemical a month. This outcome is efficient because marginal social cost equals marginal social benefit. The pollution created is not zero, but it is the efficient quantity.

 animation

The Coase Theorem

Does it matter how property rights are assigned? Does it matter whether the polluter or the victim of the pollution owns the resource that might be polluted? Until 1960, everyone thought that it did matter. But in 1960, Ronald Coase had a remarkable insight, now called the Coase theorem.

The **Coase theorem** is the proposition that if property rights exist, if only a small number of parties are involved, and if transactions costs are low, then private transactions are efficient. There are no externalities because the transacting parties take all the costs and benefits into account. Furthermore, it doesn't matter who has the property rights.

Application of the Coase Theorem In the example that we've just studied, the factories own the river and the homes. Suppose that instead, the residents own their homes and the river. Now the factories must pay a fee to the homeowners for the right to dump their waste. The greater the quantity of waste dumped into the river, the more the factories must pay. So again, the factories face the opportunity cost of the pollution they create. The quantity of chemical produced and the amount of waste dumped are the same whoever owns the homes and the river. If the factories own them, they bear the cost of pollution because they receive a lower income from home rents. If the residents own the homes and the river, the factories bear the cost of pollution because they must pay a fee to the homeowners. In both cases, the factories bear the cost of their pollution and dump the efficient amount of waste into the river.

The Coase solution works only when transactions costs are low. **Transactions costs** are the opportunity costs of conducting a transaction. For example, when you buy a house, you incur a series of transactions costs. You might pay a realtor to help you find the best place and a lawyer to run checks that assure you that the seller owns the property and that after you've paid for it, the ownership has been properly transferred to you.

In the example of the homes alongside a river, the transactions costs that are incurred by a small number of chemical factories and a few homeowners might be low enough to enable them to negotiate the deals that produce an efficient outcome. But in many situations, transactions costs are so high that it would be inefficient to incur them. In these situations, the Coase solution is not available.

Suppose, for example, that everyone owns the airspace above their homes up to, say, 10 miles. If someone pollutes your airspace, you can charge a fee. But to collect the fee, you must identify who is polluting your airspace and persuade them to pay you. Imagine the costs of negotiating and enforcing agreements with the 50 million people who live in your part of the United States (and perhaps in Canada or Mexico) and the several thousand factories that emit sulfur dioxide and create acid rain that falls on your property! In this situation, we use public choices to cope with external costs. But the transactions costs that block a market solution are real costs, so attempts by the government to deal with external costs offer no easy solution. Let's look at some of these attempts.

Government Actions in a Market with External Costs

The three main methods that governments use to cope with external costs are

- Taxes
- Emission charges
- Cap-and-trade

Taxes The government can use taxes as an incentive for producers to cut back the pollution they create. Taxes used in this way are called **Pigovian taxes**, in honor of Arthur Cecil Pigou, the British economist who first worked out this method of dealing with external costs during the 1920s.

By setting the tax equal to the marginal external cost, firms can be made to behave in the same way as they would if they bore the cost of the externality directly. To see how government actions can change the outcome in a market with external costs, let's return to the example of the chemical factories and the river.

Assume that the government has assessed the marginal external cost accurately and imposes a tax on the factories that exactly equals this cost. Figure 15.4 illustrates the effects of this tax.

The demand curve and marginal social benefit curve, $D = MSB$, and the firms' marginal cost curve, MC, are the same as in Fig. 15.2. The pollution tax equals the marginal external cost of the pollution. We add this tax to the marginal private cost to find the market supply curve. This curve is the one labeled $S = MC + tax = MSC$. This curve is the market supply curve because it tells us the quantity supplied at each price given the firms' marginal cost and the tax they must pay. This curve is also the marginal social cost curve because the pollution tax has been set equal to the marginal external cost.

Demand and supply now determine the market equilibrium price at $150 a ton and a quantity of

Economics in Action

The Greatest Market Failure?

British economist Nicholas Stern reviewed the science and economics of global warming and climate change for the United Kingdom government and his report, the *Stern Review on the Economics of Climate Change* attracted much attention. Stern calls climate change "the greatest market failure the world has ever seen."

As the figure shows, global temperature and carbon dioxide (CO_2) trends are starkly upward. Stern says that to avoid the risk of catastrophic climate change, this upward trend must be stopped.

Scientists debate the contribution of human economic activity to these trends, but most say it is the major source. Although ice-core estimates show long swings in CO_2 concentration, the recent increase is the most rapid recorded.

The cost of achieving Stern's target is high, estimated at 1 percent of the value of global production. If this cost is to be met by the people who live in the rich countries, and realistically they are the only ones who can afford to pay, it will cost about $750 per person every year.

Some economists question Stern's assumptions and conclusions and argue that the cost of reducing emissions will be much lower if we go a bit more slowly and take advantage of future technological advances

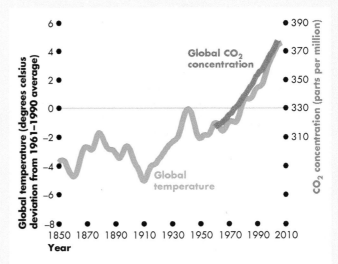

Global Warming Trends

Sources of data: Met Office Hadley Centre and Scripps Institution of Oceanography.

that will lower the cost of renewable energy sources—the sun, tide, and wind.

All economists agree that solving the global warming problem will require changes in the incentives that people face. The cost of carbon-emitting activities must rise and the cost of the search for new energy technologies must fall. A carbon tax or tradeable carbon permits are two possible ways of addressing this problem.

FIGURE 15.4   A Pollution Tax to Achieve an Efficient Outcome

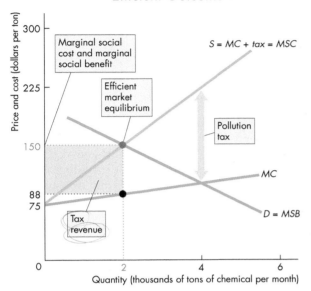

When the government imposes a pollution tax equal to the marginal external cost of pollution, the supply curve becomes the marginal private cost curve, MC, plus the tax—the curve S = MC + tax. Market equilibrium occurs at a price of $150 a ton and a quantity of 2,000 tons of chemical a month. This equilibrium is efficient because marginal social cost equals marginal social benefit. The purple rectangle shows the government's tax revenue.

myeconlab   animation

2,000 tons of chemical a month. At this quantity of chemical production, the marginal social cost is $150 and the marginal social benefit is $150, so the outcome is efficient. The firms incur a marginal private cost of $88 a ton and pay a tax of $62 a ton. The government collects tax revenue of $124,000 a month.

Emission Charges Emission charges are an alternative to a tax for confronting a polluter with the external cost of pollution. The government sets a price per unit of pollution. The more pollution a firm creates, the more it pays in emission charges. This method of dealing with pollution externalities has been used only modestly in the United States but is common in Europe where, for example, France, Germany, and the Netherlands make water polluters pay a waste disposal charge.

To work out the emission charge that achieves efficiency, the government needs information about the polluting industry that, in practice, is rarely available.

Cap-and-Trade Instead of taxing or imposing emission charges on polluters, each potential polluter might be assigned a permitted pollution limit. Each firm knows its own costs and its benefits from pollution, and making pollution limits marketable is a clever way of using this private information that is unknown to the government. The government issues each firm a permit to emit a certain amount of pollution, and firms can trade these permits. Firms that have a low marginal cost of reducing pollution sell their permits, and firms that have a high marginal cost of reducing pollution buy permits. The market in permits determines the price at which firms trade permits. Each firm buys or sells permits until its marginal cost of pollution equals the market price of a permit.

This method of dealing with pollution provides an even stronger incentive than emission charges to find lower-polluting technologies because the price of a pollution permit rises as the demand for permits increases.

Trading in lead pollution permits became common during the 1980s, and this marketable permit program enabled lead pollution to be virtually eliminated in the United States (see p. 300). But this success might not easily translate to other pollutant because most lead pollution came from gasoline, which was easy to monitor.

REVIEW QUIZ

1 What is the distinction between private cost and social cost?
2 How do external costs prevent a competitive market from allocating resources efficiently?
3 How can external costs be eliminated by assigning property rights?
4 How do taxes help us to cope with external costs? At what level must a pollution tax be set to be efficient?
5 How do emission charges and marketable pollution permits work?

You can work these questions in Study Plan 15.1 and get instant feedback.

Your next task is to study common resources and the government actions that can bring efficient use.

◆ The Tragedy of the Commons

Overgrazing the pastures around a village in Middle Ages England, and overfishing the cod stocks of the North Atlantic Ocean during the recent past are tragedies of the commons. The **tragedy of the commons** is the overuse of a common resource that arises when its users have no incentive to conserve it and use it sustainably.

To study the tragedy of the commons and its possible remedies, we'll focus on the recent and current tragedy—overfishing and depleting the stock of Atlantic cod. We begin by thinking about the sustainable use of a renewable resource.

Sustainable Use of a Renewable Resource

A *renewable natural resource* is one that replenishes itself by the birth and growth of new members of the population. Fish, trees, and the fertile soil are all examples of this type of resource.

Focusing on fish, the sustainable catch is the quantity that can be caught year after year without depleting the stock. This quantity depends on the stock and in the interesting way illustrated in Fig. 15.6.

If the stock of fish is small, the quantity of new fish born is also small, so the sustainable catch is small.

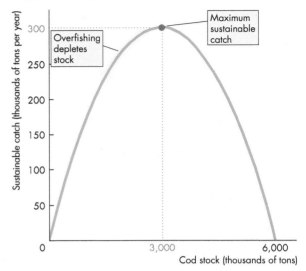

FIGURE 15.5   Sustainable Catch

As the stock of fish increases (on the *x*-axis), the sustainable catch (on the *y*-axis) increases to a maximum. Beyond that number, more fish must compete for food and the sustainable catch falls.

If the catch exceeds the sustainable catch, the fish stock diminishes.

⟨X⟩ *myeconlab* animation

Economics in Action
The Original Tragedy of the Commons

The term "tragedy of the commons" comes from fourteenth-century England, where areas of rough grassland surrounded villages. The commons were open to all and used for grazing cows and sheep owned by the villagers.

Because the commons were open to all, no one had an incentive to ensure that the land was not overgrazed. The result was a severe overgrazing situation. Because the commons were overgrazed, the quantity of cows and sheep that they could feed kept falling, the longer the overgrazing continued.

During the sixteenth century, the price of wool increased and England became a wool exporter to the world. Sheep farming became profitable, and sheep owners wanted to gain more effective control of the land they used. So the commons were gradually privatized and enclosed. Overgrazing ended, and land use became more efficient.

Economics in Action

One of Today's Tragedies of the Commons

Before 1970, Atlantic cod was abundant. It was fished for many centuries and a major food source for the first European settlers in North America. During the sixteenth century, hundreds of European ships caught large quantities of cod in the northwest Atlantic off the coast of what is now New England and Newfoundland, Canada. By 1620, there were more than 1,000 fishing boats in the waters off Newfoundland, and in 1812 about 1,600 boats. During these years, cod were huge fish, typically weighing in at more than 220 pounds and measuring 3-6 feet in length.

Most of the fishing during these years was done using lines and productivity was low. But low productivity limited the catch and enabled cod to be caught sustainably over hundreds of years.

The situation changed dramatically during the 1960s with the introducton of high-efficiency nets (called trawls, seines, and gill nets), sonar technology to find fish concentrations, and large ships with efficient processing and storage facilities. These technological advances brought soaring cod harvests. In less than a decade, cod landings increased from less than 300,000 tons a year to 800,000 tons.

This volume of cod could not be taken without a serious collapse in the remaining stock and by the 1980s it became vital to regulate cod fishing. But regulation was of limited success and stocks continued to fall.

In 1992, a total ban on cod fishing in the North Atlantic stabilized the population but at a very low level. Two decades of ban have enabled the species to repopulate, and it is now hoped that one day cod fishing will return but at a low and sustainable rate.

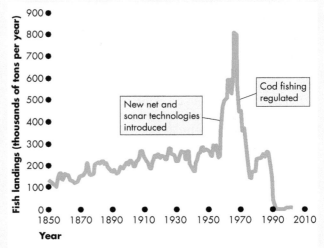

The Atlantic Cod Catch: 1850–2005

Source of data for graph: Millenium Ecosystem Assessment.
Source of information: Codfishes—Atlantic cod and its fishery,
http://science.jrank.org/

If the fish stock is large, many fish are born, but they must compete with each other for food so only a small number survive to reproduce and to grow large enough to catch.

Between a small and a large stock is a quantity of fish stock that maximizes the sustainable catch. In Fig. 15.5, this fish stock is 3,000 thousand tons and the sustainable catch is 300 thousand tons a year. The maximum sustainable catch arises from a balancing of the birth of new fish from the stock and the availability of food to sustain the fish popuation.

If the quantity of fish caught is less than the sustainable catch, the fish stock grows; if the quantity caught exceeds the sustainable catch, the fish stock shrinks; and if the quantity caught equals the sustainable catch, the fish stock remains constant and is available for future generations of fishers in the same quantity that is available today.

If the fish stock exceeds the level that maximizes the sustainable catch, overfishing isn't a problem. But if the fish stock is less than the level that maximizes the sustainable catch, overfishing depletes the stock.

The Overuse of a Common Resource

Why might a fish stock be overused? Why might overfishing occur? The answer is that fishers face only their own private cost and don't face the cost they impose on others—external cost. The *social* cost of fishing combines the *private* cost and *external* cost. Let's examine the costs of catching fish to see how the presence of external cost brings overfishing.

Marginal Private Cost You can think of the *marginal private cost* of catching fish as the additional cost incurred by keeping a boat and crew at sea for long enough to increase the catch by one ton. Keeping a fishing boat at sea for an additional amount of time eventually runs into *diminishing marginal returns* (see p. 194). As the crew gets tired, the storage facilities get overfull, and boat's speed is cut to conserve fuel, the catch per hour decreases. The cost of keeping the boat at sea for an additional hour is constant so the marginal cost of catching fish increases as the quantity caught increases.

You've just seen that the *principle of increasing marginal cost* applies to catching fish just as it applies to other production activities: Marginal private cost increases as the quantity of fish caught increases.

The marginal private cost of catching fish determines an indiviual fisher's supply of fish. A profit-maximizing fisher is willing to supply the quantity at which the market price of fish covers the marginal private cost. And the market supply is the sum of the quantities supplied by each individual fisher.

Marginal External Cost The marginal exernal cost of catching fish is the cost per additional ton that one fisher's production imposes on all other fishers. This additional cost arises because one fisher's catch decreases the remaining stock, which in turn decreases the renewal rate of the stock and makes it harder for others to find and catch fish.

Marginal external cost also increases as the quantity of fish caught increases. If the quantity of fish caught is so large that it drives the species to near extinction, the marginal external cost becomes infinitely large.

Marginal Social Cost The *marginal social cost* of catching fish is the marginal private cost plus the marginal external cost. Because both of its components increase as the quantity caught increases, marginal social cost also increases with the quantity of fish caught.

Marginal Social Benefit and Demand The marginal social benefit from fish is the price that consumers are willing to pay for an additional pound of fish. Marginal social benefit decreases as the quantity of fish consumed increases, so the demand curve, which is also the marginal social benefit curve, slopes downward.

Overfishing Equilibrium Figure 15.6 illustrates overfishing and how it arises. The market demand curve for fish is the marginal social benefit curve, *MSB*. The market supply curve is the marginal *private* cost curve, *MC*. Market equilibrium occurs at the intersection point of these two curves. The equilibrium quantity is 800 thousand tons per year and the equilibrium price is $10 per pound.

At this market equilibrium, overfishing is running down the fish stock. Figure. 15.6 illustrates why

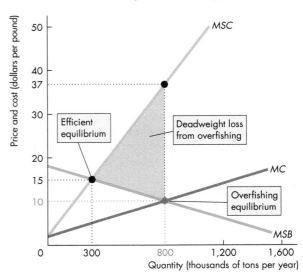

FIGURE 15.6   Why Overfishing Occurs

The supply curve is the marginal private cost curve, *MC*. The demand curve is the marginal social benefit curve *MSB*. Market equilibrium occurs at a quantity of 800 thousand tons and a price of $10 per pound.

The marginal social cost curve is *MSC* and at the market equilibrium there is overfishing—marginal social cost exceeds marginal social benefit.

The quantity at which *MSC* equals *MSB* is the efficient quantity, 300 thousand tons per year. The gray triangle shows the deadweight loss from overfishing.

⟨X⟩ myeconlab animation

overfishing occurs. At the market equilibrium quantity, marginal social benefit (and willingness to pay) is $10 per pound, but the marginal social cost exceeds this amount. The marginal external cost is the cost of running down the fish stock.

Efficient Equilibrium What is the efficient use of a common resource? It is the use of the resource that makes the marginal social benefit from the resource equal to the marginal social cost of using it.

In Fig. 15.6, the efficient quantity of fish is 300 thousand tons per year—the quantity that makes marginal social cost (on the *MSC* curve) equal to marginal social benefit (on the *MSB* curve). At this quantity, the marginal catch of each individual fisher costs society what people are willing to pay for it.

Deadweight Loss from Overfishing Deadweight loss measures the cost of overfishing. The gray triangle in Fig. 15.6 illustrates this loss. It is the marginal social cost minus the marginal social benefit from all the fish caught in excess of the efficient quantity.

Achieving an Efficient Outcome

Defining the conditions under which a common resource is used efficiently is easier than delivering those conditions. To use a common resource efficiently, it is necessary to design an incentive mechanism that confronts the users of the resource with the marginal *social* consequences of their actions. The same principles apply to common resources as those that you met earlier in this chapter when you studied the external cost of pollution.

The three main methods that might be used to achieve the efficient use of a common resource are

- Property rights
- Production quotas
- Individual transferable quotas (ITQs)

Property Rights A common resource that no one owns and that anyone is free to use contrasts with *private property*, which is a resource that *someone* owns and has an incentive to use in the way that maximizes its value. One way of overcoming the tragedy of the commons is to convert a common resource to private property. By assigning private property rights to what was previously a common resource, its owner faces the same conditions as society faces. It doesn't matter who owns the resource.

The users of the resource will be confronted with the full cost of using it because they either own it or pay a fee to the owner for permission to use it.

When private property rights over a resource are established and enforced, the *MSC* curve becomes the marginal *private* cost curve, and the use of the resource is efficient.

Figure 15.7 illustrate an efficient outcome with property rights. The supply curve $S = MC = MSC$ and the demand curve $D = MSB$ determine the equilibrium price and quantity. The price equals both marginal social benefit and marginal social cost and the quantity is efficient.

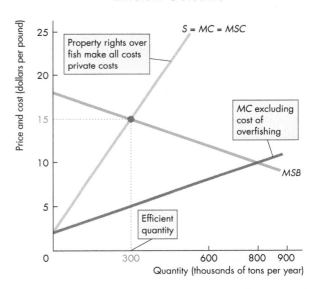

FIGURE 15.7 Property Rights Achieve an Efficient Outcome

With private property rights, fishers pay the owner of the fish stock for permission to fish and face the full social cost of their actions. The marginal cost curve includes the external cost, so the supply curve is the marginal private cost curve and the marginal social cost curve, $S = MC = MSC$.

Market equilibrium occurs at $15 per pound and at that price, the quantity is 300 thousand tons per year. At this quantity, marginal social cost equals marginal social benefit, and the quantity of fish caught is efficient.

The property rights convert the fish stock from a common resource to a private resource and it is used efficiently.

The private property solution to the tragedy of the commons *is* available in some cases. It was the solution to the original tragedy of the commons in England's Middle Ages. It is also a solution that has been used to prevent overuse of the airwaves that carry cell-phone services. The right to use this space (called the frequency spectrum) has been auctioned by governments to the highest bidders. The owner of each part of the spectrum is the only one permitted to use it (or to license someone else to use it).

But assigning private property rights is not always feasible. It would be difficult, for example, to assign private property rights to the oceans. It would not be impossible, but the cost of enforcing private property rights over thousands of square miles of ocean would be high. It would be even more difficult to assign and protect private property rights to the atmosphere.

In some cases, there is an emotional objection to assigning private property rights. Critics of it have a moral objection to someone owning a resource that they regard as public. In the absence of property rights, some form of government intervention is used, one of which is a production quota.

Production Quota A *production quota* is an upper limit to the quantity of a good that may be produced in a specified period. The quota is allocated to individual producers, so each producer has its own quota.

You studied the effects of a production quota in Chapter 6 (pp. 123–124) and learned that a quota can drive a wedge between marginal social benefit and marginal social cost and create deadweight loss. In that earlier example, the market was efficient without a quota. But in the case of common resources, the market overuses the resource and produces an inefficient quantity. A production quota in this market brings a move toward a more efficient outcome.

Figure 15.8 shows a quota that achieves an efficient outcome. The quota limits the catch (production) to 300 thousand tons, the efficient quantity at which marginal social benefit, *MSB*, equals marginal social cost, *MSC*. If everyone sticks to their own quota, the outcome is efficient. But implementing a production quota has two problems.

First, it is in every fisher's self-interest to catch more fish than the quantity permitted under the quota. The reason is that price exceeds marginal private cost, so by catching more fish, a fisher gets a higher income. If enough fishers break the quota, overfishing and the tragedy of the commons remain.

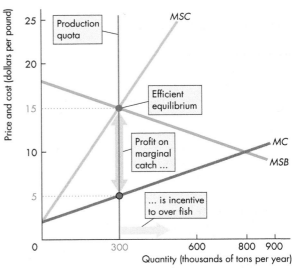

FIGURE 15.8 **A Production Quota to Use a Common Resource Efficiently**

A quota of 300 thousand tons that limits production to this quantity, raises the price to $15 per pound, and lowers marginal cost to $5 per pound. A fisher who cheats and produces more that the alloted quota increases his profit by $10 per pound. If all (or most) fishers cheat, production exceeds the quota and there is a return to overfishing.

ⓧ myeconlab animation

Second, marginal cost is not, in general, the same for all producers—as we're assuming here. Efficiency requires that the quota be allocated to the producers with the lowest marginal cost. But bureaucrats who allocate quotas do not have information about the marginal cost of individual producers. Even if they tried to get this information, producers would have an incentive to lie about their costs so as to get a bigger quota.

So where producers are difficult, or very costly, to monitor or where marginal cost varies across producers, a production quota cannot achieve an efficient outcome.

Individual Transferable Quotas Where producers are difficult to monitor or where marginal cost varies across producers, a more sophisticated quota system can be effective. It is an **individual transferable quota (ITQ)**, which is a production limit that is assigned to an individual who is then free to transfer (sell) the quota to someone else. A market in ITQs emerges and ITQs are traded at their market price.

The market price of an ITQ is the highest price that someone is willing to pay for one. That price is marginal social benefit minus marginal cost. The price of an ITQ will rise to this level because fishers who don't have a quota would be willing to pay this amount to get one.

A fisher with an ITQ could sell it for the market price, so by not selling the ITQ the fisher incurs an opportunity cost. The marginal cost of fishing, which now includes the opportunity cost of the ITQ, equals the marginal social benefit from the efficient quantity.

Figure 15.9 illustrates how ITQs work. Each fisher receives an allocation of ITQs and the total catch permitted by the ITQs is 300 thousand tons per year. Fishers trade ITQs: Those with low marginal cost buy ITQs from those with high marginal cost and the market price of an ITQ settles at $10 per pound of fish. The marginal private cost of fishing now becomes the original marginal private cost, *MC* plus the cost of the ITQ. The marginal private cost curve shifts upward from *MC* to *MC* + *price of ITQ* and each fisher is confronted with the marginal *social* cost of fishing. No one has an incentive to exceed the quota because to do so would send marginal cost above price and result in a loss on the marginal catch. The outcome is efficient.

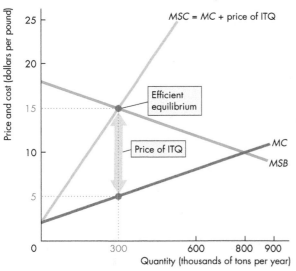

FIGURE 15.9   ITQs to Use a Common Resource Efficiently

ITQs are issued on a scale that keeps output at the efficient level. The market price of an ITQ equals the marginal social benefit minus marginal cost. Because each user of the common resource faces the opportunity cost of using the resource, self-interest achieves the social interest.

 animation

Economics in Action
ITQs Work

Iceland introduced the first ITQs in 1984 to conserve its stocks of lobster. In 1986, New Zealand and a bit later Australia introduced ITQs to conserve fish stocks in the South Pacific and Southern Oceans. The evidence from these countries suggests that ITQs work well.

ITQs help maintain fish stocks, but they also reduce the size of the fishing industry. This consequence of ITQs puts them against the self-interest of fishers. In all countries, the fishing industry opposes restrictions on its activities, but in Australia and New Zealand, the opposition is not strong enough to block ITQs.

In the United States the opposition has been harder to overcome and in 1996, Congress passed the Sustainable Fishing Act that put a moratorium on ITQs. This moratorium was lifted in 2004 and since then, ITQs have been applied to 28 fisheries from the Gulf of Alaska to the Gulf of Mexico. Economists have studied the effects of ITQs extensively and agree that they work. ITQs offer an effective tool for achieving an efficient use of the stock of ocean fish.

REVIEW QUIZ

1 What is the tragedy of the commons? Give two examples, including one from your state.
2 Describe the conditions under which a common resource is used efficiently.
3 Review three methods that might achieve the efficient use of a common resource and explain the obstacles to efficiency.

You can work these questions in Study Plan 15.2 and get instant feedback.   myeconlab

◆ *Reading Between the Lines* on pp. 312–313 looks at the use of a tax versus cap-and-trade to lower carbon emissions.

The next two chapters examine the third big question of economics: For whom are goods and services produced? We examine the markets for factors of production and discover how factor incomes and the distribution of income are determined.

Tax Versus Cap-and-Trade

Oil Spill Pushes Carbon Tax Back into Spotlight

http://www.SFGate.com
June 22, 2010

... Oil's true cost also includes the well-known litany of other hidden burdens: military spending to protect Middle East oil, the $1 billion of U.S. wealth and jobs sent overseas each day to buy oil, and pollution of all sorts, including carbon dioxide emissions. None of these costs is included in the price of the fossil fuels Americans use.

"There has to be a price, and a reward for moving to low-carbon fuels," said Rep. Pete Stark, D-Fremont. Stark may be the only one in Congress who has the temerity to propose a direct tax on carbon. ...

Congress instead is considering cap-and-trade systems for carbon emissions that do the same thing as a carbon tax, ...

The leading Senate plan ... would set an increasingly stricter limit on carbon emissions and auction emissions permits. Revenue would go to alternative energy investments and utility rebates to help low-income consumers burdened by rising energy costs. ...

Europeans pay $7 to $8 for a gallon of gas, mostly in taxes, and "they still drive," said Severin Borenstein, co-director of the UC Energy Institute. "They use much less oil per capita than we do, but they still use more than we need to get to." ...

Borenstein called for a big increase in federal funding for basic research into alternatives. "When you take a realistic look at the economic side, without major technological breakthroughs at a much faster pace than we've seen over the last couple of decades, it doesn't look very doable," he said. ...

San Francisco Chronicle article by Carolyn Lochhead. Copyright 2010 by *San Francisco Chronicle*. Reproduced with permission of *San Francisco Chronicle* via Copyright Clearance Center.

ESSENCE OF THE STORY

- The cost of oil includes external costs that include military spending to protect Middle East oil, pollution, and carbon dioxide emissions.

- Representative Pete Stark, D-Fremont, says that there has to be a price, and a reward for moving to low-carbon fuels, so he proposes a tax on carbon.

- Congress is considering cap-and-trade systems for carbon emissions.

- The leading Senate plan puts a limit on carbon emissions and auctions emissions permits.

- Revenue from the sale of permits would be spent on developing clean alternative energy and utility rebates to help low-income consumers.

- Europeans pay $7 to $8 for a gallon of gasoline and use less than Americans but more than the required target.

- Without a technological breakthrough to make clean energy cheap, it will be hard to reach a low carbon emission target.

- The news article lists some external costs of using oil. One of them, "sending jobs overseas," isn't such a cost. International trade brings gains for all, not external costs.

- The price of gasoline might be raised to incude marginal external cost with a carbon tax or a cap-and-trade carbon permit system.

- The news article says that using either of these measures would do little to curb gas consumption and Fig. 1 illustrates why.

- In the short run, the demand for gasoline, D_{SR}, is inelastic. If the U.S. gas price was raised to the European level, gas consumption would decrease by very little.

- In the long run, the demand for gasoline, D_{LR}, is elastic. Raising the U.S. gas price to the European level might eventually cut U.S. consumption to the European level.

- Figure 2 illustrates how a technological breakthrough that results in a low-cost clean fuel would work (suggests in the news article by Severin Borenstein).

- Figure 2(a) shows the short-run effects. Taxing carbon emissions or putting a price on them raises the marginal cost of gasoline to the marginal social cost, and the supply curve becomes the MSC curve. The price of gasoline rises, but the quantity consumed barely changes. The government collects the revenue shown by the purple rectangle.

- Figure 2(b) shows the long-run effect when a new technology is developed.

- The availablity of a low-cost clean fuel decreases the demand for gasoline from D_0 to D_1. The price of gasoline falls and the quantity consumed decreases.

- In the new equilibrium, the price of gasoline is lower, and so is the carbon tax or carbon price.

- Technological change is a crucial source of eventually curbing carbon emissions.

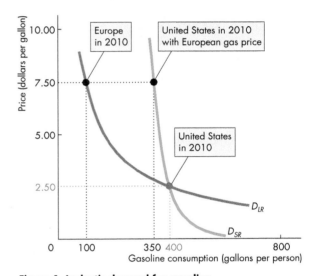

Figure 1 Inelastic demand for gasoline

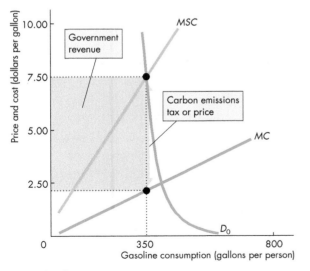

(a) In the short run

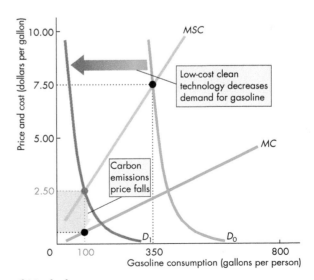

(b) In the long run

Figure 2 Short-run and long-run effects of tax and technological change

313

SUMMARY

Key Points

Negative Externality: Pollution (pp. 300–305)

- A competitive market would produce too much of a good that has external production costs.
- External costs are costs of production that fall on people other than the producer of a good or service. Marginal social cost equals marginal private cost plus marginal external cost.
- Producers take account only of marginal private cost and produce more than the efficient quantity when there is a marginal external cost.
- Sometimes it is possible to overcome a negative externality by assigning a property right.
- When property rights cannot be assigned, governments might overcome externalities by using taxes, emission charges, or marketable permits.

Working Problems 1 to 12 will give you a better understanding of the external costs of pollution.

The Tragedy of the Commons (pp. 306–311)

- Common resources create a problem that is called the tragedy of the commons—no one has a private incentive to conserve the resources and use them at an efficient rate.
- A common resource is used to the point at which the marginal private benefit equals the marginal cost.
- A common resource might be used efficiently by creating a private property right, setting a quota, or issuing individual transferable quotas.

Working Problems 13 to 19 will give you a better understanding of the tragedy of the commons.

Key Terms

Coase theorem, 303

Individual transferable
    quota (ITQ), 310

Marginal external cost, 301

Marginal private cost, 301

Marginal social cost, 301

Pigovian taxes, 304

Property rights, 302

Tragedy of the commons, 306

Transactions costs, 303

STUDY PLAN PROBLEMS AND APPLICATIONS

You can work Problems 1 to 19 in MyEconLab Chapter 15 Study Plan and get instant feedback.

Negative Externality: Pollution (Study Plan 15.1)

Use the following figure to work Problems 1 to 5.

The figure illustrates the market for cotton. Consider a small town surrounded by a large cotton farm. Suppose that the cotton grower sprays the plants with chemicals to control insects and the chemical waste flows into the river passing through the town. The marginal external cost of the chemical waste is equal to the marginal private cost of producing the cotton (that is, the marginal social cost of producing the cotton is double the marginal private cost).

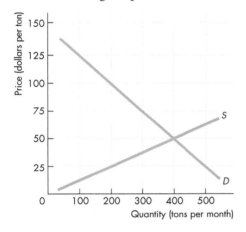

1. If no one owns the river and the town takes no action to control the waste, what is the quantity of cotton, and the deadweight loss created?

2. a. Suppose that the town owns the river and makes the cotton grower pay the cost of pollution. How much cotton is produced and what does the farmer pay the town per ton of cotton produced?

   b. Suppose that the cotton grower owns the river and rents it to the town. How much cotton is produced and how is the rent paid by the town to the grower (per ton of cotton produced) influenced by cotton growing?

   c. Compare the quantities of cotton produced in parts (a) and (b) and explain the relationship between these quantities.

3. Suppose that no one owns the river and that the city introduces a pollution tax. What is the tax per ton of cotton produced that achieves an efficient outcome?

4. Compare the outcomes when property rights exist and when the pollution tax achieves the efficient amount of waste.

5. Suppose that no one owns the river and that the government issues two marketable pollution permits: one to the cotton grower and one to the city. Each permit allows the same amount of pollution of the river, and the total pollution created is the efficient amount.

   What is the quantity of cotton produced and what is the market price of a pollution permit? Who buys and who sells a permit?

Use the following news clip to work Problems 6 to 8.

Bag Revolution

Thin plastic shopping bags aren't biodegradable and often end up in the ocean or in trees. Americans use about 110 billion bags a year. In 2007, San Francisco required all retailers with revenue over $2 million to offer only compostable or reusable bags. In all, 28 U.S. cities have proposed laws restricting the use of plastic bags.

Source: *Fortune*, May 12, 2008

6. a. Describe the externality that arises from plastic bags.

   b. Draw a graph to illustrate how plastic bags create deadweight loss.

7. a. With 70 percent of all plastic bags coming from grocery, drug and convenience stores, in July 2008, Seattle imposed a tax of 20¢ per bag from these outlets. Explain the effects of Seattle's policy on the use of plastic bags.

   b. Draw a graph to illustrate Seattle's policy and show the change in the deadweight loss that arises from this policy.

8. In 2010, the Governor of California supported a move to make California the first state in the nation to ban plastic shopping bags. He said that the bill "will be a great victory for our environment." Explain why a complete ban on plastic bags might be inefficient.

Use the following news clip to work Problems 9 to 11.

The Year in Medicine: Cell Phones

Talking on a hands-free cell phone while driving might seem safe, but think again. People who used hands-free cell phones in simulation trials exhibited slower reaction times and took longer to hit the brakes than drivers who weren't otherwise distracted. Data from real-life driving tests show that cell-phone use rivals drowsy driving as a major cause of accidents.

Source: *Time*, December 4, 2006

9. a. Explain the external costs that arise from using a cell phone while driving.
   b. Explain why the market for cell-phone service creates a deadweight loss.

10. Draw a graph to illustrate how a deadweight loss arises from the use of cell phones.

11. Explain how government intervention might improve the efficiency of cell-phone use.

12. **Pollution Rules Squeeze Strawberry Crop**

Last year, Ventura County farmers harvested nearly 12,000 acres of strawberries valued at more than $323 million. To comply with the federal Clean Air Act, growers must use 50 percent less pesticide. It is estimated that strawberry output will fall by 60 percent.

Source: *USA Today*, February 29, 2008

Explain how a limit on pesticide will change the efficiency of the strawberry industry. Would a cap-and-trade scheme be more efficient?

Tragedy of the Commons (Study Plan 15.2)

Use the following figure to work Problems 13 to 15. The figure shows the market for North Atlantic tuna.

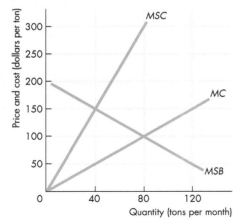

13. a. What is the quantity of tuna that fishers catch and the price of tuna? Is the tuna stock being used efficiently? Explain why or why not.
    b. What would be the price of tuna, if the stock of tuna is used efficiently?

14. a. With a quota of 40 tons a month for the tuna fishing industry, what is the equilibrium price of tuna and the quantity of tuna that fishers catch?
    b. Is the equilibrium an overfishing equilibrium?

15. If the government issues ITQs to individual fishers that limit the total catch to the efficient quantity, what is the market price of an ITQ?

16. **Whaling "Hurts Tourist Industry"**

Leah Garces, the director of programs at the World Society for the Protection of Animals, reported that whale watching is more economically significant and sustainable to people and communities than whaling. The global whale-watching industry is estimated to be a $1.25 billion business enjoyed by over 10 million people in more than 90 countries each year.

Source: BBC, June 2, 2009

Describe the tradeoff facing communities that live near whaling areas. How might a thriving whale-watching industry avoid the tragedy of the commons?

Use the following information to work Problems 17 to 19.

A natural spring runs under land owned by ten people. Each person has the right to sink a well and can take water from the spring at a constant marginal cost of $5 a gallon. The table sets out the external cost and the social benefit of water.

Quantity of water (gallons per day)	Marginal external cost (dollars per gallon)	Marginal social benefits (dollars per gallon)
10	1	10
20	2	9
30	3	8
40	4	7
50	5	6
60	6	5
70	7	4

17. Draw a graph to illustrate the market equilibrium. On your graph, show the efficient quantity of water taken.

18. If the government sets a quota on the total amount of water such that the spring is used efficiently, what would that quota be?

19. If the government issues ITQs to land owners that limit the total amount of water taken to the efficient quantity, what is the market price of an ITQ?

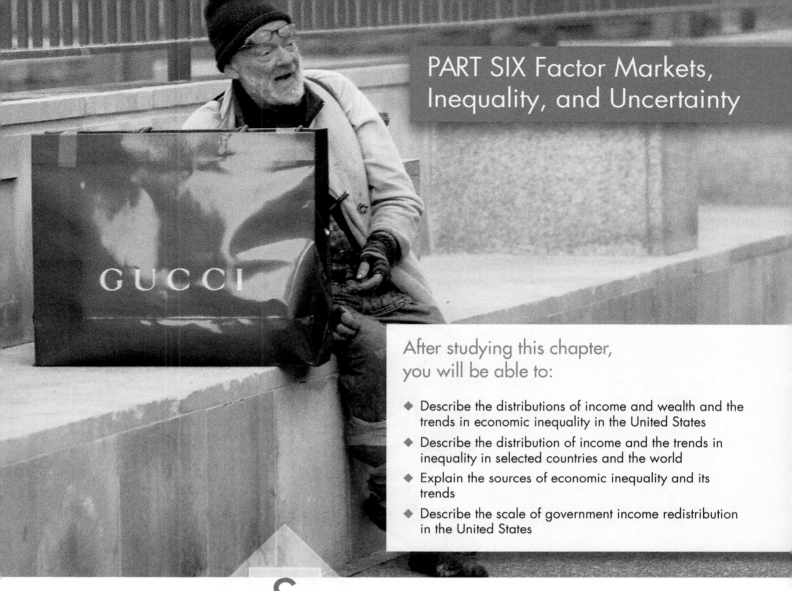

After studying this chapter,
you will be able to:

◆ Describe the distributions of income and wealth and the
trends in economic inequality in the United States

◆ Describe the distribution of income and the trends in
inequality in selected countries and the world

◆ Explain the sources of economic inequality and its
trends

◆ Describe the scale of government income redistribution
in the United States

16

ECONOMIC

INEQUALITY

Six percent of adults in Los Angeles County, some 375,000 people, experienced homelessness during the past five years. In this same county is Beverly Hills, with its mansions that are home to some fabulously wealthy movie stars. Los Angeles is not unusual. In New York City, where Donald Trump has built a luxury apartment tower with a penthouse priced at $13 million, more than 20,000 people, 9,000 of whom are children, seek a bed every night in a shelter for the homeless. Extreme poverty and extreme wealth exist side by side in every major city in the United States and in most parts of the world.

How does the distribution of income in the United States compare with that in other countries? Is income distributed more unequally or less unequally in the United States than in other countries? Are the rich getting richer and the poor getting poorer? Or are incomes becoming more equal?

In this chapter, we study economic inequality—its extent, its sources, and the things governments do to make it less extreme. We begin by looking at some facts about economic inequality in the United States. We end, in *Reading Between the Lines*, by looking at the widening gap between the incomes of top CEOs and average wage rates.

◆ Economic Inequality in the United States

The most commonly used measure of economic inequality is the distribution of annual income. The Census Bureau defines income as **money income**, which equals *market income* plus cash payments to households by government. **Market income** equals wages, interest, rent, and profit earned in factor markets, before paying income taxes.

The Distribution of Income

Figure 16.1 shows the distribution of annual income across the 117.5 million households in the United States in 2009. Note that the *x*-axis measures household income and the *y*-axis is percentage of households.

The most common household income, called the *mode* income, was received by the 6 percent of the households whose incomes fell between $20,000 and $25,000. The value of $22,000 marked on the figure is an estimate.

The middle level of household income in 2009, called the *median* income, was $49,777. Fifty percent of households have an income that exceeds the median and fifty percent have an income below the median.

The average household money income in 2009, called the *mean* income, was $67,976. This number equals total household income, about $8 trillion, divided by the 117.5 million households. You can see in Fig. 16.1 that the mode is less than the median and that the median is less than the mean. This feature of the distribution of income tells us that there are more households with low incomes than with high incomes. It also tells us that some of the high incomes are very high.

The income distribution in Fig. 16.1 is called a *positively skewed* distribution, which means that it has a long tail of high values. This distribution contrasts with the bell that describes the distribution of people's heights. In a bell-shaped distribution, the mean, median, and mode are all equal.

Another way of looking at the distribution of income is to measure the percentage of total income received by each given percentage of households. Data are reported for five groups—called *quintiles* or fifth shares—each consisting of 20 percent of households.

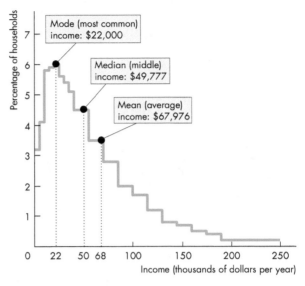

FIGURE 16.1   The Distribution of Income in the United States in 2009

The distribution of income is positively skewed. The mode (most common) income is less than the median (middle) income, which in turn is less than the mean (average) income. The distribution shown here ends at $250,000 because data above that level are not available, but the distribution goes up to several million dollars a year.

Source of data: U.S. Bureau of the Census, "Income, Poverty, and Health Insurance Coverage in the United States: 2007," *Current Population Reports*, P-60-235, (Washington, DC: U.S. Government Printing Office, 2008).

myeconlab   animation

Figure 16.2 shows the distribution based on these shares in 2009. The poorest 20 percent of households received 3.4 percent of total income; the second poorest 20 percent received 8.6 percent of total income; the middle 20 percent received 14.6 percent of total income; the next highest 20 percent received 23.2 percent of total income; and the highest 20 percent received 50.2 percent of total income.

The distribution of income in Fig. 16.1 and the quintile shares in Fig. 16.2 tell us that income is distributed unequally. But we need a way of comparing the distribution of income in different periods and using different measures. A clever graphical tool called the *Lorenz curve* enables us to make such comparisons.

FIGURE 16.2   U.S. Quintile Shares in 2009

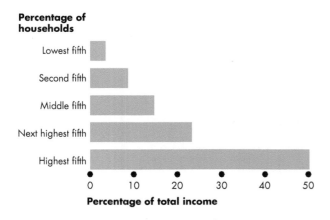

Percentage of households

In 2009, the poorest 20 percent of households received 3.4 percent of total income; the second poorest 20 percent received 8.6 percent; the middle 20 percent received 14.6 percent; the next highest 20 percent received 23.2 percent; and the highest 20 percent received 50.2 percent.

Source of data: See Fig. 16.1.

Households (percentage)	Income (percentage of total income)
Lowest 20	3.4
Second 20	8.6
Middle 20	14.6
Next highest 20	23.2
Highest 20	50.2

The Income Lorenz Curve

The income **Lorenz curve** graphs the cumulative percentage of income against the cumulative percentage of households. Figure 16.3 shows the income Lorenz curve using the quintile shares from Fig. 16.2. The table shows the percentage of income of each quintile group. For example, row *A* tells us that the lowest quintile of households receives 3.4 percent of total income. The table also shows the *cumulative* percentages of households and income. For example, row *B* tells us that the lowest two quintiles (lowest 40 percent) of households receive 12.0 percent of total income (3.4 percent for the lowest quintile plus 8.6 percent for the next lowest).

FIGURE 16.3   The Income Lorenz Curve in 2009

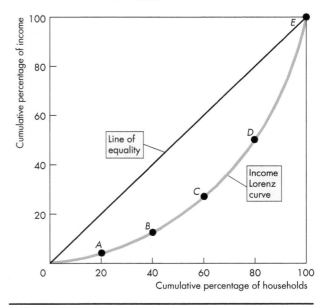

	Households		Income	
	Percentage	Cumulative percentage	Percentage	Cumulative percentage
A	Lowest 20	20	3.4	3.4
B	Second 20	40	8.6	12.0
C	Middle 20	60	14.6	26.6
D	Next highest 20	80	23.2	49.8
E	Highest 20	100	50.2	100.0

The cumulative percentage of income is graphed against the cumulative percentage of households. Points *A* through *E* on the Lorenz curve correspond to the rows of the table. If incomes were distributed equally, each 20 percent of households would receive 20 percent of total income and the Lorenz curve would fall along the line of equality. The Lorenz curve shows that income is unequally distributed.

Source of data: See Fig. 16.1.

The Lorenz curve provides a direct visual clue about the degree of income inequality by comparing it with the line of equality. This line, identified in Fig. 16.3, shows what the Lorenz curve would be if everyone had the same level of income.

If income were distributed equally across all the households, each quintile would receive 20 percent of total income and the cumulative percentages of income received would equal the cumulative percentages of households, so the Lorenz curve would be the straight line labeled "Line of equality."

The actual distribution of income shown by the curve labeled "Income Lorenz curve" can be compared with the Line of equality. The closer the Lorenz curve is to the line of equality, the more equal is the distribution of income.

The Distribution of Wealth

The distribution of wealth provides another way of measuring economic inequality. A household's **wealth** is the value of the things that it owns at a *point in time*. In contrast, income is the amount that the household receives over a given *period of time*.

Figure 16.4 shows the Lorenz curve for wealth in the United States in 1998 (the most recent year for which we have wealth distribution data). The median household wealth in 1998 was $60,700. Wealth is extremely unequally distributed, and for this reason, the data are grouped by seven unequal groups of households. The poorest 40 percent of households own only 0.2 percent of total wealth (row *A'* in the table in Fig. 16.4). The richest 20 percent of households own 83.4 percent of total wealth. Because this group owns almost all the wealth, we need to break the group into smaller parts. That is what rows *D'* through *G'* do. The richest 1 percent of households in row *G'* own 38.1 percent of total wealth.

Figure 16.4 shows the income Lorenz curve (from Fig. 16.3) alongside the wealth Lorenz curve. You can see that the Lorenz curve for wealth is much farther away from the line of equality than is the Lorenz curve for income, which means that the distribution of wealth is much more unequal than the distribution of income.

Wealth or Income?

We've seen that wealth is much more unequally distributed than is income. Which distribution provides the better description of the degree of inequality? To answer this question, we need to think about the connection between wealth and income.

Wealth is a stock of assets, and income is the flow of earnings that results from the stock of wealth. Suppose that a person owns assets worth

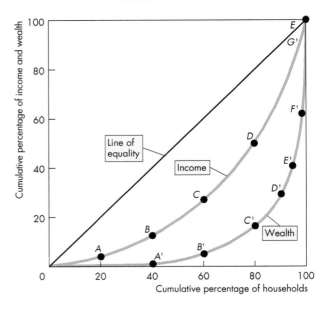

FIGURE 16.4   Lorenz Curves for Income and Wealth

	Households		Wealth	
	Percentage	Cumulative percentage	Percentage	Cumulative percentage
A'	Lowest 40	40	0.2	0.2
B'	Next 20	60	4.5	4.7
C'	Next 20	80	11.9	16.6
D'	Next 10	90	12.5	29.1
E'	Next 5	95	11.5	40.6
F'	Next 4	99	21.3	61.9
G'	Highest 1	100	38.1	100.0

The cumulative percentage of wealth is graphed against the cumulative percentage of households. Points *A'* through *G'* on the Lorenz curve for wealth correspond to the rows of the table. By comparing the Lorenz curves for income and wealth, we can see that wealth is distributed much more unequally than is income.

Sources of data: For the income distribution data, see Fig. 16.1. The Wealth distribution data are from Edward N. Wolff, "Recent Trends in Wealth Ownership, 1938–1998," Jerome Levy Economics Institute Working Paper No. 300, April 2000.

 animation

$1 million—has a wealth of $1 million. If the rate of return on assets is 5 percent a year, then this person receives an income of $50,000 a year from those assets. We can describe this person's economic condition by using either the wealth of $1 million or the income of $50,000. When the rate of return is 5 percent a year, $1 million of wealth equals $50,000 of income in perpetuity. Wealth and income are just different ways of looking at the same thing.

But in Fig. 16.4, the distribution of wealth is more unequal than the distribution of income. Why? It is because the wealth data do not include the value of human capital, while the income data measure income from all wealth, including human capital.

Think about Lee and Peter, two people with equal income and equal wealth. Lee's wealth is human capital and his entire income is from employment. Peter's wealth is in the form of investments in stocks and bonds and his entire income is from these investments.

When a Census Bureau agent interviews Lee and Peter in a national income and wealth survey, their incomes are recorded as being equal, but Lee's wealth is recorded as zero, while Peter's wealth is recorded as the value of his investments. Peter looks vastly more wealthy than Lee in the survey data.

Because the national survey of wealth excludes human capital, the income distribution is a more accurate measure of economic inequality than the wealth distribution.

Annual or Lifetime Income and Wealth?

A typical household's income changes over its life cycle. Income starts out low, grows to a peak when the household's workers reach retirement age, and then falls after retirement. Also, a typical household's wealth changes over time. Like income, it starts out low, grows to a peak at the point of retirement, and falls after retirement.

Think about three households with identical lifetime incomes, one young, one middle-aged, and one retired. The middle-aged household has the highest income and wealth, the retired household has the lowest, and the young household falls in the middle. The distributions of annual income and wealth in a given year are unequal, but the distributions of lifetime income and wealth are equal.

The data on inequality share the bias that you've just seen. Inequality in annual income and wealth data overstates lifetime inequality because households are at different stages in their life cycles.

Trends in Inequality

To see trends in the income distribution, we need a measure that enables us to rank distributions on the scale of more equal and less equal. No perfect scale exists, but one that is much used is called the Gini ratio. The **Gini ratio** is based on the Lorenz curve and equals the ratio of the area between the line of equality and the Lorenz curve to the entire area beneath the line of equality. The larger the Gini ratio, the greater is the degree of income inequality. If income is equally distributed, the Lorenz curve is the same as the line of equality, so the Gini ratio is zero. If one person has all the income and everyone else has none, the Gini ratio is 1.

Figure 16.5 shows the U.S. Gini ratio from 1970 to 2009. The figure shows breaks in the data in 1992 and 2000 because in those years, the Census

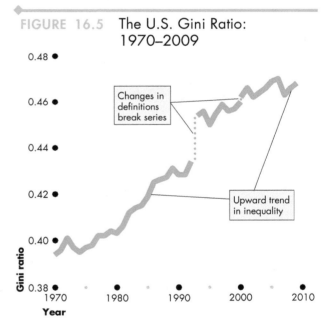

FIGURE 16.5   The U.S. Gini Ratio: 1970–2009

Measured by the Gini ratio, the distribution of income in the United States became more unequal from 1970 to 2009. The percentage of income earned by the richest households increased through these years. Changes in definitions make the numbers before and after 1992 and before and after 2000 not comparable. Despite the breaks in the data, the trends are still visible.

Source of data: See Fig. 16.1.

 animation

Economics in Action
The Rich Get Richer, but School Still Pays

The percentage of Americans who tell the Gallup poll that wealth should be distributed more evenly has been rising. In 2008, it reached 70 percent. A reason might be the trend in the incomes of the super rich. Emmanuel Saez, an economics professor at the University of California, Berkeley, used tax returns data to get the numbers graphed in Fig. 1.

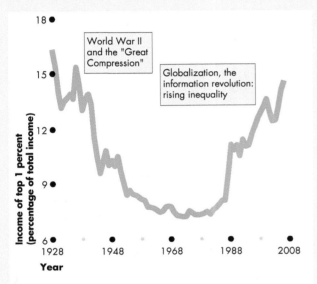

Figure 1 The Income Shares of the Top One Percent

Source of data: Adapted from Table II, "Income Inequality in the United States, 1913–1998" by Thomas Piketty and Emmanuel Saez. *Quarterly Journal of Economics*, February 2003, Vol. 118, Issue 1. © The President and Fellows of the Harvard College an MIT.

After decades of a falling share, starting in 1981, the share of income received by the richest one percent began a steady climb. By 2006 (the latest year in Professor Saez's database), the richest one percent were earning 14.6 percent of the nation's income.

Movie stars, sports stars, and the CEOs of large corporations are among the super rich. People who scratch out a living doing seasonal work on farms earn the lowest incomes. Aside from these extremes, what are the characteristics of people who earn high incomes and people who earn low incomes? Figure 2 answers this question. (The data are for 2009 but the patterns are persistent).

Education A postgraduate education is the main source of a high income. A person with a professional degree (such as a medical or law degree), earns (on average) $124,000—more than double the median income. Just completing high school raises a person's income by more than $14,000 a year; and getting a bachelor's degree adds another $36,000 a year. The average income of people who have not completed 9th grade is $22,000—less than half the median income.

Type of Household Married couples earn more, on the average, than people who live alone. A married couple earns about $72,000. In contrast, men who live alone earn about $48,000, and women who live alone earn only $33,000.

Age of Householder Households with the oldest and youngest householders have lower incomes than do those with middle-aged householders. When the householder is aged between 45 and 54, household income

Bureau changed its method of collecting the data and definitions, so the numbers before and after the breaks can't be compared. Despite the breaks in the series, the Gini ratio has clearly increased, which means that on this measure, incomes have become less equal.

The major change is that the share of income received by the richest households has increased. You can see in *Economics in Action* above how the income of the richest one percent has increased. No one knows for sure *why* this trend has occurred, but a possibility that we'll explore in the next section is that technological change has increased the value of marginal product of high-skilled workers and decreased the value of marginal product of low-skilled workers.

Poverty

Households at the low end of the income distribution are so poor that they are considered to be living in poverty. **Poverty** is a situation in which a household's income is too low to be able to buy the quantities of food, shelter, and clothing that are deemed necessary. Poverty is a relative concept. Millions of people living in Africa and Asia survive on incomes of less than $400 a year. In the United States, the poverty level is calculated each year by the Social Security Administration. In 2009, the poverty level for a four-person household was an income of $21,756. In that year, 44 million Americans—14 percent of the population—lived in households that had incomes below the

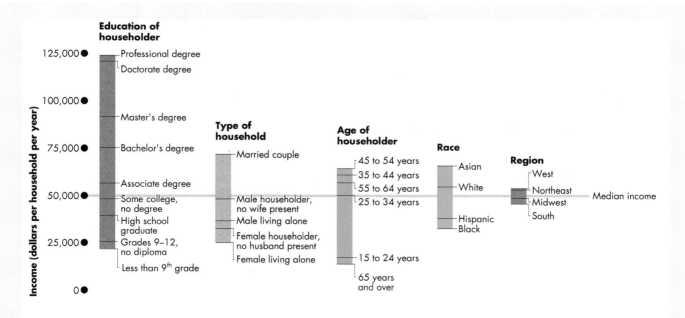

Figure 2 The Distribution of Income by Selected Household Characteristics

Source of data: See Fig. 16.1.

averages $64,000. And when the householder is aged between 35 and 44, household income averages $61,000. When the householder is aged between 15 and 24, average household income is $31,000. And for householders over 65, the average household income is also $31,000.

Race and Ethnicity White Americans have an average income of $54,000, while black Americans have an average income of $33,000. People of Hispanic origin are a bit better off, with an average income of $38,000. Asians are best off with an average income of $65,000.

Region People who live in the West and Northeast earn more, on average, than people who live in the Midwest and the South. While the region does make a difference, its magnitude is small compared to the dominating effect of education.

The bottom line: School pays and so does marriage.

poverty level. Many of these households benefited from Medicare and Medicaid, two government programs that aid the poorest households and lift some of them above the poverty level.

The distribution of poverty by race is unequal: 9.4 percent of white Americans live in poor households compared to 25 percent of Hispanic-origin Americans and 26 percent of black Americans. Poverty is also influenced by household status. More than 28 percent of households in which the householder is a female with no husband present had incomes below the poverty level.

Despite the widening of the income distribution, poverty rates are falling.

 REVIEW QUIZ

1 Which is distributed more unequally, income or wealth? Why? Which is the better measure?
2 From 1970 to 2009 did the distribution of income become more equal or more unequal? How did the richest quintile's share change?
3 What are the main characteristics of people who earn large incomes and who earn small incomes?
4 What is poverty and how does its incidence vary across the races?

You can work these questions in Study Plan 16.1 and get instant feedback.

◆ Inequality in the World Economy

Which countries have the greatest economic inequality and which have the least and the greatest equality? Where does the United States rank? Is it one of the most equal or most unequal or somewhere in the middle? And how much inequality is there in the world as a whole when we consider the entire world as a single global economy?

We'll answer these questions by first looking at the income distribution in a selection of countries and then by examining features of the global distribution of income.

Income Distributions in Selected Countries

By inspecting the income distribution data for every country, we can compare the degree of income inequality and identify the countries with the most inequality and those with the least inequality.

Figure 16.6 summarizes some extremes and shows where the United States lies in the range of degrees of income inequality.

Look first at the numbers in the table. They tell us that in Brazil and South Africa, the poorest 20 percent of households receive only 2 percent of total income while the highest 20 percent receive 65 percent of total income. An average person in the highest quintile receives 32.5 times the income of an average person in the lowest quintile.

Contrast these numbers with those for Finland and Sweden. In these countries, the poorest 20 percent receive 8 percent of total income and the highest 20 percent receive 35 percent. So an average person in the highest quintile receives 4.4 times the income of an average person in the lowest quintile.

The numbers for the United States lie between these extremes with an average person in the highest quintile receiving just under 10 times the amount received by an average person in the lowest quintile.

Brazil and South Africa are extremes not matched in any other major country or region. Inequality is large in these countries because they have a relatively small but rich European population and a large and relatively poor indigenous population.

Finland and Sweden are extremes, but they are not unusual. Income distributions similar to these are found in many European countries in which governments pursue aggressive income redistribution policies.

We look next at the global income distribution.

FIGURE 16.6 Lorenz Curves Compared

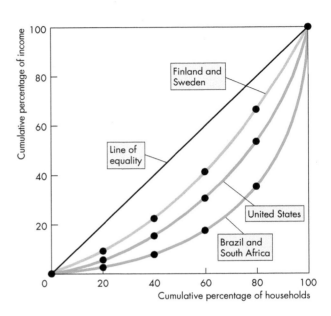

Households	Percentage of total income[1]		
	Brazil and South Africa	United States	Finland and Sweden
Lowest 20 percent	2	5	8
Second 20 percent	5	10	14
Middle 20 percent	10	16	20
Next highest 20 percent	18	22	23
Highest 20 percent	65	47	35

The table shows the percentages of total income received by each quintile. The figure shows the cumulative percentage of income graphed against the cumulative percentage of households. The data and the Lorenz curves show that income is distributed most unequally in Brazil and South Africa and least unequally in Finland and Sweden. The degree of income inequality in the United States lies between these extremes.

Sources of data: Brazil, South Africa, Finland, and Sweden, Klaus W. Deininger and Lyn Squire, Measuring Income Inequality Database, World Bank, http://go.worldbank.org/. United States, See Fig. 16.1.

[1]The data are based on income *after* redistribution. See pp. 331–333 for an account of income redistribution in the United States.

Global Inequality and Its Trends

The global distribution of income is much more unequal than the distribution within any one country. The reason is that many countries, especially in Africa and Asia, are in a pre-industrial stage of economic development and are poor, while industrial countries such as the United States are rich. When we look at the distribution of income across the entire world population that goes from the low income of the poorest African to the high income of the richest American, we observe a very large degree of inequality.

To put some raw numbers on this inequality, start with the poorest. Measured in the value of the U.S. dollar in 2005, a total of 3 billion people or 50 percent of the world population live on $2.50 a day or less. Another 2 billion people or 30 percent of the world population live on more than $2.50 but less than $10 a day. So 5 billion people or 80 percent of the world population live on $10 a day or less.

In contrast, in the rich United States, the *average* person has an income of $115 per day and an average person in the highest income quintile has an income of $460 a day.

So the average American earns 46 times the income of one of the world's 3 billion poorest people and more than 11.5 times the income of 80 percent of the people who live in developing economies. An American with the average income in the highest quintile earns 184 times that of the world's poorest people but only 15 times that of an average bottom quintile American.

World Gini Ratio We can compare world inequality with U.S. inequality by comparing Gini ratios. You saw that the U.S. Gini ratio in 2009 was about 0.47. The world Gini ratio is about 0.64. Recalling the interpretation of the Gini ratio in terms of the Lorenz curve, the world Lorenz curve lies much farther from the line of equality than the U.S. Lorenz curve.

World Trend You saw (in Fig. 16.5 on p. 321) that incomes have become more unequal in the United States—the Gini ratio has increased. The same trends are found in most economies. Increased income inequality is a big issue in two of the world's largest and poorer nations, China and India. In these two economies, urban middle classes are getting richer at a faster pace than the rural farmers.

Despite greater inequality within countries, the world is becoming *less* unequal. Figure 16.7 shows

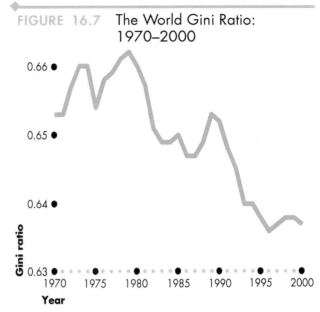

FIGURE 16.7   The World Gini Ratio: 1970–2000

Measured by the Gini ratio, the distribution of income in the entire world became more equal between 1970 and 2000.

Source of data: From "The World Distribution of Income: Falling Poverty and … Convergence, Period" by Xavier Sala-i-Martin, *Quarterly Journal of Economics*, Vol. 121, No. 2, pp. 351-397, May 2006. Reprinted by permission of MIT Press Journals.

this trend toward less inequality as measured by the world Gini ratio. How can the world income distribution become less unequal while individual countries become more unequal? The answer is that average incomes in poorer countries are rising much faster than average incomes in rich countries. While the gap between rich and poor is widening within countries, it is narrowing across countries.

REVIEW QUIZ

1   In which countries are incomes distributed most unequally and least unequally?
2   Which income distribution is more unequal and why: the income distribution in the United States or in the entire world?
3   How can incomes become *more* unequally distributed within countries and *less* unequally distributed across countries?

You can work these questions in Study Plan 16.2 and get instant feedback.

◆ The Sources of Economic Inequality

We've described some key facts about economic inequality and its trends and our task now is to explain those facts. We began this task by learning about the forces that influence demand and supply in the markets for labor, capital, and land. We're now going to deepen our understanding of these forces.

Inequality arises from unequal labor market outcomes and from unequal ownership of capital. We'll begin by looking at labor markets and three features of them that contribute to differences in income:

- Human capital
- Discrimination
- Contests among superstars

Human Capital

A clerk in a law firm earns less than a tenth of the amount earned by the attorney he assists. An operating room assistant earns less than a tenth of the amount earned by the surgeon with whom she works. A bank teller earns less than a tenth of the amount earned by the bank's CEO. Some of the differences in these earnings arise from differences in human capital.

To see the influence of human capital on labor incomes, consider the example of a law clerk and the attorney he assists. (The same reasoning can be applied to an operating room assistant and surgeon, or a bank teller and bank CEO.)

Demand, Supply, and Wage Rates An attorney performs many tasks that a law clerk cannot perform. Imagine an untrained law clerk cross-examining a witness in a complicated trial. The tasks that the attorney performs are valued highly by her clients who willingly pay for her services. Using a term that you learned an attorney has a *high value of marginal product*, and a higher value of marginal product than her law clerk. But you also learned that the value of marginal product of labor determines (is the same as) the demand for labor. So, because an attorney has a high value of marginal product, there is also has a high demand for her services.

To become an attorney, a person must acquire human capital. But human capital is costly to acquire. This cost—an opportunity cost—includes expenditures on tuition and textbooks. It also includes forgone earnings during the years spent in college and law school. It might also include low earnings doing on-the-job training in a law office during the summer.

Because the human capital needed to supply attorney services is costly to acquire, a person's willingness to supply these services reflects this cost. The supply of attorney services is smaller than the supply of law-clerk services.

The demand for and supply of each type of labor determine the wage rates that each type earns. Attorneys earn a higher wage rate than law clerks because the demand for attorneys is greater and the supply of attorneys is smaller. The gap between the wage rates reflects the higher value of marginal product of an attorney (demand) and the cost of acquiring human capital (supply).

Do Education and Training Pay? You know that an attorney earns much more than a law clerk, but does human capital add more to earning power generally and on average? The answer is that it does. Rates of return on high school and college education have been estimated to be in the range of 5 percent to 10 percent a year after allowing for inflation, which suggests that a college degree is a better investment than almost any other that a person can undertake

Human capital differences help to explain much of the inequality that we observe. High-income households tend to be better educated, middle-aged, Asian or white, and married couples (see the figure on p. 323). Human capital differences are correlated with these household characteristics. Education contributes directly to human capital. Age contributes indirectly to human capital because older workers have more experience than younger workers. Human capital differences can also explain a small part of the inequality associated with sex and race. A larger proportion of men (25 percent) than women (20 percent) have completed four years of college, and a larger proportion of whites (24 percent) than blacks (13 percent) have completed a bachelor's degree or higher. These differences in education levels among the sexes and the races are becoming smaller, but they have not been eliminated.

Career interruptions can decrease human capital. A person (most often a woman) who interrupts a career to raise young children usually returns to the labor force with a lower earning capacity than a similar person who has kept working. Likewise, a person who has suffered a spell of unemployment often finds a new job at a lower wage rate than that of a similar person who has not been unemployed.

Trends in Inequality Explained by Technological Change and Globalization

You've seen that high-income households have earned an increasing share of total income while low-income households have earned a decreasing share: The distribution of income in the United States has become more unequal. Technological change and globalization are two possible sources of this increased inequality.

Technological Change Information technologies such as computers and laser scanners are *substitutes* for low-skilled labor: They perform tasks that previously were performed by low-skilled labor. The introduction of these technologies has lowered the marginal product and the demand for low-skilled labor. These same technologies require high-skilled labor to design, program, and run them. High-skilled labor and the information technologies are *complements*. So the introduction of these technologies has increased the marginal product and demand for high-skilled labor.

Figure 16.8 illustrates the effects on wages and employment. The supply of low-skilled labor (part a) and that of high-skilled labor (part b) are S, and initially, the demand in each market is D_0. The low-skill wage rate is $5 an hour, and the high-skill wage rate is $10 an hour. The demand for low-skilled labor decreases to D_1 in part (a) and the demand for high-skilled labor increases to D_1 in part (b). The low-skill wage rate falls to $4 an hour and the high-skill wage rate rises to $15 an hour.

Globalization The entry of China and other developing countries into the global economy has lowered the prices of many manufactured goods. Lower prices for the firm's output lowers the value of marginal product of the firm's workers and decreases the demand for their labor. A situation like that in Fig. 16.8(a) occurs. The wage rate falls, and employment shrinks.

At the same time, the growing global economy increases the demand for services that employ high-skilled workers, and the value of marginal product and the demand for high-skilled labor increases. A situation like that in Fig. 16.8(b) occurs. The wage rate rises, and employment opportunities for high-skilled workers expand.

FIGURE 16.8   Explaining the Trend in Income Distribution

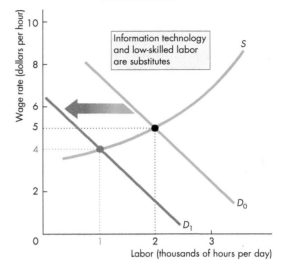

(a) A decrease in demand for low-skilled labor

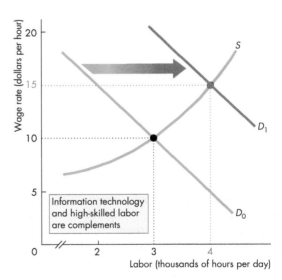

(b) An increase in demand for high-skilled labor

Low-skilled labor in part (a) and information technologies are substitutes. Advances in information technology decrease the demand for low-skilled labor and lower its wage rate. High-skilled labor in part (b) and information technologies are complements. Advances in information technology increase the demand for high-skilled labor and raise its wage rate.

myeconlab   animation

Discrimination

Human capital differences can explain some of the economic inequality that we observe. Discrimination is another possible source of inequality.

Suppose that black females and white males have identical abilities as investment advisors. Figure 16.9 shows the supply curves of black females, S_{BF} (in part a), and of white males, S_{WM} (in part b). The value of marginal product of investment advisors, shown by the two curves labeled VMP in parts (a) and (b), is the same for both groups.

If everyone is free of race and sex prejudice, the market determines a wage rate of $40,000 a year for investment advisors. But if the customers are prejudiced against women and minorities, this prejudice is reflected in the wage rate and employment.

Suppose that the perceived value of marginal product of the black females, when discriminated against, is VMP_{DA}. Suppose that the perceived value of marginal product for white males, the group discriminated in favor of, is VMP_{DF}. With these VMP curves, black females earn $20,000 a year and only 1,000 black females work as investment advisors. White males earn $60,000 a year, and 3,000 of them work as investment advisors.

Counteracting Forces Economists disagree about whether prejudice actually causes wage differentials, and one line of reasoning implies that it does not. In the above example, customers who buy from white men pay a higher service charge for investment advice than do the customers who buy from black women. This price difference acts as an incentive to encourage people who are prejudiced to buy from the people against whom they are prejudiced. This force could be strong enough to eliminate the effects of discrimination altogether. Suppose, as is true in manufacturing, that a firm's customers never meet its workers. If such a firm discriminates against women or minorities, it can't compete with firms who hire these groups because its costs are higher than those of the nonprejudiced firms. Only firms that do not discriminate survive in a competitive industry.

Whether because of discrimination or from some other source, women and visible minorities do earn lower incomes than white males. Another possible source of lower wage rates of women arises from differences in the relative degree of specialization of women and men.

FIGURE 16.9   Discrimination

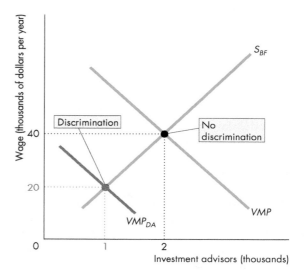

(a) Black females

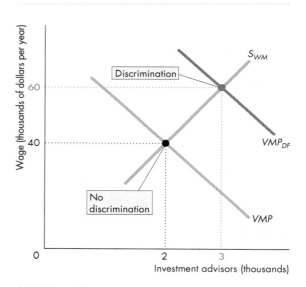

(b) White males

With no discrimination, the wage rate is $40,000 a year and 2,000 of each group are hired. With discrimination against blacks and women, the value of marginal product curve in part (a) is VMP_{DA} and that in part (b) is VMP_{DF}. The wage rate for black women falls to $20,000 a year, and only 1,000 are employed. The wage rate for white men rises to $60,000 a year, and 3,000 are employed.

Differences in the Degree of Specialization Couples must choose how to allocate their time between working for a wage and doing jobs in the home, such as cooking, cleaning, shopping, organizing vacations, and, most important, bearing and raising children. Let's look at the choices of Bob and Sue.

Bob might specialize in earning an income and Sue in taking care of the home. Or Sue might specialize in earning an income and Bob in taking care of the home. Or both of them might earn an income and share home production jobs.

The allocation they choose depends on their preferences and on their earning potential. The choice of an increasing number of households is for each person to diversify between earning an income and doing some household chores. But in most households, Bob will specialize in earning an income and Sue will both earn an income and bear a larger share of the task of running the home. With this allocation, Bob will probably earn more than Sue. If Sue devotes time and effort to ensuring Bob's mental and physical well-being, the quality of Bob's market labor will be higher than it would be if he were diversified. If the roles were reversed, Sue would be able to supply market labor that earns more than Bob's.

To test whether the degree of specialization accounts for earnings differences between the sexes, economists have compared the incomes of never-married men and women. They have found that, on the average, with equal amounts of human capital, the wages of these two groups are the same.

Contests Among Superstars

The differences in income that arise from differences in human capital are important and affect a large proportion of the population. But human capital differences can't account for some of the really large income differences.

The super rich—those in the top one percent of the income distribution whose income share has been rising—earn vastly more than can be explained by human capital differences. What makes a person super rich?

A clue to the answer is provided by thinking about the super rich in tennis and golf. What makes tennis players and golfers special is that their earnings depend on where they finish in a tournament. When Serena Williams won the Wimbledon Championship in 2010, she received £1,000,000 or $1,540,000. The runner-up in this event, Russian Vera Zvonareva,

received £500,000. So Serena earned double the amount earned by Vera. And she earned 88 times the amount received by the players who lost in the first round of the tournament.

It is true that Serena Williams has a lot of human capital. She practices hard and long and is a remarkable athlete. But anyone who is good enough to get into a tennis Grand Slam tournament is similarly well equipped with human capital and has spent a similar number of long hours in training and practice. It isn't human capital that explains the differences in earnings. It is the tournament and the prize differences that accounts for the large differences in earnings.

But three questions jump out: First, why do we reward superstar tennis players (and golfers) with prizes for winning a contest? Second, why are the prizes so different? And third, do the principles that apply on the tennis court (and golf course) apply more generally?

Why Prizes for a Contest? The answer to this question (which was noted in Chapter 5, see p. 96) is that contests with prizes do a good job of allocating scarce resources efficiently when the efforts of the participants are hard to monitor and reward directly. There is only one winner, but many people work hard in an attempt to be that person. So a great deal of diligent effort is induced by a contest.

Why Are Prizes So Different? The prizes need to be substantially different to induce enough effort. If the winner received 10 percent more than the runner up, the gain from being the winner would be insufficient to encourage anyone to work hard enough. Someone would win but no one would put in much effort. Tennis matches would be boring, golf scores would be high, and no one would be willing to pay to see these sports. Big differences are necessary to induce a big enough effort to generate the quality of performance that people are willing to pay to see.

Does the Principle Apply More Generally? Winner-takes-all isn't confined to tennis and golf. Movie stars, superstars in baseball, basketball, football, and ice hockey, and top corporate executives can all be viewed as participants in contests that decide the winners. The prize for the winner is an income at least double that of the runner up and many multiples of the incomes of those who drop out earlier in the tournament.

Do Contests Among Superstars Explain the Trend?

Contests among superstars can explain large differences in incomes. But can contests explain the trend toward greater inequality with an increasing share of total income going to the super rich as shown on p. 321?

An idea first suggested by University of Chicago economist Sherwin Rosen suggests that a winner-takes-all contest can explain the trend. The key is that globalization has increased the market reach of the winner and increased the spread between the winner and the runners-up.

Global television audiences now watch all the world's major sporting events and the total revenue generated by advertising spots during these events has increased. Competition among networks and cable and satellite television distributors has increased the fees that event organizers receive. And to attract the top star performers, prize money has increased and the winner gets the biggest share of the prize pot.

So the prizes in sports have become bigger and the share of income going to the "winner" has increased.

A similar story can be told about superstars and the super rich in business. As the cost of doing business on a global scale has fallen, more and more businesses have become global in their reach. Not only are large multinational corporations sourcing their inputs from far afield and selling in every country, they are also recruiting their top executives from a global talent pool. With a larger source of talent, and a larger total revenue, firms must make the "prize"—the reward for the top job—more attractive to compete for the best managers.

We've examined some sources of inequality in the labor market. Let's now look at the way inequality arises from unequal ownership of capital.

Unequal Wealth

You've seen that wealth inequality—excluding human capital—is much greater than income inequality. This greater wealth inequality arises from two sources: life-cycle saving patterns and transfers of wealth from one generation to the next.

Life-Cycle Saving Patterns Over a family's life cycle, wealth starts out at zero or perhaps less than zero. A student who has financed education all the way through graduate school might have lots of human capital and an outstanding student loan of $60,000. This person has negative wealth. Gradually loans get paid off and a retirement fund is accumulated. At the point of retiring from full-time work, the family has maximum wealth. Then, during its retirement years, the family spends its wealth. This life-cycle pattern means that much of the wealth is owned by people in their sixties.

Intergenerational Transfers Some households inherit wealth from the previous generation. Some save more than enough on which to live during retirement and transfer wealth to the next generation. But these intergenerational transfers of wealth do not always increase wealth inequality. If a generation that has a high income saves a large part of that income and leaves wealth to a succeeding generation that has a lower income, this transfer decreases the degree of inequality. But one feature of intergenerational transfers of wealth leads to increased inequality: wealth concentration through marriage.

Marriage and Wealth Concentration People tend to marry within their own socioeconomic class—a phenomenon called _assortative mating_. In everyday language, "like attracts like." Although there is a good deal of folklore that "opposites attract," perhaps such Cinderella tales appeal to us because they are so rare in reality. Wealthy people seek wealthy partners.

Because of assortative mating, wealth becomes more concentrated in a small number of families and the distribution of wealth becomes more unequal.

REVIEW QUIZ

1 What role does human capital play in accounting for income inequality?
2 What role might discrimination play in accounting for income inequality?
3 What role might contests among superstars play in accounting for income inequality?
4 How might technological change and globalization explain trends in the distribution of income?
5 Does inherited wealth make the distribution of income less equal or more equal?

You can work these questions in Study Plan 16.3 and get instant feedback.

Next, we're going to see how taxes and government programs redistribute income and decrease the degree of economic inequality.

Income Redistribution

The three main ways in which governments in the United States redistribute income are

- Income taxes
- Income maintenance programs
- Subsidized services

Income Taxes

Income taxes may be progressive, regressive, or proportional. A **progressive income tax** is one that taxes income at an average rate that increases as income increases. A **regressive income tax** is one that taxes income at an average rate that decreases as income increases. A **proportional income tax** (also called a *flat-rate income tax*) is one that taxes income at a constant average rate, regardless of the level of income.

The income tax rates that apply in the United States are composed of two parts: federal and state taxes. Some cities, such as New York City, also have an income tax. There is variety in the detailed tax arrangements in the individual states, but the tax system, at both the federal and state levels, is progressive. The poorest working households receive money from the government through an earned income tax credit. Successively higher-income households pay 10 percent, 15 percent, 25 percent, 28 percent, 33 percent, and 35 percent of each additional dollar earned.

Income Maintenance Programs

Three main types of programs redistribute income by making direct payments (in cash, services, or vouchers) to people in the lower part of the income distribution. They are

- Social Security programs
- Unemployment compensation
- Welfare programs

Social Security Programs The main Social Security program is OASDHI—Old Age, Survivors, Disability, and Health Insurance. Monthly cash payments to retired or disabled workers or their surviving spouses and children are paid for by compulsory payroll taxes on both employers and employees. In 2010, total Social Security expenditure was budgeted at $736 billion, and the standard monthly Social Security check for a married couple was a bit more than $1,892 in 2010.

The other component of Social Security is Medicare, which provides hospital and health insurance for the elderly and disabled.

Unemployment Compensation To provide an income to unemployed workers, every state has established an unemployment compensation program. Under these programs, a tax is paid that is based on the income of each covered worker and such a worker receives a benefit when he or she becomes unemployed. The details of the benefits vary from state to state.

Welfare Programs The purpose of welfare is to provide incomes for people who do not qualify for Social Security or unemployment compensation. They are

1. Supplementary Security Income (SSI) program, designed to help the neediest elderly, disabled, and blind people

2. Temporary Assistance for Needy Households (TANF) program, designed to help households that have inadequate financial resources

3. Food Stamp program, designed to help the poorest households obtain a basic diet

4. Medicaid, designed to cover the costs of medical care for households receiving help under the SSI and TANF programs

Subsidized Services

A great deal of redistribution takes place in the United States through the provision of subsidized services—services provided by the government at prices below the cost of production. The taxpayers who consume these goods and services receive a transfer in kind from the taxpayers who do not consume them. The two most important areas in which this form of redistribution takes place are health care and education—both kindergarten through grade 12 and college and university.

In 2010–2011, students enrolled in the University of California system paid annual tuition fees of $10,781. The cost of providing a year's education at the University of California was probably about $22,000. So households with a member enrolled in one of these institutions received a benefit from the government of more than $11,000 a year.

Economics in Action

Income Redistribution: Only the Richest Pay

A household's *market income* tells us what a household earns in the absence of government redistribution. You've seen that market income is *not* the official basis for measuring the distribution of income that we've used in this chapter. The Census Bureau's measure is *money income* (market income plus cash transfers from the government). But market income is the correct starting point for measuring the scale of income redistribution.

We begin with market income and then subtract taxes and add the amounts received in benefits. The result is the distribution of income after taxes and benefits. The data available on benefits exclude the value of subsidized services such as college, so the resulting distribution might understate the total amount of redistribution from the rich to the poor.

The figures show the scale of redistribution in 2001, the most recent year for which the Census Bureau has provided these data. In Fig. 1, the blue Lorenz curve describes the market distribution of income and the green Lorenz curve shows the distribution of income after all taxes and benefits, including Medicaid and Medicare benefits. (The Lorenz curve based on money income in Fig. 16.3 lies between these two curves.)

The distribution after taxes and benefits is less unequal than is the market distribution. The lowest 20 percent of households received only 0.9 percent of market income but 4.6 percent of income after taxes and benefits. The highest 20 percent of households received 55.6 percent of market income, but only 46.7 percent of income after taxes and benefits.

Figure 2 highlights the percentage of total income redistributed among the five groups. The share of total income received by the lowest 60 percent of households increased. The share received by the fourth quintile barely changed. And the share received by the highest quintile fell by 8.9 percent.

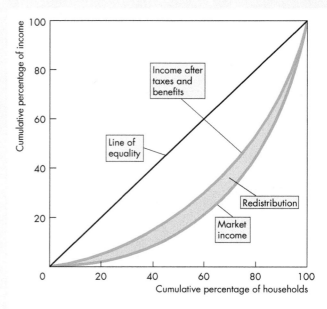

Figure 1   Income Distribution Before and After Redistribution

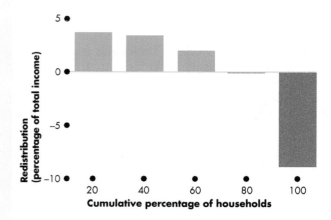

Figure 2   The Scale of Redistribution

Source of data: U.S. Bureau of the Census, "Income Poverty, and Health Insurance Coverage in the United States: 2007," *Current Population Reports*, P-60-235 (Washington, DC: U.S. Government Printing Office, 2008).

Government provision of health-care services has grown to the scale of private provision. Programs such as Medicaid and Medicare bring high-quality and high-cost health care to millions of people who earn too little to buy such services themselves.

The Big Tradeoff

The redistribution of income creates what has been called the **big tradeoff**, a tradeoff between equity and efficiency. The big tradeoff arises because redistribution uses scarce resources and weakens incentives.

A dollar collected from a rich person does not translate into a dollar received by a poor person. Some of it gets used up in the process of redistribution. Tax-collecting agencies such as the Internal Revenue Service and welfare-administering agencies (as well as tax accountants and lawyers) use skilled labor, computers, and other scarce resources to do their work. The bigger the scale of redistribution, the greater is the opportunity cost of administering it.

But the cost of collecting taxes and making welfare payments is a small part of the total cost of redistribution. A bigger cost arises from the inefficiency (deadweight loss) of taxes and benefits. Greater equality can be achieved only by taxing productive activities such as work and saving. Taxing people's income from their work and saving lowers the after-tax income they receive. This lower after-tax income makes them work and save less, which in turn results in smaller output and less consumption not only for the rich who pay the taxes but also for the poor who receive the benefits.

It is not only taxpayers who face weaker incentives to work. Benefit recipients also face weaker incentives. In fact, under the welfare arrangements that prevailed before the 1996 reforms, the weakest incentives to work were those faced by households that benefited from welfare. When a welfare recipient got a job, benefits were withdrawn and eligibility for programs such as Medicaid ended, so the household in effect paid a tax of more than 100 percent on its earnings. This arrangement locked poor households in a welfare trap.

So the agencies that determine the scale and methods of income redistribution must pay close attention to the incentive effects of taxes and benefits. Let's close this chapter by looking at one way in which lawmakers are tackling the big tradeoff today.

A Major Welfare Challenge Young women who have not completed high school, have a child (or children), live without a partner, and more likely are black or Hispanic are among the poorest people in the United States today. They and their children present a major welfare challenge.

First, their numbers are large. In 2009, there were 14 million single-mother families. This number is 12 percent of families. In 1997 (the most recent year with census data), single mothers were owed $26 billion in child support. Of this amount, $10 billion was

not paid and 30 percent of the women received no support from their children's fathers.

The long-term solution to the problem these women face is education and job training—acquiring human capital. The short-term solutions are enforcing child support payments by absent fathers and former spouses and providing welfare.

Welfare must be designed to minimize the disincentive to pursue the long-term goal of becoming self-supporting. The current welfare program in the United States tries to walk this fine line.

Passed in 1996, the Personal Responsibility and Work Opportunities Reconciliation Act strengthened the Office of Child Support Enforcement and increased the penalties for nonpayment of support. The act also created the Temporary Assistance for Needy Households (TANF) program. TANF is a block grant paid to the states, which administer payments to individuals. It is not an open-ended entitlement program. An adult member of a household that is receiving assistance must either work or perform community service, and there is a five-year limit for assistance.

REVIEW QUIZ

1 How do governments in the United States redistribute income?

2 Describe the scale of redistribution in the United States.

3 What is one of the major welfare challenges today and how is it being tackled in the United States?

You can work these questions in Study Plan 16.4 and get instant feedback.

◆ We've examined economic inequality in the United States. We've seen how inequality arises and that inequality has been increasing. *Reading Between the Lines* on pp. 334–335 looks at the increasing inequality that began during the early 1980s and continues today.

The next chapter focuses on some problems for the market economy that arise from uncertainty and incomplete information. But unlike the cases we studied in Chapters 14 and 15, this time the market does a good job of coping with the problems.

Trends in Incomes of the Super Rich

What Happened to All That Anger Over CEO Pay?

http://www.csmonitor.com
July 12, 2010

With last month's sweeping financial reform bill, Congress has finally moved to tame runaway executive pay. Sort of.

It says shareholders must vote on a CEO's pay package, though the vote is nonbinding. Has Congress thereby put an end to sky-high salaries in the executive suite?

"Totally ridiculous," says Sam Pizzigati, an editor of a newsletter on income inequality put out by the liberal Institute for Policy Studies. Shareholder votes only rarely alter corporate decisions.

Given the political anger last year over the pay and bonuses of corporate officials, especially those on Wall Street and at American International Group, such tepid reform is surprising. President Obama expressed outrage in March 2009. His administration capped executive pay at firms receiving bailout money.

That move and the recession had a small impact. In 2008, the CEOs of major U.S. firms were paid more than 300 times the wage of the average American worker. Last year, they were paid just under 300 times average pay, according to new research by Mr. Pizzigati. Now that most of those firms have paid back the government, they're setting their own compensation levels again.

Those levels would astonish the bosses of top corporations in the late 1960s. Those CEOs got about 30 times the average wage of U.S. workers.

Are today's bosses 10 times more capable? Is there a shortage of able managers? Nope and nope, says Pizzigati. "There is more management talent today than ever before." ...

ESSENCE OF THE STORY

- Congress says shareholders must hold a nonbinding vote on a CEO's pay package.

- Sam Pizzigati, editor of a liberal newsletter on income inequality, says shareholder votes rarely have force.

- The Obama Administration capped executive pay at firms receiving government bailout money.

- The Administration cap and the recession had a small impact on CEO pay.

- The CEOs of major U.S. firms were paid more than 300 times the wage of the average American worker in 2008 and just under 300 times in 2009.

- During the 1960s, CEOs got about 30 times the average wage of U.S. workers.

- Sam Pizzigati says that today's bosses are not 10 times more capable than those of the 1960s and that there is more management talent available today than ever before.

- The news article says that the incomes of top CEOs have increased from 30 times the average wage in the 1960s to 300 times in 2008.

- The facts about top CEO pay are correct and they are in line with broader changes in the incomes of the super rich.

- Economists Thomas Piketty (of l'Ecole d'économie de Paris—Paris School of Economics) and Emmanuel Saez (of U.C. Berkely) examined the tax returns of the super rich and found the trend shown in Fig. 1.

- Figure 1 shows the income share (percentage of total income) received by the top 0.01 percent of the population.

- The top 0.01 includes the top CEOs and in 2008 was made up of 15,246 families with incomes that exceeded $9,141,000.

- The average family in the top 0.01 percent received 296 times the income of the average family in the bottom quintile. This ratio was 27 in 1965. These ratios are in line with the trend reported in the news article.

- Sam Pizzigati is reported as saying that CEOs are paid too much today and, with an abundance of talent around, could and should be paid much less.

- He is right that there is an abundance of talent. Globalization has made the entire world the talent pool that large corporations tap for their CEO spot.

- But it is because of the abundance of talent that CEO pay has become so high.

- You saw on p. 329 that we can view top CEOs as the winners of a contest among potential superstars.

- Contests induce high effort and productivity from managers at all levels as they compete for the top job.

- How hard people compete (how productive they are) depends on the size of the prize and the probability of winning it.

- You can think of the contest in terms of the pyramids in Fig. 2. The talent pool is the base of the pyramid and the contest delivers a winner who gets to the top.

- When the talent pool is small, as it was in 1965, the chance of being the winner is large enough for a moderate prize to induce enough effort.

- When the talent pool gets large, as it is today, the chance of being the winner is very small, so to induce the same amount of effort, the prize is very large.

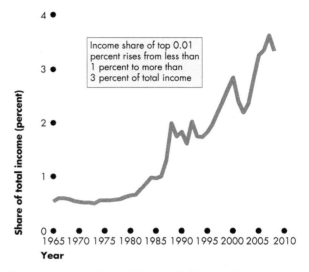

Figure 1 **Income share of the top 0.01 percent**

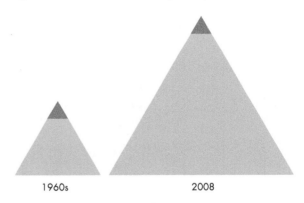

Figure 2 Bigger pyramid means bigger prizes for getting to top

Source of data: Figure 1, Emmanuel Saez, "Striking it Richer: The Evolution of Top Incomes in the United States" *Pathways*, Winter 2008 issue.

- This superstar contest idea explains the direction of change—why top CEOs' earnings have increased relative to the average wage.

- It also answers the question: Are today's managers 10 times as productive as their 1960s predecessors? The answer is no, they are not, but they are paid 10 times as much (relative to the average) to maximize the productivity of the pool of potential CEOs.

SUMMARY

Key Points

Economic Inequality in the United States (pp. 318–323)

- In 2007, the mode money income was $13,000 a year, the median money income was $50,233, and the mean money income was $67,609.
- The income distribution is positively skewed.
- In 2007, the poorest 20 percent of households received 3.4 percent of total income and the wealthiest 20 percent received 49.7 percent of total income.
- Wealth is distributed more unequally than income because the wealth data exclude the value of human capital.
- Since 1970, the distribution of income has become more unequal.
- Education, type of household, age of householder, and race all influence household income.

Working Problems 1 to 7 will give you a better understanding of economic inequality in the United States.

Inequality in the World Economy (pp. 324–325)

- Incomes are distributed most unequally in Brazil and South Africa and least unequally in Finland, Sweden, and some other European economies.
- The U.S. income distribution lies between the extremes.
- The distribution of income across individuals in the global economy is much more unequal than in the United States.
- The global income distribution has been getting less unequal as rapid income growth in China and India has lifted millions from poverty.

Working Problems 8 to 11 will give you a better understanding of economic inequality in the world economy.

The Sources of Economic Inequality (pp. 326–330)

- Inequality arises from differences in human capital and from contests among superstars.
- Trends in the distribution of human capital and in the rewards to superstars that arise from technological change and globalization can explain some of the trend in increased inequality.
- Inequality might arise from discrimination.
- Inequality between men and women might arise from differences in the degree of specialization.
- Intergenerational transfers of wealth lead to increased inequality because people can't inherit debts and assortative mating tends to concentrate wealth.

Working Problems 12 to 15 will give you a better understanding of the sources of economic inequality.

Income Redistribution (pp. 331–333)

- Governments redistribute income through progressive income taxes, income maintenance programs, and subsidized services.
- Redistribution increases the share of total income received by the lowest 60 percent of households and decreases the share of total income received by the highest quintile. The share of the fourth quintile barely changes.
- Because the redistribution of income weakens incentives, it creates a tradeoff between equity and efficiency.
- Effective redistribution seeks to support the long-term solution to low income, which is education and job training—acquiring human capital.

Working Problems 16 to 17 will give you a better understanding of income redistribution.

Key Terms

Big tradeoff, 332
Gini ratio, 321
Lorenz curve, 319
Market income, 318

Money income, 318
Poverty, 322
Progressive income tax, 331
Proportional income tax, 331

Regressive income tax, 331
Wealth, 320

STUDY PLAN PROBLEMS AND APPLICATIONS

econlab   You can work Problems 1 to 17 in MyEconLab Chapter 16 Study Plan and get instant feedback.

Economic Inequality in the United States

(Study Plan 16.1)

1. What is money income? Describe the distribution of money income in the United States in 2009.

2. The table shows money income shares in the United States in 1967.

Households	Money income (percent of total)
Lowest 20 percent	4.0
Second 20 percent	10.8
Middle 20 percent	17.3
Next highest 20 percent	24.2
Highest 20 percent	43.7

   a. Draw a Lorenz curve for the United States in 1967 and compare it with the Lorenz curve in 2007 shown in Fig. 16.3 on p. 319.

   b. Was U.S. money income distributed more equally or less equally in 2007 than it was in 1967?

Use the following news clip to work Problems 3 to 6.

Household Incomes Rise but …

As household income crept higher last year, more people in each household had to work because median earnings for those working full-time year-round actually fell. As the poverty rate edged lower, the percent of Americans living below the poverty line slipped to 12.3 percent in 2006.

   The poverty threshold is based on personal data and not on the local cost of living, so the poverty threshold is the same in rural towns and large cities. Also it does not reflect the value of household subsidies such as food stamps, tax credits, and Medicaid, which are intended to alleviate the effects of poverty. Over the years, the gap between high-income and low-income households has grown, but income inequality remained unchanged between 2005 and 2006.

Source: CNN, August 28, 2007

3. Why is the recent increase in median household income a misleading statistic when attempting to measure the change in economic inequality?

4. How does using set poverty thresholds that apply to the entire United States complicate the attempt to measure poverty?

5. Why does excluding household subsidies lead to a misleading measurement of the percentage of people actually living in poverty?

6. Why has the gap between high-income and low-income households grown in recent decades?

7. **Census: Income Fell Sharply Last Year**

   The U.S. Census Bureau reported that in 2008 the median household income fell 3.6%. The share of people living in poverty rose to 13.2% in 2008 from 12.5% in 2007. Only households led by people aged 65 or older enjoyed income gains—a 1.2% increase.

   Source: *USA Today*, September 11, 2009

   a. What does the information in this news report tell you about changes in the distribution of income in 2008?

   b. What additional information would you need to know how the changes described changed the U.S. Lorenz curve?

Inequality in the World Economy (Study Plan 16.2)

8. Incomes in China and India are a small fraction of incomes in the United States. But incomes in China and India are growing at more than twice the rate of those in the United States.

   a. Explain how economic inequality in China and India is changing relative to that in the United States.

   b. How is the world Lorenz curve and world Gini ratio changing?

Use the following table to work Problems 9 to 11.

The table shows the money income shares in Canada and the United Kingdom.

Households	Canadian money income (percent of total)	U.K. money income (percent of total)
Lowest 20 percent	7	3
Second 20 percent	13	5
Middle 20 percent	18	14
Next highest 20 percent	25	25
Highest 20 percent	37	53

9. Create a table that shows the cumulative distribution of Canadian and U.K. incomes. Is the distribution of income more unequal in Canada or in the United Kingdom?

10. Draw a Lorenz curve for Canada and compare it with the Lorenz curve in Fig. 16.3 on p. 319. In which country is income less equally distributed?

11. Draw a Lorenz curve for the United Kingdom and compare it with the Lorenz curve in Fig. 16.3 on p. 319. In which country is income less equally distributed?

The Sources of Economic Inequality (Study Plan 16.3)

12. The following figure shows the market for low-skilled labor.

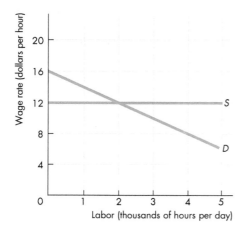

The value of marginal product of high-skilled workers is $16 an hour greater than that of low-skilled workers at each quantity of labor. The cost of acquiring human capital adds $12 an hour to the wage that must be offered to attract high-skilled labor.

Compare the equilibrium wage rates of low-skilled labor and high-skilled labor. Explain why the difference between these wage rates equals the cost of acquiring human capital.

Use the following information to work Problems 13 and 14.

In 2000, 30 million Americans had full-time professional jobs that paid about $800 a week while 10 million Americans had full-time sales jobs that paid about $530 a week.

13. Explain why professionals are paid more than salespeople and why, despite the higher weekly wage, more people are employed as professionals than as salespeople.

14. If the online shopping trend continues, how do you think the market for salespeople will change in coming years?

15. The figure shows the market for a group of workers who are discriminated against. Suppose that others workers in the same industry are not discriminated against and their value of marginal product is perceived to be twice that of the workers who are discriminated against. Suppose also that the supply of these other workers is 2,000 hours per day less at each wage rate.

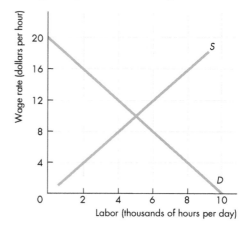

a. What is the wage rate of the workers who are discriminated against?

b. What is the quantity of workers employed who are discriminated against?

c. What is the wage rate of the workers who do not face discrimination?

d. What is the quantity of workers employed who do not face discrimination?

Income Redistribution (Study Plan 16.4)

Use the following table to work Problems 16 and 17. The table shows three redistribution schemes.

Before-tax income (dollars)	Plan A tax (dollars)	Plan B tax (dollars)	Plan C tax (dollars)
10,000	1,000	1,000	2,000
20,000	2,000	4,000	2,000
30,000	3,000	9,000	2,000

16. Which scheme has a proportional tax? Which scheme has a regressive tax? Which scheme has a progressive tax?

17. Which scheme will increase economic inequality? Which scheme will reduce economic inequality? Which scheme will have no effect on economic inequality?

ADDITIONAL PROBLEMS AND APPLICATIONS

 You can work these problems in MyEconLab if assigned by your instructor.

Economic Inequality in the United States

Use the following table to work Problems 18 and 19.
The table shows the distribution of market income
in the United States in 2007.

Households	Market income (percentage of total)
Lowest 20 percent	1.1
Second 20 percent	7.1
Middle 20 percent	13.9
Next highest 20 percent	22.8
Highest 20 percent	55.1

18. a. What is the definition of market income?
    b. Draw the Lorenz curve for the distribution of
       market income.

19. Compare the distribution of market income with
    the distribution of money income shown in Fig.
    16.3 on p. 319. Which distribution is more
    unequal and why?

Inequality in the World Economy

Use the following table to work Problems 20 to 22.
The table shows shares of income in Australia.

Households	Income share (percentage of total)
Lowest 20 percent	7
Second 20 percent	13
Middle 20 percent	18
Next highest 20 percent	24
Highest 20 percent	38

20. Draw the Lorenz curve for the income distribu-
    tion in Australia and in Brazil and South Africa
    (use the data in Fig. 16.6 on p. 324). Is income
    distributed more equally or less equally in Brazil
    and South Africa than in Australia?

21. Is the Gini ratio for Australia larger or smaller
    than that for Brazil and South Africa? Explain
    your answer.

22. What are some reasons for the differences in the
    distribution of income in Australia and in Brazil
    and South Africa?

The Sources of Economic Inequality

Use the following news clip to work Problems 23
to 26.

Bernanke Links Education and Equality

Ben Bernanke, the chairman of the Federal Reserve,
said that increased education opportunities would
help reduce the increased economic inequality that
has occurred over the last 30 years. He also said that
globalization and the advent of new technologies, the
two main causes of income inequality, will lead to
economic growth, but inhibiting them will do far
more harm than good in the long run.

Instead, the Fed chief said the best method to
improve economic opportunities is to focus on raising the level of and access to education. Workers will
become more skilful, and firms will undertake more
innovation.

It is time to recognize that education should be
lifelong and can come in many forms: early child-
hood education, community colleges, vocational
schools, on-the-job training, online courses, adult
education. With increased skills, lifetime earning
power will increase.

Source: *International Herald Tribune*,
June 5, 2008

23. Explain how the two main causes of increased
    income inequality in the United States identified
    by Mr. Bernanke work.

24. Draw a graph to illustrate how the two main
    causes of increased income inequality generate
    this outcome.

25. What are the short-term costs and long-term
    benefits associated with these two causes of
    inequality?

26. Explain Bernanke's solutions to help address
    growing income inequality.

27. **Where Women's Pay Trumps Men's**
    Men work more than women on the job, at least
    in terms of overall hours. That's just one reason
    why in most fields, men's earnings exceed
    women's earnings. But Warren Farrell found 39
    occupations in which women's median earnings
    exceeded men's earnings by at least 5 percent and

in some cases by as much as 43 percent. In fields like engineering, a company may get one woman and seven men applying for a job. If the company wants to hire the woman, it might have to pay a premium to get her. Also, where women can combine technical expertise with people skills—such as those required in sales and where customers prefer dealing with a woman—that's likely to contribute to a premium in pay.

Source: CNN, March 2, 2006

a. Draw a graph to illustrate why discrimination could result in female workers getting paid more than male workers for some jobs.

b. Explain how market competition could potentially eliminate this wage differential.

c. If customers "prefer dealing with a woman" in some markets, how might that lead to a persistent wage differential between men and women?

Income Redistribution

28. Use the information provided in Problem 16 and in Fig. 16.3 on p. 319.
    a. What is the percentage of total income that is redistributed from the highest income group?
    b. What percentages of total income are redistributed to the lower income groups?

29. Describe the effects of increasing the amount of income redistribution in the United States to the point at which the lowest income group receives 15 percent of total income and the highest income group receives 30 percent of total income.

Use the following news clip to work Problems 30 and 31.

The Tax Debate We Should be Having

A shrinking number of Americans are bearing an even bigger share of the nation's income tax burden. In 2005, the bottom 40 percent of Americans by income had, in the aggregate, an effective tax rate that's negative: Their households received more money through the income tax system, largely from the earned income tax credit, than they paid. The top 50% of taxpayers pay 97% of total income tax and the top 10% of taxpayers pay 70%. The top 1% paid almost 40% of all income tax, a proportion that has jumped dramatically since 1986.

Given the U.S. tax system, any tax cut must benefit the rich, but in terms of the change in effective tax rates: The bottom 50% got a much bigger tax cut under the Bush tax cut than the top 1%. Did the dollar value of Bush's tax cuts go mostly to the wealthy? Absolutely.

Source: *Fortune*, April 14, 2008

30. Explain why tax cuts in a progressive income tax system are consistently criticized for favoring the wealthy.

31. How might the benefits of tax cuts "trickle down" to others whose taxes are not cut?

Economics in the News

32. After you have studied *Reading Between the Lines* on pp. 334–335 answer the following questions.
    a. What are the broad facts reported in the news article about the gap in the incomes of CEOs and the average wage rate during the 1960s and in 2008?
    b. What does Sam Pizzigati say should happen to top CEO pay?
    c. How can the idea of a contest among potential CEOs explain the trend in CEO pay?
    d. If the contest among potential CEOs is the correct explanation for the trend in CEO pay, what would be the effects of a cap on CEO pay?

33. **The Best and Worst College Degrees by Salary**

    Business administration is always a strong contender for honors as the most popular college major. This is no surprise since students think business is the way to make big bucks. But is business administration really as lucrative as students and their parents believe? Nope.

    In a new survey by PayScale, Inc. of salaries by college degree, business administration didn't even break into the list of the top 10 or 20 most lucrative college degrees. A variety of engineering majors claim eight of the top 10 salary spots with chemical engineering ($65,700) winning best for starting salaries. Out of 75 undergrad college majors, business administration ($42,900) came in 35th, behind such degrees as occupational therapy ($61,300), information technology ($49,400), and economics ($48,800).

    Source: moneywatch.com, July 21, 2009

    a. Why do college graduates with different majors have drastically different starting salaries?
    b. Draw a graph of the labor markets for economics majors and business administration majors to illustrate your explanation of the differences in the starting salaries of these two groups.

Absolute advantage A person has an absolute advantage if that person is more productive than another person. (p. 36)

Allocative efficiency A situation in which goods and services are produced at the lowest possible cost and in the quantities that provide the greatest possible benefit. We cannot produce more of any good without giving up some of another good that we *value more highly*. (p. 31)

Average cost pricing rule A rule that sets price to cover cost including normal profit, which means setting the price equal to average total cost. (p. 236)

Average fixed cost Total fixed cost per unit of output. (p. 181)

Average product The average product of a factor of production. It equals total product divided by the quantity of the factor employed. (p. 176)

Average total cost Total cost per unit of output. (p. 181)

Average variable cost Total variable cost per unit of output. (p. 181)

Barrier to entry A natural or legal constraint that protects a firm from potential competitors. (p. 222)

Benefit The benefit of something is the gain or pleasure that it brings and is determined by preferences. (p. 6)

Big tradeoff The tradeoff between equality and efficiency. (pp. 105, 332)

Black market An illegal market in which the price exceeds the legally imposed price ceiling. (p. 112)

Budget line The limit to a household's consumption choices. It marks the boundary between those combinations of goods and services that a household can afford to buy and those that it cannot afford. (pp. 130)

Capital The tools, equipment, buildings, and other constructions that businesses use to produce goods and services. (p. 4)

Capital accumulation The growth of capital resources, including *human capital*. (p. 34)

Capture theory A theory that regulation serves the self-interest of the producer, who captures the regulator and maximizes economic profit. (p. 235)

Cartel A group of firms acting together—colluding— to limit output, raise the price, and increase economic profit. (p. 265)

Ceteris paribus Other things being equal—all other relevant things remaining the same. (p. 20)

Change in demand A change in buyers' plans that occurs when some influence on those plans other than the price of the good changes. It is illustrated by a shift of the demand curve. (p. 48)

Change in supply A change in seller's plans that occurs when some influence on those plans other than the price of the good changes. It is illustrated by a shift of the supply curve. (p. 53)

Change in the quantity demanded A change in buyers' plans that occurs when the price of a good changes but all other influences on buyers' plans remain unchanged. It is illustrated by a movement along the demand curve. (p. 51)

Change in the quantity supplied A change in sellers' plans that occurs when the price of a good changes but all other influences on sellers' plans remain unchanged. It is illustrated by a movement along the supply curve. (p. 54)

Coase theorem The proposition that if property rights exist, if only a small number of parties are involved, and transactions costs are low, then private transactions are efficient. (p. 303)

Collusive agreement An agreement between two (or more) producers to form a cartel to restrict output, raise the price, and increase profits. (p. 268)

Common resource A resource that is rival and nonexcludable. (p. 282)

Comparative advantage A person or country has a comparative advantage in an activity if that person or country can perform the activity at a lower opportunity cost than anyone else or any other country. (p. 36)

Competitive market A market that has many buyers and many sellers, so no single buyer or seller can influence the price. (p. 46)

Complement A good that is used in conjunction with another good. (p. 49)

Constant returns to scale Features of a firm's technology that lead to constant long-run average cost as output increases. When constant returns to scale are present, the *LRAC* curve is horizontal. (p. 187)

Consumer equilibrium A situation in which a consumer has allocated all his or her available income in the way that, given the prices of goods and services, maximizes his or her total utility. (p. 135)

Consumer surplus The excess of the benefit received from a good over the amount paid for it. It is calculated as the marginal benefit (or value) of a good minus its price, summed over the quantity bought. (p. 97)

Contestable market A market in which firms can enter and leave so easily that firms in the market face competition from *potential* entrants. (p. 276)

Cooperative equilibrium The outcome of a game in which the players make and share the monopoly profit. (p. 275)

Cross elasticity of demand The responsiveness of the demand for a good to a change in the price of a substitute or complement, other things remaining the same. It is calculated as the percentage change in the quantity demanded of the good divided by the percentage change in the price of the substitute or complement. (p. 81)

Deadweight loss A measure of inefficiency. It is equal to the decrease in total surplus that results from an inefficient level of production. (p. 101)

Demand The entire relationship between the price of the good and the quantity demanded of it when all other influences on buyers' plans remain the same. It is illustrated by a demand curve and described by a demand schedule. (p. 47)

Demand curve A curve that shows the relationship between the quantity demanded of a good and its price when all other influences on consumers' planned purchases remain the same. (p. 48)

Deregulation The process of removing regulation of prices, quantities, entry, and other aspects of economic activity in a firm or industry. (p. 235)

Diminishing marginal rate of substitution The general tendency for a person to be willing to give up less of good *y* to get one more unit of good *x*, while at the same time remaining indifferent as the quantity of good *x* increases. (p. 151)

Diminishing marginal returns The tendency for the marginal product of an additional unit of a factor of production to be less than the marginal product of the previous unit of the factor. (p. 178)

Diminishing marginal utility The tendency for marginal utility to decrease as the quantity consumed of a good increases. (p. 134)

Direct relationship A relationship between two variables that move in the same direction. (p. 14)

Diseconomies of scale Features of a firm's technology that make average total cost rise as output increases—the *LRAC* curve slopes upward. (p. 187)

Dominant strategy equilibrium An equilibrium in which the best strategy for each player is to cheat *regardless of the strategy of the other player*. (p. 267)

Duopoly A market structure in which two producers of a good or service compete. (p. 264)

Economic growth The expansion of production possibilities. (p. 34)

Economic model A description of some aspect of the economic world that includes only those features of the world that are needed for the purpose at hand. (p. 8)

Economic profit The difference between revenues and economic costs. (p. 168)

Economic rent Any surplus—consumer surplus, producer surplus or economic profit. (p. 230)

Economics The social science that studies the *choices* that individuals, businesses, governments, and entire

societies make as they cope with *scarcity* and the *incentives* that influence and reconcile those choices. (p. 2)

Economies of scale Features of a firm's technology that make average total cost fall as output increases—the *LRAC* curve slopes downward. (pp. 187)

Efficient scale The quantity at which average total cost is a minimum—the quantity at the bottom of the U-shaped *ATC* curve. (p. 250)

Elastic demand Demand with a price elasticity greater than 1; other things remaining the same, the percentage change in the quantity demanded exceeds the percentage change in price. (p. 77)

Elasticity of supply The responsiveness of the quantity supplied of a good to a change in its price, other things remaining the same. (p. 84)

Entrepreneurship The human resource that organizes the other three factors of production: labor, land, and capital. (p. 4)

Equilibrium price The price at which the quantity demanded equals the quantity supplied. (p. 56)

Equilibrium quantity The quantity bought and sold at the equilibrium price. (p. 56)

Excess capacity A firm has excess capacity if it produces below its efficient scale. (p. 250)

Excludable A good or service or a resource is excludable if it is possible to prevent someone from enjoying the benefit of it. (p. 282)

External diseconomies Factors outside the control of a firm that raise the firm's costs as the market output increases. (p. 209)

External economies Factors beyond the control of a firm that lower the firm's costs as the market output increases. (p. 209)

Externality A cost (external cost) or a benefit (external benefit) that arises from production or consumption of a private good and that falls on someone other than its producer or consumer. (p. 282)

Factors of production The productive resources used to produce goods and services. (p. 3)

Four-firm concentration ratio A measure of market power that is calculated as the percentage of the value of sales accounted for by the four largest firms in an industry. (p. 171)

Free-rider problem The problem that the market would provide an inefficiently small quantity of a public good. (p. 285)

Game theory A set of tools for studying strategic behavior—behavior that takes into account the expected behavior of others and the recognition of mutual interdependence. (p. 266)

Gini ratio The ratio of the area between the line of equality and the Lorenz curve to the entire area beneath the line of equality. (p. 321)

Goods and services The objects that people value and produce to satisfy human wants. (p. 3)

Herfindahl–Hirschman Index A measure of market power that is calculated as the square of the market share of each firm (as a percentage) summed over the largest 50 firms (or over all firms if there are fewer than 50) in a market. (p. 171)

Human capital The knowledge and skill that people obtain from education, on-the-job training, and work experience. (p. 3)

Incentive A reward that encourages an action or a penalty that discourages one. (p. 2)

Income effect The effect of a change in income on buying plans, other things remaining the same. (p. 156)

Income elasticity of demand The responsiveness of demand to a change in income, other things remaining the same. It is calculated as the percentage change in the quantity demanded divided by the percentage change in income. (p. 82)

Indifference curve A line that shows combinations of goods among which a consumer is *indifferent*. (p. 150)

Individual transferable quota (ITQ) A production limit that is assigned to an individual who is free to transfer (sell) the quota to someone else. (p. 310)

Inelastic demand A demand with a price elasticity between 0 and 1; the percentage change in the quantity demanded is less than the percentage change in price. (p. 76)

Inferior good A good for which demand decreases as income increases. (p. 50)

Intellectual property rights Property rights for discoveries owned by the creators of knowledge. (p. 291)

Interest The income that capital earns. (p. 4)

Inverse relationship A relationship between variables that move in opposite directions. (p. 15)

Labor The work time and work effort that people devote to producing goods and services. (p. 3)

Land The "gifts of nature" that we use to produce goods and services. (p. 3)

Law of demand Other things remaining the same, the higher the price of a good, the smaller is the quantity demanded of it; the lower the price of a good, the larger is the quantity demanded of it. (p. 47)

Law of diminishing returns As a firm uses more of a variable factor of production with a given quantity of the fixed factor of production, the marginal product of the variable factor of production eventually diminishes. (p. 178)

Law of supply Other things remaining the same, the higher the price of a good, the greater is the quantity supplied of it. (p. 52)

Legal monopoly A market in which competition and entry are restricted by the granting of a public franchise, government license, patent, or copyright. (p. 222)

Limit pricing The practice of setting the price at the highest level that inflicts a loss on an entrant. (p. 277)

Linear relationship A relationship between two variables that is illustrated by a straight line. (p. 14)

Long run The time frame in which the quantities of *all* factors of production can be varied. (p. 175)

Long-run average cost curve The relationship between the lowest attainable average total cost and output when the firm can change both the plant it uses and the quantity of labor it employs. (p. 186)

Long-run market supply curve A curve that shows how the quantity supplied in a market varies as the

market price varies after all the possible adjustments have been made, including changes in each firm's plant and the number of firms in the market. (p. 209)

Lorenz curve A curve that graphs the cumulative percentage of income or wealth against the cumulative percentage of households. (p. 319)

Macroeconomics The study of the performance of the national economy and the global economy. (p. 2)

Margin When a choice is made by comparing a little more of something with its cost, the choice is made at the margin. (p. 7)

Marginal benefit The benefit that a person receives from consuming one more unit of a good or service. It is measured as the maximum amount that a person is willing to pay for one more unit of the good or service. (pp. 7, 32)

Marginal benefit curve A curve that shows the relationship between the marginal benefit of a good and the quantity of that good consumed. (p. 32)

Marginal cost The *opportunity cost* of producing *one* more unit of a good or service. It is the best alternative forgone. It is calculated as the increase in total cost divided by the increase in output. (pp. 7, 31, 181)

Marginal cost pricing rule A rule that sets the price of a good or service equal to the marginal cost of producing it. (p. 235)

Marginal external benefit The benefit from an additional unit of a good or service that people other than the consumer enjoy. (p. 287)

Marginal external cost The cost of producing an additional unit of a good or service that falls on people other than the producer. (p. 301)

Marginal private benefit The benefit from an additional unit of a good or service that the consumer of that good or service receives. (p. 287)

Marginal private cost The cost of producing an additional unit of a good or service that is borne by the producer of that good or service. (p. 301)

Marginal product The increase in total product that results from a one-unit increase in the variable input, with all other inputs remaining the

same. It is calculated as the increase in total product divided by the increase in the variable input employed, when the quantities of all other inputs remain the same. (p. 176)

Marginal rate of substitution The rate at which a person will give up good *y* (the good measured on the *y*-axis) to get an additional unit of good *x* (the good measured on the *x*-axis) while at the same time remaining indifferent (remaining on the same indifference curve) as the quantity of *x* increases. (p. 151)

Marginal revenue The change in total revenue that results from a one-unit increase in the quantity sold. It is calculated as the change in total revenue divided by the change in quantity sold. (p. 196)

Marginal social benefit The marginal benefit enjoyed by society—by the consumer of a good or service (marginal private benefit) plus the marginal benefit enjoyed by others (marginal external benefit). (p. 287)

Marginal social cost The marginal cost incurred by the producer and by everyone else on whom the cost falls—by society. It is the sum of marginal private cost and marginal external cost. (p. 301)

Marginal utility The *change* in total utility resulting from a one-unit increase in the quantity of a good consumed. (p. 133)

Marginal utility per dollar The marginal utility from a good that results from spending one more dollar on it. It is calculated as the marginal utility from the good divided by its price. (p. 136)

Market failure A situation in which a market delivers an inefficient outcome. (p. 101)

Market income The wages, interest, rent, and profit earned in factor markets and before paying income taxes. (p. 318)

Markup The amount by which the firm's price exceeds its marginal cost. (p. 251)

Microeconomics The study of the choices that individuals and businesses make, the way these choices interact in markets, and the influence of governments. (p. 2)

Minimum efficient scale The *smallest* quantity of output at which the long-run average cost reaches its lowest level. (p. 188)

Minimum wage A regulation that makes the hiring of labor below a specified wage rate illegal. The lowest wage at which a firm may legally hire labor. (p. 115)

Mixed good A private good the production or consumption of which creates an externality. (p. 282)

Money income Market income plus cash payments to households by the government. (p. 318)

Money price The number of dollars that must be given up in exchange for a good or service. (p. 46)

Monopolistic competition A market structure in which a large number of firms make similar but slightly different products and compete on product quality, price, and marketin, and firms are free to enter or exit the market. (pp. 170, 246)

Monopoly A market structure in which there is one firm, which produces a good or service that has no close substitutes and in which the firm is protected from competition by a barrier preventing the entry of new firms. (pp. 170, 222)

Nash equilibrium The outcome of a game that occurs when player A takes the best possible action given the action of player B and player B takes the best possible action given the action of player A. (p. 267)

Natural monopoly A market in which economies of scale enable one firm to supply the entire market at the lowest possible cost. (p. 222)

Natural monopoly good A good that is nonrival and excludable. When buyers can be excluded if they don't pay but the good is nonrival, marginal cost is zero. (p. 282)

Negative externality An externality that arises from either production or consumption and that imposes an external cost. (p. 282)

Negative relationship A relationship between variables that move in opposite directions. (p. 15)

Nonexcludable A good or service or a resource is nonexcludable if it is impossible (or extremely costly) to prevent someone from enjoying its benefits. (p. 282)

Nonrival A good or service or a resource is nonrival if its use by one person does not decrease the quantity available for someone else. (p. 282)

Normal good A good for which demand increases as income increases. (p. 50)

Normal profit When a firm's resources are earning the same value they would earn in their best alternative. (p. 169)

Oligopoly A market structure in which a small number of firms compete. (pp. 170, 264)

Opportunity cost The highest-valued alternative that we must give up to get something. (pp. 6, 29)

Payoff matrix A table that shows the payoffs for every possible action by each player for every possible action by each other player. (p. 266)

Perfect competition A market in which there are many firms each selling an identical product; there are many buyers; there are no restrictions on entry into the industry; firms in the industry have no advantage over potential new entrants; and firms and buyers are well informed about the price of each firm's product. (pp. 170, 196)

Perfectly elastic demand Demand with an infinite price elasticity; the quantity demanded changes by an infinitely large percentage in response to a tiny price change. (p. 77)

Perfectly inelastic demand Demand with a price elasticity of zero; the quantity demanded remains constant when the price changes. (p. 76)

Perfect price discrimination Price discrimination that occurs when a firm sells each unit of output for the highest price that anyone is willing to pay for it. The firm extracts the entire consumer surplus. (p. 233)

Pigovian taxes Taxes that are used as an incentive for producers to cut back on an activity that creates an external cost. (p. 304)

Positive externality An externality that arises from either production or consumption and that creates an external benefit. (p. 282)

Positive relationship A relationship between two variables that move in the same direction. (p. 14)

Poverty A state in which a household's income is too low to be able to buy the quantities of food, shelter, and clothing that are deemed necessary. (p. 322)

Preferences A description of a person's likes and dislikes and the intensity of those feelings. (pp. 6, 32, 133)

Price cap A regulation that makes it illegal to charge a price higher than a specified level. (p. 112)

Price cap regulation A rule that specifies the highest price that the firm is permitted to set—a price ceiling. (p. 237)

Price ceiling A regulation that makes it illegal to charge a price higher than a specified level. (p. 112)

Price discrimination The practice of selling different units of a good or service for different prices. (p. 223)

Price effect The effect of a change in the price of a good on the quantity of the good consumed, other things remaining the same. (p. 154)

Price elasticity of demand A units-free measure of the responsiveness of the quantity demanded of a good to a change in its price, when all other influences on buyers' plans remain the same. (p. 74)

Price floor A regulation that makes it illegal to trade at a price lower than a specified level. (p. 115)

Price taker A firm that cannot influence the price of the good or service it produces. (p. 196)

Private good A good or service that is both rival and excludable. (p. 282)

Producer surplus The excess of the amount received from the sale of a good or service over the cost of producing it. It is calculated as the price of a good minus the marginal cost (or minimum supply-price), summed over the quantity sold. (p. 99)

Product differentiation Making a product slightly different from the product of a competing firm. (pp. 170, 246)

Production efficiency A situation in which goods and services are produced at the lowest possible cost. (p. 29)

Production possibilities frontier The boundary between the combinations of goods and services that can be produced and the combinations that cannot. (p. 28)

Production quota An upper limit to the quantity of a good that may be produced in a specified period. (p. 123)

Profit The income earned by entrepreneurship. (p. 4)

Progressive income tax A tax on income at an average rate that increases with the level of income. (p. 331)

Property rights The social arrangements that govern the ownership, use, and disposal of anything that people value. Property rights are enforceable in the courts. (pp. 302)

Proportional income tax A tax on income at a constant average rate, regardless of the level of income. (p. 331)

Public good A good or service that is both nonrival and nonexcludable. It can be consumed simultaneously by everyone and from which no one can be excluded from enjoying its benefits. (p. 282)

Public production The production of a good or service by a public authority that receives its revenue from the government. (p. 289)

Quantity demanded The amount of a good or service that consumers plan to buy during a given time period at a particular price. (p. 47)

Quantity supplied The amount of a good or service that producers plan to sell during a given time period at a particular price. (p. 52)

Rate of return regulation A regulation that requires the firm to justify its price by showing that its return on capital doesn't exceed a specified target rate. (p. 236)

Rational choice A choice that compares costs and benefits and achieves the greatest benefit over cost for the person making the choice. (p. 6)

Regressive income tax A tax on income at an average rate that decreases with the level of income. (p. 331)

Regulation Rules administered by a government agency to influence prices, quantities, entry, and other aspects of economic activity in a firm or industry. (p. 235)

Relative price The ratio of the price of one good or service to the price of another good or service. A relative price is an opportunity cost. (pp. 46)

Rent The income that land earns. (p. 4)

Rent ceiling A regulation that makes it illegal to charge a rent higher than a specified level. (p. 112)

Rent seeking The lobbying for special treatment by the government to create economic profit or to divert consumer surplus or producer surplus away from others. The pursuit of wealth by capturing economic rent. (pp. 230)

Rival A good, service, or a resource is rival if its use by one person decreases the quantity available for someone else. (p. 282)

Scarcity Our inability to satisfy all our wants. (p. 2)

Scatter diagram A graph that plots the value of one variable against the value of another variable for a number of different values of each variable. (p. 12)

Search activity The time spent looking for someone with whom to do business. (p. 112)

Short run The time frame in which the quantity of at least one factor of production is fixed and the quantities of the other factors can be varied. The fixed factor is usually capital—that is, the firm uses a given plant. (p. 175)

Short-run market supply curve A curve that shows the quantity supplied in a market at each price when each firm's plant and the number of firms remain the same. (p. 202)

Shutdown point The price and quantity at which the firm is indifferent between producing the profit-maximizing output and shutting down temporarily. The shutdown point occurs at the price and the quantity at which average variable cost is a minimum. (p. 200)

Signal An action taken by an informed person (or firm) to send a message to uninformed people. (p. 254)

Single-price monopoly A monopoly that must sell each unit of its output for the same price to all its customers. (p. 223)

Slope The change in the value of the variable measured on the y-axis divided by the change in the value of the variable measured on the x-axis. (p. 18)

Social interest theory A theory that the political and regulatory process relentlessly seeks out inefficiency and introduces regulation that eliminates deadweight loss and allocates resources efficiently. (p. 235)

Strategies All the possible actions of each player in a game. (p. 266)

Subsidy A payment made by the government to a producer. (pp. 124, 289)

Substitute A good that can be used in place of another good. (p. 49)

Substitution effect The effect of a change in price of a good or service on the quantity bought when the consumer (hypothetically) remains indifferent between the original and the new consumption situations—that is, the consumer remains on the same indifference curve. (p. 157)

Sunk cost The past expenditure on a plant that has no resale value. (p. 175)

Supply The entire relationship between the price of a good and the quantity supplied of it when all other influences on producers' planned sales remain the same. It is described by a supply schedule and illustrated by a supply curve. (p. 52)

Supply curve A curve that shows the relationship between the quantity supplied of a good and its price when all other influences on producers' planned sales remain the same. (p. 52)

Symmetry principle A requirement that people in similar situations be treated similarly. (p. 106)

Tax incidence The division of the burden of the tax between the buyer and the seller. (p. 117)

Technological change The development of new goods and of better ways of producing goods and services. (p. 34)

Total cost The cost of all the productive resources that a firm uses. (p. 180)

Total fixed cost The cost of the firm's fixed inputs. (p. 180)

Total product The maximum output that a given quantity of labor can produce. (p. 176)

Total revenue The value of a firm's sales. It is calculated as the price of the good multiplied by the quantity sold. (pp. 78, 196)

Total revenue test A method of estimating the price elasticity of demand by observing the change in total revenue that results from a change in the price, when all other influences on the quantity sold remain the same. (p. 78)

Total surplus The sum of consumer surplus and producer surplus. (p. 100)

Total utility The total benefit that a person gets from the consumption of all the different goods and services (p. 133)

Total variable cost The cost of all the firm's variable inputs. (p. 180)

Tradeoff A constraint that involves giving up one thing to get something else. (p. 6)

Tragedy of the commons The absence of incentives to prevent the overuse and depletion of a commonly owned resource. (p. 306)

Transactions costs The opportunity costs of making trades in a market. The costs that arise from finding someone with whom to do business, of reaching an agreement about the price and other aspects of the exchange, and of ensuring that the terms of the agreement are fulfilled. (pp. 103, 303)

Unit elastic demand Demand with a price elasticity of 1; the percentage change in the quantity demanded equals the percentage change in price. (p. 76)

Utilitarianism A principle that states that we should strive to achieve "the greatest happiness for the greatest number of people." (p. 104)

Utility The benefit or satisfaction that a person gets from the consumption of goods and services. (p. 133)

Voucher A token that the government provides to households, which they can use to buy specified goods and services. (p. 289)

Wages The income that labor earns. (p. 4)

Wealth The value of all the things that people own—the market value of their assets—at a point in time. (p. 320)

College campus (page 1) Image Source/Getty Images

Parrot cartoon (page 2) Copyright © 1985 The New Yorker Collection/Frank Modell from cartoonbank.com. All Rights Reserved.

Lehman Brothers (page 5) Kurt Brady/Alamy

Corn (page 27) MNPhoto/Alamy

Ethanol gasoline pump (page 27) Alex Farnsworth/The Image Works

Gas prices (page 45) Justin Sullivan/Staff/Getty Images

Oil drill (page 59) Alberto Incrocci/Getty Images

Strawberry picking (page 61) Chris O'Meara/AP Images

Rotting tomato plants (page 73) Chris O'Meara/AP Images

Rose (page 95) Corbis Super RF/Alamy

Hot dog stand cartoon (page 101) Copyright © 1988 The New Yorker Collection/Mike Twohy from cartoonbank.com. All Rights Reserved.

Ted Kennedy (page 111) Win McNamee/Staff/Getty Images

Ke$ha album (page 129) Photo courtesy of Deepa Chungi

e-reader (page 149) Chris Hackett/Getty Images

Wine cartoon (page 153) Copyright © 1988 The New Yorker Collection/Robert Weber from cartoonbank.com. All Rights Reserved.

Redbox (page 155) Justin Sullivan/Getty Images

Theater foyer (page 155) Corbis

Sony reader (page 159) Newscom

Computer server room (page 167) Jetta Productions/ Dana Neely/Blend Images/Corbis

Pizza (page 170) Michael Newman/PhotoEdit Inc.

Corn fields (page 170) Robert Glusic/Getty Images

Comcast (page 170) George Widman/AP Images

Boeing (page 170) Alastair Miller/Bloomberg News/Landov

Auto plant (page 188) Glowimages/Getty Images

Corn harvest (page 195) Woudew/Shutterstock

Motorcycle (page 205) Rena Schild/Shutterstock

Woman on Computer (page 207) Digital Vision/Getty Images

Tractor (page 207) Elena Elisseeva/Shutterstock

Google campus (page 221) Paul Sakuma/AP Images

Airline cartoon (page 234) William Hamilton

Sneaker display (page 245) Vario Images GmbH & Co. KG/Alamy

Computer store display (page 263) Paul Sakuma/AP Images

Firefighters (page 281) Patti McConville/Getty Images

Lighthouse (page 283) Kenneth C. Zirkel/Getty Images\

Kotlikoff (page 291) Kalman Zabarsky/ Boston University

The Healthcare Fox (page 291) The Healthcare Fix: Universal Insurance for All Americans by Laurence J. Kotlikoff, published by The MIT Press.

Pollution (page 299) Charlie Waite/Getty Images

Tragedy of the Commons (page 306) *River Valley with Swineherd; Hamlet Beyond* (ca 1600), Marten Ryckaert. Oil on panel. Private collection/Christie's Images/Bridgeman Art Library

Cod (page 307) Jeff Rotman/Getty Images

Homeless man (page 317) Getty Images, Inc. - Agence France Presse

The Pearson Series in Economics

Abel/Bernanke/Croushore
Macroeconomics*

Bade/Parkin
Foundations of Economics*

Berck/Helfand
The Economics of the Environment

Bierman/Fernandez
Game Theory with Economic Applications

Blanchard
Macroeconomics*

Blau/Ferber/Winkler
The Economics of Women, Men and Work

Boardman/Greenberg/ Vining/ Weimer
Cost-Benefit Analysis

Boyer
Principles of Transportation Economics

Branson
Macroeconomic Theory and Policy

Brock/Adams
The Structure of American Industry

Bruce
Public Finance and the American Economy

Carlton/Perloff
Modern Industrial Organization

Case/Fair/Oster
Principles of Economics*

Caves/Frankel/Jones
World Trade and Payments: An Introduction

Chapman
Environmental Economics: Theory, Application, and Policy

Cooter/Ulen
Law & Economics

Downs
An Economic Theory of Democracy

Ehrenberg/Smith
Modern Labor Economics

Ekelund/Ressler/Tollison
Economics*

Farnham
Economics for Managers

Folland/Goodman/Stano
The Economics of Health and Health Care

Fort
Sports Economics

Froyen
Macroeconomics

Fusfeld
The Age of the Economist

Gerber
International Economics*

Gordon
Macroeconomics*

Greene
Econometric Analysis

Gregory
Essentials of Economics

Gregory/Stuart
Russian and Soviet Economic Performance and Structure

Hartwick/Olewiler
The Economics of Natural Resource Use

Heilbroner/Milberg
The Making of the Economic Society

Heyne/Boettke/Prychitko
The Economic Way of Thinking

Hoffman/Averett
Women and the Economy: Family, Work, and Pay

Holt
Markets, Games and Strategic Behavior

Hubbard/O'Brien
Economics*
Money and Banking*

Hughes/Cain
American Economic History

Husted/Melvin
International Economics

Jehle/Reny
Advanced Microeconomic Theory

Johnson-Lans
A Health Economics Primer

Keat/Young
Managerial Economics

Klein
Mathematical Methods for Economics

Krugman/Obstfeld/Melitz
International Economics: Theory & Policy*

Laidler
The Demand for Money

Leeds/von Allmen
The Economics of Sports

Leeds/von Allmen/Schiming
Economics*

Lipsey/Ragan/Storer
Economics*

Lynn
Economic Development: Theory and Practice for a Divided World

Miller
Economics Today*
Understanding Modern Economics

Miller/Benjamin
The Economics of Macro Issues

Miller/Benjamin/North
The Economics of Public Issues

Mills/Hamilton
Urban Economics

Mishkin
The Economics of Money, Banking, and Financial Markets*

The Economics of Money, Banking, and Financial Markets, Business School Edition*

Macroeconomics: Policy and Practice*

Murray
Econometrics: A ModernIntroduction

Nafziger
The Economics of Developing Countries

O'Sullivan/Sheffrin/Perez
Economics: Principles, Applications and Tools*

Parkin
Economics*

Perloff
Microeconomics*
Microeconomics: Theory and Applications with Calculus*

Perman/Common/ McGilvray/Ma
Natural Resources and Environmental Economics

Phelps
Health Economics

Pindyck/Rubinfeld
Microeconomics*

Riddell/Shackelford/Stamos/ Schneider
Economics: A Tool for Critically Understanding Society

Ritter/Silber/Udell
Principles of Money, Banking & Financial Markets*

Roberts
The Choice: A Fable of Free Trade and Protection

Rohlf
Introduction to Economic Reasoning

Ruffin/Gregory
Principles of Economics

Sargent
Rational Expectations and Inflation

Sawyer/Sprinkle
International Economics

Scherer
Industry Structure, Strategy, and Public Policy

Schiller
The Economics of Poverty and Discrimination

Sherman
Market Regulation

Silberberg
Principles of Microeconomics

Stock/Watson
Introduction to Econometrics
Introduction to Econometrics, Brief Edition

Studenmund
Using Econometrics: A Practical Guide

Tietenberg/Lewis
Environmental and Natural Resource Economics
Environmental Economics and Policy

Todaro/Smith
Economic Development

Waldman
Microeconomics

Waldman/Jensen
Industrial Organization: Theory and Practice

Weil
Economic Growth

Williamson
Macroeconomics

---

* denotes ⟨myeconlab⟩ titles   Log onto www.myeconlab.com to learn more